Treasury of the True Dharma Eye

Dōgen's *Shōbōgenzō*

# Treasury of the True Dharma Eye
## Dōgen's *Shōbōgenzō*

### Volume VIII

Introduction, Appendices, Supplementary Notes, Works Cited

An annotated translation
by the Sōtō Zen Text Project

Sōtōshū Shūmuchō
Tokyo

University of Hawai'i Press
Honolulu

© 2023 by Sōtōshū Shūmuchō
The Administrative Headquarters of Sōtō Zen Buddhism
All rights reserved.
Printed in China

Treasury of the True Dharma Eye: Dōgen's *Shōbōgenzō*

Volume VIII: Introduction, Appendices, Supplementary Notes, Works Cited

Published in Japan by Sōtōshū Shūmuchō, Tokyo
ISBN: 978-4-911061-00-8

Published for the rest of the world by University of Hawai'i Press, Honolulu

**Library of Congress Cataloging-in-Publication Data**

Names: Dōgen, 1200–1253, author. | Sōtō Zen Text Project, translator.

Title: Treasury of the true dharma eye : Dōgen's Shōbōgenzō / an
annotated translation by the Sōtō Zen Text Project.

Other titles: Shōbō genzō. English

Description: Honolulu : University of Hawai'i Press, [2024] | Published in
Japan by Sōtōshū Shūmuchō, 2023. | Includes bibliographical
references and index. | Contents: v. 8. Introduction, appendices, supplementary
notes, works cited

Identifiers: LCCN 2024004760 (print) | LCCN 2024004761 (ebook) | ISBN
9780824899172 (v. 1 ; paperback) | ISBN 9780824899189 (v. 2 ; paperback)
| ISBN 9780824899196 (v. 3 ; paperback) | ISBN 9780824899202 (v. 4 ;
paperback) | ISBN 9780824899219 (v. 5 ; paperback) | ISBN 9780824899226
(v. 6 ; paperback) | ISBN 9780824899233 (v. 7 ; paperback) | ISBN
9780824899240 (v. 8 ; paperback) | ISBN 9780824899257 (paperback) | ISBN
9798880700264 (v. 1 ; pdf) | ISBN 9798880700271 (v. 2 ; pdf) | ISBN
9798880700288 (v. 3 ; pdf) | ISBN 9798880700295 (v. 4 ; pdf) | ISBN
9798880700301 (v. 5 ; pdf) | ISBN 9798880700318 (v. 6 ; pdf) | ISBN
9798880700325 (v. 7 ; pdf) | ISBN 9798880700332 (v. 8 ; pdf)

Subjects: LCSH: Sōtōshū—Doctrines—Early works to 1800.

Classification: LCC BQ9449.D653 E5 2024 (print) | LCC BQ9449.D653 (ebook)
| DDC 294.3/85—dc23/eng/20240318

LC record available at https://lccn.loc.gov/2024004760
LC ebook record available at https://lccn.loc.gov/2024004761

Cover art: Eihei Dōgen Zenji Gyōjōzu scroll, courtesy of Rev. Ōtani Tetsuo
Cover design by Urs App

University of Hawai'i Press books are printed on acid-free paper and meet the
guidelines for permanence and durability of the Council on Library Resources.
Printer-ready copy has been provided by Sōtōshū Shūmuchō

# CONTENTS

## VOLUME VIII

### INTRODUCTION, APPENDICES, SUPPLEMENTARY NOTES, WORKS CITED

Preface.................................................................................................. iii

Conventions ......................................................................................... iv

Abbreviations....................................................................................... vi

Introduction to the *Shōbōgenzō* ........................................................... 1

Appendices......................................................................................... 233

    1. Tables for Reference .................................................................. 235

    2. Key Dates in the Life of Dōgen and His *Shōbōgenzō* ......... 264

    3. Honzan Edition Chapters in This Translation....................... 278

    4. Index of Chapter Titles ............................................................. 281

Supplementary Notes to the Translation ........................................... 289

Works Cited........................................................................................ 565

# Preface

This volume contains reference materials produced by the Sōtō Zen Text Project in the course of its work on the translation of the *Shōbōgenzō*. Unlike the seven volumes of translation, which reflect the combined labors of the Project team, this eighth volume is largely the work of two Project members, William M. Bodiford and T. Griffith Foulk. Professor Bodiford is the author of the essay "Introduction to the *Shōbōgenzō*," which provides a detailed textual history of the *Shōbōgenzō*; he has also compiled useful appendices providing a chronology of dates associated with Dōgen and the *Shōbōgenzō*, and an index to the chapters of the *Shōbōgenzō* in the various redactions in which they are found. Professor Foulk has provided an extensive set of Supplementary Notes on some of the expressions appearing in the *Shōbōgenzō*, including information on sources and interpretations. It is our hope that these materials will prove helpful to readers who seek a more detailed understanding of the work we have translated here.

Carl Bielefeldt
Editor

iv

# Conventions

This publication is an annotated translation, in seven volumes, of one hundred three texts of Dōgen's Japanese *Shōbōgenzō,* plus an additional volume containing an introduction, supplementary notes, appendices, and list of works cited. The translation is based on the edition of the *Shōbōgenzō* published in Kawamura Kōdō 河村孝道, ed., *Dōgen zenji zenshū* 道元禅師全集, vols. 1-2 (Tokyo: Shunjūsha, 1991, 1993), cited herein as DZZ.1 and DZZ.2; volume and page numbers of this edition are noted in braces at the corresponding locations in the translation.

The Japanese text accompanying the translation here follows the punctuation and *kanazukai* of the Kawamura edition; for ease of reference to premodern sources, Kawamura's modern Japanese kanji have been replaced with traditional forms. Also, for ease of reference, the sections into which the texts of the Kawamura edition are divided have been assigned numbers in square brackets by the translators. The translation of Kawamura's longer sections is sometimes broken into separate paragraphs, and transitions to new topics between sections are sometimes marked by a string of asterisks.

Though primarily written in Japanese, the *Shōbōgenzō* includes many passages of Chinese, ranging from long quotations of texts to short phrases inserted into the Japanese sentences. Since this inclusion of Chinese is a prominent linguistic feature of the original texts, the translation seeks to indicate such passages by the use of oblique font. The reader is warned, however, that, given the ubiquity in the Japanese language of expressions adopted from Chinese, the identification of the shorter phrases as Chinese, rather than Japanese, is often rather arbitrary.

Much of the *Shōbōgenzō* is devoted to comment on material in other texts. The translation uses quotation marks to indicate terms and passages on which Dōgen is commenting. Here, again, the reader is warned that the distinction between use and mention can often be difficult to draw.

Sanskrit, Chinese, and Japanese terms appearing in the *Oxford English Dictionary* (3rd edition) are considered to have been adopted into English; other such terms are treated as foreign words and rendered in italics. Romanization of all such terms, whether treated as foreign or English, is given with diacritics.

With some exceptions, Chinese transliterations of Sanskrit terms are rendered as romanized Sanskrit. Indic proper nouns, whether transliterated or translated in the Chinese, are rendered as their presumed originals where possible; the reader is warned that some such reconstructions are unattested and speculative.

The proper noun "Zen" is used in reference to (a) the tradition that Dōgen calls the "buddhas and ancestors," and (b) the Japanese instantiation of that tradition; the Chinese name "Chan" is used in reference to the Chinese instantiation of the tradition.

Romanized readings of the Japanese text given in the notes follow wherever possible the ruby (*furigana*) in Kawamura's text; readings not provided by Kawamura are based on *Zengaku daijiten* 禅学大辞典 (1978) and/or Katō Shūkō 加藤宗厚, *Shōbōgenzō yōgo sakuin* 正法眼藏用語索引 (1962).

Citations of T. (*Taishō shinshū daizōkyō* 大正新脩大藏經) are from the *SAT Daizōkyō Text Database* (https://21dzk.l.u-tokyo.ac.jp/SAT); citations of ZZ. (*Dainihon zokuzōkyō* 大日本續藏經) are from the *CBETA Hanwen dazangjing* 漢文大藏經 (http://tripitaka.cbeta.org).

The Kawamura edition provides colophons from several sources, some following the relevant chapter, some in the head notes of the chapter, some in the collation notes (*honbun kōi* 本文校異) for that chapter in the end matter of DZZ.1 and DZZ.2. For the convenience of the reader, this translation collects these colophons (and occasionally others omitted by Kawamura) at the end of each chapter. Colophons without attribution are assumed to have been written by Dōgen.

vi

# Abbreviations

B. CBETA.B. = Supplement (*bubian* 補編): *Dazangjing bubian* 大藏經補編
BGDJ = *Bukkyōgo daijiten* 佛教語大辞典. Edited by Nakamura Hajime 中村元
C. = Chinese language
CBETA = *CBETA Chinese Electronic Tripiṭaka Collection*
*Denkōroku* = *Record of the Transmission of Illumination*, Foulk, T. Griffith, editor, 2021. Vol. 1.
DNBZ = *Dai nihon bukkyō zensho* 大日本佛教全書
DZZ = *Dōgen Zenji zenshū* 道元禅師全集. 7 vols. Kawamura Kōdō 河村孝道, et al., compilers
ESST = *Eihei shōbōgenzō shūsho taisei* 永平正法眼藏蒐書大成
ESST-D = *Dōgen zenji shinseki kankei shiryōshū* 道元禪師真蹟関係資料集
ESST-S = *Eihei shōbōgenzō shūsho taisei sōmokuroku* 永平正法眼藏蒐書大成總目録
HYDCD = *Hanyu dacidian* 漢語大詞典. 12 vols.
J. = Japanese language
J. CBETA.J. = *Jiaxing dazangjing* 嘉興大藏經
*Kenzeiki* = Kawamura Kōdō, editor, 1975, Zuichō copy and 1754 xylograph
*Kōroku* = *Dōgen oshō kōroku* 道元和尚廣録
KR = Kanseki Repository (*Kanseki Ripo* 漢籍リポ). Online: https://www.kanripo.org
M. = *Dai kanwa jiten* 大漢和辞典. Morohashi Tetsuji 諸橋轍次 editor
NDGZ = *Nichiren daishōnin gosho zenshū* 日蓮大聖人御書全集
P. = Pāli
R.CBETA.R = Reprint: *Dai Nihon zoku zōkyō* 大日本續藏經
S. = Sanskrit
SCZ = *Shōbōgenzō chūkai zensho* 正法眼藏註解全書
SK = *Sōtōshū komonjo* 曹洞宗古文書
SZ = *Sōtōshū zensho* 曹洞宗全書
T = *Taishō shinshū daizōkyō* 大正新脩大藏經
T. CBETA.T = *Taishō shinshū daizōkyō* 大正新脩大藏經
X. CBETA.X = *Xinzuan* 新纂 (revised): *Shinsan Dai Nihon zoku zōkyō* 新纂大日本續藏經
Z. CBETA.Z = *Dai Nihon zoku zōkyō* 大日本續藏經
ZGDJ = *Zengaku daijiten* 禪學大辭典
ZSZ = *Zoku Sōtōshū zensho* 續曹洞宗全書
ZT = *Zengaku taikei* 禪學大系
ZTS = *Zengaku tenseki sōkan* 禅学典籍叢刊
ZZ = *Dai Nihon zoku zōkyō* 大日本續藏經

# Introduction to the *Shōbōgenzō*

# Contents

## Introduction to the *Shōbōgenzō*

List of Tables.................................................................................4

Preface...........................................................................................5

I. The *Shōbōgenzō*.......................................................................9

  1. The *Shōbōgenzō* in Seventy-five Chapters ................................16

  2. The *Shōbōgenzō* in Twelve Chapters........................................21

  3. Supplementary Chapters Historically Associated with the
     *Shōbōgenzō*............................................................................28

  4. Earlier Draft Variants of *Shōbōgenzō* Chapters ........................42

II. Vicissitudes.............................................................................54

  5. The *Shōbōgenzō* in Sixty Chapters and Its Descendants...........54

  6. Dōgen and His *Shōbōgenzō* .....................................................71

     Dōgen's World .......................................................................72

     Dōgen Prior to China ...........................................................83

     Dōgen in China......................................................................90

     Dōgen Back in Japan ..........................................................119

     Dōgen in Echizen................................................................151

     Kamakura and Beyond .......................................................158

III. Supplements.......................................................................173

  1. The Beginnings of Zen in Japan according to Mujū Dōgyō....174

  2. The *Shōbōgenzō* Honzan Edition Today.................................180

  3. Preface to the *Treasury of the True Dharma Eye* by the
     Śramaṇa Dōgen...................................................................193

  4. The *Shōbōgenzō* in Chinese and in Japanese scripts ..............198

  5. Sources for Dōgen's Life......................................................214

  6. Dates and Calendarial Considerations .................................228

# TABLES

Table 1. Supplementary Chapters, Table of Contents  36
Table 2. *Shōbōgenzō* in Eighty-four Chapters  38
Table 3. *Shōbōgenzō* in Eighty-nine Chapters 39
Table 4. *Shōbōgenzō* in Ninety-six Chapters  40
Table 5. Himitsu Manuscript, Chapter Numbers and Positions  43
Table 6. Variant Chapters, Descriptive Table of Contents  49
Table 7. Arrangement of Chapters: Sixty versus Twelve  239
Table 8. Arrangement of Chapters: Sixty versus Seventy-five  240
Table 9. Arrangement of Chapters: Sixty versus Seventy-five, *redux*  241
Table 10. Identical Titles for Two Different Chapters  241
Table 11. Honzan Edition Chapters Out of Order in the Original  242
Table 12. Schematic Evolution of Dōgen's *Shōbōgenzō*  243
Table 13. Colophons in Exemplary Manuscripts of the *Shōbōgenzō*  243
Table 14. The Predicate in Dōgen's Colophons  244
Table 15. Common Designations of the Five Mountains  244
Table 16. Kōans Discussed in the *Zuimonki*  245
Table 17. Distribution of Kōans in the *Shōbōgenzō* in Chinese script  247
Table 18. Chronological Profiles of the Three Substantive Compilations  248
Table 19. Variant Colophons for Chapter 3, "Buddha Nature"  249
Table 20. Colophons Not Shared across Compilations  250
Table 21. Chapters Exclusive to the *Shōbōgenzō* in 75 Chapters  250
Table 22. An Identical Date for Three Different Chapters  251
Table 23. Early Compositions and Events  252
Table 24. Convocation Addresses in the *Extensive Records of Reverend Dōgen*  252
Table 25. Convocation Addresses related to Hongzhi and/or Rujing  253
Table 26. Periodization of *Shōbōgenzō* Chapters  255
Table 27. Dated *Shōbōgenzō* Chapters, Part 1: Before Kōshōji  255
Table 28. Dated *Shōbōgenzō* Chapters, Part 2: At Kōshōji  256
Table 39. Dated *Shōbōgenzō* Chapters, Part 3: Echizen Province  257
Table 30. Sequential Chapters  258
Table 31. Non-Sequential Chapters  260
Table 32. Dated *Shōbōgenzō* Chapters, Part 4: After Kamakura  260
Table 33. Successive Abbots of Kenchōji  261
Table 34. The Five Houses of Chan  262
Table 35. Dōgen within the Eisai Faction  263
Table 36. Dōgen among the Linji Lineage  264
Table 37. Dōgen within the Caodong Lineage  265
Table 38. Early Sōtō Intermingling with Nōnin's Faction  266
Table 39. Early Sōtō Temples and Lineages  267

# Introduction to the *Shōbōgenzō*

by William M. Bodiford

## Preface

In 1252, the Japanese Zen master Dōgen 道元 (1200-1253) completed the final ordering and revisions of his life work, the *Shōbōgenzō* 正法眼蔵 (*Treasury of the True Dharma Eye*). It was, and is, an audacious title. In the Chinese Buddhist literature of his time, the words "treasury of the true dharma eye" signified the very essence (eye) of reality, the truth taught by the Buddha, the ability to perceive that truth, the literature and lineage of the Buddhist teachers who perceive, teach, and convey that truth. In short, it is a title that promises to present the religious core of Buddhism. Moreover, one of the leading and most influential Buddhist teachers in China already had used this exact same phrase (C. *Zhengfayanzang*) as a title for one of his own publications. Dōgen's title, therefore, invited comparison with a very powerful predecessor, a comparison that would not be to his advantage. At this time, Dōgen was neither influential nor a leading figure in Japan (much less China). True, as the scion of an unnamed aristocratic family he did not lack political connections. And he had gained some local fame for having traveled to China. The intelligentsia probably could recognize his name, but no more than that. In fact, it was much worse than that. He had never served as abbot of a major temple in the civilized center of Japan. Instead, he dwelled in a remote area far removed from the circles of power and cultural production. His death the following year was not noted in the diaries of any contemporary aristocrats or historians. His writings did not circulate beyond the reaches of his immediate disciples. He and his writings, as was the case for so many of his contemporaries, easily could have been forgotten and lost.

Today, Dōgen's *Shōbōgenzō* has become the most often read, cited, and studied literary work of Japanese Buddhism. Its diverse audiences approach it with a wide range of expectations. Among followers of the Sōtō School of Zen, who look to Dōgen as their founding patriarch, the *Shōbōgenzō* presents the foremost voice of orthodoxy and institutional identity. It firmly links modern Sōtō religious identity to the Buddhist traditions of China while situating it within a distinctive Japanese milieu. For social historians, it provides otherwise inaccessible ethnographic details regarding Buddhist monastic practices in thirteenth-century China and Japan. For scholars of historical linguistics, it preserves a unique trove of evidence regarding the processes by which medieval Japanese language accommodated and gave new expression to Chinese idioms and wit. For scholars of religion, it addresses a host of religious and social issues that resonate throughout the milieu of premodern Japan. For all readers, its insightful comments and vivid observations, frequently expressed in novel and even poetic diction, delight the imagination and stimulate lingering reflections. Its condemnations of all forms of narrow mindedness and rejection of gender discrimination inspire us. Its expositions of old Zen stories, standing in juxtaposition with passages from well-known scriptures, weave seemingly disparate plot lines into one another in ways that transform the act of reading. For Buddhists of all backgrounds, it paints images of wisdom that inspire and instruct. For any lover of literature, its "universe of language" (Terada 1974) enchants literary imaginations. For philosophers, its wordplay, emphasis on intertextuality, and explorations of the contextual basis of knowledge suggest a timeless modernity.

For these reasons, Dōgen's *Shōbōgenzō* is the premodern Japanese text that is most often discussed by contemporary theorists. Prominent Japanese intellectuals — such as Watsuji Tetsurō 和辻哲郎 (1889–1960), Tanabe Hajime 田邊元 (1885–1962), Akiyama Hanji 秋山範二 (1893–1980), Nishitani Keiji 西谷啓治 (1900–1990), Terada Tōru 寺田透 (1915–1995), Abe Masao 阿部正雄 (1915–2006) and so forth — have published influential personal interpretations of its nuances.[1] The fact that it is the only premodern work allowed two volumes (not just one) in the *Nihon shisō taikei* (*Compendium of Japanese Thought*; 1970–1982) — an authoritative sixty-seven volume compendium of primary sources for the study of traditional Japanese thought issued by the prestigious publisher Iwanami Shoten — confirms its preeminence and cultural importance. In recent decades, its renown and influence have spread beyond Japan. The *Shōbōgenzō* already belongs to the world. I hesitate to list all the world's languages into which it has been translated, in whole or in part, because any such compilation will rapidly become out of date.

The work has achieved this great prestige in spite of (or, maybe, because of) the many difficulties it presents to readers (and to translators).

---

[1] See the bibliography for full citations. Regarding philosophical readings of Dōgen, see Heine 2020; Kasulis 2011a, 2011b; Kimura 1991; and Steineck 2018.

Sometimes passages from the *Shōbōgenzō* present us with a Rorschach test inkblot of language that can be parsed in multiple ways depending on the background and predispositions of its readers. In addition to the fundamental, inherent complexity of its core subject matter — the true nature of existence and our proper role within it — the *Shōbōgenzō* suffers from the same kinds of problems that plague almost all ancient writings. It comes from a time, culture, and society very different from our own. It is expressed in a language that people today (including native speakers of Japanese) cannot understand without lengthy study and the aid of many specialized reference materials. Its textual history and manuscript traditions have eluded our understanding, while scholars have proposed contradictory, or even untenable, theories about them. Most of all, the *Shōbōgenzō* has not been served well by the somewhat haphazard ways that its several surviving manuscript versions were compiled and edited for publication.

The Sōtō Zen Text Project translation of the *Shōbōgenzō* is based on the version of the *Shōbōgenzō* printed in the *Dōgen zenji zenshū* (DZZ: *Complete Works of Zen Master Dōgen*) published 1991 to 1993 (in 2 volumes) by Shunjūsha (Tokyo). This version is referred to as the "Kawamura edition" after the name of its principal editor, Kawamura Kōdō.[2] The Kawamura edition, as will be explained in more detail below, represents a significant advance over previous editions of the *Shōbōgenzō*. It is a far more reliable and accurate version adhering closely to the *Shōbōgenzō* that Dōgen wrote and intended for posterity. It includes sixteen supplementary chapters (several not found in any previous compilation) that provide exegetical support and context to Dōgen's *Shōbōgenzō* and that enable the study of Dōgen's methods of writing and rewriting the *Shōbōgenzō*.

The remainder of this introduction is divided into two main sections. Crucial information is repeated in each section so that they can be read independently.

Section I, The *Shōbōgenzō*, is addressed to all readers. It presents an overview of the *Shōbōgenzō* and its main features as exemplified by this translation (and the Japanese text upon which it is based). This overview is intended to enhance understanding of the translation and maximize the usefulness of its many annotations and supporting materials. It is

---

[2]  The DZZ as a whole was compiled in seven volumes by Kagamishima Genryū (1912–2001), Sakai Tokugen (1912–1996), and Sakurai Shūyū (1916–2000).

hoped that even well-informed readers already familiar with Dōgen's work will find much new information here.

Section II, Vicissitudes, discusses the evolution of the *Shōbōgenzō* and the life of its author in relationship to its production. In recent years, scholars have made great advances in their understanding of these topics. Nonetheless, many standard reference works and even recent academic publications too often repeat outdated information that specialists now know to be incorrect. Section II will summarize these issues as they relate to the *Shōbōgenzō* and our understanding of it. Anyone who wishes to understand the *Shōbōgenzō* as a product of particular historical, sociological, or cultural contexts will find this information helpful. An orientation in these topics is essential for anyone who wishes to trace the development of the *Shōbōgenzō* and chart its rise from obscurity to renown.

The introduction is followed by six supplements and four appendices. The supplements provide detailed information on specific topics of interest primarily to specialists. The appendices present supporting information in tabular form. The first appendix consists of the tables (beginning with number 7) that are discussed in Section II. It is followed by a chronological list of key events (Appendix 2), by a list of Honzan edition chapters in this translation (Appendix 3), and by an index of chapter titles (in Japanese and in their English translations; Appendix 4).

# I. The *Shōbōgenzō*

For the purposes of this introduction, it is helpful to think of the *Shōbō-genzō* as existing in two main iterations. The first one, the modern edition, was born in 1815, when Eiheiji 永平寺 — a Sōtō headquarters monastery (*honzan* 本山) founded by Dōgen — first printed his *Shōbōgenzō* and distributed copies of it to about 300 other major Sōtō temples across Japan. This event occurred during the third century of the Tokugawa regime, a period when the military government rigidly regulated society, including Buddhist institutions. Eiheiji was one of several rival Sōtō headquarters monasteries, each one supported by its own separate network of affiliated temples. Most of the rival headquarters possessed their own private manuscript copies of the *Shōbōgenzō*, in various different formats with differences (mostly minor, but some major) in content. Because many Sōtō leaders and government officials feared that disagreements based on these textual differences could upset the prescribed social order, in 1722, the Tokugawa regime had prohibited all copying, printing, or distribution of the *Shōbōgenzō*.

Eiheiji had overcome this prohibition by promising to print a new standard version of the *Shōbōgenzō* for all temples, not another private one. Its compilers at Eiheiji justified their editorial policies with the following assertions: Dōgen had written random essays; after his death, these essays were gathered into various compilations, which somehow collectively became known as "*Shōbōgenzō*"; over time, subsequent copyists rearranged the chapters, reordered them, renamed them, and introduced countless errors. Eiheiji, therefore, took the liberty of creating a new collection based on the best features of all the available manuscripts, one that includes more chapters than any other collection, arranged in a new order, in which all copyist errors have been corrected. Rather than reproducing any existing version of the *Shōbōgenzō*, this new version represents the *Shōbōgenzō* that its compilers imagined Dōgen would have wanted to write had he lived long enough to do so. There was only one caveat. Five chapters that already had aroused public controversy were expunged. The titles of these chapters still appeared, but their contents were represented by blank sheets of paper. They could be read only at Eiheiji by select individuals who received special permission.[3]

Over time, this modern *Shōbōgenzō* became known as the "Honzan" (headquarters) edition. After the Tokugawa regime fell, the expunged

---

[3] Bodiford (2019a, 238–243); Kumagai (1982, 1028–1037); Yoshida (1982).

chapters were restored, and the entire compilation became widely available in modern typeset editions, which have been reprinted endlessly.[4] This Honzan edition is the version of the *Shōbōgenzō* that is most widely known, studied, and commented upon. Its editorial justifications likewise became the standard story of the *Shōbōgenzō*, a story that remains influential even today.[5] The story of the *Shōbōgenzō* as a random collection of disparate essays, an accident of history, informs our received interpretations and commentaries. It suggests that the *Shōbōgenzō* lacks definition or boundaries, that it can and should be rearranged (expanded or abridged) according to our whims, and — most of all — that its contents and contours resulted from the accidents of history, the serendipity of circumstances, rather than authorial intention.

Today, scholars understand the story of the *Shōbōgenzō* very differently. Textual discoveries of the twentieth century have upended the old standard story summarized above. In 1927, Kohō Chisan 孤峰智燦 (1879–1967), an abbot of Yōkōji 永光寺, discovered the only surviving intact manuscript of a previously unknown (and unsuspected) version of the *Shōbōgenzō* in twelve chapters. In 1934, the historian Ōya Tokujō 大屋德城 (1882–1950) revealed the existence of an early manuscript (copied 1287) of Dōgen's *Shōbōgenzō* in Chinese script (the so-called *shinji Shōbōgenzō*) at the Kanazawa Bunko 金澤文庫 (a library founded ca. 1270s) in Kamakura. A variant version of this work had been known by scholars during the Tokugawa period but had been dismissed as spurious. Further investigations would confirm that Dōgen himself had compiled this work and assigned it the title *Shōbōgenzō*. In the late 1930s, Ōkubo Dōshū 大久保道舟 (1896–1994), an archivist at the Historiographical Institute (Shiryō Hensanjo) of the University of Tokyo, reported the existence of an early draft version of Dōgen's *Bendōwa* 辨道話 (*Talk on Pursuing the Way*). Analysis of this work confirmed that Dōgen's writing of the *Shōbōgenzō* began with his compilation and annotation of the version in Chinese (attested in the Kanazawa Bunko manuscript) and subsequently developed into his expositions in Japanese. In 1953, Ōkubo published his analysis of newly discovered holographs of *Shōbōgenzō* chapters in Dōgen's hand and in the handwriting of his disciple Ejō 懷奘 (1198–1280). Ōkubo convincingly argued that these

---

[4]   See Supplement 2: The *Shōbōgenzō* Honzan Edition Today for a description of its principal editions.

[5]   See Bodiford (2019a, 240–246) regarding the description of the *Shōbōgenzō* presented by the editors of the Honzan edition.

*Introduction to the* SHŌBŌGENZŌ 11

holographs demonstrate that Dōgen himself had edited and numbered the chapters in the *Shōbōgenzō*.[6]

These kinds of textual discoveries prompted the launch of a new program of documentary surveys of Sōtō Zen temples. In 1965, the administrative headquarters of the Sōtō school chartered an academic committee with the assignment to catalog and preserve historically important documents.[7] From 1969 to 1978, teams of Sōtō-affiliated scholars conducted systematic nationwide surveys of the many textual materials held by Sōtō temples (Azuma 1991, 49). Three researchers — Nagahisa Gakusui 永久岳水 (1890–1981), Kosaka Kiyū 小坂機融, and the aforementioned Kawamura Kōdō — investigated the manuscript history of the *Shōbōgenzō*. During on-site investigations, these three scholars cataloged and photographed more than three hundred premodern, handwritten copies of the *Shōbōgenzō*, including approximately one hundred ninety complete compilations.[8] Kosaka and Kawamura then published annotated facsimiles of their most important findings in two multivolume series: *Eihei shōbōgenzō shūsho taisei* (ESST, 25 vols.; 1974–1982) and *Eihei shōbōgenzō shūsho taisei zokushū* (ESST-Z, 10 vols.; 1992–2000). Meanwhile, in 1986, Kawamura published a massive (831-page) overview of his researches on the textual history of the *Shōbōgenzō*: its origins, compilations, transmission, and commentarial traditions. Thanks to these findings and publications, scholars worldwide now have access to the most important textual evidence for the entire *Shōbōgenzō* in all of its historical permutations. The alluring poetry of Dōgen's compositions can, for the first time, be defaced by the actual "scabs of history" (rather than by mere whimsy or speculation).[9]

---

[6] Ōkubo (1953, 312–313, 345–346); Ōkubo (1966, 282–2833, 312); also see Bodiford (2019a, 246–252).

[7] Azuma 1991, 49. In addition to this committee, researchers working on the program included members of the Center for Sōtō Studies (Shūgaku Kenkyūsho 宗學研究所), and designated faculty at Sōtō-affiliated universities (e.g., Komazawa University, Aichi Gakuin University, etc.). Cf. Kawaguchi 1979, 105; Yamahata 1971b, 147.

[8] Kagamishima (1986b, 459) and Kawamura (1986, 16 n. 2). Kawamura estimates that an additional 100 or more manuscript copies of the *Shōbōgenzō* probably exist in Japan but are held by individuals or institutions that were not accessible to their survey.

[9] Barnstone (1993, 5) lamented how textual scholarship intrudes between readers and literature with this quotation attributed to Pierre Grange (1927): "It is sinful and sad to mark the face of a poem, beautiful in translation,

The implications of these textual discoveries continue to be explored. They have given scholars much to digest. Whenever one textual finding causes any facet of a previously sacrosanct hypothesis to fall away, its absence imperils not just the specific conclusions it had supported but also related hypotheses. Corrections to any of the other hypotheses will prompt reconsideration of previous modifications, and so forth in a continuing dialectical progression. For this reason, the general public might feel that every few years the orientation of *Shōbōgenzō* scholarship seems to shift again without firm bearings. Yet, while many individual trees remain in dispute or unknown, the overall contours of the forest have emerged in clear relief.

Today, scholars know that Dōgen himself selected the title, *Shōbōgenzō*, wrote the essays, revised them, compiled them, and ordered them into a fixed series of numbered chapters. In many cases, he revised them repeatedly; in other cases, not at all. His sustained literary efforts throughout his career might imply that he must have had a guiding authorial intention for the work as a whole. If so, what was it? We do not know, or at least Dōgen does not seem to have clearly articulated it. When Dōgen died, his *Shōbōgenzō* remained unfinished. He did not live long enough to compose an author's preface to the completed work, a preface in which he could have explained the title and his goals. Some readers might detect a unified vision that runs through the entire work, but other critics will surely disagree. The compilers of the Honzan edition were not entirely wrong in regarding its contents as rather disparate. Their solution was simply to arrange the chapters in chronological order (as best they could, albeit without complete success).

In 1953, Okada Gihō 岡田宜法 (1882–1961), a pioneer in what was then the new academic field of Zen Studies (*zengaku* 禪學), adopted a different approach. In his eight-volume survey of what he termed "*Shōbōgenzō* thought" he rearranged the chapters of the Honzan edition into sixteen thematic categories. While Okada's arrangement never caught on, it nonetheless serves as a convenient survey of the wide range of issues and topics that Dōgen addresses. Here are Okada's categories: (1) interpretations of Buddhism (*bukkyōkan* 佛教觀; six chapters); (2) interpretations of religious faith (*shinkyōkan* 信仰觀; seven chapters); (3) interpretations of Zen moral precepts (*zenkaikan* 禪戒觀; three chapters); (4) interpretations of seated meditation (*zazenkan* 坐禪觀; six chapters);

---

with scabs of authentic history." Tellingly, "Pierre Grange" actually is Barnstone's own fictional nom de plume (Rodríguez García 2004, 12–13).

Introduction to the SHŌBŌGENZŌ      13

(5) interpretations of the pure regulations of monastic life (*shingikan* 清規觀; five chapters); (6) interpretations of sustained practice (*gyōjikan* 行持觀; nine chapters); (7) interpretations of karma and causality (*ingakan* 因果觀; three chapters); (8) interpretations of saṃsāra, or life, death, and rebirth (*shōjikan* 生死觀; two chapters); (9) interpretations of mind (*shinshōkan* 心性觀; ten chapters); (10) interpretations of awakening (*daigokan* 大悟觀; thirteen chapters); (11) interpretations of dharma transmission (*shihōkan* 嗣法觀; nine chapters); (12) interpretations of time and space (*jikūkan* 時空觀; two chapters); (13) interpretations of the buddha (*buttakan* 佛陀觀; seven chapters); (14) interpretations of the ancestral or patriarchal lineage (*bussokan* 佛祖觀; five chapters); (15) interpretations of scriptures (*kyōtenkan* 經典觀; six chapters), and (16) miscellaneous (*zōbu* 雜部; one chapter).

Okada's taxonomy will strike many readers as idiosyncratic, but it has the virtue of being firmly rooted in the Zen tradition. It nonetheless includes modern religious concepts (e.g., Buddhism, faith, spirituality, time and space, scriptures, etc.) that only tangentially correspond to notions from Dōgen's time. His conceptual mapping asserts that Dōgen's comments remain relevant for modern times. Okada thereby highlights a key feature: Dōgen's ability to speak to times, places, and people beyond his own experience accounts for the continued relevance of the *Shōbōgenzō* today.

Okada's taxonomy also points to another, often overlooked dimension of Dōgen's title. As mentioned above, the title *shōbōgenzō* functions as a truth claim. The words "treasury of the true dharma eye" assert the orthodoxy of the Zen tradition, of its ancestral traditions, and of the preeminence of Zen over all rival schools of Buddhism. In this sense they express a narrow sectarian slogan exclusive to the Zen school. Yet, insofar as "treasury of the true dharma eye" claims to represent the core teachings of all buddhas, this slogan also embraces the various forms, expressions, and schools of Buddhism — or, at least, Zen approaches to them. The treasury of the true dharma eye must be ecumenical and catholic. It encompasses the ideal (timeless truth of reality) and the concrete (lived moments of each day). Dōgen's essays routinely fuse together multiple layers of signification (sectarian and catholic; concrete and abstract; etc.) in defiance of Okada's neat categories.

Even if Dōgen's authorial intentions cannot be known with certainty, there exists much greater certainty regarding the kind of *Shōbōgenzō* he intended to write. His sustained literary efforts over much of his career clearly indicate that he intended to leave the reader with his *Shōbōgenzō* in his final, revised version. This final revision refers not just to its arrangement of chapters (one set of 75 and another set of 12), but also to their content (whether rewritten, corrected, expanded, or condensed). Until recently, that final version has not been available in print. Previous editors, beginning with the Honzan edition, selected chapters and inserted or deleted textual passages from a variety of manuscripts — whether early, late, or of unknown provenance — in an eclectic fashion without clear textual criteria. Typically, any passage in Dōgen's handwriting, even if only from a manuscript fragment, served as the basis for emending text from later manuscripts. That approach is now recognized as problematic, since holographs by Dōgen come in all varieties. Many (or most) come from his discarded rough drafts. They were more likely to survive because once their content had been replaced by newer revised versions, the draft manuscript continued to be valued as mementos of Dōgen's calligraphy, and over time they became dispersed across Japan, so that no single fire or calamity could claim them all. Regardless of their impeccable pedigree, the textual content of Dōgen's holographs cannot be trusted uncritically. But later manuscripts, even ones that might have been meticulously copied and scrupulously checked for errors, likewise can present problems of textual contaminations (i.e., errors) if they were corrected against manuscripts from other filiations.

Traditional editing techniques and their practice of weaving together eclectic material from disparate manuscripts have only exacerbated the difficulties of interpreting Dōgen's writings. Consider, for example, *Shōbōgenzō* chapter 28, "Making a Bow and Getting the Marrow" ("Raihai tokuzui"). This chapter stands out for its unbridled condemnation of gender discrimination. Dōgen forcefully rejects the relevance of gender identities. He cites multiple examples of religious women in China who commanded (and received) more reverence than did male teachers of lesser attainment. In the second half of this chapter, he then denounces the corrupt customs of Japan that denigrate women and exclude them from entering the grounds of major Buddhist monasteries, which are designated as "fixed realms" (*kekkai* 結界; i.e., zones excluding the impure). He even casts aspersions on the famed Buddhist patriarchs of Japan who supposedly first established exclusion zones and on the Buddhist avatars (i.e., local gods) who supposedly enforce them.

Modern readers cannot fail to be impressed by Dōgen's strident defense of the value of religious women and his condemnations of the

*Introduction to the* SHŌBŌGENZŌ                    15

social injustices in the Buddhist institutions of Japan. Yet few readers will ever know that the second half of this chapter actually does not exist within this chapter, at least not in its final revised version. The strident condemnations appear only in a single variant manuscript that preserves a discarded rough draft. In the Honzan edition of this chapter, the two separate versions are woven together seamlessly, without even a paragraph break between them. This editorial fusion of disparate manuscripts leaves no space for readers to raise key questions: Why did Dōgen switch from the Chinese examples (which represented universal norms) to the particularities of Japan? Why did he subsequently delete them? How do his rhetorical strategies here compare to those in other revised chapters with large sections of additions or deletions? We can ask these questions (and hope to answer them) only if we have texts that accurately reflect what Dōgen left behind as his final revised version of the *Shōbōgenzō*.

The textual criticism of the *Shōbōgenzō* has advanced tremendously since the 1980s, when the *Shōbōgenzō* manuscript corpora were catalogued, and photographic facsimiles of the important textual witnesses were published. Access to these materials allows scholars today to identify more reliably which specific manuscript witnesses most accurately preserve Dōgen's final revised text. Once identified, a limited, designated set of reliable witnesses can then be cross-checked against one another to produce (in theory) a printed edition that is both accurate and consistent with Dōgen's intended version. The Kawamura edition of the *Shōbōgenzō* (DZZ vols. 1 and 2) is the first one based on this approach. Even while it strives to present Dōgen's *Shōbōgenzō* in the format edited and revised by Dōgen, it does not ignore the legacy of the Honzan edition. In Chapter 28, "Making a Bow and Getting the Marrow," for example, it presents the final revised version. Then it presents the material from the discarded rough draft that appears in the Honzan version. Rather than weaving them together, however, it clearly labels the discarded material in part two as an editorial "appendix" (*furoku* 付録). In this way it maintains a textual fidelity to Dōgen's revised version while also providing readers with access to familiar material traditionally associated with the *Shōbōgenzō*.

The Kawamura edition of the *Shōbōgenzō*, on which the Sōtō Zen Text Project translation is based, consists of four categories of chapters. The chapters in each category differ from the others both in provenance and in character. Considerations of these differences should inform (and will

16 DŌGEN'S *SHŌBŌGENZŌ* VOLUME VIII

influence) how readers evaluate their content. The four categories of chapters are: 1) the *Shōbōgenzō* in seventy-five chapters (translated in Volumes I-V, chapters 1-75); 2) the *Shōbōgenzō* in twelve chapters (in Volume VI, chapters T1-12); 3) supplementary chapters historically associated with the *Shōbōgenzō*; and 4) earlier draft variants of *Shōbōgenzō* chapters (in Volume VII, numbers S1-9, V1-7, respectively).

## 1. The *Shōbōgenzō* in Seventy-five Chapters

The *Shōbōgenzō* in seventy-five chapters is the *Shōbōgenzō* that Dōgen wanted people to read. It is the *Shōbōgenzō* that exerted the strongest influence on Dōgen's disciples and the religious institutions that they and their disciples established across Japan. Senne 詮慧 (dates unknown), one of Dōgen's leading disciples and Dōgen's dharma heir, emphasized this point in the commentary that he completed in 1263 (ten years after Dōgen's death). He wrote:

> 此義先師ノ御調ナレドモ、七十五帖ノ假名ノ正法眼藏ニハ不見トコ
> タヘム輩ハ、非正嫡、先師ノ會下トハ不可謂。 (Punctuation added;
> "Tsuki kikigaki" 都機聞書, ESST.12.306; cf. Kawamura 1986, 490.)

> Any brethren who have not read the *Shōbōgenzō* in Japanese script in seventy-five chapters, in which my late master states this truth in his own words, are not [Dōgen's] legitimate [dharma] heirs and cannot even refer to themselves as having been members of my late master's assembly.

Every word of Senne's brief assertion conveys information. First, "brethren" (*tomogara* 輩) refers to fellow religious, and the phrase "late master" (*senshi* 先師) refers to Dōgen. Normally, only a dharma heir would use this term for a deceased teacher. Senne seems to imply that he knows of deceitful religious who falsely claimed to have been dharma heirs of Dōgen. (Who were they?) He explicitly refers to "Japanese script" (*kana* 假名) to distinguish the Japanese *Shōbōgenzō* in seventy-five chapters from Dōgen's other *Shōbōgenzō*, composed in Chinese (*shinji* 眞字), and thereby implicitly confirms Dōgen's authorship of both versions. His most important point is that Dōgen taught the *Shōbōgenzō* in seventy-five chapters not just to his dharma heirs (i.e., his most select, senior disciples) but to his entire monastic assembly. Only knowledge of this version would confirm one's prior membership within that assembly.

The *Shōbōgenzō* in seventy-five chapters begins with "The Realized Kōan" ("Genjō kōan") and concludes with "Leaving Home" ("Shukke").

*Introduction to the* SHŌBŌGENZŌ: *1. The seventy-five-chapter version*          17

The first words of "The Realized Kōan" set the tone for the work as a whole:

> 諸法の佛法なる時節、すなはち迷悟あり、修行あり、生あり、死あり、諸佛あり、衆生あり。萬法ともにわれにあらざる時節、まどひなく、さとりなく、諸佛なく、衆生なく、生なく、滅なし。(DZZ.1:2)

> At times when the dharmas are the buddha dharma, just then there are delusion and awakening; there is practice; there is birth; there is death; there are buddhas; there are living beings. At times when all the myriad dharmas are not self, there is no delusion; there is no awakening; there are no buddhas; there are no living beings; there is no arising there is no cessation.

This opening dialectic begins with a realm of duality (i.e., delusion), in which identifiable aspects of existence (i.e., dharmas) seem to consist of complementary opposites that people either desire as wholesome (e.g., awakening, birth, buddhas) or reject as unwholesome (e.g., delusion, death, living beings). The very next line places this realm of duality in juxtaposition with the realm of nonduality (i.e., awakening, or wisdom), in which all such dualities have lost their ability to sway our knowledge of truth. Seventy-four chapters later, after one has meandered across multiple realms of delusion and awakening, the final chapter, "Leaving Home," exalts the religious who leave home and become members of the monastic order as the ones who belong to the bloodline (as proper heirs) of the buddhas:

> あきらかにしるべし、諸佛諸祖の成道、ただこれ出家受戒のみなり、諸佛諸祖の命脈、ただこれ出家受戒のみなり。  (DZZ.2:260)

> It should be clear that the attainment of the way of the buddhas and the ancestors is only by those who leave home and receive the precepts; the vital artery of the buddhas and the ancestors is only of those who leave home and receive the precepts.

Kagamishima Genryū (1991, 22–23), the preeminent *Shōbōgenzō* scholar of his generation, saw a clear thematic development that begins with "The Realized Kōan" and leads directly to "Leaving Home." According to Kagamishima's analysis, Dōgen presents kōans (i.e., Zen stories) as expressions of nondual truth, or reality, as revealed through Zen awakening. Dōgen placed "The Realized Kōan" first to set the agenda for his *Shōbōgenzō* as a whole. Reality as revealed in Zen awakening embraces our realms of delusion even as one sees through them, knowing their unreality. Kagamishima regarded "Leaving Home" as a fitting conclusion because (as he explained, p. 23) living as a religious constitutes the realization (*genjō*) of unsurpassed awakening (*mujō bodai* 無上菩提), which itself is ultimate truth (or kōan). Thus, Dōgen's thread of discourse begins with the abstract true nature of reality and concludes with its realization in concrete religious life.

Kagamishima's assertions draw support from Senne's commentary (mentioned previously). At the beginning of his commentary, Senne wrote:

今ノ七十五帖、ツラネラルル一々ノ草子ノ名字ヲアゲテ、現成公按トモ云ベシ . . . 第一ノ見成公按ニテ、第七十五ノ出家マデヲナジ義也。 (Punctuation added; "Genjō kōan kikigaki" 現成公按聞書; ESST.11.8 and 10; cf. Kawamura 1986, 490.)

Although each of these seventy-five chapters, one after another, possesses individual chapter titles, every one of them could be titled "The Realized Kōan" . . . From [chapter] number one, "The Realized Kōan," down to [chapter] number seventy-five, "Leaving Home," they relate the identical principle.

The thrust of Senne's remark agrees with Kagamishima. Rather than addressing the *Shōbōgenzō* as a whole, however, Senne's comments actually focus on the words "realized kōan." Nowadays, most students of Zen know the word "kōan" as the Japanese designation for a Zen story or dialogue. In its original Chinese context, this word (C. *gong'an*) referred to cases in public (i.e., government) courts that served as legal precedents: the cases that establish the way things should be done and thereby clarify the laws that govern the given circumstances. In that context, "realized" (J. *genjō*; C. *xiancheng*) referred to the settled law, something previously determined. By extension, a "realized kōan" also refers to an open-and-shut case, or an obvious situation. But Senne cautions against understanding the terms "realized" or "kōan" in an exclusively secular manner. He states that "realized" should not be understood as the process of making an obscure (*inmotsu* 隠没) thing more apparent or obvious. Moreover, "kōan" refers not to the truth of a particular set of circumstances, but to the entirety of the "treasury of the true dharma eye" conveyed by the buddha and ancestors (*kōan to wa ima no shōbōgenzō o iu nari* 公按トハ今ノ正法眼藏ヲ云也; ibid. 8–9).

Neither Kagamishima nor Senne point out the most obvious thread that runs through the *Shōbōgenzō* in seventy-five chapters: it is filled with references to Chinese Zen stories (J. *kōan*). Overall, it quotes and com-

*Introduction to the* SHŌBŌGENZŌ: *1. The seventy-five-chapter version*     19

ments on more than three hundred kōans, and it thereby serves as an introduction to and overview of this important genre of Chinese Buddhist literature. In fact, "The Realized Kōan" (Chapter 1) actually consists of a sophisticated commentary on one specific kōan, but the commentary lies hidden inside the chapter's overarching dialectics.

Today, many students of Zen associate kōan commentaries with the influential Chinese classics known as the *Blue Cliff Collection* (C. *Biyanji* 碧巖集; J. *Hekiganshū*; ca. 1125?) and the *Gateless Gate* (or *Wumen's Barriers*; C. *Wumenguan* 無門關; J. *Mumonkan*; 1228). While their formats are not identical, in both of these works the commentary first quotes the Zen story in question and then explains its significance, starting with the particulars of the story and proceeding to their larger implications.

Dōgen does not follow that sequence. In "The Realized Kōan," he begins with the larger dialectics, gradually proceeds toward the implications of the kōan for the study of Buddhism, its implications for the development of oneself, and finally concludes by quoting the Zen story (i.e., the kōan of "Baoche: No Place Not Reached") that encapsulates all the issues he previously raised.[10] Only at the very end does it become clear how the issues raised previously relate to the Zen story that concludes the chapter. While the precise resonance and harmony among all the elements might not be immediately obvious to all readers, Dōgen clearly demonstrates that the kōan is not illogical nor impenetrable. The implications of "No Place Not Reached" relate not just to Baoche but to daily practice, self-development, the study of Buddhism, and the nature of reality as both dual and nondual. It is precisely Dōgen's ability to reveal kōans and explore their endless layers of meaning that provides the *Shōbōgenzō* with much of its power. Senne is probably correct in his assertion that all seventy-five chapters entail similar exercises in discerning the logic of the "realized kōan." There is much more to say about the historical significance of this "The Realized Kōan" chapter (regarding which, see Section II, Vicissitudes).

The *Shōbōgenzō* in seventy-five chapters exhibits one more important characteristic. Almost all of its individual chapters (71 out of 75) end with a colophon by Dōgen. Typically, Dōgen's colophons give the title

---

[10]  "The Realized Kōan" (DZZ.1:6) refers to Baoche as "Mayu Baoche" 麻浴寶徹 (J. Mayoku Hōtetsu), but in Chinese sources he usually is referred to as Magu Baoche 麻谷寶徹. Magu could be pronounced in Japanese as "Makoku," but it is possible that the visually similar *gu* 谷 actually represents *yu* 浴.

of the overall collection (*Shōbōgenzō*), the assigned chapter number, the assigned chapter title, as well as an assigned date and place of composition. A version of the same chapter that lacks any of these elements typically represents an earlier rough draft. The evidence of the various rough drafts that survive, suggests that Dōgen assigned a complete colophon with all the elements mentioned above only after he had revised a chapter at least once or twice. The assigned date of composition typically indicates the date of the initial draft, not the date of the final revision that survives today as a numbered chapter in the *Shōbōgenzō*.

Dōgen's colophons, moreover, do not acknowledge any scribal assistance he might have received from his disciples. Nonetheless, other (not 75-chapter) versions of the *Shōbōgenzō* contain scribal colophons showing that Dōgen's disciples frequently copied chapters. In particular, Ejō 懷弉 (1198–1280), Dōgen's senior disciple and dharma heir, served as his secretary acolyte (*shojō jisha* 書狀侍者). It was Ejō's responsibility to assist Dōgen with his paperwork and compositions. Ejō routinely produced clean copies (without mistakes or words crossed out) of Dōgen's rough drafts. Sometimes, Ejō assigned this task to others. Whether the text was copied by himself or by another assistant, Ejō always added his own scribal notes to identify what had been done (e.g., copied, proofread, or collated), where and when it was done, and who did it. Ejō's scribal notes provided him with an important record of his own work. His notes, however, were his own. They were never an intrinsic part of Dōgen's *Shōbōgenzō*. When Dōgen wrote his own clean copies, he never included Ejō's notes. For this reason, the *Shōbōgenzō* in seventy-five chapters contains colophons by Dōgen alone. It does not include any of Ejō's scribal notes.

This last statement refers only to the early manuscripts. Students of the *Shōbōgenzō* long have regarded Ejō's scribal notes as valuable historical evidence for validating individual chapters. In later manuscripts, it is not uncommon to find scribal notes attributed to Ejō for which no earlier textual witness exists. Printed editions, beginning with the Honzan edition, likewise include scribal notes by Ejō regardless of whether they existed in that specific chapter's original manuscript or not. This translation (and the Kawamura edition upon which it is based) does something similar. In this translation, however, whenever a colophon or scribal note comes from a manuscript other than the *Shōbōgenzō* in seventy-five chapters it is explicitly identified as such. The manuscript filiations of colophons are significant. Mistakes in chronology or textual significance can occur

*Introduction to the* SHŌBŌGENZŌ: *2. The twelve-chapter version* 21

when the manuscript basis of the colophons becomes confused (this issue will be discussed again below and in Section II, Vicissitudes).

Before ending this subsection, we should revisit the statements by Senne quoted above. The fact that Senne specifically refers to "the *Shōbōgenzō* in seventy-five chapters" demands our attention. It raises the question of why he mentioned this specific number. Are other numbers of chapters possible? How many *Shōbōgenzō* chapters exist? By mentioning a specific number, Senne seems to suggest that he himself knew of other versions of the *Shōbōgenzō* that had been compiled in different arrangements and numbers of chapters. The next subsection will examine the *Shōbōgenzō* in twelve chapters, and the subsection following it will examine chapters from alternative versions of the *Shōbōgenzō* with different numbers of chapters. The chapters that comprise those categories differ both in provenance and in character from the chapters found in the *Shōbōgenzō* in seventy-five chapters.

## 2. The *Shōbōgenzō* in Twelve Chapters

The *Shōbōgenzō* in twelve chapters presents the supplementary *Shōbōgenzō* that Dōgen had intended to write. He had compiled it simultaneously with the *Shōbōgenzō* in seventy-five chapters. But these two compilations exhibit major differences in format and content. Dōgen dated the completion of the version in seventy-five chapters to 1252. And most all its chapters appear to have been revised, some of them more than once. Seventy-one (out of 75) chapters conclude with a colophon by Dōgen. In the version in the twelve chapters, only one chapter — but not the solitary one that Dōgen had revised — includes his colophon.[11] Only one more chapter bears an assigned date of composition by Dōgen, but he did not live long enough to revise it or any of the others. The *Shōbōgenzō* in twelve chapters appears to have been a work in progress when Dōgen died. For this reason, it is much more difficult to discern with confidence Dōgen's authorial intent or goals for this work.

It is not just its lack of colophons by Dōgen that sets the *Shōbōgenzō* in twelve chapters apart. In contrast to the previous seventy-five chapters, its chapters seem more thematically unified. They address shared

---

[11]   Dōgen attached a dated colophon to "The Merit of the Kāṣāya" ("Kesa kudoku"), and he revised "Karma of the Three Times" ("Sanjigō"), which exists in two versions.

concerns that clearly build upon and reinforce one another. Moreover, they pick up this thread precisely at the position where the *Shōbōgenzō* in seventy-five chapters leaves off. That version concludes with "Leaving Home" ("Shukke") while the *Shōbōgenzō* in twelve chapters commences with "The Merit of Leaving Home" ("Shukke kudoku"). "Leaving Home" exalts the religious who leave home and become members of the monastic order as the ones who belong to the bloodline (as proper heirs) of the buddhas, while the "The Merit of Leaving Home" acclaims the very act of leaving home as:

これ最尊なり ． ． ． これ、佛佛祖祖正傳の正法眼藏涅槃妙心無上菩提なり (DZZ.2:293)

Above all the most honored . . . [It is] the treasury of the true dharma eye, the wondrous mind of nirvāṇa, the unsurpassed bodhi [awakening], directly transmitted by buddha after buddha and ancestor after ancestor.

Subsequent chapters add layers of applause for fundamental Buddhist monastic rites, such as "Receiving the Precepts" (Chapter 2), "The Merit of the Kāṣāya" (i.e., vestment; Chapter 3), "Offerings to the Buddhas" (Chapter 5), and so forth, until they build to a crescendo that concludes in "The Eight Understandings of the Great Person" (Chapter 12), which proclaims:

いま習學して生生に増長し、かならず無上菩提にいたり、衆生のためにこれをとかむこと、釋迦牟尼佛にひとしくして、ことなることなからむ (DZZ.2:457)

Learning and studying them now, we enhance them in life after life; we shall surely reach unsurpassed bodhi and teach them to living beings. In this, we shall be the same as the Buddha Śākyamuni, without any difference from him.

Kagamishima Genryū (1991, 23-24) describes the *Shōbōgenzō* in twelve chapters as a unified progression that begins with the promise of "The Merit of Leaving Home" and concludes with the fulfilment of "The Eight Understandings." While the *Shōbōgenzō* in seventy-five chapters presents the truth of reality as seen through the logic of the realized kōan, the twelve chapters present an exalted overview of the religious life as lived by those who attain this truth. Kagamishima observes that neither the truth of reality nor the true religious life can be achieved alone without the other.

The *Shōbōgenzō* in twelve chapters survives in its complete, final form only in one manuscript that was discovered at Yōkōji in 1927. This man-

*Introduction to the* SHŌBŌGENZŌ: *2. The twelve-chapter version* 23

uscript was produced in 1446 by an unnamed newly ordained religious (i.e., bhikṣu) who clearly took its message to heart. In his copyist colophon, he dedicates the merit of his act as follows:

之意趣者、以此良結緣、生生世世、見佛聞法、出家得道、供養三寶、濟度衆生、成等正覺。永平末流小新戒比丘 (DZZ.2:458)

My aspiration is that by these favorable karmic conditions, birth after birth and lifetime after lifetime, I will see a buddha and hear the dharma, leave home and attain the way, make offerings to the three treasures, deliver living beings, and attain perfect awakening. [Dedication by] a newly ordained bhikṣu, a humble descendant of Eihei [Dōgen].

As Kawamura Kōdō (1991, 419) points out, the dedicatory statement of this copyist, not only eloquently declares his own motives for producing this copy, but also concisely summarizes the main themes of the *Shōbōgenzō* in twelve chapters as a whole. His words demonstrate that, at least as late as the middle of the fifteenth century at some temples, this work continued to inspire and guide the religious life of Sōtō clergy.

Nonetheless, since no other complete manuscript of this *Shōbōgenzō* in twelve chapters survives intact, it must have dropped out of circulation rather quickly. This inference finds reinforcement in the fact that even mentions of a *Shōbōgenzō* in twelve chapters hardly exist elsewhere. Other references to Dōgen's *Shōbōgenzō* are widespread. A typical example would be the funeral records (*sōki* 喪記) for Tsūgen Jakurei 通幻寂靈 (1322–1391). Jakurei was a sixth-generation descendant in the dharma lineage of Dōgen. He served multiple terms as an abbot of Sōjiji, the most powerful Sōtō temple in medieval Japan, and played a key role in Sōjiji's rise to prominence. In short, Jakurei was an ecclesiastical powerhouse. No one would have been better situated to have access to Dōgen's *Shōbōgenzō*. As befitting an illustrious clerical leader, Jakurei's funeral ceremonies spanned several days and involved countless disciples and dignitaries from multiple monasteries. A key event consisted of the presentation of gifts that Jakurei had bequeathed to his disciples and selected dignitaries. These gifts included a dharma robe that Jakurei had received from his own teacher, implements once used by Dōgen, and other significant objects. Mostly, they consisted of books, beginning with his copies of the recorded sayings of two key Chinese Chan patriarchs: Hongzhi Zengjue 宏智正覺 (1091–1157; J. Wanshi Shōgaku) and Rujing 如淨 (1162–1227; J. Nyojō). The gifts also included Jakurei's personal copies of Dōgen's *Shōbōgenzō*. His copy of the *Shōbōgenzō* in seventy-five chapters was protected inside a black lacquered box. His

24　　　　DŌGEN'S *SHŌBŌGENZŌ* VOLUME VIII

copy of the *Shōbōgenzō* in Chinese script was in Jakurei's own handwriting. Several disciples received copies of random, individual chapters from the *Shōbōgenzō* in seventy-five chapters. Nowhere, however, does his funeral record mention or suggest the existence of a *Shōbōgenzō* in twelve chapters.[12]

The same pattern of omission exists in other premodern documents that mention the *Shōbōgenzō* by name. They never specify twelve chapters. This lacuna in the historical record prevents detection of any influence exerted by the *Shōbōgenzō* in twelve chapters on the development or practice of Zen in premodern times. Of course, at least seven of the twelve chapters circulated in other *Shōbōgenzō* compilations (see the next subsection). The contents of these specific chapters were not unknown, but they would not have been recognized as constituting an identifiable group, standing together and worthy of special attention. When people studied Dōgen's *Shōbōgenzō*, therefore, they mainly focused their attention elsewhere.

This situation changed dramatically during the twentieth century after the discovery of the Yōkōji manuscript in 1927.[13] First, the discovery of a *Shōbōgenzō* in twelve chapters forced a re-examination of the numbering of chapters and what significance it might convey. In the modern Honzan edition of 1815 (and in its initial expanded reprints), none of the chapters are numbered. Numerical designations had been deemed mere conveniences with neither intrinsic significance nor historical basis. The Yōkōji discovery initiated a review (and eventually a rejection) of that assumption. Second, a reconsideration of the numbering of chapters directed new attention to the *Shōbōgenzō* in seventy-five chapters. Of all the premodern manuscripts of a *Shōbōgenzō* with numbered chapters, only those that consist of the version in seventy-five chapters lack any chapters that duplicate ones among the newly discovered manuscript in twelve chapters. In other words, only the seventy-five-chapter and the twelve-chapter versions form a *Shōbōgenzō* combination without redundancies. Further investigations forced scholars to recognize the centrality of the *Shōbōgenzō* in seventy-five chapters. Third, the discovery

---

[12] *Ryūsen Tsūgen zenji sōki* 龍泉通幻禪師喪記 (1392); in ZSZ.2.Shingi 清規, 25–35.

[13] Kohō Chisan 孤峰智燦 (1879–1967), the abbot of Yōkōji, discovered the manuscript in 1927, and, in 1931, Nagahisa Gakusui announced the discovery and included a transcription of the previously unknown chapter, "One Hundred Gateways to the Illumination of the Dharma" ("Ippyakuhachi hōmyōmon") in his *Shōbōgenzō chūkai shinshū* 正法眼藏註解新集. Finally, in 1955, Kohō Chisan published a full account of the discovery (see Akitsu 2019a, 153).

of a *Shōbōgenzō* in twelve chapters prompted greater awareness of the idea that Dōgen's *Shōbōgenzō* remained an unfinished work in progress. This awareness raised additional questions: How had it evolved? What were Dōgen's editorial goals? Had those goals also evolved? In short, since the 1950s, when scholars first began studying it, the *Shōbōgenzō* in twelve chapters has revolutionized scholarly understandings of the *Shōbōgenzō*, the ways that scholars study it, and the key questions they ask about it. This revolution arose as much from the mere fact that it exists as from its contents. At the same time, because traditionally nothing was known about either its existence or its contents, it also has given rise to much speculation and conjecture.

Probably the most contentious discussion concerns the possible date (or dates) of the *Shōbōgenzō* in twelve chapters.[14] As is also the case for the *Shōbōgenzō* in seventy-five chapters, it contains colophons by Dōgen alone. It does not include any of Ejō's scribal notes. Unlike the seventy-five chapters, most of which were dated by Dōgen, only two of the twelve chapters bear dates assigned by Dōgen: "The Merit of the Kāṣāya" (1240) and "The Eight Understandings of the Great Person" (1253).

At first glance the evidence seems split. One chapter is dated rather early (1240) while the other chapter is very late, the year of Dōgen's death. None of the other chapters have dates. By way of comparison, within the *Shōbōgenzō* in seventy-five chapters, only five chapters date from before 1240, six chapters bear dates within 1240, and all other chapters date from subsequent years (but none as late as 1253). In terms of content and format, the first ten chapters of the *Shōbōgenzō* in twelve chapters share many stylistic and thematic similarities. Moreover, seven of these first ten can also be found in another compilation, known as the *Shōbōgenzō* in sixty chapters (discussed in the next subsection). Here, it suffices to note merely that the *Shōbōgenzō* in sixty chapters is an earlier, rough draft of the entire manuscript, which subsequently was split apart to form the basis for both the version in seventy-five chapters and the version in twelve chapters. Based on these factors, it seems reasonable to assume that the first ten chapters were all initially composed sometime before 1245, during the first half of the same decade in which were composed the bulk of the chapters for the *Shōbōgenzō* in seventy-five (and in sixty) chapters. (Dates of chapters are discussed in Section II, Vicissitudes.)

---

[14] Regarding the many controversies over possible dates of the *Shōbōgenzō*, see Heine 2006.

The last two chapters, "One Hundred Gateways to the Illumination of the Dharma" and "Eight Understandings of the Great Person," differ from the others in style and content. Each of them consists of extended quotations from a single Chinese Buddhist scripture. Dōgen provides no context for the quotation. He makes no effort to render the Chinese passages into a Japanese idiom, provides no explanation nor commentary. Each chapter concludes with only a very brief exhortation. These two chapters seem to consist of Chinese source material that had been selected for use in future essays — essays that Dōgen never lived to write. It seems reasonable to assume that both date from the same late period, just before Dōgen became too ill for literary exertions.

This last assumption is confirmed by Ejō's scribal notes for chapter 12, which were reproduced in the *Kenzeiki* 建撕記 (*Kenzei's Chronicle*; 1452). Kenzei 建撕 (1415–1474), an abbot of Eiheiji (the monastery founded by Dōgen), compiled an extremely influential documentary hagiography of Dōgen. Because his account continues several generations beyond Dōgen with a history of Eiheiji, I refer to it as a chronicle (not as a biography). In recent decades, scholars have discovered a great many of the original documents that Kenzei excerpted in his chronicle. The newly discovered documents generally (but not always) confirm the accuracy of Kenzei's quotations. Ejō's scribal note for chapter twelve is also attested by one other (albeit later) textual witness (i.e., the Himitsu manuscript discussed in the next subsection).

In his scribal notes for chapter 12, Ejō does not merely recount the usual details (i.e., by whom, where, and when copied) but also explains the circumstances surrounding the composition itself. He states that previously Dōgen had informed him of the following plan for the *Shōbōgenzō*. First, Dōgen would revise his previously composed chapters of the *Shōbōgenzō* in Japanese script (*kana* 假名). And that had been accomplished. Next, Dōgen would compose new chapters so that, if combined together, there would be a total of one hundred chapters. Alas, Dōgen became ill, and his illness gradually worsened. After composing a draft for this chapter, number twelve, his work on the drafts came to an end. Ejō's notes conclude with a lamentation over the misfortune that Dōgen died without having achieved his goal of a total of one hundred chapters (*Kenzeiki*, pp. 79–80).[15]

---

[15] Kawamura (1991, 408–410) analyzes Ejō's remarks as found in multiple manuscript versions of *Kenzeiki*.

Prior to the 1927 discovery of a *Shōbōgenzō* in twelve chapters, the only line in Ejō's scribal note that received much notice was his report that Dōgen had intended to compose a *Shōbōgenzō* in one hundred chapters. In the centuries after Dōgen's death, many people would attempt to accomplish this goal on his behalf. After the 1927 discovery, scholars soon recognized the correspondence between Ejō's scribal note and the fact that it refers to the twelfth chapter of the previously unknown and unsuspected *Shōbōgenzō* in twelve chapters. In 1953, Ōkubo Dōshū convincingly demonstrated that Dōgen's reference to his having already revised his "previously composed chapters of the *Shōbōgenzō* in Japanese script" must refer to his *Shōbōgenzō* in seventy-five chapters.[16] But the significance of the *Shōbōgenzō* in twelve chapters and its relationship to the seventy-five chapters remained undefined. At that time (the 1950s) and for the next several decades, the Honzan edition provided the only text of the *Shōbōgenzō* available for examination. Without access to the original manuscripts, it was impossible to deduce how Dōgen might have revised or rewritten his chapters. Even the chronology of the *Shōbōgenzō* in seventy-five chapters remained unknown. This lack of hard facts provided fertile grounds for speculation. Scholars suggested many alternative theories. Some people, for example, proposed that after finishing the *Shōbōgenzō* in seventy-five chapters at an early date, Dōgen must have composed twelve new chapters at a late date. Some people imagined that what Dōgen really said was that he had abandoned his previously composed seventy-five chapters and henceforth intended to write one hundred completely new chapters. Neither of these propositions can be supported by the manuscript evidence available today. Even though a precise dating for every chapter remains unattainable, it is undeniable that in chronological terms there is much overlap between the *Shōbōgenzō* in seventy-five chapters and the one in twelve chapters. Both compilations incorporate chapters from across the entire span of Dōgen's teaching career.

---

[16] Ōkubo (1953, 312–313, 345–346); Ōkubo (1966, 282–2833, 312); also see Bodiford (2019a, 246–252).

# 3. Supplementary Chapters Historically Associated with the *Shōbōgenzō*

The *Shōbōgenzō* in seventy-five chapters (category 1 above) and the *Shōbōgenzō* in twelve chapters (category 2 above) together comprise the eighty-seven chapters that Dōgen selected for inclusion in his *Shōbōgenzō*. He personally edited and revised all the seventy-five chapters and revised at least one of the twelve chapters. The story of these chapters reflects the development of the *Shōbōgenzō* during its author's lifetime.

After Dōgen's death in 1253, the *Shōbōgenzō* enjoyed a long afterlife. It grew and developed, and its contents evolved in ways not imagined by Dōgen. The evolved forms of the *Shōbōgenzō* still live even today. The supplementary chapters in this section reflect this afterlife. Although the accrual of additional chapters occurred over many centuries at the hands of subsequent actors, the chapters themselves (or at least most of them) were composed by Dōgen. And the karmic roots (i.e., underlying causes) for their incorporation into the *Shōbōgenzō* began with Dōgen's own organic process of revising and compiling his *Shōbōgenzō*. To understand the nature of these supplementary chapters and why people in subsequent centuries thought that they belonged in the *Shōbōgenzō*, it helps to understand how Dōgen wrote and compiled the *Shōbōgenzō*. Since this topic (as well as Dōgen's authorship of the *Shōbōgenzō* in relationship to key events in his life) is discussed in detail elsewhere (Section II, Vicissitudes; and Table 12), here I present only a brief schematic overview of the key steps in its textual evolution.

Dōgen's composition of the *Shōbōgenzō* involved a multistep process with identifiable stages of development. Below, I will summarize the individual steps and their implications. Then, I will consider how this complex process propelled the further evolution of the *Shōbōgenzō* in the centuries after Dōgen's death.

STEP 1. Hints regarding Dōgen's authorial goals exist in three important early compositions: the *Shōbōgenzō* in Chinese script and two essays in Japanese: *Talk on Pursuing the Way* (*Bendōwa*) and "The Realized Kōan" ("Genjō kōan"). The first composition has a preface dated 1235, while the two essays are dated 1231 and 1233, respectively; but all three are related. The text in Chinese consists of an anthology of three hundred Chinese Chan stories (kōans). In its earliest extant manuscript (which copied a rough draft that predates the 1235 final version), all

*Introduction to the* SHŌBŌGENZŌ: *3. Associated supplementary chapters*     29

the Chinese kōans include interlinear Japanese morphosyntactic marks that indicate how each sentence can be vocalized as Japanese. Each of the two essays in Japanese quotes a kōan from this anthology (number 122, "Xuanze: Bingding Youth," in *Bendōwa* and number 123, "Baoche: No Place Not Reached," in "Genjō kōan"), but the quotations appear in Japanese, not Chinese. With his *Shōbōgenzō* in Chinese script, Dōgen unequivocally embraces the title "treasury of the true dharma eye" for the whole of Buddhism, which he identifies with Chinese kōan discourse. In *Bendōwa*, he introduces himself and proclaims his mission to disseminate the "treasury of the true dharma eye" to Japan. He quotes the "Xuanze: Bingding Youth" kōan to assert that Buddhism is neither book learning nor intellectual speculation. "The Realized Kōan" then analyzes the "Baoche: No Place Not Reached" kōan to illustrate how genuine Buddhist practice under the guidance of a proper teacher embodies the whole of Buddhism. Taken together these three compositions suggest that Dōgen's decision to compose a *Shōbōgenzō* in Japanese script could not have been the result of mere happenstance.

STEP 2. Nonetheless, according to the dates of the chapters as specified in Dōgen's colophons to the *Shōbōgenzō* in seventy-five chapters, he did not begin writing in earnest until almost a decade later. These colophons state that Dōgen composed three chapters in 1239, six chapters in 1240, seven chapters in 1241, fifteen chapters in 1242, and so forth. For several of these chapters Dōgen's initial rough drafts survive, the handwriting for some of which has traditionally been attributed to Dōgen's hand or that of one of his disciples, especially Ejō. These manuscripts either have no colophon or only a minimal colophon. Dōgen's colophon for a draft of the chapter "Buddha Nature" ("Busshō"), for example, states only the date (1241) and the place of composition. His colophon for a draft of the chapter "Sustained Practice" ("Gyōji") likewise states only the date (1242) and place of composition. Neither manuscript bears the title "Shōbōgenzō" nor a chapter number. These surviving manuscripts (and other similar rough drafts) suggest that Dōgen wrote many chapters (perhaps as independent essays?) before he undertook the task of compiling them into a single work entitled *Shōbōgenzō* with numbered chapters.

STEP 3. After Dōgen had composed a sufficient number of chapters, he compiled them into an initial draft version of the *Shōbōgenzō* in sixty chapters. After Dōgen's death, his disciple Ejō wrote out a clean copy of the *Shōbōgenzō* in sixty chapters. Ejō's holograph does not survive,

30 DŌGEN'S *SHŌBŌGENZŌ* VOLUME VIII

but one very reliable medieval copy of it does (the Tōunji manuscript of 1510). Today, scholars can compare in detail an intact medieval manuscript of the *Shōbōgenzō* in sixty chapters with intact medieval manuscripts of its seventy-five-chapter and twelve-chapter descendants. In the initial sixty-chapter compilation every chapter is numbered sequentially, beginning with *Shōbōgenzō* 1, "The Realized Kōan." Forty-four of the chapters include colophons by Dōgen. Forty-three chapters (not always the same ones) include scribal notes by Ejō. This initial compilation served as the basis for Dōgen's final versions of the *Shōbōgenzō* in seventy-five chapters and the one in twelve chapters. Many of the individual chapters in the sixty-chapter version are textually identical to their counterparts in the seventy-five- or twelve-chapter compilations. But sometimes they differ in content. In the medieval manuscripts, these differences resulted neither from errors nor deliberate emendations by their scribes (as had been supposed by the editors of the Honzan edition). Rather they reflect additions and deletions made by Dōgen himself when he revised some of the sixty chapters for inclusion in his two subsequent compilations.

STEPS 4, 5, AND 6. To produce his final *Shōbōgenzō*, Dōgen split the sixty chapters into two groups, added thirty additional chapters, discarded two chapters, revised many chapters, and rearranged the results into the seventy-five- and twelve-chapter compilations that survive today. If we count the two discarded chapters, Dōgen actually composed initial versions of ninety chapters — only ten short of his goal of one hundred. Each one of these three steps consists of very different authorial and editorial processes. It is important to recognize their distinct features. Yet no single one of them occurred in isolation without the other two. In practice, they entailed one another. For this reason, we should analyze them as simultaneous processes. As we will see (in Section II, Vicissitudes: The *Shōbōgenzō* in Sixty Chapters and Its Descendants), Dōgen's colophons likewise provide overlapping dates.

The versions of the *Shōbōgenzō* in twelve, sixty, and seventy-five chapters constitute substantive compilations. In other words, all three were edited and arranged by their author. All subsequent expanded or comprehensive versions of the *Shōbōgenzō* with additional chapters constitute derived compilations. They derive from the author's originals but deviate from them. Within a short time after Dōgen's death, the corpora of his surviving *Shōbōgenzō* materials included his clean copy of the *Shōbōgenzō* in seventy-five chapters, Ejō's clean copy of the *Shōbōgenzō*

*Introduction to the* SHŌBŌGENZŌ: 3. *Associated supplementary chapters* 31

in sixty chapters (with his scribal notes), as well as many fragmentary copies of discarded rough drafts in the handwriting of Dōgen and his disciples. There must also have been manuscripts of the *Shōbōgenzō* in twelve chapters, perhaps even a clean copy in Dōgen's hand and one by Ejō with his scribal notes. But our knowledge of the manuscript history of the *Shōbōgenzō* in twelve chapters awaits the discovery of additional manuscripts now lost.

The production of expanded versions of the *Shōbōgenzō* in subsequent centuries reflects a lack of knowledge about Dōgen's compositional process described above and resulted from the failures of later scribes to understand the relationships among these surviving corpora. Scribes sought to preserve a comprehensive *Shōbōgenzō* by adding chapters from the sixty-chapter version to the one in seventy-five chapters (or vice-versa: adding chapters from the one in seventy-five to the one in sixty chapters). Some scribes also included other essays that had never previously been included in the *Shōbōgenzō*. Over time, they succeeded in producing so many new versions of the *Shōbōgenzō* that scholars now commonly refer to these variations by their total number of chapters (e.g., 78, 84, 89, 90, 95, or 96 chapters, etc.). No one fully understands the precise evolution of each of these variations. Even today, even after so many textual discoveries during the past century, much of the manuscript tradition remains unknown and only vaguely understood. Moreover, numerous findings of what can be known have not been well disseminated. Accurate information has not always displaced the many unsubstantiated conjectures and outdated conclusions that remain in circulation.

In concrete terms, the nine "supplementary chapters" historically associated with the *Shōbōgenzō* consist of the nine chapters included within the 1815 Honzan edition (the headquarters edition) that do not belong among the eighty-seven chapters (75 + 12) that we now recognize as those Dōgen selected for inclusion in his *Shōbōgenzō*. They constitute the third compilation of *Shōbōgenzō* chapters. Their titles and their corresponding chapter numbers in the 1815 Honzan edition appear in Table 1. As revealed by this table, they are arranged in an order that reflects their numerical sequence in the Honzan edition. (The Himitsu manuscript and its peculiar chapter numbering is discussed below and illustrated in Table 5.)

| Supplementary Chapters | Chapter position in the Honzan edition |
|---|---|
| 1. Talk on Pursuing the Way (xylograph edition of 1788) | 1 |
| 2. Procedures for the Hall of Gathered Clouds (Kōfukuji manuscript) | 5 |
| 3. The *Lotus* Turns the *Lotus* (sixty-chapter *Shōbōgenzō*) | 17 |
| 4. The Mind Cannot Be Got (or "Latter Mind Cannot be Got"; Himitsu manuscript) | 19 |
| 5. The Four Attractions of the Bodhisattva (sixty-chapter *Shōbōgenzō*) | 45 |
| 6. Instructions to the Administration Cloister (*Kenzeiki*) | 81 |
| 7. Only Buddhas with Buddhas (Himitsu manuscript) | 91 |
| 8. Birth and Death (Himitsu manuscript) | 92 |
| 9. The Way of the Buddhas (or "The Mind of the Way"; Himitsu manuscript) | 93 |

Table 1. Supplementary Chapters, Table of Contents

The inclusion of the above nine chapters in the Honzan edition resulted from actions of three key Sōtō clerics: Taiyō Bonsei 太容梵清 (1378–1439?), Manzan Dōhaku 卍山道白 (1636–1714), and Handō Kōzen 版橈晃全 (1627–1693).[17] Each of these individuals produced an influential version of the *Shōbōgenzō*, which nowadays are usually identified by their names: the Bonsei version in eighty-four chapters; Manzan version in eighty-nine chapters; and the Kōzen version in ninety-five (or ninety-six) chapters. Each new version incorporated its predecessor(s). This progression culminated in the Honzan edition of the *Shōbōgenzō*.

In 1419, Taiyō Bonsei 太容梵清 (who in 1422 would become abbot of Sōjiji) copied a *Shōbōgenzō* in eighty-four chapters, consisting of the usual seventy-five chapters plus an appended supplemental section of nine extra chapters. All nine chapters came from the *Shōbōgenzō* in sixty chapters and (in Bonsei's version) retained their original chapter numbers. It is significant that Bonsei did not make use of the *Shōbōgenzō* in twelve chapters nor any the miscellaneous chapters that now exist at Eiheiji (i.e., the Himitsu manuscript, discussed below). These omissions suggest that by Bonsei's time, the twelve chapters had already dropped

---

[17] See Akitsu 2017 regarding the career and likely dates of Taiyō Bonsei.

*Introduction to the* SHŌBŌGENZŌ: *3. Associated supplementary chapters*   33

out of circulation, and that at Eiheiji the miscellaneous chapters had not yet been collected or bound together. Bonsei's original 1419 handwritten manuscript still partially exists, although it was heavily damaged by fire in 1814. Prior to the fire, it served as the model for subsequent attempts to compile a comprehensive *Shōbōgenzō.*

In 1686, Manzan Dōhaku 卍山道白 (1636–1714) copied Bonsei's eighty-four chapters and revised them. Manzan re-arranged them into a more or less chronological sequence, re-numbered the chapters, and edited them. Then he appended a new supplemental section of five extra chapters, for an overall total of eighty-nine. Manzan's supplement included "Talk on Pursuing the Way" (*Bendōwa*; a previously unknown work without provenance), two brief sets of regulations, and two — only two — chapters from the *Shōbōgenzō* in twelve chapters. Manzan must have found a fragmentary copy of that compilation.

Finally, in 1693, Handō Kōzen 版橈晃全 (1625–1693), an abbot at Eiheiji, compiled an even larger *Shōbōgenzō* in ninety-five (or ninety-six) chapters based on Manzan's version. Kōzen retained the chronological format but revised the sequence of chapters. He incorporated into the main sequence not just Manzan's five supplemental chapters but also an additional six (or seven) chapters from a miscellaneous group that had been collected at Eiheiji. Kōzen's chronological arrangement of ninety-five chapters provided the format for the Honzan edition of 1815.

More than a century separates Kōzen's arrangement from the Honzan edition because, in 1722, all copying, compiling, printing, or distributing of the *Shōbōgenzō* was banned by a government decree.[18] This decree would not be lifted until 1796, after Gentō Sokuchū 玄透即中 (1729–1807) became abbot of Eiheiji. In 1787 and 1788, before Sokuchū went to Eiheiji, he had violated the law by printing "Sustained Practice" ("Gyōji") and *Bendōwa*. His imprimatur on the printed edition of *Bendōwa* served to authenticate that work (until the discovery of new sources in the twentieth century allowed scholars to prove its authenticity).

As mentioned above, the initial model for a comprehensive *Shōbōgenzō* began as the seventy-five chapters plus supplements (plus 9, plus 5, and plus 6 for a total of 20 extra chapters). Only two of those extra chapters can be traced directly to the *Shōbōgenzō* in twelve chapters. Nonetheless nine more (a total of 11 out of 20) have indirect counterparts in the twelve-chapter compilation: seven of the nine chapters that

---

[18]   Regarding the Honzan edition, also see Supplement 2: The *Shōbōgenzō* Honzan Edition Today.

Bonsei added from the *Shōbōgenzō* in sixty chapters, as well as two of the six miscellaneous chapters added by Kōzen. These relationships are outlined in tables 2, 3, and 4 below:

The *Shōbōgenzō* in eighty-four chapters (1418) by Taiyō Bonsei, in relationship to the twelve-chapter *Shōbōgenzō*

Based on the 75-chapter *Shōbōgenzō*, numbered 1 to 75, with an appendix of 9 chapters from the 60-chapter version:

| 60-chapter *Shōbōgenzō* numbers | 12-chapter *Shōbōgenzō* counterparts |
| --- | --- |
| 8. Karma of the Three Times | no. 8 (revised version) |
| 12. The *Lotus* Turns the *Lotus* | — |
| 28. The Four Attractions of the Bodhisattva | — |
| 39. Four Horses | no. 9 |
| 34. Bringing Forth the Mind of Bodhi | no. 4 |
| 41. The Merit of the Kāṣāya | no. 3 |
| 58. The Merit of Leaving Home | no. 1 |
| 59. Offerings to the Buddhas | no. 5 |
| 60. Refuge in the Three Treasures | no. 6 |

Table 2. *Shōbōgenzō* in Eighty-four Chapters

As illustrated by Table 2, the *Shōbōgenzō* in eighty-four chapters copied by Bonsei consisted of two distinct sections. The main section consists of the standard seventy-five chapters in their standard order. The supplementary section consists of chapters not found among the seventy-five but found in Dōgen's initial compilation in sixty chapters. All these supplementary chapters were placed together in their own separate section and retained their original chapter numbers. They consist of the two discarded chapters (numbers 12, 28), as well as the seven chapters that Dōgen had reassigned to the *Shōbōgenzō* in twelve chapters. Dōgen had revised one chapter, "Karma of the Three Times" ("Sanjigō") when he reassigned it. The fact that Bonsei's copy included the earlier, unrevised version of "Karma of the Three Times" strongly suggests that the *Shōbōgenzō* in twelve chapters had become unavailable by the early 1400s. If Bonsei had known of the twelve-chapter *Shōbōgenzō*, he would not have needed to copy this hybrid version in eighty-four chapters.

Introduction to the SHŌBŌGENZŌ: 3. Associated supplementary chapters    35

The *Shōbōgenzō* in eighty-nine chapters (1686) by Manzan Dōhaku,
in relationship to the twelve-chapter *Shōbōgenzō*

Based on the 84-chapter *Shōbōgenzō*, revised, re-arranged, and renumbered,
with an appendix of 5 supplemental chapters:

| *Supplement* | *Original source* |
| --- | --- |
| 1. Talk on Pursuing the Way | ? |
| 2. Procedures for the Hall of Gathered Clouds | Kōfukuji temple manuscript |
| 3. Instructions to the Administration Cloister | *Kenzeiki* excerpt |
| 4. Receiving the Precepts | 12-chapter *Shōbōgenzō* |
| 5. The Eight Understandings of the Great Person | 12-chapter *Shōbōgenzō* |

Table 3. *Shōbōgenzō* in Eighty-nine Chapters

As shown in Table 3, the *Shōbōgenzō* in eighty-nine chapters compiled by Manzan consisted of two distinct sections. The main section
reproduces the same eighty-four chapters found in Bonsei's copy but
mixed together and numbered consecutively from 1 to 84. By Manzan's
time, the significance of the chapter numbers either had been forgotten or no longer seemed important. The supplementary section consists of an eclectic (or random) group of chapters from several different sources. It includes two of the five new chapters that Dōgen had
composed specifically for the *Shōbōgenzō* in twelve chapters. Manzan
re-arranged and renumbered those chapters. His version of "The Eight
Understandings of the Great Person" ("Hachi dainin gaku") — like the
one in the twelve-chapter *Shōbōgenzō* — lacks the scribal note by Ejō
found in *Kenzeiki* and attached to the version of this chapter that is found
in the Himitsu manuscript. Evidently, Manzan derived it directly from
the twelve-chapter *Shōbōgenzō*. Manzan's writings, however, contain no
mention of a *Shōbōgenzō* in twelve chapters. This lacuna suggests that
he did not have access to a complete manuscript of the twelve-chapter
version (Kawamura 1991, 409–410).

# 36    DŌGEN'S *SHŌBŌGENZŌ* VOLUME VIII

The *Shōbōgenzō* in ninety-six chapters (1693) by Handō Kōzen,
in relationship to the twelve-chapter *Shōbōgenzō*

Based on the 89-chapter *Shōbōgenzō*, revised, re-arranged, and renumbered,
with an additional seven chapters (according to the Kazan manuscript):

| Title | Original source | 12-chapter Shōbōgenzō |
|---|---|---|
| 16. Latter Mind Cannot be Got | Himitsu, chapter 8 (1.4) | — |
| 87. Birth and Death | Himitsu, chapter — (1.2) | — |
| 88. The Mind of the Way (Dōshin) | Himitsu, chapter — (1.7) | — |
| 89. Deep Faith in Cause and Effect | Himitsu, chapter 87 (1.5) | no. 7 |
| 90. The Bhikṣu of the Fourth Dhyāna | Himitsu, chapter 10 (3.2) | no. 10 |
| 93. Only Buddhas with Buddhas | Himitsu, chapter — (3.7) | — |
| 94. To Mount the Seat (Shinzo) | *Taihakuhōki* 太白峰記 | — |

Table 4. *Shōbōgenzō* in Ninety-six Chapters

As shown in Table 4, Kōzen included a spurious chapter, number 94,
"To Mount the Seat" ("Shinzo" 陞座). Interestingly, he placed it before
number 95, "Talk on Pursuing the Way" ("Bendōwa"). The fact that he
placed these two chapters together (ignoring the early date assigned to
"Bendōwa") might indicate that he considered both as being of doubtful
provenance. "To Mount the Seat" was not included in the 1815 Honzan
edition. Nonetheless, it was included within the *Shōbōgenzō* in the 1929
edition of the *Sōtōshū zensho* (*Complete Works of the Sōtō School*). The
editors of the revised 1970 edition of the *Sōtōshū zensho* deleted "To
Mount the Seat" from the *Shōbōgenzō* and moved it to a separate volume
of supplemental and doubtful texts.[19] Kōzen cited the *Taihakuhōki* 太白
峰記 (*Records of Tiantong Monastery*) as his source for "To Mount the
Seat," but a work with that title is otherwise unknown. Most likely, it is

---

[19]    ZSZ.1.Shūgen hoi, "Shōbōgenzō shinzo" 正法眼藏陞座, 115–124. Also
see Kawamura 1978. See ESST.4.662–678 for two medieval manuscript
copies of "Shinzo," entitled "The Plum Blossom Inheritance Certificate"
("Baika shisho" 梅花嗣書).

*Introduction to the* SHŌBŌGENZŌ: *3. Associated supplementary chapters* 37

a generic designation for medieval period collections of secret initiation documents (*kirigami* 切紙; Kawamura 1978).

Table 4 also shows that the *Shōbōgenzō* in ninety-six chapters compiled by Kōzen consisted of a single, comprehensive whole without any divisions into sections. The chapters run in sequence from 1 to 96 without regard to provenance. None of the chapters come directly from the *Shōbōgenzō* in twelve chapters, but two of them come from variant versions that Kōzen, in his editorial notes, reports having found at Eiheiji as independent chapters. His notes reveal that Eiheiji did not possess a copy of the *Shōbōgenzō* in twelve chapters. Nothing in Kōzen's notes suggests that he was aware that such a compilation once existed or that he sought to find it (Kawamura 1991, 410).

Kōzen provides our earliest written reference to the existence of a miscellaneous group of chapters that he refers to as "bound in three volumes in the library" [of Eiheiji] (*bunzō no uchi no sansatsu ni tojitaru* 文藏のうちの三冊にとじたる; Kawamura 1991, 411). (In this quotation, the verb *tojiru*, "sewn," refers to volumes of bound books; J. *tojihon* 綴本.) He used seven miscellaneous chapters from these bound volumes to expand his compilation. In 1723, Jōten Sokuchi 承天則地 (d. 1744), a subsequent abbot of Eiheiji, ordered that these volumes be unstitched and sewn back together with new covers that would "carefully maintain them for later generations" (*hiji mitsuji shite kōdai ni tsutaubeki* 秘持密持して後代に傳うべき). Contrary to Sokuchi's intentions, several sheets of their now loose-leaf paper were lost in this process. As a result, two of its chapters ("Leaving Home" and "The Bhikṣu of the Fourth Dhyāna") became incomplete fragments (*reihon* 零本). Each bound volume in Sokuchi's version has its own table of contents. Together they list titles for twenty-eight chapters. Two of the titles and chapters are duplicates. The entire collection thus consists of twenty-six separate chapters, two of which appear twice. Its chapters are bound together in random order without regard to their respective assigned chapter number (if any). Sokuchi's words "carefully maintain" (*hiji mitsuji*) became shortened to "*himitsu*" 祕蜜 (written with the glyph for "honey" but pronounced as a synonym for "secret"), a misnomer that has been widely misunderstood to mean that the collection was a "secret" *Shōbōgenzō*. The Himitsu volumes were no more (and certainly no less) secret than usual for the contents of any storehouse at any temple in Japan. Abbots, senior temple administrators, and their assistants would have access to it, but outsiders and the general public would not.

Today, this Himitsu manuscript, with its three volumes and twenty-eight chapters, frequently appears in lists together with the *Shōbōgenzō* in twelve, in sixty, and in seventy-five chapters. Together, they form the group commonly known as the "four versions" (*shishu* 四種) of the *Shōbōgenzō*. The designation "Four Versions" might seem to imply that each of these four collections enjoys the same status. Such an implication can be misleading. It is only true to the extent that each one of these four versions includes certain chapters that cannot be found in any other source. For this reason, modern comprehensive editions of the *Shōbōgenzō* (such as this one) that include every known chapter will necessarily include chapters drawn from each of these four collections. Also, note the inconsistences in the counting of chapters. The seventy-five-chapter *Shōbōgenzō* actually contains seventy-six complete chapters (with the two chapters of "Sustained Practice" counted as one), while the so-called twenty-eight-chapter *Shōbōgenzō* in fact consists of only twenty-six separate titles.

The first three of these versions, the *Shōbōgenzō* in seventy-five, twelve, and sixty chapters, differ from the Himitsu manuscript in many fundamental respects. First and foremost, the first three versions all consist of substantive compilations that were arranged, ordered, and edited by Dōgen himself. Their provenance lies beyond doubt. Originally, each one of them would have come into existence as a clean copy written in Dōgen's own hand. The versions in seventy-five and in sixty chapters both possess robust manuscript traditions with families of supporting textual witnesses that allow scholars to evaluate their reliability and to identify their most exemplary witnesses. While the version in twelve chapters lacks an extensive manuscript tradition, a few manuscript fragments and an abundance of internal textual evidence serve to verify its pedigree and its importance. When we read or quote any passages found in these first three compilations, we can be confident that we are reading and quoting words that Dōgen actually wrote.

The Himitsu manuscript, in contrast, does not even rise to the level of a derived compilation. It was never compiled. Rather it consists of random chapters, stitched together in random order. Five of its chapters lack any chapter number. The numbered chapters are incomplete and bound together so that their chapter numbers run out of sequence, as is shown in Table 5, "Arrangement of Chapters in the Himitsu Manuscript."

Introduction to the SHŌBŌGENZŌ: 3. Associated supplementary chapters 39

## Arrangement of Chapters in the Himitsu Manuscript

| Volume 1 | Volume 2 | Volume 3 | Position |
|---|---|---|---|
| *unnumbered* | 32 | 52 | *1* |
| *unnumbered* | 34 | 10 | *2* |
| 8 | 29 | 75 | *3* |
| 8 | 45 | 47 | *4* |
| 87 | 67 | 51 | *5* |
| 42 | 69 | 42 | *6* |
| *unnumbered* | 66 | 38 | *7* |
| *unnumbered* | *unnumbered* | | *8* |
| 44 | 12 | | *9* |
| 66 | 2 | | *10* |
| 60 | | | *11* |

Table 5. Himitsu Manuscript, Chapter Numbers and Arrangement

As shown in Table 5, the chapters of the Himitsu manuscript are not in numerical order, and five of the chapters lack any numerical designation. The assigned numbers are not always reliable. For example, the manuscript contains two chapters numbered 66. The one in volume one (1.10) is titled "The Samādhi of Self Verification," while the one in volume two (2.7) is titled "Great Practice." For this reason, a specific chapter in this collection can be positively identified only by its bound position within each of the manuscript's three volumes, so that "1.4" refers to the chapter in volume 1, position 4. This positional notation follows the extrinsic designations written on the inside covers of each volume.[20] Where chapters with parallel contents also exist (among the other three versions), they reveal the general unreliability of the chapters in the Himitsu manuscript. All its chapters contain numerous copyist errors (e.g., the chapter numbered "87" should be "7").[21] In content, they preserve earlier variant drafts. Where parallel chapters do not exist, scholars

[20] ESST.1.875b, 918a, 951b. Because these positional designations are extrinsic to the chapters, they should not be conflated with the assigned chapter numbers (which are intrinsic to each chapter's identity and status).

[21] Kawamura (1991, 411) points out that the copyist(s) who produced these individual chapters could not accurately interpret the cursive calligraphy of the earlier source text(s).

40 DŌGEN'S *SHŌBŌGENZŌ* VOLUME VIII

have voiced doubts as to the authenticity of the Himitsu chapters.[22] Their provenance consists entirely of the fact that Kōzen's editorial notes state that they existed within the storeroom of Eiheiji. How or when they arrived there remains unknown and unknowable. It is frequently stated that none of the chapters in the Himitsu manuscript overlap with the *Shōbōgenzō* in sixty chapters, and that these two collections, therefore, constitute a matched pair. That assertion is incorrect. The chapter "Beyond the Buddha" ("Butsu kōjō ji") exists in both (as chapter 26 in the sixty- and seventy-five-chapter versions and as 1.1, in the Himitsu manuscript). What is correct is that the version of this chapter found in the Himitsu manuscript appears very problematic. For all the above reasons, this introduction generally refers to this collection as the "Himitsu manuscript," a designation that avoids the connotations of the term "secret" and the title "*Shōbōgenzō*," both of which can invite misunderstandings.

The supplementary chapters constitute something of a mixed bag. They come from rather disparate sources. Two chapters had been included in the *Shōbōgenzō* in sixty chapters, but Dōgen subsequently discarded them: chapter 12, "The *Lotus* Turns the *Lotus*" ("*Hokke* ten *Hokke*"), and chapter 28, "The Four Attractions of the Bodhisattva" ("Bodaisatta shishōbō"). No one knows why Dōgen discarded them or if he had intended to revise them for inclusion in his proposed one-hundred-chapter compilation. Both were included in the expanded *Shōbōgenzō* in eighty-four chapters that Taiyō Bonsei copied in 1418.

Two of the supplementary chapters consist of rules or procedures. "Procedures for the Hall of Gathered Clouds" ("Jūundō shiki") originated as a missive that Dōgen addressed to Sōshin 宗信 (dates unknown), the religious in charge of the cloud hall (a.k.a. saṃgha hall) at Kōshōji in 1239. "Instructions to the Administration Cloister" ("Jikuinmon") might have been a similar missive that Dōgen composed at Eiheiji in 1246. Neither of these documents had been composed for inclusion in the *Shōbōgenzō*. In 1686, Manzan Dōhaku (1636–1714) included both of them as supplementary chapters in his *Shōbōgenzō* in eighty-nine chapters. A copy of the first document survives by chance at Kōfukuji in Kumamoto. The second one survives as a paraphrase in *Kenzeiki*. Kenzei described the original document as having been written in Japanese, but Kenzei

---

[22] E.g., Itō Yūten (1954, 1955, 1956) regarding "Birth and Death" ("Shōji"); Kimura (2016) presents different arguments against that same chapter ("Shōji") and the Himitsu version of "Beyond the Buddha" ("Butsu kōjō ji").

*Introduction to the* SHŌBŌGENZŌ: *3. Associated supplementary chapters* 41

recorded only his own summation in Chinese. The version included in the 1815 Honzan edition renders much of Kenzei's Chinese-language summation back into Japanese syntax (i.e., *yomi-kudashi* 読み下し).

Four of the supplementary chapters, the ones from the Himitsu manuscript, are rather problematic. All four were added to the *Shōbōgenzō* in 1693 by Handō Kōzen (1625–1693). Two of them might be earlier rough drafts of other chapters that bear identical titles. In both cases, Kōzen gave them new titles to avoid comparison with the standard version of the chapters. The two chapters are (1) "The Mind Cannot Be Got" ("Shin fukatoku," Himitsu manuscript 1.3), a title identical to that of chapter 8 in the seventy-five-chapter *Shōbōgenzō*, which Kōzen therefore renamed "The Latter Mind Cannot be Got" ("Go Shin fukatoku"); and (2) "The Way of the Buddhas" ("Butsudō," Himitsu manuscript, 1.7), a title corresponding to chapter 44 in the seventy-five-chapter *Shōbōgenzō*, renamed by Kōzen "The Mind of the Way" ("Dōshin"). The other two chapters from the Himitsu manuscript, "Only Buddhas with Buddhas" ("Yui butsu yo butsu") and "Birth and Death" ("Shōji"), are even more problematic. Both exist only in the Himitsu manuscript. No other manuscript witnesses have ever been found. It is possible that they were not composed by Dōgen. If they were composed by Dōgen, then at best they present very early rough drafts of essays that Dōgen had not yet selected for revision to be included in the *Shōbōgenzō*.

Of all the supplementary chapters, "Talk on Pursuing the Way" (*Bendōwa*), stands out as being the most important and influential. It provides the earliest example of Dōgen's attempt to render a Chinese kōan in Japanese. The kōan (number 122 in the *Shōbōgenzō* in Chinese script) involves Fayan Wenyi 法眼文益 (J. Hōgen Mon'eki; 885–958) and the "Bingding Youth." This kōan encapsulates Dōgen's motivation for going to China and for his subsequent mission in Japan. Dōgen quotes this same kōan in several of his other works dating from all periods of his career. Significantly, in "Talk on Pursuing the Way" Dōgen does not just repeat the kōan in its original Chinese, but renders it as Japanese (for details, see Supplement 4). This fact demonstrates that, as early as 1231, at the very start of his teaching career, Dōgen already aspired to render Chinese vernacular Buddhism understandable to a Japanese audience by presenting it in his own Japanese idiom.

"Talk on Pursuing the Way" occupies the place of honor as chapter number 1 in the Honzan edition of the *Shōbōgenzō*, not just because of its early assigned date (1231) but also because it serves to introduce Dōgen himself (his personal background and qualifications), the contemporary situation of Buddhism in China during his training there, the key points of the Zen teaching he hopes to establish in Japan, as well has his religious goals and motives. In short, it presents an excellent introduction to Zen, to Dōgen, and to the *Shōbōgenzō* in Japanese script that Dōgen would come to write. For this reason, it is highly prized not just within Sōtō circles but by readers of all backgrounds as an essential introduction to Zen and to Japanese spirituality.

When Manzan Dōhaku added it to his *Shōbōgenzō* in eighty-nine chapters in 1686, "Talk on Pursuing the Way" lacked provenance. Many stories circulated regarding where or how he might have obtained this essay, but even today no one knows where Manzan found it. And the same is true for the 1788 xylograph edition printed by Gentō Sokuchū, which serves as the textual source for the translation in this section. Because Sokuchū subsequently became the abbot of Eiheiji, his imprimatur silenced most (but not all) doubts as to the work's authenticity. These doubts were not completely laid to rest until 1959 when the publication of an earlier draft version of "Talk on Pursuing the Way" (discussed below in the next subsection) allowed scholars to prove conclusively Dōgen's authorship of this popular introductory work.

## 4. Earlier Draft Variants of *Shōbōgenzō* Chapters

The *Shōbōgenzō* in seventy-five chapters (category 1 above) and the *Shōbōgenzō* in twelve chapters (category 2 above) comprise the eighty-seven chapters that Dōgen selected for inclusion in his *Shōbōgenzō*. He personally edited and revised all the seventy-five chapters and revised at least one of the twelve chapters. The story of the eighty-seven chapters reflects the development of the *Shōbōgenzō* during Dōgen's lifetime. The supplementary chapters (category 3 above) consist of nine additional chapters that are included in the 1815 Honzan edition. The story of these nine chapters reflects the long afterlife of the *Shōbōgenzō* following Dōgen's death. Even chapters that Dōgen himself did not select for inclusion nonetheless became part of his textual legacy and cherished by many of his readers. The impetus for incorporating extraneous chapters into the *Shōbōgenzō* derives at least in part from Dōgen's process of revising and re-ordering the chapters that he composed. Here we focus on this process. The seven variant texts in this final category each preserve

*Introduction to the* SHŌBŌGENZŌ: *4. Earlier draft variants of chapters*      43

an earlier draft of one of the chapters in the previous three categories above. They provide direct evidence regarding the crucial question of how Dōgen revised individual chapters of the *Shōbōgenzō*. They shed light on the larger issue of how the *Shōbōgenzō* — and Dōgen's teachings — evolved over time. The translations of these seven draft variants allow readers of English to investigate the precise features and characteristics of the textual evolution of the *Shōbōgenzō*.

Throughout his career, Dōgen developed his ideas, his translation techniques, his own idiom, and his teachings through the process of revising and rewriting his compositions. Sometimes, his revision is mentioned in the colophons or scribal notes attached to the chapters, such as the colophons by Dōgen for the chapters "Great Awakening" (chapter 10), "Spring and Autumn" (37), and "Washing the Face" (50) in the *Shōbōgenzō* in seventy-five chapters. Several of Ejō's scribal notes in the *Shōbōgenzō* in sixty chapters seem to imply the anticipation of a revised version, because Ejō states that he had copied Dōgen's initial draft version (*gosōhon* 御草本; *gosōan* 御草案): "Buddha Nature" (chapter 3), "Bringing Forth the Mind of Bodhi" (34), and "The Merit of the Kāṣāya" (41). In his scribal notes to "Beyond the Buddha" (26), Ejō states that he had copied an initial draft version that Dōgen had not yet revised (*misaichi gosōhon* 未再治御草本). This comment by Ejō clearly implies that normally Dōgen would have revised his draft.

In another scribal note that survives only in the Himitsu manuscript, Ejō makes this implication explicit. In a scribal colophon for "Deep Faith in Cause and Effect," chapter 7 (Himitsu manuscript, 1.5), Ejō wrote:

以御草案書寫之未及中書清、定有可再治事也、雖然書寫之

Copied this from his [i.e., Dōgen's] initial draft. He had not yet reached an intermediate draft or clean copy, and surely there would have been revisions; nevertheless, I have copied it.

When interpreted within the broader context of the extant manuscripts and of Ejō's scribal notes as a whole, it is clear that Ejō here describes Dōgen's usual method of composition. That is, Dōgen would not normally ask Ejō to copy a rough draft; but once Dōgen had revised his draft — and Ejō expected that Dōgen would always revise his draft — then Dōgen would give it to Ejō and ask him to make a clean copy. Ejō's scribal note (dated 1255) for this chapter probably can be interpreted as a lament that Dōgen's early death did not allow him to complete all the revisions he had intended for every chapter he included in the *Shōbōgenzō*. Ejō states that he nonetheless copied it in the form that Dōgen had left it.

Colophons alone cannot reveal the full extent of Dōgen's revisions. Internal textual evidence shows that in many cases the colophon and assigned date of composition might remain identical even after a chapter had been revised. The chapter "Extensive Study" ("Henzan") presents a prime example of this phenomenon. The version found in the *Shōbō-genzō* in sixty chapters (chapter 37) preserves an earlier rough draft of the version (chapter 57) found in the seventy-five-chapter compilation, even though both bear word-for-word identical colophons by Dōgen with an identical date (1244.11.27) of composition. Discrepancies between chapters in the seventy-five- or twelve-chapter versions and chapters with identical titles in other versions (especially in the *Shōbōgenzō* in sixty chapters or in the Himitsu manuscript) can be extreme. In almost every known case, these discrepancies result neither from copyist errors nor deliberate editorial manipulation — the causes that were widely assumed by scholars prior to the 1970s — but rather result from Dōgen's own hand. This internal evidence demonstrates that the eighty-seven (75 + 12) chapters represent Dōgen's final revised (or most recent) versions, while the surviving variant versions of those chapters — whether independent manuscripts or within the sixty-chapter compilation or Himitsu collection — frequently reflect earlier stages of development.

The Kawamura edition of the *Shōbōgenzō* includes seven variant texts that exemplify the variety of Dōgen's earlier draft versions (Table 6). For the sake of convenience, the earlier draft variants can be divided into three groups of three chapters each. The first group (variant chapters 1, 2, and 6) consists of initial draft chapters that survive as single, isolated manuscripts. At the time they were composed, these chapters were neither labeled nor numbered as chapters within a larger work known as the *Shōbōgenzō*. Each one survived at a location away from Eiheiji, the temple founded by Dōgen. When compared side-by-side with the final revised versions, the draft variant versions reveal the ways that Dōgen added material, deleted material, and rewrote previous passages.

*Introduction to the* SHŌBŌGENZŌ: *4. Earlier draft variants of chapters*   45

---

### Variant Chapters, Descriptive Table of Contents

---

1. Talk on Pursuing the Way (Shōbōji manuscript version, based on a 1332 copy)
   — contrast with the 1788 xylograph edition (supplementary chapter 1).
2. The Inheritance Certificate (Kōjakuji manuscript version)
   — contrast with chapter 39 in the *Shōbōgenzō* in seventy-five chapters.
3. Beyond the Buddha (Himitsu manuscript, 1.1, version)
   — contrast with chapter 26 in the *Shōbōgenzō* in seventy-five chapters.
4. Washing the Face (chapter 50 in the sixty-chapter *Shōbōgenzō*)
   — contrast with chapter 50 in the *Shōbōgenzō* in seventy-five chapters.
5. Extensive Study (chapter 37 in the sixty-chapter *Shōbōgenzō*)
   — contrast with chapter 56 in the *Shōbōgenzō* in seventy-five chapters.
6. Great Awakening (Ōsu Bunko manuscript version)
   — contrast with chapter 10 in the *Shōbōgenzō* in seventy-five chapters.
7. Karma of the Three Times (chapter 8 in the sixty-chapter *Shōbōgenzō*)
   — contrast with chapter 8 in the *Shōbōgenzō* in twelve chapters.

Table 6. Variant Chapters, Descriptive Table of Contents

The second group (variant chapter 3 along with supplementary chapters 4 and 9) consists of miscellaneous chapters collected at Eiheiji and eventually stitched together into the so-called Himitsu manuscript. Note that the label "*himitsu*" (secret) is a misnomer. It actually derives from the admonition "to carefully maintain" (*hiji mitsuji* 秘持密持) the manuscript. The variant chapters in this category include only one chapter, "Beyond the Buddha" (1.1), from the Himitsu manuscript. The previous category of Supplementary Chapters — titles found only in the Honzan edition — includes four chapters from that manuscript. Two of them, "The Mind Cannot Be Got" (1.3) and "The Way of the Buddhas" (1.7), present themselves as rough drafts of chapters (numbers 8 and 44) with identical titles in the *Shōbōgenzō* in seventy-five chapters. Upon closer examination, this version of "The Mind Cannot Be Got" also exhibits textual parallels with "Reading Other Minds" (chapter 73). Taken together, these three chapters from the Himitsu manuscript provide abundant material for a side-by-side comparison with their corresponding chapters that will enable readers to evaluate contributions of this manuscript to the *Shōbōgenzō* corpus. We should remember that chapter 28, "Making a Bow and Getting the Marrow" ("Raihai tokuzui") incorporates an appendix of supplementary material from a draft variant chapter

46 DŌGEN'S *SHŌBŌGENZŌ* VOLUME VIII

in the Himitsu manuscript (1.8). Since the chapters in the Himitsu manuscript lack individual provenance, the reputation for reliability of any one chapter cannot help but rise and fall with the others.

The third group (variant chapters 4, 5, and 7) consists of draft variant chapters found within the *Shōbōgenzō* in sixty chapters (Dōgen's initial compilation of the *Shōbōgenzō*). Over the past half century, the relative evaluation of the sixty- and seventy-five-chapter versions vis-à-vis one another has reversed. Whereas previous generations tended to regard the version in sixty chapters as the one closer to Dōgen's editorial vision, today, the weight of scholarship rests with the combination of seventy-five and twelve chapters. These three variant texts allow readers to compare the differences for themselves.

The seven earlier draft variant texts translated herein represent only about one third of the more than twenty chapters of the *Shōbōgenzō* that survive in both draft and revised versions.[23] Taken together, the seven fully represent the range of textual materials — some previously unknown, others previously mis-contextualized — that in recent decades have come to play an important role in scholarship on the *Shōbōbenzō*. Each one of these draft versions exhibits its own unique characteristics and, today, seems especially significant for reasons particular to itself. These features require individual explanation. I will begin with the three isolated manuscripts: *Talk on Pursuing the Way*, "The Inheritance Certificate," and "Great Awakening." Each one of these works relates autobiographical information about Dōgen's studies in China and the goals of his mission in Japan.

"Talk on Pursuing the Way" ("Bendōwa")

*Talk on Pursuing the Way* presents a much beloved introduction to Dōgen and his teachings. The 1788 printed edition (included as Supplementary Chapter 1), however, lacked provenance. Doubts as to its authenticity could not be allayed until the discovery of an earlier manuscript of a draft version (included here as Variant 1) in the late 1930s and its publication in 1959. The manuscript of this draft version had been copied at Yōkōji (the major monastery founded by Keizan Jōkin) in 1332 and recopied in 1515 at Shōbōji. This manuscript history provides clear provenance, but internal and external textual evidence provides the most con-

---

[23] There is no consensus regarding the precise number of chapters that exist in both draft and revised forms. Kagamishima (1989, 20–21) lists twenty-five titles, while Kawamura (1986, 544) lists forty-one titles.

*Introduction to the* SHŌBŌGENZŌ: *4. Earlier draft variants of chapters* 47

clusive proof of its authenticity. The draft manuscript of *Talk on Pursuing the Way* must be examined together with a draft manuscript of Dōgen's *Shōbōgenzō* in Chinese script.

In the 1930s, scholars became aware of an early draft copy, dated 1287, of the *Shōbōgenzō* in Chinese script preserved at the Kanazawa Bunko. It consists of a fragmentary copy of only one of three volumes. In this draft version, the Chinese script contains Japanese morphosyntactic marks (*waten* 和點) indicating how the Chinese original should be parsed, vocalized, and transcribed into Japanese.[24] This manuscript includes the kōan regarding the "Bingding Youth," which Dōgen renders as Japanese in *Talk on Pursuing the Way*. The Japanese rendition of this Chinese kōan in the Shōbōji draft version of *Talk on Pursuing the Way* clearly builds upon the Japanese marks to the same kōan in the *Shōbōgenzō* in Chinese script. The Japanese version of this same kōan in the 1788 printed edition, on the other hand, has been revised and refined in a manner that renders its appearance more Japanese than Chinese.

Taken together, the two previously unknown manuscripts with draft versions of *Talk on Pursuing the Way* and of the *Shōbōgenzō* in Chinese script allowed scholars to uncover a clear progression in Dōgen's process of translation: (1) the original Chinese text; (2) revisions to the Chinese script (logographs); (3) the insertion of Japanese morphosyntactic marks; (4) a draft rendition into Japanese script (i.e., transposing logographs and inserting phonographs); and (5) a revised, more radical rendition into Japanese script. In this final step, Japanese phonographs replace most Chinese logographs so that the original Chinese source text becomes invisible to the reader. If one examines only steps 1 and 5 side-by-side, it is difficult to demonstrate that the version in Japanese must derive from any one of several possible original Chinese versions of the kōan. When texts from all five steps appear side-by-side, however, the precise source text and the evolution in Dōgen's methods of transforming the Chinese into Japanese become demonstrable. In this way, the draft version of *Talk on Pursuing the Way* provides crucial evidence for studying how Dōgen developed his techniques for transforming Chinese dialogues into his own Japanese idiom. Moreover, the draft versions of *Talk on Pursuing the Way* and of the *Shōbōgenzō* in Chinese script thereby serve to authenticate one another. Both preserve textual parallels unique to Dōgen's expressions. These expressions inextricably link them to Dō-

---

[24]  For a general explanation of "glossed reading" (*kudoku* 訓讀), see Lurie (2011, 175–184 and 390–391 n4.5); and Whitman 2011.

gen's *Shōbōgenzō* in Japanese script. (For examples of actual sentences, see Supplement 4, "The *Shōbōgenzō* in Chinese and in Japanese scripts.")

## "The Inheritance Certificate" ("Shisho")

"The Inheritance Certificate" is the only revision of a chapter (number 39) that survives as an original manuscript in Dōgen's own handwriting. This manuscript (usually known as the "Satomi" manuscript) provides invaluable information regarding the paper, ink, handwriting, calligraphic style, colophons, and so on, of Dōgen's final revised chapters. All other chapters of the *Shōbōgenzō* extant today in Dōgen's handwriting consist of rough drafts. They survived because, once they had been replaced by newer revised versions, they could be given away as valuable mementos of Dōgen's handwriting. In this way, they became dispersed among many temples across Japan, where they were not subject to loss by a single fire. Kōjakuji (Hiroshima Prefecture) provides us with a key example of this process. This temple once owned an earlier draft of "The Inheritance Certificate" in Dōgen's own handwriting. In the seventeenth century clerics at Kōjakuji cut this chapter into individual sheets of paper that they distributed to twenty-six patrons as part of a fund-raising campaign. Fortunately, the temple first commissioned a calligraphic reproduction of the original draft manuscript and also compiled a catalog to record the names and locations for each recipient of the cuttings.

In the 1970s, Kawamura Kōdō used the information in this catalog to track down fourteen of the original cuttings. Many of them had been mounted on hanging scrolls. As scrolls, they served as objects of beauty or as calligraphic relics, not as records of Dōgen's teachings. Not all these original cuttings could be recovered intact. Some had been cut further into smaller cuttings, which in turn were distributed to persons unknown. The original manuscript consisted of 344 lines of handwriting, of which Kawamura recovered 160 lines. With the help of the seventeenth-century calligraphic reproduction, which still survives, he carefully reassembled the text of the cuttings, verified the accuracy of the calligraphic reproduction, and reconstructed the original draft manuscript. Kawamura's reconstruction serves as the basis for the translated draft variant herein. As a result, today it is now possible to compare and contrast the text of an earlier draft as written (more or less) in Dōgen's own hand with the text of a final revised version of the same chapter as written in Dōgen's own hand. Any differences must belong to Dōgen;

Introduction to the SHŌBŌGENZŌ: 4. Earlier draft variants of chapters    49

there can be no possibility of textual irregularities having been introduced by later scribes or editors.[25]

## "Great Awakening" ("Daigo")

Dōgen's colophon to the "Great Awakening" chapter — number 10 in the *Shōbōgenzō* in seventy-five chapters — assigns two dates of composition: first in 1242 and again in 1244. Until recently all known recensions of this chapter represented the same version with both dates. In 1979, Ishii Shūdō and Itō Ryūju discovered an early draft version of the "Great Awakening" chapter at the Ōsu Bunko (a library founded in the 14th century) in Nagoya. The manuscript lacks provenance: no manuscript tradition, no colophon (to assign it a place or date or composition), no chapter number, no main title to designate it as part of the *Shōbōgenzō*. Its unpolished style suggests that it must represent the 1242 draft version mentioned in the colophon to the revised chapter. Its contents extend more than twice the length of the final revised version. It comments on eight kōan episodes, while the final revised version discusses just three. These additional episodes include new details regarding Rujing's teaching of the sloughing off of body and mind (*shinjin datsuraku*). It recounts, for example, the famous story of Rujing having used this phrase when scolding a monk who dozed off — an episode that plays a crucial role in the earliest traditional biographies of Dōgen but had until now been labeled by scholars as fictitious and without textual support. It is not found in any of Dōgen's other writings. The draft version of "Great Awakening" also includes another hotly debated kōan episode involving the Sōtō patriarch Touzi Yiqing (1032–1083) and his non-Sōtō master, Fushan Fayuan (991–1067). The inclusion of their kōan dialogue in this chapter demonstrates beyond a shadow of a doubt that Dōgen accepted the legitimacy of Fushan's role as a non-Sōtō intermediary in Touzi's inheritance of a Sōtō dharma lineage. This issue became a major point of controversy in Sōtō doctrine during the seventeenth century and remains so today. These two kōan episodes represent just two examples of how this draft chapter bears directly on the validity of opposing interpretations of several passages in Dōgen's other writings. This draft chapter provides data for reconsidering the established Sōtō interpretations of key doctrines and practices.

---

[25]    For detailed information regarding the Kōjakuji manuscript and its cuttings, see Kawamura (1986, 594–596, 598–609) and ESST-S.531–550.; for facsimiles of the extant cuttings, see ESST-D.96–130.

## "Beyond the Buddha" ("Butsu kōjō ji") Himitsu Manuscript

The manuscript tradition of the *Shōbōgenzō* includes three versions of "Beyond the Buddha." Dōgen's final version can be found in the *Shōbōgenzō* in seventy-five chapters. A nearly identical version appears in Dōgen's initial compilation of the *Shōbōgenzō* in sixty chapters. Both these versions bear the same main title: "*Shōbōgenzō*, number 26." They, likewise, bear identical colophons by Dōgen with the same assigned date (1242.3.23). Another version, in the Himitsu manuscript (1.1) under consideration here, differs substantially from the other two. Only its opening section concerns the theme of "beyond the buddha." Subsequent sections address other topics, seemingly only loosely related to one another. Some passages seem parallel to other chapters, such as "Studying the Way with Body and Mind" ("Shinjin gakudō"), "Deportment of the Practicing Buddha" ("Gyōbutsu igi"), "The Old Buddha Mind" ("Kobutsushin"), "Radiance" ("Kōmyō") and "Avalokiteśvara ("Kannon"). It is difficult to know what to make of this bricolage. Some commentators have interpreted all these discussions as elucidating the meaning of "beyond the buddha." Others suggest, perhaps more persuasively, that the text represents, not a coherent essay, but a collection of notes, left behind by Dōgen and copied together at some later time under the title of the opening topic. More recently, Wakayama Yūkō (2015; 2016) compared the Himitsu version of "Beyond the Buddha" to a dharma talk (*hōgo*, number 11; DZZ.4:160–164) in Dōgen's recorded sayings that rambles over a very similar aggregation of disconnected topics. Could this chapter and corresponding dharma talk represent an initial exploration of topics that Dōgen later elaborated in subsequent individual chapters? Maybe, but maybe not. Kimura Kiyotaka (2016) cautions that "Beyond the Buddha" includes textual parallels to medieval texts in the Nichiren tradition that postdate Dōgen. All that can be said with certainty is that "Beyond the Buddha" requires further investigation.

## Variants from the *Shōbōgenzō* in Sixty Chapters

Comparisons between the *Shōbōgenzō* in sixty-chapters and the versions of the same chapters in the twelve- or seventy-five-chapter compilations can provide fundamental evidence regarding the evolution of the *Shōbōgenzō*. Dōgen selected all of these chapters for inclusion within his *Shōbōgenzō*. And he did so twice. When he revised them, he was self-consciously revising the *Shōbōgenzō*, a work that he himself regarded as his legacy. Even minor changes to these chapters, therefore, can reveal formative aspects of his thought processes and revising techniques. Previously many scholars have attempted to analyze the evolution of the *Shōbōgenzō* based on the assigned dates of chapters according to Dōgen's colophons or Ejō's scribal notes. That approach can achieve only limited (or even misleading) results, because Dōgen sometimes left the dates unchanged even after revising the contents of a chapter. The evolution of chapters from their initial versions in sixty chapters to their revised versions in the twelve- or seventy-five-chapter compilations awaits the attention and analyses of future scholars.

## "Washing the Face" ("Senmen")

"Washing the Face" is chapter number 50 in both the *Shōbōgenzō* in sixty chapters and the version in seventy-five chapters. Dōgen's colophon for this chapter in the sixty-chapter version states that Dōgen initially composed it in 1239 at Kōshōji, outside of Kyoto and subsequently revised it in 1243 at Kippōji, in Echizen. Dōgen's colophon for this chapter in the seventy-five-chapter version mentions the first two dates and then adds a third date for this version: 1250 at Eiheiji, in Echizen. The fact that the sixty-chapter version mentions only the first two dates, but not the third, helps establish that Dōgen compiled the *Shōbōgenzō* in seventy-five chapters subsequently to the version in sixty-chapters. His colophon demonstrates that Dōgen was still in the process of editing and revising the *Shōbōgenzō* in seventy-five chapters as late as the year 1250. The draft variant and final versions of "Washing the Face" present the same basic teachings, but also exhibit many, sometimes quite interesting, differences in style and content. Comparison of these two versions, therefore, provides excellent examples of how Dōgen edited and revised his *Shōbōgenzō* chapters during the late 1240s and early 1250s — the period when he put his final touches on the *Shōbōgenzō* in seventy-five chapters.

## "Extensive Study" ("Henzan")

"Extensive Study" is designated chapter 37 in the *Shōbōgenzō* in sixty chapters and as chapter 57 in the seventy-five-chapter compilation. Dōgen gave both versions identical colophons with an identical date and location of composition: 1244 below Mount Zenjihō. Although the dates are identical, the final version must have been subsequently revised. In this example — as is also the case for many other chapters — the

52 DŌGEN'S *SHŌBŌGENZŌ* VOLUME VIII

assigned date of composition pertains only to the initial draft. It does not indicate when the composition was completed. There are quite a few differences between the two texts, but for the most part Dōgen's revisions consist of stylistic improvements that do not substantially change the content. These changes, therefore, reveal Dōgen's efforts as a wordsmith with a keen interest in language.

"Karma of the Three Times" ("Sanjigō")

"Karma of the Three Times" is designated chapter 8 both in the *Shōbōgenzō* in sixty chapters and in the twelve-chapter compilation. It presents a rare example of a chapter in the *Shōbōgenzō* in twelve chapters for which an earlier draft variant and a revised version both survive. Neither version has a colophon by Dōgen with an assigned date of composition, however. This lacuna suggests that Dōgen had not yet completed the final touches to this chapter. Of the seven chapters from the sixty-chapter compilation that Dōgen set aside for inclusion in his expanded *Shōbōgenzō* (i.e., the twelve-chapter compilation), this is the only chapter that Ejō copied during Dōgen's lifetime, albeit only a few months before Dōgen's death. The fact that Ejō made a copy when he did might indicate that at that time Dōgen was feeling well enough to write and had intended to work further on this chapter. But without additional collaborative evidence this inference cannot carry more weight than mere speculation.

In contrast to the rather extensive revisions Dōgen made to "Washing the Face" and "Extensive Study," he made relatively few changes to "Karma of the Three Times." The draft variant is somewhat shorter than the revised version and lacks, most notably, the sustained criticism of Chan Master Jingcen of Changsha that Dōgen added to the end of the revised version. Some people have interpreted this criticism as evidence that Dōgen revised his moral compass. It must be noted, however, that the same criticism can be found in Dōgen's *Hōkyōki* (*Baoqing Records*; DZZ.7:20), which dates to 1225, when Dōgen was in China. Finally, it should be noted that the draft variant of "Karma of the Three Times" from the *Shōbōgenzō* in sixty chapters is the version that appears in the Honzan edition as chapter 83. The editors of the 1815 Honzan edition did not yet know of and did not have access to the *Shōbōgenzō* in twelve chapters. This draft variant, therefore, could just as easily have been included among the previous category of supplementary chapters.

The chapters in each of the four categories discussed above differ in provenance, in their significance within Dōgen's *oeuvre*, and in the magnitude of their historical influence. The *Shōbōgenzō* in seventy-five chapters provides us our most reliable record of Dōgen's teachings. Until it was displaced by the 1815 Honzan edition, it was the *Shōbōgenzō* that exerted the strongest influence on Dōgen's disciples and the religious institutions that they and their disciples established across Japan. The *Shōbōgenzō* in twelve chapters presents an unfinished vision that extols the virtues of Buddhist monasticism. Although it did not exert much influence in premodern times, its discovery in the twentieth century sparked a major reassessment of Dōgen's teachings, his legacy, and our understanding of the textual structure of his *Shōbōgenzō*. The supplementary chapters present a disparate variety of materials that came to be included in the 1815 Honzan edition. They include draft variants that Dōgen had discarded, rules or procedures, as well as otherwise unknown chapters from the Himitsu manuscript. One of them — "Talk on Pursuing the Way" — stands out as a widely beloved and highly influential introduction to Dōgen and his teachings. Finally, the translated draft variants provide fundamental evidence regarding the thought processes and revising techniques that shaped the evolution of the *Shōbōgenzō*. Taken together — especially in light of the historically accurate textual edition upon which they are based — these chapters present the most complete and reliable version of the *Shōbōgenzō* available in translation.

## II. Vicissitudes

Any well-considered reading, analysis, and understanding of the *Shōbō-genzō* requires the evaluation of numerous factors, most of which lie beyond the scope of this introduction. Due to limitations of space, we can describe here only textual features that relate directly to the translation itself. Above, Section I — The *Shōbōgenzō* — focused on the contents, structure, provenance, and manuscript traditions of the various chapters or categories of chapters upon which the translation is based. Here, Section II — Vicissitudes — explores the historical roots that gave rise to categories of chapters discussed above. Subsection 5, the *Shōbōgenzō* in sixty chapters and its descendants, focuses on the textual evidence regarding how the three compilations of the *Shōbōgenzō* in sixty, in seventy-five, and in twelve chapters relate to one another. Subsection 6, Dōgen and His *Shōbōgenzō*, focuses on key episodes in Dōgen's life that relate to his *Shōbōgenzō* and its interpretation.

### 5. The *Shōbōgenzō* in Sixty Chapters and Its Descendants

As explained above, today we know of three compilations of the *Shōbō-genzō* that were arranged, ordered, and edited by Dōgen himself. From the smallest to the largest, they consist of the *Shōbōgenzō* in twelve, sixty, or seventy-five chapters. These compilations can be termed substantive because they serve as the basis for all subsequent compilations (such as those in 78, 84, 89, 90, 95, or 96 chapters, etc.) derived from them.

Prior to the 1927 discovery of an early manuscript copy (dated 1446) of the *Shōbōgenzō* in twelve chapters, most Sōtō clerics had assumed that the book of essays by Dōgen entitled "*Shōbōgenzō*" must have been edited and compiled posthumously by his disciples. Two key disciples were given primary credit for having collected Dōgen's miscellaneous Buddhist sermons in Japanese (*kana hōgo* 假名法語) and preserved them in bound volumes. It was thought that Dōgen's disciple Ejō 懷弉 (1198–1280), who was Dōgen's appointed successor as abbot of Eiheiji, must have compiled the *Shōbōgenzō* in seventy-five chapters about two years after Dōgen's death. Next, they imagined that about seventy-four years later another important abbot of Eiheiji, Giun 義雲 (1253–1333), compiled the *Shōbōgenzō* in sixty-chapters. According to this "Ejō and Giun" theory, the title of the work, its numbers of chapters, and the order of its chapters all must have been historical accidents.[26]

The discovery of the *Shōbōgenzō* in twelve chapters prompted a thorough examination of the manuscript and textual evidence and forced scholars to abandon the "Ejō and Giun" model. That model has been replaced by a new one, according to which Dōgen himself first compiled the *Shōbōgenzō* in sixty-chapters. Thereafter, he split this compilation into two new compilations. He added thirty additional chapters, discarded two previous chapters, and combined two separate chapters into one, thereby producing one *Shōbōgenzō* in twelve chapters and another in seventy-five chapters (see Table 12, Schematic Evolution of Dōgen's *Shōbōgenzō*).

According to this model, Dōgen himself selected the title "*Shōbōgenzō*," wrote the chapters, edited the chapters, arranged the chapters into sequences, and numbered the chapters from "1" to "12" or from "1" to "75." This new model has been widely adopted by scholars, but the traditional "Ejō and Giun" model remains widely known and accepted by Sōtō adherents and the public at large. Many people who know about both models tend to interpret the "Dōgen as compiler" model in terms of elements borrowed from the earlier "Ejō and Giun" theory in ways that can seem incongruous. Dissonance arises because the "Ejō and Giun" model assumed that Ejō and Giun merely reshuffled an identical set of chapters that remained unchanged, while the "Dōgen as compiler" model rests on the evidence that Dōgen revised chapters and wrote new chapters in the process of constructing his new compilations. It is not just the arrangement of chapters that evolved but also their contents. This subsection presents the main components of the "Dōgen as compiler" model, so that readers can better understand the relationships between these three substantive compilations and can more easily evaluate the various scenarios that have been proposed to interpret their significance.

The Sōtō Zen Text Project translation of the *Shōbōgenzō*, especially the colophons to each chapter and the variant texts, provides ample evidence for evaluating this model. The scope of the evidence to be considered and its relative importance, however, varies in accordance with methodological approaches and the scope of the questions being asked. Reliable results require that scholars consider the colophons within the context of their respective manuscript traditions (e.g., sixty-chapter versus seven-

---

[26] The introductory sections of the Honzan edition (T.2582.82:7a–b, 9b–10b) present this theory as historical fact. See Bodiford 2019, 240–246.

ty-five-chapter compilations). As we will see, even when the same chapter exists in more than one compilation, sometimes its colophon differs from one compilation to the other. It can become somewhat tedious to distinguish the respective colophons in every case, but when their textual affiliations become unclear or confused it is impossible to evaluate the characteristics of their respective manuscript traditions. This subsection, therefore, presents each issue in a modular format so that one can peruse issues selectively.

First, compare the numbering and ordering of chapters. If one compares the arrangement of the chapters in the *Shōbōgenzō* in sixty chapters with their arrangement in its twelve-chapter and seventy-five-chapter descendants, several features instantly stand out. Seven chapters appear in both the sixty- and the twelve-chapter versions. Table 7 (Sixty versus Twelve) compares their arrangement in each compilation. Three chapters align in relative order with their counterparts. In the twelve-chapter version, the remaining four chapters have been arranged in an order that supports these three. In the sixty-chapter compilation, they lack any thematic order. Consider, for example, "The Merit of the Kāṣāya" ("Kesa kudoku") and "The Merit of Leaving Home" ("Shukke kudoku"). These two chapters concern related topics. The *kāṣāya* refers to the robe, or vestment, that a religious receives as part of the ritual of leaving home to join the fraternity, or brotherhood, of the monastic community. Despite their related content, the sixty-chapter version separates them by seventeen other, unrelated chapters. In the twelve-chapter version, the order of these two chapters is reversed, and they appear much closer together. They are separated by the addition of another chapter, "Receiving the Precepts" ("Jukai"), which refers to the assumption of monastic vows and morality that one performs as part of this same ritual of leaving home. In short, leaving home, receiving the precepts, and donning a *kāṣāya* constitute the three key acts that transform ordinary people into religious professionals. In the twelve-chapter version, the first three chapters on these topics reinforce one another. This kind of coherence cannot be found in the sixty-chapter version.

Second, the arrangement of chapters in the *Shōbōgenzō* in seventy-five chapters largely mirrors the previous arrangement used for the sixty chapters. As indicated in Table 8 (Sixty versus Seventy-five), the arrangement of the first twenty-seven chapters is practically identical in both compilations. The only differences consist of the elimination of two chapters and the consolidation of two chapters. The version in sixty

*Introduction to the* SHŌBŌGENZŌ: *5. The sixty-chapter version and its descendants* 57

chapters loses its chapter 8, "Karma of the Three Times" ("Sanjigō") — which is reassigned to the *Shōbōgenzō* in twelve chapters — and its chapter 12, "The *Lotus* Turns the *Lotus*" — which is discarded. Also, its chapters 16 and 17, "Sustained Practice" ("Gyōji," parts 1 and 2), are consolidated in the seventy-five-chapter version as a single, albeit two-part, chapter number 16 (16A and 16B). These changes allow the seventy-five-chapter version to include different chapters as its number 8, 12, and 17. Even taken together, these deletions and additions do not fundamentally modify the reader's overall experience of this first third of the *Shōbōgenzō*. The fact that Dōgen preserved the same sequence of chapters for the first third of the total in two different iterations of the *Shōbōgenzō* helps to confirm that this arrangement reflects a deliberate authorial intent.

A similar kind of preserved sequence also exists near the end of the *Shōbōgenzō* in seventy-five chapters. As shown in Table 9 (Sixty versus Seventy-five, *redux*), the exact same sequence of seven chapters reoccurs in the sixty and the seventy-five-chapter compilations. In this second example, however, the addition of other chapters plays a much larger role. Within the sequence presented by this table, the *Shōbōgenzō* in seventy-five chapters boasts five additional chapters (numbers 66, 67, 68, 69, 71) not previously included in its sixty-chapter predecessor. The addition of so many additional chapters definitely interrupts the sequence. Although the same chapters from the sixty-chapter version appear in the same order as in that compilation, readers of the seventy-five-chapter revised compilation cannot help but feel the sensation of reading a more comprehensive, expanded work. In tone and content, however, these additional chapters — "The King of Samādhis Samādhi" ("Zanmai ō zanmai"), "Turning the Dharma Wheel" ("Ten hōrin"), "Great Practice" ("Dai shugyō"), "The Samādhi of Self Verification" ("Jishō zanmai"), and "The Pātra Bowl" ("Hou") — retain the cohesiveness of the original. In other words, they build on the same themes and motifs without introducing dissonance. This internal consistency of the *Shōbōgenzō* in seventy-five chapters — while not as strong as that exhibited by its twelve-chapter sibling — constitutes the third noteworthy feature of these chapter arrangements.

This sequence of seven chapters (in Table 9) displays another notable peculiarity. The chapter titled "Bringing Forth the Unsurpassed Mind" (Chapter 53) in the initial compilation received a new numerical designation (Chapter 65) and a new title: "Bringing Forth the Mind of Bodhi."

58 DŌGEN'S *SHŌBŌGENZŌ* VOLUME VIII

Its contents remain unchanged, only the title differs. This change seems peculiar, because the initial sixty-chapter compilation also includes another chapter (34) with that same title, which subsequently was included in the *Shōbōgenzō* in twelve chapters with its original title unchanged. As a result, the two separate chapters that began with distinct titles subsequently acquired an identical title even as their contents remained different (see Table 10, Identical Titles for Two Different Chapters).

At first glance, the identical titles invite confusion. The two chapters do not overlap in content. Why should they have identical titles? The chapters are not totally unrelated. The term "unsurpassed mind" (*mujō shin* 無上心) is an alternative designation for mind of bodhi (*bodai shin* 菩提心; S. *bodhicitta*). Nonetheless, the first chapter (number 34) introduces this concept in a rather straight-forward manner (similar to that of the twelve-chapter compilation as a whole), while the second chapter (number 53) comments on a series of kōans (in the usual manner of the seventy-five-chapter compilation). Perhaps Dōgen thought that the act of merely re-locating each chapter in a different compilation of the *Shōbōgenzō* would eliminate any possible confusion. Or perhaps he wanted to explicitly bring these two chapters into an intertextual dialogue. Or, who knows?

What subsequently happened is that the 1815 Honzan edition confused them and compounded the confusion by changing the dates assigned to them. In the initial *Shōbōgenzō* in sixty chapters, only the second one (number 53) bears a colophon and date (1244.2.14). Naturally, this colophon and date also appear in the same chapter (number 63) with the revised title in the seventy-five-chapter compilation. The first chapter (number 34) lacks a colophon and thus lacks a date. The same is true for the version of it (number 4) that appears in the twelve-chapter compilation. In the early 1690s, when Handō Kōzen compiled his comprehensive version of the *Shōbōgenzō* in ninety-five (or ninety-six) chapters, he reused the original chapter titles from the version in sixty chapters and copied Dōgen's colophon (with the date 1244.2.14) into both.[27] Then, the editors of the 1815 Honzan edition assigned them a strict chronological order, side-by-side, in the positions of numbers 69 and 70, as if both chapters had been composed on the same day. As a result, generations of

---

[27] See page 180 of the table of the colophons and editorial notes (*okugaki shikigo taishō* 奧書識語對照; ESST-S.172–186) from the Kazan 可山 manuscript (ca. 1691) and Kangan 寬巖 manuscript (ca. 1693), which represent draft versions of the compilation by Kōzen.

readers have wondered how Dōgen could have written two very different chapters on the same topic during the span of a single day. The manuscript tradition, however, provides no basis for copying the colophon from chapter 53 into chapter 34.

This example highlights the problem of chronology, a baffling topic made even more perplexing by widespread scribal irregularities such as the present case. By the time of the 1815 Honzan edition, copyists had begun to combine chapters and colophons from disparate sources. In the medieval manuscripts, not every chapter bears a colophon. By the middle of the seventeenth century, it became increasingly common for subsequent scribes to remedy this deficiency by whatever means they could. It is no wonder that the colophons in the Honzan edition sometimes deviate from the manuscripts deemed most reliable by scholars today. When evaluating the dates, therefore, it is also important to evaluate the dates of the dates. Dates found only in later manuscripts lack the authority conveyed by undated chapters in earlier manuscripts. But even dates in early manuscripts cannot be accepted uncritically. The assigned date of composition sometimes indicates only the date of the initial draft, not the date of the final revision that survives today as a numbered chapter in the *Shōbōgenzō*. (E.g., Dōgen's original and revised colophons to the chapter "Buddha Nature," which survives in a holograph by Ejō; see Table 19.)

In the discussion below, I rely only on dates found in the Tōunji manuscript (dated 1510) of the *Shōbōgenzō* in sixty chapters, the Ryūmonji manuscript (dated 1547) of the version in seventy-five chapters, and the Yōkōji manuscript (dated 1446) of the version in twelve chapters. These three exemplary textual witnesses provide unimpeachable colophons for most but not every chapter (see Table 13, Number of Colophons in Exemplary Manuscripts). (The Ryūmonji and Yōkōji manuscripts also constitute the source texts [*teihon* 底本] for the Kawamura edition used as the basis for this translation.)

It is impossible to know with any degree of certainty why Dōgen first compiled one version of the *Shōbōgenzō* and later split it into two versions. The dramatic improvement in the cohesion and the more logical arrangement achieved in the subsequent twelve-chapter version suggest the possibility that a primary motivation might have been to achieve these refinements. In other words, perhaps the creation of a *Shōbōgenzō* in seventy-five chapters was driven by Dōgen's growing realization that the chapters now known as the *Shōbōgenzō* in twelve chapters belonged together. At the same time, the most compelling impetus for revising the arrangement of chapters (regardless of compilation) must have come from Dōgen's ongoing literary production of additional chapters that had to be accommodated within an expanded arrangement. Eventually Dōgen composed about eighty-eight to ninety chapters (depending on how they are counted). Initially, he arranged earlier and later chapters together in thematic sequences, not in chronological order. As the overall number of chapters increased, his earlier arrangement in sixty chapters became inadequate.

These considerations imply a chronological (not just thematic) evolution of the *Shōbōgenzō*. The dates provided by the colophons in the exemplary manuscripts do not reveal the precise chronology of each of the steps outlined in Table 12 (Schematic Evolution). At best, the most reliable dates can only provide parameters for evaluating possible scenarios (and eliminating improbable ones).

Table 18 (Chronological Profiles of the Three Substantive Compilations) summarizes the dates assigned to chapters in the three substantive compilations. The typical timeline of *Shōbōgenzō* chapters disregards differences among the individual compilations. All chapters are mixed together regardless of their source. In Table 18, however, each compilation presents its own individual chronological profile. The leftmost column consists of years, and each year lists separately the chapters of each compilation. For each compilation, first it indicates the total number of chapters dated to that year, and then lists the assigned chapter numbers of those respective chapters. To avoid confusion, it is important to keep in mind that this table uses the chapter numbers of each compilation to designate the individual chapters. Some chapters retain their assigned chapter number in more than one compilation, while in other instances the assigned chapter number for this or that chapter differs in different compilations. For example, among the chapters dated to 1242, the designation "4" corresponds to "Studying the Way with Body and Mind" in both the sixty- and seventy-five-chapter versions of the *Shōbōgenzō*. The same cannot be said for the chapter designation "17." In the sixty-chapter compilation, "17" corresponds to the second half of "Sustained Practice," while in the seventy-five-chapter compilation the same numerical designation corresponds to "Such" (i.e., chapter 29 in the sixty-chapter compilation).

If our understanding of the evolution of the *Shōbōgenzō* was based on only a single one of these substantive compilations (without knowl-

Introduction to the SHŌBŌGENZŌ: 5. *The sixty-chapter version and its descendants* 61

edge of the other two), the evidence would lead to different conclusions. When comparing the three chronological profiles with one another, it is possible to arrive at more than one conclusion. The explanation below will first discuss the chronological profiles of each substantive compilation as a whole. Then it will examine issues presented by the chronology of individual chapters. Sometimes the colophons of individual chapters clearly indicate that the seventy-five-chapter compilation must be later than the one in sixty chapters, but not in all cases.

The *Shōbōgenzō* in twelve chapters survives in its complete format in only a single extant manuscript witness, which was discovered at Yōkōji (Ishikawa Prefecture) in 1927. The manuscript, dated 1446, is a copy of an earlier manuscript (now lost) which was dated 1420. Aside from these two scribal dates, it has no known manuscript tradition. Based on the evidence of this manuscript, the *Shōbōgenzō* in twelve chapters exhibits a lengthy but largely undefined chronological profile. Dōgen assigned dates to only two chapters: number 3, "The Merit of the Kāṣāya," dated 1240; and number 12, "The Eight Understandings of the Great Person," dated 1253. None of the other chapters bears a colophon by Dōgen. Ten chapters thus lack assigned dates. The general lack of colophons suggests that Dōgen had not yet applied his final touches to this compilation. It probably remained unfinished at the time of his death. We can only speculate regarding the dates for its ten undated chapters. Based on stylistic considerations, chapters 1 to 10 probably form a related group, within which these chapters date from the early to middle 1240s. Stylistically, chapter 11, "One Hundred Gateways to the Illumination of the Dharma," more likely dates from shortly before chapter 12. The dearth of hard data precludes any firm conclusions, but the evidence of this manuscript suggests that Dōgen's work on this *Shōbōgenzō* spans the period from 1240 to 1253.

The *Shōbōgenzō* in sixty chapters survives in its complete format in at least six manuscript witnesses. Its exemplary manuscript, owned by Tōunji (Miyagi Prefecture), was produced in 1510 by Kinkō Yōken 金岡用兼 (1437–1513). Its provenance is well documented. It is a copy of an earlier manuscript, dated 1480, which was produced by Kōshū 光周 (1434–1492), which in turn was copied from a 1389 manuscript produced by Sōgo 宋吾 (1343–1406). Based on the evidence of this manuscript, the *Shōbōgenzō* in sixty chapters exhibits a two-part chronological profile. Dōgen assigned dates to 44 of its chapters. He dated numbers 1 and 2 to 1233 and dated the other chapters between 1238 and 1245. The bulk of the chapters occupy the three-year period from 1241 to 1243. He dated 5 chapters to 1241, 14 chapters to 1242 (the year when production peaked), and 13 chapters to 1243. The following two years, 1244 and 1245, account for only 3 chapters each year. Dōgen's colophons provide no evidence of any work on the *Shōbōgenzō* after 1245. But 16 other chapters lack any colophons and, hence, also lack dates. The lack of colophons for these chapters suggests that Dōgen ceased work on the *Shōbōgenzō* in sixty chapters while it remained unfinished. One might assume that the bulk of its other chapters also date to the period between 1241 and 1245, but definitive deductions remain out of reach. Ultimately, the evidence of this manuscript suggests that Dōgen's work on this *Shōbōgenzō* spans the period from 1233 to 1245.

The Shōbōgenzō in seventy-five chapters survives in its complete format in at least twenty-four manuscript witnesses. Its exemplary manuscript, owned by Ryūmonji (Ishikawa Prefecture), was produced in 1547 by Tessō Hōken 喆凼芳賢 (d. 1551). Its provenance is well documented. It is a copy of an earlier manuscript dated 1430, which in turn was based on a 1333 manuscript produced by Tsūgen 通源 (dates unknown). This 1333 manuscript by Tsūgen is the textual ancestor of a multi-branched family of many other extant manuscripts of the Shōbōgenzō in seventy-five chapters.[28] One of these, owned by Kenkon'in (Aichi Prefecture), is earlier (ca. 1488) than the Ryūmonji manuscript, but none of these can rival the overall quality of the Ryūmonji copy. Based on the evidence of this manuscript, the *Shōbōgenzō* in seventy-five chapters exhibits a more extended, two-part chronological profile. Dōgen assigned dates to 71 of its chapters. He dated numbers 1 and 2 to 1233 — just as is the case in the earlier compilation in sixty chapters, which shares the same first two chapters. He dated the other chapters between 1239 and 1252. The bulk of the chapters occupy the three-year period from 1242 to 1244. He dated 15 chapters to 1242, 23 chapters to 1243 (the year when pro-

---

[28] The Ryūmonji manuscript is remarkably similar to the Kenkon'in 乾坤院 manuscript (copied ca. 1488; Aichi Pref.) and the Shōbōji 正法寺 manuscript (copied ca. 1512; Iwate Pref.), both of which derive from the same copy by Tsūgen but via different intermediary copies. When textual or paratextual elements agree in all three of the manuscripts, one can assume with great confidence that they accurately represent the version by Tsūgen (Bodiford 2019, 222–223, 280–282). Also see Hirose (1982) and (1988, 517–572) for an overview of the medieval diffusion of the *Shōbōgenzō*. Note that the copyist Tsūgen discussed here is not related to the Sōtō patriarch Tsūgen Jakurei 通幻寂靈 (1322–1391).

Introduction to the SHŌBŌGENZŌ: 5. *The sixty-chapter version and its descendants* 63

duction peaked), and 11 chapters to 1244. The number of chapters assigned to non-peak years also exceeds the numbers reported for the sixty-chapter version. He dated 6 chapters to 1240, 7 chapters to 1241, and 5 chapters to 1245. Most significantly, his colophons also date chapters to the years 1246, 1250, and 1252. None of these later dates appear in any manuscript witness of the *Shōbōgenzō* in sixty-chapters. All of them appear in every manuscript witness of the *Shōbōgenzō* in seventy-five chapters. This pattern indicates that Dōgen continued to work on the seventy-five-chapter compilation long after he had ceased working on the one in sixty chapters. Thus, Dōgen's work on this *Shōbōgenzō* spans the period from 1233 to 1252.

Based on the chronological profiles of each substantive compilation as a whole, one can reasonably conclude that the sixty-chapter compilation provided the basis for the ones in seventy-five and in twelve chapters. When one examines the chronological evidence for individual chapters, however, the evidence can be mixed. We will begin with chapters that agree with the overall chronological pattern. Within the *Shōbōgenzō* in seventy-five chapters, Dōgen's colophons for chapter 50, "Washing the Face" (dated 1250), and for chapter 1, "The Realized Kōan" (dated to 1252), especially command attention. The first, "Washing the Face," is atypical in that it lists three sets of dates in three locations: 1239 at Kōshōji, near Kyoto; 1243 at Kippōji, in Echizen; and 1250 at Eiheiji. Whether by accident or by design, the *Shōbōgenzō* in sixty chapters retains this chapter (also numbered 50) in its intermediate stage of revision. Its colophon mentions only the first two dates (1239 and 1243) and locations. In style and content, it lacks the final round of revisions found in the 1250 version. Comparisons of the 1243 intermediate version (translated herein as variant chapter 4) against the 1250 final revision, provide important clues regarding the purport of Dōgen's statement to Ejō that he (Dōgen) "would rewrite all the chapters of the *Shōbōgenzō* in Japanese script that he had previously composed" (*aogiraku wa izen eramu tokoro no kana no shōbōgenzō tō mina shoshi aratame* 仰者以前所撰假名正法眼藏等皆書改; *Kenzeiki*, p. 79). Some have speculated that this statement referred to Dōgen's future aspirations to rewrite the chapters of the *Shōbōgenzō* in seventy-five chapters — or even to discard them in favor of newer chapters not yet written. The manuscript evidence (here and elsewhere) suggests nothing of the kind, but rather demonstrates the opposite. It shows that Dōgen revised the earlier compilation of sixty chapters and wrote new ones to produce two new compilations in twelve

64 DŌGEN'S *SHŌBŌGENZŌ* VOLUME VIII

and in seventy-five chapters (Kawamura 1986, 470; cf. Kawamura 1991, 408–411).

The second noteworthy colophon, that for "The Realized Kōan," is crucial because it provides a terminus for Dōgen's work on the *Shōbōgenzō* in seventy-five chapters. "The Realized Kōan" begins both the sixty- and seventy-five-chapter compilations both sequentially (chapter number 1) and chronologically (dated to 1233). (Although, if giving precise dates, chapter 2, "Mahā-prajñā-pāramitā," is a few months earlier.) In the sixty-chapter version, it has only its single early date. In all manuscripts of the *Shōbōgenzō* in seventy-five chapters, however, Dōgen's colophon to "The Realized Kōan" also carries the very last date: 1252. This latter date appears with the somewhat cryptic designation "compiled and ordered" (*shūroku* 拾勒). This term does not appear elsewhere in Dōgen's writings. The verb "compiled" (*shū*) refers to the act of collecting and gathering together. It cannot refer only to a single chapter or item. The verb "order" (*roku*) is much rarer. It typically refers to two somewhat disparate processes. In ordinary contexts it designates the act of preparing a final prooftext to be inscribed on a stone stele or memorial. In the postscripts to larger works, it can refer to the act of determining the number of chapters (*rokujō kansū* 勒成卷數). Examples of this second usage appear repeatedly in the Buddhist literature of China and Japan.[29] Its precise meaning for Dōgen cannot be discerned with absolute certainty. In light of the fact that no other later date occurs anywhere else in the *Shōbōgenzō* in seventy-five chapters, "compiled and ordered" seems very likely to indicate the year when Dōgen completed (or at least ceased) his work on this compilation.

Dōgen's colophons to "Washing the Face" and "The Realized Kōan" highlight a second key element in the chronological evolution of the *Shōbōgenzō*. As its compilations evolved, its individual chapters also evolved. It is not always clear how these two evolutionary processes fit together. "Washing the Face" and "The Realized Kōan" atypically provide dates for both their conception and completion. Other colophons do not, and Dōgen did not always append a colophon. In some cases,

---

[29] The phrase *rokujō* 勒成 followed by a specified number of scrolls (*kan* 卷) occurs well over a hundred times in the Taishō canon (e.g., T.220.5:1a24-25, 7:991c8-9, 1055b27, 1065c10; T.1804.40:1b10; T.2122.53:496c16; T.2189.56:144a19; T.2196.56:492b27; T.2826.85:1236a20-21; etc.)
Note especially the use of the abbreviated phrase *roku kansū* 勒卷數 in the *Asabashō* 阿娑縛抄 (T.3190.94:504b24, 504c10) and *Mon'yōki* 門葉記 (T.3216.96:757ab).

Introduction to the SHŌBŌGENZŌ: 5. *The sixty-chapter version and its descendants* 65

one can attempt to overcome these limitations by comparing individual chapters — not just their colophons but also their contents — across compilations or with independent manuscripts that preserve earlier drafts. The chapter "Buddha Nature" (number 3) provides perhaps the best-known subject of this kind of analysis. In 1953, Ōkubo Dōshū published his analysis of the variant colophons for "Buddha Nature" found not only in the sixty- and seventy-five-chapter compilations but also in a holograph by Ejō that Ōkubo had discovered at Eiheiji (see Table 19, Variant Colophons for Chapter 3, "Buddha Nature," which abbreviates the colophons for clarity).

According to Ōkubo's analysis of the paper, ink, and handwriting, the Eiheiji manuscript is an authentic holograph by Ejō. It was written in 1258, when Ejō collated (*kōgō* 校合) his earlier clean copy (*shosha* 書寫; dated 1243) of "Buddha Nature" with a subsequent version that Dōgen had extensively revised.[30] This 1258 holograph is especially remarkable because Ejō produced a diplomatic copy of Dōgen's corrections, cross-outs (i.e., deletions), and additions. It shows that Dōgen had revised practically every section of "Buddha Nature" — vocabulary, phrases, sentences, and longer passages.[31] Nonetheless, he did not change its date. The original colophon (which Dōgen crossed out) and the revised colophon by Dōgen both bear the exact same date. In the revised colophon, Dōgen changed the verb "record" (*ki* 記) to the more verbose phrase "present to the assembly" (*jishu* 示衆). Neither he nor Ejō ever explain the significance (if any) of this particular alteration. (The precise meaning of "present to the assembly" has become a much-discussed topic — see below.) Dōgen's revised version of "Buddha Nature" appears in both the sixty-chapter and seventy-five-chapter compilations of the *Shōbōgenzō*. Dōgen's revised colophon appears in both. Only the 1261 scribal notes by Ejō in the sixty-chapter compilation provide any indication that Dōgen had ever revised the chapter. But if the 1258 holograph by Ejō had not been discovered, the precise nature of Dōgen's revisions would have remained unknown and their existence unsuspected.

In regard to the chronological evolution of the *Shōbōgenzō*, it is important to note that "Buddha Nature" is dated to 1241. Its contents, however, as they appear both in the sixty- and the seventy-five-chapter

---

[30] Ōkubo (1953, 349–352; 1966, 315–318). Also see Bodiford (2019, 255–259).

[31] ESST-D.659–690 (facsimile). See Tsunoda (2001) for a detailed and essential transcription.

66 DŌGEN'S *SHŌBŌGENZŌ* VOLUME VIII

compilations, must date from sometime after 1243. It seems that Dōgen assigned dates retroactively to many (if not most) chapters only after they had been revised. For this reason, one cannot naïvely assume that the dates in the colophons are reliable. The reliability (or unreliability) of the dates in Dōgen's colophons constitutes an unresolved issue — one that has been all but unexamined — in the textual study of the *Shōbōgenzō*. It demands closer attention. Consider, for example, chapters that lack colophons (i.e., lack dates) in the sixty-chapter compilation but subsequently acquire colophons when they were re-assigned to the seventy-five-chapter compilation (see Table 20, Colophons Not Shared across Compilations).

Table 20 lists in chronological order eight chapters that appear in the sixty- and seventy-five-chapter compilations. Six of these chapters lack colophons (and, hence, lack dates) in the sixty-chapter compilation, but acquired them in the seventy-five-chapter version. The dates for these chapters range between the years 1240 and 1243, a period that falls within the chronological profile (1233 to 1245) of the *Shōbōgenzō* in sixty chapters. If those six chapters had been completed by the dates assigned to them, then one might expect that Dōgen would have written colophons for each of them at the time when he compiled the *Shōbōgenzō* in sixty chapters. The fact that Dōgen had not written colophons until after these chapters were reassigned to the compilation in seventy-five chapters suggests that perhaps each of them might have been under revision until some later date. This hypothesis rests on the observed pattern among independent manuscripts that chapters without colophons tend to be rough drafts. Note, however, that this hypothesis cannot account for the fact that two chapters — "One Bright Pearl" (1238) and "Sūtra Reading" (1241) — that already had colophons in the sixty-chapter compilation somehow lost them in the *Shōbōgenzō* in seventy-five chapters. These chapters constitute the prime example of how the chronology of individual chapters can present mixed evidence that sometimes contradicts the overall chronological pattern. Until additional evidence can be discovered, this issue will remain unsettled.

Similar considerations can apply to the twenty-five chapters that Dōgen included in the *Shōbōgenzō* in seventy-five chapters but are not in the sixty-chapter version. Table 21, "Chapters Exclusive to the *Shōbōgenzō* in Seventy-five Chapters," lists these chapters in chronological order. It also includes three additional chapters — "Extensive Study," "Washing the Face," and "The Realized Kōan" — that bear revised colophons, dated later than their sibling version included within the sixty-chapter compilation. Two of these twenty-five chapters (numbers 12 and 34) lack colophons. Twenty of the remaining twenty-three additional chapters bear colophons with assigned dates from before 1245 (i.e., the last year in the chronological profile of the sixty-chapter compilation). Based on the assigned dates alone, it seems logical that these additional chapters also possibly could have been included in the *Shōbōgenzō* in sixty chapters. One can only speculate why they would have been excluded. The most likely hypothesis would be that they remained under revision until some later date. This hypothesis is supported by the fact that among these twenty additional chapters, the extant manuscript tradition includes at least eleven in the form of rough drafts. (Among these eleven drafts, "The Inheritance Certificate" is translated herein as variant chapter 2.) These eleven chapters, at least, were not finished at the time of the dates assigned to them in their colophons. It is not known precisely when they were finished, but evidently it was not early enough for them to be included within the *Shōbōgenzō* in sixty chapters.

The difficulties inherent in any attempt to construct a precise chronology of chapters in the *Shōbōgenzō* can be illustrated by three chapters that share the exact same (assigned) date of composition (see Table 22, An Identical Date for Three Different Chapters). They are "The Merit of the Kāṣāya," "Sometimes," and "Transmitting the Robe." In their final form, each one bears the assigned date of "first day of winter, senior metal year of the rat, the first year of Ninji," which corresponds to the first day of the tenth lunar month (i.e., the seventeenth of October) in 1240. In the *Shōbōgenzō* in sixty chapters, however, one of them is absent and another lacks a colophon and, thus, lacks a date. According to the hypothesis discussed above, one might assume that, at the time the *Shōbōgenzō* in sixty chapters was compiled, among these three chapters only "The Merit of the Kāṣāya" (number 41) had been completed. In regard to the other two chapters, "Sometimes" (number 20) would have been awaiting final touches, while "Transmitting the Robe" (as yet unnumbered) would have been an incomplete rough draft. If this is so, then how did they all receive the same date? One possibility is that all three might have originated at the same time as separate sections of a single longer composition that Dōgen would have subsequently shortened and split into separate works. Both the *kāṣāya* (*kesa* 袈裟) and the robe (*e* 衣) refer to the vestments of Zen clergy. It is easy to imagine how these two topics might have been discussed at the same time or even in relationship to one another. The plausibility of this hypothesis is enhanced by the existence of other chapters in the manuscript tradition that had been substantially shortened from much longer rough drafts (e.g., the variant version of "Great Awakening" translated herein). But even if a common origin seems plausible for the two chapters about vestments, it is not clear how a chapter with a completely different theme like "Sometimes" might fit into this process.

Another possible explanation for the shared dates of these chapters concerns Dōgen's use of different predicates in each of these colophons. Although the dates are identical, Dōgen states that "The Merit of the Kāṣāya" was "presented to the assembly" (*jishu* 示衆), while "Sometimes" was "written" (*sho* 書) and "Transmitting the Robe" was "recorded" (*ki* 記). It is easy to imagine that each of these predicates ("present," "write," "record") must designate different acts or even refer to different types or styles of compositions. If each of these verbs refers to different aspects of a much longer process, then perhaps those different aspects might have overlapped in time.

Kawamura Kōdō, however, in his massive study of the evolution of the *Shōbōgenzō* (1986, 39–40; 543–551) argues that these three verbs function interchangeably in Dōgen's colophons. He cautions against the widespread tendency to associate the first one ("present") with oral instructions and to associate the latter ones ("write," "record") exclusively with scribal instruments. Kawamura (1986, 39, 546) cites the term "present in writing" (*shoji* 書示) in the colophon to "Great Awakening" (chapter 10) as an example of the equivalence of these verbs for Dōgen. This colophon records two dates, an original draft in 1242 and a revised version in 1244. Kawamura points out that Dōgen deliberately revised the language used in his colophon as well. Dōgen wrote "presented to the assembly" (*jishu*) for the first occurrence, and then in regard to the second occurrence he wrote: "presented (*ji*) in writing to the great assembly (*shu*) of humans and gods" (*shoji o ninten daishu* 書示 於人天大衆). Kawamura regards the first version as a terse form of the verbose expression used in the latter version. He points out that Dōgen's goal in composing the *Shōbōgenzō* precisely consisted of disseminating Buddhism via written media to as wide an audience as possible. Thus, "present to the assembly" (*jishu*) should be understood as a clear statement that these writings should be made available to all members of the monastic community.

Introduction to the SHŌBŌGENZŌ: 5. *The sixty-chapter version and its descendants* 69

Kawamura further suggests (pp. 546–548) that, as Dōgen revised and rewrote chapters of the *Shōbōgenzō*, he would change the wording of his earlier colophons from "write" (*sho*) or "record" (*ki*) to "present to the assembly" (*jishu*) to convey this goal more clearly. Kawamura speculates that, had Dōgen lived longer, eventually he would have used the expression "present to the assembly" as his formulaic terminology (*shijigo* 指事語) in all colophons instead of "write" or "record." He cites the examples of Dōgen's revised colophons to "Buddha Nature" (chapter 3) in the holograph by Ejō (see Table 19) and the revised colophons to "The Mind Cannot Be Got" (chapter 8; see the supplementary chapter 4 translated herein). In these examples, Dōgen replaced the terms "record" (chapter 3) or "write" (chapter 8) with the phrase "present to the assembly." Finally, Kawamura argues that "present to the assembly" could not have referred to a lecture (such as a *teishō* 提唱) before an audience. He points out that Dōgen's colophon for "The King of Samādhis Samādhi" (chapter 66) uses the phrase "present to the assembly" while the corresponding chapter in the Himitsu manuscript (1.10) contains a scribal note by Ejō in which Ejō reports that he copied Dōgen's manuscript on that very same evening. If Ejō had copied on the same day that Dōgen had composed it (i.e., *jishu*), then it must have been written in the format that Ejō copied. In structure and format "The King of Samādhis Samādhi" chapter consists of a polished essay, not the transcript of an oral lecture.

Kawamura presents a strong case. His examples comprise persuasive evidence. When one examines all the colophons of the sixty- and seventy-five-chapter compilations in this translation, however, his examples do not account for the overall number of colophons in the respective manuscript traditions (see Table 14, The Predicate in Dōgen's Colophons). On the one hand, Kawamura is certainly correct that Dōgen routinely wrote "present to the assembly" in his colophons. Within the *Shōbōgenzō* in seventy-five chapters it occurs in 57 of the colophons — by itself in 56 colophons plus once in the colophon for "Great Awakening" (chapter 10) where it is followed by the expanded version of "presented in writing to the great assembly of humans and gods" (as described above). In his colophon for "Washing the Face" (chapter 50) Dōgen wrote it three times, once for each revised iteration. It occurs more often (in 75% of chapters) in the seventy-five-chapter compilation than in the sixty-chapter version (only in 58% of chapters). Clearly it was Dōgen's favored locution, but it certainly was not his inevitable choice. If we recalculate the percentages in terms of the total numbers of colophons (see Table 13), rather than chapters, in each compilation, then the figures contradict Kawamura's hypothesis. Dōgen wrote "present to the assembly" in 85 percent of the colophons for the sixty-chapter compilation, but only in 78 percent of the colophons for the version in seventy-five chapters. Moreover, in colophons for the chapters that are found in both compilations, Dōgen did not invariably replace the verbs "record" or "write" with "present to the assembly." In his colophons to "The Cypress Tree" (chapter 40), for example, in the *Shōbōgenzō* in sixty chapters, he wrote "present to the assembly" and then he replaced that phrase with "record" for the version in the seventy-five-chapter compilation. The colophon in this chapter suggests either that Dōgen did not consciously distinguished between these two predicates, or, perhaps, that sometimes he preferred "record."

The fact that the percentage of colophons with "present to the assembly" is lower for the compilation in seventy-five chapters, serves to highlight the importance of examining the colophons within the context of their respective manuscript traditions. When sorted by compilation, the colophons not only exhibit different chronological profiles but also reveal previously undetected patterns (such as this decline in Dōgen's expected formulaic terminology). More important, this kind of pattern among sorted colophons demonstrates that these differences began with Dōgen (not with later copyists). The differences in the colophons suggest that even minor textual variations within the contents of the chapters (not just major differences, such as exhibited by the variant chapters listed in Table 12) likewise might be the result of Dōgen's hand.

What might have been Dōgen's intentions in writing "record"? If Kawamura is correct in his suggestion that "present to the assembly" implies accessibility (which seems plausible), then "record" must imply something else. In this regard, it seems significant that many of the chapters within which his colophons state "record" concern topics related to dharma transmission: "Ocean Seal Samādhi" (number 13), "Prediction" (21), "Making a Bow and Getting the Marrow" (28), "Transmitting the Robe" (32), and "The Inheritance Certificate" (39), for example. Significantly, in 1547, Tessō Hōken stated in his scribal colophon to "The Inheritance Certificate" that this chapter must be kept secret and revealed to disciples only after they had received dharma transmission. Hōken's remarks accurately describe the customary secrecy that surrounded succession rituals in medieval Japan. Even if this culture of secrecy cannot

Introduction to the SHŌBŌGENZŌ: 6. *Dōgen and his* Shōbōgenzō          71

be traced back to Dōgen himself, its roots must be very early. Gikai (1219–1309), Eiheiji's third abbot and the disciple of Ejō, kept a record of the dharma transmission procedures taught to him by Ejō. In this record, he states that it was during the time when he was inside the abbot's quarters alone with Ejō that he first saw "The Inheritance Certificate" and heard the details of dharma transmission.[32] His language here is ambiguous. It could refer either to an actual inheritance certificate or to the chapter with that title. Surviving manuscripts demonstrate that Gikai wrote copies of Dōgen's *Shōbōgenzō*. It might seem surprising if he had not also copied "The Inheritance Certificate" chapter prior to his own dharma transmission, but it also would make it noteworthy. Gikai's note, especially in light of the comment by Hōken, at least raises the possibility that Dōgen wrote "record" for chapters that were not to be made accessible to everyone.

Currently, the evidence regarding the precise chronology of *Shōbōgenzō* chapters and/or the implications of the colophons that Dōgen wrote for them remains inconclusive. He wrote the *Shōbōgenzō* to convey to his disciples in Japan the authentic Buddhism that he had acquired in China. He did not write it with the intention of calling attention to his editorial decisions, program of composition, or biographical progress as an author. It would not be fair to fault him for his failure to describe these elements in unambiguous detail. However lamentable or egregious Dōgen's faults, they can frustrate but cannot prevent scholars from interpreting the *Shōbōgenzō* as a chronological, biographical, and historical source. It is to those topics that we now must turn our attention.

## 6. Dōgen and His *Shōbōgenzō*

Dōgen cannot be understood today without acknowledging his exalted status within the Sōtō School, one of the largest Buddhist denominations in Japan. Within this ecclesiastical framework, no one outranks the "Eminent Ancestor" (*kōso* 高祖), Dōgen. Even more so than the "Great Ancestor" (*taiso* 太祖), Keizan Jōkin 瑩山紹瑾 (1264–1325), Dōgen constitutes the font of Sōtō's religious ideals, sectarian identity, and institutional structures. Dōgen's monastery, Eiheiji (founded in 1244), and Keizan's monastery, Sōjiji 總持寺 (founded in 1321), stand together as the two headquarter temples of the Sōtō administration (and stand apart

---

[32]  *Goyuigon kiroku* 御遺言記録 (DZZ.7:190).

as rivals for influence over Sōtō affairs). It is impossible for scholars to evade the weight of this impressive legacy and the way it bends the reading of historical sources toward the germination of the many important developments that were to sprout after Dōgen's death. To understand Dōgen's relationship to his *Shōbōgenzō* and to read the *Shōbōgenzō* as a biographical and historical source, however, one must strive to discern Dōgen in his own time as a relatively powerless, almost anonymous, religious cleric, who lived in mostly precarious circumstances, with neither institutional security nor any assurance of success. Dōgen's lifespan teetered on the cusp of several major historical developments that would transform Japanese culture and come to define its medieval age. Below, we will briefly mention three key social transformations, all of which began before Dōgen was born and reached their culminations only long after his death. The benefit of hindsight frames these outcomes as foregone conclusions, but Dōgen participated in these developments without foresight of their sweep or subsequent impact.

### *Dōgen's World*

Fifteen years before Dōgen's birth, Minamoto Yoritomo 源頼朝 (1147–1199) inaugurated a military administration (*bakufu* 幕府) in Kamakura that would eventually lead to a system of shared governance by the aristocrats of the royal court in Kyoto and the ascendant warriors allied to the shogun. Throughout Dōgen's lifetime, the warrior administration remained beset by instability and violence. In 1203, the second shogun, Minamoto Yoriie 源頼家 (1182–1204), was deposed after only one year in office and assassinated the following year. The third shogun, Minamoto Sanetomo 實朝 (1192–1219), likewise was assassinated by Yoriie's son, a Buddhist cleric named Kugyō 公曉 (1200–1219), who was immediately arrested and put to death for his crime. Kugyō had trained in Buddhism at Onjōji 園城寺, a major Tendai monastery at the foot of Mount Hiei near Kyoto. Dōgen initially trained in Buddhism at the Tendai headquarters Enryakuji 延暦寺, which occupied Mount Hiei itself. Based upon this proximity, the eminent scholar Yanagida Seizan (1922–2006) speculated that Kugyō and Dōgen must have been close friends. Yanagida concluded that Kugyō's tragic fate accounts for the denunciations of political involvements found in Dōgen's writings.[33]

---

[33] Yanagida 1980 (and English translation, Yanagida 1982).

Introduction to the SHŌBŌGENZŌ: 6a. Dōgen's World

The machinations of the warrior government nonetheless provided Dōgen with the opportunity to snare the patron who helped cement his worldly success. In 1221, armies of the Kamakura warriors attacked Kyoto to suppress an uprising by royalists. In this battle (known to history as the Jōkyū Disturbance), they captured three former chiefs (*jōkō* 上皇) of the royal family and sentenced them to exile. They killed the warrior leaders who had allied with the royals and confiscated their estates (*shōen* 莊園). Thereupon, they established an administrative office, the Rokuhara Tandai 六波羅探題, in the center of Kyoto to exercise the authority of the shogun over the city and all lands to its west. This office took its name from its location, which was at the site formerly occupied by the Rokuharamitsuji 六波羅蜜寺, directly across the street from the main gateway to Kenninji 建仁寺, the temple where Dōgen at that moment resided as a young student of Zen. Hatano Yoshishige 波多野重義 (d. 1258), a general who lost an eye in this battle, and his sons worked at the Rokuhara Tandai. In subsequent years, Dōgen presented two chapters of his *Shōbōgenzō* at or near this location.[34] Hatano was rewarded for his role in the battle of 1221 with lands confiscated from royalists in the province of Echizen. In 1243, Hatano set aside a portion of this land adjacent to the family fortress he had constructed there and presented it to Dōgen. Today, the Hatano fortress no longer survives; Dōgen's Eiheiji alone dominates the site. In 1247, the head administrator of the military government, Hōjō Tokiyori 北條時頼 (1227–1263), attacked his rivals (especially those affiliated with the Miura 三浦 clan) in the so-called Battle of Hōji 寶治. Two Hatano sons were killed in this battle. Shortly thereafter, Dōgen journeyed to Kamakura and stayed there for more than half a year. Many people have speculated regarding the possible significance of this visit. For his part, Dōgen merely stated that he visited his patron (i.e., Hatano Yoshishige) and preached to him the doctrine of karma: those who cultivate goodness attain favorable fortunes while those who commit evil will fall into hell.[35] With or without favorable karma, it is difficult to imagine how Dōgen could have propagated his teachings except for the Hatano (or other warrior patrons of similar stature).

One hundred ten years before Dōgen's birth, the Chinese government loosened restriction on the overseas activities of its merchant marine. As

---

[34] "The Old Buddha Mind" ("Kobutsushin" 古佛心) and "Full Function" ("Zenki" 全機).

[35] *Dōgen oshō kōroku* 道元和尚廣録 (Extensive Records of Reverend Dōgen), 3, *jōdō* 上堂 251; DZZ.3:166; cf. Leighton and Okumura 2004, 246.

74 DŌGEN'S *SHŌBŌGENZŌ* VOLUME VIII

maritime technology steadily improved, Chinese settlements (*tōbō* 唐房, 唐坊) sprang up at key locations on the Japanese coastline, especially at Hakata 博多 landing (*tsu* 津) near Dazaifu. These merchant communities served as key nodes in private networks that moved people, goods, technology, knowledge, and cultural practices across the seas between China, Japan, and Korea.[36] Over time, the interests of Chinese traders frequently coalesced with the religious aspirations of Buddhist clergy in Japan to their mutual benefit. Extant sources do not allow us to chart the full scope of these intersections, but they appear regularly in historical records from as early as the tenth century, even when overseas trade remained (in legal theory at least) more tightly regulated.

The following three examples are well known: The cleric Chōnen 奝然 (938–1016) returned from China in 985 with many rare goods, including a complete set of the first xylographic edition of the Chinese Buddhist canon (printed 983) and the now-famous Udāyana image of Śākyamuni Buddha (which Chōnen himself had commissioned). A few years later, Chōnen expressed his gratitude to the Emperor of China by sending many boxed sets of Japanese craft goods as well as about 420 kilograms of Japanese sulfur.[37] In 1069, the cleric Jōjin 成尋 (1011–1081) arranged passage to China with the sulfur trader Chen Yong 陳詠, who also provided translation services (*tsūji* 通事). Three years later, Jōjin's disciples, who had accompanied him to China, found another sulfur trader who ferried them back to Japan. The Song Empire of China lacked domestic sources of sulfur, but desperately needed the substance to manufacture gunpowder and other essential compounds.[38] In 1192, two years after he had returned to Japan, Eisai 榮西 (1141–1215; a.k.a. Yōjō-bō 葉上房) sent a shipload of Japanese lumber to Tiantong temple (one of the Five Mountains; see Table 15), where his master Xu'an Huaichang 虛庵懷敞 (dates unknown, J. Kian Eshō) used it to restore the monastery's re-

---

[36] Von Glahn (2014; and 2019); Enomoto (2007; and 2010); Murai (2018). Popular accounts tend to exaggerate the role played by members of the Taira clan, especially Taira Kiyomori 平清盛 (1118–1181), in the development and promotion of overseas trade with China. For a dissenting view, see Yamauchi 2012.

[37] "Ribenguo chuan" 日本國傳 in *Songshi* 宋史 491.5b–6a (https://www.kanripo.org/text/KR2a0032/491). See Wang (1994, 90–91 n100) for a translation of the complete list of gifts.

[38] See Yamauchi (2011) for a concise overview of the importance of sulfur for China and the role of Japanese Buddhist monks in its exportation from Japan.

*Introduction to the* SHŌBŌGENZŌ: *6a. Dōgen's World*                                        75

nowned but dilapidated Thousand Buddha Pavilion (Qianfoge 千佛閣).[39] At this time, a construction boom, precipitated in part by an influx of newcomers who fled south as the Jin 金 Kingdom conquered territories to the North, caused shortages of domestic timber, and imports from Japan were especially valued. The economic exchanges facilitated by Chōnen and Jōjin attract historical notice because of their earlier dates. Eisai's shipment of timber is notable because it marks the period when similar economic exchanges began to become commonplace.

A glimpse of how these exchanges functioned in practice can be gained by examining another well-known example, that of Enni (i.e., Enni-bō 圓爾房; a.k.a. Ben'en 辯圓; 1201–1280), who sent lumber to his master Wuzhun Shifan 無準師範 (1177–1249; J. Bujun Shihan) for the restoration of Jingshan temple (see Table 15) after a 1242 fire.[40] Missives exchanged at this time by Enni and Shifan (etc.) survive (as original documents or as later copies), and recent advances in scholarship have shed new light on their contents.[41] The historian Enomoto Wataru (2008) demonstrated that a portion of the lumber sent by Enni was seized by Chinese authorities as a tax or customs duty. The lumber was provided to Enni by Kujō Michiie 九條道家 (1193–1252), an aristocratic patron of Enni. And, most significant of all, the lumber was not free. Defu 德敷 (J. Tokushiki), the supervisor of Jingshan, arranged a payment of thirty thousand strings of cash to be sent to Enni (and through him, no doubt, to Michiie). The temple was happy to pay the fee because high-quality lumber from Japan cost much less than lower-grade timber from the depleted forests of China. As Nakamura Tsubasa (2010, 1697) explains, Enni used his connections in China and with Chinese traders in Japan to attract a powerful patron (Michiie) and to broker a trade to the economic advantage of both sides. Viewed from the opposite perspective, Michiie

[39] "Tiantongshan qianfogeji" 天童山千佛閣記, in *Gongkuiji* 攻媿集 (1198), by Lou Yao 樓鑰 (1163–1213); (https://www.kanripo.org/text/KR4d0243/). For analyses of this work, see Ishii Shūdō (1982, 95–100) and Satō Shūkō (2014, 114–122).

[40] The extant sources provide contradictory information regarding the Buddhist names used by Enni (Nishio 2002, 390–391; Nishio 2011, 32). Initially his ordination name (*hōki* 法諱) seems to have been Ben'en, while he was known by the monastic sobriquet Enni-bō. In China he used Enni as his ordination name (as a replacement for Ben'en). For this reason, the combination "Ben'en Enni" or "Enni Ben'en" is incorrect.

[41] E.g., Nishio 2001; Nishio 2002; Nishio 2003; Nishio 2011, 2–55; Hashimoto 2007; Enomoto 2008; Nakamura 2010.

used his political status (as one of the most powerful leaders in Japan) to employ a well-connected cleric (Enni) in a profitable arrangement that also extended his influence over domestic Buddhist circles and into the networks of overseas Chinese traders.

The examples above provided models to be replicated countless times over the next two centuries. Chinese overseas trade networks flourished, ship voyages became more frequent, and hundreds of Buddhist clerics traveled between Japan and China (Enomoto 2007, 11–19; Enomoto 2010, and Enomoto 2013). In subsequent centuries Buddhist temples in Japan became important nodes in Chinese trade networks. Japan exported vast quantities of craft goods (especially swords and lacquerware) and commodities (gold, copper, sulfur, mercury, timber) while importing Chinese coins and prestige goods (*karamono* 唐物, such as printed books, calligraphy, paintings, and ceramics). Massive importation of Chinese coins led to the rapid monetization of Japanese domestic trade, which stimulated commerce. Power blocks (i.e., so-called *kenmon* 權門) in Japan and in China came to depend on the economic fruits of overseas trade (von Glahn 2014, 258; von Glahn 2019, 58; Schottenhammer 2017, 148). Even the regular rebuilding of the Shrines at Ise relied on funds provided by trade ships sent to China under the imprimatur of Buddhist temples in Japan. The shrines fell into desolation in the fifteenth century after the final Buddhist trade mission to China failed (Kojima 1985, 193–224) and licensed trade ceased.

Dōgen witnessed only the initial early effervescence of these trade arrangements, well before they became regularized and their impacts were widely felt. Nonetheless, Dōgen could not have traveled so freely to China and back but for the existence of regular (and relatively safe) maritime shipping. This shipping also provided clerics access to information and goods. Japanese aristocrats and warrior leaders alike collected rarities from China. Hatano Yoshishige (Dōgen's patron) would have passed near Tsuruga 敦賀 (a town facing the China sea) when he journeyed between Kyoto and his newly acquired lands in Echizen. Tsuruga landing also participated in the Chinese trade because the coastal sea route from Hakata to Tsuruga with a short portage from there to Lake Biwa constituted the fastest way to transport Chinese goods to Kyoto. The proximity of the Hatano lands to Tsuruga suggests that Hatano would have recognized the cultural and material value in Dōgen's knowledge of China. In 1250, when Hatano purchased a printed edition of the Chinese Buddhist canon for Dōgen, it most likely arrived via Tsuruga. When

Introduction to the SHŌBŌGENZŌ: 6a. Dōgen's World

Dōgen journeyed to China, he would have been regarded not simply as a religious pilgrim but also as a likely "connection" (C. *guanxi* 关系) for future deals. And Dōgen's own decision to study the Buddhism of China can be seen as a precursor to the "China fever" (*chūgokunetsu* 中国熱; i.e., a fascination with all things Chinese) that swept over much of Japanese elite society in the late thirteenth century (Nakamura 2014, 38).

In 1194, six years before Dōgen's birth, the royal court in Kyoto issued an injunction against the "Superior Eisai, who went to China, and Superior Nōnin of Kyoto" (*nittō shōnin Eisai zaikyō shōnin Nōnin* 入唐上人榮西在京上人能忍) for their attempts to introduce what the court referred to as the "lineage of Bodhidharma" (Darumashū 達磨宗) — what nowadays we refer to as the Zen school. The injunction declared that, as requested by Tendai clerics, henceforth those teachings will be taboo (*chōji* 停止).[42] Today, this injunction serves to remind us of three key points. First, the trade route from Hakata to China led directly to the main centers of Chinese monastic Buddhism. The most prestigious of these monasteries, commonly known as the "Five Mountains" (see Table 15), comprised large enterprises tightly regulated by the state, which housed well-disciplined and well-educated elite clergy. Japanese Buddhists who journeyed to China typically found themselves at one of these state-authorized monasteries, where they could study contemporary Chinese doctrines and ceremonies involving monastic discipline (i.e., vinaya), Tiantai 天台 (J. Tendai), Pure Land, Chan, poetry, Confucianism, and so forth. Second, their newly acquired access to the latest developments in Chinese Buddhism provided Japanese clerics from all social backgrounds with new forms of political and religious capital that could threaten the established Buddhist norms of Japan. Even clerics who never traveled to China — such as Nōnin 能忍 (d. 1195; a.k.a. Dainichi-bō 大日房) — could wield this newly imported knowledge to advance their own agendas. Third, while the knowledge acquired by Japanese pilgrims to China embraced multiple elements, Zen stood out. It was the most novel Buddhist practice and, perhaps for that reason, had been prohibited by the Japanese court. The force of this prohibition was so great that Zen, however defined, could not become an established feature of Japan's religious landscape until well after Dōgen's death.

---

[42] *Hyakurenshō* 百錬抄, fasc. 10, entry for Kenkyū 建久 5 (1194).7.5. In *Shintei zōho kokushi taikei* 新訂増補国史大系 14.164. Modern scholars use "Darumashū" as a designation for Nōnin's followers.

The prohibition of Zen appeared just one year after the restoration the Thousand Buddha Pavilion at Tiantong, a project for which Eisai had shipped lumber from Japan. Within Japan, he had begun to establish himself as a master instructor in esoteric Buddhism. Over time, his many disciples came to constitute an identifiable initiation lineage, which subsequently became known as the Yōjōryū 葉上流 line of Japanese Tendai. The centrality of esoteric ritual for Eisai can be gauged by surveying the contents of the books he wrote. Of the nineteen extant compositions by Eisai, fifteen focus on esoteric Buddhism, two focus on Zen, and one focuses on monastic discipline. His works on esoteric Buddhism date from all periods of his career, from ca. 1170s (after his first visit to China) and the late 1180s (during his second sojourn in China) to 1211 (four years before his death). It is not the case that going to China caused him to abandon esoteric Buddhism and adopt Zen (Mano 2011, 828–831; Yoneda 2008, 345–343). Rather, Eisai wrote that he had taught esoteric Buddhism while in China and had performed an esoteric consecration ritual to initiate his Chinese Chan master (*Eisai sei kanjōshiki ju tō zenji* 榮西製灌頂式授唐禪師).[43] In other words, Eisai and Xu'an Huaichang alternated the roles of student and master as each one initiated the other into his own specialized lore.

Eisai valued Chan practice precisely because it could augment esoteric rituals and because he expected the promulgation of Chinese-style monastic discipline to revitalize Buddhism in Japan.[44] For this reason, he strongly protested the court's prohibition against his Zen teachings. In 1198 — the same year he received his "most profound" (*saishin* 最深) esoteric initiation from his master Kikō 基好 (dates unknown; a.k.a. Shūzen-bō 習禪房) — Eisai wrote *Kōzen gokokuron* 興禪護國論 (*Promoting Zen to Protect the Realm*), his best-known composition (Taga 1965, 281). In this Zen apology, Eisai quotes numerous scriptures and treatises to emphasize the importance of Zen practice, especially during the present age of Buddhist decline (*mappō* 末法). He points out that Dengyō 傳教 (i.e., Saichō 最澄; 766–822), the founding patriarch of Japanese Tendai, had incorporated the Zen lineages of Daoxuan 道璿 (702–760; J. Dōsen) and of Xiaoran 翛然 (fl. 804; J. Shunen) in his teachings. Rather than the introduction of something foreign, therefore, Eisai argued that

---

[43]  *Hotsu bodaishinron kuketsu* 菩提心論口決; T.2293.70:32a–b. Also see Nakao 2005, 51–52; Nakao 2014, 30; Nakao 2020, 48–51.

[44]  Nakao 2005, 54–65; Nakao 2020, 55–79.

*Introduction to the* SHŌBŌGENZŌ: *6a. Dōgen's World* 79

he aimed merely to restore what previously existed and had been lost.[45] He also attempted to distinguish the Zen that he had mastered in China from the so-called "Darumashū" of the charlatan Nōnin. He attacked people who mistakenly refer to the Zen lineage by the designation "Dharumashū" (*mōshō zenshū myōwatsu darumashū* 妄稱禪宗名曰達磨宗) in the harshest possible terms:

其人無惡不造之類也。如聖教中言空見者是也。不可與此人共語同座。應避百由旬矣。(*Kōzen gokokuron* 興禪護國論; T.2543.80:7c–8a)

There is no evil that such people will not do. They are the ones the noble teachings denounce for their false views of emptiness. One must not talk with such people nor even sit beside them. One must avoid them by a distance of a thousand *yojana*.

After the court in Kyoto prohibited the teaching of Zen, Eisai found support elsewhere. In 1195 (one year after the royal injunction), he founded Shōfukuji 聖福寺 on the waterfront at Hakata landing, probably with the support of the local Chinese traders.[46] Four years later, Eisai was in Kamakura, where he performed esoteric prayer rituals on behalf of Minamoto Yoritomo and acquired a new disciple, Taikō Gyōyū 退耕行勇 (1163–1241; a.k.a. Shōgon-bō 莊嚴房). Gyōyū had trained in China for five years (1184–1188) and subsequently became a cleric at the Hachimangūji 八幡宮寺 that Yoritomo had erected in 1180.[47] In Kamakura, Eisai secured the patronage of Yoritomo's wife, Hōjō Masako 北條政子 (1157–1225). With support from Masako, Eisai founded a series of temples: Jufukuji 壽福寺 (1200) in Kamakura, Kenninji (1202) in Kyoto, and Zenjōin 禪定院 (1211) on Mount Kōya (subsequently renamed the Kongō Zanmaiin 金剛三昧院 in 1219).[48] These temples provided an essential institutional basis for the teaching of contemporary Chinese-style Buddhist practices in Japan.

While Masako wielded considerable influence, her patronage of Eisai cannot be interpreted as a de facto endorsement by the military administration in Kamakura. Yoritomo had constructed the town of Kamakura

---

[45]  *Kōzen gokokuron* 興禪護國論; T.2543.80:4a. Also see Groner 1984, 7, 22–25 (regarding Daoxuan), and 43–44 (regarding Xiaoran). Eisai quotes Saichō's *Naishō buppō sōshō kechimyakufu* 內證佛法相承血脈譜; see *Dengyō daishi zenshū* 傳教大師全集, 1.211–215.

[46]  For a detailed review of the extant sources regarding the founding of Shōfukuji, see Kawazoe (1988, 11–26).

[47]  Regarding Taikō Gyōyū, see Nakao 1981; Nakao 1987.

[48]  Regarding Masako, see Nakao 2020, 113–119; Nakamura 2014, 38–45.

around three principal Buddhist temples: the aforementioned Hachi-mangūji (established 1180), Shōchōjuin 勝長壽院 (established 1184), and Yōfukuji 永福寺 (established 1192). The overseers (*bettō* 別當) and the religious at these three temples were appointed from Onjōji, Enra-kuji, or Tōji 東寺 — three of the most powerful Buddhist institutions of the day — located in or near Kyoto. This arrangement continued unal-tered throughout Masako's lifetime and beyond (Taira 2020, 350–355). The three central temples provided prayer rituals to promote the military policies of the Kamakura administration, while the religious at Eisai's temples preformed prayer rituals for the recompence of Yoritomo and the health of Masako. The military administration ignored whether Eisai taught Zen or not (Nakamura 2014, 44; Nakao 2020, 113–119).

Many of Eisai's disciples, or the disciples of his disciples, also jour-neyed to China. The first-hand knowledge that they conveyed to Bud-dhists in Japan provided a vital foundation for the development of Zen. They imparted information, not just about Buddhist teachings and Zen lore, but also about practical matters such as travel routes, legal proce-dures, monastic routines, local customs and vernacular language. Dōgen learned these topics directly from many of these people. They included not only Myōzen 明全 (1184–1225; a.k.a. Butsuju-bō 佛樹房) — who nowadays is well-known as Dōgen's teacher — but also two of Taikō Gyōyū's disciples: Daikatsu Ryōshin 大歇了心 (d. 1257; a.k.a. Hannya-bō 般若房) and Ryūzen 隆禪 (dates unknown; a.k.a. Butsugen-bō 佛眼房). Clerics such as these and other members of Eisai's faction dominated the nascent Zen groups of Japan throughout Dōgen's lifetime (Nakao 2004).

Within just a few generations, however, Eisai's lineage died out. Eisai himself continued to be celebrated as the first patriarch of Zen in Japan, but the accomplishments of his disciples and, in many cases, even their names became lost to history. Consider, for example, the *Genkō shakusho* 元亨釋書 (*Genkō Era Account of Buddhism*; 30 vols.) by Kokan Shiren 虎關師鍊 (1278–1346), the first (1322) encyclopedic history of Buddhism and Zen in Japan.[49] It devotes an entire chapter to Eisai's biography and states that "subsequent generations all regard him as a great patriarch of Zen" (*gose kai sui zenmon shi daiso* 後世皆推禪門之大祖), but the biogra-phy does not identify a single one of Eisai's disciples. The names of two of Eisai's disciples — Taikō Gyōyū and Eichō 榮朝 (1165–1247; a.k.a.

---

[49]  For overviews of the *Genkō shakusho*, see Bielefeldt 1997; and Bodiford 2009, 131–138, 142–144.

Introduction to the SHŌBŌGENZŌ: 6a. Dōgen's World          81

Shakuen-bō 釋圓房) — do appear elsewhere in the *Genkō shakusho* but it explicitly links only one of them (Eichō) to Eisai.[50]

Some sense of how this forgetting occurred can be acquired by looking at the story of early Zen in Japan as told by Mujū Dōgyō 無住道曉 (1226–1312; a.k.a. Ichien-bō 一圓房), a member of one of the very last generations in Eisai's lineage. Dōgyō wrote brief but influential accounts of the beginnings of Zen in Japan (see Supplement 1). He identifies five key individuals: Eisai, Dōgen (a.k.a. Buppō-bō 佛法房), Enni, Hōjō Tokiyori, and Lanxi Daolong 蘭溪道隆 (1213–1278; J. Rankei Dōryū). Daolong is a Chinese Buddhist teacher who came to Japan in 1246. According to Dōgyō's account (which is translated in a subsequent section below), Eisai, Dōgen, and Enni heralded the coming of Zen, while Daolong constituted its arrival. In brief, Dōgyō asserts the following five key points. (1) Buddhists in Japan prior to the time of Eisai parroted the words "*zen*" 禪 (i.e., meditation), which appears in the scriptures they chanted, but they never actually practiced any form of seated meditation. (2) Eisai's followers outwardly practiced monastic discipline (*kairitsu* 戒律; i.e., *vinaya*), Tendai, esoteric Buddhism (*shingon* 眞言), and Pure Land Buddhism, but, being careful not to oppose the norms of Japan, they practiced Zen only in secret while waiting for a future time when it might become acceptable to society at large. (3) Dōgen built the first wide platforms for seated meditation (i.e., *zazen* 坐禪), and (4) Enni was the first to promulgate Chinese procedures (*sahō* 作法) for seated meditation. Nonetheless, (5) the proper practice of Zen in a Chinese manner according to the Chinese liturgy began only after 1253 (the year of Dōgen's death), when Daolong became the first abbot of the newly constructed Kenchōji 建長寺 in Kamakura. Thanks to Hōjō Tokiyori, the head administrator of the military government and the founding patron of Kenchōji, this temple followed all the same ritual ceremonies as in China. Tokiyori — who must have been a reincarnation (*saitan* 再誕) of Eisai — thereby fulfilled Eisai's destiny.

Today, many of Dōgyō's assertions seem problematic at best. Regardless of the historical veracity of his account, it nonetheless provides us with valuable insights into how Eisai was perceived. Within a century of his death Eisai had become little more than a figurehead whose legacy belonged to others. Significantly, Dōgyō did not belong to a rival sect. He was a member of Eisai's own lineage. If a member of Eisai's own

---

[50]    *Genkō shakusho* 元亨釋書; 2; DNBZ.101.159b; for Taikō Gyōyū and Eichō, see ibid.; vols. 6 and 7; DNBZ.101.208a, 208b, 216b.

faction understood him in these terms, then similar (or even lower) evaluations probably circulated among other Buddhist groups. Dōgyō's account also provides valuable insights into the social milieu within which Eisai — as well as Dōgen and Enni — built their careers. The more we know about the activities of Eisai and his faction, the better we can contextualize Dōgen's teachings and his audience. For example, when Dōgen denounces people who designate themselves as the "Zen school" (as he does in chapter 44, "The Way of the Buddhas"), is he arguing for a catholic, all-inclusive Buddhism, or is he merely parroting the government's taboo, or both? Did others in the Eisai faction say the same thing? Without knowledge of this social network it, is impossible to gauge fully how Dōgen's catholic vision might have been similar to or different from his compatriots. At the very least, Dōgen and his compatriots in Eisai's faction navigated similar constraints and social expectations.

In other words, Dōgen and Dōgyō (etc.) shared the same milieu not just in societal terms but also because Dōgen likewise belonged to Eisai's faction (see Table 35, Dōgen within the Eisai Faction). Dōgen had studied Zen at Eisai's Kenninji under the direction of Eisai's disciple Myōzen. While there, he would have encountered Daikatsu Ryōshin, the disciple of Taikō Gyōyū. In 1226, while Dōgen remained in China, Gyōyū (who was in Kamakura at the time) received word of Myōzen's sudden death the previous year. He lamented: "How utterly pitiful! We have lost half our ancestral house!" (*kashakko, shitsu soka isseki* 可惜許、失祖家一隻).[51] This incident demonstrates the high esteem with which he regarded Myōzen, and it confirms that members of Eisai's faction exchanged tidings with one another even across the seas. Gyōyū's disciple Ryūzen figures prominently in Dōgen's adventures in China, since they studied together at Tiantong. He is mentioned by name in "The Inheritance Certificate" ("Shisho") chapter of the *Shōbōgenzō*, in Dōgen's *Hōkyōki* (*Baoqing Records*), in Dōgen's collection of Chinese gāthā (*geju* 偈頌) style verses, and in the *Zuimonki* 隨聞記 (*Occasional Transcripts*) by Dōgen's disciple Ejō 懷弉 (1198–1280).[52] The "Zen person Nin 忍 of

[51] *Kaizan gyōjō narabi ashikaga reifu* 開山行狀并足利靈府 (Jōmyōji 浄妙寺 Temple manuscript, Kamakura), transcribed in Nakao 1987b; see p. 47. For a discussion of this passage, also see Nakao 1986, 193–195.

[52] See "Shisho" (DZZ.1:429); *Hōkyōki* (DZZ.7:10); *Dōgen oshō kōroku* 道元和尚廣録 (Extensive Records of Reverend Dōgen), vol. 10 (DZZ.4:268; cf. Leighton and Okumura 2004, 620); *Zuimonki* 2 (DZZ.7:65). Note that the *Zuimonki* manuscript is corrupt. It mistakingly gives Ryūzen's monastic sobriquet (Butsugen-bō 佛眼房) as "Gokon-bō" 五根房. In his 1758

*Introduction to the* SHŌBŌGENZŌ: *6b. Dōgen prior to China* 83

Mount Kōya" mentioned in another one of Dōgen's gāthā verses likely refers to a disciple of Gyōyū or of Ryūzen at the Kongō Zanmaiin.[53] Note that Dōgen composed this verse after he had returned from China. Clearly, his ties to Eisai's faction continued unbroken before, during, and after his journey there.

### Dōgen Prior to China

I identify and review the primary sources for Dōgen's biography elsewhere (see Supplement 5). His extant writings contain few details about his early life. His *Extensive Records* record four major convocation addresses (numbers 363, 409, 478, 524) that commemorated the death anniversaries of his parents. The middle two, both dedicated to his mother, occurred during the twelfth months of 1250 and 1251. The last one, delivered during the ninth month of 1252, is dedicated to his father. The first one, which occurred during the Spring of 1250, is dedicated to his "nurturing father" (*ikufu* 育父), an unusual term that possibly could refer to a stepfather. If it in fact referred to a stepfather, then that would explain the discrepancy in paternal memorial dates. The parents are not named, but each of the father figures is identified as a state councilor (*ashō* 亞相) from the Minamoto aristocracy.[54] In Ejō's *Zuimonki*, Dōgen provides more background information. He reminds Ejō that Buddhist notions of universal filial piety differ from Confucian ones, which exclusively concern only one's own parents (*Zuimonki* 3; DZZ.7:98). From a young age (*yōshō* 幼少), he loved Chinese literature, and even now (ca. 1236) recalls examples of "splendid diction" (*bigen* 美言) from works such as the *Wenxuan* 文選 (*Selected Literature*; *Zuimonki* 3; DZZ.7:90).[55]

---

printed edition, Menzan Zuihō 面山瑞方 (1683–1769) revised this name to Gogen-bō 五眼房, which also is incorrect. By Menzan's time, details about Ryūzen had been forgotten.

[53] *Dōgen oshō kōroku* 10 (DZZ.4:272; cf. Leighton and Okumura 2004, 622).

[54] *Kōroku* 5 and 7 (DZZ.3:232, 272; DZZ.4:60, 164). For a review of past speculation regarding the possible identities of Dōgen's parents, see Nakaseko 1979, 49–65. The title *ashō* normally is an alternative for *dainagon* 大納言, but in this context it can also refer to a junior (*gon* 權) *dainagon*, which would greatly expand the list of possible candidates for Dōgen's paternity.

[55] *Wenxuan* (J. *Monsen*; 60 chapters) is a literary anthology from the sixth century that includes works by 130 authors and surveys all genres of Chinese belles-lettres. Tutors in China used it as a textbook since the eighth century.

Beginning in his youth, he studied Chinese history and statecraft (*kidendō* 紀傳道) and had been an avid reader (even to a fault) for his entire life (*Zuimonki* 3; DZZ.7:92).[56]

Simply judging from the number and variety of Chinese classics that he quotes, it is clear that Dōgen must have received the kind of thorough tutorials in Chinese learning that normally would be available only to the scion of an aristocrat. Kagamishima (1965, 265–268) finds that Dōgen's *Shōbōgenzō* includes twelve quotations from eight different Chinese classics: *Book on Filial Piety*; *Analects of Confucius*; *Records of the Grand Historian*; *Master Zhuang*; *Master Wen*; *Master Guan*; *Master Shi*; and the *Six Stratagems*.[57] Significantly, Ejō's *Zuimonki* — a much shorter work — includes thirteen quotations, six of which come from four additional Chinese titles: *Spring and Autumn Annals of Master Lü*; *Sayings of the Confucius School*; *Essentials of Politics*; and the aforementioned *Selected Literature*.[58] Dōgen criticizes other Buddhist teachers who quote Chinese classics as source texts for authoritative truth statements, but he freely cites Chinese works as illustrative examples of secular thinking and general human proclivities (Kagamishima 1965, 193–208). *Sanso gyōgōki* (SZ.Shiden.1.1a) places Dōgen's Chinese education into a chronological sequence: 1203 (his fourth year) Dōgen memorized the *Hundred Songs* (*Baiyong* 百詠), by the Tang-dynasty court poet Li Jiao 李嶠 (644–713); 1206 (his seventh year) Dōgen began studying the *Spring and Autumn Annals* (*Chunqiu* 春秋) with the *Zuozhuan* 左傳 commentary, as well as the *Book of Songs* (*Shijing* 詩經). This precise chronology seems to reflect the educational norms of China, but similar examples can be found among the biographies of other notable scions of aristocrats in Japan.[59]

Dōgen writes nothing about his induction into Buddhist monastic life. Ejō's *Zuimonki* provides our only example of how Dōgen described his

---

[56]   The *Zuimonki* (Chōenji manuscript) writes "*kiden*" 紀傳 with the homophone 記典 (headnote at DZZ.7:92).

[57]   Respectively: *Xiaojing* 孝經 (J. *Kōkyō*); *Lunyu* 論語 (J. *Rongo*); *Shiji* 史記 (J. *Shiki*); *Zhuangzi* 莊子 (J. *Sōshi*); *Wenzi* 文子 (J. *Monshi*); *Guanzi* 管子 (J. *Kanshi*); *Shizi* 尸子 (J. *Shishi*); and *Liutao* 六韜 (J. *Rikutō*).

[58]   Respectively: *Laozi* 老子 (J. *Rōshi*); *Lushi chunqiu* 呂氏春秋 (J. *Ryoshi shunju*); *Kongzi jiayu* 孔子家語 (J. *Koshi kego*); *Zhenguan zhengyao* 貞觀政要 (J. *Jōgan seiyō*); and *Wenxuan* 文選 (J. *Monsen*).

[59]   For Japanese examples, see Nakaseko 1979, 66–72; regarding the Chinese system, see Miyazaki (1976, 16) which states that boys memorized more than 400,000 characters of texts at the rate of 200 characters a day over a period of eight years.

early religious career. In the vaguest possible terms, Dōgen mentions only his first Buddhist inclinations and his much later decision to leave Mount Hiei (the main monastic headquarters of Tendai Buddhism) and enter Kenninji in Kyoto. Not a single word in his description hints about the intervening events or dates:

> 我、初めてまさに無常によりて、聊か道心を發し、あまねく諸方を とぶらひ、終に山門を辭して、學道を修せしに、建仁寺に寓せし に、中間に正師にあはず、善友なきによりて、迷て邪念をおこし て。(Zuimonki 5; DZZ.7:120)

As a result of [encountering] impermanence, I initially brought forth something of the mind of the way and inquired everywhere. Until I left the Mountain Gate [i.e., Mount Hiei] and lodged at Kenninji to train in the study of the way, during that time, never having encountered a true teacher and lacking a wise friend, I was deluded and gave rise to false thoughts.

The term "wise friend" (*zen'u* 善友) refers to a Buddhist master who guides disciples to the truth, and the word "impermanence" (*mujō* 無常) frequently alludes to an untimely death. *Sanso gyōgōki* (SZ.Shiden.1.1a) makes this last point explicit. It states that, in 1207 (his eighth year) Dōgen suffered the loss of his mother. Accordingly, it goes on to say, in 1208 (his ninth year) Dōgen began to study Vasubandhu's *Abhidharma Storehouse Treatise*, one of the fundamental introductions to Buddhist cosmology and basic doctrines.

Dōgen himself does not state when he encountered impermanence or who died. He does not say when he entered religious life. His description skips over those details to immediately voice his dissatisfaction with Mount Hiei. The above passage in the *Zuimonki* continues with Dōgen's explanation of the reason why he felt disappointed by his Buddhist instructors on Mount Hiei:

> 教道の師も、先づ學問先達にひとしくよき人也、國家に知れ、天下 に名譽せん事を教訓す。よて教法等を學するにも、先、此國の上 古の賢者に、ひとしからん事を思ひ、大師等にも同からんと思て、 因、高僧傳、續高僧傳等を、披見せしに、大國の高僧、佛法者の樣 を見しに、今の師の教への如には非ず。又我がをこせる心は、皆經 論・傳記等には、厭い惡み、きらへる心にて、有りけりと思より、 漸く心つきて思に、道理をかんがふれば、名聞を思とも、當代下劣 の人に、よしと思はれんよりも、上古の賢者、向後の善人を可恥。 ひとしからん事を思とも、此國の人よりも、唐土天竺の先達、高僧 を可恥。かれにひとしからんと思べし。乃至諸天冥衆、諸佛菩薩等を 恥、かれにひとしからんとこそ、思べきに、道理を得て後には、此國

の大師等は、土かわらの如く覺て、從來の身心皆改ぬ。　　(Zuimonki 5; DZZ.7:120–121)

My teachers in the Way [on Mount Hiei] instructed me that, first I should equal the learning of my superiors, so that I would become renowned among the ruling houses and famous throughout the realm. Accordingly, even when studying the doctrines, above all, I strove to equal the paragons of Japan's antiquity, even aspiring to equal those awarded the title of Great Teacher (*daishi* 大師). While reading the [Chinese] *Lives of Eminent Monks* and *Continued Lives of Eminent Monks*, however, what I read about eminent monks in great kingdoms, their behavior in the Buddha dharma, disagreed with what I was being taught.[60] Moreover, I came to know that, in all the [Buddhist] scriptures, commentaries, and biographies, the ambitions that I had nurtured are despised and to be avoided. I comprehended the truth that aspirations for fame among the inferior people of the present age actually would shame me before the paragons of antiquity and wise [friends] of generations to come. If I wish to equal someone, then rather than the people in this kingdom [i.e., Japan], I should shame [i.e., measure] myself by the superiors and eminent monks of China and India. They are the ones I should strive to equal. Likewise, I should shame myself by striving to equal the unseen multitudes of gods, bodhisattvas, and buddhas. After having grasped this truth, I began to regard the great teachers of this kingdom as mere rubble and broken tiles, and I thereby completely reformed my previous body and mind [i.e., behavior and attitude].

The *Sanso gyōgōki* does not repeat or even allude to this explanation from the *Zuimonki*. Instead, it introduces a completely different interpretation of the reason why Dōgen became frustrated by his Buddhist training on Mount Hiei. According to its version, after Dōgen had mastered all the Buddhism taught on Mount Hiei and had read the entire Buddhist canon twice, he became stumped by doubts. Dōgen asked:

如本自法身法性者。諸佛爲甚麼。更發心修行。
(*Sanso gyōgōki*；SZ.Shiden.1.1b)

Since [the buddhas] fundamentally constitute the dharma nature of the dharma body, for what purpose should the buddhas nonetheless bring forth the mind of awakening and practice?

---

[60] *Lives of Eminent Monks* (*Gaosengzhuan* 高僧傳), T.2059; 518, 14 vols., by Huijiao 慧皎 (497–554), and *Continued Lives of Eminent Monks* (*Xugaosengzhuan* 續高僧傳), T.2060; 645, 30 vols., by Daoxuan 道宣 (596–667). Also see Wright 1954; and Kieschnik 1997.

*Introduction to the* SHŌBŌGENZŌ: *6b. Dōgen prior to China*　　　87

This question raises a fundamental issue that in later years Dōgen addressed repeatedly in his writings, but not in the same terminology as used here. The *Sanso gyōgōki* seems to have rephrased the issue in language that would have been more familiar to mainstream Buddhists in Japan. We will return to this question and Dōgen's response below, in a context that allows consideration of the Zen idiom that Dōgen used to frame this issue.

In the previous passage from the *Zuimonki* quoted above, Dōgen states that, after having failed to find a proper teacher on Mount Hiei, next he entered Kenninji in Kyoto. Kenninji maintained close ties to China. In 1211, when Shunjō 俊芿 (1166–1227; a.k.a. Gazen-bō 我禪房) returned to Japan after twelve years in China, Eisai invited him to Kenninji, where he taught full time for a year and a half. Three years later, in 1215, Daikatsu Ryōshin 大歇了心 (d. 1257; a.k.a. Hannya-bō 般若房), a disciple of Taikō Gyōyū, returned from his sojourn in China and resided for a year or more at Kenninji.[61] Possibly other Buddhist clerics who returned from China likewise came through Kenninji. Shunjō maintained close ties to the Eisai faction. Eisai had initiated Shunjō into esoteric procedures, and Shunjō taught Chinese vinaya practices at Kenninji. Eisai's disciple, Enrin 圓琳 (b. 1187; a.k.a. Ichiyō-bō 一葉房), who subsequently would serve as the eighth-generation abbot of Kenninji, for example, received instructions in bodhisattva precept initiation procedures from Shunjō at Kenninji in 1212.[62] In subsequent years, Shunjō founded his own temple, Sennyūji 泉涌寺, about two and a half kilometers south of Kenninji. Construction was not completed until 1226 but, both before and after that date, he composed detailed pure regulations for the Buddhist liturgy.[63] Significantly, many early liturgical documents from Sennyūji include phonetic glosses to indicate the pronunciations used in China for ritual chants and terms.[64] At least one manuscript, *Kyōkaigishō* 教誡

---

[61]　This date appears in *Kaizan gyōjō narabi ashikaga reifu* 開山行狀并足利靈府, a chronological biography of Taikō Gyōyū, which is transcribed in Nakao (1987); see p. 45a.

[62]　Notomi (1974, 117–118) cites several manuscripts from the Kanazawa Bunko that document the overlapping connections between Shunjō and members of the Eisai faction.

[63]　E.g., *Seishu gishiki tsuiroku* 清衆規式追録 (1221) and *Sennyūji sōshoku shidai* 泉涌寺僧職次第 (1227). See Ōmiwa and Nishitani 2011, 82.

[64]　Sennyūji documents label these glosses as "Song pronunciation" (*sōon* 宋音); see Nishitani 2014, 10.

儀鈔 (*Notes on Monastic Decorum*), copy dated 1297, mentions a ritual practice that Shunjō had taught to Dōgen. If Dōgen in fact studied liturgy under Shunjō (which seems quite possible), then Shunjō also would have taught him how to pronounce Chinese words in the Chinese manner (as *huayan* 華言, instead of the historic Japanese *yamatogoe* 和音).[65] The *Zuimonki* records the following assertion by Dōgen that affirms his ability to converse in Chinese:

> 我、幼少の昔、記典等をを好み、學して、其が今も、入宋傳法するまでも、内外の書籍をひらき、方言を通ずるまでも、(Zuimonki 3; DZZ.7:92)

Long ago, in my youth, I enjoyed studying the curriculum of the histories and biographies (*kidendō* 紀傳道; i.e., statecraft).[66] And even now, even until I entered Song China and received transmission of the dharma, I perused Buddhist and non-Buddhist books to the point of becoming fluent in the local speech.

It is not completely clear what Dōgen might have meant by "peruse books" (*shoseki o hiraku* 書籍を開く). Perhaps he read them aloud while nearby companions corrected his pronunciation. In his *Tenzo kyōkun* (*Admonitions for the Chef*), Dōgen recounts a conversation with a monastic cook that he dates to the fourth of the fifth month of 1223, less than one month after his arrival in China. Maybe the dialogue was facilitated by an interpreter. The nearby merchant (*washitō* 倭使頭) who sold goods from Japan, for example, must have been able to speak both Chinese and Japanese.[67] Or maybe Dōgen and the cook exchanged written notes.[68] If

---

[65] Notomi 1974. Regarding the conversational ability of Japanese Buddhist clerics who visited Song China, also see Enomoto 2003; and especially Tachi 2014.

[66] The traditional education in Dōgen's time consisted of four curriculums (*shidō* 四道): history and statecraft (*kidendō* 紀傳道); Confucian classics (*myōgyōdō* 明經道); administration (*myōbōdō* 明法道); and mathematics (*sandō* 算道).

[67] The word *wa* 倭 in the merchant's designation does not refer to his place of origin, residence, or family background. It refers to his trade specialization (Enomoto 2001), which required bilingual skills. Eisai, for example, described the merchant who facilitated his travels in China, Li Dezhao, as bilingual (*ryōchō tsūji ri tokushō* 兩朝通事李德昭; *Kōzen gokokuron* 興禪護國論 9; T.2543.80:15b). See Enomoto (2010, 115–116; 134–136) regarding the importance of merchants as translators for Japanese Buddhists in China. Also see Enomoto 2003; and Tachi 2014.

[68] Many Japanese Buddhists in China are known to have communicated by exchanging written notes. For example: the *Song History* (*Songshi* 宋史

*Introduction to the* SHŌBŌGENZŌ: *6b. Dōgen prior to China*    89

Dōgen himself, on the other hand, truly could converse verbally in Chinese at such an early date, then he must have rehearsed his conversation skills over many previous months, if not years, before he departed from Japan. His language studies would have begun while he was at Kenninji with a likeminded cohort who wished to emulate the Buddhist practices of China.

The *Sanso gyōgōki* (SZ.Shiden.1.2a) dates Dōgen's arrival at Kenninji to 1217 (his eighteenth year). The *Kenzeiki* (p. 10) provides the same date and then adds that at this point Dōgen already had spent six years in training on Mount Hiei. The *Sanso gyōgōki* merely states that Dōgen became the disciple of Myōzen, but the *Kenzeiki* mistakenly identifies Myōzen as the second abbot of Kenninji. Most manuscript versions of the *Kenzeiki* (p. 8; but not the 1552 copy by Zuichō) compound the mistake by identifying "Myōzen" as an alternative name for Taikō Gyōyū. Actually, in 1115, when Eisai died, Gyōyū became the second abbot of Kenninji, but he continued to serve simultaneously as abbot of Jufukuji in Kamakura. Once his disciple Daikatsu Ryōshin returned from China later that same year, Ryōshin took over as the deputy leader of Kenninji under Gyōyū.[69] Somewhat later (date unknown), Dōshō 道聖 (d.1241, a.k.a. Santai-bō 三諦房), another of Eisai's disciples, became the official third abbot of Kenninji.[70] Meanwhile, the *Kenzeiki* (p. 11) reports that on 1221.9.13 Dōgen received dharma transmission from Myōzen in the Linji (J. Rinzai) lineage of Eisai.[71]

---

491.5b and 13a) account of Japan states that Chōnen 奝然 (938–1016) wrote well even though he could not speak Chinese (*Diaoran shan lishu er butong huayan* 奝然善隸書而不通華言), and that Jakushō 寂照 (926?–1034) does not understand Chinese speech but recognizes the words and writes them extremely well (*Jizhao buxiao huayan er shi wenzi shanxie shenmiao* 寂照不曉華言而識文字繕寫甚妙) (https://www.kanripo.org/text/KR2a0032/491). Likewise, Jōjin 成尋 (1011–1081) wrote that once, when his Chinese interpreter was not present, he wrote notes in reply to questions (*e tsūji shukkyo i hissho un* 依通事出去以筆書云; *Santendai godaisanki* 參天台五臺山記 6; CBETA.B.174.32.392c16).

[69]   *Kaizan gyōjō narabi ashikaga reifu* 開山行狀并足利靈府, transcribed in Nakao 1987; see p. 45a.

[70]   Biographical records for Dōshō, if extant, have not been reprinted. We do not know if he also studied in China.

[71]   Today, Eiheiji owns a copy of a document (*Shishi sōjōge* 師資相承偈) originally dated 1221.9.12 that purports to confirm this dharma transmission ritual (SK.1.5).

## *Dōgen in China*

Extant records cannot provide us with precise numbers of Japanese Buddhists who journeyed to China because many travelers went unrecorded; and, even when documents happen to mention a pilgrim by name, usually it cannot be known if any named individual refers only to a solo traveler or to the head of an entourage. This kind of inexactitude can be seen in the directive (*inzen* 院宣), issued in the name of the royal prelate Go-Takakura-in 後高倉院 (1179–1223), on the twenty-first of the second month of 1223, to permit travel to Hakata landing by the Kenninji cleric Myōzen, so that he might journey to China with two or three of his disciples (SK.1.5–6). That same day, the military administrative office in Kyoto (Rokuhara Tandai) issued a more precise permit (*gechijō* 下知牒) that named: Myōzen, Dōgen, Kakunen 廓然, and Kōshō 高照 (or Ryōshō 亮照?; SK.1.6). While Dōgen alone commands our attention today, at that time, he represented only one-fourth of Myōzen's party; and, except for the whims of fate, any of these four pilgrims might have succeeded where the others failed. Because Myōzen later died in China (another accident of history), Dōgen wrote two brief précis of Myōzen's activities there.[72] Since Dōgen accompanied Myōzen, his two accounts also inform us of his own movements.

Myōzen departed Kyoto on the twenty-second of the second month and arrived in China about two months later.[73] No reports state what they did along the way between these two dates. Eisai's account of his journey to China (*Eisai nittō engi* 榮西入唐縁起) provides some clues, since Myōzen and his party were following in Eisai's footsteps.[74] In Eisai's

---

[72] One consists of a colophon (untitled, unsigned, undated) written in very small handwriting at the end of Myōzen's ordination certificate; see *Myōzen gusoku kaichō* 明全具足戒牒 (SK.1.1–5, esp. 4–5); *Myōzen oshō ryakuden* 明全和尚略傳 (ESST-D.31–33); or *Myōzen kaichō okugaki* 明全戒牒奥書 (DZZ.7:234–235). The other consists of a calligraphic copy of an unsigned original dated 1227.10.5 said to have been a holograph by Dōgen titled *Shari sōdenki* 舍利相傳記 (DZZ.7:216–218).

[73] For the date of departure, see *Myōzen kaichō okugaki* (DZZ.7:234) and *Shari sōdenki* (DZZ.7:216). For their arrival, see *Myōzen kaichō okugaki* (DZZ.7:234) and "Washing the Face" (50; "Senmen"; DZZ.2:49).

[74] My summary of Eisai's time in Hakata follows Enomoto 2005. Eisai kept a diary of his time in China; and, in *Zuimonki* (3; DZZ.7:87), Dōgen mentioned a biography of Eisai written by Minamoto Akikane 源顯兼 (d.

Introduction to the SHŌBŌGENZŌ: 6c. Dōgen in China

case, he arrived at the Chinese settlement (*tōbō* 唐房) adjacent to Hakata landing on the eighth of the second month of 1168 and arrived in China more than two months later, on the twenty-fourth of the fourth month. Eisai spent most of that time in Japan. His ship did not raise anchor until the third day of the fourth month and did not reach open seas (*hōyō* 放洋) until the eighteenth. While waiting for his departure, Eisai conducted prayer rituals at every available religious site without omission (*mufukeireki* 無不經歷). Specifically, he prayed at the two main Tendai temple complexes, Anrakuji 安樂寺 and Daisenji 大山寺, located just outside of Dazaifu, and at the shrine to the god Sumiyoshi 住吉 located near the Chinese settlement on the coast. Eisai's account provides a glimpse of the religious landscape inhabited by Dōgen and his compatriots.

Dazaifu, a town located about 14 kilometers inland, served as the home of the local military administrative offices (*Chinzei bugyō* 鎮西奉行) that, in theory at least, supervised the maritime trade conducted by Chinese seamen. The sprawling Anrakuji temple complex dominated Dazaifu. Along with numerous subtemples and ritual halls, it was home to the mausoleum of Sugawara Michizane 菅原道眞 (845–903), a Japanese government minister who died in exile at Dazaifu and who, as Tenjin 天神, a local avatar of the god Daijizaiten 大自在天, became worshiped across Japan as a patron of Chinese learning. Long after Dōgen's time, Zen monks helped popularize the "Totō Tenjin" 渡唐天神 legend that Michizane's avatar had journeyed to China and studied Zen at Jingshan (one of the Five Mountains).[75] But even Dōgen, with his childhood upbringing in Chinese learning, revered Michizane. His recorded sayings (*Kōroku* 10; DZZ.4:280) include a verse in Chinese that Dōgen dedicated to him. Daisenji, the home of the Great Bodhisattva (*daibosatsu* 大菩薩) Hōman 寶滿, guarded the northeast, a baleful direction, and thereby performed the same function for Dazaifu as Mount Hiei performed for the capital.[76] In Daizaifu, it chartered Chinese trade ships and brokered

---

1215); Yoneda 2008a, 204–208. Neither source exists today, but Myōzen (and maybe Dōgen) would have known both.

[75] See Era Hiromu (1967) regarding the organization of the Buddhist priesthood at Anrakuji. For the legend of Michizane as a Zen monk, see Borgen 1994, 325–334; Yoshizawa 2011. After the Meiji period separation of buddhas and gods, Anrakuji was destroyed, and Michizane's shrine became Dazaifu Jinja. In 1947, it adopted the name Dazaifu Tenmangū.

[76] After the Meiji period separation of buddhas and gods, Daisenji transformed into Kamado Jinja 竈門神社.

the exchange of goods with clients in central Japan such as Mount Hiei.[77] The great god (*daijin* 大神) Sumiyoshi protected sailors and fishermen. The famous Buddhist pilgrim Ennin 圓仁 (794–864) mentioned Sumiyoshi several times in his diary of his nine-year travels to China and back (838–847). The seamen who transported Ennin had shrines to Sumiyoshi on each ship, and they worshiped Sumiyoshi upon boarding, to obtain more favorable winds, for a safe return, and so forth. Eisai's account demonstrates that three hundred years later Sumiyoshi continued to protect pilgrims on their journey to China.[78]

Dōgen mentioned his time aboard ship only once, in this passage found in Ejō's *Zuimonki*:

入宋の時き、船中にして痢病をせしに、惡風出來て、船中さわぎし時、病忘て止まりぬ (*Zuimonki* 6; DZZ.7:144)

When I journeyed to Song China, while I was sick with diarrhea aboard ship, violent winds arose, throwing the ship into confusion. I forgot my sickness, and it stopped.

Myōzen and his party arrived at Qingyuan 慶元 (J. Hyōgen; previously Mingzhou 明州; i.e., the old walled, central section of present-day Ningbo), the town that served as the center for maritime trade with Japan and Korea, and which also stood as the central urban hub for a network of major Buddhist temples in its environs. Initially, they resided at Jingfusi 景福寺 (J. Keifukuji) in the center of the city.[79] This temple also appears in the biographies of two other Japanese pilgrims: Shunjō (who entered Jingfusi shortly after his arrival in China and studied vinaya there for three years, 1200–1202) and Enni (who, like Myōzen et al., entered Jingfusi immediately upon arrival in Qingyuan in 1235).[80] The fact that three rather disparate pilgrims stayed at the same temple suggests a pattern, but its significance is not certain. One can only imagine why Jingfusi might have been a suitable facility by considering the larger social circumstances faced by these pilgrims.

---

[77] Von Glahn 2014, 275–277; Yamamura 2021, 251.

[78] *Nittō guhō junrei gyōki* 入唐求法巡禮行記; fascs. 1, 2, 4; CBETA.B.95.18.26, 27, 31, 33, 34, 117, 123. Also see Reischauer (1955, 94, 98, 114, 117, 122, 139, 407).

[79] *Myōzen kaichō okugaki* 明全戒牒奥書 (DZZ.7:234).

[80] Regarding Shunjō, see *Fukaki hōshiden* 不可棄法師傅; DNBZ.115.521b; cf. Ōmiwa and Nishitani 2011, 82. Regarding Enni, see *Shōichi kokushi nenpu* 聖一國師年譜; DNBZ.95.132a.

*Introduction to the* SHŌBŌGENZŌ: *6c. Dōgen in China* 93

In China, all Buddhist monastics (especially foreign guests) had to carry official identity papers (*gongping* 公憑) and travel permits (*gongyimian* 公移免) and receive legal permission to assume residence at any specific state regulated monastery or temple. The legal and bureaucratic vocabulary required to navigate these procedures — not to mention possible extralegal necessities, such as "favor funds" (*renqingqian* 人情錢; i.e., bribes) — exceeded the linguistic abilities of even the most fluent Japanese pilgrims. They required the assistance of maritime traders who could interpret both the language and the legal procedures. This type of assistance would be factored into the fees charged for the voyage from Japan to China.[81] It is possible that Jingfusi, which specialized in teaching vinaya and monastic decorum, processed newly arrived overseas clergy on behalf of the government (Satō Shūkō 1995, 104). Or, maybe it was simply the most convenient location nearby government offices for both internal affairs and maritime trade (*shibosi* 市舶司). Jingfusi no longer exists, but its previous location is occupied by the local shrine of the city god (*chenghuangmiao* 城隍廟) of Ningbo City (Nishitani 2013, 66; Nishitani 2018, 184–185). A short distance of about 1.3 kilometers separates the shrine from the local landings near the confluence of the Yong 甬 and Yuyao 餘姚 Rivers, where merchants would anchor their ships. From that location, government officials and/or Buddhist clergy could easily summon maritime traders when their interpretation services were needed.

As mentioned above, Dōgen recounted a conversation with a monastic cook that he dates to the fourth of the fifth month of 1223, shortly after he and Myōzen arrived in China. According to Dōgen, this conversation occurred onboard a merchant ship. The *Kenzeiki* (p. 12) dutifully notes this event without comment, but Menzan Zuihō inserted a note into his 1754 revised edition that prefaces the conversation with the explanation that: "Dōgen remained aboard ship throughout the fifth month" (*gogatsu no chū shi nao fune ni ari* 五月ノ中師猶ヲ船ニアリ). Although this inference might have seemed plausible to Menzan, it seems highly unlikely as a practical matter and completely ignores the fact that Dōgen's legal status in China depended entirely on his position as the disciple (i.e., servant) of Myōzen, the only traveler with official permits. Although many scholars have repeated Menzan's interpretation, it is simpler to assume

---

[81]  Enomoto 2004, especially p. 70; Enomoto 2010, 115–116. Enomoto (2004) points out that fake ordination certificates were not uncommon.

94 DŌGEN'S *SHŌBŌGENZŌ* VOLUME VIII

that Dōgen met the cook on a day when he had walked over from Jing-fusi to summon an interpreter or for some other errand.[82]

Nine days later, on the thirteenth, Myōzen enrolled into Tiantong, a large Buddhist monastery where Eisai had received dharma transmission from his Chinese master. Tiantong is tucked between two mountains in a remote location about twenty-five kilometers east-southeast from the shrine of the city god of Ningbo City (where Jingfusi once stood). At that time, Wuji Liaopai 無際了派 (J. Musai Ryōha; 1150–1224) served as the abbot of Tiantong. As a student within an assembly directed by Liaopai, Dōgen found himself within a Linji (J. Rinzai) context (see Table 36, Dō-gen among the Linji Lineage). Liaopai, moreover, represented a different branch of the Linji House. Rather than the Huanglong 黄龍 (J. Ōryū) lineage that Dōgen had mastered under Myozen, Liaopai belonged to the ascendant Yangqi 楊岐 (J. Yōgi) lineage.[83] Liaopai's master was Zhuoan Deguang 拙庵德光 (J. Setsuan Tokkō; 1121–1203), the teacher who had accepted Nōnin as his dharma heir. Nōnin is the Japanese founder of the so-called "Darumashū" that Eisai had denounced in such harsh terms. One can easily imagine that Dōgen must have had many questions about the similarities and differences among the Huanglong and Yangqi lin-eages and the reasons why Eisai had denounced Nōnin. In his writings, however, Dōgen focused on the larger picture: the Five Houses of Chan (see Table 34), which he later outlined in *Bendōwa* (1231). Although nowadays basic information about Chan is readily available either on-line or in countless introductory essays, it can be informative to examine Dōgen's statements within the context of his own existential circum-stances.

*Bendōwa* (*Talk on Pursuing the Way*), consists of Dōgen's autobi-ographical self-introduction along with an introduction to Zen. Dōgen introduces Zen as the authentic Buddhism that Bodhidharma brought to China. Successive generations of Chinese teachers transmitted Bodhidharma's lineage in a single line down to Caoxi Huineng 曹溪慧能 (J. Sōkei Enō; 638–713). Huineng produced two outstanding disciples: Nanyue Huairang 南嶽懷讓 (J. Nangaku Ejō; 677–744) and Qingyuan Xingsi 青原行思 (J. Seigen Gyōshi; d. 740). Thereafter, the descendants

---

[82]  Satō Shūkō (1995, 105), based on different reasons also rejects the no-tion that Dōgen remained aboard ship.

[83]  Of the so-called 24 lineages of Zen in Japan (*zenshū nijūshiryū* 禪宗二十四流), 21 derive from the Yangqi branch. This list, however, does not in-clude all the Chan lineages introduced to Japan.

*Introduction to the* SHŌBŌGENZŌ: *6c. Dōgen in China*                95

of Nanyue and Qingyuan proliferated and produced the branch lineages that came to be known as the Five Houses (*wujia* 五家; J. *goke*) of Chan: the Linji 臨濟 (J. Rinzai) House; the Weiyang 潙仰 (J. Igyō) House; the Caodong 曹洞 (J. Sōtō) House; the Yunmen 雲門 (J. Unmon) House; and the Fayan 法眼 (J. Hōgen) House. This family tree (diagramed in Table 34, The Five Houses of Chan) reflects not just Dōgen's view but the way that the Chinese Chan tradition portrayed itself in its genealogical accounts. Dōgen concluded his explanation by stating that today (ca. 1231) only the Linji House is widespread in China.

This last assertion certainly reflects Dōgen's situation in China and the branch lineages of Zen that were introduced to Japan during his lifetime. Table 36, "Dōgen among the Linji Lineage," aligns the key ancestors of the Yangqi branch of the Linji House in China (nearer the left margin) with Dōgen's contemporaries who introduced those Chinese lineages to Japan (along the right margin). It also includes Dōgen, who interacted with many of these people and who initially studied under Linji teachers of the Yangqi branch while in China — although he subsequently introduced a lineage of the Caodong (J. Sōtō) House to Japan. Eisai is missing (since he belonged to the Huanglong branch of the Linji House; see Table 35), but three of the six Japanese who appear in this table also belonged to the Eisai faction: Dōgen, Enni, and Muhon Kakushin 無本覺心 (1207–1298; a.k.a. Shinchi-bō 心地房). Kakushin had been a disciple of Taihō Gyōyū (see Table 35), but he subsequently received initiation in the bodhisattva precepts from Dōgen.[84] Kakua 覺阿 (b. 1141) preceded Dōgen by half a century, but he is included because the *Genkō shakusho* (*Genkō Era Account of Buddhism*; 1322) evaluated Kakua and Dōgen as a matched pair of failures: it states that Kakua lacked followers within Japan, while Dōgen, stuck in the wilds of northern Japan, lacked influence within the central district of the capital.[85]

Lanxi Daolong 蘭溪道隆 (J. Rankei Dōryū; 1213–1278) came to Japan in 1246. He and Enni both descended from the same lineage of Huqiu Shaolong 虎丘紹隆 (J. Kukyū Shōryū; 1077–1136). His ship to Hakata landing carried many other Buddhists, from both Korea and China, and several from Japan, including Gettō Chikyō 月翁智鏡 (dates unknown), a disciple of Shunjō and the future fourth abbot of Sennyūji. Chikyō

---

[84]  *Ju Kakushin kaimyaku* 授覺心戒脈 (DZZ.6:228, 230–231).

[85]  It refers to Kakua and Dōgen as "A-Gen" 阿元; see *Genkō shakusho* 元亨釋書; 6; DNBZ.101.76a.

invited Daolong to Kyoto in 1247.[86] A short time later, Daikatsu Ryōshin invited Daolong to Kamakura to stay at Jufukuji 壽福寺 (founded by Eisai), where Ryōshin served as abbot. Thereafter, Daolong became the abbot at one temple after another: in 1248, at Jōrakuji 常樂寺 (founded by Taikō Gyōyū); in 1253, at the newly-constructed Kenchōji 建長寺; and in 1265, at Kenninji (founded by Eisai) in Kyoto. His ascension to the abbotship of Kenninji marked both the culmination and the termination of the Eisai faction. Prior to 1265, all the abbots of Kenninji had been members of the Eisai faction, but after Daolong none were. Dōgen resided in Kamakura from the eighth month of 1247 to the third month of 1248, precisely at the same time that Daolong began to make a name for himself. They must have met at least once, but no reliable evidence exists regarding any possible connections between them. The *Kenzeiki* (pp. 64–65) reproduces an exchange of missives, dated to 1247, between Dōgen in Echizen and Daolong in Kyoto, but they are spurious.[87]

Within Table 36, Dahui Zonggao 大慧宗杲 (J. Daie Sōkō; 1089–1163) stands apart as the most famous and influential Chan master of the Song dynasty.[88] Dahui (a.k.a. Miaoxi 妙喜; J. Myōki) had composed his own collection of Chan stories (*gong'an* 公案; J. kōan), which he titled *Treasury of the True Dharma Eye* (C. *Zhengfayanzang*; J. *Shōbōgenzō*).[89] The fact that Dōgen adopted the same title for his own collection of essays indicates that Dōgen recognized Dahui's importance. Nonetheless, Dahui might not have seemed as important to Dōgen as he was to be deemed by history. Table 36 shows that Dahui represented only one of several Chan/Zen lineages introduced to Japan during Dōgen's time. Any one of these lineages could have become more prominent, at least in Japan. And the only person in Japan who claimed any affiliation to Dahui's lineage was Nōnin, a teacher who gained that affiliation by proxy. In 1189, Nōnin sent two disciples (Renchū 練中 and Shōben 勝辨) as his proxies to China. Those disciples met Dahui's disciple Zhuoan Deguang at Aśoka temple (one of the Five Mountains), showed Deguang a verse

---

[86] Tachi 2014, 262–264 and 281 notes 33–34; Nakamura 2014, 579ff.

[87] DZZ.7:270–273; and 393–394 ("kaidai" 解題 by Itō Shūken).

[88] Regarding Dahui and his influence, see Schlütter 2008, especially 104–136. The influence of Dahui and his descendants grew even stronger in subsequent centuries (see Ishii Shūdō's 9-part series of articles 1970–1978).

[89] Dahui composed *Zhengfayanzang* (3 vols.) in 1141 as a collection of 663 *gong'an* with comments by himself (Miaoxi) on 140 of them. It was first printed in 1147 and reprinted in 1237 and repeatedly thereafter.

*Introduction to the* SHŌBŌGENZŌ: *6c. Dōgen in China*     97

in Chinese that Nōnin had composed, and Deguang thereupon certified Nōnin as his dharma heir. Dōgen, on the other hand, journeyed to China himself and received direct instruction from Deguang's disciple Wuji Liaopai. The *Sanso gyōgōki* (SZ Shiden 1.2a) adds that Dōgen also interviewed Zheweng Ruyan 浙翁如琰 (J. Setsuō Nyotan; 1151–1225), another one of Deguang's disciples. Even without Ruyan, one can see how Dōgen could have come to regard his own direct knowledge of Dahui's lineage as being more detailed and accurate than what was conveyed by Nōnin's followers.

In "The Way of the Buddhas" (chapter 44; "Butsudō") Dōgen admits that, before he became the disciple of Rujing, he actively sought to investigate the "arcane import of the five lineages" (*goshū no genshi* 五宗の玄旨) of Chan. After he became Rujing's disciple, however, he learned the "key point that 'five lineages' constitutes a corrupt designation" (*goshū no ranshō naru mune* 五宗の亂稱なる旨; DZZ.1:477). This comment highlights the inherent tension between the ideal of universal truth and the necessity of expressing it via disparate historical circumstances. Dōgen's quest to resolve this tension entailed two main components: mastering the Zen stories (kōan) of each of the Five Houses (to be discussed in a separate section) and inspecting the dharma succession documents of all Five Houses.

Dōgen described the second component of his quest in "The Inheritance Certificate" (number 39; "Shisho"), which recounts how he managed to view several inheritance certificates, one of which he also reproduces, during his Chinese residency. Dōgen's narrative unfolds as if he merely chanced upon a series of fortuitous coincidences. At the same time, he repeatedly reminds his readers how rare and difficult it is to see one of these documents — remarks that leave little doubt that he quested for them.[90] In one case, he collaborated with another monastic officer (Prior Shiguang) over a period of months for an opportunity to view the document. In another case, he relied on the intercession of Ryūzen (Butsugen-bō), a compatriot in Eisai's faction who had already been at Tiantong for several years. During these episodes, he repeatedly inquired how the documents could exhibit different features if they all descend from a single progenitor. In response, the chapter presents an overarching theme of unity amidst diversity. In all, Dōgen describes six individual inheritance certificates, in more or less detail, which appear in the following narrative sequence:

[90]  Cf. Satō Shūkō 1995, 109.

1. Certificate of the Fayan House. From a spiritual descendant of Fayan Wenyi 法眼文益 (Hōgen Mon'eki; 885–958), shown to Dōgen by a cleric named Weiyi 惟一 (J. I'ichi), who held the status of "West Hall" (C. *xitang* 西堂; J. *seidō*) at Tiantong. Rujing recommended Weiyi to Dōgen, and Dōgen states that seeing this certificate resolved all his doubts (DZZ.1:426–427).[91]

2. Certificate of the Yunmen House. From a spiritual descendant of Yunmen Wenyan 雲門文偃 (Unmon Bun'en; 864–949), shown to Dōgen by a cleric named Zongyue 宗月 (J. Shūgatsu) who served as head seat (C. *shouzuo* 首座; J. *shuso*) at Tiantong. Dōgen states that he gained his initial, slight understanding after hearing Zongyue explain the discrepancies among certificates (DZZ.1:427–428).

3. Certificate of the Linji House, Yangqi Branch (1). From a spiritual descendant of Foyan Qingyuan 佛眼清遠 (J. Butsugen Seion; 1067–1121), shown to Dōgen by a cleric named Chuan 傳 (J. Den) who served as canon prefect (C. *zhangzhu* 藏主; J. *zōsu*), a librarian, at Tiantong. After Ryūzen (Butsugen-bō) interceded on behalf of Dōgen, Chuan allowed Dōgen to view the certificate during autumn of 1223. Note that Dōgen's mentor Shunjō (1166-1227; a.k.a. Gazen-bō) belonged to this lineage. Dōgen would have especially valued this connection (DZZ.1:429).

4. Certificate of the Linji House, Yangqi Branch (2). From Zhuoan Deguang (J. Setsuan Tokkō; 1121–1203), a disciple of Dahui Zonggao (J. Daie Sōkō), who had bestowed it on Wuji Liaopai (J. Musai Ryōha; 1150–1224), the abbot of Tiantong. It was shown to Dōgen by a cleric named Shiguang 師廣 (J. Shikō) who served as prior (C. *dousi* 都寺; J. *tsūsu*) at Tiantong. Shiguang first promised Dōgen during the autumn of 1223 that he would arrange a viewing. He could not do so until the twenty-first day of 1224. This is the only occasion for which Dōgen provides a precise date in his narrative. He also provides a transcription of the main contents of the certificate. Dōgen does not say so, but most likely he was allowed to write out a copy. As mentioned above, Nōnin claimed lineage affiliation with Deguang. Dōgen's transcription of a cer-

---

[91] Satō Shūkō (1995, 109–110) notes that the Weiyi in this episode could not have been Huanxi Weiyi 環溪惟一 (J. Kankei I'ichi; 1202–1281) as is frequently assumed.

*Introduction to the* SHŌBŌGENZŌ: *6c. Dōgen in China*    99

tificate written by Deguang provides proof that Dōgen knew the "arcane import" (*genshi* 玄旨) of Nōnin's lineage (DZZ.1:430–432).

5. Certificate of unidentified provenance (Weiyang House). Unidentified certificate shown to Dōgen by a cleric named Yuanzi 元鼒 (J. Genshi; in some manuscripts mistakenly written Yuankao 元鼒; J. Genkō) who served as the leader of Wanniansi 萬年寺 in the Tiantai range of mountains. Dōgen states that this event occurred "around [during (?)] the time of Baoqing" (*hōkyō no koro* 寶慶のころ) — the interpretation of which will be discussed below — when Dōgen toured Buddhist monasteries in the regions adjacent to Mount Tiantai. Dōgen explains that Yuanzi showed him the certificate (and offered him dharma transmission) after the two of them had discussed the "Fine Successor" *gong'an* (J. kōan) involving Dawei Lingyou 大潙靈祐 (J. Dai'i Reiyū; 771–853) and his disciple Yangshan Huiji 仰山慧寂 (J. Kyōzan Ejaku; ca. 802–887). Mount Dawei is better known as Mount Weishan 潙山 (J. Isan) and, in combination with Yansgshan, its presence in this episode clearly implies that this inheritance certificate must have come from a spiritual descendant of the Weiyang House (DZZ.1:432).[92] Keizan's *Denkōroku* (p. 532) makes this point explicit.

6. Certificate of the Caodong House. Summary of the key features of the inheritance certificate that Dōgen himself received when he joined the Caodong House as the dharma heir of Rujing. Dōgen especially notes that the Caodong House preserves the ritual of mixing blood that had been performed by Caoxi Huineng (J. Sōkei Enō) and Qingyuan Xingsi (J. Seigen Gyōshi), during the eighth century when they first formed this lineage. Significantly, in this passage Dōgen does not use the term "Caodong House" but refers to the "followers of Dongshan" (*tōzan monka* 洞山門下), that is, Dongshan Liangjie 洞山良价 (J. Tōzan Ryōkai; 807–869) and his successors (DZZ.1:433–434).

---

[92] The "Fine Successor" *gong'an* (C. *lingsi hua* 令嗣話; J. *ryōshiwa*; *reishiwa*) can be found in the *Shōbōgenzō* in Chinese script (no. 103; DZZ.5:180). In this context, the adjective *ling* 令 (J. *ryō*; *rei*; denoting "splendid") frequently functions as a third-person honorific prefix for kinship terms. Normally it could be translated simply as "[your] son" (synonyms include: *linglang* 令郎; *lingzi* 令子; *lingyin* 令胤; *lingxi* 令息), but "fine successor" better captures the way that Lingyou uses it in the second-person as "you, my fine son." Note that the correct pronunciations for Lingyou's residence should be "Dawei" or "Weishan" (not "Dagui" nor "Guishan").

Historians of China find a treasure-trove of information in "The Inheritance Certificate" (chapter 39; "Shisho"). No other accounts of these kinds of documents exist prior to the ground-breaking 1963 study by Holmes Welch (1921–1981), who at that time unfortunately was unaware of Dōgen's writings.[93] Actual copies of succession documents from this early period do not survive.[94] Dōgen's descriptions provide the only evidence. Historians cannot even guess when the custom of inheritance documents began, but Dōgen's detailed reports demonstrate that it was well established by the early thirteenth century. Dōgen's descriptions do not stop with the actual documents. He also provides ethnographic descriptions of their use and misuse both within and outside of monastic settings. He provides remarkably explicit accounts of ritual matters that he himself regarded as the most secret of secrets. He quotes at length admonitions by Rujing that condemn widespread abuses of dharma transmission and that thereby inform us about what many people actually did (DZZ.1:429–430). Nowhere else can one find information about these vital social contexts. Dōgen also described emotional and spiritual nuances that help the reader appreciate the religious significance of the concrete link to the buddha knowledge (and to the Buddha as a living presence) that these documents can provide. In a key episode, Dōgen learns that his spiritual quest will be fulfilled via a dream vision, in which he encounters the Chan Master Damei Fachang 大梅法常 (J. Daibai Hōjō; 752–839), a famous disciple of Mazu Daoyi 馬祖道一 (J. Baso Dōitsu; 709–788), who presented Dōgen with a plum blossom. Dōgen interpreted this dream as an auspicious sign from the buddhas and believed that its prophecy would definitely be fulfilled (DZZ.1:433). Finally, according to Ishii Shūdō (2015e, 639), a leading specialist in the history of Buddhism during the Song dynasty, the "The Inheritance Certificate" chapter provides one of our only two incontrovertible dates

---

[93] Welch 1963, titled "Dharma Scrolls and the Succession of Abbots in Chinese Monasteries," remains an essential source. The informants quoted by Welch refer to these documents as "dharma scrolls" (C. *fajuan* 法卷), but the actual documents (at least the one photographed by Welch) are titled *Treasury of the True Dharma Eye* (C. *Zhengfayanzang*).

[94] The inheritance certificate that Rujing supposedly bestowed on Dōgen, the so-called *Shisho no zu* 嗣書ノ圖 (dated 1227) owned by Eiheiji and designated a national treasure (*kokuhō* 國寶), is not authentic (Ishii Shūdō 2015, 645–646).

*Introduction to the* SHŌBŌGENZŌ: *6c. Dōgen in China* 101

for Dōgen's activities in China: 1224.1.21, when Dōgen viewed the inheritance certificate of Wuji Liaopai.[95]

The question of chronology looms large in Dōgen's writings. "The Inheritance Certificate" chapter is no exception. The narrative sequence (1–6) presented above of Dōgen's perusal of inheritance certificates in many ways exemplifies the difficulties of translating Dōgen's accounts into a temporal order. Logically, the first two episodes must have occurred later in time (probably after episode 5), because the questions that Dōgen addressed to his mentors, Weiyi and Zongyi, concern the discrepancies among the inheritance certificates that Dōgen already had examined. Of these two episodes, the one with Zongyi (number 2) would have occurred before the one with Weiyi (number 1), because Dōgen stated that, thanks to Zongyi, he gained a slight understanding, and that the episode with Weiyi resolved all his doubts. Moreover, Weiyi had been recommended to Dōgen by his master Rujing. At the time of the fourth episode (1224.1.21), Wuji Liaopai was still alive and abbot of Tiantong Temple. Dōgen did not meet Rujing until later, after Liaopai's death. It seems likely, therefore, that the first episode, with Weiyi, actually must have occurred next to last, after Dōgen became the disciple of Rujing and had acquired complete confidence in the inheritance certificate (number 6) that Rujing would soon bestow. If this logical sequence does in fact accord with the actual chronology, then why would Dōgen have written a different narrative sequence? Here one can only speculate. Many of Dōgen's chapters (such as "The Realized Kōan") begin by stating the truth of the matter (the answer) and proceed by presenting the larger context (the problem) to which it relates. According to this pattern, the episode with Weiyi should come first because it resolved the doubts that were prompted by the disparate certificates of the earlier episodes.

The fourth episode above illustrates how even precise dates must be interpreted in light of their relationship to contemporaneous events. Advances in our knowledge of the biographies of Rujing and of Wuji Liaopai have forced scholars to abandon their previously accepted timelines for key events in Dōgen's career.[96] Scholars once thought that the birth and death dates for Rujing (1162–1227.7.17) and for Wuji Liaopai

---

[95] Ishii gives the other incontrovertible date as 1225.5.27 when Myōzen died. My entire description of the Shisho chapter and its significance is heavily indebted to Ishii 2015.

[96] For convenient summaries, see Itō Shūken (1983 and 1984) and Satō Shūkō (1985, 1995, and 1997).

(1150–1224) occurred one year later than the years indicated by the best sources available today. This chronological shift for their dates forced some episodes that involved Dōgen likewise to shift to an earlier point in his life. Ishii Shūdō (2015e, 638-639) exaggerates, but only slightly, when he emphasizes the scarcity of incontrovertible dates for Dōgen's activities in China. It is not that reliable dates do not exist, but rather that some older scholars nonetheless prefer the previous, now discredited descriptions for dates tied to a one-year later sequence. As we shall see below, their preference derives not simply from familiarity, but because the newer, earlier dates entail adopting new narrative sequences that alter the possible significance attached to any or all events on all dates. Ultimately, revised biographical narratives open new spaces that permit (or invite) alternative textual interpretations of the *Shōbōgenzō*.

Now we can return to the fifth episode, the certificate of unidentified provenance (nonetheless associated with the Weiyang House) that Yuanzi showed to Dōgen at the Wanniansi in the Tiantai range of mountains. When did it occur? Dōgen wrote "around [during (?)] Baoqing." The Baoqing Era officially began with the lunar New Year 1225 and lasted three years until the last day of 1227. "Around" (*koro*) that time, therefore, traditionally has been interpreted as indicating that Dōgen toured the Tiantai Mountains and beyond sometime toward the end of 1224 or shortly after the beginning of 1225. Either time frame would have worked with the previous chronology, but neither fits the revised chronology. In this episode, Yuanzi offered dharma transmission to Dōgen, which could not have occurred unless, at the time of this episode, Dōgen had not yet become the disciple of Rujing. Wuji Liaopai died during the first half of 1224, most likely during the fourth month, and Rujing became the abbot of Tiantong shortly thereafter. In other words, by the middle of 1224, Dōgen and Rujing had encountered one another. After Rujing arrived at Tiantong, Dōgen's dialogue with Yuanzi could not have occurred as he reported it. Moreover, the *Kenzeiki* (p. 19) states that after completing this tour, Dōgen returned to Tiantong, and then Liaopai died (*hensan no nochi Tendō ni kaeshitamau tokoro ni Ha Wuji oshō nyūmetsusu* 徧參ノ後、天童ニ歸給處ニ、派無際和尚入滅ス). Based on these facts (and a host of other supporting circumstances), in 1984, Itō Shūken proposed that Dōgen's tour must have occurred during the Spring of 1224, with a departure shortly after the fourth episode (dat-

*Introduction to the* SHŌBŌGENZŌ: *6c. Dōgen in China*     103

ed 1224.1.21).[97] If Itō's theory is correct, then Dōgen either must have mistaken the era name or used "Baoqing" as a future era name (*mirai nengō* 未來年號) for the entire year in which the era was announced (a not uncommon practice in medieval Japan; see Supplement 6: Dates and Calendarial Considerations). And the Japanese suffix *koro* 頃 should be understood as "during" (not "around").[98]

Dōgen's quest to master the Five Houses of Chan spanned the first two years of his residency in China. Meanwhile, he began to study and master the routines of monastic life. In major monasteries, such as Tiantong, where Dōgen stayed, the summer retreat provided three months (typically, from 4.15 to 7.15) of structured training: daily devotions, sessions of seated meditation, regularly scheduled instruction, and assigned manual labor. Shortly after the end of Dōgen's first retreat (ca. 1223.7.20), the same monastic cook whom he had encountered aboard a ship on the fourth of the fifth month came to Tiantong to check on him. Very much impressed by this cook, Dōgen also sought instruction from the resident cook at Tiantong. Dōgen wrote that, thereafter in his spare time, he routinely inquired of the monastic officers at various temples about their duties (*Tenzo kyōkun*; DZZ.6:2, 12, 14). Sometime during that same autumn, Dōgen visited Aśoka temple, located about 20 kilometers due east from the shrine of the city god of Ningbo city, on the other side of the mountain from Tiantong. At Aśoka, large murals that depict the thirty-three patriarchs of India and China gave Dōgen his first visceral sense of Buddhist history as a lived human endeavor (chapter 3, "Busshō"; DZZ.1:31). During the tenth month, the middle of winter, Dōgen was back in Qingyuan (Ningbo) where he met three monks from the Korean peninsula (chapter 32, "Den'e"; DZZ.1:370; and chapter 3, "Kesa kudoku"; DZZ.2:330–331).[99] Dōgen does not provide a reason for being in Qingyuan. Since Qingyuan is the location of the government offices, the simplest explanation would be that he visited those offices

---

[97]  Itō Shūken 1984, 109–110. Satō Shūkō (1995, 116–117, 120) provides additional evidence in support of Itō.

[98]  The suffix *koro* frequently adds a degree of imprecision (*oyoso* およそ), but it can also denote a season (e.g., *sakura no koro* 桜のころ) or a broad duration of time such as "during my youth" (*wakarishi koro* 若かりしころ).

[99]  Dōgen dates this event with an era designation (Jiading 嘉定 17; i.e., 1224) and a sexagesimal digit (senior wood year of the monkey; *kōshin* 甲申; i.e., 1223) that disagree. Sexagesimal digits generally are more likely to be correct, and the year 1223 seems to be supported by other sources.

104 DŌGEN'S *SHŌBŌGENZŌ* VOLUME VIII

either to request permission to travel or to report his return from a pilgrimage (so that he could be re-admitted to Tiantong).[100] The fact that on this occasion in Qingyuan he exchanged information with other monks from outside China (who also would require special permission to travel within China) lends credibility to this theory.

If Dōgen visited Qingyuan at the beginning or end of a pilgrimage, then where was his destination? Aśoka temple was too near. It would not require overnight lodging to reach. Dōgen probably could have traveled to Aśoka temple and back with only a letter of permission from the abbot of Tiantong. The *Sanso gyōgōki* (as well as *Denkōroku* and *Kenzeiki*) states that Dōgen had an interview with Zheweng Ruyan (another disciple of Deguang), who served as abbot of Jingshan outside of Lin'an (present-day Hangzhou). Jingshan is just far enough distant (forty kilometers outside of Hangzhou, a total distance of 186 kilometers from Ningbo) to fit perfectly into the late autumn to early winter time-frame of 1223. A round-trip visit would require several days of travel, but it would not be too arduous, because most of the route could be traversed via coastal sea transport. Dōgen's writings, however, make no mention of such a journey. If it occurred, Dōgen's own account of it has not survived.[101]

Dōgen's journey to the Wannian temple in the Tiantai range of mountains (whenever it occurred) definitely was an arduous adventure. Dōgen mentions this journey only in passing, to set the stage for the fifth episode of his quest for inheritance certificates. He describes neither his itinerary nor his purpose. More details of his physical travels could have distracted from the narrative of his spiritual journey, but they also would help locate his encounter with the Buddhism of China beyond the walls of Tiantong. He merely wrote: "while I was wandering to Mount Tai and Mount Yan" (*Taisan Ganzan tō ni unyū suru* 台山雁山等に雲遊する; DZZ.1:432).

At first glance, a reader might interpret these words as two specific locations: Guoqingsi 國清寺 (J. Kokuseiji) on Mount Tiantai 天台山 (J. Tendaisan), where Tiantai 天台 (J. Tendai) Buddhism began, about

---

[100] Itō Shūken (1984, 107); Satō Shūkō (1995, 114).

[101] See *Sanso gyōgōki* (SZ Shiden 1.2); *Denkōroku* (p. 527); and *Kenzeiki* (p. 18). The printed version of *Denkōroku* reports that Ruyan asked Dōgen when he arrived in China, and Dōgen replied: "The 4th month of last year" (*kakusai shigatsu* 客歳四月), which would imply that they met during 1224. In the Kenkon'in manuscript (ca. 1488), however, Dōgen's answer appears as "four months ago" (*shigekkan* 四月間), which must be 1223. See Azuma 1970, 107; cf. Ito Shūken (1984, 197) and Satō Shūkō (1995, 113–114).

*Introduction to the* SHŌBŌGENZŌ: *6c. Dōgen in China* 105

ninety-five kilometers southeast of Ningbo, and Nengrensi 能仁寺 (J. Nōninji) in the Yandang 雁蕩 (J. Gantō) mountains about 177 kilometers south-southeast of Ningbo. That interpretation certainly is not impossible, but the combination of "Tiantai-Yandang" frequently denotes all the mountainous regions of the Zhedong 浙東 District (present-day southeast Zhejiang Province).[102] Chushi Fanqi 楚石梵琦 (1296–1370) made this usage explicit when he mentioned "Tiantai-Yandang" in farewell remarks to a monk on a journey to Zhedong, and in remarks to another monk on a journey to the counties of Taizhou 台州 and Wenzhou 温州 in that same district.[103] He also used the same designations as Dōgen: "Mount Tai and Mount Yan."[104] In a more abstract sense, these mountainous regions, renown for scenic beauty and for being remote, signify the Buddhist practice of pilgrimage itself, in which young monks seek to find a teacher and to find the truth.[105] This is the nuance conveyed by Cishou Huaishen 慈受懷深 (1077–1132) when he exhorted his students with these words:

本來無證亦無修、人人盡是阿羅漢、何必天台鴈蕩求。[106]

---

[102] E.g.: *Huanglong huinan chanshi yulu* 黃龍慧南禪師語錄; 1; T.1993.47:635b; *Dahui pu jue chanshi yulu* 大慧普覺禪師語錄; 12; T.1998A.47:862c; the biography of Wuzhun Shifan in *Daming gaoseng zhuan* 大明高僧傳; 8; T.2062.50:932b-c; *Liaoan qingyu chanshi yulu* 了菴清欲禪師語; 6 (CBETA.X.1414.71.359c // Z.2:28.357c // R.123.714a); *Chushi fanqi chanshi yulu* 楚石梵琦禪師語錄; 17 (CBETA.X.1420.71.639a // Z.2:29.127b // R.124.253b); and *Yuan zhiji chanshi yulu* 愚菴智及禪師語錄; 8 (CBETA.X.1421.71.688c // Z.2:29.176d1 // R.124.352b).

[103] See *Chushi fanqi chanshi yulu* 16 (CBETA.X.1420.71.633a // Z.2:29.121b // R.124.241b) and (CBETA.X.1420.71.633a // Z.2:29.121b // R.124.241 b).

[104] *Chushi fanqi chanshi yulu* 17; CBETA.X.1420.71.639b // Z.2:29.127c-d // R.124.254a-b.

[105] E.g., *Chanzong zaduhai* 禪宗雜毒海; 4 (CBETA.X.1278.65.74a // Z.2:19.73b // R.114.145b); *Gulin qingmao chanshi shiyi jisong* 古林清茂禪師拾遺偈頌; 1 (CBETA.X.1413.71.273c // Z.2:28.271c // R.123.542a); the biography of Baiyou Miaozhi 白猷妙智 (1337–1408) in *Buxu gaosengzhuan* 補續高僧傳; 25 (CBETA.X.1524.77.532a // Z.2B:7.186b // R.134.371b); the biography of Anchi Yeguo 菴赤冶果 in *Wudeng quanshu* 五燈全書; 79 (CBETA.X.1571.82.424c // Z.2B:14.320a // R.141.639a); and the question by Shizhou Ying 十洲瀛 in *Zheng yuan lüe ji buyi* 正源略集補遺; 1 (CBETA.X.1588.85.105b // Z.2B:18.248c // R.145.496a).

[106] *Cishou huaishen chanshi guanglu* 慈受懷深禪師廣錄; 1 (CBETA.X.1451. 73.102a // Z.2:31.276d // R.126.552b).

Originally there is nothing to verify and nothing to practice! Each and every one of you is an arhat. What else must you seek in the Tiantai Yandang [mountains]?

Similarly in his remarks at the end of a summer retreat (when monks would become free to travel), Wuzhun Shifan 無準師範 (J. Bujun Shihan; 1177–1249) addressed this question to his "cloud and river" (*unsui* 雲水) trainees:

水雲何處覓行蹤、踏破天台鴈蕩峰。[107]

What place do you rivers and clouds [trainees] seek via the footprints trampled on the mountain peaks of the Tiantai Yandang?

The fact that such remote mountainous regions came to signify the practice of Buddhist pilgrimage gave rise to an idiomatic saying repeated verbatim in the discourse records of several Chan teachers: "The Tiantai Yandang where no people go" (*Tiantai Yandang juerenxing* 天台鴈蕩絕人行).[108]

Dōgen followed in the footsteps of countless other monks by wandering amid the Tiantai Yangdang. His use of this broader designation, Tai and Yan mountains rather than a specific place name situates his journey in a spiritual landscape. The fact that he went to Wanniansi, however, likely was by a design both spiritual and practical. Wanniansi is the temple where Eisai had trained and first met his Chan master, Xuan Huaichang, before the two of them moved to Tiantong. The date 1224.7.5 marked the tenth memorial for Eisai (who died 1215.7.5). For this commemoration, Myōzen "donated roles of notes [paper currency] and a thousand strings of [metal] cash" (*juan chujuan qianmin* 捐楮卷千緡; i.e., enormous sums of money) to the halls of Tiantong, sponsored a special memorial meal for the monastic community, and also commissioned a biography of Eisai to be written by Yu Chu 虞樗 (J. Ku Cho), a Song government official.[109] A commemoration event on this scale re-

---

[107] *Wuzhun shifan chanshi yulu* 無準師範禪師語録; 5 (CBETA.X.1382.70. 269a11-13 // Z.2:26.475b13-15 // R.121.949b13-15).

[108] E.g., *Yingan tanhua chanshi yulu* 應菴曇華禪師語録; 1 (CBETA.X.1359.69. 509a // Z.2:25.405b-c // R.120.809b-810a); *Hengchuan xinggong chanshi yulu* 橫川行珙禪師語録; 1 (CBETA.X.1411.71.189c // Z.2:28.188a // R.123.375a); and *Neishao zhong chanshi yulu* 內紹種禪師語録; 1 (CBETA.J.B306.34.414c).

[109] *Ribenguo Qianguang fashi citangjì* 日本國千光法師祠堂記 (1225). In *Zoku gunsho ruijū* 續群書類從, 9A, sec. 225.36.273. Also see Satō Shūkō 1991, 64–65; Satō Shūkō 2014, 125–127, 133n27.

*Introduction to the* SHŌBŌGENZŌ: *6c. Dōgen in China*       107

quired a great deal of planning and financial support. Myōzen must have collected large sums of Chinese cash while still in Japan (where it was also used as currency) with the assistance of Eisai's other disciples. This large memorial donation might very well have been one of main goals for which Myōzen and his disciples visited China. Dōgen and Ryūzen must have assisted with the preparations.[110] In his writings, however, Dōgen never mentions any of it. His account of Myōzen's activities in China merely states that Myōzen's virtue was lauded by everyone in Liangzhe 兩浙 (present-day Zhejiang Province) and across all of China.[111] It is possible that Dōgen overstates Myōzen's fame, and it is also possible that Dōgen himself helped spread word of Myōzen's virtue by delivering a missive from Myōzen to Wanniansi regarding plans for a similar commemoration event to be sponsored there.[112] If so, tidings of such an event would explain how Dōgen so easily obtained an audience with Yuanzi, the abbot of the monastery, and why Yuanzi treated him with such deference. Myōzen's commemoration of Eisai and his gifts to the temple(s) where Eisai trained certainly constituted exemplary virtue.

Dōgen wrote that his tour included at least one night at Mount Damei 大梅 (a.k.a. Baofusi 保福寺), where in a dream vision he received an auspicious plum blossom from Damei Fachang (752–839), the purported founder of that temple. The name *damei* means "large plum blossom," and it is possible that many plum trees grew near or in Baofusi. If Dōgen's journey occurred during the early spring (as suggested by Itō Shūken), then he would have visited Mount Damei during the middle of the season when the plum trees were in full bloom.[113] Dōgen could not have found an easy route to this location. Mount Damei lies about seventy-three kilometers northeast of Wanniansi, but the intervening landscape consists entirely of mountains. And even without mountains, pilgrims rarely travel in a straight line. The pilgrimage trail would have led from one mountain hermitage to another, zigzagging around precipices and obstructions, ascending steep climbs and descending treacherous declines. Dōgen's route most likely took him across the famous stone bridge (J. *shakkyō* 石橋; C. *shiliang* 石梁) on the road between Guoqingsi and Wanniansi, which straddles a steep waterfall. When the light is at the

---

[110]  Satō Shūkō 1991, 64–65; and Satō Shūkō 1995, 109–110.

[111]  *Shari sōdenki* 舍利相傳記 (DZZ.7:216–217).

[112]  Cf. Satō Shūko 1995, 119; also see p. 115 where Satō suggests a similar motive for Dōgen to visit Hangzhou.

[113]  Satō Shūkō 1995, 117.

108 DŌGEN'S *SHŌBŌGENZŌ* VOLUME VIII

proper angle, the virtuous can look into the mist that rises from the water crashing on the rocks below and see the arhats. In 1249, after the arhats at Eiheiji in Japan dazzled worshipers with flowery rays of lights, Dōgen wrote that elsewhere such an apparition can be seen only from the stone bridge in the Tiantai mountains (DZZ.7:286). He would have been in a position to know with his own eyes.[114]

Mount Damei lies only about twenty-four kilometers southwest of Tiantong and the same distance southeast of Qingyuan (Ningbo). The direction toward Tiantong consists entirely of mountains while the route into town leaves the mountains after the first few kilometers and enters a broad plain. Which route Dōgen traversed cannot be known, but he probably would have needed to inform government officers in Qingyuan of his intention to return to Tiantong. Neither the distance nor total days covered during this journey is known. If it began shortly after the twenty-first of the first month of 1224, then it probably would have concluded within three months. The start of the summer retreat on or about the fifteenth day of the fourth month normally dictated that monks must be in residence no later than the end of the third month.[115] The abbot of Tiantong, Wuji Liaopai, died sometime round that same date or shortly thereafter.

When Liaopai died, Rujing, the person who would be appointed as his successor, was serving as the abbot of Jingci (J. Jōji), one of the Five Mountains (see Table 15). Before the end of the summer retreat (7.15), Rujing retired from his responsibilities at Jingci and thereafter performed his inauguration ceremony at Tiantong. As explained previously, this transition occurred during the middle of 1224 (not 1225 as had been assumed previously). It is not known if Rujing arrived at Tiantong in time for Eisai's memorial (on 1224.7.5) or after the summer retreat had already ended. Either way, when he arrived at Tiantong he definitely would have heard much about Myōzen (and his disciples) as well as Eisai. The rebuilt Thousand Buddha Pavilion (Qianfoge), for which Eisai had donated lumber from Japan in 1192, stood just outside the monastery where it would greet visitors first, before they entered the main complex.

On 1225.4.15, Rujing presided over the start of the summer retreat. At the end of that month, during the early morning hours of the first day of the fifth month, he noticed a monk who was sitting asleep in the Cloud

---

[114] Satō Shūken 1995, 119.
[115] Itō Shūken 1984, 109–110.

*Introduction to the* SHŌBŌGENZŌ: *6c. Dōgen in China* 109

Hall where all the trainees sat together to practice seated meditation (*za-zen*). Dōgen heard a thunderclap (*hekireki* 霹靂) when Rujing struck the sleeping monk and scolded him with these now famous words: "Study-ing Zen is mind and body sloughed off" (*canchan zhe xinshen tuoluo ye* 參禪者心身脫落也; J. *sanzen wa shinjin datsuraku nari*).[116] Later that same morning, Dōgen visited Rujing in the abbot's quarters, Miaogaotai, offered burning incense, and performed obeisance. Rujing thereupon ac-knowledged Dōgen's awakening and accepted Dōgen as his dharma heir. This moment held such importance for Dōgen that he described it twice in "Face to Face Conferral" (chapter 51; "Menju"), each time with a pre-cise date (1225.5.1). At the beginning of this chapter, he wrote:

大宋寶慶元年乙酉五月一日、道元、はじめて先師天童古佛を妙高臺
に燒香禮拜す。先師古佛、はじめて道元をみる。そのとき、道元に
指授面授するにいはく、佛佛祖祖、面授の法門、現成せり。これす
なはち靈山の拈華なり、嵩山の得髓なり、黃梅の傳衣なり、洞山の
面授なり。これは佛祖の眼藏面授なり。吾屋裏のみあり、餘人は夢
也未見聞在なり。 (DZZ.2:54–55)

On the first day of the fifth month of the junior wood year of the rooster, the first year of Baoqing in the Great Song, I, Dōgen, first burned incense and paid obeisance at the Miaogaotai to my former master, the Old Bud-dha of Tiantong. My former master, the Old Buddha, first saw Dōgen. At that time, in giving Dōgen personal instruction and face-to-face con-ferral, he said: 'The dharma gate conferred face-to-face by buddha after buddha and ancestor after ancestor is fulfilled. This is precisely holding up the flower on Vulture Peak; it is getting the marrow on Mount Song; it is transmitting the robe at Huangmei; it is the face-to-face conferral of Dongshan. This is the face-to-face conferral of the treasury of the eye of the buddhas and ancestors. It exists only within our house; others have never seen or heard of it even in their dreams.

And he concluded this chapter (number 51) with:

道元、大宋寶慶元年乙酉五月一日、はじめて先師天童古佛を禮拜面
授す。やや堂奧を聽許せらる、わづかに身心を脫落するに、面授を
保任することありて、日本國に本來せり。 (DZZ.2:60)

On the first day of the fifth month of the junior wood year of the rooster, the first year of Baoqing in the Great Song, I, Dōgen, first paid obeisance to and had a face-to-face conferral from my former master, the Old Bud-dha of Tiantong. I was granted a certain access to the interior of the hall; having somewhat sloughed off body and mind, having been entrusted with a face-to-face conferral, I came back to the Land of Japan.

---

[116] "Great Awakening" (chapter 10; "Daigo"), variant version, DZZ.2:609.

Shortly after this ceremony, Dōgen gave Rujing a written note in which he requested permission to visit him for private, one-on-one instructions. Rujing replied in the affirmative. Their consultations in the abbot's quarters commenced two months later, on the second of the seventh month of 1225 (*Hōkyōki*; DZZ.7:2). Dōgen compiled a record of some of their questions and answers, which subsequently became the basis for the *Hōkyōki*. Presumably access to Rujing's private instructions in the abbot's quarters was what Dōgen alluded to with the phrase "access to the interior of the hall."

On a later date during that same summer retreat, Rujing presented Dōgen with an inheritance certificate in the Caodong 曹洞 (J. Sōtō) House. This document does not survive.[117] Dōgen did not explicitly mention this event in his other writings, but it is clearly implied in "Buddhas and Ancestors" (chapter 52; "Busso"). In this chapter, Dōgen reproduced the entire Caodong lineage (see Table 37), beginning with the seven ancient buddhas ending with Śākyamuni Buddha, the twenty-eight generations of ancestors in India, and concluding with Rujing as the twenty-third ancestor of China. Dōgen would not have known the precise orthography for each of these names or the precise format for listing them unless he had received the actual certificate. He already had learned that each of the five houses wrote inheritance certificates according to its own idiosyncratic tradition. For this reason, his statement that he studied these names with Rujing during the summer retreat of 1225 carries special significance. It is also noteworthy that he concluded this chapter (number 52) in a format similar to the conclusion that he wrote for the previous chapter:

道元、大宋國寶慶元年乙酉夏安居時、先師天童古佛大和尚に參侍して、この佛祖を禮拜頂戴することを究盡せり。(DZZ.2:68)

In the summer retreat of the junior wood year of the rooster, the first year of Baoqing, in the Land of the Great Song, attending my former master, the Most Reverend Old Buddha of Tiantong, I, Dōgen, exhaustively investigated the act of doing obeisance and paying respect to these buddhas and ancestors.

The dates and interpretation of Dōgen's awakening (*shinjin datsuraku*), of his recognition (*menju*), and of his inheritance certificate stand out as the most noticeable revisions forced by the chronological shift in the timeline of Dōgen's activities in China. Previously, when scholars

---

[117] The so-called *Shisho no zu* 嗣書ノ圖 (dated 1227) owned by Eiheiji and designated a national treasure (*kokuhō* 國寶), is not authentic. See Ishii Shūdō (2015, 645–646) for a brief summary of the extant scholarship.

*Introduction to the* SHŌBŌGENZŌ: *6c. Dōgen in China*        111

assigned the arrival of Rujing to the year 1225, they crafted divergent — and extremely influential — interpretations of these events. Before examining those interpretations, it will be helpful to review the mistaken chronology on which they were based.

Until the 1980s, the *Kenzeiki* — specifically the revised version (1754) by Menzan Zuihō — provided the authoritative timeline for Dōgen's activities. Its authority began to wane only after 1975, when Kawamura published transcriptions of five premodern manuscripts (including the copy by Zuichō dated 1552) in parallel panels alongside Menzan's edition. The copy by Zuichō provides very few dates for Dōgen's activities and little information about the key events described above. It includes only three events:

| | |
|---|---|
| – | Rujing appointed abbot of Tiantong by the Song Emperor Ningzong 寧宗 [1168–1224; r. 1194–1224]        (p. 20) |
| – | Dōgen attains the Dharma by comprehending the "body and mind sloughed off" saying (*hikkyō tokuhō wa shinjin datsurakuwa o motte yō to nashitamau nari* 畢竟得法ハ身心脱落話ヲ以テ爲要給也)        (p. 24) |
| 1225.9.18 | [Dharma] transmission concluded on Baoqing 1, month 9, day 18        (p. 25) |

In the *Kenzeiki* copy by Zuichō, no other events occurred within the above sequence. They appear on separate pages of the printed version only because Kawamura aligned each episode with the contents of Menzan's edition. Due to limitations of space, I must omit many of the emendations that Menzan included in his sequence of events:

| | |
|---|---|
| – | Rujing receives an imperial appointment to Tiantong temple, and Dōgen thereupon rushes back to Tiantong.        (p. 20) |
| 1225.5.1 | Dōgen [having arrived at Tiantong] thereupon pays obeisance to Rujing; Rujing tells him, "The dharma gate conferred face-to-face by buddha after buddha and ancestor after ancestor is fulfilled."        (p. 20–21) |
| 1225.5.7 (*sic*) | Myōzen dies.        (p. 21–22) |
| – | As a result, Dōgen sends a note to Rujing requesting permission to visit him for private instructions; Rujing replies in the affirmative.        (p. 22) |
| – | Rujing scolds a monk sitting asleep by saying, "To study Zen you must slough off body and mind"' (*sanzen wa subekaraku shinjin datsuraku subeshi* 參禪は須く身心脱落すべし); Dōgen attains a great awakening.        (p. 24) |

112 DŌGEN'S *SHŌBŌGENZŌ* VOLUME VIII

| | |
|---|---|
| 1225.9.18 | Rujing confers the great precepts transmitted by the buddhas and ancestors. [cf. DZZ.6:189]  (p. 25) |
| – | Dōgen journeys to Zhexi 浙西 [i.e., Jingshan temple], etc.  (p. 30) |
| 1227 winter | Rujing confers a robe, his portrait, and books as proof that Dōgen has received dharma transmission.  (p. 31) |

Note that Menzan depicts a version of events in which Dōgen met Rujing for the very first time on the first of the fifth month of 1225 (as opposed to Dōgen's statement, quoted above, that he presented a stick of incense to Rujing for the first time on that date). Menzan imagined a love-at-first-glance scenario, in which Rujing acknowledged Dōgen as his dharma successor without any previous contact between them. Then at some unknown later date between the beginning of the fifth month and the eighteenth of the ninth month, Dōgen attained great awakening (*daigo* 大悟).

The significance assigned to that supposed first meeting (1225.5.1) increased exponentially and changed qualitatively after 1944, when Etō Sokuō (1888–1958) published his ground-breaking study of Dōgen titled *Shūso toshite no dōgen zenji* 宗祖としての道元禪師. Its English-language translation (by Ichimura Shōhei, 2001) is titled: *Dōgen Zenji as Founding Patriarch (of the Japanese Sōtō Zen School)*. Etō Sokuō founded "*shūgaku*" 宗學, an academic enterprise designed to highlight the unique features of Dōgen's approach to Zen and to explicate them in modern terms, including insights from philosophy, religious studies, and theology. In 1953, he became the president of Komazawa University and, in 1954, became the founding director of its Shūgaku Research Center. Etō's agenda exerted enormous influence over the study of Dōgen throughout the second half of the twentieth century.[118]

Etō argued that Dōgen's unique approach to Zen was born on the first day of the fifth month of 1225, at the moment when Rujing accepted him as a dharma heir upon their very first meeting. According to Etō, this unlikely moment of unconditional acceptance sparked in Dōgen an awakening to the power of faith. As Dōgen's faith deepened, he came to understand it in terms of the words that he later attributed to Rujing: [Faith consists of] "holding up the flower on Vulture Peak . . . getting the marrow on Mount Song . . . transmitting the robe at Huangmei . . . the face-to-face conferral of Dongshan." According to Etō, it matters

---

[118] For an overview of the intellectual environment within which Etō's *shūgaku* emerged, see Sahashi 1995.

*Introduction to the* SHŌBŌGENZŌ: *6c. Dōgen in China* 113

not whether Rujing actually said these words or Dōgen only imagined them. Dōgen's faith deepened, and all his doubts disappeared on a later occasion, when he heard Rujing utter the words "slough off body and mind."[119] The philosopher Sugio Gen'yū (1928–2012) amplified Etō's interpretation in 1977, by arguing that the "slough off body and mind" episode must be fictional, a dramatic embellishment added by later biographers, that could have played no role in a religion of faith. He admitted that Rujing might have uttered those words but pointed out that Dōgen himself never described Rujing using them to scold (*shitta* 叱咤) a sleeping monk. Thus, he drew a sharp distinction between the "body and mind sloughed off saying" (*shinjin datsurakuwa* 身心脱落話) and the "sloughed off upon scolding" (*shittaji datsuraku* 叱咤時脱落) episode, which he rejected. Sugio's arguments swayed many leading scholars for a period during the 1970s and 1980s.[120]

This kind of theological or philosophical interpretation of the key events of 1225.5.1 became untenable after scholars began to understand that Dōgen must have met Rujing almost a year earlier, in 1224.[121] Instead of love at first sight, Dōgen had been a trainee within the assembly under the direction of Rujing for eight or ten months prior to the fifth month of 1225. They would have had ample opportunity to observe and even to talk to one another.

Dōgen's writings, moreover, contain many passages that support the so-called "sloughed off upon scolding" narrative. On two separate occasions in Ejō's *Zuimonki* (2 and 3; DZZ.7:70 and 101–102), Dōgen described in detail how Rujing would strike monks if they fell asleep during sessions of seated meditation. Dōgen's remarks in a major convocation address (number 136; *Extensive Records* 2) at Daibutsuji leave little room to doubt the centrality of the words "body and mind sloughed off" in his own awakening:

要知瞿曇比丘因由麼。一由聞得天童脱落話而成佛道。二由大佛拳頭力得入諸人眼睛裏 (DZZ.3:82)

Do you want to know the causes of the Bhikṣu Gautama? First, he is caused when I hear Tiantong's [i.e., Rujing's] talk of "sloughing off" and

---

[119]   Etō 1944, 345 (chapter 7); cf. the translation by Ichimura: Etō 2001, 547–549.

[120]   Sugio 1977. Also see Kagamishima 1985, 316–317; and Ishii Shūdō 2008, 74–77.

[121]   Sugio later (1986, 22–23) presented a modified theory.

attain the way of the buddhas. Second, he is caused when the power of Daibutsu's [i.e., Dōgen's] fist enters your eye.

Note how Dōgen links the talk of "sloughing off" and the striking with fists by using these two elements in parallel. And finally, in "Great Awakening" (chapter 10; "Daigo"; early draft variant version, DZZ.2:609), Dōgen explicitly links the words "body and mind sloughed off" used by Rujing in his lectures with the strikes used by Rujing in the meditation hall, which could be heard by those asleep as well as by those awake.

Aside from its temporal implausibility, Menzan's interpretation of "Face to Face Conferral" ("Menju"), ignores the fact that Dōgen described a special ritual. Dōgen wrote that, for the first time, he went unsummoned and alone into Miaogaotai (the abbot's quarters), ceremonially offered incense, and paid obeisance. Clearly this was a special occasion with special significance. A similar locution is found in Gikai's *Goyuigon*, in the section where he records how he received dharma transmission from Ejō. For his entry dated the second day of 1255, Gikai wrote:

建長七年乙卯正月二日、義介初拝第二世堂頭和尚。初夜之後參方丈、於羅漢前間行之。於羅漢前香台燒香大展三拝。 (DZZ.7:190)

On Kenchō 7, junior wood year of the rabbit, first month, second day, I, Gikai, first paid obeisance to the Reverend Second Abbot [Ejō]. After the first night [meditation period], I went to the abbot's quarters and performed it in the space before the arhats. I offered incense on the stand in front of the arhats and preformed full prostrations three times.

Gikai and Ejō alike were two senior disciples of Dōgen who had trained together for many years. They had performed obeisance to one another on many previous ceremonial occasions. Nonetheless, on 1255.1.2, Gikai performed this kind of obeisance for the first time. He likely modeled his language in this passage on the expression that Dōgen used in his account.[122] In 1997, Satō Shūkō provided the most convincing argument against Menzan's interpretation. Satō examined the language used by Rujing both on 1225.5.1 and in his reply to Dōgen's request for private consultations. Rujing's response to Dōgen on both occasions clearly reflects a new elevation of Dōgen's status, one that could only have occurred after his awakening.[123]

---

[122] Itō Shūken 1984, 112–113.

[123] Satō Shūkō 1997, 77–81. Also see Itō Shūken 2015.

*Introduction to the* SHŌBŌGENZŌ: *6c. Dōgen in China* 115

The Caodong lineage that Dōgen presents in "Buddhas and Ancestors" (chapter 52; "Busso") differs in many key respects from the way that lineage is understood by historians. "Buddhas and Ancestors" presents the Caodong House in isolation, but the historical record includes a significant intervention by Fushan Fayuan 浮山法遠 (J. Fuzan Hōon; 991–1067), a member of the Linji House (see Table 37, Dōgen within the Caodong Lineage). Keizan's *Denkōroku* (and the Chinese sources upon which it is based) states that Touzi Yiqing 投子義青 (J. Tōsu Gisei; 1032–1083) originally was the disciple of Fayuan (a.k.a. Yuanjian 圓鑑; J. Enkan). Touzi attained awakening under Fayuan and then spent another three years training under him. During this three-year period, Fayuan taught Touzi the teachings of Taiyang Jingxuan 大陽警玄 (J. Taiyō Kyōgen; 943–1027), a master of the Dongshan lineage.[124] Fayuan and Jingxuan had been close colleagues. When Taiyang lamented one day that he had already become elderly and feared that he would not live long enough to find a suitable disciple to whom he could transmit his lineage, Fayuan promised to act as a go-between. Accordingly, when Touzi proved to be a suitable candidate, Fayuan selected him to become the successor to the Caodong dharma lineage of Taiyang Jingxuan.[125]

During the early modern period, the historicity of this account became very controversial within Sōtō Zen circles (see Bodiford 1991). Some people denounced it as a violation of the teaching of "face to face conferral" (*menju* 面授) that Dōgen taught in his *Shōbōgenzō*. They believed that Dōgen would have rejected the legitimacy of this kind of dharma transmission by proxy (*daifu* 代附). The early draft variant version of "Great Awakening" (chapter 10; DZZ.2:608), however, includes Dōgen's commentary on the circumstances (kōan) of Touzi's awakening under Fayuan. This version of "Great Awakening" raises new questions about Dōgen's teaching of "face to face conferral," his views of dharma transmission by proxy, and the possible reasons why he first included this story and subsequently deleted it.[126]

---

[124] The appellation Taiyang 大陽 (J. Taiyō) derives from the name of Taiyangsi. Nowadays, in China, the name of this temple frequently is written as 太陽寺; but in premodern Buddhist texts, it always is written as 大陽寺. Regardless of the written form, the pronunciation of the first character will be "tai" (not "da").

[125] See *Denkōroku*, ancestor 44, pp. 442–456.

[126] Kagamishima, "kaidai" 解題; DZZ.4:324–326.

Myōzen died at Tiantong on the twenty-seventh of the fifth month of 1225. His death is reported in the biography of Eisai written by Yu Chu that Myōzen had commissioned on behalf of Eisai's tenth memorial. Dōgen also reported it in his account of Myōzen's activities in China. Dōgen states that Myōzen came down with a sudden fever on the eighteenth of that month, he died ten days later on the twenty-seventh, his corpse was cremated on the twenty-ninth, and the cremation resulted in many relics (*Shari sōdenki*; DZZ.7:217). Dōgen does not say who conducted the funeral service, but most likely it was Rujing. During this period, Dōgen would have been responsible for nursing Myōzen during his illness, preparing the firewood for the cremation, and disposing of Myōzen's material effects. Dōgen also would have supervised the erection of a stone stele (dated 1225.8.9) inscribed with the biography of Eisai that Myōzen had commissioned. It is likely that these responsibilities account for the long delay between Dōgen's acceptance by Rujing (1225.5.1) and the start of his private consultations with Rujing (1225.7.2).[127] In "Buddha Nature" (chapter 3; "Busshō"; DZZ.1:31), Dōgen reports that he visited Aśoka temple for a second time, and that his visit occurred during the summer retreat of 1225. Dōgen mentioned a recent visit to Aśoka temple in his *Hōkyōki* (DZZ.7:24), which means that Rujing must have known of his visit and given permission for Dōgen to violate the monastic sequestering rules of the summer retreat.

Why would Rujing have allowed Dōgen to visit Aśoka temple during the summer retreat? One can only speculate. Aśoka temple was (and is) famous for its Buddha relics, and it also accepted funerary relics of Buddhist clerics.[128] Dōgen wrote that he carried Myōzen's cremation relics back to Japan (*Shari sōdenki*; DZZ.7:217), but it is also possible that he deposited some of Myōzen's many relics at Aśoka temple.[129] Relics of all kinds, but especially funerary ones, figure large in all forms of Buddhism, especially Chan.[130] Zhuoan Deguang (J. Setsuan Tokkō), the master who had conferred dharma transmission on Nōnin via proxy, served as abbot of Aśoka temple when he acknowledge Nōnin. As part

---

[127] Satō Shūkō 1987, 85–86.

[128] Regarding the influence of Aśoka temple across Japan on the promotion of relic worship in general and of its own specific model of reliquaries, *hōkyōintō* 寶篋印塔, known as "Chinese Aśoka Stūpa" (*daitō ikuōtō* 大唐育王塔), see Enomoto (2010, 131–133); Nishitani (2018, 97–126); and Ōtsuka (2017, 218–249).

[129] Satō Shūkō 1997, 84.

[130] Faure 1991, 132–208; Faure 1996, 144–178; Robson 2017.

*Introduction to the* SHŌBŌGENZŌ: *6c. Dōgen in China* 117

of his dharma transmission procedures, Deguang sent a collection of relics to Nōnin. By all accounts, these relics contributed much momentum to Nōnin's success in propagating his Zen teachings.[131] Once again, Dōgen's tracks in China crisscrossed with ones related to Nōnin's lineage.

Dōgen's *Extensive Records* (10; DZZ.4:246–270) includes fifty Chinese gāthā-style verses (*jisong* 偈頌; J. *geju*) that Dōgen wrote while in China. All of them are dated to the year 1226 (one year after Dōgen's awakening and one year prior to his return to Japan), but there is no way to judge if this date is accurate. In *Hōkyōki* (DZZ.7:6), Rujing dictated a set of rules that, among other injunctions, forbad Dōgen from travels. For this reason, it is unlikely that he traveled to Jingshan as suggested by Menzan. But judging from the prefacing remarks that Dōgen wrote for each of his verses, he must have enjoyed some degree of freedom during 1226. Two of the poems (numbers 28, 45) were written when he visited Pujisi 普濟寺 (J. Fusaiji; a.k.a. Mount Putuoshan 普陀山), the famous island shrine dedicated to the bodhisattva Avalokiteśvara. Putuoshan Island lies about eighty-three kilometers from Ningbo. A visit there probably would have required an overnight trip. Dōgen exchanged poems with a wide variety of people. He wrote twenty-one verses for government officials, fifteen for literati scholars, twelve for fellow Buddhist monks, and exchanged one verse with his compatriot, Ryūzen (Butsugen-bō).[132] Frequently he wrote verses in reply to those that he received from these individuals. And sometimes he seems to have done so more than once with the same individuals. By 1226, therefore, he had begun to participate in the local community.

Dōgen's *Extensive Records* includes verses written in Chinese from all periods of his career throughout the rest of his life. None of his verses is dated from before the year 1226. Why did he start writing them at that point in his life? He certainly lived during an age when mastery of Chinese prosody, with its complex rhyme structures and regulated parallel vocabulary, was *de rigueur* for high-level Buddhist clerics.[133] Perhaps Rujing encouraged or even tutored Dōgen in his Chinese compositions.[134] The *Hōkyōki* (DZZ.7:44) contains one entry of instructions by Rujing in

---

[131]  Faure 1987, 35–45.

[132]  See, respectively, verse nos. 1, 8, 10-11, 15-17, 24–25, 35-41, 43, 46, 48-50; nos. 2–7, 9, 12-14, 18, 30–31, 47; and no. 42.

[133]  See Nishio Kenryū 2011, 156–176, 237–303; and Tamamura 1941.

[134]  Frédéric Girard (2007, 10–13) advances a similar hypothesis and cites Rujing's encouragement (see *Hōkyōki*, DZZ.7:40–42).

which Rujing refers to himself as being in his sixty-fifth year, which corresponds to 1226. Dōgen's private consultations with him must have lasted at least until then. In "The Real Marks of the Dharmas" (chapter 43; "Shohō jissō"), Dōgen quotes passages and a verse from a public lecture that Rujing presented during the third month of 1226. Dōgen praises Rujing's words for their "splendid diction and unusual phrases" (*bigen kiku* 美言奇句) which will forever be inscribed on his body and mind, bones and marrow (DZZ.1:469). Clearly Dōgen admired Rujing's literary style and sought to emulate it (and emulate him).

Rujing died on the seventeenth of the seventh month of 1227. Dōgen does not mention Rujing's death or his funeral in any of his extant writings. As mentioned elsewhere (see the section regarding Dates), documents attributed to Dōgen provide contradictory information regarding the year when he returned to Japan. If Dōgen was still in China at the time of Rujing's death and still in the same location as Rujing, so that he would have known firsthand of Rujing's final hours, final words, and death verse, then it would be strange for him not to mention these details. But it would not be at all unusual if many of Dōgen's records, private papers, missives, and short essays became lost. No information survives regarding the overseas adventures of the vast majority of the hundreds of other Japanese Buddhist monks who journeyed to China.[135]

---

[135] Regarding the fraught estimates for the total number of the hundreds (*sūhyaku ni oyobu* 数百に及ぶ) of Buddhist monks who visited China, see Enomoto 2007,11, 18–19; Enomoto 2010, 136–137; and Enomoto 2021, 50–61. In each new iteration of his calculations, the estimates increase substantially.

## Dōgen Back in Japan

In a short essay on Dōgen's career, Ikeda Rosan (1994) notes how conveniently it can be divided into four decades, each one of which began with a change in status or location. Ikeda listed them as follows: in 1213, Dōgen became a Buddhist monk; in 1223, Dōgen went to China; in 1233, Dōgen founded Kōshōji 興聖寺 just south of Kyoto; and, in 1243, Dōgen left Kyoto and moved to Echizen (present-day Fukui Pref.). This mnemonic scheme works remarkably well. One might question the dates 1213 and 1223, both of which derive from Menzan's revised version of the *Kenzeiki* (pp. 6–7, 33). Early evidence is lacking for the first one, and the second one fudges the evidence. In 1233, Dōgen conducted a summer retreat at Kannon Dōri Cloister 觀音導利院. At that same location or nearby, he subsequently constructed additional buildings and, in 1236, formally founded Kōshōji.[136] For a short overview of Dōgen's activities (such as this one), probably the most convenient feature of this four-part sequence lies in the way its skips over the mysterious period following Dōgen's return from China (whenever that occurred; see Supplement 6) and the summer retreat he convened in 1233. By 1233, Dōgen had attracted a community of followers, found a location for them to practice together, and had begun providing them with copies of his earliest compositions (see Table 23, Early Compositions and Events). The acts that might have achieved this combination of results can be discerned only dimly or not at all via the extant sources.

Dōgen assigned a significant date to each one of his early compositions: *Talk on Pursuing the Way* on the Harvest Moon; *Universal Promotion of the Principles of Seated Meditation* on the Midyear Moon; "The Realized Kōan" on the Harvest Moon; "Advice on Studying the Way" on Clear Brightness; *Shōbōgenzō* in Chinese script on First Yang. And he officially founded Kōshōji on the Lateyear Moon (see Table 23). The named days and moons derive from traditional Chinese calendrical lore, and each one of them can evoke associations with pan-Asian traditional customs (such as special greetings, foods, prayer rituals, etc.). "Clear Brightness," for example, evokes images of spring cleaning and purification, when one invokes the aid of gods and ancestors, while "First

---

[136] The *Kenzeiki* copy by Zuichō merely quotes the colophon to "Mahā-prajñā-pāramitā" ("Maka hannya haramitsu"; cf. DZZ.1:12–13) and notes that its location later became Kōshōji. Menzan's version omits the colophon and states that Dōgen fulfilled his long-standing vow to erect Kōshōji in 1233.

Yang" actually falls on the winter solstice (*tōji* 冬至), when *yang* is most depleted, and one should eat nutritional foods to ward off illness. Because of historical and regional variations, however, it is impossible to know with certainty which (if any) of these kinds of specific associations might have applied to Dōgen's community. Each of the named moons refers to a full moon, when one celebrates recent accomplishments and honors those who assisted in them. "Summer retreat day" refers to the annual Buddhist training period, which typically would begin at noon on the fifteenth of the fourth month and end at noon on the fifteenth of the seventh month. Because it begins and ends on days with a full moon, one might assume that "Summer Retreat day" most likely refers to the first day of the retreat, but that is not necessarily the case. It can refer to any day during the retreat.

The pattern of dates that coincide with holidays is itself more noteworthy than any specific holiday. It is difficult to imagine that Dōgen actually composed so many early works only on special days of the year. The actual writing, editing, and rewriting must have taken many days, if not weeks. His *Advice on Studying the Way* (*Gakudō yōjinshū* 學道用心集) actually confirms this point, since it includes a section with a second date: 1234.3.9 (DZZ.5:20). On the holidays mentioned in the dates of his early compositions, Dōgen likely wrote the date and signed his name to a composition that he had recently completed and then ceremonially made the manuscript available to his disciples or presented it to its designated recipient. In this way, the holiday and the event or release would lend significance to one another, rendering each of them more memorable.

"Mahā-prajñā-pāramitā" (chapter 2) opens with the name Avalokiteśvara, the bodhisattva who appears in the *Heart Sūtra* and the namesake for the Kannon Dōri Cloister where Dōgen's community had gathered for their first summer retreat. It is a very short essay that consists mostly of long quotations from Buddhist scriptures in their original Chinese format (without being rendered into Japanese word order). Dōgen also quotes Rujing's now famous "Wind Bell" gāthā-style verse, also without any explanation in Japanese.[137] The "Wind Bell" verse uses onomatopoeia to great effect:

---

[137] The newsletter of the San Francisco Zen Center is titled *Wind Bell* (see Wenger, 2001). Also see Girard (2007) regarding the diffusion of Rujing's "Wind Bell" verse within Japanese Buddhist circles during Dōgen's lifetime.

Tic ding-dong! Whoosh! Tic ding-dong!

(C. *di dingdong liao di dingdong*; J. *teki teitō ryō teki teitō* 滴丁東了滴丁
東; DZZ.1:11; T.2002A.48:132b14-16)

One can easily imagine the quiet of a meditation hall interrupted by
the faint chimes of a wind bell in the whistling breeze. This quotation
suggests that Dōgen possessed his own compilation of Rujing's verses
(and prose works?) prior to the arrival of the version of Rujing's recorded sayings that colleagues in China sent to him in 1242.[138]

The 1233 version of *Universal Promotion of the Principles of Seated
Meditation* (the Tenpuku holograph) is dated to the very last day of the
summer retreat. It might represent the revised version of an earlier draft.
In *Talk on Pursuing the Way* (DZZ.2:481), Dōgen reports that he had
composed a work with an identical title during the Karoku Era (1225 to
1227). A summer retreat (with long daily sessions of meditation) six or
more years later than the Karoku draft might seem like an ideal occasion
for a revision (assigned to a later date). Its possible relationship to any
earlier draft, however, cannot be determined. Only one other version of
this work exists. It is undated, and internal evidence suggests that it must
be later, not earlier, than the 1233 version.[139]

*Talk on Pursuing the Way* (*Bendōwa*), as described earlier, begins with
Dōgen's self-introduction and a brief overview of Zen. He wrote it in
1231, two years prior to the summer retreat he convened at Kannon Dōri
Cloister. It surely played a role in attracting the followers who participated in that first retreat. Dōgen likely wrote not just to recruit new followers but also for disciples who had already joined him. His *Extensive
Records* (volume 8) contains early dharma talks (*hōgo* 法語) that predate *Bendōwa*. In one talk (number 12, dated 1231.7), he praised the nun
Ryōnen 了然 for her dedication, unmatched by any of his other followers

---

[138] In the *Hōkyōki* (DZZ.7:40), Dōgen asked Rujing about this verse but did
not reproduce it there.

[139] The other version of the *Fukan zazen gi* is found in Dōgen's *Extensive Records* 8 (DZZ.4:177–180). It is virtually identical to the one printed in 1358
by Donki 曇希 (1297-1350?) within an abridged version of Dōgen's recorded sayings titled *Eihei Gen zenji goroku* 永平元禪師語録 (reprinted 1648;
DZZ.5:105–108). Evidence for its later date consists of its greater length,
vocabulary, and closer adherence to the Chinese rules of double-harness (C.
*pinli* 駢儷; J. *benrei*) style with matched lines of four and six glyphs (*siliu
wen* 四六文; J. *shirokubun*). See Bielefeldt (1988) for a detailed historical,
textual, and religious examination of the *Fukan zazen gi*.

(DZZ.4:166).[140] In this and in another *hōgo* (number 4; DZZ.4:146, 148) addressed to the same nun, Dōgen quotes obtuse kōans in Chinese. Her familiarity with these topics indicates that she must have been studying Zen for some time. *Bendōwa* concludes with a long formulaic section of didactic question and answers. Some of the exchanges seem purely rhetorical, but others might reflect actual concerns raised by his followers. By this time, many Japanese monks, like Dōgen, had returned from residencies in China. Not all of them taught Zen, and among teachers of Zen not everyone taught in the same manner.[141] The questions and answers in *Bendōwa* provide rare evidence for the wide range of religious attitudes of Buddhists in urban Japan circa 1231.

Dōgen quotes only a single kōan in *Bendōwa* to demonstrate the value of Zen training to his audience of new recruits and veterans. Although it constitutes one of the half dozen Zen stories that play a key role in Dōgen's teachings, it is relatively ignored in the scholarly literature. In the question-and-answer section of *Bendōwa*, the literary interlocutor asks why people should practice Zen or anything else. Since Buddhism teaches the inherent awakening of living beings, there should be no need to know or do anything more. Dōgen first dismisses this point of view as erroneous and cites the story of "Xuanze: Bingding Youth" to verify his point. After quoting the story, Dōgen explains its key point, or moral, by asserting the importance of sustained practice that does not stop at a "single knowing or half understanding." The story can be paraphrased as follows:

> A monk named Bao'en Xuanze (J. Hōon Gensoku) resided in the assembly of Master Fayan Wenyi (J. Hōgen Mon'eki; 885–958) but never requested instruction. One day, Wenyi asked him why not, and Xuanze replied that he already had attained the truth from a previous master. He explained, that when he had asked that teacher, "What is my authentic self?" the teacher had replied, "A *bingding* youth seeking fire."

---

[140]   A calligraphic copy of this *hōgo* (Kasuisai 可睡齋 manuscript) reproduces the signature as: "early autumn, junior metal year of the rabbit, at An'yōin Cloister, Dōgen" (*shinbo mōshū jū An'yōin Dōgen* 辛卯孟秋住安養院道元). See Ishii Shūdō, ed., 2015, 11 (facsimile), 431 (transcription). Also see Ishii Shūdō 2015, 609–614; Ishii Shūdō 2020a and 2020b.

[141]   Enomoto (2021, 52) calculates that, prior to ca. 1230, fewer than one fourth of Japanese monks who traveled to China identified with Zen. In addition to Tendai, quite a few were associated with Shunjō or with Nara. Regardless of their affiliation in Japan, however, in China, all of these clerics would have participated in similar monastic routines and studies.

*Introduction to the* SHŌBŌGENZŌ: *6d. Dōgen back in Japan*     123

Wenyi told Xuanze, "That's a good answer, but you probably did not understand it." Xuanze insisted that he had understood it perfectly well. He explained that, since the sexagesimal branches *bing* and *ding* both refer to fire, the "*bingding* youth seeking fire" means that he had already attained what he sought. Wenyi rebuked him, "I knew it. You haven't understood it. If that were all there is to Buddhism, it would not have survived until now."

Feeling that he had been insulted, Xuanze stormed out in anger. Later he regretted his anger, repented of his haste, and returned to apologize to Wenyi. He bowed down and asked, "What is my authentic self?" Wenyi replied: "A *bingding* youth seeking fire." Xuanze thereupon attained awakening.

In other words, only after Xuanze abandoned his "single knowing or half understanding" could he discover that the practice of seeking fire (i.e., *zazen*) constitutes his true self. Dōgen quoted this story repeatedly over the course of his teaching career. In addition to *Bendōwa* (1231), it also appears in the *Shōbōgenzō* in Chinese script (number 122; DZZ.5:192), dated 1235, in his recorded sayings from Kōshōji (ca. 1240.10?) and again in his sayings from Eiheiji (ca. 1248.12; see *Kōroku* 1, *jōdō* 15, and 4, *jōdō* 299; DZZ.3:12–14, 196); and in his pure rules for monastic administrators (*Eiheiji chiji shingi* 永平寺知事清規; DZZ.6:102), dated 1246.

Dōgen repeated the Bingding Youth story so often that his later biographers seem to have associated it as much with Dōgen as with Xuanze. As noted by Ishii Shūdō (1988, 527), this story underlies the formulaic episode that appears in later biographies of Dōgen as the story of his doubts on Mount Hiei. As stated in the *Sanso gyōgōki* (quoted above in the section on Dōgen Prior to China), supposedly Dōgen left Mount Hiei because he had begun to doubt the meaning and necessity of Buddhist practice (*Sanso gyōgōki*; SZ.Shiden.1.1b). Dōgen addressed this issue not in the terms used in *Sanso gyōgōki* (i.e., dharma nature; dharma body) but in the Zen idiom of "Xuanze: Bingding Youth." The second half of this story, the stereotypical figure of the arrogant know-it-all who can learn only after a change of heart, also reappears in biographies of Dōgen. The *Denkōroku* (pp. 528–529), for example, states that Dōgen initially was so disappointed by the Buddhist teachers in China that he quickly decided to return to Japan. Supposedly he changed his opinion and began to study in earnest only after he met Rujing. If that story ac-

124 DŌGEN'S *SHŌBŌGENZŌ* VOLUME VIII

curately describes Dōgen's change of heart in China, then his experience could only have reinforced his affinity with this kōan.

The *Denkōroku* (pp. 555–556) tells a similar story about Ejō. It recounts how Ejō first met Dōgen shortly after his return from China. At first, they seemed to be in agreement, but Ejō left after Dōgen rebuked him for a point of error. Several years later, Ejō abandoned his pride and returned to become Dōgen's disciple. According to the *Denkōroku*, he formally joined Dōgen during the first year of the Bunryaku 文暦 Era, which began the fifteenth of the eleventh month of 1234. This date probably derives from Ejō's own words. An entry dated the first month of 1255 in the *Goyuigon* (DZZ.7:196) quotes Ejō as informing Gikai that he first joined Dōgen's assembly just over twenty years previously (i.e., the end of 1234).

At some point shortly thereafter, Ejō began to transcribe notable remarks by Dōgen that he (and others) heard, in the work now known as the *Zuimonki* (*Transcriptions*). The *Zuimonki* can be of great value for readers of the *Shōbōgenzō* because it sometimes conveys Dōgen's colloquial explanations of Zen vocabulary items that nowadays have become technical terms for theorists of Dōgen's thought.[142] For example, Ejō recorded Dōgen's explanation of "undefiled" (*fuzenna* 不染汚) practice as follows:

> 只、身心を佛法になげすてて、更に悟道得法までも、のぞむ事なく、修行しゆく、是を不染汚の行人と云也。有佛の處にもとどまらず、無佛の處をもすみやかにはしりすぐ、と云、この心なるべし。
> (*Zuimonki* 6; DZZ.7:147)

One who, simply casting body and mind into the buddha-dharma, continues to train without any expectations, even of awakening to the way and attaining the dharma — this is called an undefiled practitioner. This is the meaning of not staying where the Buddha is while rushing away from where the Buddha is not.

Ejō arrived shortly after Dōgen wrote *Advice on Studying the Way* (*Gakudō yōjinshū* 學道用心集), a collection of practical advice regarding the proper approach to daily practice. Not surprisingly, the term "study the way" (*gakudō*) appears frequently (78 times) in the *Zuimonki*. Ejō's focus on this term serves as a reminder that, among Buddhists at this time in Japan, there existed no commonly shared norms regarding what the practice of Buddhism might entail. Even Ejō, an advanced practitioner

---

[142] See Ishii Shūdō (1988, 123) for this observation and the example that illustrates it.

who had been trained on Mount Hiei, in Pure Land, and in the Zen lineage of Nōnin (the so-called Darumashū), nonetheless did not know how to practice Buddhism in the manner demanded by Dōgen. Accordingly, he kept careful notes.

Another key feature of the *Zuimonki*, frequently overlooked, consists of the information it conveys regarding how Dōgen taught kōans. In the quotation above, for example, Dōgen explains the meaning of the kōan known as "Zhaozhou: The Buddha Is and the Buddha Is Not" (*Jōshū: ubutsu mubutsu* 趙州有佛無佛). As shown in Table 16, "Kōans Discussed in the *Zuimonki*," Dōgen mentions at least sixteen kōans in the *Zuimonki*, and each one of these kōans appears in Dōgen's *Shōbōgenzō* in Chinese script. Only very rarely did he explicitly identify the kōans by title or by the name of its protagonist. Instead, he used key words (analogous to pivot words, *tengo* 轉語) that bear such an intrinsic relationship to the kōans that they invoke its connotations to listeners who recognize them. This manner of speaking clearly indicates the great importance of kōan study within Dōgen's assembly. Dōgen could not have used these words in such a casual way and expect to be understood unless he also expected his students to have memorized each of the kōans in which they appear. His students had to learn not just technical Buddhist vocabulary written in Chinese but also the vernacular Chinese expressions that so often enliven the dramatic dialogues typical of most kōans.

These passages in the *Zuimonki* also clearly indicate that Dōgen taught and explained Chinese kōans in Japanese. Of course, a Japanese teacher in Japan would speak Japanese to Japanese students. Nonetheless this point bears emphasis. As mentioned previously, Mujū Dōgyō (Ichienbō) strongly identified Zen with the adoption of Chinese cultural norms and Chinese liturgy. Even during Dōgen's lifetime, the adoption of Chinese liturgy entailed the use of Song-period Chinese pronunciations. In the centuries subsequent to Dōgen, this identification of Zen and Chinese literary learning grew even stronger, as Zen temples became centers for the printing of Chinese books, the teaching of Chinese Confucian classics, and the production of literary works written exclusively in classical Chinese — the latter commonly known in Japan as the literature of the Five Mountains (*gozan bungaku* 五山文學). Within the context of Japan, "Five Mountains" served as a collective designation for all the major Zen monasteries sponsored by the political elites, without regard to the actual number of institutions included. The cultural prestige of these temples rested in no small measure on the quality of their Chinese

126 DŌGEN'S *SHŌBŌGENZŌ* VOLUME VIII

literary output. Dōgen wrote a great many literary works in Chinese. Unlike the vast majority of his Zen successors in Japan, however, he also produced prodigious quantities of literary works written in Japanese. The *Zuimonki* partially reveals the context within which Dōgen strove to explain Zen in Japanese terms. He seems to have expected his students to rely on kōans for acquiring a proper understanding of Buddhist doctrine and practice.

Dōgen also taught kōans as a meditative exercise. In this regard he resembled other Zen teachers of his time, including his own teacher, Rujing.[143] Several of the early dharma talks in Dōgen's *Extensive Records* provide practical advice regarding kōan meditation techniques. Consider, for example, these instructions (talk number 2) addressed to an otherwise unknown Superior Enchi 圓智, identified as the abbot of Ganshitsuji 巖室寺 in Tōtomi Province (present-day Shizuoka Pref.):

智禪人、請此掛額上月久日深、於佛祖道中雪上加霜。若不住此工夫邊、又是錦面添花。誠夫道無礙也。貴賤・尊卑・老少・愚鈍、共行俱來。紫磨金色、巍巍尊堂［堂］、從道得來。(*Kōroku* 8; DZZ.4:142)

Zen practitioner [En]chi, please attach this [kōan] to your forehead as months lengthen and days deepen, adding frost atop the snow on the way of the buddhas and ancestors. If you do not persist in this effort, then you've heaped flowers atop brocade. Truly the way is unobstructed. The wealthy and poor, noble and base, elders and youths, dull and clever, practice together and progress alike. Purple-golden hued [Buddhas] — magnificent, venerable, and imposing — come from attaining the way.

Another talk (number 5; DZZ.4:148-150) is noteworthy for what Dōgen says about kōan practice and about the student practitioner to whom the talk is addressed. The practice occurred from the spring of 1234 until the autumn of 1235 and consisted of private consultations in the abbot's quarters (*nisshitsu* 入室), during which the student would request instruction in old cases (*shin'eki kosoku* 請益古則), and in response Dōgen would raise new items (*konen shinjō* 舉拈新條). He lists several examples: Juzhi's One Finger (Juzhi *yizhi* 俱胝一指; J. Gutei *isshi*); Heshan's Beating a Drum (Heshan *dagu* 禾山打鼓; J. Kazan *tagu*); Linji's Shout

---

[143] Regarding Rujing, see his discussion of "Zhaozhou: Dog Has No Buddha-nature" (*Zhaozhou: gouzi foxing wu* 趙州狗子佛性無) in *Rujing heshang yulu* 如淨和尚語錄 2; CBETA.T.2002A.48:127b12-16. Kagamishima (1973; rpt. 1982, 124; also 1983, 120) and Ishii Shūdō (1985, rpt. 1991a, 404) alike find no distinction between Rujing's remarks and the approach advocated by Dahui Zonggao (1089–1163).

(Linji *he* 臨濟喝; J. Rinzai *katsu*); and Deshan's Staff (Deshan *bang* 德山棒; Tokusan *bō*) — all of which appear in the *Shōbōgenzō* in Chinese script (numbers 245, 186, 27, and 31). Dōgen states that all these teaching methods (*giryō* 伎倆) lead to one and the same verification. The vocabulary and procedures mentioned herein provide no evidence that might distinguish Dōgen's methods of teaching kōans from those of any other of his contemporaneous Zen masters.

Dōgen addressed this talk to a Lord Ya, who is probably the individual named Ya Jokō 野助光 in one of Dōgen's Chinese gāthā-style verses (*Kōroku* 10; DZZ.4:274). Both the talk and the verse refer to Ya as someone from the town of Dazaifu, in Kyushu. In the talk, Dōgen not only addresses Ya as a lord (*kō* 公), but describes him as a government official (*tafu* 大夫; i.e., *shitafu* 士大夫) and a scholar (*gakushi* 學士) from the Confucian literati groves (*jurin* 儒林). He is not a Buddhist monk, but Dōgen nonetheless praises him as someone whose spiritual aspirations exceed those of most monks.

Because the family name Ya is written with only a single glyph, many people have assumed that Ya must be a Chinese surname and, therefore, that Ya must have been a Chinese merchant (or son of a Chinese merchant) who resided in the Chinese community of Dazaifu (or Hakata). By extension, the same identification can be applied to the otherwise unknown lay person named Yō Kōshū 楊光秀, who was the recipient of the "Realized Kōan" (chapter 1; "Genjō kōan") in 1233.[144] There is no evidence to support (or deny) this hypothesis, but the larger historical context invites skepticism. While the expatriate Chinese merchant community at Hakata and Dazaifu did not suffer social segregation, Dōgen's description of Ya as a government official, a scholar, and as a member of the Confucian groves all point toward an individual of elite status, which people of overseas origin were unlikely to attain even in Dazaifu.[145]

The phrase "Confucian groves" especially demands attention since many early historical accounts use it to describe the genealogical lineage of Sugawara Michizane, who was widely worshiped across Japan, and especially in Dazaifu, as a patron god of Chinese learning. Michizane used this term to describe his own ancestors in the Chinese verses he

---

[144] E.g., see Kagamishima 1988, 323–234.

[145] Regarding the social status of Chinese at Hakata, see von Glahn (2014, 274) and Enomoto (2001). Nakaseko (1979, 306–307) groups Ya Jokō and Yō Kōshū together with other government officials among Dōgen's students.

128 DŌGEN'S *SHŌBŌGENZŌ* VOLUME VIII

composed, and it appears in a widely-quoted Chinese verse written in support of Michizane by the royal ruler Daigo 醍醐 (885–930; r. 897–930).[146] In Dazaifu, descendants of Michizane served as the hereditary overseers (*bettō*) of Anrakuji, and a collateral branch served as the hereditary administrators (*bunjin* 文人) of his mausoleum (Era Hiromu 1967, 79–81). The term *bunjin* originally referred to academicians, especially instructors at an academy (which had been the official role of the Sugawara clan). Documents from shortly after Dōgen's time, reveal that the *bunjin* of Anrakuji had adopted the surname Ono 小野 (*ibid.* pp. 82–83). If reduced to a single glyph, the surname Ono could be rendered as "Ya" (an alternative pronunciation of its second glyph). The use of a single glyph to represent a longer Japanese surname would not be uncommon for academicians. Michizane, for example, was commonly known as Kan 菅 *shōjō* 丞相 (Chamberlain Kan). Clearly the use of a surname written with a single glyph alone cannot automatically establish non-Japanese identity.

Extant sources cannot reveal if Ya Jokō or Yō Kōshū were affiliated with Anrakuji or not. What can be known for certain is that both resided in Dazaifu, both were early disciples of Dōgen, and both studied kōans under Dōgen's direction. These facts raise at least two key questions, one historical and the other philosophical (or doctrinal).

The historical question asks, what, if any, was Dōgen's connection to Dazaifu (or Hakata)? In the colophon to "The Realized Kōan," Dōgen identified Yō Kōshū as a lay person who resides in Chinzei 鎮西, which typically referred to Dazaifu as the location of the administrative offices (Chinzei *bugyō*) of the Kamakura military government. Mujū Dōgyō, in his account of the beginnings of Zen in Japan (translated in a separate section below), uses the word "Chinzei" as a designation for Shōfukuji — the Zen temple that Eisai founded in Hakata. During his final years, Eisai routinely rotated among his temples (Kenninji in Kyoto, Jufukuji in Kamakura, and Shōfukuji in Hakata). Enni likewise traveled between Jōtenji 承天寺 in Hakata and Tōfukuji 東福寺 in Kyoto. Lanxi Daolong

---

[146] For Michizane's own usage, see *Kanke kōshū* 菅家後集 (*Gunsho ruijū* 群書類從, vol. 9, 194a; cf. Borgen 1994, 299). For the poem written by Daigo, see Borgen (1994, 223): "From of old your family has been one of scholars" 門風自古是儒林. This line is quoted in numerous historical, legendary, and fictional accounts of Michizane's lives, the earliest of which predate Dōgen's time. Note that, in the two examples above, Borgen renders the literal "Confucian groves" (*jurin*) into English as the more-easily understood (but generic) "scholars."

*Introduction to the* SHŌBŌGENZŌ: *6d. Dōgen back in Japan* 129

also initially presided over two temples: Engakuji 圓覺寺 in Hakata and Kenchōji in Kamakura. Their examples suggest the possibility of an established pattern among early Zen pioneers. Could Dōgen likewise have first taught Zen in Dazaifu, perhaps traveling between Kenninji and Shōfukuji? If so, his dual residency would explain how his community in Kyoto attracted disciples from Dazaifu (some 525 kilometers distant). Except for these two disciples, however, the only other evidence that links Dōgen to Dazaifu consists of its role as a port of exit and return for his overseas journey to China.[147]

The doctrinal question relates to the very different kinds of information that the extant sources convey about Dōgen's two early disciples from Dazaifu. The fact that one of them (Ya, or possibly Ono?) entered the abbot's quarters (*nisshitsu*) to request instruction in old cases (*shin'eki kosoku*) while the other one (Yō, or possibly Yanagi?) received Dōgen's Japanese-language explanation of "The Realized Kōan" (chapter 1) raises the question of how different (or how related) these two methods of kōan instruction might have been. Previous scholarship tended to address this issue in somewhat simplistic or reductionist terms, which more often than not relied on anachronistic evidence derived from later Zen masters such as Hakuin Ekaku 白隱慧鶴 (1686–1769) or Menzan Zuihō. Today, those kinds of simplistic distinctions have been confounded by a growing body of scholarship that explores the importance of Dōgen's *Shōbōgenzō* in Chinese script not just for his teaching of kōans but for his teachings as a whole.[148] Indeed, one can now reasonably question whether it would have been possible for Dōgen to have composed his *Shōbōgenzō* in Japanese script in the way that he did without the benefit of his initial work on a *Shōbōgenzō* in Chinese script.

Dōgen's preface (translated in Supplement 3) to the *Shōbōgenzō* in Chinese script is dated 1235.11.3. The manuscript tradition of this work reveals variant contents, which indicate that Dōgen must have revised it at least once. It is not clear if the date of the preface applies to the

---

[147] *Kenzeiki* (p. 32) reports a legend promoted by Daijiji (in Kumamoto; founded 1282) that Dōgen returned from China via Kawashiri 河尻 (in present-day Kumamoto). While it is theoretically possible for a ship blown off-course to make landfall anywhere, regardless of where it first sighted land, the final destination of Dōgen's ship would have been Hakata. See von Glahn 2014.

[148] For a useful summary of recent findings, see Ishii Shūdō 2009. Because scholarship has advanced so rapidly, publications from earlier dates (while nonetheless essential) must be treated with caution.

initial draft or to the final revised version. Either way, its gestation must have occurred over a period of many years. As mentioned previously, kōan 122, "Xuanze: Bingding Youth," plays a key role in *Talk on Pursuing the Way* (*Bendōwa*), dated 1231, while kōan 123, "Baoche: No Place Not Reached," plays an even more central role in "The Realized Kōan" ("Genjō kōan"), dated 1233. The early dates assigned to these two essays indicate that Dōgen already selected and translated at least two of the three hundred kōans in his *Shōbōgenzō* several years earlier than the 1235 date of its preface. It is also significant that the chronological sequence of these essays agrees with the sequential order of the kōans in Dōgen's compilation. By a remarkable coincidence (or by design?), kōan 121, "Magu: A Hoe Hoes the Weeds," appears in chapter 1 of Ejō's *Zuimonki* (DZZ.7:56). These three kōans form a tripartite lesson, within which each one reinforces and amplifies the other two. The first and third both involve Magu Baoche 麻谷寶徹 (J. Mayoku Hōtetsu; dates unknown), whose teachings provide the interpretive frame for the story of Xuanze and the Bingding Youth.[149]

Dōgen plainly states the moral of this lesson in the *Zuimonki*: "The Way never ceases. Upon awakening (*satori*), one still must practice the Way." Then Dōgen adds an aside: "Consider the story of Abbot Liangsui inquiring of Magu." The story of Liangsui 良遂 (J. Ryōsui; dates unknown) and Magu is not necessarily obscure. It appears in the recorded sayings of several well-known Chinese masters. But it is not the kind of story that even dedicated students of Zen might recognize by name. Dōgen mentions it in none of his other compositions, and other well-known collections of kōans do not include it.[150] Without access to Dōgen's *Shōbōgenzō* in Chinese script, it would be extremely doubtful if Ejō or the other members of Dōgen's community could have understood his instructions in this comment. Dōgen's aside, therefore, bears major implications. It indicates that Dōgen compiled his kōan collection not just for his own use but also for the benefit of his students.

The fact that certain kōans (e.g., numbers 121, 122, 123) appear in sequential order indicates that the collection is not random but follows a design. A brief examination of some of its more notable features provides clues as to the nature of that design.

---

[149] Magu 麻谷 is also known as Mayu 麻浴, but in Japanese Sōtō both variants are pronounced identically as "Mayoku."

[150] Ishii Shūdō 1988, 554.

First, as indicated by the statistics in Table 17, "Distribution of Kōans in the *Shōbōgenzō* in Chinese script," Dōgen selected kōans that, taken together, present a comprehensive overview of the Zen tradition. It begins with Śākyamuni, continues in a single lineage down to the Sixth Ancestor, Caoxi Huineng (J. Sōkei Enō), and then branches into the two main lineages of Nanyue Huairang (J. Nangaku Ejō) and Qingyuan Xingsi (J. Seigen Gyōshi). Most important, it encompasses each of the Five Houses. Along with the descriptions of the multiple inheritance certificates found in the chapter (number 39; "Shisho") of that same name, it demonstrates Dōgen's mastery of the "arcane import" (*genshi*) of all traditions of Zen. The inclusion of so many kōans that involve people from the Qingyuan Branch, and especially from the Caodong (J. Sōtō) lineage, stands out. Nonetheless, overall, it presents a remarkably balanced and nonsectarian collection. Table 17 fails to represent another key feature of this collection: Dōgen presents kōans that emphasize the underlying unity among the seemingly diverse and disparate styles of Chan. The tripartite lesson mentioned above, for example, joins together Magu Baoche (a disciple of Mazu Daoyi) from the Nanyue Lineage with Fayan Wenyi of the Fayan House in the Qingyuan Lineage. In this example, and in many others, Dōgen demonstrates that all of the Five Houses, regardless of lineage, teach the same underlying truth and alike emphasize the primacy of seated meditation (*zazen*).

Second, to convey this message, Dōgen carefully selected which kōans to include. Table 17 presents one aspect of Dōgen's selection process; but, for it to be readily apparent, one must add dates to the names. The list below includes all the names of Chinese people from Table 17 with their dates in alphabetical order.

# 132 DŌGEN'S *SHŌBŌGENZŌ* VOLUME VIII

| Major Figures in the *Shōbōgenzō* in Chinese script | *numbers of kōan* |
|---|---|
| Baizhang Huaihai 百丈懷海 (J. Hakujō Ekai; 720–814) | 5 |
| Caoshan Benji 曹山本寂 (J. Sōzan Honjaku; 840–901) | 9 |
| Caoxi Huineng 曹溪慧能 (J. Sōkei Enō; 638–713) | 2 |
| Dongshan Liangjie 洞山良价 (J. Tōzan Ryōkai; 807–869) | 11 |
| Fayan Wenyi 法眼文益 (J. Hōgen Mon'eki; 885–958) | 5 |
| Linji Yixuan 臨濟義玄 (J. Rinzai Gigen; d. 866) | 9 |
| Luohan Guichen 羅漢桂琛 (J. Rakan Keichin; 867–928) | 5 |
| Mazu Daoyi 馬祖道一 (J. Baso Dōitsu; 709–788) | 5 |
| Nanquan Puyuan 南泉普願 (J. Nansen Fugan; 748–834) | 9 |
| Nanyue Huairang 南嶽懷讓 (J. Nangaku Ejō; 677–744) | 4 |
| Qingyuan Xingsi 青原行思 (J. Seigen Gyōshi; d. 740) | 4 |
| Weishan Lingyou 潙山靈祐 (J. Isan Reiyū; 771–853) | 19 |
| Xuansha Shibei 玄沙師備 (J. Gensha Shibi; 835–908) | 12 |
| Xuefeng Yicun 雪峰義存 (J. Seppō Gison; ca. 822–908) | 10 |
| Yangshan Huiji 仰山慧寂 (J. Kyōzan Ejaku; 802–887) | 8 |
| Yaoshan Weiyan 藥山惟儼 (J. Yakusan Igen; 744–827) | 6 |
| Yunmen Wenyan 雲門文偃 (J. Unmon Bun'en; 864–949) | 12 |
| Zhaozhou Congshen 趙州從諗 (J. Jōshū Jūshin; 778–897) | 18 |
| 18 individuals　　*total number of kōans* | 153 |

The eighteen Chinese individuals listed in Table 17 account for more than half of the kōans in Dōgen's compilation. Most of them lived during the eighth and ninth centuries, the period idealized in many traditional histories. Dōgen also idealized these people and what he perceived as their Buddhist truth. They are his heroes or role models. Missing from this list are all the people that Dōgen himself encountered in China as well as their immediate predecessors. Only a handful of people date from later centuries, with the four most recent ones consisting of two representatives of the Caodong lineage, Taiyang Jingxuan 大陽警玄 (J. Taiyō Kyōgen; 943–1027) and Furong Daokai 芙蓉道楷; (J. Fuyō Dōkai; 1043–1118), as well as two representatives of the Linji House from about the same period, Yexian Guixing 葉縣歸省 (J. Sekken Kisei; dates unknown) and Langya Huijue 瑯瑘慧覺 (J. Rōya Ekaku; dates

*Introduction to the* SHŌBŌGENZŌ: *6d. Dōgen back in Japan* 133

unknown), with one kōan each (numbers 242, 243, 269, and 6, respectively).[151]

Third, several of the extant manuscripts of the *Shōbōgenzō* in Chinese script feature Japanese morphosyntactic marks (*waten* 和點) to gloss the meaning of vocabulary, provide pronunciations, and indicate syntax. One manuscript labels them as "Dōgen's marks" (Eihei *goten* 永平御點; see DZZ.5:300). This assertion might well have some historical basis, as suggested by the fact that the oldest extant manuscript (copied 1287, owned by Kanazawa Bunko) has the most extensive markings, and a reader who follows its markings can generate a Japanese vocalization of the text that agrees to a remarkable extent with Dōgen's Japanese version of the "Xuanze: Bingding Youth" kōan found in the draft version of *Bendōwa*. The linguistic correlation between these two texts provides the strongest available evidence that Dōgen authored *Bendōwa* (see the examples in Supplement 4). To understand fully the significance of these morphosyntactic markings, two crucial points must be kept in mind. First, during Dōgen's lifetime no rules governed the use of textual marks and few norms existed. Aristocratic families and Buddhist lineages alike maintained their own (i.e., in-house) idiosyncratic methods to convey distinctive individual hermeneutic cultures. Second, the act of marking a text could dictate novel readings to force interpretations unrelated to surface denotations.[152] Medieval textual marks allowed for freedom of interpretation in ways not possible in the somewhat mechanistic, word-by-word process of *yomi-kudashi* (i.e., vocalizing Chinese texts according to the word order of Japanese syntax) practiced in modern Japan. In short, the intellectual energy required to interpret an entire compilation of Chinese kōans (C. *gong'an*) with a complex system of glosses and Japanese morphosyntactic marks laid the basis for, and perhaps helped provide the impetus for, Dōgen's efforts to convey Buddhist truths in Japanese (Nomura 1965).

Textual marks, however, are fragile. Readers can ignore them, and copyists can omit them. Beginning in the eighteenth century, scholars of Confucian persuasions and advocates of national learning (*kokugaku*) developed multiple rival ways of reading and marking Chinese script to

---

[151]  Ishii Shūdō 1988, 550.

[152]  For a detailed analysis of forced reading techniques found in medieval Buddhist commentaries from Mount Hiei, see Maeda 1900. While Maeda finds parallels in the writings of Shinran, Kagamishima (1965, 71–72) finds similar parallels in Dōgen. Also see Kim 1985.

interpret them either more in accordance with Chinese norms (for advocates of Chinese Learning; *kangaku* 漢學) or as expressions of Japanese sentiments (for nativists; *kokugaku* 國學).[153] None of their approaches accepted medieval Japanese morphosyntactic marks, which came to be seen as faulty. Copyists of early manuscripts began to omit old-style marks or to "correct" (i.e., replace) them with academically acceptable ones. Works by Dōgen suffered this same fate. Later manuscript copies of his *Shōbōgenzō*, whether in Chinese or in Japanese script, either lack Japanese morphosyntactic marks or feature newly added ones that reflect the contemporary academic sensibilities of each individual scribe.

What happens to Dōgen's Chinese script when shorn of its earlier morphosyntactic marks? Some scholars have suggested that Dōgen's *Shōbōgenzō* in Chinese script consists merely of Chinese literary excerpts, without any creative or authorial contribution by Dōgen. If one sets aside the acts of selection and arrangement discussed above and focuses only on individual kōan entries, then indeed many entries will seem indistinguishable from similar material found in Chinese sources. Presumably, Dōgen quoted Chinese originals still extant in compositions by Chinese authors or compilers. That presumption generally proves to be correct. It is also the case that Dōgen sometimes edited his sources, or even combined material from different sources, to produce kōans that reflected his vision of what the great masters of China should have taught.[154]

These editorial interventions comprise the fourth key feature of the *Shōbōgenzō* in Chinese script. In this respect, Dōgen is far from unique. Individual kōan stories, especially popular ones, frequently appear in many variant forms. Pronouns change, obscure terms give way to current expression, and so on. Their content also evolves in ways that tend to reflect the personalities of individual teachers and the social conditions of their times. Dōgen likewise edited his kōans (see the examples in Supplement 4). The most important and the most radical example of

---

[153] See Bodiford (2013) for an analysis of how variant applications of reading marks to early printed versions of the *Kojiki* 古事記 (Ancient Accounts) produced alternative visions of early Japan.

[154] For examples, see Supplement 4: The Shōbōgenzō in Chinese and in Japanese scripts. Also see Kagamishima 1965, 40–62; Kim 1985. Note that overzealous copyists and editors sometimes "correct" quotations by rewriting them according to an external source.

*Introduction to the* SHŌBŌGENZŌ: *6d. Dōgen back in Japan*          135

this process can be seen in kōan number 8: "Nanyue: Polish a Tile and Strike the Cart" (*Nangaku masen tasha* 南嶽磨塼打車; DZZ.5:128).[155]

The story of Nanyue polishing a tile constitutes one of the most famous kōans in Dōgen's oeuvre. Dōgen repeats it several times in his *Shōbōgenzō* in Japanese script: in "Needle of Seated Meditation" (chapter 12; "Zazen shin"; DZZ.1:165), in "Sustained Practice," part 1 (chapter 16A; "Gyōji"; DZZ.1:151), and in "The Old Mirror" (chapter 19; DZZ.1:237). It describes how Mazu Daoyi was rebuked by his teacher, Nanyue Huairang, for his single-minded devotion to seated meditation. The nature of that rebuke, its timing, and its implications all differ from the Chinese original in the way that Dōgen tells it. Dōgen's revision of this story constitutes one of the key features of his teachings.[156]

According to the standard Chinese version, every day Mazu sat in meditation. One day, Nanyue stood before Mazu with a tile in his hands that he rubbed with a stone. When asked, he told Mazu that he was busy polishing the tile to make a mirror. When Mazu asked, "How can you expect to make a mirror by polishing a tile?" Nanyue replied by rebuking Mazu: "How can you expect to become a buddha by practicing seated meditation?" In other words, formal methods of practice are unnecessary.[157]

Dōgen turns this story on its head by inserting at the beginning of the kōan the statement that Mazu already had "intimately received the mind seal" (*mitsuju shin'in* 密受心印; i.e., confirmation) from Nanyue.[158] In Dōgen's version, Nanyue serves to affirm that one must continue to practice seated meditation (*zazen*) daily even after attaining awakening. In *Zuimonki* 3, Dōgen explains his point in simple terms:

> 南岳の磚を磨して、鏡を求めしも、馬祖の作佛を求めしを、戒めたり。坐禪を制するには非る也。坐、すなはち佛行なり。坐即不爲也。是、即、自己の正躰也。此外、別に佛法の可求無き也。(DZZ.7:100)

---

[155] Ishii Shūdō 1988, 125–129; Ishii Shūdō 2009, 130–131; Ishii Shūdō 2012, 103–118.

[156] For a comprehensive analysis, see Bielefeldt 1988, 131–160. Also see Kagamishima 1965, 67–71; Kim 1985, 74–79.

[157] *Jingde chuandeng lu* 景德傳燈録; 5; T.2076.51:240c. See Bielefeldt (1988, 141) for a translation of the entire episode from this source.

[158] For an examination of the phrase *mitsuju shin'in* 密受心印 in Chinese Chan sources and in Dōgen's works, see Ishii Shūdō 2012.

136    DŌGEN'S *SHŌBŌGENZŌ* VOLUME VIII

Nanyue polished the tile to admonish Mazu for seeking a mirror and for seeking to attain buddhahood. He did not admonish him to restrict his practice of seated meditation. Sitting is buddha activity. Sitting is not striving. It is the true body of your own self. Apart from it no other buddha-dharma can be attained.

Dōgen's interpretation of this episode relies entirely on the new version of the kōan that he authored in his *Shōbōgenzō* in Chinese script. As pointed out by Ishii Shūdō, this revision went beyond merely creating a new version of the story. Dōgen not only created a version that does not exist in Chinese sources but one that could not possibly have existed. Dōgen's version runs against the grain of the overall teachings of Nanyue and Mazu. For this reason, Ishii suggests that Dōgen's *Shōbōgenzō* in Japanese script derives, not just some of its textual sources from Dōgen's earlier version in Chinese, but also its fundamental inspiration.[159]

Previously, we noted that most of the eighteen individuals listed in Table 17 lived during the eighth and ninth centuries. The textual sources for the kōans in which they appear, however, derive from later time periods. Ishii Shūdō identified four main Chinese sources.[160] These titles constitute the main Chan works that Dōgen studied during his early career prior to 1235. Note that these correlations ignore Dōgen's revisions to the wording. For example, kōan 8, "Nanyue: Polish a Tile and Strike the Cart," clearly derives from *Jingde chuandeng lu* (*Jingde Era Transmission of the Flame*), even though it is equally obvious that Dōgen edited it to produce a new kōan with a modified message.

| Major Chinese Sources for the *Shōbōgenzō* in Chinese script | *numbers of kōan* |
|---|---|
| *Zongmen tongyao ji* 宗門統要集 (J. *Shūmon tōyōshū*; ca. 1100) | 129 |
| *Jingde chuandeng lu* 景德傳燈録 (J. *Keitoku dentōroku*; ca. 1011) | 42 |
| *Hongzhi lu* 宏智録 (J. *Wanshiroku*; ca. 1197) | 42 |
| *Yuanwu yulu* 圜悟語録 (J. *Engo goroku*; ca. 1136) | 38 |
| 18 individuals    *total number of kōans* | 252 |

---

[159]   Ishii Shūdō 2021, 103–106.

[160]   Ishii Shūdō (1988, 572) builds on but differs from the data reported by Kagamishima 1987.

*Introduction to the* SHŌBŌGENZŌ: *6d. Dōgen back in Japan*          137

The first two of these works exerted enormous influence on the Chan tradition as a whole, not just during Dōgen's lifetime but for generations thereafter. The *Zongmen tongyao ji* (*Collection of the Essential Teachings of Our Lineage*) delimited the basic sets of stories that were adapted as kōans in many (or most) subsequent compilations. Because it was re-printed repeatedly (1100, 1133, 1135, 1146, 1179, etc.), it became one of the most widely read and copied kōan collections in history.[161] The *Jingde chuandeng lu* (*Jingde Era Record of the Transmission of the Flame*) is the first of the major "flame histories," which served to define Chan identity for future generations. It presents a unified version of the Chan lineage, within which even collateral branches receive recognition. In addition to well-known kōans, it provides basic biographical information for major figures, as well as excerpts from several of their key literary compositions. The second two works consist of the recorded sayings of Hongzhi Zengjue 宏智正覺 (J. Wanshi Shōgaku; 1091–1157), represent-ing the Caodong House, and of Yuanwu Keqin 圜悟克勤 (J. Engo Koku-gon; 1063–1135), representing the Linji House. Almost all the kōans ad-opted from their recorded sayings come from sections devoted to poetic verses dedicated to old kōans (i.e., *songgu* 頌古; J. *juko*; or *niangu* 拈古; J. *nenko*). The quotations of kōans that accompany verse comments will frequently be abbreviated or revised to fit better the verse or its special occasion. The names of Hongzhi Zengjue and Yuanwu Keqin should be added to the list of Dōgen's heroes (see the discussion of the distribu-tion of kōans in the *Shōbōgenzō* in Chinese script above). He studied the kōans that they cited and sometimes modeled his comments on theirs.

Today, Yuanwu Keqin is perhaps best known for his comments on kōans in the *Blue Cliff Collection* (*Biyanji* 碧巖集; J. *Hekiganshū*). None of the kōans used by Dōgen come from that work (Ishii Shūdō 1988, 552). Likewise, none come from the *Gateless Barrier* (*Wumenguan* 無門 關; J. *Mumonkan*), which did not circulate widely in China and was not introduced to Japan until after Dōgen's death.[162] Neither work is quot-ed in any of Dōgen's compositions (although those works might quote earlier kōans that Dōgen also quotes). After Buddhist temples in Japan began regularly to reprint the *Blue Cliff Collection* and *Gateless Barrier* (beginning in the 14th century), they supplanted the *Zongmen tongyao*

---

[161]  A study of this work by Ishii Shūdō (2000) is available in English trans-lation.

[162]  A study of this work by Ishii Shūdō (2004) is available in English trans-lation.

*ji*, which fell into obscurity. While the *Blue Cliff Collection* and *Gateless Barrier* each possesses its own individual features, together they came to define what Buddhist practitioners and academic scholars alike regard as the exemplary models for kōan commentaries. When examining Dōgen's comments on the many kōans that he quotes in his works, it helps to remember that he was mostly unaware of those other two works. He developed his own style of kōan commentary, not necessarily in opposition to their models but in their absence.

Significantly, at least eight kōans in the *Shōbōgenzō* in Chinese script come from the *Zhengfayanzang* (*Treasury of the True Dharma Eye*; ca. 1163) by Dahui Zonggao (1089–1163). These eight kōans must have come from this work, since it contains the only known example of each of them.[163] It is possible that Dōgen derived a few more kōans from Dahui's *Zhengfayanzang*, but those that also exist in the *Zongmen tongyao ji* are counted only under that title. The number of textual borrowings is less significant than the fact that Dōgen directly quoted passages (even one would be remarkable) from Dahui's work. It indicates that he could not have selected the title "*Shōbōgenzō*" in ignorance of its previous appropriation by Dahui. Why would Dōgen have chosen the same title for his own collection of kōans as that already used by Dahui? It seems especially odd since Dōgen sometimes harshly criticizes Dahui.[164]

Dōgen officially opened Kōshōji with an inaugural address on the fifteenth of the tenth month of 1236 (*Kōroku* 1; DZZ.3:2). The inauguration ceremony occurred almost one full year after the date assigned to his *Shōbōgenzō* in Chinese script. Thereafter, Dōgen began to implement the monastic norms and ceremonies conducted at Buddhist temples in China. This task could not have been easy. It requires the proper facilities, implements, codified days and hours, codified procedures, celebrants to lead, participants to follow, and a great deal of time and energy for preparation and rehearsal. If the extant records provide any indication, the process of filling the monastic offices and defining their duties required many months. At the end of 1236, on the twenty-ninth of the twelfth month, Ejō took center stage to conduct the "wield the whisk" (*hinpotsu* 秉拂) ceremony that inaugurated him as the head seat (*shuso* 首座), or leader of the assembly (*Zuimonki* 5; DZZ.7:119). One month later, Dōgen composed the *Tenzo kyōkun* (*Admonitions for the Chef*; DZZ.6:24), on the duties of the officer in charge of meals, supplies, and finances,

---

[163]  Ishii Shūdō 1988, 33.

[164]  For a convenient summary, see Bielefeldt 1985, 36–39.

Introduction to the SHŌBŌGENZŌ: 6d. Dōgen back in Japan   139

among countless additional tasks. In this work, Dōgen vividly describes his conversations with monastic cooks in China, but at this time his recollections must have been nearly nine (or more) years old.[165] On the twenty-fifth of the fourth month of 1239, Dōgen composed rules for the cloud hall (*undō* 雲堂; a.k.a. saṃgha hall), a version of which eventually made its way into the Honzan edition of the *Shōbōgenzō*. Certainly, similar monastic practices and assigned responsibilities must have been implemented even before Kōshōji officially opened, but now every monastic officer faced higher expectations. They were to fulfill their obligations in ways that more closely approximated Chinese models.

Presumably, Dōgen also assumed many new responsibilities. Chief among them, or at least the one most associated with Zen literature, was the convocation address (*jōdō* 上堂). This type of lecture constitutes an essential component of the discourse records or "recorded sayings" (*yulu*; J. *goroku*) that abbots of major monasteries in China produced. In earlier centuries, "sayings" might have referred to supposedly spontaneous remarks, a transcription of colloquial dialogues rather than literary prose. By Dōgen's time, however, discourse records had become highly formalized literary works. The ones produced in Japan followed Chinese conventions, including language. Rather than "recorded sayings," it is more accurate to think of these works as collected compositions in Chinese.[166] Convocations would follow a defined format and occur on a regularly scheduled basis as designated by the monastic calendar, as well as on special occasions. The monastic community would assemble in the Dharma (i.e., preaching) Hall, and the abbot would then ascend the high seat and present a brief statement in Chinese. Typically, the statement consists of a quotation (most often a kōan) raised (*kyo* 舉; i.e., recounted) for consideration. Then, the abbot would present a question, comment, or verse (all in Chinese). Theoretically, the abbot's remarks could be followed by questions from the audience, but normally they would not be recorded. The abbot's address was always recorded as if it had been presented entirely in Chinese. In monasteries where the abbot came from China, that might have occurred. In the case of Japanese abbots, we can only guess how they might have conveyed their statement and comments. Perhaps, abbots would first compose the Chinese

---

[165]   Dōgen's many quotations from his time in China suggest the existence of a now-lost diary (*zaitōki* 在唐記).

[166]   For an overview, see Bodiford 2012a. For an abbreviated list of annual events, see Bodiford 1993, 160–161.

language version, present it as a formal statement, and then explain it to the audience.

The acolyte (*jisha* 侍者) was responsible for preserving the written accounts of monastic events and correspondences, including all sermons and pronouncements by the abbot. Every type of monastic communication would (or should) follow established Chinese conventions. Most likely, only Dōgen possessed the knowledge to train his acolyte(s) at Kōshōji in these tasks. This job would require knowledge of Chinese monastic culture as well as a high level of competence in Chinese language, both classical literature and colloquial idioms. The acolyte would be expected to make clean copies of each new item, label it, date it, catalog it, and preserve it in ordered boxes. Each year's activities might have produced hundreds of sheets of new records. Tamamura Takeji (1941: 142–156), the scholar who pioneered academic research on the literature of Japanese Zen temples, wrote that an almost infinite number of "recorded sayings" survive even today in temple storehouses. The identity of Dōgen's acolyte at Kōshōji cannot be known with certainty. Dōgen's disciple Senne 詮慧 (d. after 1263) is the most likely candidate, since he compiled the final record of Dōgen convocation addresses from Kōshōji. It is possible that Senne replaced a predecessor who proved unsatisfactory. Records from Dōgen's first four years at Kōshōji are extremely fragmentary or nonexistent. As stated above, for example, *Extensive Records* reports that Dōgen presented an inaugural address (on 1236.10.15), but the content of the address is missing. Only thirty-one convocation addresses survive from the years 1236 to 1240 — and probably none from 1236 (see Table 24).

Beginning in 1241, the records of Dōgen's convocation addresses become more complete and more regular. Many of these addresses explicitly name the occasion on which they occurred. Those that do not can be located on the monastic calendar in between the ones with dates. Some presentations, however, must have been recorded out of sequence. In 1980, Itō Shūken greatly advanced our understanding these records by carefully weighing the available evidence, adjusting the sequence of certain convocation addresses, correlating them with traditional calendrical lore, and then identifying many of them according to modern calendar dates. Table 24, "Convocation Addresses in the *Extensive Records of Reverend Dōgen*," provides a rough summary of Itō's conclusions. He could

Introduction to the SHŌBŌGENZŌ: 6d. Dōgen back in Japan        141

not resolve all the chronological obscurities, but his findings provide the current standard for the likely dates of Dōgen's convocation addresses.[167]

Because reliable dates can rarely be found for Dōgen, it is tempting to correlate the topics discussed in his convocation addresses (for which the dates now are known or can be guessed) with the occurrence of similar topics in chapters of his *Shōbōgenzō* (for which the dates might be in dispute or unknown). Sometimes the correlations can be very revealing, and recent scholars routinely apply this technique. It nonetheless remains important to consider how correlations can sometimes be misleading. Consider, for example, the "Xuanze: Bingding Youth" kōan which also appears in two of Dōgen's convocation addresses: numbers 15 (ca. winter 1240?) and 299 (winter 1248). Fortunately, the text of *Bendōwa* carries a date (1231). If it were undated, however, one might want to correlate the kōan between these sources and consider whether *Bendōwa* should be assigned to a date around 1240, by which time the same kōan likely had first appeared in Dōgen's recorded sayings from Kōshōji.

The contents and relative dates from the convocation addresses can sometimes be used to test the likelihood of hypotheses regarding the evolution of ideas or rhetorical tropes within the *Shōbōgenzō*. Because the *Extensive Records* provides more convocation entries over a longer span of dates, it should provide more reliable statistical data. At the same time, each one of Dōgen's major works exhibits its own distinctive characteristics. For example, the two individuals mentioned and quoted most often by Dōgen are: Hongzhi Zengjue (1091–1157; J. Wanshi Shōgaku) and his own teacher, Rujing (1162–1227; J. Nyojō). Neither appear in the *Shōbōgenzō* in Chinese script. Rujing is cited more often than Hongzhi in the *Shōbōgenzō* in Japanese script, but in the *Extensive Records*, this ranking is reversed: Hongzhi is quoted or mentioned more often than Rujing.[168] It has been suggested that Dōgen's attitude toward Rujing evolved in response to his changing social fortunes. Some chapters in the *Shōbōgenzō* do not mention him at all, while other chapters exalt his status. Do these differences derive from the nature of the topics addressed in different chapters, or can they be linked to historical de-

---

[167]  Unless stated otherwise, all the dates given herein regarding the *Extensive Records* derive from the work of Itō Shūken 1979; Itō Shūken 1980; with additional information from Ishii Shūdō (1991b, 328–330). Itō could not assign dates to entries nos. 1–31, during the years 1237 to 1240.

[168]  Kagamishima 1987, 1; Ishii Shūdō 1991, 328–330, 334–335, 336.

142 DŌGEN'S *SHŌBŌGENZŌ* VOLUME VIII

velopments? No one can say with certainty, but the *Extensive Records* provides an alternative set, with a more reliable chronological profile. Its evidence, even if inconclusive, cannot be ignored. Table 25 compares the number of convocation addresses that mention or quote Hongzhi or Rujing each year. If converted to rough percentages, the data reveal the following trend:

| | | |
|---|---|---|
| Overall convocation addresses | Hongzhi 13% | Rujing 11% |
| Kōshōji period (ca. 1240 to 1243) | Hongzhi 5% | Rujing 4% |
| Echizen period I (ca. 1245 to 1247) | Hongzhi 15% | Rujing 10% |
| Echizen period II (ca. 1248 to 1252) | Hongzhi 15% | Rujing 15% |

These numbers can be interpreted in at least two ways, which suggest contradictory conclusions. On the one hand, they confirm that the number of convocations at which Dōgen mentioned Rujing increased over time. So did those for Hongzhi, who rose in prominence much earlier and more rapidly. Rujing finally caught up with Hongzhi's numbers only during the final years of Dōgen's career. On the other hand, the numbers can be seen as further evidence that the incomplete, fragmentary records for convocations at Kōshōji fail to provide accurate information. If the records had been more complete, then one might expect that they likely would provide statistics in agreement with the subsequent years, which seem remarkably consistent. According to this contrary interpretation, instead of revealing changes during the middle period (when both Hongzhi and Rujing rose in prominence), the records actually reveal a glaring gap during the earlier period, when convocations related to Hongzhi and Rujing failed to be recorded.

Considered in isolation, the *Extensive Records* suggest that little occurred between 1236, when Dōgen founded Kōshōji, and 1241, when his convocation addresses began to be delivered (and recorded) regularly. Nothing could be further from the truth. Inactivity was not the case. Dōgen's colophons to individual chapters of the *Shōbōgenzō* tell a very different story. The dates in colophons present their own difficulties of interpretation (see The *Shōbōgenzō* in Sixty Chapters and Its Descendants), but they also convey valuable raw data — especially when examined within the context of the separate manuscript traditions of each compilation — that cannot be ignored. They provide a starting point (not the final product) for constructing a chronology of *Shōbōgenzō* chapters. While Dōgen's convocation addresses (*jōdō*) occurred during three clearly demarcated periods, there exists no widely accepted schema for the periodization of the chapters in his *Shōbōgenzō*. Every scholar will group the chapters differently depending on whatever criteria work best for a given topic or issue.

The most basic (or generic) periodization of *Shōbōgenzō* chapters (see Table 26) simply groups them by location (or facility) and the assigned dates (if any) in the colophons for each chapter. The locations delimit temporalities: before Kōshōji (1233 to 1236), at Kōshōji (1236.10.15 to 1243.7.15), in Echizen Province (1243.7.15 to 1247.8.1), and back in Echizen Province again (1248.3.14 to 1253.8.3) after a trip to Kamakura. The periodization herein includes the dates assigned to the compositions and to revisions. This approach might seem reasonable, but it can be misleading in several respects. The dates can be misleading because some chapters lack colophons and/or dates; other chapters were (or could have been) revised without notation and with their original date unchanged; some chapters share identical dates; and it is possible that some colophons (with dates) now appear in chapters other than the ones for which they were written. Aside from issues presented by the dates found in the colophons of chapters in the *Shōbōgenzō*, a larger conceptual issue also exists, which any periodization schema necessarily embodies. Consider the different chronological profiles found in Tables 23 and 26. Both tables present data for the period prior to 1236 (when Kōshōji was founded). Table 23, "Early Compositions and Events," includes four essays that reflect the religious audience and activities of Dōgen during the years 1231 to 1233. The first section of Table 26, "Periodization of *Shōbōgenzō* Chapters," includes only two of those essays, but now groups them into a larger framework that reflects the religious audience and activities of Dōgen not just during those early years but also during the years 1238 to 1253. Contrary to the implications of Table 26, during the years 1231 to 1233, Dōgen had not yet begun to write his *Shōbōgenzō*. The essays of those years were composed as independent works. In 1235, he completed his *Shōbōgenzō* in Chinese script. Already at that time, he must have had an inkling of his ambition to compose a comprehensive *Shōbōgenzō* in Japanese script. But he did not attempt to do so. Manuscripts for the initial drafts of chapters do not include chapter numbers and do not include the overall designation *Shōbōgenzō*. Table 26 nonetheless retrospectively (i.e., anachronistically) includes his earlier works in a different literary creation that was to incorporate them only at some later date. If that later date could be determined, it would be possible to present the data from Table 26 in a more accurate manner.

Table 27 (Before Kōshōji) highlights the two compositions that later became chapters in the *Shōbōgenzō*. It looks to the subsequent developments while drawing attention away from other contemporaneous developments. In this regard, "The Realized Kōan" is noteworthy because its colophon in the seventy-five-chapter compilation differs from the one in the sixty-chapter version. Only the one in the seventy-five-chapter compilation carries the additional date "1252," with the designation "compiled and ordered" (*shūroku*; see The *Shōbōgenzō* in Sixty Chapters and Its Descendants). In chronological sequence, "Mahā-prajñā-pāramitā" came first, but when Dōgen arranged them as chapters, he placed "The Realized Kōan" first. These two initial chapters might seem rather disparate in style and focus. Nonetheless, one can discern paired metaphors: the importance of fanning oneself even as the ubiquitous wind blows everywhere (chapter 1) and the wind bell that voices the wisdom of emptiness (chapter 2).

According to the dates in Table 26, Dōgen did not begin to write essays in Japanese regularly until the years 1240 (7 essays) and 1241 (8 essays). His output at Kōshōji peaked in 1242 (15 essays). This is the same period during which Dōgen's number of convocation addresses at Kōshōji also peaked (at 48 during 1241 according to Itō Shūken; see Table 24). Scholars who study Dōgen often state as a truism that Dōgen's literary output of *Shōbōgenzō* chapters decreased in inverse proportion to the number of his convocation addresses. This inverse ratio might hold true for the later years of Dōgen's career, but it does not apply to the early 1240s at Kōshōji. If his combined increased literary output in these two different genres correlates with economic security and social stability, then this period must have been one of great success for Dōgen and for his community of disciples. Before examining further the *Shōbōgenzō* chapters composed at Kōshōji, therefore, we must consider their audience.

In spring of 1241 or on the eighteenth of the fourth month of 1242, Ekan 懐鑒 (d. 1251) and Gikan 義鑒 (a.k.a. Gikai 義介; 1219–1309) and their companions joined Dōgen's community. The *Sanso gyōgōki* (SZ. Shiden.1.6b) provides the earlier date. It states that Gikai's teacher Ekan decided to become Dōgen's disciple, and that Gikai accompanied him. The later date derives from a collection of funerary records, which includes the eulogy for Gikan written by his disciple, Keizan Jōkin. Kei-

*Introduction to the* SHŌBŌGENZŌ: *6d. Dōgen back in Japan*    145

zan's remarks include a brief chronology of Gikai's life. The existence of this work was all but unknown prior to 1971, but scholars now regard it as the most reliable historical source for Gikai's life. It merely lists the date that he became a resident of Kōshōji as 1242.4.18.[169]

The *Kenzeiki* does not mention this event; but, in his 1754 revised version (pp. 145–146), Menzan Zuihō includes a detailed supplemental note about it. Menzan identifies Ekan (a.k.a. Kakuzen-bō 覺禪房) as the disciple of Kakuan 覺晏 (a.k.a. Butchi-bō 佛地房; dates unknown), who was the dharma heir of Nōnin. Menzan further explained that Kakuan produced four disciples (or dharma heirs?): Ekan, Ejō, Eshō 懷照, and the nun Egi 懷義 (each with the same initial character, *e*, as a generational designation). Kakuan had urged all of them to study under Dōgen, and everyone but Egi did so.[170] Next, Menzan lists the names of Ekan's numerous disciples, beginning with Gikai: Gien 義演, Giin 義尹, Gijun 義準, Gisen 義荐, and Giun 義運 (each with the same initial character, *gi*, which in Nōnin's lineage designates the generation after *e*). Gikai used two names. Within the context of Nōnin's lineage, he referred to himself as Gikan, but in relation to Dōgen he used the name Gikai. The latter designation is the name used by biographers within the Sōtō tradition. He served as the third abbot of Eiheiji, the founder of Daijōji 大乘寺 (in Kaga), and the master of Keizan Jōkin. Gien (d. 1314) served as Dōgen's acolyte at Eiheiji, compiled chapters 5–7 of Dōgen's *Extensive Records*, and became the fourth abbot of Eiheiji. Giin refers to Kangan Giin 寒巖 義尹 (1217–1300), the founder of Daijiji 大慈寺 (in Higo), about whom Menzan likely was mistaken. Giin's biography suffered many embellishments, but it provides no evidence that links him to Nōnin's lineage. Gijun became one of Ejō's dharma heirs and founded a temple that later disappeared. The names Gisen and Giun do not appear in the historical record. Either Menzan was mistaken about them, or the evidence has been lost.

Even without every name in Menzan's list, Nōnin's faction contributed at least five key individuals (Ejō, Ekan, Gikai, Gien, and Gijun) to

---

[169] See "Shōsatsu shiki" 抄箚式 (p.6). In *Eihei daisandai Daijō kaisan daioshō senge sōjikiki* 永平第三代大乘開山大和尚遷化喪事規記. Reprinted under the title "Tettsū Gikai zenji sōki" 徹通義介禅師喪記 within a compilation created by the editors of ZSZ, *Sōkishū* 喪記集, in ZSZ.2.Shingi 清規, 1–7.

[170] The name Eshō 懷照 does not appear elsewhere in the historical record, but "The Retreat" (chapter 72; "Ango"; DZZ.2:233) mentions the name Eshō 懷昭, which is written with similar glyphs.

Dōgen's nascent Sōtō Zen community. In future generations, the line that descended from Gikai (who maintained the strongest ties to Nōnin's legacy) formed the mainstream of Sōtō. The year 1242, when Ekan and Gikai arrived at Kōshōji, happened to be the same period in which Dōgen produced numerous convocation addresses and (if the assigned dates are to be believed) composed more essays in Japanese than ever before. Could it be simply a coincidence that these events converged at this time? Perhaps. If Dōgen's increased literary productivity reflected the general success of his community, then it certainly would have become more attractive to potential rivals, such as Ekan and his disciples. Another perspective might suggest that the addition of new people who already had advanced training in kōan literature and other Zen matters could have made a good situation even better. They would bring their expertise to enhance the management of Kōshōji's affairs, their advanced training in Zen meant that Dōgen could more easily discuss and teach advanced topics, and the curiosity and commitment they brought would inspire his best efforts. Yet another perspective might see Ekan and his disciples as students in need of remedial education. They could have presented a threat, especially if either Dōgen or his earlier students regarded them and their teachings as deviant. As mentioned previously, Eisai denounced Nōnin's teachings in the strongest possible terms: "One must not talk with such people nor even sit beside them" (T.2543.80:7c–8a).

If Ekan and Gikai comprised the audience for the novel genre of Japanese-language essays about Buddhism that Dōgen pioneered, then how did this audience shape Dōgen's teachings? Bernard Faure aptly framed this issue:

> We may well wonder to what extent Dogen [sic] was influenced by, rather than influenced, his new disciples. In other words, who converted whom is perhaps not so clear as the tradition would have us believe. (Faure 1987, 26)

The possible responses to this quandary multiply over time. The "who" and the "whom" morph into new possible combinations in light of additional sources and newer lines of inquiry, and the stage on which historians plot their activities continually expands to include additional factors.[171] Just as the consideration of Dōgen's position within the larger Eisai faction reveals previously ignored aspects of his activities in

---

[171] Abe et al. (13 vols.; 2013–2019) provides a representative sample of new textual materials and cutting-edge scholarship. Sueki et al. 2021, reprints several of the more important essays from volume 13 of *ibid.* in an affordable paperback edition.

China, so likewise Nōnin now must be understood within the broader religious impact felt in Japan by the importation of Chinese Buddhist knowledge, practices, and material culture. And, for that matter, Rujing also must be seen within the milieu of Southern Song society, inside his circle of associates, who consisted almost entirely of masters of the Yangqi branch of the Linji House. As shown in Table 38, "Early Sōtō Intermingling with Nōnin's Faction," interlineage relations began before Dōgen. None of the people could have escaped the larger cultural flows and religious tides of their times. Rather than viewing interlineage relationships as aberrations, we should examine the larger social contexts in which they occur.

In China, Dōgen began his training under Wuji Liaopai, a disciple of Zhuoan Deguang (the person who granted dharma succession to Nōnin). As described in "The Inheritance Certificate" (chapter 39; "Shisho"), Dōgen investigated Nōnin's lineage through him. Rujing had also studied under Zhuoan Deguang, and he told Dōgen about it. Dōgen quotes this conversation (see "Sustained Practice"; chapter 16B; "Gyōji"; DZZ.1:197), but Rujing must have told him more than what Dōgen repeats here. The nonconformist, iconoclastic Rujing depicted by Dōgen does not appear in Rujing's own recorded sayings. His teachings therein can hardly be distinguished from those of his many Linji associates.[172] The dissonance between these two versions of Rujing surely results from the different authors who represent him. But which version is less accurate? Maybe the authors on both sides slanted their depictions. The disciples of Rujing who compiled his recorded sayings could have been more inclined toward conformity than he was. Likewise, some of the characteristics of Rujing that Dōgen most admired, but that cannot be found in Rujing's sayings, do exist in the sayings of his earlier Linji teacher, Songyuan Chongyue 松源崇嶽 (1132–1202).[173] In this regard, Kagamishima Genryū noted an intriguing statement in the Final Instructions (*yuikai* 遺誡) of Lanxi Daolong, a second-generation descendant of Songyuan.[174] Daolong began his admonitions with this dictum:

松源一派。有僧堂規。專要坐禪。其餘何言。(*Daikaku shūiroku* 大覺拾遺録; DNBZ.95.111b)

---

[172] Kagamishima 1973 (rpt. 1982, 124–125); Kagamishima 1978; Kagamishima 1983, 115–122.

[173] Hasegawa 1988.

[174] Kagamishima 1983, 18–19, 72–73; Ishii Shūdō 2006, 118–119.

The Songyuan faction has a rule for the Saṃgha Hall: You must solely practice seated meditation (*zazen*). What more can I say.

While the terminology differs, the gist seems remarkably similar to the otherwise unattested admonition that Dōgen repeatedly attributes to Rujing:

不用燒香禮拜念佛修懺看經、祗管打坐始得。(*Kōroku* 9, *juko* 頌古 85; DZZ.4:240)

Make no use of burning incense, prostrations, buddha-mindfulness, repentances, or *sūtra* recitation. Just sit (*shikan taza*) [in *zazen*]; then will you get it.[175]

These examples serve as reminders that convocation addresses capture only certain teachings, those that can be made public. Instructions intended for in-house consumption survive elsewhere in the recollections of individual disciples, who might or might not record them.

Eisai's *Kōzen gokokuron* (*Promoting Zen to Protect the Realm*) depicts Nōnin as an outsider and as a deviant. Eisai's evaluation once was widely accepted among modern historians, who knew little more than the fact that Nōnin's lineage no longer existed. Today, Eisai's dismissal must be seen as a partisan attack. Nōnin's lineage actually flourished, and for decades (or longer) contended for mainstream status. Its main temple (Sanbōji 三寶寺) continued to exist until the fifteenth century.[176] When the leaders of other new Buddhist movements wished to denounce the growing popularity of Zen as a rival, they directed their ire at Nōnin (no one else). The founder of the Chinzei branch of the Pure Land School, Benchō 辨長 (1162–1238; a.k.a. Shōkō-bō 聖光房), for example, boasted of having bested Nōnin in debate by quizzing him regarding the Five Houses of Chan.[177] Nichiren denounced Nōnin repeatedly: in (a) *The Teaching, Capacity, Time, and Country*; in (b) *The Rationale for Writing*

---

[175] Translation based on Foulk 2012, 94. See Foulk 2012 and Foulk 2015 for detailed analyses of this quotation.

[176] Documents state that warfare destroyed Sanbōji in 1469. Fortunately, by then its most important artifacts had been moved elsewhere for safekeeping. See Nakao 1986, 147. For an overview of Nōnin's activities, see Nakao 2005, 101–105. Takahashi Shūei (2013) provides a review of scholarship related to Nōnin's school. Furuse (2021) and Tachi (2021) report the latest findings. My comments herein rely on Nakao 2005.

[177] *Shōkō shōninden* 聖光上人傳 (1287); *Zoku gunsho ruijū*, Denbu 傳部, 9A.32.

*On Establishing the Correct Teachings for the Peace of the Land*; in (c) *The Opening of the Eyes* (Part Two); and in (d) *Letter from Sado.*[178] Significantly, Nichiren routinely attacks only two people: Dainichi-bō (a.k.a. Nōnin) and Hōnen-bō 法然房 (a.k.a. Genkū 源空; 1133–1212), the founder of the Pure Land movement. He regarded them equally as the two main enemies of the *Lotus Sūtra*. If we judge Nōnin by the enemies he made, he must have been very skilled at providing the Buddhist innovations of Song-dynasty China in a format accessible to broad segments of Japanese society. If we judge him by his disciples, then it is clear that many of them must have been devoted students of Zen. Keizan (who began his studies under Ejō) certainly described Ejō's previous training in those terms (*Denkōroku* 1.553–554).

Table 28 (At Kōshōji) lists the thirty-eight chapters with assigned dates from Dōgen's time at Kōshōji. The chapters from this five-year period comprise thirty-six out of seventy-five, or thirty-two out of sixty, or one out of twelve of his three substantive compilations of the *Shōbōgenzō*. Excepting the version in twelve chapters (for which only two chapters can be dated), these thirty-eight chapters comprise about half of the chapters in each of Dōgen's other two compilations. They constitute more than forty percent of the ninety chapters total that Dōgen composed. When compared to Okada's 1953 taxonomy of sixteen thematic categories in the *Shōbōgenzō*, these thirty-eight chapters correspond to every category but two. The large number of chapters and the broad range of topics that they address leave little doubt that Dōgen must have adopted essays in Japanese as a new genre for propagating his teachings. Nonetheless, it remains unclear when or where he began to think of these essays (or a select subset of them) as his *Shōbōgenzō*.

Of Okada's sixteen categories, the two that remained unrepresented at Kōshōji consist of "karma and causality" and "Zen precepts." If one assumes that Dōgen might have selected topics for his essays based on contemporaneous circumstances, then it is noteworthy that the arrival of many students from Nōnin's lineage apparently did not elicit any

---

[178] See (a) *Kyōkijikokushō* 教機時國抄 (NDGZ.442); (b) *Ankokuron gokan yurai* 安國論御勘由來 (NDGZ.423); (c) *Kaimokushō* 開目抄 (NDGZ.607; cf. T.2689.84:232b); and (d) *Sado gosho* 佐渡御書 (NDGZ.959–960); translated in *The Writings of Nichiren Daishonin* (1999): (a) 52; (b) 162–163; (c) 286; and (c) 303–304. Nichiren consistently refers to Nōnin by his residence designation "Dainichi-bō." In *Kyōkijikokushō* he also denounces Nōnin's disciple Kakuan, whom he refers to as "Butsuda" 佛陀 (rendered as "Budda"), which is a mistake for Kakuan's residence designation "Butchi-bō" 佛地房.

150    DŌGEN'S *SHŌBŌGENZŌ* VOLUME VIII

ethical concerns related to either of these categories. Eisai had accused Nōnin's followers of antinomianism, writing that: "There is no evil that such people will not do" (T.2543.80:7c–8a). From among Dōgen's dated chapters, Okada's categories of "karma and causality" and "Zen precepts" will not be addressed until 1244 and 1246, respectively. These are relatively late dates, but well before he went to Kamakura (after which, according to some theories, moral concerns became more noticeable).[179]

Table 28 (At Kōshōji) lists the chapters in chronological order, with their assigned dates in the left-most column and their assigned chapter number(s) in the columns to the right. In all, twenty-seven (out of thirty-eight) share the same chapter number in both the sixty- and the seventy-five-chapter compilations. This correspondence constitutes prime evidence for Dōgen's role in having compiled both compilations (Kawamura 1986, 14–16). But the chapter numbers and chronological sequence rarely correspond. Dōgen seems to have jumped from topic to topic without a plan. Only a few chronological sequences seem to suggest a shared concern. In 1239, the chapters "Washing the Face" (number 50) and "Washing and Purifying" (number 54) both concern monastic procedures, specifically hygiene. Three chapters composed in 1240 and 1241 address the "arcane import" and ritual procedures related to dharma transmission: "Transmitting the Robe" (number 32), "Buddhas and Ancestors" (number 52), and "The Inheritance Certificate" (number 39). Also note that three chapters, one of which is clearly unrelated to the other two, share the identical date of 1240.10.1 (also see Table 22). This anomaly casts doubts on the reliability of the assigned dates overall.

During the eighth month of 1242 at Kōshōji, Dōgen received a copy of Rujing's recorded sayings that had been sent to him from China. At a convocation that month (*Kōroku* 1, number 105; DZZ.3:60), Dōgen raised the books over his head to show them to the entire assembly. Then he led the assembly in performing full prostrations, three times, toward the books. What did he intend by this remarkable public display of fidelity toward his master's words? Nine years previously, without the benefit of that compilation from abroad, Dōgen had quoted Rujing's Wind Bell

---

[179] Okada assigns 3 chapters each to these categories. "Karma and causality" includes: "Great Practice" (no. 68; dated 1244.3.9), "Deep Faith in Cause and Effect" (no. 3; d.u.), and "Karma of the Three Times" (no. 8; d.u.). "Zen precepts" includes: "Leaving Home" (no. 75; dated 1246.9.15); "The Merit of Leaving Home" (no. 1; d.u.), and "Receiving the Precepts" (no. 2; d.u.).

*Introduction to the* SHŌBŌGENZŌ: *6e. Dōgen in Echizen*     151

verse in "Mahā-prajñā-pāramitā" (chapter 2; 1233). Dōgen's quotation matches the version in Rujing's record.[180] One year later (1243.9) in Echizen, Dōgen again quoted a verse by Rujing, about the purchase of a calf, a golden-faced Gautama ("The Real Marks of the Dharmas"; number 43; DZZ.1:467). This verse does not exist in Rujing's recorded sayings. Dōgen followed the quotation with a brief declaration that, even now, eighteen years after he heard Rujing's lecture, he still vividly remembers Rujing's "splendid diction and unusual phrases" (*bigen kiku*). Clearly in both cases the lived experience trumped the written record (or lack thereof).

In this statement, the expression "splendid diction and unusual phrases" (*bigen kiku*) deserves attention. Dōgen wrote this remark, not just in praise of the verse by Rujing that he quoted, but also to praise Rujing's manner of teaching. At the same time, it also describes Dōgen's own literary goals, the manner of composition that he learned from Rujing and strove to express in his *Shōbōgenzō*. "Splendid diction" (*bigen* 美言; literally "beautiful words") refers to memorable maxims, adages, or epigrams, in the sense of pithy, witty quotations that succinct convey the point. These are the kinds of remarks that Dōgen (as stated in *Zuimonki* 3; DZZ.7:90) had tried to memorize as a child, when he studied the classics of Chinese literature. In the context of Zen, they would consist of the famous sayings collected in kōans. "Unusual phrases" (*kiku* 奇句) refers to novel, creative expressions that are unique to the occasion, situation, or person. Used in combination, a creative application of a known saying (or cliché) can bring that saying to life and reveal new nuances or meanings that were always there but previously unrecognized.

*Dōgen in Echizen*

Two of the essays (or chapters?) from the Kōshōji period (Table 28) stand out, not for their content, but because of their location. Dōgen lectured on "Full Function" (number 22) during the last month of 1241 at the residence of Hatano Yoshishige in the Rokuharamitsu district of Kyoto (near the Rokuhara Tandai military offices). Four months later, on the twenty-ninth of the fourth month of 1243, Dōgen lectured again in the Rokuharamitsu district, this time on "The Old Buddha Mind" (number 9). Although the colophon does not mention Hatano by name, the location alone leaves no doubt that Dōgen (and entourage) had visited

---

[180]   Compare DZZ.1:11 and T.2002A.48:132b.

152 DŌGEN'S *SHŌBŌGENZŌ* VOLUME VIII

him. In China during this same period, it had become commonplace for abbots of temples to visit wealthy patrons to thank them for (or to solicit) their support. Certain entries in the recorded sayings of Rujing (such as a convocation address delivered upon returning from a shipload of rice; *michuan* 米船; J. *meisen*) suggest that Rujing also engaged in this practice.[181] Whether modeled after Rujing or someone else, Dōgen did likewise. He had found his patron, and Dōgen's presence in Rokuharamitsu served to introduce him to Hatano's men (i.e., his administrative staff) and to Hatano's family. Dōgen clearly passed the audition.

The *Kenzeiki* (p. 44) reports that Dōgen lamented to Yoshishige about how much he wished to escape from the hustle and bustle of the urban capital and find a secluded place in the mountains with clear spring waters. In response, Yoshishige offered him the use of a secluded ancient temple (*ankan koji* 安閑古寺) site located within the new (since 1221) Hatano domain in Echizen. Dōgen accepted, and along with his assembly, departed Kōshōji for Echizen on the sixteenth of the seventh month of 1243, the day after the end of the summer retreat (p. 45). The Hatano family remained the patrons of Eiheiji until the sixteenth century, including the time (ca. 1452) when Kenzei wrote his chronicle. Yoshishige's descendants would have read and approved the wording for this episode. We cannot ignore their interest in having their ancestor portrayed solely in altruistic terms. But, while Kenzei's account might not relate the larger context in which the relocation occurred, it nonetheless seems the no less sensible.

Among Dōgen's compatriots within the Eisai faction, many already had secured their own temples backed by the patronage of powerful families. As early as 1221, Eichō (a.k.a. Shakuen-bō; 1165–1247) founded Chōrakuji 長樂寺 in rural Kōzuke Province with the patronage of Serada Yoshisue 世良田義季 (d. 1247).[182] This is where Enni (1201–1280) first began his Zen training. In 1237, Taikō Gyōyū (a.k.a. Shōgon-bō; 1163–1241) founded Jōrakuji 常樂寺 in Kamakura with the patronage of the Hōjō family. And in 1239, Ryūzen (a.k.a. Butsugen-bō), Dōgen's companion at Tiantong in China, became the abbot of Kongō Zanmaiin (which also had been founded by the Hōjō) on Mount Kōya (Nakao 1988). Dōgen was not unaware of these developments. He presented

---

[181]  Kagamishima 1973, 122. The shipload of rice is mentioned in vol. 1: T.2002A.48:123a19-21.

[182]  A.k.a. Tokugawa Yoshisue 得川義季, the warrior who posthumously became the namesake for the Tokugawa 德川 family of shoguns.

*Introduction to the* SHŌBŌGENZŌ: *6e. Dōgen in Echizen*     153

one of his Chinese-style gāthā verses to the "Zen adept Nin" of Mount Kōya, a person who presumably was a disciple of Ryūzen.[183] Significantly, while all of these temples served as centers for Zen training, none of them openly proclaimed Zen. Both Chōrakuji and Jōrakuji ostensively were Pure Land chapels.[184] The Kongō Zanmaiin identified with Eisai's esoteric lineage. If Hatano Yoshishige offered Dōgen financial, political (and military) support for a temple where Zen could be taught openly, then how could Dōgen have refused? In return, Yoshishige would become identified with a locally powerful religious institution that would serve to strengthen his authority and prestige over the lands and people he ruled. After the temple was built, he did in fact became known as the "Lord of the Great Buddha Temple" (*Daibutsuji dono* 大佛寺殿), using the temple's initial designation.[185]

Dōgen arrived in Echizen Province by the beginning of the intercalary seventh month (1243.int7.1). He founded Daibutsuji on the eighteenth of the seventh month of 1244 (*Kōroku* 2; DZZ.3:70). He conducted the first summer training retreat there the following year, and his first convocation address in Echizen occurred on the same day (1245.4.15) that the retreat began (*Kōroku* 2, *jōdō* 127; DZZ.3:70). In other words, even after Dōgen had founded Daibutsuji and inaugurated his term as abbot, he waited until the following year before he conducted his first convocation. Perhaps the Dharma Hall was not ready until then. If Dōgen had faced similar circumstances at Kōshōji, it is possible that his first convocation there occurred in 1237, the year after the temple was founded.[186] On the fifteenth of the sixth month of 1246, Dōgen changed the name of Daibutsuji to "Eiheiji" (*Kōroku* 2, *jōdō* 177; DZZ.3:116). This is the name by which it is still known today.

Because Eiheiji still exists in its original location, one can easily see exactly where Dōgen was based during the second half of his career in Japan. Thanks to archeologists, it is also possible to see the hilltop location where the Hatano residence and fortifications once stood (1.5 km northwest of the temple). In contrast, the locations of Dōgen's other temples remain uncertain. Today, a Kōshōji exists in Uji (near Kyoto),

---

[183]   Geju 偈頌 51, "Yo Yasan Nin zennin" 與野山忍禪人 (DZZ.4:272).

[184]   Chōrakuji later became a Zen temple within the Japanese Gozan network.

[185]   Supplemental note by Menzan Zuihō in his 1754 version of *Kenzeiki*, p. 147.

[186]   Itō Shūken 1979, 247.

154 DŌGEN'S *SHŌBŌGENZŌ* VOLUME VIII

but it was first "restored" (i.e., erected) in 1603, long after the location
of the original temple by that name (in Fukakusa, also near Kyoto) had
been forgotten. Likewise, when Dōgen first arrived in Echizen, he identified his location as Kippōji (also pronounced Yoshiminedera): "Temple
on Fortunate Peak."[187] Today, a temple with that name exists nearby (5
km from Eiheiji and 6.5 km from the Hatano site), but it dates only from
1905. The location of Zenjihō 禪師峰 (a.k.a. Yamashibu), where Dōgen
also spent time, is even more obscure. A temple named Zenjibuji 禪師
峰寺 (written with the same characters) exists within the wider area (9
km from present-day Kippōji, 14 km from Eiheiji, and 15.5 km from the
Hatano site), but despite the word "peak" in its name it lies within a level
plain (inside the urban center of present-day Ōno City). The topography
does not match, and its distance from Zenjihō would have rendered it
too impractical. Rather than identifying Kippō and Zenjihō with later
toponyms, it might be reasonable to regard them as Dōgen's own designations for temporary locations near the Hatano residence.

The layout, number of buildings, and design of Daibutsuji (a.k.a. Eiheiji) cannot be known. Moreover, no records indicate who might have
supervised the construction. According to Mujū Dōgyō (a.k.a. Ichien-bō)
and his story of early Zen in Japan, the Saṃgha Hall at Kōshōji outside
Kyoto featured rows of wide platforms (*kōjō* 廣牀), just like the ones used
in China. No one in Japan had ever seen anything like it before. Accordingly, both secular and religious people came to marvel at it and bow to
Dōgen. This kind of novel design required architectural knowledge and
experienced craftsmen. Ever since the 1180s, when Chōgen 重源 (a.k.a.
Shunjō-bō 俊乗房; 1121–1206) had employed a team of foremen and
craftsmen from China to reconstruct Tōdaiji 東大寺 in Nara, knowledge
of design techniques and manual skills in Chinese Buddhist construction
(known as *daibutsuyō kenchiku* 大佛樣建築 by historians) gradually had
become more available in Japan. The availability of craftsmen in the
central regions around Kyoto where Kōshōji was built, however, did not
necessarily apply to rural areas such as Echizen. Moreover, Zen temples
required their own architectural features (referred to as *zenshūyō kenchiku* 禪宗樣建築) that in 1244 might have been beyond the abilities even
of craftsmen in the capital.[188]

---

[187]   Kippōji can be written either 吉峰寺 or 吉嶺寺, without any change in
pronunciation. Sometimes Dōgen replaced the character for "temple" (*ji*)
with *shōja* 精舍, a Buddhist translation of the Sanskrit *vihāra*.

[188]   For a detailed account of Chōgen at Tōdaiji, see Nishida 1970. Regard-

Introduction to the SHŌBŌGENZŌ: 6e. *Dōgen in Echizen*      155

The *Sanso gyōgōki* (SZ.Shiden.1.7b) states that, after Dōgen died and Ejō succeed him as abbot of Eiheiji, Ejō assigned Gikai the task of designing Eiheiji in accordance with Song Chinese norms (*sōchō fūzoku* 宋朝風俗) and completing the construction of the monastic complex. Evidently during Dōgen's lifetime neither of these goals had been achieved. The extent to which Gikai accomplished them (or not) likewise cannot be measured. Throughout its history, Eiheiji suffered several major fires (especially destructive ones occurred in 1340, 1473, 1574, 1641, 1714, and 1786).[189] Its present-day layout and design features cannot be traced back earlier than the beginning of the nineteenth century, when Gentō Sokuchū (1729–1807) supervised major renovations (Yokoyama 1967, 96). While we cannot know the precise appearance of Daibutsuji (a.k.a. Eiheiji) during Dōgen's time, it is safe to assume that its scale was much smaller and its design much less imposing than the Eiheiji that exists today.

The relocation of an entire monastic community from a peripheral site near the center of civilized society to an ancient temple site among uncleared mountains in a rural district, the necessity of daily provisions for them, and the endless decisions regarding the construction of new facilities would tax the patience of any leader. Dōgen must have confronted new difficulties and worries daily. From the beginning of the intercalary seventh month of 1243, when his own words ("The Three Realms are Only Mind"; number 41; DZZ.1:448) place him and his community at Kippōji in Echizen, until the fifteenth of the fourth month of 1245, when he conducted the first summer retreat at Daibutsuji, for a period of more than a year and a half, Dōgen did not produce a single Chinese statement for a convocation address (see Table 24). He must have been busy with other matters. Those matters included not just temple affairs, but literary exertions. During that same period of a year and a half, Dōgen somehow found the time to produce more than thirty chapters of the *Shōbōgenzō*. During the entire period from his first arrival in Echizen until 1247.8.1, when he journeyed to Kamakura, Dōgen produced thirty-three dated chapters. Most of them date to his initial months in Echizen (see Table 29).

---

ing the features of medieval Zen architecture, which likely became available only after Dōgen's time, see Sakurai Toshio 1985; Sasaki 2014.

[189]   For a concise list, see the timeline in Sakurai Shūyū 1982, vol. 2, pp. 1526–1560. Note that the fire of 1297 is disputed by historians.

156    DŌGEN'S *SHŌBŌGENZŌ* VOLUME VIII

Table 29 (Echizen Province) lists thirty-three chapters and three revisions with assigned dates from Dōgen's time in Echizen prior to his journey to Kamakura (which occurred during the eighth month of 1247). The inclusion of dated revisions demands special attention. It is not clear precisely how often or when Dōgen revised chapters. He provided revised colophons for only a few of his revisions. In the revised colophons (and especially in Ejō's holograph copy of "Buddha Nature"; see Table 19), Dōgen provides the two titles, one for the work overall (*Treasury of the True Dharma Eye*) and the chapter titles, as well as a chapter number. In other words, these revisions leave no doubt that, by the second half of 1243, Dōgen had begun to conceive of his individual essays as a unified work, titled *Shōbōgenzō*. The fact that during the process of revision he also re-numbered some chapters, tinkering with their arrangement, further indicates that the unity of this larger work must have consisted of something beyond a mere collection of otherwise unrelated essays.

Table 29 arranges the chapters in chronological order, with their assigned dates in the left-most column and their assigned chapter number(s) in the columns to the right. The chapter numbers show that fifteen titles are unique to the seventy-five-chapter compilation, while twenty-one titles also appear in the sixty-chapter compilation. Of the shared works, seven share identical chapter numbers while fourteen have different numbers. The most startling feature of the chapter numbers — especially when contrasted with the dated chapters from Kōshōji (in Table 28) — lies in the many cases where the chronological order agrees with the sequential numerical order of the chapters. Whereas the titles ascribed to Dōgen's Kōshōji period seemed to have been composed in a random order and then re-arranged as numerically dated sequenced chapters, the opposite procedure seems to have been followed in Echizen. Among the numerical designations for the compilation in sixty chapters, there are three groups of sequential chapters (46–50; 51–55; and 56–60). The numerical sequences for the compilation in seventy-five chapters is even more remarkable. It continues with just a few interruptions from 41 to 75.

This temporal and serial correspondence becomes even more evident if the chapters with irregular numbers are removed, as in Table 30, leaving only sequential chapters. This sequential list admits minor irregularities, where chapters are out of sequence only by a single digit. It also ignores numerical gaps between chapters. Finally, it adds three undated chapters from the sixty-chapter (and/or twelve-chapter) compilation(s) that not only fit the numeric order but also share linguistic features with

*Introduction to the* SHŌBŌGENZŌ: *6e. Dōgen in Echizen* 157

"The Retreat" (which is dated). All four chapters ("The Retreat" plus the 3 undated ones) contain long excerpts from Chinese Buddhist texts with very little exposition in Japanese. In many cases, even textual passages that at first glance look Japanese (being written in a mixture of Japanese script and Sinitic characters), upon closer examination actually consist of excerpts from Chinese sources with the word order adapted to Japanese syntax (in so-called Sino-Japanese or *yomi-kudashi* style). The preponderance of Chinese-language material, whether unaltered originals or rendered in a Sino-Japanese format, suggests works in progress which await additional translation and commentary by Dōgen. These four chapters (one dated to 1245) seem to provide a clear point of overlap between the three substantive compilations.

Examination of the dates in Tables 29 and 30 reveals anomalies. The chapters numbered 46, 48, 49, 50 appear in sequence only if all four can be regarded has sharing the same assigned date (1243.10.20). That is not necessarily the case. Two of the colophons provide incomplete information, which does not automatically preclude the same day. As a practical matter, however, it seems very unlikely that all four should share the same date. The same anomaly applies to chapters 58–59 (1243.12.17) and 65–66 (1244.2.15). In these instances, Dōgen actually assigned identical dates to more than one chapter. The assigned dates for chapters 64–66 allow a span of only three days for four chapters. These tight temporal sequences might help explain why certain chapters (e.g., "The Retreat" plus the three undated ones) appear incomplete. In many cases, the precise significance of the assigned dates remains difficult to interpret.

The somewhat unexpected correspondence of temporal and serial sequences among the chapters dated to Echizen before the eighth month of 1247 also directs attention toward chapters that defy this pattern. Do they exhibit any shared characteristics that set them apart? Table 31, "Non-Sequential Chapters," lists these chapters in two groups. The first group consists of five chapters from the seventy-five-chapter compilation. Three of them are dated revisions. If a revision bears its own date, later than its initial date, then it naturally should fall out of sequence. Two of the chapters, however, lack any indication that they had been revised. Could they have been? "Principles of Seated Meditation" (number 11; 1243.11) seems to be related to the *Universal Promotion of the Principles of Seated Meditation* (*Fukan zazen gi*; 1233.7.15). If so, then its production could have gestated over a period of years. The second group consists of four chapters that exhibit temporal and serial correspondence

158  DŌGEN'S *SHŌBŌGENZŌ* VOLUME VIII

according to their relative positions in the seventy-five-chapter compilation but lack similar coordination within the compilation of sixty chapters. Their irregularity has no relationship to differences in the total number of chapters. In other words, it differs from the pattern exhibited by chapters 61–65 in the seventy-five-chapter compilation, which correspond to chapters 51–55 in the sixty-chapter version. Their chapter numbers increase from 37 to 44 and then decrease from 44 to 43 to 42. This pattern might possess its own internal logic, but it was discarded.

Dōgen continued to work on the *Shōbōgenzō* until the end of his life. By the end of 1245, he had abandoned the compilation in sixty chapters. No chapters from that version carry an assigned date later than the sixth month of 1245. Beginning in that same year, Dōgen began to conduct convocations at Daibutsuji and continued to do so, after its name was changed to Eiheiji on the fifteenth of the sixth month of 1246. Before he departed for Kamakura, his production of convocation addresses peaked at seventy-four in 1246. That year marked the turning point, when datable convocations start to become more common than new chapters of the *Shōbōgenzō* (which nonetheless might have existed as undated drafts).

*Kamakura and Beyond*

At the time that Dōgen adopted the name "Eihei" (Lasting Tranquility) for his new temple, the tides of political power had already begun to shift in the outside world. The system of shared governance — in which the royal court in Kyoto and the military administration in Kamakura exercised distinct yet overlapping functions — presents multilayered levels of authority that defy easy explanation or ready understanding. In terms of Dōgen's career, one needs to know only that, while his Eiheiji celebrated "lasting tranquility," the most powerful individual in the realm, Kujō Michiie (1193–1252), would soon suffer a change in fortunes. His fall from power scrambled the religious landscape of Japan. Buddhist leaders, especially those who lacked well-established social positions, suddenly had to adapt to unexpected political uncertainties. Here is a simplified version of those events.[190]

---

[190]  My summary of Kujō Michiie and Hōjō Tokiyori is indebted to Harada 2006 and Nakamura 2014. I remain responsible for any errors introduced by oversimplifying a complex series of developments.

*Introduction to the* SHŌBŌGENZŌ: *6f. Kamakura and beyond* 159

Michiie served as chief advisor to the court (as *daijō daijin* 太政大臣, or "chancellor"), and his son, Kujō Yoritsune 九條頼經 (1218–1256), served as shogun in Kamakura. With the aid of his son, Michiie exercised power behind the scenes in both realms. He expected his power to increase in the fourth month of 1244, when Yoritsune abdicated his position as shogun to his five year old son (Michiie's grandson), Yoritsugu 頼嗣 (1239–1256). This move gave Yoritsune greater flexibility to cultivate allies within the warrior administration. His ambitious plan was thwarted when the Hōjō reasserted their heretofore diminished authority as the hereditary power behind the shogun. In the third month of 1246, Hōjō Tokiyori assumed governing authority (*shikken* 執權) from his ailing older brother. Shortly thereafter (1246.7), Tokiyori accused Yoritsune of plotting against the Hōjō, arrested Yoritsune's men, and expelled Yoritsune from Kamakura. This move, known to history as the "palace upheaval" (*miya sōdō* 宮騷動), signaled Tokiyori's intention to rule without interference from the court (or from the shogun appointed by the court). Later that year, Michiie lost his position in the government. It marked the beginning of the end of his influence.

Hōjō Tokiyori further cemented his hold on power the following year (1247.6.7) in the Battle of Hōji (*Hōji kassen* 寶治合戰). Tokiyori suspected two of his retainers, Miura Mitsumura 三浦光村 (1205–1247) and his older brother Miura Yasumura 三浦泰村 (1184–1247), of having been allied with Kujō Yoritsune. He moved to depose them. In the end, they and their associates were defeated, and their men (some five hundred) committed suicide. This conflict took lives on both sides. The *Azuma kagami* 吾妻鏡 (*History of the East*; entry for 1247.6.22) lists the names of over one hundred Hōjō retainers who were killed during five days of skirmishes, including two Hatano men (Yoshishige's sixth and seventh sons).[191] This battle eliminated all possible military opposition to Tokiyori's power. The court in Kyoto had no other likely allies in Kamakura who might help moderate the dictates of Tokiyori. Since Michiie had been a major patron of Buddhist temples, religious leaders whom he had favored (such as Enni) became less secure. All temples (the third establishment in medieval Japan) discovered that their patrons among the aristocrats of the court could no longer guarantee their security with the same level of confidence as before. The most powerful temples from the area around Kyoto already had connections in Kamakura through their

---

[191] *Azuma kagami* 36 (see Hayakawa 1915, 3.369).

160 DŌGEN'S *SHŌBŌGENZŌ* VOLUME VIII

involvement in Kamakura's three principal temples. But the majority of temples did not and found their influence diminished.

Faced with these uncertain developments, numerous Buddhists who previously would have felt no inclination to do so now traveled to Kamakura in the hope of an interview with Tokiyori to request his support. Notable individuals include: Shin'a 眞阿 (the founder of Jōkōmyōji 淨光明寺) in 1251; Nichiren in 1253; Enni in 1254; Ninshō 忍性 (1217–1303; a.k.a. Ryōkan-bō 良觀房) in 1261; and Eison 叡尊 (1201–1290; a.k.a. Shien-bō 思圓房) in 1262. The most significant pilgrim was one of the first: Lanxi Daolong. As mentioned previously, he traveled to Kamakura in 1248 and, having won Tokiyori's support, subsequently became the abbot of the new temple, Kenchōji, that Tokiyori constructed in 1253. The construction of Kenchōji marked a turning point, after which the military administration openly promoted the establishment of Zen temples as independent institutions without ties to earlier temple networks.

Dōgen traveled to Kamakura even earlier, on the third of the eight month of 1247, about two months after the Battle of Hōji. On the fourteenth of the second month of 1248, one day after his return to Eiheiji, Dōgen presented a special convocation address in which he discussed his Kamakura trip at some length. He described the purpose of his journey merely as: "to preach the Dharma to my lay patron(s)" (*Kōroku* 3, *jōdō* 251; DZZ.3:166). In light of the fact that the Hatano family had lost two men in the fighting, one can easily imagine that they sought religious solace. The practice of Buddhist temples offering funeral services for lay people probably had not yet developed in Japan, but Buddhist memorial services and prayer ceremonies for the deceased certainly would have been performed. Dōgen, however, provides no further details. No other contemporaneous sources provide information. The previously cited *Azuma kagami* mentions Dōgen nowhere in its fifty-one extant chapters. Evidently his visit attracted little or no notice. We cannot know what he said or did in Kamakura.

Nonetheless, later accounts invariably interpret Dōgen's visit to Kamakura within the political framework of the many other Buddhists who sought patronage from the military administration and, especially, in light of the one (Lanxi Daolong) who obtained it. The *Kenzeiki* (p. 62) provides the most notable example of this approach. It states:

寶治元年八月三日、鎌倉御下向之事
　　最明寺殿
＜最明寺殿ハ時頼ト云也＞、法名道宗、堅ク依被請申、御下向。ヤ
カテ受菩薩戒給。其外之道俗男女、受戒ノ衆不知數ト云云。 堅ク留
メ申シ建立寺院メ開山祖師可奉仰申再三言上アリシレトモ、越州ニ

# Introduction to the SHŌBŌGENZŌ: 6f. Kamakura and beyond

小院ノ檀那アリトテ堅ク辭シテ蘭溪禪師ヲ請シ出シ給ウベシトテ我
レハ竊カ二鎌倉ヲ出、越前永平寺ヱ歸リマシマス。其時ノ建立寺院
ハ今建長寺也。

On the third day, eighth month, during the first year of Hōji, [Dōgen] journeyed down to Kamakura.
The Lord of Saimyōji (i.e., Tokiyori), whose Dharma name is Dōsō 道
宗 [*sic*], insisted on the visit.[192] In due course, he received the bodhisattva precepts [from Dōgen]. The numbers of Buddhist monastics and laypeople, male and female, who also received the precepts were beyond
counting. [Tokiyori] insisted twice and a third time that Dōgen stay and
become the founder of a temple that he would construct. Dōgen adamant-
ly refused, saying that he already had a patron in Echizen with a small
hermitage. Dōgen suggested that you [Tokiyori] should offer that temple
to Zen master Lanxi, while I [Dōgen] quietly depart from Kamakura and
return to Eiheiji in Echizen. The temple that [Tokiyori] offered to construct is the present-day Kenchōji.

Menzan, in his 1754 revised edition, adds in a supplemental note (p. 150)
that Dōgen resided at Tokiyori's residence during his time in Kamakura.

This version of Dōgen's journey to Kamakura reflects the worldview
of fifteenth-century Japan, when Kenzei wrote his account. He could not
imagine any other reason for Dōgen to visit Kamakura except to minister
to the new hegemon. He also could not imagine Dōgen being anything
other than an esteemed guest. Note how the *Kenzeiki* portrays Dōgen as
having the upper hand. He is not the one who asked for a temple but the
one who declined the offer of a temple. Normally, if two people make
the same journey, but only one of them (Lanxi Daolong) establishes residency and receives a newly constructed temple, while the other one
(Dōgen) returns home empty handed, then neutral observers will evaluate them differently. The one with the temple is successful, while the
one who returned home would be seen as a loser. The *Kenzeiki* account
attempts to deflect that judgment. Nonetheless, the reek of failure lurks
beneath as a subplot even today. Historians and the general public alike
routinely evaluate events in terms of economic advantage or loss. When
calculating in those terms, however, it is important to remember what
was known and when it became known. Dōgen arrived in Kamakura just
as Michiie's decline began, long before its inevitability became certain.
Tokiyori's rise to power, rather than being an obvious missed opportunity, could have seemed to be just another example of the fickleness of

---

[192]  The actual Dharma name is Dōsū 道崇 (a.k.a. Kakuryō-bō 覺了房).

162     DŌGEN'S *SHŌBŌGENZŌ* VOLUME VIII

fate, upon which one should not rely. Whether by design or by failure Dōgen had no ties to either Michiie or Tokiyori.

Dōgen's convocation address on the fourteenth of the second month of 1248 provides the only source of information on his trip to Kamakura. It raises issues that permit or invite divergent interpretations. It is unusual in several respects. It mentions precise dates (instead of the usual seasons, moons, or holidays). It addresses questions (or complaints) voiced by members of the assembly since Dōgen's return. Rather than pondering eternal truths, it merely recounts recent events. And it offers a mea culpa of sorts. Because it is so unusual, one cannot help but assume that something serious must have prompted it. But the precise circumstances to which it responds can only be guessed.

Dōgen's remarks begin by providing the precise dates of his departure and his return. Then he acknowledges that people have questions regarding the purpose of his journey. Some wish to know if he values secular people (i.e., political intrigues) more than religious people (i.e., the clergy in his assembly). Other people want to know if he taught some special doctrine that he has withheld from the assembly. This second concern might strike some readers as odd, but it seems perfectly reasonable within the context of the broadly shared culture of esoteric Buddhism and its emphasis on secret initiations. Dōgen does not address the first question, perhaps because his return constitutes a response. In regard to the second question, Dōgen emphasizes that he taught only what everyone in the assembly already knows: those who cultivate goodness will ascend (to the heavens) and those who commit evil will fall (into the hells). Causal activities engender results. One must sift through the rubble to extract the jewels. Then Dōgen admits that, although he is unable to explain the causes or the results, his striving to cultivate the way being somewhat mistaken, now he pitifully has become a water buffalo (*Kōroku* 3, *jōdō* 251; DZZ.3:166).

Several items immediately call attention to themselves. First, one might ask if Dōgen previously had been teaching the doctrine of karma and retribution? Scattered references to it appear in some early sources, such as the *Hōkyōki* and *Zuimonki* (DZZ.7:12; 07:14; 07:20; 07:67; 07:138), but it hardly seems like a dominant theme. On the other hand, warriors like Tokiyori expected (but rarely gave) strict adherence to codes of conduct. They would be expected to appreciate a fire-and-brimstone moral sermon. Second, what kind of water buffalo? Third, how

Introduction to the SHŌBŌGENZŌ: 6f. Kamakura and beyond    163

was he mistaken? Does admission of error constitute an apology? If so, for what faults must he apologize?

The issue of the water buffalo impinges on the third issue. Water buffalos by definition enjoy the paddy fields in bucolic or agricultural settings. In kōan literature, bovines (ox, buffalo, or cow) frequently appear either as the goal to be sought or as an example of relaxed liberation, as in these two examples: "to seek for the ox, you must follow its tracks" (*xunniu xufangji* 尋牛須訪跡; J. *jingyū suhōseki*); "walking along, riding a water buffalo" (*buxing qishuiniu* 步行騎水牛; J. *hokō kisuigyū*).[193] Dōgen concluded his remarks with the statement that his return to Eiheiji intensified his love of its mountains. Maybe this love constitutes the "somewhat mistaken" (*tashō shaku* 多少錯) sentiments that resulted in his transformation into a water buffalo, in which case it is not a mistake at all. It could be interpreted as a compassionate (i.e., Buddhist) embrace of the human world of suffering (especially if cast as an act of going beyond the dichotomy of saṃsāra versus nirvāṇa).

This third issue elicits diverse responses but no concrete evidence to determine which answer might be best. First, one must interpret Dōgen's remarks as an admission of his mistake. Only then can one ponder what possible mistakes he could have committed. One possibility is that Dōgen was wrong to leave his temple for more than half a year without adequate plans. Perhaps troubles arose while Dōgen was away about matters that he should have performed before departure. Another possibility is that Dōgen had not adequately disciplined the members of his assembly. Perhaps trouble arose while he was away because some people felt that they could misbehave without suffering consequences. This speculation derives, not just from the content of Dōgen's remarks on his return, but also from the story of a monk named Genmyō 玄明 who supposedly was expelled after Dōgen returned.

According to the *Kenzeiki* (p. 63), after Dōgen returned to Eiheiji, Tokiyori sent him a notice that the warrior government had donated six tracts of land to Eiheiji, and that these lands would generate produce (i.e., rents in kind) valued at 2,000 *koku* per annum. (A *koku* is a large amount, the precise value of which varied over time.) Dōgen refused the gift and sent the notice back to Kamakura. Subsequently he discovered that, unbeknown to him, a foolish monk named Genmyō had actually

---

[193]    The first example appears 30 times in CBETA while the second one, a line from a verse attributed to Fu Dashi 傅大士 (J. Fu Daishi; 497–569), appears 179 times.

solicited the gift on behalf of Eiheiji. Genmyō expected that by doing so, he would thereby gain Dōgen's favor. Instead, Dōgen expelled him from Eiheiji and then removed the section of the saṃgha hall where Genmyō had sat, cut out the floor, and excavated the earth beneath it down to a depth of seven feet.

This story sounds preposterous, but it might have some historical foundation. The *Goyuigon* (entry dated 1255.1.6; DZZ.7:192-194) includes a record of the following exchange between Gikai and Ejō:

> 義介先年同一類之法内所談云、於佛法中諸惡莫作、諸善奉行。故佛法中諸惡元來莫作、故一切行皆修善也。所以擧手動足一切所作、凡一切諸法生起皆佛法、云云。
> 此見正見乎。
> 和尚答云、先師門徒中有起此邪見之一類、故在世之時義絶畢。被放門徒明白也。依立此邪義也。若欲慕先師佛法之輩、不可共語同坐、是則先師遺誡也。

Gikai: My Dharma fellows of past years, would say: "Within the buddha dharma 'to do no evil, practice the good' actually means that evils already have been refrained from and every action cultivates goodness. Therefore, raising a hand or moving a leg, whatever one does, all dharmas that arise constitute the buddha dharma." Is this view correct?

Ejō: Among our master's [Dōgen's] followers there was a group who espoused such pernicious views. That is why he cut off all contact with them while he was still alive. Clearly the reason he expelled them was because they maintained those pernicious views. Whoever wishes to honor our late master's buddha dharma will not converse or sit with such [people]. This was our master's final admonition.

According to this dialogue, Dōgen had definitely expelled members of his assembly who violated or misrepresented the basic moral teachings of Buddhism. Could this kind of incident lie behind his remarks when he returned from Kamakura? Note that he held the convocation on the day after his return. Maybe the day when he returned was the one on which he expelled his irredeemable followers. If it had been done immediately after his return from Kamakura, while other people were unawares, then it could have given rise to baseless rumors, such as the story about Genmyō. And it could have raised the questions to which Dōgen alluded in his remarks.

A third possible kind of fault for which Dōgen must apologize might involve doctrinal errors. According to this line of thought, Dōgen's experiences in Kamakura forced him to realize that his approach to seated meditation was mistaken. However much people practice seated meditation, it is not enough. Buddhist practice must also engage the broader world of human society, within which social evils must be restrained and social goodness must be promoted. If Dōgen experienced a change of heart, then one might imagine that, after he returned to Eiheiji, he must have begun to revise his previously written chapters of the *Shōbōgenzō* to reflect more accurately his reformed teachings. Moreover, if this was the case, then people who wish to honor Dōgen's final admonitions (as Ejō commanded them to do) should study his later chapters and regard them as being more authoritative than his earlier works. This interpretation thus aims to change the way that people study Dōgen and thereby also change the way that Buddhists (especially Buddhists in Japan) practice his teachings.[194]

In some respects, the interpretation of Dōgen's mistake(s) as doctrinal in nature seems premised on the assumption that the *Shōbōgenzō* in twelve chapters must have assumed its final form only after 1248, when Dōgen returned to Eiheiji. It also regards the content of those twelve chapters as differing from the chapters in the seventy-five- and sixty-chapter compilations, not just in tone or content, but also in regard to their fundamental orientation toward Buddhist practice.

Little direct evidence exists regarding Dōgen's work on the *Shōbōgenzō* after his return from Kamakura. Table 32 (After Kamakura) lists only three dated works, two revised chapters from the *Shōbōgenzō* in seventy-five chapters and one new chapter from the compilation in twelve chapters. These dates indicate that Dōgen worked on both compilations and possibly devoted more work to the one in seventy-five chapters. The chapters can be differentiated, not just in regard to their respective compilations, but also based on the nature of the work each involved. "Washing the Face" (number 50) constitutes an earlier chapter that was revised for the third time. This third revision exists only in the seventy-five-chapter compilation. Its presence clearly indicates that Dōgen continued to improve this compilation even after he stopped working on the one in sixty chapters. The fact that Dōgen revised "Washing the Face" three times demonstrates that he could take a long time before becoming fully satisfied. "The Realized Kōan" is unique because it carries both a very early date and one of the latest dates. The later date, again found only within the seventy-five-chapter compilation, consists of the

---

[194] Matsumoto Shirō (2000, 160) notes that, unless people acknowledge Dōgen's confession of errors (*shippai no kokuhaku* 失敗の告白), there cannot be any hope for future progress in the study of Dōgen.

166 DŌGEN'S *SHŌBŌGENZŌ* VOLUME VIII

year (1252) and the verbal phrase: "compiled and ordered" (*shūroku*). This predicate demands a collective subject or object, neither of which is stated. Implicitly at least, this colophon seems to apply to the seventy-five-chapter compilation as a whole. It indicates that Dōgen had completed the compilations and assigned chapter numbers in their final form. "The Eightfold Awareness of the Great Person" presents an initial draft, one which is almost devoid of any comments or Japanese translations by Dōgen. In light of Dōgen's tendency to revise chapters over time, one might question whether a rough draft would accurately convey his intended message.

In this regard, it is important to remember that the Yōkōji manuscript of the *Shōbōgenzō* in twelve chapters (the only extant complete manuscript) does not contain any colophons or scribal notes by Ejō. Only two of its chapters have colophons by Dōgen. It is Ejō (as reported in the *Kenzeiki*, p. 79–80) who labeled "The Eightfold Awareness of the Great Person" a rough draft. Kawamura (1986, 529) compiled a list of scribal colophons by Ejō from various recensions of the *Shōbōgenzō* (which derive from either the version in sixty chapters or the Himitsu manuscript) that label the following chapters as Dōgen's rough drafts (*gosōan* 御草案):

Kawamura's List of Rough Drafts in the *Shōbōgenzō* in Twelve Chapters

3. The Merit of the Kāṣāya
4. Bringing Forth the Mind of Bodhi
6. Refuge in the Treasures of Buddha, Dharma, and Saṃgha
7. Deep Faith in Cause and Effect
9. Four Horses
10. The Bhikṣu of the Fourth Dhyāna
12. The Eightfold Awareness of the Great Person

The practice of mixing together colophons from different manuscripts can be problematic. Sometimes — as was the case with chapters 69 and 70 in the Honzan edition (see the discussion of "Bringing Forth the Mind of Bodhi" above) — a colophon written for one chapter ends up being inserted into a different chapter. Kawamura's list, therefore, should not be regarded as definitive but can be seen as illustrative of the similar literary characteristics exhibited by these chapters. Each one seems to be unfinished.

After returning to Eiheiji, Dōgen began to present more convocation addresses than ever before. As shown in Table 24, Dōgen presented 280 convocation addresses from 1248 to 1252. He averaged fifty-six con-

*Introduction to the* SHŌBŌGENZŌ: *6f. Kamakura and beyond*  167

vocations per year during this period (as opposed to forty-one per year during his earlier period in Echizen, and thirty-one per year for his final three years at Kōshōji). At the beginning of 1250, Hatano Yoshishige presented Eiheiji with a copy of the entire Buddhist canon (*Kōroku* 5, *jōdō* 361; DZZ.3:232). In previous centuries, a complete collection of Buddhist scriptures could have been found only at a handful of major monasteries; but, during Dōgen's lifetime, renewed trade with China provided greater access to imported scriptures.[195] After Eiheiji received its copy of the canon, Dōgen began to include quoted passages of much greater length culled from a wider variety of sūtras.

Some of these quotations can be interpreted as indirect evidence for assigning later dates of composition to the *Shōbōgenzō* in twelve chapters as a whole, or to certain of its chapters. The evidence is far from conclusive, however.[196] Convocations 381 and 383 (*Kōroku* 5; DZZ.4:244–256), from the middle of 1250, quote passages critical of Śāriputra (one of the disciples of the Buddha) that correspond to statements found in "The Bhikṣu of the Fourth Dhyāna." Convocation 446 (*Kōroku* 6; DZZ.4:32–38), from the middle of 1251, draws distinctions between buddhas and bodhisattvas in ways similar to those found in "Bringing Forth the Mind of Bodhi." Convocation 510 (*Kōroku* 7; DZZ.4:90), from the middle of 1252, discusses the "Baizhang: Not in the Dark about Cause and Effect" kōan (number 102), which also appears in "Deep Faith in Cause and Effect." Similar correspondences also exist from earlier periods. Convocation 182 (*Kōroku* 2; DZZ.3:120–122), from the middle of 1246, quotes information on the previous lives of Śākyamuni Buddha, which also appears in "Offerings to the Buddhas." These correspondences require interpretation. It is exceedingly difficult to demonstrate a clear temporal pattern or habit in which the topics addressed in convocations and in chapters routinely occur at the same time. One can more easily demonstrate the opposite.

Consider "Karma of the Three Times," for example. This chapter lacks any assigned date, but it is numbered as chapter 8 in both the sixty- and twelve-chapter compilations. Its low number within the sixty-chapter

---

[195] The historian Ōtsuka Norihiro (2017, 90–129) compiled a list of all the copies of the Buddhist canon imported into Japan from 1172, when Buddhists began to cross the China Sea more frequently, until the fall of the Hōjō family in 1333. He counted 59 sets, a rate of about 2.7 copies per year. His count is incomplete (it does not include the one given to Eiheiji).

[196] For a detailed analysis of parallel quotations in convocation addresses and chapters, see Ishii Seijun 1991.

168 DŌGEN'S *SHŌBŌGENZŌ* VOLUME VIII

compilation suggests that it must have been composed at Kōshōji. Its literary style agrees with other chapters from that same period. In terms of content, it discusses themes that are also mentioned in early works, such as the *Hōkyōki* (DZZ.7:20) and *Zuimonki* 2 (DZZ.7:79ff). At the same time, it also mentions topics (i.e., the crimes of Devadatta; a quotation by Kumārajīva) that are also quoted in Convocations number 437 (regarding Devadatta; *Kōroku* 6; DZZ.4:26–28) and numbers 485 and 517 (regarding Kumārajīva; *Kōroku* 7; DZZ.4:66, 96–98). These three convocations likely date from the final years of Dōgen's life (ca. 1251.6, 1252.2, and 1252.7). This wide range of corresponding dates — from before Kōshōji, during Kōshōji, to late Eichizen (on multiple occasions) — speaks more to Dōgen's long-term concern with these issues throughout his career than it does to the date(s) when this chapter might have been composed. It is possible that Dōgen revised it after his final convocations, but it is also possible that he selected those topics for his convocations because he had already written about them in this chapter.

A similar wide range of corresponding dates relate to the chapter "Deep Faith in Cause and Effect." The "Baizhang: Not in the Dark about Cause and Effect" kōan (number 102) appears in the *Shōbōgenzō* in Chinese script (dated 1235), is mentioned in "Great Practice" (chapter 68; dated 1244.3.9), and is mentioned in convocations numbers 62, 94, 205, and 510, which date from circa 1241, 1242, 1246, and 1252 (see *Kōroku* 1, 3, 7; DZZ.4:42, 54–56; DZZ.3:138; and DZZ.4:90). A similar pattern exists for the "Xuanze: Bingding Youth" kōan (number 122; see the discussion in Dōgen Back in Japan). Such cases, in which Dōgen returns to the same topic or same kōan multiple times, provide another avenue for exploring his multiple evolutions (literary, doctrinal, pedagogical, etc.) across his teaching career.

Taken as a whole, Dōgen's multiple iterations of his *Shōbōgenzō* in Japanese script quote approximately 319 kōans. Of these, sixty-four can also be found in his *Shōbōgenzō* in Chinese script. In eight instances, however, the source text for the version quoted in the Japanese *Shōbōgenzō* does not agree with the version quoted in the Chinese one.[197] Moreover, the source texts that Dōgen quotes most often in the *Shōbōgenzō* in Japanese script also differ in certain respects from the primary ones he used for his Chinese compilation. As explained above, for that work, the most often cited sources are of two comprehensive compilations, as well as the re-

---

[197] Tsunoda 1995 (in Kagamishima), 15–44. Tsunoda published an earlier version of this study in 1993, but the 1995 version supersedes it with important revisions.

*Introduction to the* SHŌBŌGENZŌ: *6f. Kamakura and beyond* 169

corded sayings of Hongzhi Zengjue (J. Wanshi Shōgaku; 1091–1157) and of Yuanwu Keqin (J. Engo Kokugon; 1063–1135).[198] Once again, here is the previous list:

| Major Chinese Sources for the *Shōbōgenzō* in Chinese script | *numbers of kōan* |
|---|---|
| *Zongmen tongyao ji* 宗門統要集 (J. *Shūmon tōyōshū*; ca. 1100) | 129 |
| *Jingde chuandeng lu* 景德傳燈録 (J. *Keitoku dentōroku*; ca. 1011) | 42 |
| *Hongzhi lu* 宏智録 (J. *Wanshiroku*; ca. 1197) | 42 |
| *Yuanwu yulu* 圜悟語録 (J. *Engo goroku*; ca. 1136) | 38 |
| *total number of kōans* | 252 |

For the *Shōbōgenzō* in Japanese script, I rely on the data provided by Kagamishima Genryū (1987). He identifies seven main sources, which include the four works listed above, as well as two more comprehensive compilations and one additional recorded sayings text. Dōgen's *Shōbōgenzō* in Chinese script is not included in Kagamishima's list, and Kagamishima does not clearly state whether or not the quotations that he identifies as being derived from the four sources listed above are in addition to — or already encompass — the quotations that can also be found in Dōgen's *Shōbōgenzō* in Chinese script. This aspect of Kagamishima's data awaits future verification.

---

[198]  Ishii Shūdō (1988, 572) builds on but differs from the data reported by Kagamishima 1987.

| Major Chinese Sources for the *Shōbōgenzō* in Japanese script | *numbers of kōan* |
| --- | --- |
| *Jingde chuandeng lu* 景德傳燈録 (J. *Keitoku dentōroku*; ca. 1011) | 64 |
| *Rujinglu* 如淨録 (J. *Nyojōroku*; ca. 1227) | 27 |
| *Tiansheng guangdenglu* 天聖廣燈録 (J. *Tenshō kōtōroku*; ca. 1036) | 26 |
| *Zongmen liandeng huiyao* 宗門聯燈會要 (J. *Shūmon rentō eyō*; ca. 1185) | 21 |
| *Hongzhi lu* 宏智録 (J. *Wanshiroku*; ca. 1197) | 21 |
| *Zongmen tongyao ji* 宗門統要集 (J. *Shūmon tōyōshū*; ca. 1100) | 21 |
| *Yuanwu yulu* 圜悟語録 (J. *Engo goroku*; ca. 1136) | 11 |
| *total number of kōans* | 170 |

In comparison to the previous list of sources for the *Shōbōgenzō* in Chinese script, several differences appear. First, Dōgen cited a much wider range of sources for his compositions in Japanese. The number of kōans in both texts is practically identical, especially if we include five alternative kōans found in the earlier draft of the compilation in Chinese. In the case of the Chinese version, only four source texts account for 252 kōans (out of 305). For the *Shōbōgenzō* in Japanese script, seven source texts together can account for no more than 170 (out of 319). Second, the number of kōans derived from the *Jingde chuandeng lu* (*Jingde Era Record of the Transmission of the Flame*) increased dramatically, from forty-two to sixty-four. Third, the number of kōans derived from each of the other three main sources for the previous work decreased. Third, the recorded sayings of Rujing (*Rujinglu* 如淨録; ca. 1227), which play no role in the compilation in Chinese, came to occupy second place with twenty-seven kōans in the *Shōbōgenzō* in Japanese script. Fifth, the number of kōans derived from the *Zongmen tongyao ji* (*Collection of the Essential Teachings of Our Lineage*) decrease dramatically, from 129 in the previous work to only twenty-one quotations in the Japanese version. Actually, as Kagamishima notes himself (p. 1–2), the *Zongmen liandeng huiyao* (*Outline of the Linked Flames of Our Lineage*) largely derives from the *Zongmen tongyao ji*. Usually, the wording of kōans will agree in both

Introduction to the SHŌBŌGENZŌ: 6f. *Kamakura and beyond*     171

texts except for minor orthographic differences. For this reason, it would be permissible to designate the *Zongmen tongyao ji* as the actual source for the kōans now identified with the *Zongmen liandeng huiyao*. Even if their respective kōans were merged together, however, the decrease in the numbers of kōans derived from this source would remain dramatic: from 129 in the previous work to only forty-two quotations in the Japanese version. This emendation would be significant, however, even if only because it would drop the recorded sayings of Rujing from second to third place.

As mentioned previously, at one time, the *Zongmen tongyao ji* was one of the most widely read and copied collections of kōans. Scholars in Japan therefore identify it with Linji (J. Rinzai) orientations. Sometimes, they extend this assumption by suggesting that its earlier prominence and subsequent decline as a source for quotations by Dōgen must be indicative of an evolution or change in Dōgen's attitudes toward kōans in general and toward the Linji House in particular. One can neither affirm nor deny this kind of conclusion since it rests more on the interpretation of data than on the data themselves. As an interesting aside, there exist other data to suggest that Dōgen himself might not have been overly concerned with the textual pedigree of the kōans he quoted. In "Deep Faith in Cause and Effect" (number 9 of the 12-chapter compilation), Dōgen quotes a kōan and then asserts: "This episode is found in the *Tiansheng guangdenglu* (*Tiansheng Era Record of the Spread of the Flame*; DZZ.2:388)." Dōgen is wrong. The actual source is his own *Shōbōgenzō* in Chinese script (number 102, Baizhang: Not in the Dark about Cause and Effect), and that version derives directly from the *Zongmen tongyao ji*.[199] This mistake suggests that during the move from Kōshōji to Kippōji to Daibutsuji, at some point in time, Dōgen must have lost his copy of this text. If he still possessed a copy, then he most likely would have verified his quotation against the original.

On the sixth day of 1253, Dōgen assigned a title and chapter number to "The Eightfold Awareness of the Great Person" (number 12). As far as can be determined, it was the very last chapter he wrote for the *Shōbōgenzō*. Thereafter, very little is known. Ejō, in his scribal notes to this chapter (*Kenzeiki*, pp. 79–80), states that Dōgen's illness had worsened so much that it prevented him from writing. Ejō does not mention the nature of the illness or when it might have begun. In an entry dated 1253.7.8 (*Goyuigon*; DZZ.7:184), Gikai states that Dōgen's illness sud-

---

[199]   Kagamishima 1987, 16n3; Ishii Shūdō 1988, 224.

denly became worse, so much so that Gikai rushed to be by his side. Gikai's very last meeting with Dōgen occurred on the sixth of the eighth month of 1253 at an inn in Wakimoto 脇本, a station (about thirty kilometers southwest of Eiheiji) along the path to Kyoto. Gikai thereupon returned to Eiheiji, while Ejō accompanied Dōgen to Kyoto, where they sought medical attention for his illness.

*Kenzeiki* (p. 83) reports that Dōgen died seventeen days later, on the twenty-third of that month. Ejō sent notifications to Eiheiji and to Hatano Yoshishige. Then he carried his master's corpse to a small temple near the Higashiyama District where he cremated it (p. 84). About two weeks later, on the sixth of the ninth month, Ejō departed Kyoto with Dōgen's ashes; a few days later, on the twelfth, he performed a nirvāṇa ceremony (*nyūnehan no gishiki* 入涅槃之儀式) for Dōgen in the abbot's quarters of Eiheiji, where he presented offerings of incense, flowers, and candles. On a later date, he subsequently erected a memorial stūpa for Dōgen, called the Jōyōan 承陽庵, in the west corner of Eiheiji's grounds (p. 85).

Ejō lived another twenty-seven years (until 1280), served as Eiheiji's second abbot, acted as the custodian of Dōgen's surviving manuscripts, and produced disciples who would lay the foundation for the institutional success of Dōgen's teachings. Ejō and his disciples copied many of Dōgen's compositions, but not all of them. Other hands also contributed. Within a decade (1263), another one of Dōgen's disciples, Senne, composed his massive commentary on the *Shōbōgenzō* in seventy-five chapters. It was the first but not the last attempt to explain what Dōgen wrote. The afterlife of the *Shōbōgenzō* had begun.

# Supplements

These supplements provide detailed information on specific topics of interest primarily to specialists.

Supplement 1: The Beginnings of Zen in Japan according to Mujū Dōgyō introduces an influential traditional account of Dōgen's milieu, which until recently has tended to distort historical evaluations of early Zen and of Dōgen. The *Shōbōgenzō* constitutes evidence for an alternative view of Zen in Japan.

Supplement 2: The *Shōbōgenzō* Honzan Edition Today introduces the modern edition of the *Shōbōgenzō* (ca. 1815) and its evolution, especially its most recent revised versions. The revised edition of 2020 is especially noteworthy because it includes Dōgen's *Shōbōgenzō* in Chinese script, the topic of supplements 3 and 4. Appendix 3 provides a list of the chapters of the Honzan edition and their location in this translation.

Supplement 3: Preface to the *Treasury of the True Dharma Eye* by the Śramaṇa Dōgen translates the preface to the *Shōbōgenzō* in Chinese script composed by Dōgen in 1235, summarizes its textual history, and considers why its authenticity has been in doubt.

Supplement 4: The *Shōbōgenzō* in Chinese and in Japanese scripts introduces the interlingual techniques that Dōgen used when he transcribed kōans. Several examples, presented in an accessible manner, illustrate how Dōgen's initial *Shōbōgenzō* of 1235 provided the foundation for, and developed into, the later *Shōbōgenzō* for which he became renowned.

Supplement 5: Sources for Dōgen's Life introduces the primary sources cited in the introduction, identifies significant textual versions (if any), and discusses the issue of sectarian bias or deliberate dishonesty.

Supplement 6: Dates and Calendarial Considerations briefly introduces the main systems of recording dates found in the historical sources. It reviews the conflicting dates for Dōgen's return from China to illustrate how the calendarial notations can sometimes disagree and to explain the practice of notation by a "future era name" (*mirai nengō* 未來年號).

## Supplement 1:

## The Beginnings of Zen in Japan according to Mujū Dōgyō

Until recently, historians viewed the development of Zen in Japan through a narrative frame based on the writings of Mujū Dōgyō 無住道曉 (1226–1312) and Kokan Shiren 虎關師錬 (1278–1346). Dōgyō (a.k.a. Ichien-bō 一圓房) was one of the last members of the Eisai faction (see Table 35). He wrote two collections of Buddhist tales: *Sand and Pebbles* (*Shasekishū* 沙石集; ca. 1279–1283; 12 chapters) and *Casual Discussions* (*Zōdanshū* 雜談集; 1305; 10 chapters), which provide rich information and insights into the religious life of thirteenth-century Japan.[200] Dōgyō was a disciple of Enni 圓爾 (i.e., Enni-bō 圓爾房; a.k.a. Ben'en 辯圓; 1201–1280), a more senior member of the Eisai faction who also introduced a new Zen lineage he had acquired in China. Kokan Shiren, another disciple of Enni, reproduced the same interpretive approach as Dōgyō but in dry, scholarly language, in an encyclopedic history of Buddhism in Japan: the *Genkō shakusho* 元亨釋書 (*Genkō Era Account of Buddhism*; 30 chapters), completed in 1322. Both authors exalt Eisai as the founding patriarch of Zen in Japan but fail to mention his disciples. Both authors mention Dōgen but depict him as ineffective and without any legacy. Both authors treat Japanese Zen primarily as a transplant of Chinese Buddhist norms (language, customs, literary arts, and institutional structures) into virgin Japanese soil.

This narrative framework is not entirely without basis, of course. Its uncritical acceptance, however, has resulted in a tendency to ignore the contributions of Eisai's disciples (many of whom have become forgotten) and to regard Dōgen and his teachings as being outside of the mainstream Zen of Japan. Here is a brief synopsis of the story of the beginnings of Zen in Japan as told by Mujū Dōgyō.

Eisai, Dōgen, and Enni heralded the coming of Zen, while Lanxi Daolong constituted its arrival. In brief, Dōgyō asserts the following five key points. (1) Buddhists in Japan prior to the time of Eisai parroted the word "zen" 禪 (i.e., meditation), which appears in the scriptures they chanted, but they never actually practiced any form of seated meditation. (2) Eisai's followers outwardly practiced monastic discipline (*kairitsu* 戒律; i.e., *vinaya*), Tendai, Esoteric (*shingon* 眞言), and Pure Land Bud-

---

[200]   See Morrell (1985) for a translation and study of *Sand and Pebbles*.

# Introduction to the SHŌBŌGENZŌ: Supplement 1    175

dhism but, being careful not to oppose the norms of Japan, practiced Zen only in secret, while waiting for a future time when Zen might become acceptable to society at large. (3) Dōgen built the first wide platforms for seated meditation (*zazen* 坐禪), and (4) Enni was the first to promulgate Chinese procedures (*sahō* 作法) for seated meditation. Nonetheless, (5) the proper practice of Zen in a Chinese manner according to the Chinese liturgy began only after 1253 (the year of Dōgen's death), when Lanxi Daolong became the first abbot of the newly constructed Kenchōji 建長 寺 in Kamakura. Thanks to Hōjō Tokiyori, the head administrator of the military government and the founding patron of Kenchōji, this temple followed all the same ritual ceremonies as in China. Tokiyori — who must have been a reincarnation (*saitan* 再誕) of Eisai — thereby fulfilled Eisai's destiny.

Dōgyō's account succinctly presents a framework that allowed subsequent generations, professional historians as well as the general public, to exalt Eisai without consideration of the human context in which he lived, how he accomplished his goals, or the disciples who inherited his legacy. I refer to this account in the singular because it constitutes a unified vision, but Dōgyō articulated it in three separate digressions embedded within stories he wrote about other topics. Points 1 and 2 appear in *Sand and Pebbles* 10B, "Auspicious Deaths: Kenninji" (*Kenninji no monto no naka ni rinjū medetaki no koto* 建仁寺ノ門徒ノ中ニ臨終目出事). Points 3 and 4 appear in *Casual Discussions* 8, "Adhering to the Rule and Seated Meditation" (*Jiritsu zazen no koto* 持律坐禪ノ事). Point 5 appears in *Casual Discussions* 3, "Sentiments of a Foolish Old Man" (*Gurō jukkai* 愚老述懷). Below, I translate the key excerpts as a unified sequence so that readers can more easily discern the contours of Dōgyō's vision of the beginnings of Zen in Japan.

Excerpt 1. *Sand and Pebbles* 10B: Auspicious Deaths: Kenninji

故建仁寺ノ本願僧正榮西ノ流ハ、法々ノ是非揀擇〔ナ〕ク、戒律ヲモ
學シテ威儀ヲ守り、天台・眞言・禪門共ニ翫バル。念佛ヲモス〔ス〕
メラレタリ。... 鎭西ノ聖福寺、洛陽ノ建仁寺、關東壽福寺、彼創草
ノ禪院ノ始ナリ。然ドモ、國ノ風儀ニソムカズシテ、戒門・天台・眞
言ナンドカネテ、一向ニ唐様ヲ行ゼラレズ。時ヲ待ツ故ニヤ。深キ心
アルベシ。殊ニハ眞言ヲ面トシテ、禪門ハ内行ナリキ。 (*Shasekishū*,
p. 453)

The students of the late Saṃgha Prefect Eisai, the founder of Kenninji, did not pick and choose among this dharma or that dharma [i.e., Buddhist practice] but maintained proper deportment by studying the rules of discipline while practicing Tendai, Shingon (esoteric rituals), and Zen together.[201] They even promoted nenbutsu (i.e., Pure Land chanting) . . . Zen cloisters [in Japan] began with temples that he [Eisai] founded: Shōfukuji in Chinzei [Hakata], Kenninji in Rakuyō [Kyoto], and Jufukuji in Kantō [Kamakura].[202] These temples did not contravene the norms of our kingdom [Japan] but combined training in morality (*vinaya*), Tendai, and esoteric Buddhism, without practicing anything in a Chinese manner. They waited for the right time. With a profound understanding, they presented a Shingon exterior while inwardly practicing Zen.

Excerpt 2: *Casual Discussions* (8.5): Adhering to the Rule and Seated Meditation

坐禪ノ事自昔至今マニ、諸寺・諸山ニ法華ヲ翫ビ、懺法を讀ム事、天下同ケレドモ、半行半坐、不如法歟。半坐ハ坐禪也。行道・聲明ナドハスレドモ、坐禪ノ行コレナシ。經ノ文ノ坐禪ハ、口に誦スレドモ、身ニハ行ゼズ。「常ニ好坐禪修攝其ノ心」トモ云。「常貴坐禪、得諸ノ深定」トモ説キ、「或ハ在林樹下、專精ニシテ而坐禪ス。乃至菩薩ハ志堅固ニ、坐禪若ハ讀經」等ト説給ヘリ。

　　此經、コトニ如説ノ修行ハ、坐禪可有歟。坐禪ノ事、法華等の經ニ、處處ニコレレドモ、人コレヲ事とセズ。口に誦シテ身ニ行セズ。凡夫ノ習ヲロカナリ。サルママニ、語ハ如鸚鵡、心ハ似猿猴。

　　中比建仁寺ノ本願、入唐シテ、禪門・戒律ノ儀傳ラレシモ、只校床ニテ事事シキ坐禪ノ儀無リケリ。國ノ風儀ニマカセテ、天台・眞言ナドアヒナラベテ、一向ノ禪院ノ儀式、時至テ佛法房の上人、深草ニテ如大唐、廣林ノ坐禪始テ行ズ。其ノ時坐禪メヅラシキ事ニテ、有信俗等拜シ貴ガリケリ。其ノ時ノ僧ノカタリ侍シ。

　　其ノ後東福寺ノ開山度宋シ、徑山ノ下ニ久住シ、坐禪等ノ作法、被行ケリ。コトニ隆老唐僧ニテ、建長寺、如宋朝ノ作法、行ハレシヨリ後、天下ニ禪院ノ作法流布セリ。時ノ至ルナルベシ。
(*Zōdanshū*, pp. 256–257)

---

[201]  The label "shingon" 眞言 refers to the broadly shared esoteric Buddhist traditions of Japan, including but not limited to the Shingon School.

[202]  Chinzei 鎭西 in a broad sense refers to Kyushu as whole and in a narrow sense to Dazaifu (where the Chinzei military administrative officers were located), but Shōfukuji was located in Hakata on the coast near Dazaifu.

Seated Meditation (*zazen*): From antiquity to the present, although all temples and mountain [monasteries] alike throughout the realm have taught the *Lotus Sūtra* and chanted its repentance rituals, what about the dharma procedures for half-walking and half-sitting [*samādhi*]?[203] "Half sitting" refers to seated meditation. They practiced walking chants but did not perform seated meditation. Their mouths chanted the passages in the *Sūtra* about seated meditation, but their bodies did not practice it. The *Sūtra* says "[The bodhisattva] always delights in seated meditation to concentrate the mind."[204] And it says, "Or beneath a tree in the forest, concentrating the spirit and practicing seated meditation . . . The bodhisattva, with resolute determination, practicing seated meditation or reciting the sūtra . . . ."[205]

Since this scripture especially emphasizes practicing in such manner, the monks should have practiced seated meditation. But even though the *Lotus Sūtra* repeatedly mentions seated meditation, none of them practiced it. They chanted with their mouths but did not practice with their bodies. They acted foolishly. In this way, their speech resembled that of parrots, and their minds resembled those of monkeys.

In recent times, the founder of Kenninji [Eisai] went to China and transmitted the procedures of Zen training and moral behavior, but he only used a narrow platform without ritual procedures for seated meditation. Conforming to the norms of our kingdom [Japan], he situated Zen within Tendai and Shingon. The ritual procedures exclusive to Zen cloisters were implemented later, when the Superior Buppō-bō [Dōgen] in Fukakusa [at Kōshōji] first installed Chinese-style broad platforms for seated meditation. At that time, because seated meditation was so novel, the faithful and secular alike honored him with their bows. I was told so by a monk who was there at that time.

Later, the founder of Tōfukuji [Enni], who had dwelled for a long time at Jingshan in Song [China], implemented the proper procedures for seated meditation. But it was not until after the Chinese monk, Old Daolong [Lanxi Daolong], implemented the Song-style rituals at Kenchōji that the

---

[203] These repentance rituals (*senbō* 懺法) involve contemplation of the Bodhisattva Samantabhadra (Fugen Bosatsu 普賢菩薩), a ritual strongly associated with the *Lotus Sūtra*. The half-walking and half-sitting *samādhi* (*hangyō hanza zanmai* 半行半坐三昧) constitutes a fundamental framework for traditional Tendai forms of mental cultivation. See Stevenson 1986.

[204] *Lotus Sūtra*, chapter 14, "Practice of Ease and Joy" (Anyuexing pin 安樂行品); T.262.9:37b10.

[205] *Lotus Sūtra*, chapter 19, "Merit of the Preacher of the Dharma" (Fashi gongde pin 法師功德品); T.262.9:49b5-7.

178 DŌGEN'S *SHŌBŌGENZŌ* VOLUME VIII

rituals of Zen cloisters began to spread throughout the realm. Finally, the right time had arrived.

Excerpt 3: *Casual Discussions* (3.5): Sentiments of a Foolish Old Man

［最明寺の禪門　（北條時頼のこと）］　...　威勢如國王、建長寺建立シ、唐僧渡リ如唐國、禪院作法盛ナル事、併ラ彼ノ興行也。建仁寺ノ本願ノ再誕トモ云ヘリ。在世ニ生テ、定テ見佛聞法ノ益モ御座ケレバ、貴事ナルベシ。

　　　天下ヲ自在ニ成敗セラレシカバ、只如國王。王ト云ハ自在ノ義也。承久ノ後ハ、關東ノ計トシテ、院・國王ヲモ、遠キ嶋ヘ奉移、公家ニハ關東ヲ御心ニマカセズ。サレバ只王ノ德用ナルベシ。(*Zōdanshū*, p. 118)

[In regard to Hōjō Tokiyori] . . . his meritorious achievements consist of his king-like authority in having constructed Kenchōji and in having the monk from China [Lanxi Daolong] propagate the ritual procedures of the Zen cloisters just like those in Song China. We can regard him as the reincarnation of the founder of Kenninji [Eisai]. And we can revere the fact that, even while living in this world, he definitely possessed the blessings of seeing the buddhas and hearing the dharma.

The one who himself dictates success or failure within the realm alone equals a king. The word "king" means "autonomy." After the Jōkyū Disturbance (1221), Kantō [i.e., the Hōjō] dictated that royal prelates and the king [of Japan] be exiled to distant islands.[206] Among the court aristocrats, no one could disobey the wishes of Kantō. Therefore, he [the head of the Hōjō family] alone exercised the virtues of a king.

---

[206] In 1221, armies of the Kamakura warriors attacked Kyoto to suppress an uprising by royalists. In this battle (the Jōkyū Disturbance), they captured three former chiefs (*jōkō* 上皇) of the royal family and sentenced them to exile: Go-Toba-In 後鳥羽院 (1180–1239) to Oki-no-shima Island, where he died; Juntoku-In 順德院 (1197–1242) to Sado Island, where he died; and Tsuchimikado-In 土御門院 (1196–1231) to Tosa. The suffix "*in*" (cloister) in the above posthumous titles indicate that all three were Buddhist prelates. In addition, the current head of the royal family (identified by Dōgyō as the "king of the realm," a one-year old infant who occupied the throne for only 78 days) was deposed and became known simply as the "deposed ruler of the Kujō line" (*Kujō haitei* 九條廢帝). In 1870, the Meiji government awarded him the title of "Heavenly Sovereign Chūkyō" 仲恭天皇. In the other posthumous titles, they likewise replaced the suffix "cloister" (*in*) with "heavenly sovereign" (*tennō* 天皇), the translation of which came to be rendered by the European term "emperor."

Enomoto Wataru, a historian of the premodern maritime cultural exchanges between China and Japan, compiled a chronological list of the successive abbots of Kenchōji in Kamakura — the temple that Hōjō Tokiyori founded and to which he appointed Lanxi Daolong to serve as abbot. Enomoto's findings flesh out the background to Dōgyō's vision of the beginnings of Zen in Japan and allow us to recognize why it once seemed so compelling. According to Enomoto's calculations, of the first twenty-four abbots at Kenchōji, from 1263 (the year when Kenchōji was completed) to about 1337 (shortly after the fall of the Kamakura warrior administration), thirteen came from China (C) and five were Japanese who had trained (tr.) in China. Together these two groups occupied the abbotship more than seventy percent of the time. The abbots of Japanese origin who never visited China served relatively short tenures (see Table 33, Successive Abbots of Kenchōji).[207] Definitive evidence does not exist, but one might reasonably assume that most of the Chinese abbots spoke no local language (*xiangtan* 郷談; i.e., Japanese).[208]

Enomoto's data demonstrate that the arrival of Lanxi Daolong and his inaugural term as abbot of Kenchōji truly signaled the advent of something new in the religious landscape of Japan. Dōgyō (and historians who relied on his vision) could look at Kenchōji in isolation and easily interpret the label "Zen" as a Chinese-style of Buddhist practice, conducted according to Chinese liturgies and ritual procedures, taught by Chinese teachers (or by teachers who had learned in China), within which Chinese language and literary arts would play prominent roles. This interpretation of Zen captures the avant-garde novelty exuded by many newly constructed Zen temples in medieval Japan. At the same time, however, it risks allowing the glare of medieval Zen's Chinese exoticism to cast into the shadows the complex, broader religious landscape it occupied. Its brilliant sparkle can obscure the less glamorous but nonetheless essential soil into which the transplant took root and became translated into something accessible to local people who could not travel across the seas. We cannot divine Dōgen's motives; but, whether he intended it or not, his undertaking to write a *Shōbōgenzō* in Japanese script constituted a herculean effort to write a counternarrative of the beginnings of Zen in Japan.

---

[207]  Enomoto 2013, 25–26.

[208]  Tachi (2014, 262–272) surveys of the surviving evidence.

## Supplement 2:
## The *Shōbōgenzō* Honzan Edition Today

This Introduction begins with the suggestion that the *Shōbōgenzō* exists in two main iterations: the modern one printed at Eiheiji circa 1815, and an alternative one based on certain individual manuscript traditions initiated by Dōgen. Next, it introduces and explains those manuscript traditions, especially those in seventy-five chapters and twelve chapters. Academic circles recognize these eighty-seven (i.e., 75 + 12) chapters as the *Shōbōgenzō* compiled by Dōgen. Accordingly, contemporary academic studies of Dōgen focus primarily on the seventy-five- and twelve-chapter compilations. The modern edition of 1815, commonly known as the Honzan edition, however, remains the more widely recognized *Shōbōgenzō* among the public at large. Until the 1970s, it was the only version readily available. And even after publications of the alternative version in eighty-seven chapters became available, many people within traditional Sōtō settings (e.g., temples and Zen study groups), as well as scholars of literature and the arts, continued to cherish the Honzan edition. Because of its wide use over such a long period of time by clergy, laypeople, and scholars alike, today it remains very relevant.

The Honzan edition, however, is not a single edition. Since its initial printing, it has evolved in both subtle and sometimes significant ways. At first, it evolved in reaction to and as corrections of certain limitations imposed by the political climate and the xylographic technology that produced it. Later, it evolved in response to changing social conditions (and educational policies) in attempts to better meet the expectations of its readers. Despite (or because of) its evolutionary development, the Honzan edition always exerts an aura of authority as an authorized (i.e., official) version of the *Shōbōgenzō*. This aura of authority remains undiminished even in reprints of the Honzan edition issued by commercial publishers unrelated to the Sōtō school. The present supplement briefly reviews the main versions of the Honzan edition, especially the most recent revisions: one published in 2019 by Eiheiji and a very different one published in 2020 by the Headquarters (Shūmuchō) of the Sōtō school.

Somewhat ironically, the origins of the initial Honzan edition can be traced back to an order issued in 1722 by Sōtō administrators (acting under the authority of the Tokugawa military government) that forbad the copying, editing, or printing of any part of the *Shōbōgenzō* (*Shōbōgenzō kaihan kinshirei* 正法眼藏開版禁止令; see Kumagai 1982, 1028). By that time, manuscript copies of the *Shōbōgenzō* had become prized treasures, owned only by certain temples where only high-ranking clerics could see them. Many varieties of manuscripts existed, some of which disagreed in the number and the contents of their chapters. Over the previous three decades, factions of reform-minded clergy, especially Manzan Dōhaku 卍山道白 (1636–1714), had denounced certain administrative practices at Sōtō temples (see Bodiford 1991). Manzan, as well as his allies and opponents alike, had cited Dōgen's writings in support of, or in opposition to, monastic reforms. Spirited debates on these issues sparked fears among both the military government and the high-ranking prelates within Sōtō temples that unfettered access to alternative (or deliberately altered) versions of the *Shōbōgenzō* could only foment conflicts. Eventually, in 1796, the government agreed to authorize Eiheiji to print the *Shōbōgenzō* in the hope that a single, genuine (*shinpon* 眞本; i.e., authoritative) version of the text would help end controversies over Dōgen's words (Kumagai 1982, 1031–1035).

Accordingly, Eiheiji produced a new *Shōbōgenzō*, designed with features that could not be rivalled by any previous compilation. It was not only the largest compilation (with ninety-five chapters) but also the most editorially sophisticated, with its own scholarly apparatus, including an introduction that explained the origins of the manuscripts and its editorial policies for correcting them, with annotations and collation notes in every chapter, and with its own unique sequence of chapters. Its editorial notes denounced earlier manuscript versions as being faulty, unreliable, and filled with errors.[209] Rather than privileging any particular manuscript (or manuscript tradition) as Dōgen's intended version, therefore, it presented itself as an ideal *Shōbōgenzō*, the one that Dōgen would have compiled if he had lived long enough to do so. For its actual content, it relied mainly on an unfinished compilation by an earlier abbot of Eiheiji, Handō Kōzen 版橈晃全 (1627–1693), as corrected and edited by Daigu Shunryō 大愚俊量 (1759–1803) and Sodō Ontatsu 祖道穩達 (ca. 1748–1813). Another abbot of Eiheiji, Gentō Sokuchū 玄透即中 (1729–1807), supervised the production work and the fundraising campaign to finance it.

The xylographic *Shōbōgenzō* produced by Eiheiji consists of four folding cases (*chitsu* 帙) that hold twenty bound fascicles (*satsu* 册; five per case), comprised of ninety-five individual chapters (*maki* 卷), with one to eight chapters per fascicle. An additional (21st) fascicle consists of

---

[209] T.2582.82:7a–b. Also see Bodiford 2020, 240–242.

three supplemental works: a historical introduction (*en'yū* 縁由), an explanation of editorial policies (*hanrei* 凡例), and a descriptive table of contents (*kanmoku retsuji* 卷目列次). The format of this *Shōbōgenzō* adheres to many of the orthographic conventions found in the manuscripts it reproduced. Most pages lack any paragraph breaks or other textual segmentation. No spaces separate words, but commas in the white spaces between lines of text indicate the divisions between clauses and/or sentences (the reader determines which). Identical Chinese characters sometimes appear in variant graphic forms. Japanese phonetic characters (*kokuji* 國字; i.e., *kana*) are standardized as true forms (*magana* 眞假名; i.e., *katakana*), not cursive (*zokugana* 俗假名; i.e., *hiragana*) forms.[210] None of the individual chapters are numbered (an editorial policy based on the theory that Dōgen had never numbered them).[211] And five of the chapters consist only of the chapter title followed by blank sheets of paper (*hakushi* 白紙). Senior clerics with proper authorization could copy the text of these abridged chapters by hand at Eiheiji, but otherwise they would remain secret. The following chapters were represented by blank pages:

> "Buddhas and Ancestors" (Busso 佛祖)
> "The Inheritance Certificate" (Shisho 嗣書)
> "Transmitting the Robe" (Den'e 傳衣)
> "Receiving the Precepts" (Jukai 受戒)
> "The Samādhi of Self Verification" (Jishō zanmai 自證三昧)

Each of these chapters contains information related to dharma transmission rituals, the administration of which remained the subject of controversy due to the reforms advocated by Manzan Dōhaku. In 1906, Fukuyama Hakurin 福山白麟 (d. 1925), the abbot of Myōgonji 妙嚴寺 (Aichi Pref.) donated funds to produce xylographs for the abridged chapters so that the entire Honzan edition could be printed in a uniform format. The original printing blocks (1,110 xylographs total) still exist and occasionally are used to produce commemorative sets of the original Honzan edition of the *Shōbōgenzō*.[212]

---

[210] For this nomenclature, see T.2582.82:8c. Here *magana* does not refer to *man'yōgana*.

[211] *Kyūrai teisū aru koto nashi* 舊來定數有ルコト無シ (T.2582.82:8c).

[212] The most recent example seems to have been in 1974 when 100 sets were printed by hand rubbings to commemorate the seven hundredth memorial of Ejō (Sano 1983, 22).

*Introduction to the* SHŌBŌGENZŌ: *Supplement 2* 183

The five abridged chapters had already become available to the public in 1885. That is the year that Ōuchi Seiran 大内青巒 (1845–1918), an extremely influential Sōtō layperson and founder of the Kōmeisha 鴻盟社 publishing company, issued a typeset version of the Honzan edition in a handy, single volume format. This 1885 version reproduced the format and orthography of the original xylographs for ninety chapters without any changes and, in addition, included the text for what had been the five blank chapters.[213] In 1926, Kōmeisha issued a revised version titled *Shōbōgenzō: honzanban shukusatsu* 正法眼藏: 本山版縮刷 (Small-type Honzan edition of the *Shōbōgenzō*). This revised version eliminated the preface by Ōuchi Seiran that had graced the initial 1885 version, placed commas between words, and replaced commas with periods at the end of sentences. It converted Japanese phonetic characters to the standard cursive forms (*hiragana*) taught in primary schools. It moved the so-called variant version of "Washing the Face" ("Senmen") from the margins of that chapter to its end as an appendix.[214] Finally, it added a simple table of contents (*mokuji* 目次) for the ninety-five chapters. In other respects, it simply reproduced the original 1885 transcription. This revised version of the Honzan edition was reprinted in 1943 and again in 1952. It remained in print at least until the 1980s and became one of the two most widely studied versions of the *Shōbōgenzō*. Many Sōtō clerics preferred its simplicity, which allowed them to read and interpret the text in its xylographic format (which had become the traditional one).

The Kōmeisha versions of the Honzan *Shōbōgenzō* exhibit one unintended feature of note. The chapters themselves remained unnumbered, but the addition of the simple table of contents allows readers to easily detect an irregularity in their layout. The printed sequence of chapters in the Honzan edition (both in the original xylographic version and in the Kōmeisha typeset versions) does not fully correlate with the descrip-

---

[213] Aokage Sekkō 青蔭雪鴻 (1832–1885), the abbot of Eiheiji, provided a calligraphic forward. Ōuchi (p. 12–13) states that Aokage had approved his request to include the text of the five blank chapters because when clerics copied them by hand, they frequently made mistakes, which caused their content to be misunderstood. The 1906 xylograph edition of the five blank chapters reproduced the text from Ōuchi's 1885 edition (Akitsu 2019b).

[214] The original Honzan edition admitted the existence of two versions of "Senmen" (*ganrai nihon ari* 元來二本アリ; T.2582.82:8b). The longer version (from the seventy-five-chapter compilation) constituted the main chapter, with the shorter version (from the sixty-chapter compilation) printed in the margins around it.

184 DŌGEN'S *SHŌBŌGENZŌ* VOLUME VIII

tive table of contents provided by the original editors of that work. It is not clear what might have caused this irregularity. The xylographs were carved in no particular order over a period of years from 1769 to 1811 (and 1906). After the leaves of paper were pressed to the inked blocks, they would be placed into stacks for each fascicle. For the sixteenth, nineteenth, and twentieth fascicles, they were assembled out of order, such that the unnumbered chapters that would have occupied positions 70, 92, 90, and 91 are out of sequence. This mistake caused the intervening chapters (70 to 85 as well as 89 to 94) likewise to shift positions (see Table 11, Chapters Out of Order in the Original Honzan Edition). When Ōuchi Seiran transcribed the original printed text into his typeset edition in 1885, he reproduced this irregular order.

In 1931, the Honzan edition in ninety-five chapters appeared in volume 82 of the *Revised Buddhist Canon of the Taishō Era* (*Taishō shinshū daizōkyō* 大正新脩大藏經). This version was transcribed directly from the xylographic original by Kishizawa Ian 岸澤惟安 (1865–1955), a Sōtō cleric who came to epitomize the new type of Zen master known as "Genzōka" 眼藏家: a specialist in the study and explication of the *Shōbōgenzō*. Kishizawa collated the text against eight alternative versions, seven of which were hand-copied manuscripts he owned.[215] He added numbers to the chapters and corrected their sequence to agree with the descriptive table of contents (*kanmoku retsuji*). He formatted the variant version of "Washing the Face" as an appendix of that chapter. In other respects, he retained the same conventions as in the first printed version, including its *katakana* phonetic characters and ambiguous punctuation. Today, the *Taishō Canon* is available on-line as "The SAT (Saṃgaṇikīkṛtaṃ Taiśotripiṭakaṃ) Daizōkyō Text Database."[216] The Honzan edition can be found (and searched) under Taishō serial number 2582.

Etō Sokuō (1888–1958) produced the most widely read Honzan edition for the Iwanami Bunko series of inexpensive paperbacks in 1939 (volume 1), 1942 (volume 2), and 1943 (volume 3). Iwanami reprinted the three-volume set regularly through the 1980s. Etō's version was the first to adopt modern editorial policies, such as regularizing the orthography (e.g., eliminating variant forms of Chinese characters and standardiz-

---

[215] See the collation key at the bottom of T.2582.82:7. Kishizawa (1943, 823) later wrote that he undertook this task at the urging of Ōuchi Seiran.

[216] Sponsored by the University of Tokyo: <https://21dzk.l.u-tokyo.ac.jp/SAT/>.

Introduction to the SHŌBŌGENZŌ: *Supplement 2*

ing the spelling of Japanese phonetic characters, etc.), adding extensive phonetic glosses, and modern forms of punctuation. He numbered the chapters and corrected their order. With the assistance of Ōkubo Dōshū (1896–1994), he provided extensive collation notes, including some based on medieval manuscripts that had been unknown to the editors of the original Honzan edition. Etō added a separate compilation (*besshū* 別輯) of supplementary chapters, including two previously unknown ones from the *Shōbōgenzō* in twelve chapters (the existence of which had not even been suspected when the Honzan edition was compiled). Finally, he added a glossary of names and terms. Ultimately, Etō's extensive efforts to improve and update the Honzan edition served to demonstrate its limitations. His separate compilation and collation notes document the existence of earlier, more reliable textual sources that were unknown to the people who had compiled this standard edition of Dōgen's work.

In 1969 and in 1970–1972, two alternatives to the Honzan edition appeared in quick succession, the first one edited by Ōkubo Dōshū, followed by a second one edited by Mizuno Yaoko (1921–2010).[217] Both editions purport to reproduce Dōgen's text as found in earlier, medieval period manuscripts. Ostensively, both seemed to represent the *Shōbōgenzō* in seventy-five chapters and in twelve chapters, but while the chapters of each were so arranged, neither edition derived entirely from original manuscripts in those lineages. In many respects, both editions emulated the Honzan edition, selecting chapters or even sentences eclectically (as did the Honzan edition) without consistent criteria, so long as their contents agreed with the Honzan version.[218] Their internal adherence to the previously printed (i.e., Honzan) versions testified to the continued influence that the Honzan edition exerted over the expectations of readers. In 1990, a revised version of the Mizuno edition (in 4 volumes) replaced the earlier version by Etō Sokuō in the Iwanami Bunko series of paperbacks. Shortly thereafter (1991–1993), Shunjūsha published a new edition of the *Shōbōgenzō* edited by Kawamura Kōdō as volumes 1 and 2 of its *Complete Works of Dōgen* (*Dōgen zenji zenshū*).

---

[217] See Ōkubo (1969–1970), *Dōgen zenji zenshū*, vol. 1; and Mizuno (1970–1972) in *Dōgen, Nihon shisō taikei*, vols. 12–13.

[218] Bodiford (2019a, 264–273) surveys the sources and editorial policies used by Ōkubo and by Mizuno. Eclecticism, like all scholarly methods, is practiced in many ways, each variation of which entails strengths and weaknesses. Epp (1976) provides an insightful overview in terms of Biblical studies.

This Kawamura edition remains the only published version to rely primarily on manuscripts affiliated to the *Shōbōgenzō* in seventy-five chapters and in twelve chapters. This is the edition that is the basis of the Sōtō Zen Text Project translation.

The editions by Ōkubo (1969) and Mizuno (1970–1972) share one noteworthy feature. Both editors endeavored to reproduce the phonetic glosses found in medieval manuscripts of the *Shōbōgenzō*. These glosses provide invaluable linguistic data for phonological investigation of thirteenth-century Chinese, as well as the ways that Chinese loan words were used by Japanese. While the unfamiliar phonetic glosses might have demonstrated that the editors consulted medieval manuscripts, they proved to be a source of endless frustration for readers. In many (or most) cases, both in religious contexts and in everyday settings, the lexicographical pronunciation of these words today differs from the medieval glosses. As a result, readers who attempt to find an unfamiliar word in a dictionary cannot rely on the pronunciation provided in either the Ōkubo or Mizuno editions. The name "Eisai" serves as an example that will be familiar even to people who do not read Japanese. In recent years, some scholars have adopted the pronunciation "Yōsai" at least in part because both Ōkubo (1969, 1.433) and Mizuno (1972, 2.105) reproduce the characters for his name, 榮西, with the medieval gloss やうさい (*yōsai*). The Kawamura edition (1991–1993), as well as the two recent revised Honzan editions (2019; and 2020), reverted to phonetic glosses that reflect the lexicographical pronunciations (e.g., *eisai*) that one can find in ordinary dictionaries.[219]

### *2019 Revised Honzan Edition*

In 2019, Eiheiji published under its imprimatur *Shōbōgenzō: honzanban teiho* 正法眼藏: 本山版訂補 (Honzan Edition of the *Shōbōgenzō*, Revised and Expanded).[220] The work was commissioned in 2002, by Miyazaki Ekiho 宮崎奕保 (1901–2008), who then served as abbot of Eiheiji, as part of the seven-hundred-fiftieth commemoration of Dōgen' death. The words "Honzan edition" in its title explicitly identifies it not just with Eiheiji but also with the weight of past traditions. Its editors — Kawamura

---

[219]   E.g., the 2020 Revised Honzan edition states (*hanrei* 凡例; unnumbered page) that it determined phonetic glosses based on their potential for enabling readers to find words in a dictionary (*dokusha ga tōgai goku o shiraberu kanōsei* 読者が当該語句を調べる可能性).

[220]   My description is based on Tsunoda 2020.

*Introduction to the* SHŌBŌGENZŌ: *Supplement 2*                    187

Kōdō (a specialist in historical manuscripts) and Tsunoda Tairyū (a specialist in Dōgen's teachings) — worked to update those traditions, even if only partially. They argued that a new edition to commemorate Dōgen should follow the eighty-seven-chapter (75 plus 12) format that he had devised. Accordingly, they reprinted the same text as in the chapters of the original Honzan edition, but re-arranged the chapters into three sections: seventy-five chapters, twelve chapters, and a supplemental section (*shūi* 拾遺), which consists of the additional chapters included in the original Honzan edition not among the eighty-seven selected by Dōgen. The result somewhat resembles the two earlier editions by Ōkubo and by Mizuno. It includes seven variant chapters, which have the same titles as in the previous (1991–1993) Kawamura edition but are arranged somewhat differently, appearing immediately after their namesake versions as appendices. Its printed text eschews the modern (i.e., simplified) Chinese characters dictated by the Japanese government's language policies in favor of their traditional (i.e., complex) forms — which remain the format commonly used during formal religious rituals at Buddhist temples. The phonetic Japanese characters all have been converted to the now standard *hiragana* forms, and the phonetic spellings corrected to agree with the forms in dictionaries of literary Japanese. It includes extensive notes and phonetic glosses (with traditional Sōtō pronunciations). It is bound as a single volume, so that clerics at monastic retreats or lectures can easily carry it and consult it. This edition will encourage traditionalists within temples to familiarize themselves with the chapter layout of Dōgen's *Shōbōgenzō*.

*2020 Revised Honzan Edition*

In 1990, on the one hundredth anniversary of the adoption of the *Shushō-gi* 修證義 (The Meaning of Practice and Verification) as an official statement of Sōtō teachings, the Headquarters (Shūmuchō) of the Sōtō school adopted a plan to publish its own revised versions of the *Denkōroku* 傳光録 (The Record of Transmitting Illumination), by Keizan Jōkin, and the *Shōbōgenzō*, by Dōgen. These three works share a significant karmic connection. Ōuchi Seiran had compiled the initial draft version of the *Shushōgi*, and he had printed the first modern typeset editions of the *Denkōroku* and *Shōbōgenzō* (both in 1885). The Sōtō Headquarters wanted to publish new versions of these works in a format that would be more accessible and readable by modern audiences while maintaining fidelity to their original content.[221] The updated *Denkōroku* was published in 2005, and the updated *Shōbōgenzō* in 2020.[222] Both publications kept the text and the format of the 1885 versions. In other words, in 2020, the Shūmuchō published a revised version of the 1885 Honzan edition. The title on its cover reads simply: *Shōbōgenzō*.

As was the case with Etō Sokuō's Iwanami version, the 2020 revised edition implements modern editorial principles. In many key respects, however, it implements them differently. The type is large and easy to read, with many paragraph breaks. It eliminates orthographic irregularities, uses simplified forms of Chinese characters, and provides modern punctuations. It numbers the ninety-five chapters and corrects their order. Almost all words have phonetic glosses on their first appearance, and all Buddhist and unfamiliar Chinese terms are explained in brief notes at the top of the page. Typos and misprints in Ōuchi's original are corrected without comment. It does not include any collation notes. Instead, textual notes clearly identify the original sources for all quotations (fully utilizing the sixty years of advances in bibliographic scholarship since Etō). It does not include any variant versions of chapters, not even the second version of "Washing the Face" ("Senmen") that the xylographic Honzan edition had printed in the margins. It deletes without comment the supplemental material included in the original Honzan edition and its previous reprints — i.e., its historical introduction, explanation of editorial policies, and descriptive table of contents — each of which included much nineteenth-century misinformation. Like all previous reprints, it retains the brief acknowledgements at the end of each chapter (*bokoku shikigo* 募刻識語) that list the names of temples and individual patrons who donated funds to finance the carving of the original xylographs. The support of Fukuyama Hakurin, the abbot of Myōgonji, for example, is acknowledged at the end of each of the five previously blank chapters. Overall, the 2020 revised version of the Honzan edition provides readers with an accurate and easy to read rendition of the text carved during the years from 1769 to 1811 (and 1906). Even scholars will find its citations of source texts convenient and helpful.

The most noteworthy features of this 2020 revised Honzan edition lie not in its text, however, but in its supplements. Of course, it includes

---

[221]  See the unnumbered preface (*aisatsu*) by Oniyūda Shun'ei 鬼生田俊英, the administrative head of the Shūmuchō, in volume 1.

[222]  The Sōtō Headquarters distributes these publications to temples but not usually to the general public.

the expected explanatory overview of Dōgen, an explanation of his key teachings, and a précis of the *Shōbōgenzō* and its manuscript traditions. It also provides two additional supplements that might be unexpected. First, a separate compilation (*besshū*) includes the complete text of Dōgen's *Shōbōgenzō* in Chinese script. The textual notes in this section cross-reference all the instances in Dōgen's writings (not just in the *Shōbōgenzō*, but also in his *Extensive Record*, in his monastic rules, and in other minor works) where he quotes or alludes to the kōans in this collection. The inclusion of Dōgen's kōan collection in this authorized edition of the *Shōbōgenzō* constitutes a complete rehabilitation of the so-called *shinji Shōbōgenzō*. Rather than being disregarded as a spurious work, it is now recognized (as stated in the explanation, 3.357–358) that Dōgen's teachings cannot be fully understood without careful consideration of his *Shōbōgenzō* in Chinese script. Nonetheless, this work remains relatively unknown and understudied. As explained in the introduction to this translation (see Dōgen Back in Japan), only in recent decades have scholars begun to understand the many ways in which the significance of the *Shōbōgenzō* in Chinese script extends beyond its role as a source text. Its inclusion in a new edition of the *Shōbōgenzō* published by the Headquarters of the Sōtō school can be expected to encourage increased attention to Dōgen's initial *Shōbōgenzō*, not just among scholars but also among the Sōtō clergy.

Second, a supplemental section composed by members of the Division for the Protection and Promotion of Human Rights (Jinken Yōgo Suishin Honbu 人権擁護推進本部) within the Sōtō Headquarters, discusses the sensitive topics of language and representation. In recent decades, people in all parts of the world have struggled to reconcile their higher ideals with the less noble aspects of social realities, including (but certainly not limited to) conventional modes of speech. The Human Rights Division conducts regular workshops and events for clerics and laypeople, whether affiliated to the Sōtō school or not, to promote more inclusive and equitable modes of behavior. In this section of the revised Honzan *Shōbōgenzō*, they discuss the work through this lens.

Readers of a translated text that was originally written hundreds of years ago in a land far away might be able to ignore or even overlook problematic expressions. The social context that renders words and phrases questionable might not even be recognizable through the translation. For readers in Japan, however, some of the potentially hurtful expressions that were commonplace during Dōgen's time remain in use (or at least in memory). And some of their social contexts unfortunately remain all too familiar. Even readers far removed in time and space from thirteenth-century Japan can recognize the kinds of issues discussed in this section. I will not mention any specific terms, but merely list a few of the broad categories addressed by the Human Rights Division. All of them reflect universal issues: labels used to refer to social classes, especially terms used in regard to disadvantaged categories of people; terms related to physical attributes and perceived types of disabilities; expressions of ageism and sexism; labels based on regional or national origins; and designations based on religious stereotypes. In addition to the above, Buddhist teachings of karma also can present issues, especially in political or social contexts if used to rationalize (or used as an excuse for ignoring) injustices. The discussion of these kinds of perennial concerns in this context should serve, not as casual indictments of the past, but as reminders that we must demand better of ourselves and our communities.

*Honzan Edition Chapters in this Translation*

The Honzan edition constitutes the most widely known version of the *Shōbōgenzō*, not only in Japan but throughout the world. It is the basis for all previous translations of the *Shōbōgenzō* into the languages of the world. Even translations based on the Ōkubo edition (1969) or Mizuno edition (1970–1972), which once were highly favored by scholars, indirectly reflect the contents of the Honzan edition because of the editorial policies adopted by both Ōkubo and Mizuno (Bodiford 2019a, 264–273). For this reason, whenever one compares the Honzan edition (in whatever version) to the Kawamura edition, or compares the wording used in other translations to the translation herein, one must bear in mind that some disagreements reflect unavoidable differences between the original source texts. They do not necessarily agree.

Textual discrepancies can be minor or major. Even in instances where the same words appear in the same order, editors might have rendered the sentence breaks or paragraph breaks in different locations. The ways that editors add punctuation to the text of the *Shōbōgenzō* has evolved as a result of advances in bibliographic and grammatical studies. In other passages, the actual wording might differ. Differences in wording arise from two main circumstances.

First, the Honzan edition is an eclectic compilation that combined materials from different sources. It was collated with late copies of manuscripts, which had sometimes been amended by their copyists. Moreover, the editors of the Honzan edition included material even in cases when it did not exist in the manuscript source that they had selected for any particular chapter. The best-known example of this practice can be found in "Making a Bow and Getting the Marrow" (chapter 28; H8; "Raihai tokuzui"). The extra textual material added by the editors of the Honzan edition nowadays has become a standard part of this chapter.[223] This hybrid version appears in the Kawamura edition as well, but the extra material is labeled an "appendix" (*furoku* 付録). In almost all other instances, the Kawamura edition more faithfully reproduces the text as found in its source texts (i.e., the manuscripts from Ryūmonji and Yōkōji).[224]

The second reason that the text of the Kawamura edition may vary from the Honzan edition is that, in some cases, the Honzan edition relies on a chapter with an identical title that comes from a manuscript tradition other than the seventy-five- or twelve-chapter compilations. One must bear in mind that the *Shōbōgenzō* in twelve chapters was unknown (and its existence was not even suspected) when the editors of the Honzan edition compiled their text. Chapters in the Honzan edition with the same titles as those in the twelve-chapter compilation actually derive from different sources, which can differ in content. The most significant example of this issue is the chapter "Karma of the Three Times" ("Sanjigō"). A chapter with this title exists in the *Shōbōgenzō* in sixty chapters. That version is reproduced in the Honzan edition. Its editors could not know that Dōgen subsequently revised that chapter (but without providing a colophon or date) when he included it in his *Shōbōgenzō* in twelve chapters. As a result, the same title exists in two versions. This translation includes both versions, with the earlier draft from the sixty-chapter compilation labeled as a variant (V7). Mizuno (1972, 6) reproduces earlier draft versions of chapters (not the ones from the Yōkōji manuscript) as if they represent the authentic twelve chapters, which they do not. Her chapter 8 actually corresponds to variant 7 in this translation. Her

---

[223]   This material derives from a discarded draft version in the Himitsu manuscript: hi–(1.8).

[224]   Each volume of the Kawamura edition includes a table of collations (*honbun kōi* 本文校異; DZZ.1:495–509; 2:625–653) that should be consulted — and checked for errors (of which, there are a few).

editorial decision reflects the weight of the Honzan edition, which in the minds of many readers continued to represent what the *Shōbōgenzō* should say. Likewise, in the 2019 revised Honzan edition with its revised (75 plus 12) arrangement, ten of the chapters within the twelve-chapter section derive from alternative manuscript traditions. They might not differ from their namesakes in the twelve-chapter compilation as obviously as is the case with the chapter "Karma of the Three Times," but readers cannot assume that their contents are completely identical.

Finally, note that the vast majority of textual studies of the *Shōbōgenzō* and commentaries on its proper interpretation rely exclusively on the Honzan edition. When one examines the same textual passages exclusively from the seventy-five- and twelve-chapter compilations, some of the conclusions advanced in those earlier interpretations will be called into question. This factor helps explain why the versions of the seventy-five- and twelve-chapter texts compiled separately by Ōkubo and by Mizuno were both edited in an eclectic manner that tended to replicate the contents of the Honzan edition. The revised Honzan editions of 2019 and 2020 express similar textual conservatism.

Appendix 3, "Honzan Edition Chapters in This Translation," lists the ninety-five Honzan chapters with corresponding titles in this translation. Note that it places angle brackets < > around corresponding chapter numbers from texts that were unknown by its editors.

# Supplement 3:
## Preface to the *Treasury of the True Dharma Eye* by the Śramaṇa Dōgen

Of Dōgen's many compositions, only one has a preface signed with his name. It is dated 1235.11.3 and is attached to his *Shōbōgenzō* in Chinese script (DZZ.5:124). The preface is very brief. It is translated here in full, and the translation is followed by a somewhat lengthier overview.

正法眼藏序

> 觀音導利興聖寶林寺

正法眼藏也、大師釋尊已拈擧矣。拈得盡也未。直得二千一百八十餘歲、法子法孫、近流遠派、幾箇萬萬、前後三三。

諸人要明來由麼。昔日靈山百萬衆前、世尊拈花瞬目、迦葉破顏微笑。當時世尊開演之曰、吾有正法眼藏涅槃妙心、附囑摩訶大迦葉。

迦葉直下二十八代菩提達磨尊者、親到少林、面壁九年。撥草瞻風、得可附髓。震旦之傳、肇于之也。六代曹谿、得青原・南嶽。師勝資強、嫡嫡相嗣。

正法眼藏、不昧本來。祖祖開明之者、三百箇則、今之有也。代以得人、古之美也。

> 于時嘉禎乙未一陽佳節
> 住持觀音導利興聖寶林寺
> 入宋傳法沙門道元序

### Preface to the *Treasury of the True Dharma Eye*[225]
#### Kannon Dōri Kōshō Hōrin Monastery

The "treasury of the true dharma eye" refers to what the Great Master, Venerable Śākyamuni has already raised. How could its having been raised ever end? It has been directly attained for two thousand one hundred eighty plus years by dharma heirs and dharma descendants, in mainstream lineages and branch lineages, numbering in the thousands and tens of thousands, "before and after, three and three."

---

[225] For my translation, I consulted Kawamura's (1974, 97–98) transcriptions of the Shinpōji 眞法寺 and Jōkōji 成高寺 (also ESST.1.65b–67a) manuscripts (both of which include medieval reading marks and glosses) as well as Ishii Shūdō (1988, 38). The standard edition is DZZ.5:124–125.

194 DŌGEN'S *SHŌBŌGENZŌ* VOLUME VIII

Do you want to know its origins? "One day long ago, before an assembly of a million on Vulture Peak, the World Honored One held up a flower, and blinked his eyes. Kāśyapa broke into a smile. This is what the World Honored One proclaimed at that moment: 'I have a treasury of the true dharma eye; I bequeath it to Mahā, the Great, Kāśyapa.'"

A direct descendant of Kāśyapa in the twenty-eighth generation, Venerable Bodhidharma himself arrived at Shaolin and faced a wall for nine years. Ignoring the grasses, looking up to the wind, he attained Huike and bequeathed the marrow. Its transmission within Cīnasthāna began from there. The Sixth Ancestor, Caoxi, gained Qingyuan and Nanyue. [Thereafter,] superlative masters and stout disciples successively inherited it from legitimate heir to legitimate heir.

The treasury of the true dharma eye is not being in the dark about the fundamental. Herein are three hundred cases clarified by ancestor after ancestor. That with which they have gained people over the generations is the splendors of the ancients.

First Yang Festivities, junior wood year of the ram, the first year of Katei
Prefaced by Dōgen
The Śramaṇa who Transmits the Dharma from the Song,
Abbot of Kannon Dōri Kōshō Hōrin Monastery

Dōgen's preface begins by identifying the *shōbōgenzō* ("treasury of the true dharma eye") as the teaching of Śākyamuni Buddha at Vulture Peak in India and, as the teaching that generations of his religious descendants have taught and continue to teach ever since. Next, he quotes the kōan "World Honored One: Holding up a Flower, and a Smile" (C. *Shizun nianhua xeixiao* 世尊拈花微笑; J. *Seson nenge mishō*) in its entirety.[226] After the briefest possible summary of the history of the Zen lineage, Dōgen reaches his main point: The three hundred Zen stories he compiled all convey the "splendors of the ancients." That is, they constitute the splendid words and deeds by which the ancestors of old conveyed

---

[226] *Shōbōgenzō*, case no. 253 (DZZ.5:258). Dōgen quotes this same kōan in "The Way of the Buddhas" (44; "Butsudō"), "Secret Words" (45; "Mitsugo"), "Face to Face Conferral" (51; "Menju"), "The Udumbara Blossom" (64; "Udonge"), and twice in his *Extensive Record* (*Kōroku* 6 and 9, *jōdō* 428 and *juko* 1; DZZ.4:12 and 182).

Introduction to the SHŌBŌGENZŌ: *Supplement 3* 195

the *shōbōgenzō* (i.e., the truth) to their own disciples (i.e., the lineage of Zen ancestors).

Today, scholars without exception accept that Dōgen compiled the *Shōbōgenzō* in Chinese script. Most scholars recognize that his editing and transcribing this initial *Shōbōgenzō* led to (or at least played a major role in) his production of a *Shōbōgenzō* in Japanese script. The widespread scholarly acceptance of the *Shōbōgenzō* in Chinese script, however, does not always extend to its preface. This divergence partially results from historical accident, and partially reflects traditional images of Dōgen's style of teaching (for which, supposedly, a collection of kōans could have been only for Dōgen's own use, not for his students).

The preface written by Dōgen first appeared in print in 1765 (ESST.14.647a–b), in the edition of *Nenpyō sanbyakusoku funōgo* 拈評 三百則不能語 (*Evaluations of Three Hundred cases of the Ineffable*) by Shigetsu Ein 指月慧印 (1689–1764), printed by Shigetsu's disciple Katsudō Honkō 瞎道本光 (1710–1773). Shigetsu evaluated (i.e., commented on) the three hundred kōans (which he divided into 301 entries) in Dōgen's *Shōbōgenzō* in Chinese script. He did not, however, always reproduce the text of the kōans as written by Dōgen. Occasionally he substituted more familiar versions, some of which clearly came from sources compiled after Dōgen's death (Kagamishima 1954, 440–441, 442n1). Because of these textual irregularities, scholarly Sōtō clerics did not accept that Shigetsu had commented on a kōan collection that could actually have been compiled by Dōgen. They dismissed the so-called "three hundred cases" (*sanbyakusoku*) as spurious. The preface by Dōgen presented additional issues, since it bore a second date (1764) and seemed to have been copied from a separate work. It too was rejected as spurious (Ōkubo 1970, 2.524).

The editors of the original Honzan edition copied a preface from a separate work for their new *Shōbōgenzō*, which they placed at the very beginning of the supplemental (*hanrei narabi kanmoku* 凡例並卷目) fascicle. Instead of the discredited text (translated above), they selected a preface (T.2582.82:7a) written by Giun 義雲 (1253–1333), the fifth abbot of Eiheiji. Giun did not write his preface for a copy of Dōgen's *Shōbōgenzō*, a fact that the editors of the Honzan edition omit. His preface originally appeared in Giun's own *Shōbōgenzō hinmokuju* 正法眼藏 品目頌 (ESST.20.3), a composition of sixty Chinese gāthā-style verses (*geju* 偈頌), one verse in praise of each chapter of Dōgen's *Shōbōgenzō* in sixty chapters. Its repurposed use in the Honzan edition served to re-

196 DŌGEN'S *SHŌBŌGENZŌ* VOLUME VIII

inforce the theory (advanced by the editors of the Honzan edition) that Giun had compiled the *Shōbōgenzō*. In the eyes of many, it also implied that the version in sixty chapters represented the most reliable one (i.e., the one authorized by Eiheiji).

The *Shōbōgenzō* in Chinese script was all but forgotten until 1934, when the historian Ōya Tokujō (1882–1950) revealed the existence of an incomplete manuscript (only the second of three fascicles) of it at the Kanazawa Bunko (a library founded ca. 1270s) in Kamakura. This manuscript had been copied (from and collated with two variant versions) in 1287, only thirty-five years after Dōgen's death. In 1940, Tamamuro Taijō (1902–1966), a Sōtō historian, published a transcription of the Kanazawa Bunko text and pointed out that it exhibits several unusual linguistic features closely related to Dōgen's own idiosyncratic style of writing. By the 1950s, subsequent studies had demonstrated the authenticity of the *Shōbōgenzō* in Chinese script.[227] Generations of students, clergy, and scholars since that time have accepted this conclusion.

The Kanazawa Bunko manuscript, however, was incomplete. It did not include Dōgen's preface. Ōkubo Dōshū, therefore, excluded the preface from the main section of his edition of the *Complete Works of Dōgen* (*Dōgen zenji zenshū*; 1969–1970). He relegated it to a separate appendix of spurious works.[228] Just a few years later, Kawamura Kōdō began to publish the results of his investigations into the manuscript history of the *Shōbōgenzō*. He had discovered six additional manuscript copies of the *Shōbōgenzō* in Chinese script, four complete versions and two incomplete.[229] The four complete manuscripts all include Dōgen's preface, and all of them have the same wording as found in the 1765 xylograph. Two of them include phonetic glosses and reading marks, which suggest the interpretation followed in the translation above (and which differ from the one proposed by Ōkubo 1970, 2.524). The manuscript evidence uncovered by Kawamura convincingly established the authenticity of

---

[227] See Ishii Shūdō (1988, 581–582) regarding Tamamuro's contributions. Regarding the linguistic features of the *Shōbōgenzō* in Chinese script, see Ishii Shūdō (2009); Kagamishima (1954); and Nomura (1965).

[228] Ōkubo (1970, 2.524). Ōkubo reprinted the 1765 xylographic version and added punctuation and *kundoku* 訓読 morphosyntactic marks to indicate how to render it into Japanese. Ōkubo's *kundoku* produces a rather different interpretation than the one indicated by my translation.

[229] Ishii Shūdō (2009, 119) lists the extant manuscripts and also lists (p. 120) Kawamura's fourteen most important publications regarding them between 1971 and 2002.

Dōgen's preface. This conclusion nonetheless leaves unresolved at least two concerns that cannot be assuaged by textual evidence alone.[230] They are: Why among all of Dōgen's compositions would he have chosen to write a preface only for a minor work such as this one? How could he have given the distinction of a preface to a composition which does not include a saying of (or does mention the name of) Rujing?

---

[230] Comments by Ishii Shūdō (1988, 41–42) implicitly raise these concerns. Note that the chapter cited here originally was published in 1983 and does not necessarily reflect his later conclusions.

## Supplement 4:
## The *Shōbōgenzō* in Chinese and in Japanese scripts

When Dōgen compiled his *Shōbōgenzō* in Chinese script in the early 1230s, Buddhist clergy in Japan had been practicing, and teaching, the reading and the writing of literary Chinese and Chinese characters (logographs and phonographs) for centuries. All aspects of Chinese language constituted integral features of Japanese culture.[231] Because people both in Japan and in China shared an educational framework based on similar textual practices and studied the same works of classical literature, difficulties in verbal communication between them could be attributed to unfamiliar pronunciations (*yuan yiyin bujie* 縁異音不解), rather than blamed on foreign languages.[232] When Dōgen referred to the speech he heard in China, he used the word *hōgen* 方言 (regional speech), while Lanxi Daolong and other Chinese teachers in Japan struggled with what they described as *xiangtan* 郷談 (the local talk).[233] Today, both of these terms might be translated as "dialect" (but, today, no one would use them to refer to Chinese or Japanese). The use of these regional designations reflects social realities that later came to be erased by modern notions of national languages and their officially codified orthographies. Nonetheless, one of the most important features of Dōgen's *Shōbōgenzō* consists of the fact that he also wrote a version in Japanese (whether he imagined it as a unique language or not). Writing in Japanese, employing the orthographic flexibility of Japanese script, enabled Dōgen to explore,

---

[231] See Lurie (2011) regarding both the practice of Chinese language technologies in Japan and debates over how to conceptualize its practice. Pages 323–334, "Overcoming the Bilingual Fallacy," are especially pertinent for Dōgen. Here I refer to Chinese language rather than to sinoscript (or sinographic) culture, because the aural vocalization of spoken Chinese also figures into Buddhist interactions. Recent publications on sinoscript culture are too numerous to cite at length; in addition to Lurie, I have drawn on Denecke (2014); King (2015); and Whitman (2011). Also see Lee (2010) regarding the ideology of national language within the context of Japanese modernization.

[232] For "unfamiliar pronunciations," see *Zongnan jiaye* 終南家業, 1 (CBETA.X.59.1109.727b11-13 // Z.2:10.361d16-18 // R.105.722b16-18) and Tachi (2014, 261). Regarding the power of sinoscript to facilitate communication across disparate languages, see Denecke (2014).

[233] For Dōgen, see *Zuimonki* 3 (DZZ.7:92), for Lanxi Daolong, see Tachi (2014, 264).

Introduction to the SHŌBŌGENZŌ: *Supplement 4*                    199

elucidate, and transform Chinese script into his own novel idiom. As strange as it may seem, his writing of a *Shōbōgenzō* in Japanese script began with his writing of a *Shōbōgenzō* that today is now commonly known as the *shinji Shōbōgenzō*: "the *Shōbōgenzō* in Chinese script."[234] Dōgen, however, used one and the same title for both works. He might even have conceived of them as a singular project.

Dōgen's life-long efforts to express the *Shōbōgenzō* in a Japanese idiom parallels the oeuvre of several of his renowned Buddhist contemporaries, such as Shinran 親鸞 (1173–1263) and Nichiren 日蓮 (1222–1282) — teachers who, like Dōgen, proselytized among people from all levels of society far removed from the well-educated, aristocratic elites of the central capital. However, in many respects, Dōgen stands alone. Two features are especially relevant here. First, Dōgen developed his own Japanese idiom primarily in an effort to explicate the Chinese vernacular (or pseudo-vernacular) as recorded in the conversational style of Chan records. He repeatedly translates passages from Chinese texts because he wants people to learn to read them as he does. Dōgen explores nuances in the Chinese originals that otherwise would escape notice. Second, Dōgen left a paper trail that, while often incomplete, is unrivaled in documenting with tantalizing details his methods and techniques for transcribing, translating, and/or transcreating the Chinese originals. This documentary trail begins with his *Shōbōgenzō* in Chinese script.

Limitations of space will permit only brief glimpses of the process by which the *Shōbōgenzō* in Chinese script gave birth to the transformed *Shōbōgenzō* for which Dōgen became renowned. A few simple examples should suffice to allow readers of English to observe the key steps. The examples necessarily discuss Chinese and Japanese scripts (whether logographs or phonographs) but require knowledge of neither. For readers with the requisite linguistic skills, the examples can serve as appetizers or previews for future investigations of this type, which too often have been overlooked by scholars outside of Japan.

---

[234] The word *shinji* 眞字 (also pronounced *mana*; also written 眞名) refers to proper glyphs in a block calligraphic style, such as those with individually written lines (e.g., *kaisho* 楷書 as opposed to cursive writing, *sōsho* 草書). In Japanese contexts, it can refer to Chinese characters (*kanji* 漢字 as opposed to Japanese ones, *waji* 和字). In premodern texts, among Japanese glyphs, it can refer to Chinese characters used phonetically (e.g., *man'yōgana* 萬葉假名), and, among phonographs, it can refer to *katakana* カタカナ (as opposed to *hiragana* ひらが な). Normally. it does not refer to the Chinese language or to Chinese grammar.

The transformation of Chinese records into the *Shōbōgenzō* involves more procedures than can be considered here. The main steps consist of: (1) selecting an appropriate kōan; (2) editing (or revising) the kōan; (3) arranging the kōan into sequences or clusters with other kōans; (4) segmenting the kōan into clauses and/or sentences; (5) marking clauses and sentences with morphosyntactic glosses (*waten* 和點) to indicate vocalizations, lexical significations, and syntactical inversions; (6) transcribing the kōan into Japanese script in a way that eliminates the need for most (but not necessarily all) of the previous morphosyntactic marks; (7) revising the transcription and rewriting much (but not all) of the kōan into Japanese script, sometimes including Japanese expressions. Each of these steps can be repeated more than once, in more than one fashion, and each of them can involve complex strategies that will be ignored in the discussion that follows.[235] Steps involving multiple kōans (numbers 1 and 3) also must be ignored (these steps are discussed briefly in the subsection Dōgen Back in Japan; also see Table 17). Also note that while segmenting (step 4) must precede marking (step 5), the process of adding the morphosyntactic glosses effectively renders the kinds of punctuation marks (e.g., commas and periods) commonly used today unnecessary. To modern eyes the texts might continue to look unpunctuated before and after.

All the examples below concern case 122 of the *Shōbōgenzō* in Chinese script, "Xuanze: Bingding Youth" (C. *Xuanze bingding tongzi* 玄則丙丁童子; J. *Gensoku byōjō dōji*). This kōan is especially important for Dōgen. It figures prominently in *Talk on Pursuing the Way* (*Bendōwa*), and its existence in the Chinese *Shōbōgenzō*, played a vital role in establishing the authenticity of the *Bendōwa* as a work by Dōgen. As mentioned several times elsewhere in the Introduction, the existence of the *Bendōwa* was completely unknown prior to 1686, when Manzan Dōhaku (1636–1714) included it as a supplemental chapter within his newly compiled *Shōbōgenzō* in eighty-nine chapters. It became available to the public in 1788, when Gentō Sokuchū (1729–1807) printed it as an independent work by Dōgen. Thereafter, the possible provenance of the *Bendōwa* became a question that generated much speculation, but no evidence could be found to substantiate any of the theories. Etō Sokuō (1888–1958) provided a key clue with the posthumous publication (in 1959) of his study and reprint of a previously unknown draft copy of the *Bendōwa* dated

---

[235] Regarding Dōgen's citation strategies, see Kagamishima (1965, 33–83) and Kim (1985).

*Introduction to the* SHŌBŌGENZŌ: *Supplement 4*   201

1332 (commonly known as the Shōbōji manuscript).[236] Comparisons of the "Bingding Youth" kōan in the Kanazawa Bunko manuscript of the *Shōbōgenzō* in Chinese script (dated 1287), in the 1332 Shōbōji manuscript draft version, and in the 1788 xylograph edition by Gentō Sokuchū left no doubt that all three versions represent different stages of evolution (or revision) by the same authorial hand. The examples, therefore, reveal, not just key steps in the evolution of the *Bendōwa*, but also the evidentiary links that demonstrate the textual filiation of its manuscripts. In 1965, Nomura Zuihō published a particularly detailed examination of the linguistic characteristics of the Japanese markup in the Kanazawa Bunko manuscript.[237]

We will begin with the Chinese source text. The "Bingding Youth" kōan exists in several different Chinese Chan texts, each with its own version, but the one quoted by Dōgen exists in only one source: the recorded sayings of Hongzhi Zengjue (1091–1157; J. Wanshi Shōgaku). As reproduced under the title, "Bingding Youth Kōan: Modern Transcriptions," at the very end of this section, it provides our reference text. The reproduction presents the kōan in numbered lines, with each line appearing in four parallel registers (*a*, *b*, *c*, and *d*), as follows:

- a. the original kōan as found in the CBETA version of Hongzhi's recorded sayings[238]
- b. the same kōan as it appears in *Shōbōgenzō*, case 122 (DZZ.5:192)[239]
- c. text *b* rendered into Japanese form (*yomi-kudashi* 読下し; DZZ.5:193)
- d. text *c* spelled out in Roman letters (according to modified Hepburn Romanization)

---

[236]  See Etō (1959, 326–338). This copy is found within another manuscript titled *Shōbōgenzō zatsubun* 正法眼藏雜文, which survives as a copy dated 1515. Etō (pp. 28–32) reviews the theories regarding the origins of the text printed by Gentō Sokuchū.

[237]  My analysis draws on Nomura (1965) as well as Ogawa (2003, 54–59) and Ishii Shūdō (2009, 122–124), both of whom likewise rely on Nomura.

[238]  *Hongzhi chanshi guanglu* 宏智禪師廣録; 1 (CBETA.T.2001.48:3a6-16). In this passage the wording in the Taishō edition matches that of the Song edition of the *Hongzhilu* 宏智録 (reprinted ca. 1201) except for the following variant glyphs: *er* 爾 written as 你; *ceng* 曾 as 曽; *feng* 峰 as 峯; and *ge* 箇 as 个 (see Ishii Shūdō, editor, 1984–1986, 1.11a and 12a).

[239]  DZZ.5 reproduces the text found in the Jōkōji 成高寺 manuscript (copied 1481), which differs in some details (noted below) from the text of the Kanazawa Bunko manuscript.

202 DŌGEN'S *SHŌBŌGENZŌ* VOLUME VIII

Note that all the transcriptions conform to modern orthographic conventions (such as punctuation).[240] In the examples that follow, the text of the kōan will be cited by the line number (and, when necessary, register letter).

It is possible to compare the version of the kōan in the Chinese source text against Dōgen's version of the same kōan by quickly scanning registers *a* and *b*. First, note the blank spaces in register *a*. They reveal places where Dōgen added additional Chinese glyphs, while the boldface type in register *b* represents Dōgen's additions. Next, look for the opposite situation (i.e., blanks spaces in register *b*) where Dōgen omitted words. Finally, there also exist places with boldface type in register *b*, but without a blank space in register *a*. Those instances represent places where Dōgen replaced the original word with a different word. Here are the results:

15 added glyphs    (in lines 1, 2, 5, 7 and 10)
1 omitted glyph    (in line 17)
6 revised glyphs   (in lines 1, 4, 7, 13, and 17)[241]

These numbers reveal in quantifiable fashion that Dōgen did not merely copy passages from Chinese sources. Closer examination reveals that these emendations must have been the result of conscious revisions, not accidental mistakes. None of them changes the content of the kōan or the meaning of the lines, but all of them render the kōan easier to read, especially for people who might be unfamiliar with this genre of literature and its vocabulary. In other words, Dōgen revised the Chinese wording, not for himself, but for a Japanese audience who lacked his familiarity with this material.

In line 1b, for example, Dōgen replaced the abbreviated name "Ze" 則 (J. Soku) with the full name of the kōan's protagonist: Xuanze 玄 則 (J. Gensoku). If readers do not already know the name Xuanze, they will not recognize "Ze" by itself. Next, he revised Xuanze's title from "comptroller" (*kan'in* 監院; i.e., the post that he held at the time of this story) to "Zen master" (*zenji* 禪師). In Japan during the 1230s, hardly

---

[240] Nonetheless, the Japanese rendering (by the editors of DZZ) in register *c* sometimes incorporate unconventional interpretations that derive from the manuscript traditions. These irregularities do not play a role in any of the examples.

[241] For the purposes of this count, I ignore the distinction between the glyphs for the verb "to say" (*iwaku*), which in lines 4 and 7 shift from *un* 云 to *etsu* 曰, glyphs frequently regarded as synonyms in Japan.

Introduction to the SHŌBŌGENZŌ: *Supplement 4*

anyone would recognize the title "comptroller." That office had not yet been introduced from China. The title "Zen master" helps clarify that this kōan recounts how Xuanze mastered Zen. In subsequent lines (4b, 7b, 13b, 17b) Dōgen replaced "Ze" (J. Soku) with "master" (*shi* 師).

Other emendations clarify the flow of the story or make explicit otherwise subtle nuances. In line 2, for example, the pronoun "this" (*shi* 此) actually refers to "here." Dōgen removed its ambiguity by revising it to "this place" (*shiken* 此間).[242] Likewise, he inserted personal pronouns to explicitly identify who is being referred to (lines 2, 7) or who is speaking (line 5). Also in line 5, Dōgen changed the phrase about having attained "ease and joy" (*anraku* 安樂) to the more spiritually significant "a state of ease and joy" (*anrakusho* 安樂處).[243] In line 10, he inserted the word "resembles" (*ji* 似) to make explicit the comparison that is only implied in the Chinese original. Similarly, the addition of the conjunctive "thereupon" (*dai* 乃) in line 13 confirms that Xuanze's agitation arose at that very moment. But, in line 17b, Dōgen deleted the locative particle *yo* 於, which in line 17a serves a similar temporal function. In this case, however, the phrase "as these words were spoken" (*genka* 言下) alone conveys the temporality. When rendered into Japanese syntax, the phrase *genka* would be followed by the Japanese temporal particle *ni* に, whether the Chinese sentence included its particle *yo* 於 or not. In other words, the Chinese *yo* 於 would seem superfluous to Japanese readers.

Clearly, steps 1, 2, and 3 (especially 3) require authorial intervention in the original text. While those steps focus entirely on the Chinse text and its logographs, the next set of steps (5, 6, and 7) involve reconceptualizing the text to reveal, not just how it should be interpreted, but also how that interpretation can be vocalized with Japanese words: verbs, adverbs, adjectives, and relational particles that signify syntax. Successful vocalization requires aural balance: certain sounds harmonize while others might clash. Synonyms can be used if aurally appropriate whether they color the nuances or not. While the first set of steps (1, 2, and 3) manipulate visual signs (logographs), the second set of steps manipulate signs that are both visual and aural (phonographs). Japanese writing technologies not only include multiple kinds of phonographs, but also allow Chinese logographs to convey Japanese vocalizations that can be unrelated to the ways that the logographs might be pronounced as Chinese words.

---

[242] In modern Japanese the same characters 此間 represent the phrase *kono aida* (i.e., recently; the other day).

[243] The Kanazawa Bunko manuscript lacks this emendation.

204 DŌGEN'S *SHŌBŌGENZŌ* VOLUME VIII

The following three examples have been selected for their relative simplicity. Each example tracks a single clause or sentence through steps 5, 6, and 7 by relying on three different source texts, a different text for each step:

> step 5. application of Japanese marks (i.e., vocalizations) to the revised Chinese kōan
>> e. 1287 Kanazawa Bunko manuscript[244]
> step 6. transcribing the kōan into Japanese linguistic format according to its vocalization
>> f. 1322 Shōbōji manuscript[245]
> step 7. revising the transcription for improved Japanese style and ease of reading
>> g. 1788 xylograph by Gentō Sokuchū[246]

Do not be misled by the fact that the manuscripts or xylograph date from after the time of Dōgen's death. Each of them preserves content that reflects a different stage in Dōgen's own process of composition.

Example 1. "I shouldn't deceive the Reverend" (line 4b)

e. 某甲不敢瞞和尚 *soregasi fukanman oshō*

f. 某甲和尚ヲ欺クヘカラス *soregashi oshō wo azamuku-bekarazu*

g. それかし。和尚をあさむくへからす。 *soregashi, washō wo azamuku-bekarazu*

In example 1, the morphosyntactic marks in the (*e*) Kanazawa Bunko manuscript provide minimal instructions. They consist of seven Chinese logographs, above which in a smaller size there are Japanese square phonographs (*katakana* カタカナ). These phonographs gloss the pronunciations of the first five logographs. The sentence begins with a first-person pronoun, "I," written as 某甲. Normally one might pronounce these two glyphs as *bōkō*, but here the small-size phonograph *shi* シ above the 甲 indicates that the combination should be pronounced as *soregashi*, a

---

[244]   Facsimile in Ishii Shūdō, editor, (2015, 35–36) and diplomatic transcription (*honkoku* 翻刻), p. 445.

[245]   Facsimile in *Shōbōgenzō zatsubun: Shōbōji-bon* 正法眼藏雑文: 正法寺本 (2010, 22–23) and diplomatic transcription, pp. 110–111.

[246]   Facsimile in ESST.4.752a–753a.

*Introduction to the* SHŌBŌGENZŌ: *Supplement 4* 205

slightly humble Japanese designation for oneself. A separate phonetic gloss sits above the next 3 logographs 不敢瞞. It says *fu* フ (不) *kan* カム (敢) *man* マム (瞞), which merely indicates the usual Chinese pronunciation for each glyph. In short, only the first word (*bōkō*) is vocalized as Japanese (*soregashi*).

The next two steps (indicated by lines *f* and *g*), however, transpose the vocalizations and the word positions into Japanese formats. First, notice how the last word (*oshō* 和尚) in the first line (*e*) occupies the central position in the next two lines (*f* and *g*). This change reflects the different sentence structures of Chinese (i.e., subject, verb, object) and Japanese (i.e., subject, object, verb). Second, the verb has changed from *man* 瞞 to *gi* 欺. Both of these logographs convey the sense of "deceive" (i.e., conceal the truth, mislead, etc.). Interestingly, the phonetic gloss above the verb indicates that it should be vocalized as *azamu-* アサム (i.e., "deceive"). The Chinese logograph *man* 瞞 also could be vocalized this way (and in line 4d, it is), but dictionaries indicate that its usual pronunciation as a Japanese word should be *damasu* (i.e., a synonym for "deceive"). Third, note that the logographs *fu* 不 ("not") and *kan* 敢 ("dare") disappear in line *f*. In the Japanese vocalizations (lines *f* and *g*), they have been replaced by a verbal suffix (*-bekarazu*) that conveys the same basic sense. Finally, in the last line (*g*), all the logographs except the object, "reverend," have been replaced by cursive phonographs (*hiragana* ひらがな). The last sentence looks as if it could have been composed in Japanese, rather than written as a transcription (*yomi-ku-dashi*) from Chinese. Regardless of the different visual appearances of each line, all three of them can be vocalized identically as: *soregashi oshō wo azamuku-bekarazu.* Moreover, they convey the same meaning: "I shouldn't deceive the Reverend."

Why did Dōgen leave the word "reverend" in Chinese logographs instead of Japanese phonographs? We cannot know. Perhaps, as a Buddhist term, it deserves (and requires) the weight expressed by Chinese logographs to convey its spiritual significance.[247] The phonetic gloss above it in line *g*, provides a slightly unusual pronunciation. Instead of the expected *oshō*, it indicates *washō* ワシヤウ (i.e., an archaic variant pronunciation). It seems out of place, especially since that pronunciation

---

[247] See Robert (2066) regarding how sinitic scripts can function as a kind of "hieroglossia" (i.e., a dead language used to impart sacrality).

206 DŌGEN'S *SHŌBŌGENZŌ* VOLUME VIII

is not typical of medieval manuscript copies of writings by Dōgen. Perhaps Gentō Sokuchū added this gloss when he edited his xylograph.[248]

Example 2.　"Previously, when I was with the Chan Master of Qingfeng, I fully understood what is ease and joy in the buddha dharma" (line 5b)

e. 某甲曾テ在ニ青峯ノ處ニ、得箇タリ安樂ヲ *soregashi katsute shinpō no tokoro ni arishi ni, anraku [no tokoro] wo etari*

f. 曾テ青峯禪師ノ處ニ**有**リシ**時**、**佛法**ニ**置**テ安樂ノ處ヲ**了達**セリ、 *katsute seihō **zenji** no tokoro ni arishi **toki, buppō ni okite** anraku no tokoro wo **ryōdachi** seri*

g. かつて。青峰の禪師のところにありしとき。佛法におきて。安樂 のところを。了達せり。 *katsute **(mukashi)** seihō no zenji no tokoro ni arishi toki, buppō ni okite anraku no tokoro wo ryōdachi seri*

Example 2 consists of a complex sentence with two main clauses. We will note only a few key features. Before comparing the three sentences, first we must note an irregularity in the Kanazawa Bunko manuscript (line *e*). As mentioned previously, line 5b, shows that Dōgen changed the phrase "ease and joy" (*anraku* 安樂) to "a state of ease and joy" (*anrakusho* 安樂處). The Kanazawa Bunko manuscript does not include this emendation. I have taken the liberty of adding the word "*tokoro*" (i.e., the phonetic gloss for *sho* 處 given in the first half of this line) inside square brackets within the Romanized transcription of line *e*. This emendation appears in other manuscripts of *Shōbōgenzō*, case 121, and it also appears in the Japanese vocalizations of this kōan in the *Bendōwa* (lines *f* and *g*).

Overall, the first line (*e*) serves to illustrate the complexity of Japanese morphosyntactic marks. Note how the last two logographs (安樂) in line *e* appear (as "*anraku*") at the very beginning of the second clause in the Romanized transcription. The Japanese vocalization follows the word order indicated by the markup, regardless of the actual position of the logographs on the page.

Line 5b shows that Dōgen added the first person pronoun *soregashi* to the beginning of the first line (*e*). In *Bendōwa*, however, he deleted

---

[248] The editors of *Bendōwa* (DZZ.2:477) did not retain this gloss in their printed edition.

that word. Instead, he completely rewrote the rest of the sentence. The words in boldface type identify 8 Chinese logographs that he added to the second line (*f*) and one glyph that he revised (i.e., *zai* 在 changed to *yū* 有, both of which can be vocalized in Japanese as *ari*). The simple addition of the word "Chan master" (*zenji* 禪師) marks "Qingfeng" 青峯 (J. Seihō) as a person (not a toponym) and thereby renders the addition of *soregashi* unnecessary. The most significant emendations appear in the second half of the sentence. He prefaced the phrase "ease and joy" (*anraku* 安樂) with another phrase of three logographs (*chi buppō* 置佛 法), which the markup indicates should be vocalized in Japanese order as "*buppō in okite*" (i.e., in regard to the buddha dharma). At the end of the sentence he added the verbal phrase "fully understand" (*ryōdachi* 了 達).[249] Taken together, these additions emphasize that, at this point in the story, Xuanze had attained only an intellectual understanding of what he falsely imagined as Buddhist teachings.

Finally, just as in the previous example, the last line (*g*) is written entirely in cursive phonographs except for the key terminology, most of which consists of Buddhist terms. Visually, the second and third lines present seemingly opposite appearances, one (line *f*) looks Chinese while the other (line *g*) looks Japanese. Nonetheless, both lines would be vocalized identically as: *katsute seihō zenji no tokoro ni arishi toki, buppō ni okite anraku no tokoro wo ryōdachi seri.* Moreover, they convey the same meaning: "Previously, when I was with the Chan Master of Qingfeng, I fully understood what is ease and joy in the buddha dharma."

Nonetheless, the last line (*g*) exhibits one oddity, probably added by Gentō Sokuchū. Floating over its initial word, *katsute* かつて (written in cursive phonographs), there is a gloss: *mukashi* ムカシ (written in square phonographs). In this case, with two sets of phonographs, the gloss does not indicate the vocalization, but indicates the intended nuance or meaning. The word *katsute* can be somewhat ambiguous, indicating a range of temporalities: once, sometime, previously, long ago. The word *mukashi* indicates one of these: long ago. In light of the overall context of the sentence, this gloss seems superfluous.[250]

---

[249] In modern Japanese the glyphs 了達 normally are pronounced as "*ryōtatsu*" (not *ryōdachi*).

[250] The editors of *Bendōwa* (DZZ.2:478) did not retain this gloss in their printed edition.

208 DŌGEN'S *SHŌBŌGENZŌ* VOLUME VIII

Example 3: "At these words, the Honorable Ze had a great awakening to the buddha dharma" (line 17b)

e. 師言ノ下ニ大悟ス *shi, kotoba no shita ni daigo su*

f. 則公言下ニ大ニ佛法ヲ悟リキ **soku kō**, *genka ni ooki ni* **buppō** *wo satoriki*

g. 則公。このことはのしたに。おほきに。佛法をさとりき。 *soku kō, kono kotoba no shita ni, ooki ni buppō wo satoriki.*

The third and final example concerns the very last sentence in this kōan, the moment when Xuanze finally abandoned his shallow understanding and attained awakening. The first line (*e*) provides hardly any markup, just two relational particles (*no* ノ and *ni* ニ), a verbal ending (*su* ス), and a single phonetic gloss (*kotoba* コトハ). The verbal ending indicates that the final word, "great awakening" (*daigo* 大悟) functions as a verb (not as a noun) and the phonetic gloss indicates that "as these words were spoken" (*genka* 言下) should be vocalized as: *kotoba no shita*.

Dōgen initially had revised the first line (*e*) by changing the abbreviated name Ze 則 (J. Soku) to "master" (*shi* 師). In the *Bendōwa* (line *f*), he revised the text again. He reverted to the abbreviated name Ze but, to avoid confusion, he added an honorific suffix (*kō* 公) that clearly marks Ze as a person's name (i.e., not an ordinary word). He also inserted the phrase "buddha dharma" (*buppō* 佛法) into the middle of "great awakening" (*daigo* 大悟) to produce the new construction: "greatly awaken to the buddha dharma." Finally, he added the verbal ending *riki* リキ, which indicates that this new construction as a whole should be vocalized as: *ooki ni buppō wo satoriki.*[251] The addition of the term "buddha dharma" in this line balances the "buddha dharma" that was added to line 5 in the second example above. The two occurrences of this value-laden term alert the reader to the contrast between "fully understand" and "greatly awaken." In this same line (*f*), the phrase "as these words were spoken" lack any markup. Accordingly, it appears as *genka* in the Romanized transcription. Based on the first (*e*) and third (*g*) lines, however, one could make a strong case that it should appear as: *kotoba no shita ni.*

Finally, just as in the previous two examples, the last line (*g*) is written entirely in cursive phonographs, except (in this case) for two key words: the name "Honorable Ze" and "buddha dharma." Visually, these two

---

[251] In this context, *satoriki* represents the past tense of the verb *satoru*, the nominal form of which is *satori*.

Introduction to the SHŌBŌGENZŌ: *Supplement 4* 209

sets of logographs stand out from the surrounding textual field. Their visual prominence emphasizes that the story is about two key factors: Xuanze (i.e., oneself) and the buddha dharma. The entire *Shōbōgenzō* is about one's own relationship to the buddha dharma. If one accepts that the phrase "as these words were spoken" in the second line (*f*) should be verbalized as *kotoba no shita ni*, then just as in the previous two examples, the second and third lines (*f* and *g*) could be vocalized practically identically as: *soku kō, kono kotoba no shita ni, ooki ni buppō wo satoriki.*

In this case, I write "practically" because of a peculiarity involving the two logographs *genka* 言下. When written as logographs, this phrase idiomatically conveys "as [these] words were spoken" but the pronoun "these" is only implied. The Japanese vocalization "*kotoba no shita ni*" seems perfectly understandable as long as the logographs are present or their presence is implied. If the logographs are replaced by Japanese phonographs, then it makes more sense to vocalize them as: "*kono kotoba no shita ni*," with the addition of the pronoun "*kono*" この. As a result, in the third example, the lines (*f* and *g*) from *Bendōwa* actually would not be vocalized identically. Nonetheless, they would be very close. Moreover, they convey the same meaning: "At these words, the Honorable Ze had a great awakening to the buddha dharma."

In each of these three examples (and in every line of this kōan as well as countless others throughout Dōgen's oeuvre), parallel passages whether written primarily in Chinese script (as in the *f* lines) or primarily in Japanese script (as in the *g* lines) can express exactly the same semantic content and the same aural experience.[252] The choice of either script does not necessarily alter the vocalization. Frequently, readers can choose for themselves how to vocalize the text. Authors (or editors) can use markup to help guide their choice. *Shōbōgenzō*, case 122, illustrates the interlingual quality of the text in the way that it presents the key phrase of this kōan: "*bingding* youth seeks fire" (C. *bingding tongzi laiqiu huo* 丙丁童子來求火; J. *byōjō dōji raigu ka*).[253]

---

[252] Ilya Gershevitch (1979, 138), a specialist in Old Persian, coined the term "alloglottography" to refer to examples such as this one in which an *allos* (other) *glotta* (tongue; language) is used for the *graphy* (writing) of one's own *glotta* (p. 154 n65; e.g., vocalizing sentences in Chinese as Japanese).

[253] See Lurie (2011, 180) regarding the interlingual (in contrast to bilingual) qualities of the scribal technologies of Japan, in which linguistic differences need not be reflected in writing.

210  DŌGEN'S *SHŌBŌGENZŌ* VOLUME VIII

This phrase appears twice: when the Chan Master of Qingfeng first says it to Xuanze (line 8a) and again when Fayan says the exact same words to Xuanze (line 16a). The first time resulted in Xuanze thinking to himself that he had attained a deep understanding. The second time prompted Xuanze's great awakening. Qualitatively, these two occasions could not be more different from one another. Yet, both revolve around the identical phrase. In the Kanazawa Bunko manuscript, the markup for the first instance produces this vocalization in Japanese word order (subject - object - verb):

e. 丙丁童子來テ求ヒ火ヲ *byōjō dōji kitarite hi wo motomu*

The second instance lacks any markup, which typically would result in simply vocalizing the logographs in their original Chinese word order (*bōyomi* 棒讀):

e. 丙丁童子來求火 *byōjō dōji raigu ka*

The markup for the first instance allows the reader to vocalize and understand the line as a Japanese expression. The lack of markup in the second instance places the reader in the moment of Xuanze's awakening.

The above examples provide rare glimpses of Dōgen's craft as an author who worked within an interlingual framework. They not only reveal the reversibility of the text (in which passages in Chinese script transpose themselves into Japanese script and, sometimes, revert back again), but also confirm the intimate relationship between *Shōbōgenzō*, case 121, and *Bendōwa* — both in its draft version and in its final revised form. In this way, they also affirm the inseparable relationship between Dōgen's initial *Shōbōgenzō* in Chinese script and the later one for which he became renowned. They caution scholars not to automatically assume that Dōgen composed within two separate literary or bilingual linguistic frameworks when writing this or that *Shōbōgenzō*. The *Shōbōgenzō* in Chinese script reveals at least seven main steps in the process by which Dōgen transformed Chinese source texts into Japanese literary works. The *Shōbōgenzō* in Japanese script most certainly entailed all seven of these steps. And, in most (but not all) chapters, it builds upon them with additional steps (revisions and literary transpositions) that expand the range of the kōan discourse to include subjects and themes beyond the boundaries of its original source texts. The fact that we can detect the roots of this process within the language examples above serves to illustrate how the selection, compilation, and revisions of the kōans that

*Introduction to the* SHŌBŌGENZŌ: *Supplement 4*    211

were included in his initial *Shōbōgenzō* initiated a literary and religious journey that continued throughout the rest of Dōgen's life.

Bingding Youth Kōan: Modern Transcriptions (*Shōbōgenzō* in Chinese script, number 122)

1.  a　　則監院、在法眼會中、一日、眼問、
    b　**玄**則**禪師**、在法眼會中、一日、眼**云**、
    c　**玄**則**禪師**、法眼の會中に在りしに、一日、眼云く、
    d　**Gen**soku **zenji**, Hōgen no echū ni arishi ni, ichinichi, Gen iwaku:
2.  a　爾在此　多少時　、則云　　　　　　　　三年、
    b　你在此**間**多少時耶、師曰、**在和尚會、已得三年、**
    c　你、此**間**に在りて多少の時ぞ、師曰く、**和尚の會に在りて、す**でに三年を得たり、
    d　Nanji, koko ni arite ikubaku no toki zo? Shi iwaku, **oshō no e ni hanberite**, **sude ni** sannen o etari.
3.  a　眼云、爾是後生、尋常何不問事、
    b　眼云、你是後生、尋常何不問事、
    c　眼云く、你はこれ後生なり、尋常に何ぞ問事せざる、
    d　Gen iwaku: Nanji wa kore goshō nari, yonotsune ni nanzo monji sezaru?
4.  a　則云、某甲不敢瞞和尚、
    b　**師**曰、某甲不敢瞞和尚、
    c　**師**曰く、某甲、敢て和尚を瞞かず、
    d　**Shi** iwaku: Soregashi, aete oshō o azamukazu.
5.  a　　　曾在青峰處、得箇安樂　、
    b　**某甲**曾在青峰處、得箇安樂**處**、
    c　**某甲**、かつて青峰の處に在りしに、箇の安樂の**處**を得たり、
    d　**Soregashi**, katsute Seihō no tokoro ni arishi ni, kono anraku **no tokoro** o etari.
6.  a　眼云、爾因甚語得入、
    b　眼云、你因甚語得入、
    c　眼云く、你、甚なる語によりてか、入ることを得し、
    d　Gen iwaku: Nanji, ikanaru kotoba ni yorite ka, iru koto o eshi?
7.  a　則云、曾問　　、如何是學人自己、
    b　**師**曰、曾問**青峰**、如何是學人自己、
    c　**師**曰く、かつて**青峰**に問う、如何なるかこれ學人の自己なると、
    d　**Shi** iwaku: Katsute **Seihō** ni tou, "Ika naru ka kore gakunin no jiko naru?" to.

8. a 峰云、丙丁童子來求火、眼云、好語、
   b 峰云、丙丁童子來求火、眼云、好語、
   c 峰云く、丙丁童子、來たりて火を求むと、眼云く、好き語なり、
   d Hō iwaku: "Byōjō dōji, kitarite hi o motomu" to. Gen iwaku:
   Yoki kotoba nari.

9. a 祇恐爾不會、則云、丙丁屬火、
   b 祇恐你不會、師云、丙丁屬火、
   c ただ恐らくは、你、會せざらんことを、師云く、丙丁は火に屬す、
   d Tada, osoraku wa, nanji, esezaran koto o. Shi iwaku: Byōjō wa
   hi ni zokusu.

10. a 將火求火、　將自己覓自己、
    b 將火求火、似將自己覓自己、
    c 火をもって火を求む、自己をもって自己を覓むるに似たり、
    d Hi o motte hi o motomu. Jiko o motte jiko o motomuru ni **nitari**.

11. a 眼云、情知爾不會、
    b 眼云、情知你不會、
    c 眼云く、情に知りぬ、你、會せざりしことを、
    d Gen iwaku: Makoto ni shirinu, nanji, esezarishi koto o.

12. a 佛法若如此、不到今日、
    b 佛法若如是、不到今日、
    c 佛法もしかくのごとくならば、今日に到らじ、
    d Buppō moshi kaku no gotoku naraba, konnichi ni itaraji.

13. a 則、　躁悶便起、
    b **師、乃**操悶便起、
    c **師、乃ち**操悶して便ち起ちぬ、
    d **Shi**, **sunawachi** sōmon site sunawachi tachinu.

14. a 至中路却云、他是五百人善知識、
    b 至中路却云、他是五百人善知識、
    c 中路に至りて却って云く、他はこれ五百人の善知識なり、
    d Chūro ni itarite kaette iwaku: ta wa kore gohyakunin no zenchishiki
    nari.

15. a 道我不是、必有長處、却迴懺謝便問、
    b 道我不是、必有長處、却回懺悔便問、
    c 我が不是を道う、必ず長處あらん、却回して懺悔して便ち問う、
    d Waga fuze o iu, kanarazu chōsho aran. Kyōi shite sange site
    sunawachi tou:

*Introduction to the* SHŌBŌGENZŌ: *Supplement 4*     213

16. a 如何是學人自己、眼云、丙丁童子來求火、
   b 如何是學人自己、眼云、丙丁童子來求火、
   c 如何なるかこれ學人の自己なる、眼云く、丙丁童子、來たりて
     火を求む、
   d Ika naru ka kore gakunin no jiko naru? Gen iwaku: Byōjō dōji,
     kitarite hi o motomu.

17. a 則、**於**言下大悟、
   b **師**、   言下大悟、
   c **師**、   言下に大悟す、
   d **Shi**, genka ni daigo su.

# Supplement 5:
## Sources for Dōgen's Life

This supplement introduces the basic primary sources cited in Subsection 6 of the Introduction, "Dōgen and His *Shōbōgenzō*," briefly reviews their limitations, and (if necessary) identifies the version cited herein. The basic primary sources must be examined and fleshed out by peripheral materials, which are too numerous to review. Here I limit my remarks to the most often cited sources, the ones that typically appear in discussions of Dōgen's life and his literary career.

The *Shōbōgenzō* — with its great length, its multi-layered complexity, and the well-established provenance of so many of its manuscripts — provides an unparalleled wealth of resources for the study of Dōgen, his message and his times. However abundant its textual riches, the *Shōbōgenzō* presents kaleidoscopes of fragmentary episodes, sometimes extremely patchy ones without clear chronological sequence or geographic guideposts, which cannot be molded into a shapely narrative. The production of such a narrative — whether with a hagiographic focus on the revelation of spiritual truth or with a biographic focus on psychological and social motives — nonetheless underpins most traditional and modern readings of the text.[254] Aside from his *Shōbōgenzō* in Japanese script, which exists as versions in twelve, sixty, and seventy-five chapters as discussed above (see section I), Dōgen also composed a *Shōbōgenzō* in Chinese script, with a preface (dated 1235). The existence of a preface (translated in Supplement 3) is significant for two reasons. First, it indicates a degree of completeness. Author's typically assign a preface only after a work is finished. Second, it clearly indicates that Dōgen himself selected the title *Shōbōgenzō* (*Treasury of the True Dharma Eye*). The fact that both works (whether the Japanese version in twelve, sixty, and seventy-five chapters or the Chinese version) have an identical title suggests that they are intimately related to one another. At the very least, they share a common beginning. Whether labeled as being in Chinese or Japanese, each version employs both scripts but with an emphasis on one mode of writing or the other. Moreover, the manner in which Dōgen selected, arranged, revised, and added morphosyntactic glosses (*waten* 和點) to the kōans in his initial *Shōbōgenzō* in Chinese script provided the literary foundation for his *Shōbōgenzō* in Japanese script.

---

[254] For an older but still useful overview of this issue, see Bielefeldt 1985.

Introduction to the SHŌBŌGENZŌ: *Supplement 5*        215

Depending on how and what one counts as an individual kōan episode (*soku* 則), the *Shōbōgenzō* in Japanese script incorporates about 319 kōans, while the one in Chinese transcribes 300 kōans (Kagamishima 1987, 1).[255] Taiyō Bonsei 太容梵清 (1378–1439?), the compiler of the *Shōbōgenzō* in eighty-four chapters, referred to the version in Japanese as "the *Shōbōgenzō* of 1,000 [kōan] episodes" (*sensoku Shōbōgenzō* 千則正法眼藏) and the version in Chinese as "the *Shōbōgenzō* of 300 episodes" (*sanbyakusoku Shōbōgenzō* 三百則正法眼藏; see Yokoyama 2018, 94). The first designation, with its hyperbole, is not found elsewhere, but the latter designation became widely used. Because of their fraternal relationship, the *Shōbōgenzō* in Chinese script necessarily figures prominently in any evaluation of the one in Japanese. The relationship between these two versions is discussed in more detail elsewhere (see Dōgen back in Japan; and Supplement 4: The *Shōbōgenzō* in Chinese and in Japanese scripts). Today, the most reliable typeset editions of these works can be found in *Dōgen zenji zenshū* (DZZ) published by Shunjū-sha.[256]

Dōgen's *Hōkyōki* 寶慶記 (*Baoqing Records*) records brief transcriptions by Dōgen of his private conversations with his teacher Rujing 如淨 (1162–1227). The transcriptions begin on 1225.7.2 (the first dated entry) and end sometime in 1226 (a period that corresponds to the first two years of the Chinese Baoqing Era). This is the period immediately after Rujing had accepted Dōgen as his dharma heir. Careful consideration of the *Hōkyōki*'s well-established provenance, contents, and linguistic features, demonstrate that there is no basis for the speculations by some scholars who disparaged its textual reliability.[257] It is equally obvious

---

[255] The *Nenpyō sanbyakusoku funōgo* 拈評三百則不能語, a commentary on the *Shōbōgenzō* in Chinese script, by Shigetsu Ein 指月慧印 (1689–1764), published posthumously in 1767, counts a total of 301 kōan by dividing no. 239 (DZZ.5:252) into two separate entries. Medieval manuscripts of the text as well as the *Zhengfayanzang* 正法眼藏 (fascicle 1) by Dahui Zonggao 大慧宗杲 present it as a single entry. See Ishii Shūdō 1988, 12; cf. CBETA.X.67.1309.581a4-10 // Z.2:23.25d13-26a1 // R118.50b13-51a1.

[256] See DZZ vols. 1–2 (edited by Kawamura Kōdō) and DZZ.5:124–275 (edited by Ishii Shūdō.) Note that the *Shōbōgenzō* in sixty chapters is not available as a typeset edition. For this work, see the Tōunji manuscript (facsimile in ESST.6).

[257] This issue is too complex to summarize adequately here. In its simplest terms, scholars who deemed that Dōgen did not teach the proper understanding of the karma of the three times (*sanjigō* 三時業) until the very end of his

216 DŌGEN'S *SHŌBŌGENZŌ* VOLUME VIII

that Dōgen (not Rujing) selected which comments to record and how to transcribe them in written form. For this reason, it can be regarded as an early precursor to the "transcription" (*kikigaki* 聴書) genre of Sōtō Zen literature. For many years, most people read the Iwanami Bunko paperback edition edited by the renowned scholar Ui Hakuju 宇井伯壽 (1882–1963), first published in 1938. Nowadays, scholars cite the text of the autograph by Ejō owned by Zenkyūin 全久院 (Aichi Pref.), which is the source for most recent printed editions.[258]

Dōgen wrote *Bendōwa* 辨道話 (*Talk on Pursuing the Way*) for a wide audience. It presents his earliest attempt (dated 1231) to introduce himself and his approach to Zen. It exists in two iterations, an earlier rough draft and a later polished version, which first appeared in print in 1788. Because of its accessible style and its importance for any understanding of how Dōgen saw himself and his mission, *Bendōwa* remains the most widely read work by Dōgen.

Dōgen's *Tenzo kyōkun* 典座教訓 (*Admonitions for the Chef*) includes recollections of his activities and conversations in China. Although the instructions are dated to 1237, it is possible that his recollections might (or might not) be based on his contemporaneous notes.

*Dōgen oshō kōroku* 道元和尚廣録 (*Extensive Records of Reverend Dōgen*) consists of a massive (ten-volume) collection of various works by Dōgen written in Chinese. Its first seven volumes consist of major convocation addresses (*jōdō* 上堂) that Dōgen presented as a regularly scheduled monastic ritual during the years 1241 to 1243 and 1245 to 1252 (see Table 24). Sometimes, his *jōdō* reference current events; and, because they followed the liturgical calendar in chronological order, it is possible to deduce the dates of many of these addresses. Many of his *jōdō* cite or quote Zen stories (kōan). Overall, the *Extensive Records* (*Kōroku*) comments on 298 kōans (Kagamishima 1987, 3). It also includes 125 Chinese gāthā (*geju* 偈頌) style verses composed by Dōgen during all stages of his career (in China, in Kyoto, in Echizen, and in Kamakura). His verses composed in China indicate that Dōgen kept contemporaneous written

---

life tended to dismiss the appearance of this term in early texts such as the *Hōkyōki* (DZZ.7:20) or the *Zuimonki* 2 (DZZ.7:79) as indications that these works must have suffered later manipulation. Then those scholars marshal circumstantial evidence to support their suppositions of textual unreliability. The result is a very forced reading.

[258] This version is reproduced in DZZ.7; and in Ōkubo 1969–1970, vol. 2; and is accompanied by photographic facsimiles in Ishii Shūdō, ed., 2015.

Introduction to the SHŌBŌGENZŌ: *Supplement 5*

notes of his literary activities overseas. Because many of his verses were addressed to or exchanged with other individuals who might be named or identified by their titles, they provide us with invaluable information regarding the larger social networks with which Dōgen interacted.

The *Extensive Records* is a posthumous work compiled and edited by several of Dōgen's principal disciples: Ejō, Senne, Gien 義演 (d. ca. 1313), and possibly others. Because each disciple worked on different sections of the work, sometimes it is possible to detect stylistic differences amongst them. Nowadays, scholars cite the text found in a manuscript version owned by Eiheiji that was copied in 1598 under the supervision of Monkaku 門鶴 (d. 1615).[259] Earlier scholars (and some religious teachers even today) cite the text found in the 1672 xylograph edited by Manzan Dōhaku 卍山道白 (1636–1714) titled *Eihei kōroku* 永平廣録 (*The Extensive Records of Eihei*).[260] Because the Manzan edition appeared in print just as Sōtō clerics began to employ Dōgen's words to advance or oppose sectarian reforms, quotations from it frequently appear in established commentaries and interpretations of Dōgen's teachings. The Monkaku version, however, preserves a more reliable text. Comparison of the two versions reveals that Manzan rearranged passages, introduced misreadings, and added punctuation incorrectly.[261] The Manzan Dōhaku edition should be avoided as a source for studying Dōgen.

Ejō 懷弉 (1198–1280) played a major role in the establishment of Dōgen's legacy. His long lifespan and role as Dōgen's chief disciple and hand-picked successor as abbot of Eiheiji helped ensure that a stable monastic community absorbed Dōgen's teachings across several decades even after Dōgen's death. Many individual chapters in the *Shōbōgenzō* in sixty chapters contain scribal colophons by Ejō. Previously, people had assumed that these scribal colophons must indicate that Ejō himself had compiled, edited, and assigned the titles to the *Shōbōgenzō*. That assumption is mistaken. Ejō's scribal notes actually reveal valuable information about how Dōgen revised and compiled the *Shōbōgenzō*. (For

---

[259]  This version is reproduced in DZZ.3–4; in Ōkubo 1969–1970, vol. 2; and in Ōtani and Watanabe 1989.

[260]  This edition is reproduced in SZ.2; and in Ōtani 1991. In this context "Eihei" refers to Dōgen. To avoid confusion, note that Leighton and Okumura 2004 adopted the widely-recognized title *Eihei kōroku* even though their English translation is based on the Monkaku version of the text.

[261]  Ishii Shūdō 2020a and 2020b.

218 DŌGEN'S *SHŌBŌGENZŌ* VOLUME VIII

a detailed overview of this topic, see above, The *Shōbōgenzō* in Sixty Chapters and Its Descendants.)

Ejō's *Zuimonki* 随聞記 (*Occasional Transcripts*; 6 chapters) records conversations that Ejō and others had with Dōgen at the very beginning of his teaching career, during the years from 1235 to 1237 or so. The conversations range over a great many topics in an informal style that frequently seems closer to spoken idiom than the jargon-laden diction typical of Buddhist texts (whether written in Chinese or Japanese). Dōgen's remarks include many autobiographical details about his life before becoming a religious, about his experiences in China, and his views regarding current affairs. It is important to remember, however, that Dōgen is not the author. The topics, key phrases, and manner of transcribing (i.e., *kikigaki*) the speech all reflect the concerns of Ejō. The years 1235–1237 correspond to the period when Ejō first joined Dōgen's fledgling Zen community. As pointed out by Ishikawa Rikizan (1943–1997), Ejō must have struggled to accept Dōgen as his teacher. Ejō not only was older than Dōgen but already had been certified as a master of Zen in Nōnin's so-called Darumashū lineage. The *Zuimonki* repeatedly addresses topics — such as the necessity of seated meditation (*zazen*), the centrality of moral discipline, how to practice the way (*gakudō* 學道; a term that occurs 78 times), and the merit of relics and icons — about which Dōgen and the Darumashū disagreed.[262] Ishikawa describes the *Zuimonki* as a record of Ejō's religious conversion.[263] Significantly, the *Zuimonki* quotes or cites by name fifteen of the kōans found in Dōgen's *Shōbōgenzō* in Chinese script.

The title "*Zuimonki*" was added posthumously by one of Ejō's disciples (unidentified). Ejō himself occupies an ambiguous position in the text. His name appears (whether as a subject or speaker) typically in the third person, but also four times in second person or honorific form (as if written about by his disciple), and only once clearly in the first person.[264] The *Zuimonki* survives in multiple versions. Traditionally, the text

---

[262] Ishikawa (1982; 1983; 1989) examined the *Zuimonki* as a historical source in three different articles, which unfortunately share an identical title.

[263] Ishikawa 1982, 39.

[264] The first person "Ejō" 懷弉 appears in *Zuimonki* 5 (DZZ.7:117); the honorific "Jō *kō*" 弉公 appears in *Zuimonki* 2, 3, 5, and 6 (DZZ.7:65, 80, 119, & 140); the third person "Jō" 弉 appears seven times in *Zuimonki* 2 and 6 (DZZ.7:67, 67, 68, 74, 80, 137, & 150); cf. Ishikawa 1989, 81. These inconsistencies (many of which were eliminated from the Menzan edition)

*Introduction to the* SHŌBŌGENZŌ: *Supplement 5*

from the 1770 xylograph, which was edited, corrected, and rearranged by Menzan Zuihō 面山瑞方 (1683–1769), constituted the standard edition.[265] In 1929, Watsuji Tetsurō (1889–1960) edited Menzan's edition for the Iwanami Bunko series of inexpensive paperback classics and gave it an imprimatur of authority by attaching the subtitle "Dōgen's Recorded Sayings" (*Dōgen goroku* 道元語録), which it definitely is not. Watsuji's edition, in turn, served as the basis for countless other reprints and translations into the languages of the world.[266] Nowadays, scholars cite the version of the text found in a manuscript, owned by Chōenji 長圓寺 (Aichi Pref.), copied in 1644 (from an earlier version dated 1380).[267] The Chōenji version preserves features (medieval language, original order of the chapters; etc.) that more closely reflect Ejō's milieu.

*Goyuigon kiroku* 御遺言記録 (*Dōgen's Final Testament*) records conversations that Gikai 義介 (1219–1309; a.k.a. Gikan 義鑒) had with Dōgen at the very end of his teaching career, during the fourth to the eighth month of 1253, just before Dōgen departed Eiheiji and traveled to Kyoto for medical attention. The title is somewhat misleading, however, since Gikai occupies center stage in this account. While Ejō's concerns with the Darumashū lurk beneath the surface of the *Zuimonki*, out of sight for most readers, Gikai's concerns with his Darumashū background figure prominently in his transcription of Dōgen's remarks. The bulk of the text actually consists of Gikai's transcription of the private initiations he subsequently received from Ejō from the beginning of 1254 to the Spring of 1255, when Ejō formally conferred dharma transmission. A third section describes the proper procedures for conferring precepts.[268] The format of these procedures is usually attributed to Keizan Jōkin. Taken together

suggest that people other than Ejō contributed to the transcriptions.

[265] This edition is reproduced in Watsuji (1929) and in countless reprints based on Watsuji.

[266] The translation by Masunaga (1971) and its reprints must be the world's most widely read book about Dōgen. WorldCat (www.worldcat.org) lists over a thousand libraries that own a copy.

[267] This version is reproduced in DZZ.7; in Nishio et al. 1965; and in Ōkubo 1969–1970, vol. 2. It was discovered in 1941 by Ōkubo Dōshū. For an overview of the textual history of the *Zuimonki*, see Ikeda (1993).

[268] This text is available in DZZ.7; and is accompanied by photographic facsimiles in Ishii Shūdō, ed., 2015. The version in Ōkubo 1969–1970, vol. 2, renamed "Eihei shitchū kikigaki" 永平室中聞書, should be avoided. It omits the final section along with later colophons that record its provenance, thereby obscuring the character of the document as a whole.

the first two sections of *Goyuigon kiroku* serve to emphasize the legitimacy of the way that Gikai handled his Darumashū affiliation, the pre-eminence of Ejō among Dōgen's disciples, and Gikai's own authority as Ejō's dharma heir who also received endorsement by Dōgen.[269] In this way, the work clearly reveals Gikai's insecurities and the fact that he must have faced opposition from among his fellow monastics even during Dōgen's lifetime.[270] But Gikai's unmistakable personal agenda need not blind readers to the historical information he conveys. *Goyuigon kiroku* provides detailed information about topics — such as the course of Dōgen's final illness and early dharma transmission practices — that can be found nowhere else. It confirms the historicity of Dōgen's journey to Kamakura and provides insight into the early reception of Dōgen's teachings and into early monastic practices.[271]

Gikai may very well have composed a biography of Dōgen. The very first line of the *Goyuigon kiroku* concludes with a brief sentence written in very small script that says: "My late master's accounts are as recorded in a separate collection" (*senshi kiroku nyo besshū kishi* 先師記録如別集記之; DZZ.7:180). Before discussing this topic, we should first turn our attention to Gikai's disciple, Keizan Jōkin 瑩山紹瑾 (1264–1325), who definitely did write such a biography.

Keizan's *Denkōroku* 傳光録 (*Record of the Transmission of Illumination*) narrates the lineage of religious ancestors across Asia who (according to Zen scriptures) conveyed the wisdom of the Buddha, from one generation to the next, down to Ejō. It originated as the transcription of a series of lectures that began in 1300. Its final section includes detailed biographies of Rujing 如淨 (1162–1227; J. Nyojō), Dōgen, and Ejō. In regard to Dōgen and Ejō, the *Denkōroku* provides hagiographical accounts likely incorporating oral traditions that its author could have heard from his teachers: Gikai and several of Ejō's disciples, who like Gikai had studied under Dōgen, such as Jakuen 寂圓 (1207–1299; C. Jiyuan) and Gien 義

---

[269] Ishikawa 1981 remains the essential analysis of the *Goyuigon kiroku* as a historical source, but this article must be read along with Ishikawa 1990, which was written at the same time but published later. Ishikawa points out issues regarding provenance, but see Satō Shunkō 2005; Kasai Kōyū 1994.

[270] For an overview of Gikai's position within early Sōtō, see Bodiford 2021, 21–22, 24. For more detailed analysis, see Ishii Shūdō 1986; Itō 1985; Ōtani 1976; and Ōtani 2006.

[271] E.g., regarding Kamakura, see DZZ.7:182: *sennen gekō u kantō shi in* 先年下向干關東之因.

演 (d. ca. 1313). Keizan certainly knew Dōgen's written works (including obscure ones like *Hōkyōki*) and other works regarding Dōgen written by his disciples, such as *Zuimonki* and *Goyuigon kiroku*.[272]

The *Denkōroku* remained virtually unknown until 1857 when Busshū Sen'ei 佛洲仙英 (1794–1864) introduced it to the world as a xylograph in two volumes, which he had extensively edited. In 1885, Ōuchi Seiran 大内青巒 (1845–1918), an extremely influential lay Buddhist reformer, published a modern typeset edition in one volume that subsequently became the standard version. For his edition Ōuchi revised the text further to give it what Japanese in the late nineteenth century referred to as a "contemporary style" (*jibuntai* 時文體), similar to the idiom used in Japanese translations from European languages (*ōbunmyaku* 歐文脈), somewhere between the formality of Sino-Japanese style (*kanbunchō* 漢文調) and vernacular style (*genbun itchi* 言文一致), while making eclectic use of elements from both. Also, without regard for the format of the received text, Ōuchi rewrote as Chinese all passages that he regarded as quotations from earlier texts and rewrote in Japanese format all Chinese passages that he regarded as Keizan's own words.[273] The revisions by Busshū and by Ōuchi ultimately caused careful scholars to raise doubts regarding the authenticity of the *Denkōroku*. Ōkubo Dōshū, for example, rejected the *Denkōroku* as a source in his influential 1953 study of Dōgen's life.[274] Today, doubts regarding the origins of the *Denkōroku* no longer trouble scholars, thanks principally to the discovery of multiple early manuscripts of the *Denkōroku* — especially the Kenkon'in 乾坤院 manuscript (ca. 1430) and Ryūmonji 龍門寺 manuscript (ca. 1547) — and the collection, publication, and study of medieval documents from Sōtō temples across Japan.[275] Nonetheless, the usual printed versions of the *Denkōroku* should not be used uncritically but must be checked against the early manuscripts.[276]

---

[272]  An English translation of *Denkōroku* by the Sōtō Zen Text Project is now available; see Foulk 2021. Many of its detailed annotations also pertain to the *Shōbōgenzō*. All citations of the *Denkōroku* herein are to this version.

[273]  For a detailed overview, see Bodiford 2021.

[274]  Ōkubo 1953, 21–22.

[275]  Tajima Hakudō revealed the existence of the Kenkon'in manuscript in 1960 (see Tajima 1960a; Tajima 1960b), and Yamahata Shōdō (1973) reported the discovery of the Ryūmonji manuscript 13 years later.

[276]  This task is gradually becoming easier thanks to the publication of the series *Keizan zenji 'denkōroku': shohon no honkoku to hikaku* 瑩山禅師「伝光

The *Sanso gyōgōki* 三祖行業記 (*Accounts of the Accomplishments of the Three Patriarchs*) consists of concise biographies of Dōgen, Ejō, and Gikai.[277] This text lacks provenance. It is not known when, where, or by whom it was compiled. It must date from after Gikai's death (1309) and before 1399, when Tenshō Yūnen 天性融然 (d. 1427) reproduced the bulk of it in the Japan section of his *Busso shōdenki* 佛祖正傳記 (*Accounts of the Legitimate Transmission of the Buddhas and Ancestors*), a history of the Sōtō lineage.[278] The biographies in the *Sanso gyōgōki* contain many precise details that — in regard to Dōgen — derive from the *Shōbōgenzō*, the recorded sayings of Rujing, *Hōkyōki*, and *Tenzo kyōkun*, and that — in regard to Ejō and Gikai — derive from *Goyuigon kiroku* and missives that Gikai addressed to Keizan. It seems almost certain that the biography of Dōgen must date from an early period, while Gikai was alive, while the biographies of Ejō and Gikai were written later, after Gikai's death. Itō Shūken (1985) argued that Gikai must be the author of Dōgen's biography (hence the line quoted previously about "my late master" in *Goyuigon kiroku*), and that Keizan must be the author of the biographies of Ejō and Gikai. Itō presents persuasive textual evidence but cannot account for other details where his proof texts disagree (see Yoshida 1992a, 87–89). Even if Itō's premise is correct, it does not explain who combined these different biographies or when. The earliest extant manuscripts are rather late (probably sixteenth century), and all of them exhibit numerous scribal errors. In spite of these defects, the *Sanso gyōgōki* cannot be totally ignored since it conveys information from Dōgen's time and contains some details that can be found nowhere else. For example, prior to the discovery of the draft version of the *Shōbōgenzō* chapter "Great Awakening" ("Daigo"; Ōsu Bunko manuscript; variant chapter number 6), the *Sanso gyōgōki* provided the earliest written account of Dōgen attaining awakening (*shinjin datsuraku* 身心脱落) upon hearing Rujing scold a sleeping monk. Independent verification of this

録」： 諸本の翻刻と比較 by Tsurumi University: Part 1 (2015); Part 2 (2016); Part 3 (2016); Part 4 (2018); Part 5 (2019); Part 6 (2020); Part 7 (2021); etc.

[277]  This text is also known as *Sandaison gyōjōki* 三大尊行状記 (*Accomplishments of the Three Great Venerables*). Yoshida 1992a provides an overview of the various manuscript filiations, with side-by-side, collated transcriptions of the two main variant versions. Transcriptions of the other variants can be found in Akitsu 2021; Azuma 1985; and Yoshida 1992b. For convenience, I cite the standard version in SZ.Shiden 史傳 1.

[278]  Yoshida 1992a, 90; Sugawara 2015, 52–53. Cf. *Busso shōdenki*, ZSZ. Jishi-Shiden 寺誌・史傳, 312–315.

controversial story greatly enhanced scholarly evaluations of the *Sanso gyōgōki* as a historical source. But even its details that lack verification remain important because they form the normative narrative within the Gikai lineage (see Table 39).

The *Kenzeiki* 建撕記 (*Kenzei's Chronicle*), which presents a biography of Dōgen and the history of Eiheiji, was written in 1452 by Kenzei 建撕 (1415–1474), an abbot of Eiheiji. The *Kenzeiki* plays an inescapable role in considerations of Dōgen's *Shōbōgenzō* since (as described previously) it provides our earliest textual witness for the scribal colophon by Ejō in "Eight Understandings" ("Hachi dainin gaku"; chapter number 12); it is the source for "Instructions to the Administration Cloister" ("Ji kuin mon"), the supplemental chapter, appearing in the Honzan edition, that Dōgen composed at Eiheiji in 1246.[279] Traditionally, everyone read the revised and annotated (*teiho* 訂補) edition published by Menzan Zuihō in 1754 or the illustrated version of Menzan's annotated edition (*Teiho kenzeiki zue* 訂補建撕記圖會), published in 1817. In either format, until 1975, all descriptions of Dōgen whether scholarly or popular relied almost entirely on Menzan's revised version of the *Kenzeiki*. Our understanding of the *Kenzeiki* and of Dōgen's biography changed dramatically in 1975, when Kawamura Kōdō published a collated compilation of manuscript versions of the *Kenzeiki* that predate Menzan's edition. Of these manuscripts, scholars cite the copy by Zuichō 瑞長, dated 1552. The Zuichō version and the other early manuscripts of the *Kenzeiki* reveal, not only that Menzan had extensively modified the original text, but also that Kenzei's biography of Dōgen primarily served to introduce Kenzei's history of Eiheiji. Kenzei's history of Eiheiji, then, presents an alternative version of many early Sōtō developments from the perspective of the Jakuen lineage. Kenzei's account helps to explain how the numerically small and financially weak Jakuen faction came to dominate Eiheiji after Gien 義演 (d. ca. 1313), its fourth abbot.[280] Kenzei's biography of Dōgen presents the narratives that became normative within

---

[279]  The *Kenzeiki* (Kawamura 1975, 85–96) is also the source for the collection of *waka* style Japanese verses attributed to Dōgen entitled *Dōgen zenji wakashū* 道元禅師和歌集 (DZZ.7).

[280]  The essential examination of the *Kenzeiki* as a historical source remains the three-part series by Ishikawa Rikizan (1978b; 1979; 1980). Bodiford (1993, 65–80) discusses the early history of the Jakuen lineage and its control over Eiheiji. Bodiford (2006, 15–18; reprint 2012, 217–220) explains the significance of the shift away from Menzan's edition of the *Kenzeiki* that Kawamura (1975) provoked.

224    DŌGEN'S *SHŌBŌGENZŌ* VOLUME VIII

the Jakuen lineage (see Table 39) and which, in Menzan's revised form, subsequently became normative for the world.

The *Kenzeiki* organizes Dōgen's life into a chronological sequence. It repeats details from the sources discussed above and supplements them with quotations drawn from a host of other documents, only some of which still survive. For example, it quotes six portrait eulogies (*shinsan* 眞贊) written by Dōgen, of which today two are extant. Of the many incidents the *Kenzeiki* reports, about sixteen can be verified by contemporaneous documents that survive or by independent copies of those documents. In most cases, the *Kenzeiki* reproduces the contents of those documentary sources with a high degree of accuracy, although not always with identical orthography.[281] For this reason, instances of documentary deviation or contradiction command our attention. The most conspicuous (and notorious) example concerns the question of whether Dōgen ever met Eisai. Their lifespans overlapped, and the *Zuimonki* quotes Dōgen's descriptions of Eisai (descriptions which must be second-hand). Menzan's revised editions of the *Zuimonki* and *Kenzeiki* clearly suggest that Dōgen actually met Eisai. The Chōenji version of the *Zuimonki*, however, presents a different sequence of events that leaves no room for their encounter.[282] The Zuichō copy of the *Kenzeiki* presents similar chronological evidence that disallows any meeting, but then contradicts itself, as if Kenzei did not want to accept what his own chronology demonstrates.[283] This self-contradiction raises the specter of deliberate dishonesty.

Aside from deliberate dishonesty, documents mislead readers due to an almost infinite number of factors. Scholars scrutinize surviving documents for authenticity and, if authentic, for signs of discrepancies or errors. Textual irregularities might indicate omissions, transpositions, mistakes, emendations, and so on, and each of these instances potentially reflects scribal bias. Scribes can exhibit personal biases as well as societal and institutional ones. Surely each of Dōgen's disciples harbored individual agendas and assumptions. Overt institutional rivalries probably did not develop until later, perhaps much later. The first several generations of disciples after Dōgen who founded successful new temples (i.e., branch lineages) did so in distant provinces, where they operated inde-

---

[281]    Ishikawa (1979) provides several side-by-side comparisons.

[282]    Kagamishima 1973 (reprinted 1985, 12–16).

[283]    Ishikawa 1980, 166–168; cf. Kagamishima 1973 (reprinted 1985, 1–4); cf. Kawamura 1975, 8–11.

*Introduction to the* SHŌBŌGENZŌ: *Supplement 5*       225

pendently and served the religious needs of local patrons. Their rivalries did not encompass other Sōtō institutions; intra-Sōtō affiliations carried little weight. Nonetheless even at isolated temples, copyists might insert honorific terms or prestigious titles for the patriarchs of their own lineage. Forgeries were commonplace in medieval times, but many of the scribes in medieval Sōtō temples seem to have reproduced earlier texts (whether authentic or fabricated ones) rather accurately, without excessive emendation. The deliberate self-contradictions in *Kenzeiki* serve as a caution not to naïvely assume honesty in historical documents. It also demands that we consider the sectarian conflicts among early Sōtō Zen communities.

Scribal culture changed radically during the early modern period (after ca. 1630). Copyists became bolder and less hesitant to emend documents. Increased access to formal education, especially Chinese learning, and the explosive growth in the publishing of Buddhist books propelled the development of new techniques of textual criticism, such as evidentiary learning (*kōshōgaku* 考證學). Soon, it became routine for scholarly editors (such as Manzan Dōhaku, Menzan Zuihō, et al.) to compare manuscript witnesses against external standards and attempt to enhance the copies they produced by adding punctuation, correcting errors, adding dates, adding honorific titles, emending nonstandard orthographies, filling in lacuna, rearranging passages that seem to be out of sequence, checking Chinese quotations against the most recently published versions, and so forth. Each enhancement provided opportunities for biases and for cross-textual contamination. Meanwhile, government policies imposed greater centralization over Buddhist temple networks, which exacerbated institutional rivalries and exposed disparities in monastic practices, rituals, and teachings. Monastic leaders began to rely on textual scholarship in their efforts to promote or resist efforts to reform practices and teachings. Each side in a debate typically accused the other of misreading and/or amending their proof texts.[284] Today, every textual witness is assumed to be guilty unless proven innocent.

In this context, the distribution of manuscript traditions among Sōtō temples of disparate lineage affiliations can provide an indirect measurement of the relative likelihood of deliberate textual manipulation. Texts extant in widely dispersed manuscript traditions generally reflect widely shared points of agreement. Either as an accident of history or by de-

---

[284]   E.g., see Bodiford 1991, 440–445; Bodiford 1993, 48–49; Bodiford 2010, 242–248.

sign, manuscripts composed at one temple might survive or be re-copied only at another temple and not elsewhere. Any one of the temples listed in Table 39, "Early Sōtō Temples and Lineage Affiliations," potentially could have (and in some cases did) become the headquarters of its own Sōtō faction (or of all Sōtō factions). To succeed in this goal, a Sōtō temple during the medieval period needed to hold copies of writings by Dōgen or by Keizan or both. Juun Ryōchin 壽雲良椿 (d. 1516), an abbot of Shōbōji 正法寺 explained this condition in scribal colophons inserted at the end of each fascicle of the *Shōbōgenzō* in seventy-five chapters that he acquired in 1512, after his temple's previous copy was lost in a fire.[285] Fires posed a perennial threat. Many temples and their libraries disappeared in flames. Some temples destroyed by fire, such as Daijiji 大慈寺 and Yōkōan 永興 菴 (a.k.a. Yōkōji 永興寺), could not be restored.[286] Only rescued copies of their manuscripts survive to bear witness to their existence.

Below I list all the biographical sources discussed above that can be associated with the early temples mentioned in Table 39. The titles appear in rough chronological order (by date of the original composition) under the name of each temple. An asterisk (*) indicates that the entry is based on colophons or other records, but that the source itself no longer exists at that temple. These lists can be somewhat misleading. First, they cannot include titles of sources that actually existed at a temple but that are not mentioned in extant records. Second, the mention of a source by itself reveals little without information on its provenance and age. Third, even if its provenance and age are known, its contents must be examined in comparison with other manuscript witnesses of the same source and related documents.

---

[285] For an analysis and transcription of these colophons, see Mizuno 1975; cf. Sakurai 1974. Photocopies of the originals can be found in ESST.1.452b, 473b, 512b, 522b, 537a, 563a, 578a, 605b, 618a, 635a, 647a, 665a, 675b, 689b, 704a, 718b, 731b, 749a, 759a, 773a, 784a, 796a, and 808a. Colophons in some manuscripts of the *Denkōroku* tell the same story, since it would be copied along with the *Shōbōgenzō* (see Bodiford 2021, 58–59).

[286] Yōkōan (Kyoto) is more commonly known as Yōkōji 永興寺, a name that can be easily confused with Yōkōji 永光寺 (Noto). In Japanese, the names are written differently but pronounced the same.

Introduction to the SHŌBŌGENZŌ: Supplement 5     227

# List of Key Sources

DŌGEN 道元 (1200–1253):

*Hōkyōki* 寶慶記 (*Baoqing Records*; ca. 1225–1226):
Hōkyōji 寶慶寺 (Echizen); Eiheiji 永平寺 (Echizen)*; Daijiji 大慈寺 (Higo)*; Daijōji 大乘寺 (Kaga)*; Yōkōji 永光寺 (Noto)*; Kōfukuji 廣福寺 (Higo)

*Bendōwa* 辨道話 (*Talk on Pursuing the Way*; 1231):
Shōbōji 正法寺 (Mutsu)

*Shōbōgenzō* (in Chinese; 1235):
—

*Tenzo kyōkun* 典座教訓 (*Admonitions for the Chef*; 1237):
Eiheiji 永平寺 (Echizen)

*Shōbōgenzō* (in 60 chapters; 1233–1245):
Eiheiji 永平寺 (Echizen)*

*Shōbōgenzō* (in 75 chapters; 1233–1252):
Yōkōan 永興菴 (Kyoto)*; Hōkyōji 寶慶寺 (Echizen); Eiheiji 永平寺 (Echizen); Yōkōji 永光寺 (Noto); Shōbōji 正法寺 (Mutsu); Sōjiji 總持寺 (Noto)

*Shōbōgenzō* (in 12 chapters; 1240–1253):
Yōkōji 永光寺 (Noto)

*Dōgen oshō kōroku* 道元和尚廣録 (*Extensive Records of Reverend Dōgen*; 1236–1243, 1245–1252):
Eiheiji 永平寺 (Echizen)

EJŌ 懷弉 (1198–1280):

*Zuimonki* 随聞記 (*Occasional Transcripts*; ca. 1235–1237):
Hōkyōji 寶慶寺 (Echizen)*; Eiheiji 永平寺 (Echizen)*; Daijōji 大乘寺 (Kaga)*; Yōkōji 永光寺 (Noto)*

GIKAI 義介 (1219–1309):

*Goyuigon kiroku* 御遺言記録 (*Dōgen's Final Testament*; 1253, 1254–1255):
Eiheiji 永平寺 (Echizen); Daijiji 大慈寺 (Higo); Daijōji 大乘寺 (Kaga)*; Yōkōji 永光寺 (Noto)*; Kōfukuji 廣福寺 (Higo)*

KEIZAN JŌKIN 瑩山紹瑾 (1264–1325):

*Denkōroku* 傳光録 (*Record of the Transmission of Illumination*; ca. 1300–1301):
Daijōji 大乘寺 (Kaga)*; Sōjiji 總持寺 (Noto)

228 DŌGEN'S *SHŌBŌGENZŌ* VOLUME VIII

*Sanso gyōgōki* 三祖行業記 (*Accounts of the Accomplishments of the Three Patriarchs*; ca. 1280–1390):

Eiheiji 永平寺 (Echizen); Daijōji 大乘寺 (Kaga)*; Sōjiji 總持寺 (Noto)

KENZEI 建撕 (1415–1474):

*Kenzeiki* 建撕記 (*Kenzei's Chronicle*; 1452):

Eiheiji 永平寺 (Echizen)*

# Supplement 6:
## Dates and Calendarial Considerations

Most dates require no explanation. In this introduction, years follow European common era (CE) designations, while months and days follow their local East Asian lunisolar format. Occasionally, this simple format does not work. It might imply the wrong year, an error that can be easily corrected. If the sources present contradictory or incorrect dates, however, the contradictions cannot be corrected but must be explained in terms of historical calendarial practices. Our sources record dates according to five independent methods or in combinations thereof: lunar months and days, solar seasons, sexagesimal cycles, the era names of Japan, and the era names of China.

The traditional lunisolar calendar synchronizes the lunar months with the solar seasons. Months normally should start on the day of the new moon so that the fifteenth day of the month will correspond to a full moon. By convention seasons change on the fifteenth day of the month so that spring runs from 1.15 (i.e., the fifteenth day of the first month) to 4.15, summer runs from 4.15 to 7.15, autumn runs from 7.15 to 10.15, and winter runs from 10.15 to 1.15 of the following year. Months can be either small (with 29 days) or large (30 days). To keep the seasons and months in alignment, every second or third year is an embolismic year, in which an intercalary month (i.e., blue moon; *urū* 閏) appears within one of the four seasons. An intercalary month repeats the same numerical designation as the month prior to it. In numerical notations an intercalary month would be indicated by the abbreviated prefix "int". For example, the third day of the intercalary seventh month in 1243, (written as "1243.int7.3") occurred twenty-nine days later than the date 1243.7.3. These calculations ensure that the winter solstice (*tōji* 冬至) always occurs during the eleventh lunar month.

*Introduction to the* SHŌBŌGENZŌ: *Supplement 6* 229

Lunisolar years do not correspond precisely with their European counterparts. In Asia, the start of each new year accords with the astrological position not just of the sun but also of the moon. In practice, the new year might start three to five weeks later than would be the case for the corresponding year in Europe. Events during the end of the winter season or the twelfth lunisolar month might actually correspond to the following year in Europe. For example, according to the lunisolar calendar, the dates 1243.11.6 and 1243.11.13 and 1243.11.19 all occurred during the same month of the same year. These are the assigned dates for the *Shōbōgenzō* chapters "Plum Blossoms" (53, "Baika"), "The Ten Directions" (55, "Jippō"), and "Seeing Buddha" (56, "Kenbutsu"). In Europe, however, these chapters span different months and years. According to the Gregorian calendar, the lunisolar date 1243.11.13 corresponds to the first day of the year 1244. Nonetheless, it would be misleading to say that Dōgen assigned the date of New Year Day to "The Ten Directions." It is also misleading to say that it was dated to the year 1243. In cases such as this one, when a lunisolar date represents different years in Asia and Europe (but only in these cases) I provide dual dates. Thus, the previous three dates will appear as "1243.11.6"; and as "1243.11.13 [1244.1.1]"; and as "1243.11.19 [1244.1.7]." The dates inside square brackets correspond to the Gregorian calendar (which is used as it more closely aligns to the seasons).

Sexagesimal (i.e., base 60 numerical system) binomial designations commonly apply to years, months, days, and other large sets.[287] A set of ten initial signs (known as trunks, or stems, *kan* 干) combine with twelve secondary signs (known as branches, *shi* 支) to generate sixty digits, which repeat in an infinite progression. Mnemonic (and magical) associations facilitate use of this system, while simultaneously imbuing it with astrological and divinatory significance. The ten trunks denote the five phases (wood, fire, earth, metal, water) of generation, with each phase consisting of a yang (ascending or senior) mode and a yin (descending or junior) mode. The twelve branches entail multiple systems of associations, the most common of which consist of totemic animals (or classes of animals): murine (rat or mouse); bovine (ox, buffalo, or cow); tiger; leporidae (rabbit or hare); dragon; snake; horse; bovidae (sheep or goat); chicken (hen or rooster); dog; swine (hog, pig, or boar). Because the sexagesimal digits repeat in continuous cycles, they provide an accurate

---

[287] Cycles of 60 remain the standard worldwide for counting seconds and minutes; this convention is related to the use of a set of 360 (a multiple of 60) degrees to calculate angles within a circle.

method for calculating days, months, and years without reference to calendarial designations, which, when used by themselves, can be confusing because of their inherent irregularities (e.g., small or large months as well as intercalary months or blue moons). Sexagesimal digits provide especially reliable designations for years, which otherwise are numbered according to specific eras, the names of which frequently change.

Traditionally, only the king could name an era or replace it with a new one (*kaigen* 改元). Every premodern Asian kingdom (or dynasty), therefore, employed its own unique sequence of era names. During Dōgen's lifetime, the customs governing the use of era names differed in Japan and China. In Japan, new era names could be implemented upon proclamation even during the middle of a calendar year. The year 1243, for example, spans two different eras. The beginning of the year corresponds to the fourth year of the Ninji 仁治 (Humane Rule) Era, while the subsequent part of the year corresponds to the first year of the Kangen 寬元 (Magnanimous Foundation) Era. The royal court proclaimed the change of era names on 1243.2.26. People near the capital (Kyoto) probably adopted the new era name within a few days or so. Adoption by people in more distant regions would have been delayed but not for too long. Whether named Ninji 4 or Kangen 1, the sexagesimal designation remained the same: junior water year of the rabbit. In subsequent years, when people wrote accounts of events during the junior water year of the rabbit, one might use the designation "Kangen" for the entire year, including events that occurred prior to 2.26, when the year actually was still known as "Ninji." Japanese historians refer to this kind of irregularity as notation by a "future era" (*mirai nengō* 未來年號). The appearance of a future era name in recollections written long after the event in question typically attracts only editorial comment or correction. That same future era name in a document that purports to have been written at the same time as the event it records suggests that the document must be fraudulent (Hattori 1983).

During the Song dynasty, when Dōgen visited China, the Song government promulgated and implemented new era names on different dates. The year 1224 — a pivotal year for Dōgen in China — provides a convenient example of this difference between Japanese and Chinese customs. In Japan, on 1224.11.20 the court replaced the Jōō 貞應 (Upright Response) Era with a new one named the Gennin 元仁 (Fundamentally Humane) Era. Thus, in Japan, 1224 spans the third year of Jōō and the first year of Gennin. In China, on 1224.8.3, the Song Emperor Ningzong 寧宗 (1168–1224) died. Once the succession was determined, on 11.5,

*Introduction to the* SHŌBŌGENZŌ: *Supplement 6*          231

the Song court proclaimed the start of a new era named Baoqing 寶慶 (J. Hōkyō; Precious Felicity). Nonetheless, the first year of Baoqing does not include the year 1224, despite the fact that the new title "Baoqing" had been proclaimed in 1224 and the installation of a new emperor was celebrated in 1224. In China, the new era officially began on the first day of the lunar New Year, 1225. For historians today, the Chinese custom of implementing the new era at the beginning of the new year seems less confusing: changes of eras coincide with changes of years. For someone used to Japanese customs, however, it easily could have caused confusion.

This kind of confusion can be detected in the contradictory ways that documents attributed to Dōgen report the era names for when he returned from China to Japan. The so-called "Account of Composing the Universal Promotion of the Principles of Seated Meditation" (*Fukan zazen gi senjutsu yurai* 普勸坐禪儀撰述由來), an undated and untitled fragment thought to be a holograph by Dōgen, clearly states: "Previously, during the Karoku Era, when I returned to my kingdom from the land of the Song [China]" (*yo sen karokuchū jūsōdo kihongoku* 予先嘉禄中從宋土歸本國; DZZ.5:2).[288] In Japan, the Karoku Era began 1225.4.20 and officially ended 1227.12.10. In Kyushu, where Dōgen would have landed in Japan, people might have learned about the end of Karoku a few days late. At the very least, this document states that Dōgen must have been back in Japan no later than the twelfth lunar month of 1227. In his "Talk on Pursuing the Way" (*Bendōwa*), however, Dōgen states that, "at the beginning of the Shaoding Era in the Great Song, I returned to my native land" (*daisō jōtei no hajime hongō ni kaerishi* 大宋紹定のはじめ本郷にか へ り し; DZZ.2:461).[289] In China, the Shaoding Era began on the lunar Near Year, 1228. It is possible that the Karoku Era date refers to Dōgen's arrival in Kyushu in 1227, while the Shaoding Era date 1228 refers to his subsequent journey to Kyoto (i.e., his hometown). But it is also possible that "Shaoding" is an instance of a future era name (*mirai nengō*). The Song Chinese administration announced "Shaoding" on 11.6 during the third year of Baoqing (1227). If Dōgen departed China shortly thereafter, he could have learned of the era name "Shaoding"

---

[288] Menzan Zuihō assigned the title *Fukan zazen gi senjutsu yurai* and thereby linked its contents to the *Fukan zazen gi*. See Bielefeldt (1988, 16–22) for a detailed overview.

[289] The same sentence is written somewhat irregularly in the draft version as: *daisō jōtei no hajime hongō ni omomukishi* 大宋紹定の初本郷に趣きし (DZZ.2:537).

232 DŌGEN'S *SHŌBŌGENZŌ* VOLUME VIII

before his departure with plenty of time to arrive in Japan before the end of "Karoku."[290] Ultimately, however, the textual evidence provides no certainty whether Dōgen returned to Japan before the end of 1227 or after the beginning of 1228.

Dōgen's writings contain many other examples of vague or seemingly contradictory dates (Satō Shunkō 1995, 97–98). Possibly, his own recollection of events was imprecise. Most of the surviving records in which he describes his own activities were composed long after the fact. Only his *Hōkyōki* (Baoqing Records) purports to convey a contemporaneous record of events. Sometimes, Dōgen recounts details with such precision — as when he quotes a public sermon by Rujing, including the exact wording of a Chinese verse, in "The Real Marks of the Dharmas" ("Shohō jissō"; DZZ.1:467–469) — that one cannot help but assume that, on some occasions at least, he must have kept contemporaneous notes. Significantly, Dōgen provides a rather complete date for this public sermon by Rujing: Spring, the third month, the second year of Baoqing (1226).

The distinction between Dōgen's casual or vague descriptions of dates and his use of a precise date raises the question of whether or not precise dates might indicate that an event held greater significance for him. Aside from the assigned dates in its colophons, the *Shōbōgenzō* provides precise dates for only two events: 1224.1.21 (when Dōgen was allowed to view the inheritance certificate of Wuji Liaopai; "Shisho"; DZZ.1:431) and 1225.5.1 (when Dōgen entered the abbot's quarters, performed obeisance, and burned incense before Rujing; "Menju"; DZZ.2:54 and 60). The *Hōkyōki* (*Baoqing Records*) provides only one precise date: 1225.7.2 (when Dōgen first entered the abbot's quarters for private instructions from Rujing). And Dōgen's major convocation addresses mention only three precise dates, all three of which appear in the same address (number 251): 1247.8.3 (when Dōgen left Eiheiji for Kamakura), 1248.3.13 (when Dōgen returned to Eiheiji), and 1248.3.14 (when Dōgen presented said address; DZZ.3:166). Dōgen's reticence regarding the precise dates for events in his own life did not apply to his teacher Myōzen. In *Shari sōdenki* 舍利相傳記 (*Account of the Conveyance of Myōzen's Relics*), Dōgen recounts a series of precise dates: when Myōzen departed Kenninji for Dazaifu (1223.2.22), enrolled in Tiantong (1223.5.13), became ill (1225.5.18), died (5.27), and was cremated (5.29; DZZ.7:216).

---

[290] The time required to cross the East China Sea could vary widely, but 10 to 20 days would be expected if nothing went amiss.

# Appendices

# Appendix 1. Tables for Reference

These tables present overviews of the information discussed in Section II, Vicissitudes. The first group (numbers 7–11) focuses on the order and relationship among chapters in various versions of the *Shōbōgenzō*. The second group (numbers 12–17) focuses on terminological issues or textual content. The third group (numbers 18–33) concerns chronological issues. The last group (numbers 34–39) diagrams Zen lineages, with an emphasis on showing how different lineages relate to one another.

ARRANGEMENT OF CHAPTERS: SIXTY VERSUS TWELVE

| 60-chapter *Shōbōgenzō* | 12-chapter *Shōbōgenzō* |
|---|---|
| 8. Karma of the Three Times | no. 8 (*revised version*) |
| *<skip 26 chapters>* | |
| 34. Bringing Forth the Mind of Bodhi | no. 4 |
| 39. Four Horses | no. 9 |
| *<skip 1 chapter>* | 1. The Merit of Leaving Home |
| 41. The Merit of the Kāṣāya | 3. The Merit of the Kāṣāya |
| *<skip 17 chapters>* | |
| 58. The Merit of Leaving Home | no. 1 |
| 59. Offerings to the Buddhas | 5. Offerings to the Buddhas |
| 60. Refuge in the Three Treasures | 6. Refuge in the Three Treasures |
| | 8. Karma of the Three Times |
| | 9. Four Horses |

Table 7. Arrangement of Chapters: Sixty versus Twelve

Three chapters in each compilation align with their counterparts, but only in the twelve-chapter compilation do the other four chapters support one another and the other three. In the 60-chapter compilation, in contrast, these chapters appear disconnected and in random order.

# ARRANGEMENT OF CHAPTERS: SIXTY VERSUS SEVENTY-FIVE

| 60-chapter *Shōbōgenzō* | 75-chapter *Shōbōgenzō* |
| --- | --- |
| 1. The Realized Kōan | 1. The Realized Kōan |
| 2. Mahā-prajñā-pāramitā | 2. Mahā-prajñā-pāramitā |
| 3. Buddha Nature | 3. Buddha Nature |
| 4. Studying the Way with Body and Mind | 4. Studying the Way with Body and Mind |
| 5. This Mind Itself Is the Buddha | 5. This Mind Itself Is the Buddha |
| 6. Deportment of the Practicing Buddha | 6. Deportment of the Practicing Buddha |
| 7. One Bright Pearl | 7. One Bright Pearl |
| 8. Karma of the Three Times | → *reassigned as 12, no. 8* |
| 9. The Old Buddha Mind | 9. The Old Buddha Mind |
| 10. Great Awakening | 10. Great Awakening |
| 11. Principles of Seated Meditation | 11. Principles of Seated Meditation |
| 12. The *Lotus* Turns the *Lotus* | → *discarded* |
| 13. Ocean Seal Samādhi | 13. Ocean Seal Samādhi |
| 14. Sky Flowers | 14. Sky Flowers |
| 15. Radiance | 15. Radiance |
| 16. Sustained Practice, Part 1 | 16. Sustained Practice, Part 1 |
| 17. Sustained Practice, Part 2 | Practice, Part 2 → *renumbered* |
| 18. Avalokiteśvara | 18. Avalokiteśvara |
| 19. The Old Mirror | 19. The Old Mirror |
| 20. Sometimes | 20. Sometimes |
| 21. Confirmation | 21. Confirmation |
| 22. Full Function | 22. Full Function |
| 23. The Moon | 23. The Moon |
| 24. Painted Cake | 24. Painted Cake |
| 25. Sound of Stream, Form of Mountain | 25. Sound of Stream, Form of Mountain |
| 26. Beyond the Buddha | 26. Beyond the Buddha |
| 27. Talking of a Dream within a Dream | 27. Talking of a Dream within a Dream |

Table 8. Arrangement of Chapters: Sixty versus Seventy-five

The first twenty-seven chapters share an almost identical order, except for the elimination of two chapters and the consolidation of two chapters into one.

*Appendix 1: Tables for reference* 237

ARRANGEMENT OF CHAPTERS: SIXTY VERSUS SEVENTY-FIVE, *REDUX*

| 60-chapter *Shōbōgenzō* | 75-chapter *Shōbōgenzō* |
| --- | --- |
| 51. Song of the Dragon | 61. Song of the Dragon |
| 52. Intention of Ancestor Coming from West | 62. Intention of Ancestor Coming from West |
| 53. Bringing Forth the Unsurpassed Mind | 63. Bringing Forth the Mind of Bodhi |
| 54. The Udumbara Blossom | 64. The Udumbara Blossom |
| 55. The Entire Body of the Tathāgata | 65. The Entire Body of the Tathāgata |
|  | *<skip 4 additional chapters>* |
| 56. Empty Space | 70. Empty Space |
|  | *<skip 1 additional chapter>* |
| 57. The Retreat | 72. The Retreat |

Table 9. Arrangement of Chapters: Sixty versus Seventy-five, *redux*

An identical set of seven chapters appears in the same sequence near the end of each compilation. The addition of five new chapters amongst them introduces no major thematic dissonance.

IDENTICAL TITLES FOR TWO DIFFERENT CHAPTERS

| 60-chapter *Shōbōgenzō* | 12-chapter *Shōbōgenzō* |
| --- | --- |
| 34. Bringing Forth the Mind of Bodhi | 4. Bringing Forth the Mind of Bodhi |

| 60-chapter *Shōbōgenzō* | 75-chapter *Shōbōgenzō* |
| --- | --- |
| 53. Bringing Forth the Unsurpassed Mind | 63. Bringing Forth the Mind of Bodhi |

Table 10. Identical Titles for Two Different Chapters

Two separate chapters that began with distinct titles subsequently acquired an identical title even as their contents remained different.

## CHAPTERS OUT OF ORDER IN THE ORIGINAL HONZAN EDITION

Row 1: *expected position according to the descriptive table of contents*
(*kanmoku retsuji* 卷目列次)
Row 2: *actual position in the original Honzan edition*

| Row 1 | Row 2 | |
|---|---|---|
| | | Fascicle: *ketsu* 結 (16) |
| 70 | 85 | Bringing Forth the Mind of Bodhi |
| 71 | 70 | The Complete Body of the Tathāgata |
| 72 | 71 | The King of Samādhis Samādhi |
| 73 | 72 | The Thirty-seven Factors of Bodhi |
| 74 | 73 | Turning the Dharma Wheel |
| | | Fascicle *ka* 果 (17) |
| 75 | 74 | The Samādhi of Self Verification |
| 76 | 75 | Great Practice |
| 77 | 76 | Space |
| 78 | 77 | The Pātra Bowl |
| 79 | 78 | The Retreat |
| | | Fascicle: *ji* 自 (18) |
| 80 | 79 | Reading Other Minds |
| 81 | 80 | The King Requests Saindhava |
| 82 | 81 | Instructions to the Administrative Hall |
| 83 | 82 | Leaving Home |
| 84 | 83 | Karma of the Three Times |
| 85 | 84 | Four Horses |
| | | Fascicle: *jō* 成 (20) |
| 89 | 90 | Deep Faith in Cause and Effect |
| 90 | 93 | The Bhikṣu of the Fourth Dhyāna |
| 91 | 94 | Only Buddhas with Buddhas |
| 92 | 89 | Birth and Death |
| 93 | 91 | The Buddha Way |
| 94 | 92 | Receiving the Precepts |

Table 11. Honzan Edition Chapters Out of Order in the Original

The sequence of chapters in the sewn fascicles of the xylographic Honzan edition (and in the Kōmeisha typeset versions of it) does not correlate with its descriptive table of contents (*kanmoku retsuji* 卷目列次).

Appendix 1: Tables for reference

In the sixteenth, nineteenth, and twentieth fascicles, the unnumbered chapters that would have occupied positions 70, 92, 90, and 91 are out of sequence. This mistake caused the intervening chapters (70 to 85; 89 to 94) to shift positions. Other typeset editions correct this error.

SCHEMATIC EVOLUTION OF DŌGEN'S SHŌBŌGENZŌ

| 1. Early Compositions | *Bendōwa*, "Genjō kōan," *Shōbōgenzō* in Chinese, etc. | | |
| 2. Initial Compilation | — 60-chapter *Shōbōgenzō* — | | |
| 3. Split into Two Halves | reuse 51 chapters | reuse 7 chapters | discard 2 chapters |
| 4. Additional Chapters | add 25 chapters | add 5 chapters | discard rough drafts |
| 5. Final Compilations | 75-chapter *Shōbō-genzō* | 12-chapter *Shōbōgenzō* | |

Table 12. Schematic Evolution of Dōgen's *Shōbōgenzō*

An initial set of sixty numbered chapters was split into two separate compilations, two of the sixty previous chapters were discarded, two chapters previously numbered individually were combined into one, and thirty (5 + 25) additional chapters were added, to thereby produce one *Shōbōgenzō* in twelve chapters and another in seventy-five chapters.

COLOPHONS IN EXEMPLARY MANUSCRIPTS OF THE SHŌBŌGENZŌ

| | 60 Chapters | 75 Chapters | 12 Chapters |
|---|---|---|---|
| Authors | *Tōunji manuscript* | *Ryūmonji manuscript* | *Yōkōji manuscript* |
| Dōgen: assigned dates | 44 | 71 | 2 |
| Ejō: scribal notes | 43 | — | — |

Table 13. Number of Colophons in Exemplary Manuscripts of the *Shōbōgenzō*

These three exemplary textual witnesses provide the most reliable colophons (but not every chapter has one). Colophons not found herein but introduced from other manuscripts demand suspicion.

## 240 DŌGEN'S *SHŌBŌGENZŌ* VOLUME VIII

### THE PREDICATE IN DŌGEN'S COLOPHONS

| *chapter version* | *total* | *assigned chapter number (in each respective compilation)* |
|---|---|---|
| presented to the assembly (*jishu* 示衆) | | |
| *60* | 35: | 2, 3, 4, 5, 7, 14, 15, 19, 22, 24, 25, 26, 27, 29, 30, 31, 32, 35, 37, 38, 40, 41, 42, 43, 44, 45, 46, 47, 50, 51, 52, 53, 56, 57 |
| *75* | 56: | 2, 3, 4, 5, 8, 9, 11, 14, 15, 17, 19, 22, 24, 25, 26, 27, 29, 31, 35, 36, 37, 38, 41, 42, 43, 44, 45, 46, 47, 48, 49, 50, 51, 52, 54, 55, 56, 57, 58, 59, 60, 61, 62, 63, 64, 65, 66, 67, 68, 69, 70, 71, 72, 73, 74, 75 |
| recorded (*ki* 記) | | |
| *60* | 3: | 12, 13, 21 |
| *75* | 7: | 6, 13, 21, 28, 32, 39, 40 |
| written (*sho* 書; *kakite* かきて) | | |
| *60* | 4: | 1, 17, 23, 33 |
| *75* | 5: | 1, 16, 20, 23, 33 |

Table 14. The Predicate in Dōgen's Colophons

Although "present to the assembly" appears more often (56 times) in the seventh-five-chapter version than in the sixty-chapter one, as a percentage of all colophons it actually is less common (seventy-eight versus eighty-five percent of the total).

### COMMON DESIGNATIONS OF THE FIVE MOUNTAINS

*near Qingyuan* 慶元 (*a.k.a. Mingzhou* 明州; *present-day Ningbo* 寧波)

| | |
|---|---|
| Aśoka Temple: | Ayuwangshan 阿育王山, Maofeng Guanglisi 鄮峰廣利寺 |
| Tiantong: | Taibaishan 太白山 (or Mount Tiantong), Tiantong Jingdesi 天童景德寺 |

*near Lin'an* 臨安 (*present-day Hangzhou* 杭州)

| | |
|---|---|
| Jingci: | Nanshan 南山, Jingci Baoen Guangxiaosi 淨慈報恩光孝寺 |
| Jingshan: | Jingshan 徑山, Xingsheng Wanshousi 興聖萬壽寺 |
| Lingyin: | Beishan 北山, Jingde Lingyinsi 景德靈隱寺 |

Table 15. Common Designations of the Five Mountains

Each of the Five Mountains can be referred to by a variety of titles, but herein I use their common designations (see Ishii Shūdō 1980, 330).

*Appendix 1: Tables for reference* 241

## ZEN KŌANS DISCUSSED IN THE *ZUIMONKI*

1. The Way never ceases. Upon awakening (*satori*) one still must practice the Way. Consider the story of Abbot Liangsui inquiring of Magu (道は無窮なり。さとりても、猶行道すべし。良遂座主、麻谷に参し、因縁を思ふべし; *Zuimonki* 1; DZZ.7:56): Magu: A Hoe Hoes the Weeds (麻谷鋤頭鋤草; no. 121; DZZ.5:192).

2. When you listen in such a manner, you will clarify both your truths and your doubts (如是聞時、道理も不審も明めらるる也; *Zuimonki* 1; DZZ.7:63): Dasui: Kalpa Fire Clarity (大隋劫火洞然; no. 24; DZZ.5:138).

3. One time Ejō asked the master [Dōgen], "What is the truth of not being in the dark about cause and effect?" The master replied, "Immovable cause and effect" (或時、弉、師に問て云、如何是、不昧因果底の道理。師云、不動因果也; *Zuimonki* 2; DZZ.7:67): Baizhang: Not in the Dark about Cause and Effect (百丈不昧因果; no. 102; DZZ.5:180).

4. The master [Dōgen] said, "If everyone's like this, Nanquan slays the cat. The assembly could not speak. Thereupon, the cat was slain. Later, Zhaozhou removed his straw sandals, placed them on his head, and left — also a top ranked procedure" (師云、惣て如是ならば、南泉猫兒を截事。大衆已に不道得。即、猫兒を斬却了ぬ。後に趙州、脱草鞋、載出し、又、一段の儀式也; *Zuimonki* 2; DZZ.7:67): Nanquan: Slay the Cat (南泉斬却描兒; no. 181; DZZ.5:218).

5. If it was not a pivot word, then he could not have said that the mountains and rivers, the great earth, are clear and bright mind (若、一轉語に非ずば、山河大地妙淨明心とも云べからず; *Zuimonki* 2; DZZ.7:67): Dawei: Marvelous Clear and Bright Mind (大潙妙淨明心; no. 168; DZZ.5:212).

6. If he says that the buddha is a toad or an earthworm, then believe that they are the buddha and discard your commonplace wisdom (若、佛と云は、蝦蟆蚯蚓ぞ、と云はゞ、蝦蟆蚯蚓を、是を佛と信じて、日比の智惠を捨也; *Zuimonki* 2; DZZ.7:73): Zhangchao: Cease Illusory Inferences (長抄莫妄想緣; no. 20; DZZ.5:136).

7. If, when, facing your teacher, you are genuinely earnest, then no matter what, you can shoot however high and can angle however deep (若は知識に向はん時、實の志をもて、なさんずる時、高とも射べし、深くとも釣ぬべし; *Zuimonki* 3; DZZ.7:95): Lingyun: Fish in the Rivers, Birds in the Mountains (靈雲水魚山鳥; no. K40; DZZ.5:228).

8. Nanyue polished the tile to admonish Mazu for seeking a mirror and for seeking to attain buddhahood (南岳の磚を磨して、鏡を求めしも、馬祖の作佛を求めしを、戒めたり; *Zuimonki* 3; DZZ.7:100): Nanyue: Polish a Tile and Strike the Cart (南嶽磨塼打車; no. 8; DZZ.5:128).

9–10. Seeing blossoms and thereupon clarifying mind, hearing a sound and thereby awakening to the Way, and so forth, also are attaining yourself (見色明心聞聲悟道ごときも、猶、身を得也; *Zuimonki* 3; DZZ.7:103): Lingyun: Peach Blossom and Awaken (靈雲桃花悟道; no. 155; DZZ.5:206) and Yunmen: Hear the Sound and Awaken (雲門聞聲悟道; no. 257; DZZ.5:258).

11. Just like that youth who attended to Reverend Juzhi in ancient times, without seeming to study or to train, without being aware, simply by being perpetually nearby, one attains awakening (昔、俱胝和尚に使へし、一人の童子の如きは、いつ學しいつ修したりとも見へず、不覺ども、久參に近づいしに、悟道す; *Zuimonki* 5; DZZ.7:117): Juzhi: Raise Up One Finger (俱胝竪起一指; no. 245; DZZ.5:254).

12–13. Haven't you read about the one who awakened to the way upon hearing the sound of bamboo or the one who clarified mind with peach blossoms (見ずや、竹の聲に道を悟り、桃の花に心を明めし; *Zuimonki* 5; DZZ.7:118): Xiangyan: Strike Bamboo and Awaken (香嚴擊竹大悟; no. 17; DZZ.5:134) and Lingyun: Peach Blossom and Awaken (no. 155; DZZ.5:206).

14. [Dōgen said:] Present a lecture to your compatriots regarding "Dongshan: Three Pounds of Flax" (洞山の麻三斤を舉揚して、同衆に示すべしと云て; *Zuimonki* 5; DZZ.7:119): Dongshan: Buddha is Three Pounds of Flax (洞山佛麻三斤; no. 172; DZZ.5:212).

15. Regardless of the criticisms of others and regardless of resentments of others, how can we practice our Way? Those who have exhausted themselves can attain it (他のそしりにあはず、他のうらみにあはず、いかでか我が道を行ぜん。徹得困の者、是を得べし; *Zuimonki* 6; DZZ.7:144): Dawei: I've Exhausted Myself for You (大潙爲你徹困; no. 44; DZZ.5:148).

16. This is the meaning of not staying where the Buddha is while rushing away from where the Buddha is not (有佛の處にもとどまらず、無佛の處をもすみやかにはしりすぐ、と云、この心なるべし; *Zuimonki* 5; DZZ.7:147): Zhaozhou: The Buddha Is and the Buddha Is Not (趙州有佛無佛; no. 80; DZZ.5:166).

Table 16. Kōans Discussed in the *Zuimonki*

*Appendix 1: Tables for reference*   243

Dōgen mentions at least sixteen kōans, but he rarely identifies them. He must have expected his students to recognized them simply by their vocabulary. Note: I identify kōans by their titles and serial numbers in the *mokuji* 目次 (DZZ.5, *hanrei* 凡例) of the *Shōbōgenzō* in Chinese script. Upper-case "K" identifies a kōan found only in the draft version owned by the Kanazawa Bunko. The associations listed here rely on Kawamura (1986, 4–14) and Ishii Shūdō (1988, 553–554).

DISTRIBUTION OF KŌANS IN THE *SHŌBŌGENZŌ* IN CHINESE SCRIPT

BUDDHA TO HUINENG: 15 kōans overall, *including* 5 with Śākyamuni Buddha and 2 with Caoxi Huineng

HUINENG LINEAGE:

*Nanyue lineage:* 133 kōans overall, *including* 18 with Zhaozhou Congshen; 9 with Nanquan Puyuan; 5 with Mazu Daoyi; 5 with Baizhang Huaihai; 4 with Nanyue Huairang

*Qingyuan lineage:* 157 kōans overall, *including* 12 with Xuansha Shibei; 10 with Xuefeng Yicun; 6 with Yaoshan Weiyan; 5 with Luohan Guichen; 4 with Qingyuan Xingsi

FIVE HOUSES OF CHAN (ZEN):

*Linji House:* 24 kōans overall, *including* 9 with Linji Yixuan

*Weiyang House:* 36 kōans overall, *including* 19 with Weishan Lingyou and 8 with Yangshan Huiji

*Caodong House:* 39 kōans overall, *including* 11 with Dongshan Liangjie and 9 with Caoshan Benji

*Yunmen House:* 16 kōans overall, *including* 12 with Yunmen Wenyan

*Fayan House:* 8 kōans overall, *including* 4 with Fayan Wenyi

Table 17. The Distribution of Kōans in the *Shōbōgenzō* in Chinese script

Dōgen selected kōans from all Five Houses that, taken together, present a comprehensive overview of the Chan tradition. This table relies on Ishii Shūdō (1988, 554).

## 244     DŌGEN'S *SHŌBŌGENZŌ* VOLUME VIII

### CHRONOLOGICAL PROFILES OF THE THREE SUBSTANTIVE COMPILATIONS

| year | version | total | assigned chapter number (*in each respective compilation*) |
|---|---|---|---|
| 1233 | *60* | 2: | 1, 2 |
| | *75* | 2: | 1, 2 |
| 1238 | *60* | 1: | 7 |
| 1239 | *60* | 2: | 5, 50 |
| | *75* | 3: | 5, 50, **54** |
| 1240 | *60* | 3: | 25, 31, 41 |
| | *75* | 6: | 20, 25, **28**, **29**, 31, **32** |
| | *12* | 1: | 3 |
| 1241 | *60* | 5: | 3, ~~12~~, 19, 30, 35 |
| | *75* | 7: | 3, 6, **8**, 19, 35, **39**, **52** |
| 1242 | *60* | 14: | 4, 10, 13, 15, 17, 18, 21, 22, 24, 26, 27, 29, 33, 40 |
| | *75* | 15: | 4, 10, 13, 15, 16, 17, 18, 21, 22, 24, 26, 27, 33, 36, 40 |
| 1243 | *60* | 13: | 9, 14, 23, 32, 37, 38, 43, 44, 45, 46, 47, 50.v2, 51 |
| | *75* | 23: | 9, 11, 14, 23, 38, 41, **42, 43, 44, 45**, 46, **47**, 48, 49, 50.v2, **51, 53**, 55, 56, 57, 58, 59, 61 |
| 1244 | *60* | 3: | 10.v2, 52, 53 |
| | *75* | 11: | 10.v2, **37, 60**, 62, 63, 64, 65, **66, 67, 68, 69** |
| 1245 | *60* | 3: | 42, 56, 57 |
| | *75* | 5: | 70, 71, 72, **73, 74** |
| 1246 | *75* | 1: | 75 |
| 1250 | *75* | 1: | 50.v3 |
| 1252 | *75* | 1: | 1.v2 |
| 1253 | *12* | 1: | 12 |

*Chapters without dates*

| | | | |
|---|---|---|---|
| -- | *60* | 16: | 6, 8, 11, 16, 18, 20, ~~28~~, 34, 36, 39, 48, 49, 54, 55, 59, 60 |
| -- | *75* | 4: | 7, **12**, 30, **34** |
| -- | *12* | 10: | 1, 2, 4, 5, 6, 7, 8, 9, 10, 11 |

Table 18. Chronological Profiles of the Three Substantive Compilations

*Appendix 1: Tables for reference* 245

Each compilation presents a distinctive chronological profile: 1233–1245 (60-chapter version); 1233–1252 (75-chapter version); and 1240–1253 (12-chapter version). Note that boldface (e.g., **12**, **34**) indicates chapters found only in the seventy-five-chapter compilation; strikethrough (e.g., ~~12~~, ~~28~~) indicates discarded chapters; and versions (e.g., v1, v2) indicate dated revisions of the same chapter.

### VARIANT COLOPHONS FOR CHAPTER 3, "BUDDHA NATURE"

| *author* | *colophon (abbreviated for clarity)* |
| --- | --- |
| | **1. *Shōbōgenzō* in Sixty Chapters** |
| Dōgen | Presented to the assembly (*jishu*), 1241, tenth moon, fourteenth day |
| Ejō | Copied (*shosha*), 1261, summer <br> [Dōgen's] original draft, riddled here and there with overwrites, inserted phrases, and rewritten passages. |
| | **2. *Shōbōgenzō* in Seventy-five Chapters** |
| Dōgen | Presented to the assembly (*jishu*), 1241, tenth moon, fourteenth day |
| | **3. Independent Manuscript: Holograph by Ejō** |
| Dōgen (*deleted*) | ~~Recorded (*ki*), 1241, tenth moon, fourteenth day~~ |
| Ejō | Copied (*shosha*), 1243, first moon, nineteenth day |
| Dōgen (*revised*) | Presented to the assembly (*jishu*), 1241, tenth moon, fourteenth day |
| Ejō | [This is] Dōgen's revised colophon. <br> Collated (*kōgō*), 1258, fourth moon, twenty-fifth day |

Table 19. Variant Colophons for Chapter 3, "Buddha Nature"

The copies (1258 and 1261) by Ejō provide unparalleled data regarding Dōgen's revisions to his earlier draft. For the unabridged colophons, see Bodiford (2019, 255–259), and for a transcription of Ejō's entire holograph complete with strikethroughs (i.e., Dōgen's deletions), see Tsunoda (2001).

# 246 DŌGEN'S *SHŌBŌGENZŌ* VOLUME VIII

### COLOPHONS NOT SHARED ACROSS COMPILATIONS

| *Sixty Chapters* | *Seventy-five Chapters* |
| --- | --- |
| 7. One Bright Pearl, 1238 | 7. One Bright Pearl, *no colophon* |
| 20. Sometimes, *no colophon* | 20. Sometimes, 1240 |
| 6. Deportment of the Practicing Buddha, *no colophon* | 6. Deportment of the Practicing Buddha, 1241 |
| 30. Sūtra Reading, 1241 | 30. Sūtra Reading, *no colophon* |
| 36. The Arhat, *no colophon* | 36. The Arhat, 1242 |
| 11. Principles of Seated Meditation, *no colophon* | 11. Principles of Seated Meditation, 1243 |
| 48. Dharma Nature, *no colophon* | 48. Dharma Nature, 1243 |
| 49. Dhāraṇī, *no colophon* | 49. Dhāraṇī, 1243 |

Table 20. Colophons Not Shared across Compilations

These eight chapters have colophons in one compilation but lack them in the other one even in instances when the chronological profiles of the two compilations overlap.

### CHAPTERS EXCLUSIVE TO THE *SHŌBŌGENZŌ* IN SEVENTY-FIVE CHAPTERS

| | | |
| --- | --- | --- |
| 1239 | 54. | Washing and Purifying |
| 1240 | 28. | Making a Bow and Getting the Marrow |
| | 29. | The Mountains and Waters Sūtra |
| | 32. | Transmitting the Robe |
| 1241 | 8. | The Mind Cannot Be Got |
| | 39. | The Inheritance Certificate |
| | 52. | Buddhas and Ancestors |
| 1243 | 42. | Talking of the Mind, Talking of the Nature |
| | 43. | The Real Marks of the Dharmas |
| 1243 | 44. | The Way of the Buddhas |
| | 45. | Secret Words |
| | 47. | Sūtras of the Buddhas |
| | 51. | Face-to-Face Conferral |
| | 53. | Plum Blossoms |
| | 57. | Extensive Study (revised version) |

*Appendix 1: Tables for reference*  247

1244  37. Spring and Autumn
     60. The Thirty-seven Factors of Bodhi
     66. The King of Samādhis Samādhi
     67. Turning the Dharma Wheel
     68. Great Practice
     69. The Samādhi of Self Verification
1245  73. Reading Other Minds
     74. The King Requests Saindhava
1246  75. Leaving Home
1250  50. Washing the Face (*3d revision*)
1252   1. The Realized Kōan (*compiled-ordered*)

*— colophon and date lacking —*

—  12. Needle of Seated Meditation
—  34. The Teachings of the Buddhas

Table 21. Chapters Exclusive to the *Shōbōgenzō* in Seventy-five Chapters

Twenty of these chapters bear colophons with assigned dates prior to 1245.

AN IDENTICAL DATE FOR THREE DIFFERENT CHAPTERS

| *Sixty Chapters* | *Seventy-five Chapters* | *Twelve Chapters* |
|---|---|---|
| 20. Sometimes<br>  *no colophon* → | 20. Sometimes<br>  (written; *sho*) | |
| – (*not included*) | 32. Transmitting the<br>Robe (recorded; *ki*) | |
| 3. The Merit of the<br>Kāṣāya (presented to<br>the assembly;<br>*jishu*)→ | | 3. The Merit of the<br>Kāṣāya (presented<br>to the assembly;<br>*jishu*) |

Table 22. An Identical Date for Three Different Chapters

Could Dōgen have composed all three chapters on the same date (1240.10.1)?

248     DŌGEN'S *SHŌBŌGENZŌ* VOLUME VIII

EARLY COMPOSITIONS AND EVENTS

| Composition or Event | Date | Holiday |
|---|---|---|
| *Talk on Pursuing the Way* | 1231.8.15 | Harvest Moon (*chūshū* 中秋) |
| "Mahā-prajñā-pāramitā" | 1233.4.15 to 7.15 | Summer Retreat day (*ango jitsu* 安居日) |
| *Universal Promotion of the Principles of Seated Meditation* | 1233.7.15 | Midyear Moon (*chūgen* 中元) |
| "The Realized Kōan" | 1233.8.15 | Harvest Moon (*chūshū* 中秋) |
| *Advice on Studying the Way* | 1234.2.28 | Clear Brightness (*seimei* 清明) |
| — Ejō arrived | 1234.11 | |
| *Shōbōgenzō* in Chinese script | 1235.11.3 | First Yang (*ichiyō kasetsu* 一陽佳節) |
| — Dōgen founded Kōshōji | 1236.10.15 | Lateyear Moon (*kagen* 下元) |

Table 23. Early Compositions and Events

Dōgen assigned a significant date, a holiday or full moon, to each one of his early compositions.

CONVOCATION ADDRESSES IN THE *EXTENSIVE RECORDS OF REVEREND DŌGEN*

| Year | Entry numbers | Sub-total | Notable Events |
|---|---|---|---|
| 1236 | – | – | *Kōshōji founded*, 1236.10.15 |
| 1237 | ? | ? | first summer retreat |
| 1238 | ? | ? | |
| 1239 | ? | ? | |
| 1240 | ? | 31 | total of 31 convocations, 1237 to 1240 |
| 1241 | 32 to 65, 76 to 89 | 48 | |
| 1242 | 90 to 115 | 26 | Darumashū joined; Rujing's recorded sayings received |
| 1243 | 66 to 75, 116 to 126 | 21 | departed for Echizen, 1243.7.16 |

| 1243.7 | – | – | *Echizen Province* |
|---|---|---|---|
| 1244 | – | – | Daibutsuji founded, 1244.7.18 |
| 1245 | 127 to 141 | 15 | first summer retreat, 1245.4.15 |
| 1246 | 142 to 215 | 74 | Daibutsuji renamed Eiheiji, 1246.6.15 |
| 1247 | 216 to 250 | 35 | Dōgen departed for Kamakura, 1247.8.2 |
| 1248 | – | – | *After Kamakura* |
| 1248.3 | 251 to 275, 277 to 302 | 51 | Dōgen returned to Eiheiji, 1248.3.13 |
| 1249 | 303 to 360 | 58 | |
| 1250 | 361 to 411, 413 | 52 | Chinese Buddhist Canon received |
| 1251 | 276, 412, 414 to 480 | 69 | |
| 1252 | 481 to 531 | 51 | |
| 1253 | – | – | *Dōgen departed for Kyoto*, 1253.8.5 |

Table 24. Convocation Addresses in the *Extensive Records of Reverend Dōgen*

These dates rely on Itō Shūken (1979; 1980) with refinements by Ishii Shūdō (1991b, 328–330). Itō could not determine plausible dates for entries 1–31, during the years 1237 to 1240.

CONVOCATION ADDRESSES RELATED TO HONGZHI AND/OR RUJING

| Year | annu- al total | Hongzhi subtotal; | Hongzhi entry nos. | Rujing subtotal; | Rujing entry nos. |
|---|---|---|---|---|---|
| *by* 1240 | 31 | 5 | 10, 13, 14, 15, 20 | 1 | 18 |
| 1241 | 48 | 3 | 52, 77, 78 | 2 | 33, 48, |
| 1242 | 26 | 2 | 90, 101 | 2 | 105, 115 |
| 1243 | 21 | – | | – | |
| 1244 | – | – | | – | |
| 1245 | 15 | 1 | 135 | 3 | 128, 135, 136 |
| 1246 | 74 | 12 | 142, 143, 152, 155, 158, 174, 180, 183, 186, 187, 203, 206 | 6 | 147, 149, 167, 179, 184, 194 |

| Year | annu- al total | Hongzhi subtotal; | Hongzhi entry nos. | Rujing subtotal; | Rujing entry nos. |
|---|---|---|---|---|---|
| 1247 | 35 | 5 | 216, 222, 226, 227, 236 | 3 | 238, 239, 249 |
| 1248 | 51 | 9 | 257, 261, 263, 264, 266, 269, 285, 296, 299 | 4 | 272, 274, 291, 292 |
| 1249 | 58 | 13 | 303, 307, 320, 322, 326, 327, 329, 330, 337, 340, 341, 344, 345 | 10 | 306, 316, 318, 319, 341, 342, 347, 348, 358, 360 |
| 1250 | 52 | 5 | 377, 397, 400, 403, 404 | 8 | 375, 379, 384, 390, 391, 394, xxx,xxx |
| 1251 | 69 | 9 | 417, 419, 421, 425, 426, 429, 434, 465, 468 | 12 | 276, 432, 436, 437, 449, 450, 451, 454, 456, 463, 469, 470 |
| 1252 | 51 | 5 | 492, 494, 498, 501, 514 | 9 | 501, 502, 503, 514, 515, 522, 523, 530, 531 |
| Totals | 531 | 69 | related to Hongzhi | 60 | related to Rujing |

Table 25. Convocation Addresses related to Hongzhi and/or Rujing

Hongzhi Zengjue (1091–1157) and Rujing (1162–1227) are the two individuals mentioned and quoted most often by Dōgen. This relies on Ishii Shūdō (1991b, 334–335, 336).

*Appendix 1: Tables for reference*　　　251

PERIODIZATION OF *SHŌBŌGENZŌ* CHAPTERS

1. Before Kōshōji
　　1233　　2 chapters　　subtotal: 2 chapters

2. At Kōshōji
　　1238　　1 chapter
　　1239　　3
　　1240　　7
　　1241　　8　　　　　1 revision
　　1242　15
　　1243　　4　　　　　subtotal: 38 chapters and 1 revision

3. Echizen Province
　　1243　18 chapters　　1 revision
　　1244　　9　　　　　2
　　1245　　5
　　1246　　1　　　　　subtotal: 33 chapters and 3 revisions

4. After Kamakura
　　1250　　–　　　　　1 revision
　　1252　　–　　　　　1
　　1253　　1 chapter　subtotal:　1 chapter and 2 revisions

Total: 74 chapters and 6 revisions

Table 26. Periodization of *Shōbōgenzō* Chapters

Chapters simply arranged by locations and ordered by the assigned dates of composition and revision in the colophons by Dōgen.

DATED *SHŌBŌGENZŌ* CHAPTERS, PART 1: BEFORE KŌSHŌJI

|  |  | *seventy-five* | *sixty* |
|---|---|---|---|
| 1233 summer | Mahā-prajñā-pāramitā | 2 | 2 |
| 1233.8.15 | The Realized Kōan | 1 | 1 |
|  | — revised 1252 | 1 | – |

Table 27. Dated *Shōbōgenzō* Chapters, Part 1: Before Kōshōji

Only two chapters date from this early period, when Dōgen first recruited students and before he had begun to order his essays as a *Shōbōgenzō* in Japanese script.

# DATED *SHŌBŌGENZŌ* CHAPTERS, PART 2: AT KŌSHŌJI

| | | *seventy-five* | *sixty* | *twelve* |
|---|---|---|---|---|
| 1238.4.18 | OneBright Pearl | 7 | 7 | |
| 1239.5.25 | This Mind Itself Is the Buddha | 5 | 5 | |
| 1239.10.23 | Washing the Face | 50 | 50 | |
| 1239.11.6 | Washing and Purifying | 54 | – | |
| 1240.3.7 | Making a Bow and Getting the Marrow | 28 | – | |
| 1240.4.20 | Sound of the Stream, Form of the Mountain | 25 | 25 | |
| 1240.8.15 | Do No Evils | 31 | 31 | |
| 1240.10.1 | Sometimes | 20 | 20 | |
| 1240.10.1 | The Merit of the Kāṣāya | – | 41 | 3 |
| 1240.10.1 | Transmitting the Robe | 32 | – | |
| 1240.10.18 | The Mountains and Waters Sūtra | 29 | – | |
| 1240.int10.30 | — revised: Making a Bow and Getting the Marrow | – | – | |
| 1241.1.13 | Buddhas and Ancestors | 52 | – | |
| 1241.3.27 | The Inheritance Certificate | 39 | – | |
| 1241.summer | The *Lotus* Turns the *Lotus* | – | 12 | |
| 1241.9.9 | The Old Mirror | 19 | 19 | |
| 1241.9.30 | Sūtra Reading | 30 | 30 | |
| 1241.10.11 | Deportment of the Practicing Buddha | 6 | 6 | |
| 1241.10.14 | Buddha Nature | 3 | 3 | |
| 1241.11.16 | Spiritual Powers | 35 | 35 | |
| 1241.12.12 | — revised: The Inheritance Certificate [1242.1.21] | – | – | |
| 1242.1.28 | Great Awakening | 10 | 10 | |
| 1242.3.20 | Such | 17 | 29 | |
| 1242.3.23 | Beyond the Buddha | 26 | – | |
| 1242.4.5 | Sustained Practice | 16A, 16B | 16, 17 | |
| 1242.4.20 | The Ocean Seal Samadhi | 13 | 13 | |
| 1242.4.25 | Confirmation | 21 | 21 | |
| 1242.4.26 | Avalokiteśvara | 16 | 16 | |
| 1242.5.15 | The Arhat | 36 | 36 | |
| 1242.5.21 | The Cypress Tree | 40 | 40 | |
| 1242.6.2 | Radiance | 15 | 15 | |
| 1242.9.9 | Studying the Way with the Body and Mind | 4 | 4 | |
| 1242.9.21 | Talking of a Dream within a Dream | 27 | 27 | |
| 1242.10.15 | Sayings | 33 | 33 | |
| 1242.11.5 | Painted Cake | 24 | 24 | |
| 1242.12.17 | Full Function [1243.1.16] | 22 | 22 | |

| | | seventy-five | sixty | twelve |
|---|---|---|---|---|
| 1243.1.6 | The Moon | 23 | 23 | |
| 1243.3.10 | Sky Flowers | 23 | 23 | |
| 1243.4.29 | The Old Buddha Mind | 9 | 9 | |
| 1243.7.7 | Twining Vines | 38 | 38 | |

Table 28. Dated *Shōbōgenzō* Chapters, Part 2: At Kōshōji

Dōgen composed at least thirty-eight chapters while teaching his initial monastic community. As indicated by the columns on the right, he assigned the same chapter numbers to twenty-seven of them in both the sixty- and seventy-five-chapter compilations.

DATED *SHŌBŌGENZŌ* CHAPTERS, PART 3: ECHIZEN PROVINCE

| | | seventy-five | sixty | twelve |
|---|---|---|---|---|
| 1243.int7.1 | The Three Realms Are Only Mind | 41 | 32 | |
| 1243 | Talking of the Mind, Talking of the Nature | 42 | – | |
| 1243.9 | The Real Marks of the Dharmas | 43 | – | |
| 1243.9.16 | The Way of the Buddhas | 44 | – | |
| 1243.9.20 | Secret Words | 45 | – | |
| 1243.9 | Sūtras of the Buddhas | 47 | – | |
| 1243.10.20 | The Insentient Preach the Dharma | 46 | 46 | |
| 1243.10 | Dharma Nature | 48 | 48 | |
| 1243 | Dhāraṇī | 49 | 49 | |
| 1243.10.20 | — revised: Washing the Face | 50 | 50 | |
| 1243.10.23 | Face to Face Conferral | 51 | – | |
| 1243.11 | Principles of Seated Meditation | 11 | 11 | |
| 1243.11.6 | Plum Blossoms | 53 | – | |
| 1243.11.13 | The Ten Directions [1244.1.1] | 55 | 45 | |
| 1243.11.19 | Seeing Buddhas [1244.1.7] | 56 | 47 | |
| 1243.11.27 | Extensive Study [1244.1.15] | 57 | 37 | |
| 1243.12.17 | The Eye [1244.2.4] | 58 | 44 | |
| 1243.12.17 | Everyday Matters [1244.2.4] | 59 | 43 | |
| 1243.12.25 | Song of the Dragon [1244.2.12] | 61 | 51 | |
| 1244.1.27 | — revised: Great Awakening | 10 | 10 | |
| 1244.2.4 | The Intention of the Ancestral Master's Coming from the West | 62 | 52 | |
| 1244.2.12 | The Udumbara Blossom | 64 | 54 | |

DŌGEN'S *SHŌBŌGENZŌ* VOLUME VIII

| | | seventy-five | sixty | twelve |
|---|---|---|---|---|
| 1244.2.14 | Bringing Forth / the Mind of Bodhi / the Unsurpassed Mind | 63 | 53 | |
| 1244.2.15 | The Complete Body of the Tathāgata | 65 | 55 | |
| 1244.2.15 | The King of Samādhis Samādhi | 66 | – | |
| 1244.2.24 | The Thirty-seven Factors of Bodhi | 60 | – | |
| 1244.2.27 | Turning the Dharma Wheel | 67 | – | |
| 1244.2.29 | The Samādhi of Self Verification | 69 | – | |
| 1244.3.9 | Great Practice | 68 | – | |
| 1244 | — revised Spring and Autumn | 37 | – | |
| 1245.3.6 | Space | 70 | 56 | |
| 1245.3.12 | The Pātra Bowl | 71 | 42 | |
| 1245.6.13 | The Retreat | 72 | 57 | |
| 1245.7.4 | Reading Other Minds | 73 | – | |
| 1245.10.22 | The King Requests Saindhava | 74 | – | |
| 1246.9.15 | Leaving Home | 75 | – | |

Table 29. Dated *Shōbōgenzō* Chapters, Part 3: Echizen Province

Dōgen composed at least thirty-three chapters and revised three after relocating his monastic community. During this period, he definitely began to order his essays as a *Shōbōgenzō* in Japanese script.

## SEQUENTIAL CHAPTERS

| | | seventy-five | sixty | twelve |
|---|---|---|---|---|
| 1243.int7.1 | The Three Realms Are Only Mind | 41 | 32 | |
| 1243 | Talking of the Mind, Talking of the Nature 42 | – | | |
| 1243.9 | The Real Marks of the Dharmas | 43 | – | |
| 1243.9.16 | The Way of the Buddhas | 44 | – | |
| 1243.9.20 | Secret Words | 45 | – | |
| 1243.9 | Sūtras of the Buddhas | 47 | – | |
| 1243.10.20 | The Insentient Preach the Dharma | 46 | 46 | |
| 1243.10 | Dharma Nature | 48 | 48 | |
| 1243 | Dhāraṇī | 49 | 49 | |
| 1243.10.20 | — revised: Washing the Face | 50 | 50 | |
| 1243.10.23 | Face to Face Conferral | 51 | – | |
| 1243.11.6 | Plum Blossoms | 53 | – | |
| 1243.11.13 | The Ten Directions [1244.1.1] | 55 | 45 | |
| 1243.11.19 | Seeing Buddhas [1244.1.7] | 56 | 47 | |
| 1243.11.27 | Extensive Study [1244.1.15] | 57 | 37 | |
| 1243.12.17 | The Eye [1244.2.4] | 58 | 44 | |

*Appendix 1: Tables for reference* 255

| | | *seventy-five* | *sixty* | *twelve* |
|---|---|---|---|---|
| 1243.12.17 | Everyday Matters [1244.2.4] | 59 | 43 | |
| 1243.12.25 | Song of the Dragon [1244.2.12] | 61 | 51 | |
| 1244.2.4 | The Intention of the Ancestral Master's Coming from the West | 62 | 52 | |
| 1244.2.12 | The Udumbara Blossom | 64 | 54 | |
| 1244.2.14 | Bringing Forth / the Mind of Bodhi / the Unsurpassed Mind | 63 | 53 | |
| 1244.2.15 | The Complete Body of the Tathāgata | 65 | 55 | |
| 1244.2.15 | The King of Samādhis Samādhi | 66 | – | |
| 1244.2.27 | Turning the Dharma Wheel | 67 | – | |
| 1244.2.29 | The Samādhi of Self Verification | 69 | – | |
| 1244.3.9 | Great Practice | 68 | – | |
| 1245.3.6 | Space | 70 | 56 | |
| 1245.3.12 | The Pātra Bowl | 71 | 42 | |
| 1245.6.13 | The Retreat | 72 | 57 | |
| – | The Merit of Leaving Home | – | 58 | 1 |
| – | Offerings to the Buddhas | – | 59 | 5 |
| – | Refuge in the Treasures of Buddha, Dharma, Saṃgha | – | 60 | 6 |
| 1245.7.4 | Reading Other Minds | 73 | – | |
| 1245.10.22 | The King Requests Saindhava | 74 | – | |
| 1246.9.15 | Leaving Home | 75 | – | |

Table 30. Sequential Chapters

The same chapters from Echizen Province (as in the previous table), with the ones out of sequence by more than one place removed and three undated ones inserted. These three share similarities with "The Retreat" and, in the sixty-chapter compilation, follow it in numerical sequence.

256  DŌGEN'S *SHŌBŌGENZŌ* VOLUME VIII

NON-SEQUENTIAL CHAPTERS

*Among the Seventy-five-Chapter Version*          seventy-five  sixty

| 1243.11 | Principles of Seated Meditation | 11 | 11 |
| ca. 1243ff | — revised: Buddha Nature | 3 | 3 |
| 1244.1.27 | — revised: Great Awakening | 10 | 10 |
| 1244 | — revised Spring and Autumn | 37 | – |
| 1244.2.24 | The Thirty-seven Factors of Bodhi | 60 | – |

*Among the Sixty-Chapter Version*

| 1243.12.27 | Extensive Study | 57 | 37 |
| 1243.12.17 | The Eye | 58 | 44 |
| 1243.12.17 | Everyday Matters | 59 | 43 |
| 1245.3.12 | The Pātra Bowl | 71 | 42 |

Table 31. Non-Sequential Chapters

The numerous chapters with sequential dates and numbers direct attention toward chapters that do not fit this pattern.

DATED *SHŌBŌGENZŌ* CHAPTERS, PART 4: AFTER KAMAKURA

|  |  | seventy-five | sixty | twelve |
|---|---|---|---|---|
| 1250.1.11 | — revised: Washing the Face | 50 | – | – |
| 1252 | — revised: The Realized Kōan | 1 | – | – |
| 1253.1.6 | The Eightfold Awareness of the Great Person | – | – | 12 |

Table 32. Dated *Shōbōgenzō* Chapters, Part 4: After Kamakura

Little direct evidence relates to Dōgen's work on the *Shōbōgenzō* after his return from Kamakura. The existence of two dated revisions and one new draft confirm that he had continued working on it.

*Appendix 1: Tables for reference* 257

## Successive Abbots of Kenchōji

| | name | background | term(s) as abbot |
|---|---|---|---|
| 1 | Lanxi Daolong 蘭溪道隆 | C | 1249–62; 1264–74; 1278 |
| 2 | Wuan Puning 兀菴普寧 | C | 1262–64 |
| 3 | Daxiū Zhengnian 大休正念 | C | 1274–78 |
| 4 | Yiweng Shaoren 義翁紹仁 | C | 1278–79 |
| 5 | Wuxue Zuyuan 無學祖元 | C | 1278–79; 1282 |
| 6 | Ikō Dōnen 葦航道然 | tr. | 1286–91; 1294–96 |
| 7 | Jingtang Jueyuan 鏡堂覺圓 | C | 1291–94 |
| 8 | Gidon Kūshō 癡鈍空性 | | 1296–(?) |
| 9 | Sōden Dōkai 桑田道海 | | (?)–1299 |
| 10 | Yishan Yining 一山一寧 | C | 1299–1303; 1306–07; 1302–03 |
| 11 | Youjian Zitan 酉澗子曇 | C | 1303–06 |
| 12 | Muin Enhan 無隱圓範 | tr. | 1307 |
| 13 | Nanpo Shōmyō 南浦紹明 | tr. | 1307–08 |
| 14 | Kōhō Kennichi 高峰顯日 | | 1309–10 |
| 15 | Yakuō Tokuken 約翁德儉 | tr. | 1310–15 |
| 16 | Dongli Dehui 東里德慧 | C | 1315–16~ |
| 17 | Taiko Segen 太古世源 | | (?)–1318 |
| 18 | Dongming Huiri 東明慧日 | C | 1318–19; 1322–27; 1336–37(?) |
| 19 | Lingshan Daoyin 靈山道隱 | C | 1319–20 |
| 20 | Nanzan Shiun 南山士雲 | | 1320–22 |
| 21 | Tōzan Tokusen 東山德璇 | | 1322 |
| 22 | Qingzhuo Zhengcheng 清拙正澄 | C | 1327–30 |
| 23 | Pengji Chujun 朋極楚俊 | C | 1330–32; 1333 |
| 24 | Kengai Kōan 嶮崖巧安 | | 1332–33 |

Table 33. Successive Abbots of Kenchōji

Of the first twenty-four abbots at Kenchōji, from 1263 to 1337, thirteen came from China (C) and five were Japanese who had trained (tr.) in China. Together these two groups occupied the abbotship more than seventy percent of the time (Enomoto 2013, 25–26).

## The Five Houses of Chan

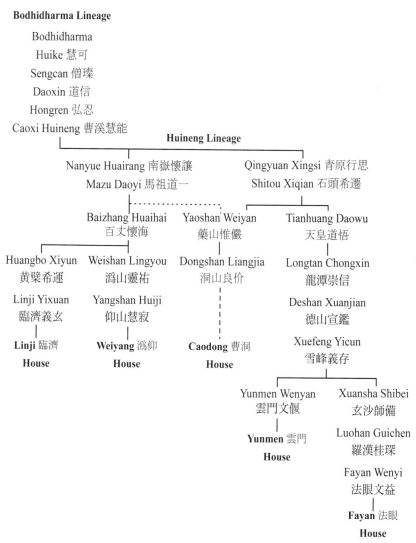

Table 34. The Five Houses of Chan

Traditional genealogical histories of the Chan tradition depict it in terms of five houses, each with its own ancestors and styles of teaching.

*Appendix 1: Tables for reference*     259

## Dōgen within the Eisai Faction

Linji Yixuan 臨濟義玄 (J. Rinzai Gigen; d. 866)     **Linji Lineage**
  Yuezhu Zujian 月珠祖鑑 (dates unknown)
  Baoying Huiyong 寶應慧顒 (d. 953)
  Fengxue Yanzhao 風穴延沼 (897-973)
  Shoushan Shengnian 首山省念 (926-994)
  Fenyang Shanzhao 汾陽善昭 (946-1023)
  Shishuang Chuyuan 石霜楚圓 (986-1039)

    ↓     **Huanglong Branch**
Huanglong Huinan 黃龍慧南 (Oryu Enan; dates unknown)
  Huitang Zuxin 晦堂祖心 (1025-1100)
  Changling Shouzhuo 長靈守卓 (1066-1124)
  Wushi Jiechen 無示介諶 (1080-1148)
  Xinwen Tanfen 心聞曇賁 (dates unknown)
  Xuan Huaichang 虛庵懷敞 (J. Kian Esho; dates unknown)

    ↓
Myōan Eisai 明庵榮西 (1141–1215), Yōjō-bō 葉上房     **Eisai Faction**
  ⌐→ Taikō Gyōyū 退耕行勇 (1163-1241), Shōgon-bō 莊嚴房
    ⌐→ Daikatsu Ryōshin 大歇了心 (d. 1257), Hannya-bō 般若房
    ⌐→ Ryūzen 隆禪 (dates unknown), Butsugen-bō 佛眼房
    └→ Muhon Kakushin 無本覺心 (1207–1298), Shinchi-bō 心地房
  ⌐→ Ten'an Gen'yū 天庵源祐 (dates unknown)
    └→ Saiō Shōku 濟翁證救 (d. 1260), Kudoku-bō 功德房
  ⌐→ Eichō 榮朝 (1165–1247), Shakuen-bō 釋圓房
    ⌐→ Zōsō Rōyo 藏叟朗譽 (1194–1277), Higan-bō 悲願房
    └→ Enni 圓爾 (a.k.a. Ben'en 辯圓; 1201–1280), Enni-bō 圓爾房
      └→ Mujū Dōgyō 無住道曉 (1226–1312), Ichien-bō 一圓房
  ⌐→ Myōzen 明全 (1184–1225), Butsuju-bō 佛樹房
    └→ **Dōgen** 道元 (1200–1253), Buppō-bō 佛法房
  ⌐→ Dōshō 道聖 (d. 1241), Santai-bō 三諦房
  ⌐→ Enrin 圓琳 (b. 1187), Ichiyō-bō 一葉房
  ⌐→ Gonrin 嚴琳 (dates unknown), Renjitsu-bō 蓮實房
  └→ Zenkyō 禪慶 (dates unknown), Zen'yō-bō 禪陽房

Table 35. Dōgen within the Eisai Faction

Eisai's faction provided the social and institutional basis for the initial establishment of Zen practice in Japan, but several of its members (such as Dōgen) introduced other Zen lineages from China.

# 260 DŌGEN'S *SHŌBŌGENZŌ* VOLUME VIII

## DŌGEN AMONG THE LINJI LINEAGE

Linji Yixuan 臨濟義玄 (d. 866)　　　　　　　　**Linji Lineage**
　Yuezhu Zujian 月珠祖鑑 (dates unknown)
　Baoying Huiyong 寶應慧顒 (d. 953)
　Fengxue Yanzhao 風穴延沼 (897–973)
　Shoushan Shĕngnian 首山省念 (926–994)
　Fenyang Shanzhao 汾陽善昭 (946–1024)
　Ciming Chuyuan 慈明楚圓 (986–1024)
　　　↓　　　　　　　　　　　　　**Yangqi Branch**
Yangqi Fanghui 楊岐方會 (992–1049)
　Baiyun Shouduan 白雲守端 (1025–1073)
　Wuzu Fanghui 五祖法演 (d. 1204)　　　*Buddhists of Japan*
　│　　　　　　　　　　　　　* also within Eisai faction
　├→ Yuanwu Keqin 圜悟克勤 (1063–1135)
　│　　　├→ Xiatang Huiyuan 瞎堂慧遠 (1103-1176)　　→ *Kakua*
　│　　　├→ Dahui Zonggao 大慧宗杲 (1089–1163)
　│　　　　└→ Zhuoan Deguang 拙庵德光 (1121–1203)　　→ *Nōnin*
　│　　　　　　├→ Wuji Liaopai 無際了派 (1150–1224)　→ ***Dōgen****
　│　　　　　　└→ Zheweng Ruyan 浙翁如琰 (1151–1225)
　│　　└→Huqiu Shaolong 虎丘紹隆 (1077–1136)
　│　　　　Yingan Tanhua 應庵曇華 (1103–1163)
　│　　　　　├→ Poan Zuxian 破菴祖先 (1136–1211)
　│　　　　　│　Wuzhun Shifan 無準師範 (1177–1249)　　→*Enni**
　│　　　　　└→ Mian Xianjie 密庵咸傑 (1118-1186)
　│　　　　　　　Songyuan Chongyue 松源崇嶽 (1132–1202)
　│　　　　　　　Wuming Huixing 無明慧性 (1162–1237)
　│　　　　　　　　　　　　　　　　→*Lanxi Daolong*
　├→ Foyan Qingyuan 佛眼清遠 (1067–1121)
　│　　　Xuetang Daoxing 雪堂道行 (1089–1151)
　│　　　Huian Huiguang 晦庵慧光 (dates unknown)
　│　　　Mengan Yuancong 蒙庵元聰 (1136–1209)　　→*Shunjō*
　└→ Kaifu Daoning 開福道寧 (1053–1113)
　　　Dahong Zuzheng 大洪祖證 (dates unknown)
　　　Yuelin Shiguan 月林師觀 (1143–1217)
　　　Wumen Huikai 無門慧開 (1183–1260)　　→*Muhon Kakushin**

Table 36. Dōgen among the Linji Lineage

Dōgen's milieu included prominent members of the Yangqi branch (near the left margin) as well as their disciples (along the right margin) who introduced their lineages to Japan.

*Appendix 1: Tables for reference*

## Dōgen within the Caodong Lineage

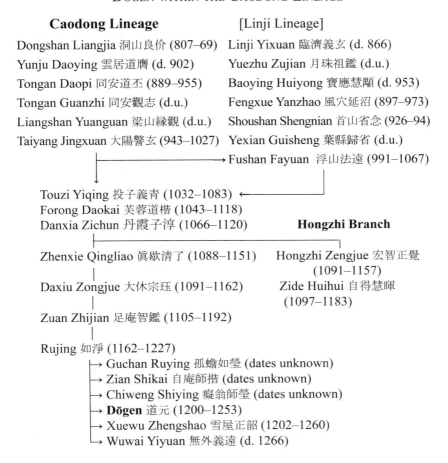

Table 37. Dōgen within the Caodong Lineage

The episode by which Touzi Yiqing restored the Caodong lineage of Taiyang Jingxuan via the intervention of Fushan Fayuan was controversial in its time and remains so today.

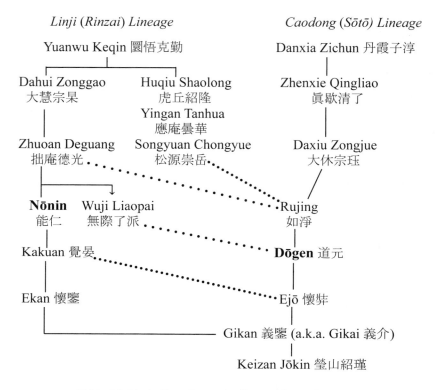

Table 38. Early Sōtō Intermingling with Nōnin's Faction

Overlapping, interlineage relationships were not exceptional, but occurred repeatedly.

## EARLY SŌTŌ TEMPLES AND LINEAGE AFFILIATIONS

| *lineage chart* | *main temple* | *location* |
|---|---|---|
| Dōgen | | |
| └→ Senne | | |
|     └→ Kyōgō | Yōkōan | Kyoto |
| └→ Ejō | | |
|     ├→ Jakuen | Hōkyōji | Echizen |
|        └→ Giun . . . Kenzei | Eiheiji | Echizen |
|     ├→ Gien | | |
|     ├→ Kangan Giin | Daijiji | Higo |
|     └→ Gikai | | |
|        └→ Keizan Jōkin | | |
|           ├→ Meihō Sotetsu | Yōkōji | Noto |
|              └→ Daichi | Kōfukuji | Higo |
|           ├→ Mutei Ryōshō | Shōbōji | Mutsu |
|           └→ Gasan Jōseki | Sōjiji | Noto |

Table 39. Early Sōtō Temples and Lineages

Any one of these temples potentially could have become the headquarters of its own faction (or of all Sōtō factions). Manuscript traditions distributed across temples of disparate lineage affiliations likely represent broadly shared institutional memories.

# Appendix 2. Key Dates in the Life of Dōgen and His *Shōbōgenzō*

### A. Events Prior to Dōgen

| | |
|---|---|
| 1168.4 | Eisai (1141–1215; a.k.a. Yōjō-bō) travels to China |
| 1170 | Kakua (b. 1141) travels to China |
| 1173 | Kakua returns from China |
| 1184 | Taikō Gyōyū (1163–1241; a.k.a. Shōgon-bō) travels to China |
| 1185 | Minamoto Yoritomo (1147–1199) establishes a military administration in Kamakura |
| 1187 | Eisai travels to China again |
| 1191.7 | Eisai returns from China |
| 1194 | Zen of Eisai and Nōnin banned by royal decree in Kyoto |
| 1195 | Eisai founds Shōfukuji in Hakata near the town of Dazaifu (in Kyushu) |
| 1198 | Eisai composes *Kōzen gokokuron*, his defense of Zen practice in Japan |
| 1199 | Shunjō (1166–1227; a.k.a. Gazen-bō) travels to China |

### B. Events during Dōgen's Life

| | |
|---|---|
| 1200 | Dōgen born |
| 1200 | Eisai establishes Jufukuji in Kamakura |
| 1202 | Eisai establishes Kenninji in Kyoto |
| 1204.7.18 | Minamoto Yoriie (1182–1204), the second shogun, assassinated by the Hōjō |
| 1211 | Eisai establishes the Zenjōin (a.k.a. Kongō Zanmaiin) on Mount Kōya |
| 1211 | Ryūzen (a.k.a. Butsugen-bō) becomes a student of Taikō Gyōyū at Kongō Zanmaiin |
| 1211 | Shunjō returns from China, initially resided at Kenninji |
| 1215.7.5 | Eisai dies |
| 1217 | Dōgen enters Kenninji and begins to study Zen under Myōzen (1184–1225) |
| 1219.1.27 | Minamoto Sanetomo (1192–1219) assassinated by Kugyō (1200–1219) |
| 1221.5 | Jōkyū Disturbance: conflict between the court in Kyoto and the military in Kamakura |
| 1221.6 | Rokuhara Tandai military administrative offices established in Kyoto |
| 1221.9.12 | Dōgen certified as Myōzen's dharma heir [SK.1.1–5 *Shishi sōjōge*] |

*Appendix 2: Key dates for Dōgen and his* SHŌBŌGENZŌ      265

| | |
|---|---|
| 1223.2.22 | Myōzen and his disciples, including Dōgen, depart Kyōto for Dazaifu and thence to China [DZZ.7:216 *Shari sōdenki*] |
| 1223.4 | Myōzen and Dōgen arrive in Qingyuan [DZZ.2:49 *Shōbōgenzō* 50 "Senmen"] and enter Jingfusi [DZZ.7:234 *Myōzen kaichō okugaki*] |
| 1223.5.4 | Dōgen encounters a monastic cook (*tenzo*) from Aśoka Temple on a merchant boat docked at Qingyuan landing [DZZ.6:012 *Tenzo kyōkun*] |
| 1223.5.13 | Myōzen and Dōgen enroll at Tiantong [DZZ.7:216 *Shari sōdenki*] |
| ca. 1223.7.15 ~ | Dōgen visited at Tiantong by the monastic cook (*tenzo*) from Aśoka Temple [DZZ.6:014 *Tenzo kyōkun*] |
| ca. 1223.7.15 ~ | Dōgen requests Temple Comptroller Guang at Tiantong to show him the inheritance certificate that Zhuoan Deguang (1121–1203) had bestowed on Wuji Liaopai [DZZ.1:431 *Shōbōgenzō* 39 "Shisho"] |
| ca. 1223.7.15 ~ | Dōgen discusses Buddhist practice with the very elderly monastic cook (*tenzo*) at Tiantong [DZZ.6:10, 12 *Tenzo kyōkun*] |
| 1223 autumn | Ryūzen requests Canon Prefect Chuan at Tiantong to show his inheritance certificate to Dōgen [DZZ.1:429 *Shōbōgenzō* 39 "Shisho"] |
| 1223 autumn | Dōgen visits Aśoka Temple and examines its murals of the thirty-three ancestors [DZZ.1:30 *Shōbōgenzō* 3 "Busshō"] |
| 1223.10 | Dōgen encounters two Buddhist monks from Korea, in Qingyuan [DZZ.1:370 *Shōbōgenzō* 32 "Den'e"] [DZZ.2:330–331 *Shōbōgenzō* 3 "Kesa kudoku"] |
| 1224.1.21 | Temple Comptroller Guang shows Dōgen the inheritance certificate that Zhuoan Deguang had bestowed on Wuji Liaopai [DZZ.1:430–431 *Shōbōgenzō* 39 "Shisho"] |
| ca. 1224.2 ~ | Dōgen examines the inheritance certificate of the head of Wanniansi on Mount Tiantai [DZZ.1:432 *Shōbōgenzō* 39 "Shisho"] |
| 1224.3 | Dōgen stays at the Daimeishan Hushengsi before returning to Tiantong [DZZ.1:432 *Shōbōgenzō* 39 "Shisho"] |
| 1224.4 | Wuji Liaopai dies |
| ca. 1224.5–7 | Rujing (1162–1227) installed as abbot of Tiantong |
| 1224.7.5 | Myōzen sponsors a memorial feast at Tiantong on behalf of Eisai on the tenth anniversary of his death [*Ribenguo Qianguang fashi citangji*] |
| 1225.5.1 | Dōgen has an awakening (*shinjin datsuraku*) [DZZ.1:54–55, 60 *Shōbōgenzō* 51 "Menju"] [cf. DZZ.2:68 *Shōbōgenzō* 52 "Busso"] [cf. DZZ.2:609–611 *Shōbōgenzō* 10 "Daigo" draft] [cf. DZZ.3:83 *Kōroku* 2, no. 136] |

| | |
|---|---|
| 1225.5.18 | Myōzen becomes ill [DZZ.7:217 *Shari sōdenki*] [*Nihonkoku Senkō hosshi shidōki*] |
| 1225.5.27 | Myōzen dies [DZZ.7:217 *Shari sōdenki*] [DZZ.7:234 *Myōzen kaichō okugaki*] |
| 1225.5.29 | Myōzen's funeral [DZZ.7:217 *Shari sōdenki*] [DZZ.7:234 *Myōzen kaichō okugaki*] |
| 1225 summer | Dōgen visits Aśoka Temple during the middle of the summer retreat [DZZ.1:30 *Shōbōgenzō* 3 "Busshō"] [cf. DZZ.7:24 *Hōkyōki* 19] |
| 1225.7.2 | Dōgen begins consultations with Rujing [DZZ.7:2 *Hōkyōki* 1] |
| 1225.9.18 | Dōgen receives bodhisattva precept initiation from Rujing [DZZ.6:188 *Busso shōden bosatsukai sahō*] |
| 1226.3 | Taikō Gyōyū at Jufukuji in Kamakura receives notification of Myōzen's death [Nakao 1986, 193–194] |
| 1226.3 | Dōgen listens to Rujing present a public sermon [DZZ.1:467–469 *Shōbōgenzō* 43 "Shohō jissō"] |
| 1227.7.17 | Rujing dies |
| 1227.10.5 | Dōgen composes an account of Myōzen's death and cremation [DZZ.7:216 *Sari sōdenki*] |
| 1231.7 | Dōgen presents the nun Ryōnen with a dharma talk (no. 12: *Ji Ryōnen-ni hōgo*) [DZZ.4:164, 166 *Kōroku* 8] |
| 1231.8.15 | Dōgen composes *Bendōwa* (initial draft) at Kannon Dōriin Cloister in Fukakusa [DZZ.2:555] |
| ca. 1233.4.15~ | Dōgen composes "Maka hannya haramitsu" at Kannon Dōriin Cloister [DZZ.1:13] |
| 1233.7.15 | Dōgen writes (or revises?) *Fukan zazen gi* [DZZ.5:12] |
| 1233.8.15 | Dōgen composes "Genjō kōan" and presents it to a scholar official in Chinzei (Dazaifu, Kyushu) [DZZ.1:7] |
| 1234.2.28 | Dōgen composes *Gakudō yōjinshū* [DZZ.5:20] |
| 1234 winter | Ejō (1198–1280), a former disciple of Kakuan, becomes Dōgen's student [*Sanso gyōgōki*, p. 4b; *Kenzeiki*, p. 35] |
| 1235.11.3 | Dōgen completes his *Shōbōgenzō* in Chinese script at Kannon Dōri Kōshō Hōrinji Temple (a.k.a. Kōshōji) [DZZ.5:124 *Shōbōgenzō jo*] |
| 1235 | Enni (1202–1280), a disciple of Eichō (1165–1247), travels to China |
| 1236.10.15 | Dōgen formally founds Kōshō Zenji (a.k.a. Kōshōji) in Fukakusa [DZZ.3:2 *Kōroku* 1] |
| 1236.12.29 | [1237.2.3] Ejō becomes head seat at Kōshōji [DZZ.7:117 *Zuimonki* 5] |
| 1237 spring | Dōgen composes *Tenzo kyōkun* at Kannon Dōri Kōshō Hōrin Zenji (a.k.a., Kōshōji) [DZZ.6:24] |
| 1237 | Taikō Gyōyū (Eisai's successor) founds Jōrakuji in Kamakura |

## Appendix 2: Key dates for Dōgen and his SHŌBŌGENZŌ 267

| | |
|---|---|
| 1238.4.18 | Dōgen composes "Ikka myōju," *Shōbōgenzō* 7, at Kannon Dōri Kōshō Hōrinji (a.k.a. Kōshōji) [DZZ.1:81] |
| 1239.4.25 | Dōgen composes *Jū undō shiki* at Kōshōji [DZZ.2:486] |
| 1239.5.25 | Dōgen composes "Soku shin ze butsu," *Shōbōgenzō* 5, at Kannon Dōri Kōshō Hōrinji (a.k.a. Kōshōji) [DZZ.1:58] |
| 1239.10.23 | Dōgen composes "Senjō," *Shōbōgenzō* 54, at Kannon Dōri Kōshō Hōrinji (a.k.a. Kōshōji) [DZZ.2:91] |
| 1239.10.23 | Dōgen composes "Senmen," *Shōbōgenzō* 50, at Kannon Dōri Kōshō Hōrinji (a.k.a. Kōshōji) [DZZ.2:53] |
| 1239 | Ryūzen becomes abbot of Kongō Zanmaiin Cloister on Mount Kōya |
| 1240.3.7 | Dōgen composes "Raihai tokuzui," *Shōbōgenzō* 28, draft, at Kannon Dōri Kōshō Hōrinji (a.k.a. Kōshōji) [DZZ.1:308] |
| 1240.4.20 | Dōgen composes "Keisei sanshoku," *Shōbōgenzō* 25, at Kannon Dōri Kōshō Hōrinji (a.k.a. Kōshōji) [DZZ.1:284] |
| 1240.8.15 | Dōgen composes "Shoaku makusa," *Shōbōgenzō* 31, at Kannon Dōri Kōshō Hōrinji (a.k.a. Kōshōji) [DZZ.1:352] |
| 1240.10.1 | Dōgen composes "Kesa kudoku," *Shōbōgenzō* 41 at Kannon Dōri Kōshō Hōrinji (a.k.a. Kōshōji) [DZZ.2:331] |
| 1240.10.1 | Dōgen composes "Uji," *Shōbōgenzō* 20, at Kōshō Hōrinji (a.k.a. Kōshōji) [DZZ.1:246] |
| 1240.10.1 | Dōgen composes "Den'e," *Shōbōgenzō* 32, at Kannon Dōri Kōshō Hōrinji (a.k.a. Kōshōji) [DZZ.1:370] |
| 1240.10.18 | Dōgen composes "Sansui kyō," *Shōbōgenzō* 29, at Kannon Dōri Kōshō Hōrinji (a.k.a. Kōshōji) [DZZ.1:328] |
| 1240.int.10.30 | — "Raihai tokuzui," draft, copied [DZZ.1:315] |
| 1241.1.3 | Dōgen composes "Busso." *Shōbōgenzō* 52, at Kannon Dōri Kōshō Hōrinji (a.k.a. Kōshōji) [DZZ.2:68] |
| 1241.3.27 | Dōgen composes "Shisho," *Shōbōgenzō* 39, at Kannon Dōri Kōshō Hōrinji (a.k.a. Kōshōji) [DZZ.1:435] [cf. DZZ.2:567 Kōjakuji ms.] |
| 1241 summer | Dōgen composes "*Hokke* ten *Hokke*," at Kannon Dōri Kōshō Hōrinji (a.k.a. Kōshōji), and presents to a Zen adept named Etatsu [DZZ.2:497] |
| 1241 summer | Dōgen composes "Shin fukatoku," *Shōbōgenzō* 8, at Kannon Dōri Kōshō Hōrinji (a.k.a. Kōshōji) [DZZ.1:86] |
| 1241.9.9 | Dōgen composes "Kokyō," *Shōbōgenzō* 19, at Kannon Dōri Kōshō Hōrinji (a.k.a. Kōshōji) [DZZ.1:239] |
| 1241.9.15 | Dōgen composes "Kankin," *Shōbōgenzō* 29, at Kannon Dōri Kōshō Hōrinji (a.k.a. Kōshōji) [DZZ.1:342] |
| 1241.10.14 | Dōgen composes "Busshō," *Shōbōgenzō* 3, (initial version) at Kannon Dōri Kōshō Hōrinji (a.k.a. Kōshōji) [DZZ.1:44] |

| | |
|---|---|
| 1241.10 | Dōgen composes "Gyōbutsu iigi," *Shōbōgenzō* 6, at Kannon Dōri Kōshō Hōrinji [DZZ.1:75] |
| 1241.11.16 | Dōgen composes "Jinzū," *Shōbōgenzō* 35, at Kannon Dōri Kōshō Hōrinji (a.k.a. Kōshōji) [DZZ.1:402] |
| 1241.12.12 | [1242.1.21] Dōgen revises "Shisho," *Shōbōgenzō* 39 (Kōjakuji ms.) [DZZ.1:435] [cf. DZZ.2:568 Kōjakuji ms.] |
| 1241 | Enni returns from China |
| 1242.1.28 | Dōgen composes "Daigo," *Shōbōgenzō* 10 (initial version), at Kannon Dōri Kōshō Hōrinji (a.k.a. Kōshōji) [DZZ.1:99] |
| 1242.3.20 | Dōgen composes "Inmo," *Shōbōgenzō* 17, at Kannon Dōri Kōshō Hōrinji (a.k.a. Kōshōji) [DZZ.1:203] |
| 1242.3.23 | Dōgen composes "Butsu kōjō ji," *Shōbōgenzō* 26, at Kannon Dōri Kōshō Hōrinji (a.k.a. Kōshōji) [DZZ.1:294] |
| 1242.4.5 | Dōgen composes "Gyōji," *Shōbōgenzō* 16, at Kannon Dōri Kōshō Hōrinji (a.k.a. Kōshōji) [DZZ.1:202] |
| 1242.4.12 | Ekan and his Darumashū students, including Gikai (1219–1309), join Dōgen's community at Kōshōji [*Sanso gyōgōki*, p. 6b] |
| 1242.4.20 | Dōgen composes "Kaiin zanmai," *Shōbōgenzō* 13, at Kannon Dōri Kōshō Hōrinji (a.k.a. Kōshōji) [DZZ.1:126] |
| 1242.4.25 | Dōgen composes "Juki," *Shōbōgenzō* 21, at Kannon Dōri Kōshō Hōrinji (a.k.a. Kōshōji) [DZZ.1:258] |
| 1242.4.26 | Dōgen composes "Kannon," *Shōbōgenzō* 18 [DZZ.1:219] |
| 1242.5.10 | — Ejō copies "Kannon," *Shōbōgenzō* 18 [DZZ.1:220] |
| 1242.5.15 | Dōgen composes "Arakan," *Shōbōgenzō* 36, at Kannon Dōri Kōshō Hōrinji (a.k.a. Kōshōji) [DZZ.1:408] |
| 1242.5.21 | Dōgen composes "Hakujushi," *Shōbōgenzō* 40 (at Kōshōji) [DZZ.1:442] |
| 1242.6.2 | Dōgen composes "Kōmyō," *Shōbōgenzō* 15, at Kannon Dōri Kōshō Hōrinji (a.k.a. Kōshōji) [DZZ.1:144] |
| 1242.8.5 | Rujing's *Recorded Sayings* received at Kōshōji [DZZ.3:60 *Kōroku* 1, *jōdō* 105; cf. *Kenzeiki*, p. 43] |
| 1242.9.9 | Dōgen composes "Shinjin gakudō," *Shōbōgenzō* 4, at Hōrinji (a.k.a. Kōshōji) [DZZ.1:52] |
| 1242.9.21 | Dōgen composes "Muchū setsumu," *Shōbōgenzō* 27, at Kannon Dōri Kōshō Hōrinji (a.k.a. Kōshōji) [DZZ.1:301] |
| 1242.10.5 | Dōgen composes "Dōtoku," *Shōbōgenzō* 33, at Kannon Dōri Kōshō Hōrinji (a.k.a. Kōshōji ) [DZZ.1:379] |
| 1242.11.2 | —Ejō copies "Dōtoku," *Shōbōgenzō* 33 [DZZ.1:379] |
| 1242.11.5 | Dōgen composes "Gabyō," *Shōbōgenzō* 24, at Kannon Dōri Kōshō Hōrinji (a.k.a. Kōshōji) [DZZ.1:273] |
| 1242.11.7 | Dōgen composes "Bukkyō" (The Teachings of the Buddhas), *Shōbōgenzō* 34, at Kōshō Shōja (a.k.a. Kōshōji) [DZZ.1:391] |

Appendix 2: Key dates for Dōgen and his SHŌBŌGENZŌ 269

| | |
|---|---|
| 1242.11.7 | —Ejō copies "Gabyō," *Shōbōgenzō* 24, at Kōshōji [DZZ.1:273] |
| 1242.12.17 | [1243.1.16] Dōgen composes "Zenki," *Shōbōgenzō* 22, at the Rokuhara Tandai in Kyoto [DZZ.1:261] |
| 1243.1.6 | Dōgen composes "Tsuki," *Shōbōgenzō* 23, at Kannon Dōri Kōshō Hōrinji (a.k.a. Kōshōji) [DZZ.1:267] |
| 1243.1.13 | —Ejō copies "Kokyō," *Shōbōgenzō* 19, at Sendanrin [DZZ.1:239] |
| 1243.1.18 | —Ejō copies "Gyōji," *Shōbōgenzō* 16 and 17 [DZZ.1:202] |
| 1243.1.19 | — Ejō copies revised and corrected version of "Busshō," *Shōbōgenzō* 3 [DZZ.1:44] |
| 1243.1.19 | — Ejō copies "Zenki," *Shōbōgenzō* 22 [DZZ.1:261] |
| 1243.2.2 | —Ejō copies "Shinjin gakudō," *Shōbōgenzō* 4 [DZZ.1:52] |
| 1243.2.25 | —Ejō copies "Shisho," *Shōbōgenzō* 39, at Kōshōji [DZZ.1:435] |
| 1243.3.8 | —Ejō proofreads his copy of "Gyōji," *Shōbōgenzō* 16 [DZZ.1:202] |
| 1243.3.10 | Dōgen composes "Kūge," *Shōbōgenzō* 14, at Kannon Dōri Kōshō Hōrinji (a.k.a. Kōshōji) [DZZ.1:137] |
| 1243.3.23 | —Ejō copies "Muchū setsumu," *Shōbōgenzō* 27 [DZZ.1:301] |
| 1243.3.27 | —Ejō copies "Shoaku makusa," *Shōbōgenzō* 31, at Kōshōji [DZZ.1:352] |
| 1243.4.8 | — Ejō copies "Keisei sanshoku," *Shōbōgenzō* 25, at Kōshōji [DZZ.1:284] |
| 1243.4.14 | —Ejō copies "Inmo," *Shōbōgenzō* 29 [DZZ.1:203] |
| 1243.4.29 | Dōgen composes "Kobutsushin," *Shōbōgenzō* 9, at Rokuhara Tandai in Kyoto [DZZ.1:91] |
| 1243.5.55 | Dōgen composes "Bodaisatta shishōbō," *Shōbōgenzō* 28 [DZZ.2:515] |
| 1243 summer | —Ejō copies "Uji," *Shōbōgenzō* 20 [DZZ.1:246] |
| 1243.7.7 | Dōgen composes "Kattō," *Shōbōgenzō* 38, at Kannon Dōri Kōshō Hōrinji (a.k.a. Kōshōji) [DZZ.1:422] |
| 1243.7.14 | — Ejō copies "Tsuki," *Shōbōgenzō* 23 [DZZ.1:267] |
| 1243.7.16 ~ | Dōgen moves his community to Echizen Province (Fukui Prefecture) [*Kenzeiki*, p. 45] |
| 1243.int7.1 | Dōgen composes "Sangai yui shin," *Shōbōgenzō* 41, at Zenjihō in Echizen [DZZ.1:448] |
| 1243.int7.3 | —Ejō copies "Hakujushi," *Shōbōgenzō* 40, at Kippōji in Echizen [DZZ.1:442] |
| 1243.int7.23 | —Ejō copies "Ikka myōju," *Shōbōgenzō* 7, at Kippōji in Echizen [DZZ.1:81] |
| 1243.int7.27 | —Ejō copies "Sangai yui shin," *Shōbōgenzō* 41 [DZZ.1:448] |

| | |
|---|---|
| 1243 | Dōgen composes "Sesshin sesshō," *Shōbōgenzō* 42, at Kippōji in Echizen [DZZ.1:456] |
| 1243.9 | Dōgen composes "Shohō jissō," *Shōbōgenzō* 43, at Kippōji in Echizen [DZZ.1:470] |
| 1243.9.16 | Dōgen composes "Butsudō," *Shōbōgenzō* 44, at Kippōji in Echizen [DZZ.1:488] |
| 1243.9.20 | Dōgen composes "Mitsugo," *Shōbōgenzō* 45, at Kippōji in Echizen [DZZ.1:494] |
| 1243.9.24 | Dōgen revises (third time) "Shisho," *Shōbōgenzō* 39 [DZZ.1:435] |
| 1243.9 | Dōgen composes "Bukkyō" (Sūtras of the Buddhas), *Shōbōgenzō* 47, at Kippōji in Echizen [DZZ.2:25] |
| 1243 | Dōgen composes "Darani," *Shōbōgenzō* 49, at Kippōji in Echizen [DZZ.2:36] |
| 1243.10.15 | —Ejō copies "Mujō seppō," *Shōbōgenzō* 46, at Kippōji in Echizen [DZZ.2:13] |
| 1243.10.16 | —Ejō copies "Mitsugo," *Shōbōgenzō* 45 (Himitsu 2.4), at Kippōji in Echizen [DZZ.1:494] |
| 1243.10.20 | Dōgen composes "Mujō seppō," *Shōbōgenzō* 46, at Kippōji in Echizen [DZZ.2:13] |
| 1243.10 | Dōgen composes "Hosshō," *Shōbōgenzō* 48, at Kippōji in Echizen [DZZ.2:30] |
| 1243.10.20 | Dōgen revises "Senmen," *Shōbōgenzō* 50, at Kippōji in Echizen [DZZ.2:53] |
| 1243.10.23 | Dōgen composes "Menju," *Shōbōgenzō* 51, at Kippōji in Echizen [DZZ.2:60] |
| 1243.10.23 | —Ejō copies "Butsudō," *Shōbōgenzō* 44 (Himitsu 1.9), at Kippōji in Echizen [DZZ.1:488] |
| 1243.10.23 | —Ejō copies and collates Dōgen's holograph of "Shisho," *Shōbōgenzō* 39 [DZZ.1:435] |
| 1243.11 | Dōgen composes "Zazen gi," *Shōbōgenzō* 11, at Kippōji in Echizen [DZZ.1:101] |
| 1243.11.6 | Dōgen composes "Baika," *Shōbōgenzō* 53, at Kippōji in Echizen [DZZ.2:77–78] |
| 1243.11.13 | [1244.1.1] Dōgen composes "Jippō," *Shōbōgenzō* 55, at Kippōji in Echizen [DZZ.2:97] |
| 1243.11.19 | [1244.1.7] Dōgen composes "Kenbutsu," *Shōbōgenzō* 56, at Mount Zenjihō in Echizen [DZZ.2:111] |
| 1243.11.27 | [1244.1.15] Dōgen composes "Henzan," *Shōbōgenzō* 57, at Mount Zenjihō in Echizen [DZZ.2:117] |
| 1243.12.17 | [1244.2.4] Dōgen composes "Ganzei," *Shōbōgenzō* 58, beneath Mount Zenjihō in Echizen [DZZ.2:123] |
| 1243.12.17 | [1244.2.4] Dōgen composes "Kajō," *Shōbōgenzō* 59, beneath Mount Zenjihō in Echizen [DZZ.2:129] |

## Appendix 2: Key dates for Dōgen and his SHŌBŌGENZŌ 271

| | |
|---|---|
| 1243.12.25 | [1244.2.12] Dōgen composes "Ryūgin," *Shōbōgenzō* 61, at Mount Zenjihō in Echizen [DZZ.2:154] |
| 1243.12.25 | [1244.2.12] —Ejō copies "Henzan," *Shōbōgenzō* 37, at Mount Zenjihō [DZZ.2:597] |
| 1243.12.28 | [1244.2.15] — Ejō copies "Ganzei," *Shōbōgenzō* 58, at Mount Zenjihō in Echizen [DZZ.2:123] |
| 1243.12 | [1244.1–2] — Ejō copies "Kaiin zanmai," *Shōbōgenzō* 13 [DZZ.1:126] |
| 1244.1.1 | —Ejō copies "Kajō," *Shōbōgenzō* 59, at Mount Zenjihō in Echizen [DZZ.2:129] |
| 1244.1.11 | —Ejō copies "Sesshin sesshō," *Shōbōgenzō* 42 (Himitsu 3.6) [DZZ.1:456] |
| 1244.1.20 | —Ejō copies "Juki," *Shōbōgenzō* 21, at Kippōji in Echizen [DZZ.1:258] |
| 1244.1.27 | Dōgen revises "Daigo," *Shōbōgenzō* 10, at Kippōji in Echizen [DZZ.1:99] |
| 1244.1.27 | —Ejō copies "Kūge," *Shōbōgenzō* 14, at Kippōji in Echizen [DZZ.1:137] |
| 1244.2.1 | —Ejō copies "Jinzū," *Shōbōgenzō* 35, at Kippōji in Echizen [DZZ.1:402] |
| 1244.2.4 | Dōgen composes "Soshi seirai i," *Shōbōgenzō* 62 [DZZ.2:159] |
| 1244.2.12 | Dōgen composes "Udonge," *Shōbōgenzō* 64, at Kippōji in Echizen [DZZ.2:172] |
| 1244.2.14 | Dōgen composes "Hotsu bodai shin," *Shōbōgenzō* 63, at Kippōji in Echizen [DZZ.2:168]; a.k.a. "Hotsu mujō shin," *Shōbōgenzō* 53 |
| 1244.2.15 | Dōgen composes "Nyorai zenshin," *Shōbōgenzō* 65, at Kippōji in Echizen [DZZ.2:176] |
| 1244.2.15 | Dōgen composes "Zanmai ō zanmai," *Shōbōgenzō* 66, at Kippōji in Echizen [DZZ.2:181] |
| 1244.2.15 | —Ejō copies "Zanmai ō zanmai," *Shōbōgenzō* 66 (Himitsu 1.10) [DZZ.2:181] |
| 1244.2.24 | Dōgen composes "Sanjūshichi hon bodai bunpō," *Shōbōgenzō* 60, at Kippōji in Echizen [DZZ.2:150] |
| 1244.2.27 | Dōgen composes "Ten hōrin," *Shōbōgenzō* 67, at Kippōji in Echizen [DZZ.2:184] |
| 1244.2.29 | Dōgen composes "Jishō zanmai," *Shōbōgenzō* 69, at Kippōji in Echizen [DZZ.2:207] |
| 1244.3.1 | —Ejō copies "Ten hōrin," *Shōbōgenzō* 67 (Himitsu 2.5), at Kippōji in Echizen; thereafter, Ejō corrects and collates it with the second revised version and recopies it [DZZ.2:184] |

| | |
|---|---|
| 1244.3.3 | —Ejō copies "Kattō," *Shōbōgenzō* 38, at Kippōji in Echizen [DZZ.1:422] |
| 1244.3.9 | Dōgen composes "Dai shugyō," *Shōbōgenzō* 68, at Kippōji in Echizen [DZZ.2:195] |
| 1244.3.9 | —Ejō copies "Sanjūshichi hon bodai bunpō," *Shōbōgenzō* 60 (Himitsu 1.11) at Kippōji in Echizen [DZZ.2:150] |
| 1244.3.13 | —Ejō copies "Dai shugyō," *Shōbōgenzō* 68 (Himitsu 2.7), at Kippōji in Echizen [DZZ.2:195] |
| 1244.3.20 | —Ejō copies "Daigo," *Shōbōgenzō* 10, at Kippōji in Echizen [DZZ.1:99] |
| 1244.3.21 | Dōgen composes *Tai taikohō* [DZZ.6:94] |
| 1244.3.21 | — Ejō copies "Maka hannya haramitsu," *Shōbōgenzō* 2, at Kippōji in Echizen [DZZ.1:13] |
| 1244.4.12 | — Ejō copies "Jishō zanmai," *Shōbōgenzō* 69 (Himitsu 2.6) at Kippōji in Echizen [DZZ.2:207] |
| 1244.5.14 | —Ejō copies "Busso," *Shōbōgenzō* 52, at Kippōji in Echizen [DZZ.2:68] |
| 1244.6.3 | —Ejō copies "Sansui kyō," *Shōbōgenzō* 29 (Himitsu 2.3), at Kippōji in Echizen [DZZ.1:328] |
| 1244.6.7 | —Ejō copies "Menju," *Shōbōgenzō* 51, at Kippōji in Echizen [DZZ.2:60] |
| 1244.7.18 | Dōgen founds Daibutsuji [DZZ.3:70 *Kōroku* 2] |
| 1244.10.16 | —Ejō copies "Kenbutsu," *Shōbōgenzō* 56, at Daibutsuji [DZZ.2:111] |
| 1244.12.13 | [1245.1.19] — Ejō copies "Kōmyō," *Shōbōgenzō* 15, at Daibutsuji in Echizen [DZZ.1:144] |
| 1244 | Dōgen revises "Shunjū," *Shōbōgenzō* 37, in Echizen [DZZ.1:415] |
| 1245.2.8 | —Ejō copies *Gakudō yōjinshū* [DZZ.5:51] |
| 1245.3.6 | Dōgen composes "Kokū," *Shōbōgenzō* 70, at Daibutsuji [DZZ.2:212] |
| 1245.3.12 | Dōgen composes "Hou," *Shōbōgenzō* 71, at Daibutsu Shōja (a.k.a. Daibutsuji) [DZZ.2:216] |
| 1245.3.13 | Dōgen composes "Ango," *Shōbōgenzō* 72, at Daibutsuji [DZZ.2:240] |
| 1245.6.15 | Dōgen composes *Echizen Eiheiji chiji shingi* [DZZ.6:166] |
| 1245.6.26 | —Ejō collates "Butsudō," *Shōbōgenzō* 44 [DZZ.1:488] |
| 1245.7.4 | Dōgen composes "Tajintsū," *Shōbōgenzō* 73, at Daibutsuji [DZZ.2:252] |
| 1245.7.8 | —Ejō copies "Kankin," *Shōbōgenzō* 29, at Daibutsuji [DZZ.1:342] |
| 1245.7.12 | —Ejō copies "Soku shin ze butsu," *Shōbōgenzō* 5, at Daibutsuji in Echizen [DZZ.1:58] |

Appendix 2: Key dates for Dōgen and his SHŌBŌGENZŌ       273

| | |
|---|---|
| 1245.7.17 | —Ejō copies "Hou," *Shōbōgenzō* 42, at Daibutsuji [DZZ.2:216] |
| 1245.10.22 | Dōgen composes "Ō saku sendaba," *Shōbōgenzō* 74, at Daibutsuji [DZZ.2:258] |
| 1245.12.24 | [1246.1.20] —Ejō copies "Jippō," *Shōbōgenzō* 55, at Daibutsuji [DZZ.2:97] |
| 1246 | Lanxi Daolong (1213–1278) travels from China to Japan |
| 1246.6.15 | Dōgen changes the name of Daibutsuji to Eiheiji [DZZ.3:116 *Kōroku* 2, *jōdō* 177] |
| 1246.6.23 | Hōjō Tokiyori (1227–1263) expells Kujō Yoritsune (1218–1256), from Kamakura |
| 1246.8.6 | Dōgen composes *Jikuinmon* at Eiheiji [DZZ.2:516] |
| 1246.9.15 | Dōgen composes "Shukke," *Shōbōgenzō* 75, at Eiheiji [DZZ.2:264] |
| 1247.6.5 | Hōjō Tokiyori (1227–1263) wages war against the Miura clan |
| 1247.8.3 | Dōgen journeys to Kamakura [DZZ.3:166 *Kōroku* 3, *jōdō* 251] |
| 1247 | Taikō Gyōyū (Eisai's successor) founds Jōrakuji in Kamakura |
| 1248 | Langxi Daolong travels to Kamakura |
| 1248.3.13 | Dōgen returns to Eiheiji [DZZ.3:166–168 *Kōroku* 3, *jōdō* 251] |
| 1249.1.1 | Dōgen composes *Jūroku rakan genzuiki* at Eiheiji [DZZ.7:287] |
| 1249.1 | Dōgen composes *Shuryō shingi* [DZZ.6:84] |
| 1249 | Muhon Kakushin (a.k.a. Shinchi-bō; 1207–1298) travels to China |
| 1250.1 | Hatano Yoshishige presents the Buddhist Canon to Eiheiji [DZZ.3:232 *Kōroku* 5, *jōdō* 361] |
| 1250.1.11 | Dōgen again revises "Senmen," *Shōbōgenzō* 50, at Eiheiji [DZZ.2:53] |
| 1252 | Dōgen completes the revisions and orders the chapters (*shūroku*) of the *Shōbōgenzō* in seventy-five chapters (75-SBGZ) [DZZ.1:7] |
| 1253.1.6 | Dōgen designates "Hachi dainin gaku," *Shōbōgenzō* 12, as the twelfth chapter of his *Shōbōgenzō* in twelve chapters [DZZ.2:458 headnote] |
| 1253.3.9 | —Ejō copies "Sanjigō," *Shōbōgenzō* 8 (60-SBGZ), at Eiheiji [DZZ.2:623] |
| 1253.7.14 | Ejō installed as the abbot of Eiheiji [*Kenzeiki*, p. 81] |
| 1253.8.5 | Dōgen journeys to Kyoto for medical attention [*Kenzeiki*, p. 81] |
| 1253.8.28 | Dōgen dies [*Kenzeiki*, p. 83] |

274    DŌGEN'S *SHŌBŌGENZŌ* VOLUME VIII

## C. Manuscripts Copied after Dōgen

| | |
|---|---|
| 1253.12.10 | [1256.1.7] —Ejō copies *Hōkyōki*, Zenkyūin ms. [DZZ.7:48] |
| 1254.9.9 | —Giin copies *Busso shōden bosatsukai sahō* [DZZ.6:190] |
| 1255.4.9 | —Ejō copies "Hotsu bodai shin," *Shōbōgenzō* 34, at Eiheiji [DZZ.2:342] |
| 1255 summer | —Ejō copies "Kesa kudoku," *Shōbōgenzō* 41 [DZZ.2:331] |
| 1255 summer | —Ejō copies "Shime," *Shōbōgenzō* 39 [DZZ.2:418] |
| 1255 summer | —Ejō copies "Jinshin inga," *Shōbōgenzō* 87 [DZZ.2:394] |
| 1255.7.5 | —Ejō copies and proofreads "Kesa kudoku," *Shōbōgenzō* 41 [DZZ.2:331] |
| 1255.7.14 | —Gien copies "Hachi dainin gaku," *Shōbōgenzō* 12, and Ejō then collates Gien's copy with his own copy [DZZ.2:458] |
| 1255.8.28 | 3d anniversary memorial service for Dōgen |
| 1258.4.25 | —Ejō collates revised and corrected versions of "Busshō," *Shōbōgenzō* 3 [DZZ.1:44] |
| 1259 summer | —Ejō copies an unrevised version of "Butsu kōjō ji," *Shōbōgenzō* 26 [DZZ.1:294] |
| 1260 summer | —Ejō copies and collates "Zanmai ō zanmai," *Shōbōgenzō* 66 [DZZ.2:181] |
| 1261 summer | —Ejō copies and collates a revised version of "Busshō," *Shōbōgenzō* 3 [DZZ.1:44] |
| 1263 | —Gishō (d.u.) copies *Gakudō yōjinshū* [DZZ.5:52] |
| 1263 | Senne (d.u.) completes *Kikigaki* commentary on the *Shōbōgenzō* in seventy-five chapters [ ESST.11–14] |
| 1275.5.25 | —Ejō (?) copies "Kesa kudoku," *Shōbōgenzō* 41 [DZZ.2:331] |
| 1275.6.16 | —Ejō copies "Arakan," *Shōbōgenzō* 36 [DZZ.1:408] |
| 1275.7.11 | —Ejō (?) copies "Keisei sanshoku," *Shōbōgenzō* 25 [DZZ.1:284] |
| 1279.3.6 | —Giun (1253–1333) copies "Kokū," *Shōbōgenzō* 56, at Zenkōji in Nakahama, Echizen [DZZ.2:212] |
| 1279.3.10 | —Ejō copies "Ryūgin," *Shōbōgenzō* 51, at Eiheiji [DZZ.2:154] |
| 1279.3.10 | —Ejō copies "Hotsu mujō shin," *Shōbōgenzō* 53 (60-SBGZ), at Eiheiji [DZZ.1:168] |
| 1279.4.16 | —Giun copies "Kie buppōsōbō," *Shōbōgenzō* 60 at Zenkōji in Nakahama, Echizen [DZZ.2:386] |
| 1279.5.20 | —Giun copies "Ango," *Shōbōgenzō* 57, at Zenkōji in Nakahama, Echizen [DZZ.2:240] |
| 1279.5.21 | "Kuyō shobutsu," *Shōbōgenzō* 59, copied at Eiheiji [DZZ.2:371] |

*Appendix 2: Key dates for Dōgen and his* SHŌBŌGENZŌ          275

| | |
|---|---|
| 1279.6.22 | —Ejō copies "Soshi seirai i," *Shōbōgenzō* 52, at Eiheiji [DZZ.2:159] |
| 1279.6.23 | "Nyorai zenshin," *Shōbōgenzō* 55, copied at Eiheiji [DZZ.2:176] |
| 1280.8.28 | Twenty-third anniversary memorial service for Dōgen |
| 1280.8.24 | Ejō dies |
| 1287 | *Shōbōgenzō* in Chinese script copied, Kanazawa Bunko ms. |
| 1292.8.13 | *Busso shōden bosatsukai sahō* copied by Keizan Jōkin (1264–1325) |
| 1299.11.23 | — Giun copies *Hōkyōki* [DZZ.7:50] |
| 1300 | Keizan Jōkin presents lectures for *Denkōroku* |
| 1303–1308 | Kyōgō writes *Shōbōgenzō okikigakishō* (a.k.a. *Goshō*) commentary on the *Shōbōgenzō* in seventy-five chapters [ESST.11–14] |
| 1326.10.12 | Daichi (1290–1366) copies Gikai's *Goyuigon kiroku* [DZZ.7:206] |
| 1329 | Giun composes set of Chinese verses on each chapter (*Bonmokuju*) of the *Shōbōgenzō* in sixty chapters [EST20] |
| 1332 | *Bendōwa* copied (Shōbōji ms. draft version) [DZZ.2:556] |
| 1333 | *Shōbōgenzō* in seventy-five chapters copied by Tsūgen [DZZ.2:635] |
| 1357 | *Eihei shoso gakudō yōjinshū* printed by Donki |
| 1358 | *Eihei Gen zenji goroku* printed by Donki |
| 1389 | *Shōbōgenzō* in sixty chapters copied by Sōgo (1343–1406) |
| 1400 | *Shōbōgenzō* in sixty chapters copied by Zenkō |
| 1419 | Taiyō Bonsei (d. 1427) copies a comprehensive *Shōbōgenzō* in eighty-four chapters [ ESST.4] |
| 1420 | *Shōbōgenzō* in twelve chapters copied (Yōkōji ms.) |
| 1430 | *Shōbōgenzō* in seventy-five chapters copied (Kenkon'in ms., Rurikōji ms., etc.) |
| 1446 | *Shōbōgenzō* in twelve chapters copied — Yōkōji ms. in three fascicles [ESST.1] |
| 1459 | *Denkōroku* copied (Kenkon'in ms.) |
| 1472 | Kenzei (1415–1474), compiles *Kenzeiki* |
| 1472 | *Shōbōgenzō* in seventy-five chapters copied by Bokudō Ryōjun (d. 1500) (Shōbōji ms.) |
| 1479–1480 | *Shōbōgenzō* in sixty chapters copied by Kōshū (1434–1492) (Tōunji ms.) |
| 1481 | *Shōbōgenzō* in Chinese script copied (Jōkōji ms.) |
| 1488 | *Shōbōgenzō* in seventy-five chapters copied (Kenkon'in ms.) [ESST.1] |
| 1490–1491 | *Shōbōgenzō* in eighty-three chapters copied (Rurikōji ms.) [ESST.5] |

| | |
|---|---|
| 276 | DŌGEN'S *SHŌBŌGENZŌ* VOLUME VIII |

| | |
|---|---|
| 1510 | *Shōbōgenzō* in sixty chapters copied by Kinkō Yōken (1437–1513) (Tōunji ms.) [ESST.6] |
| 1512 | *Shōbōgenzō* in seventy-five chapters copied (Shōbōji ms.) [ESST.1] |
| 1515 | *Bendōwa* (Talk on Pursuing the Way) copied (Shōbōji ms.) ESST.4] |
| 1547 | *Denkōroku* (Record of the Transmission of Illumination) copied by Tessō Hōken (d. 1551) (Ryūmonji ms.) |
| 1547 | *Shōbōgenzō* in seventy-five chapters copied by Tessō Hōken (d. 1551) (Ryūmonji ms.) [ESST.2] |
| 1598 | Monkaku (d.1615) supervises the copying of the *Dōgen oshō kōroku* [DZZ.3 and DZZ.4] |
| 1637 | *Denkōroku* copied by Kidō Sōe (d. 1645) (Chōenji ms.) |
| 1644 | *Zuimonki* copied by Kidō Sōe (d. 1645) from an earlier manuscript dated 1380 (Chōenji ms.) [ESST.4] |
| 1645 | *Shōbōgenzō* in eighty-four chapters (Bonsei version) copied by Kidō Sōe (d. 1645) (Chōenji ms.) [ESST.4] |
| 1651 | *Shōbōgenzō* in eighty-four chapters (Bonsei version) copied by Gesshū Sōko (1630–1698) (Ennōji ms.) [ESST.5] |
| 1672.8.28 | Manzan Dōhaku (1636–1715) prints revised edition of Dōgen's extensive record (re-titled *Eihei kōroku*) |
| 1677 | *Shōbōgenzō* in seventy-five chapters copied (Kōunji ms.) [ESST.3] |
| 1686 | Manzan Dōhaku edits, revises, re-orders, and expands the *Shōbōgenzō* into eighty-nine chapters (Daijōji ms.) [ESST.7] |
| 1690 | *Shōbōgenzō* in seventy-five chapters copied (Hōkyōji ms.) [ESST.2] |
| 1690–1693 | Handō Kōzen (1625–1693) revises, re-orders, and expands the *Shōbōgenzō* to ninety-five (or ninety-six) chapters |
| 1714 | *Shōbōgenzō* in seventy-five chapters copied (Eiheiji ms.) [EST.24] |
| 1715 | *Shōbōgenzō* in Chinese script copied (Jōkōji ms.) |
| 1751 | *Shōbōgenzō* in sixty chapters copied (Myōshōji ms.) [ESST.7] |
| 1752 | *Shōbōgenzō* in Chinese script copied (Jōkōji ms.) [ESST.1] |

D. Early Modern Printed Editions of the *Shōbōgenzō* and Related Works

| | |
|---|---|
| 1651 | *Zuimonki* xylograph printed [ESST.4] |
| 1672 | "Zazen shin" xylograph printed by Manzan Dōhaku (1636–1715) as part of his revised edition of Dōgen's |

*Appendix 2: Key dates for Dōgen and his* SHŌBŌGENZŌ        277

|        | extensive record of sayings (titled *Eihei kōroku*) |
|--------|------|
| 1684   | "Ango" xylograph printed by Manzan Dōhaku (1636–1715) [ESST.4] |
| 1700   | "Menju" xylograph printed by Manzan Dōhaku (1636–1715) [ESST.4] |
| 1722.12 | Prohibition issued by the military government forbidding the copying, editing, or printing of any part of the *Shōbōgenzō* and of other sensitive Sōtō historical texts (*Shōbōgenzō kaihan kinshi no rei*) |
| 1770   | *Zuimonki* xylograph edited and printed by Menzan Zuihō (1683–1769) |
| 1787   | "Gyōji" xylograph printed by Gentō Sokuchū (1729–1807) [ESST.4] |
| 1788   | *Bendōwa*, revised version, xylograph printed by Gentō Sokuchū (1729–1807) [ESST.4] |
| 1815   | Honzan edition of the *Shōbōgenzō* (90 printed chapters plus 5 blank chapters) printed and distributed from xylographs carved 1796 to 1808 |
| 1827   | *Eihei Gen oshō juko*, 1 volume xylograph printed by Kakudō Soshū (d. 1834) |
| 1858   | "Zanmai ō zanmai," *Shōbōgenzō* 66, xylograph printed by Ryūtaiji [ ESST.4] |
| 1906   | Honzan edition of the *Shōbōgenzō*: xylographs carved and printed for 5 previously blank chapters |

E. MODERN PRINTED EDITIONS OF THE *SHŌBŌGENZŌ*

| 1885   | Honzan edition of the *Shōbōgenzō* (95 chapters) printed by Ōuchi Seiran (1845–1918) |
|--------|------|
| 1926   | *Shōbōgenzō: honzanban shukusatsu*: revised reprint of 1885 edition |
| 1931   | Honzan edition of the *Shōbōgenzō*, edited by Kishizawa Ian (1865–1955), in Taishō edition of the Buddhist Canon (T.2582) |
| 1939–1943 | Honzan edition of the *Shōbōgenzō*, edited by Etō Sokuō (1888–1958), Iwanami paperback edition in 3 volumes |
| 1969   | *Shōbōgenzō*, chapters arranged in 75-plus-12 configuration, with supplemental and variant chapters, edited by Ōkubo Dōshū (1896–1994), in *Dōgen zenji zenshū* (Chikuma Shobō) |
| 1971   | *Kohon kōtei Shōbōgenzō zen*: stand-alone reprint of 1969 Ōkubo edition |
| 1970–1972 | *Shōbōgenzō*, chapters arranged in 75-plus-12 configuration, with *Bendōwa*, edited by Mizuno Yaoko (1921–2010), in *Nihon shisō taikei*, vols. 12–13 (Iwanami |

| | Shoten) |
|---|---|
| 1990 | reprint of 1970–1972 Mizuno edition, with supplemental chapters, Iwanami paperback edition in 4 volumes |
| 1991–1993 | *Shōbōgenzō*, versions in 75 and in 12 chapters, with supplementary and variant chapters, edited by Kawamura Kōdō, 2 volumes, in *Dōgen zenji zenshū* (Shunjūsha) |
| 2019 | Revised Honzan edition (*Shōbōgenzō: honzanban teiho*), with chapters arranged in 75-plus-12 configuration, with supplementary and variant chapters (Eiheiji; with Daihōrinkaku) |
| 2020 | Revised Honzan edition (*Shōbōgenzō* in 95 chapters), also includes *Shōbōgenzō* in Chinese script, 3 volumes (Sōtōshū Shūmuchō) |

# Appendix 3. Honzan Edition Chapters in This Translation

In the first column on the left, "H" indicates the numerical position in the Honzan edition. In the next column, plain numbers indicate the compilation in seventy-five chapters while "T" indicates the twelve-chapter compilation (with the ones that were previously unknown inside angle brackets < >), "S" indicates supplementary chapters, and "V" indicates variant texts. Alternative textual sources used in the compilation of the Honzan edition appear in the column on the far right, in which the prefix "60" indicates the sixty-chapter compilation, and the prefix "hi" indicates the Himitsu manuscript (see Table 5 for an explanation).

H: *position according to the descriptive table of contents* (kanmoku retsuji 卷目列次)

| | | *corresponding chapter in this translation* | *alternative source text* |
|---|---|---|---|
| H.1 | S1 | Talk on Pursuing the Way | |
| H.2 | 2 | Mahā-prajñā-pāramitā | 60.2 |
| H.3 | 1 | The Realized Kōan | 60.1 |
| H.4 | 7 | One Bright Pearl | 60.7 |
| H.5 | S2 | Procedures for the Hall of Gathered Clouds | |
| H.6 | 5 | This Mind Itself Is the Buddha | 60.5 |
| H.7 | 54 | Washing and Purifying | |
| H.8 | 28 | Making a Bow and Getting the Marrow | hi.1.8 |
| H.9 | 25 | Sound of the Stream, Form of the Mountain | |
| H.10 | 31 | Do No Evils | 60.31 |
| H.11 | 20 | Sometimes | 60.20 |
| H.12 | <T3> | The Merit of the Kāṣāya | 60.41 |

*Appendix 3: Honzan edition chapters in this translation* 279

| H.13 | 32 | Transmitting the Robe | |
|------|----|------------------------|--|
| H.14 | 29 | The Mountains and Waters Sūtra | |
| H.15 | 52 | Buddhas and Ancestors | |
| H.16 | 39 | The Inheritance Certificate | |
| H.17 | S3 | The *Lotus* Turns the *Lotus* | 60.12 |
| H.18 | 8 | The Mind Cannot Be Got | |
| H.19 | S4 | Latter the Mind Cannot Be Got | hi.1.3 |
| H.20 | 19 | The Old Mirror | 60.19 |
| H.21 | 30 | Sūtra Reading | 60.30 |
| H.22 | 3 | Buddha Nature | |
| H.23 | 6 | Deportment of the Practicing Buddha | 60.6 |
| H.24 | 34 | The Teachings of the Buddhas | |
| H.25 | 35 | Spiritual Powers | 60.35 |
| H.26 | 10 | Great Awakening | 60.10 |
| H.27 | 12 | Needle of Seated Meditation | |
| H.28 | 26 | Beyond the Buddha | 60.26 |
| H.29 | 17 | Such | 60.29 |
| H.30 | 16 | Sustained Practice | |
| H.31 | 13 | The Ocean Seal Samadhi | 60.13 |
| H.32 | 21 | Predictions | 60.21 |
| H.33 | 18 | Avalokiteśvara | 60.18 |
| H.34 | 36 | The Arhat | 60.36 |
| H.35 | 40 | The Cypress Tree | 60.40 |
| H.36 | 15 | Radiance | 60.15 |
| H.37 | 4 | Studying the Way with the Body and Mind | 60.4 |
| H.38 | 27 | Talking of a Dream within a Dream | 60.27 |
| H.39 | 33 | Sayings | 60.33 |
| H.40 | 24 | Painted Cake | 60.24 |
| H.41 | 22 | Full Function | 60.22 |
| H.42 | 23 | The Moon | 60.23 |
| H.43 | 14 | Sky Flowers | |
| H.44 | 9 | The Old Buddha Mind | 60.9 |
| H.45 | S5 | The Four Attractions of the Bodhisattva | 60.28 |
| H.46 | 38 | Twining Vines | |
| H.47 | 41 | The Three Realms Are Only Mind | 60.38 |
| H.48 | 42 | Talking of the Mind, Talking of the Nature | |
| H.49 | 44 | The Way of the Buddhas | |
| H.50 | 43 | The Real Marks of the Dharmas | |
| H.51 | 45 | Secret Words | |
| H.52 | 47 | Sūtras of the Buddhas | |
| H.53 | 46 | The Insentient Preach the Dharma | 60.46 |
| H.54 | 48 | Dharma Nature | 60.48 |
| H.55 | 49 | Dhāraṇī | 60.49 |
| H.56 | 50 | Washing the Face | |

| | | | |
|---|---|---|---|
| H.57 | 51 | Face to Face Conferral | |
| H.58 | 11 | Principles of Seated Meditation | 60.11 |
| H.59 | 53 | Plum Blossoms | |
| H.60 | 55 | The Ten Directions | |
| H.61 | 56 | Seeing Buddhas | 60.47 |
| H.62 | 57 | Extensive Study | |
| H.63 | 58 | The Eye | 60.44 |
| H.64 | 59 | Everyday Matters | 60.43 |
| H.65 | 61 | Song of the Dragon | 60.51 |
| H.66 | 37 | Spring and Autumn | |
| H.67 | 62 | The Intention of the Ancestral Master's Coming from the West | |
| H.68 | 64 | The Udumbara Blossom | 60.54 |
| H.69 | 63 | Bringing Forth the Unsurpassed Mind | 60.53 |
| H.70 | <T4> | Bringing Forth the Mind of Bodhi | 60.34 |
| H.71 | 65 | The Complete Body of the Tathāgata | 60.55 |
| H.72 | 66 | The King of Samādhis Samādhi | |
| H.73 | 60 | The Thirty-seven Factors of Bodhi | |
| H.75 | 69 | The Samādhi of Self Verification | |
| H.76 | 68 | Great Practice | |
| H.77 | 70 | Space | 60.56 |
| H.78 | 71 | The Pātra Bowl | 60.42 |
| H.79 | 72 | The Retreat | 60.57 |
| H.80 | 73 | Reading Other Minds | |
| H.81 | 74 | The King Requests Saindhava | |
| H.82 | S6 | Instructions to the Administrative Hall | |
| H.83 | 75 | Leaving Home | |
| H.84 | V.7 | Karma of the Three Times | 60.8 |
| H.85 | <T9> | Four Horses | 60.39 |
| H.86 | <T1> | The Merit of Leaving Home | 60.58 |
| H.87 | <T5> | Offerings to the Buddhas | 60.59 |
| H.88 | <T6> | Refuge in the Treasures of Buddha, Dharma, and Saṃgha | 60.60 |
| H.89 | <T7> | Deep Faith in Cause and Effect | hi.1.5 |
| H.90 | <T10> | The Bhikṣu of the Fourth Dhyāna | hi.3.2 |
| H.91 | S7 | Only Buddhas with Buddhas | hi.3.7 |
| H.92 | S8 | Birth and Death | hi.1.2 |
| H.93 | S9 | The Mind of the Way [Butsudō, renamed "Dōshin"] | hi.1.7 |
| H.94 | T2 | Receiving the Precepts | hi.2.10 |
| H.95 | T12 | The Eightfold Awareness of the Great Person | hi.2.9 |

# Appendix 4. Index of Chapter Titles

This index lists chapter titles in alphabetical order, both in Japanese and in English translation. The leftmost column gives the chapter location in this translation as follows: plain numbers refer to the compilation in seventy-five chapters, "T" indicates the twelve-chapter compilation, "S" indicates supplementary chapters, and "V" indicates variant texts. In the other columns, the prefix "60." indicates the sixty-chapter compilation, the prefix "hi." indicates the Himitsu manuscript (see Table 5 for an explanation), and "H." indicates the numerical position in the Honzan edition.

| | | | | |
|---|---|---|---|---|
| Ango; The Retreat | 72 | 60.57 | – | H.79 |
| Arakan; The Arhat | 36 | 60.36 | – | H.34 |
| Arhat, The; Arakan | 36 | 60.36 | – | H.34 |
| Avalokiteśvara; Kannon | 18 | 60.18 | – | H.33 |
| Baika; Plum Blossoms | 53 | – | – | H.59 |
| Bendōwa; Talk on Pursuing the Way | S1 | – | – | H.1 |
| Bendōwa; Talk on Pursuing the Way | V1 | – | – | – |
| Beyond the Buddha; Butsu kōjō ji | 26 | 60.26 | – | H.28 |
| Beyond the Buddha; Butsu kōjō ji | V3 | – | hi.1.1 | – |
| Bhikṣu of the Fourth Dhyāna, The; Shizen biku | T10 | – | hi.3.2 | H.90 |
| Birth and Death; Shōji | S8 | – | hi.1.2 | H.92 |
| Bodaisatta shishōbō; The Four Attractions of the Bodhisattva | S5 | 60.28 | – | H.45 |
| Bringing Forth the Mind of Bodhi; Hotsu bodai shin | 63 | 60.53 | – | H.69 |
| Bringing Forth the Mind of Bodhi; Hotsu bodai shin | T4 | 60.34 | – | H.70 |
| Bringing Forth the Unsurpassed Mind; Hotsu mujō shin | 63 | 60.53 | – | H.69 |
| Buddha Nature; Busshō | 3 | 60.03 | – | H.22 |
| Buddhas and Ancestors; Busso | 52 | – | hi.3.1 | H.15 |
| Bukkyō; Sūtras of the Buddhas | 47 | – | hi.3.4 | H.52 |
| Bukkyō; The Teachings of the Buddhas | 34 | – | hi.2.2 | H.24 |
| Busshō; Buddha Nature | 3 | 60.03 | – | H.22 |
| Busso; Buddhas and Ancestors | 52 | – | hi.3.1 | H.15 |
| Butsu kōjō ji; Beyond the Buddha | 26 | 60.26 | – | H.28 |
| Butsu kōjō ji; Beyond the Buddha | V3 | | hi.1.1 | – |

| | | | |
|---|---|---|---|
| Butsudō; The Way of the Buddhas | 44 | – | hi.1.9 H.49 |
| Butsudō (Dōshin); The Way of the Buddhas | S9 | – | hi.1.7 H.93 |
| Complete Body of the Tathāgata, The; | | | |
| Nyorai zenshin | 65 | 60.55 | – H.71 |
| Cypress Tree, The; Hakujushi | 40 | 60.40 | – H.35 |
| Daigo; Great Awakening | 10 | 60.10 | – H.26 |
| Daigo; Great Awakening | V6 | – | – – |
| Dai shugyō; Great Practice | 68 | – | hi.2.7 H.76 |
| Darani; Dhāraṇī | 49 | 60.49 | – H.55 |
| Deep Faith in Cause and Effect; Jinshin inga | T7 | – | hi.1.5 H.89 |
| Den'e; Transmitting the Robe | 32 | – | hi.2.1 H.13 |
| Dhāraṇī; Darani | 49 | 60.49 | – H.55 |
| Dharma Nature; Hosshō | 48 | 60.48 | – H.54 |
| Do No Evils; Shoaku makusa | 31 | 60.31 | – H.10 |
| Dōshin (Butsudō); Mind of the Way | S9 | – | hi.1.7 H.93 |
| Dōtoku; Sayings | 33 | 60.33 | – H.39 |
| Eightfold Awareness of the Great Person, The; | | | |
| Hachi dainin gaku | T12 | – | hi.2.9 H.95 |
| Everyday Matters; Kajō | 59 | 60.43 | – H.64 |
| Extensive Study; Henzan | 57 | – | – H.62 |
| Extensive Study; Henzan | V5 | 60.37 | – – |
| Eye, The; Ganzei | 58 | 60.44 | – H.63 |
| Face to Face Conferral; Menju | 51 | – | hi.3.5 H.57 |
| Four Attractions of the Bodhisattva, The; | | | |
| Bodaisatta shishōbō | S5 | 60.28 | – H.45 |
| Four Horses; Shime | T9 | 60.39 | – H.85 |
| Full Function; Zenki | 22 | 60.22 | – H.41 |
| Gabyō; Painted Cake | 24 | 60.24 | – H.40 |
| Ganzei; The Eye | 58 | 60.44 | – H.63 |
| Genjō kōan; The Realized Kōan | 1 | 60.01 | – H.3 |
| Go Shin fukatoku; Latter the Mind | | | |
| Cannot Be Got | S4 | – | hi.1.3 H.19 |
| Great Awakening; Daigo | 10 | 60.10 | – H.26 |
| Great Awakening; Daigo | V6 | – | – – |
| Great Practice; Dai shugyō | 68 | – | hi.2.7 H.76 |
| Gyō Butsu igi; Deportment of the | | | |
| Practicing Buddha | 6 | 60.06 | – H.23 |
| Gyōji; Sustained Practice, part 1 | 16A | 60.16 | – H.30 |
| Gyōji; Sustained Practice, part 2 | 16B | 60.17 | – H.30 |
| Hachi dainin gaku; The Eightfold Awareness | | | |
| of the Great Person | T12 | – | hi.2.9 H.95 |

## Appendix 4: Index of chapter titles

| | | | | |
|---|---|---|---|---|
| Hakujushi; The Cypress Tree | 40 | 60.40 | – | H.35 |
| Henzan; Extensive Study | 57 | – | – | H.62 |
| Henzan; Extensive Study | V5 | 60.37 | – | – |
| *Hokke* ten *Hokke*; The *Lotus* Turns the *Lotus* | S3 | 60.12 | – | H.17 |
| Hosshō; Dharma Nature | 48 | 60.48 | – | H.54 |
| Hotsu bodai shin; Bringing Forth the Mind of Bodhi | T4 | 60.34 | – | H.70 |
| Hotsu bodai shin; Bringing Forth the Mind of Bodhi | 63 | 60.53 | – | H.69 |
| Hotsu mujō shin; Bringing Forth the Unsurpassed Mind | 63 | 60.53 | – | H.69 |
| Hou; The Pātra Bowl | 71 | 60.42 | – | H.78 |
| Ikka myōju; One Bright Pearl | 7 | 60.07 | – | H04 |
| Inheritance Certificate, The; Shisho | 39 | – | hi.2.8 | H.16 |
| Inheritance Certificate, The; Shisho | V2 | – | – | – |
| Inmo; Such 17 | 60.29 | – | H.29 | |
| Insentient Preach the Dharma, The; Mujō seppō | 46 | 60.46 | – | H.53 |
| Instructions to the Administrative Hall; Ji Kuinmon | S6 | – | – | H.81 |
| Intention of the Ancestral Master's Coming from the West, The | 62 | 60.52 | – | H.67 |
| Ippyakuhachi hōmyōmon; One Hundred Gateways | T11 | – | – | – |
| Ji Kuinmon; Instructions to the Administrative Hall | S6 | – | – | H.81 |
| Jinshin inga; Deep Faith in Cause and Effect | T7 | – | hi.1.5 | H.89 |
| Jinzū; Spiritual Powers | 35 | 60.35 | – | H.25 |
| Jippō; The Ten Directions | 55 | 60.45 | – | H.60 |
| Jishō zanmai; The Samādhi of Self Verification | 69 | – | hi.2.6 | H.75 |
| Jukai; Receiving the Precepts | T2 | – | hi.2.10 | H.94 |
| Juki; Prediction | 21 | 60.21 | – | H.32 |
| Jū undo shiki; Procedures for the Hall of Gathered Clouds | S2 | – | – | H.5 |
| Kaiin zanmai; The Ocean Seal Samadhi | 13 | 60.13 | – | H.31 |
| Kajō; Everyday Matters | 59 | 60.43 | – | H.64 |
| Kankin; Sūtra Reading | 30 | 60.30 | – | H.21 |
| Kannon; Avalokiteśvara | 18 | 60.18 | – | H.33 |
| Karma of the Three Times; Sanjigō | T8 | – | – | – |
| Karma of the Three Times; Sanjigō | V7 | 60.08 | – | H.84 |
| Kattō; Twining Vines | 38 | 60.38 | – | H.46 |

# 284 DŌGEN'S *SHŌBŌGENZŌ* VOLUME VIII

| | | | | |
|---|---|---|---|---|
| Keisei sanshoku; Sound of the Stream, Form of the Mountain | 25 | 60.25 | – | H.9 |
| Kenbutsu; Seeing Buddhas | 56 | 60.47 | – | H.61 |
| Kesa kudoku; The Merit of the Kāṣāya | T3 | 60.41 | – | H.12 |
| Kie buppōsōbō; Refuge in the Treasures | T6 | 60.60 | – | H.88 |
| King of Samādhis Samādhi, The; Zanmai ō zanmai | 66 | – | hi.1.10 | H.72 |
| King Requests Saindhava, The; Ō saku sendaba | 74 | – | – | H.81 |
| Kobutsushin; The Old Buddha Mind | 9 | 60.09 | – | H.44 |
| Kokū; Space | 70 | 60.56 | – | H.77 |
| Kokyō; The Old Mirror | 19 | 60.19 | – | H.20 |
| Kōmyō; Radiance | 15 | 60.15 | – | H.36 |
| Kūge; Sky Flowers | 14 | 60.14 | – | H.43 |
| Kuyō shobutsu; Offerings to the Buddhas | T5 | 60.59 | – | H.87 |
| Latter the Mind Cannot Be Got; Go Shin fukatoku | S4 | – | hi.1.3 | H.19 |
| Leaving Home; Shukke | 75 | – | hi.3.3 | H.83 |
| *Lotus* Turns the *Lotus*, The; *Hokke* ten *Hokke* | S3 | 60.12 | – | H.17 |
| Mahā-prajñā-pāramitā; Maka hannya haramitsu | 2 | 60.02 | – | H.2 |
| Maka hannya haramitsu; Mahā-prajñā-pāramitā | 2 | 60.02 | – | H.2 |
| Making a Bow and Getting the Marrow; Raihai tokuzui | 28 | – | hi.1.8 | H.8 |
| Menju; Face to Face Conferral | 51 | – | hi.3.5 | H.57 |
| Merit of Leaving Home, The; Shukke kudoku | T1 | 60.58 | – | H.86 |
| Merit of the Kāṣāya, The; Kesa kudoku | T3 | 60.41 | – | H.12 |
| Mind Cannot Be Got, The; Shin fukatoku | 8 | – | hi.1.4 | H.18 |
| Mind Cannot Be Got, The; Shin fukatoku | S4 | – | hi.1.3 | H.19 |
| Mind Itself Is the Buddha, This; Soku shin ze butsu | 5 | 60.05 | – | H.6 |
| Mind of the Way, The; Dōshin (Butsudō) | S9 | – | hi.1.7 | H.93 |
| Mitsugo; Secret Words | 45 | – | hi.2.4 | H.51 |
| Moon, The; Tsuki | 23 | 60.23 | – | H.42 |
| Mountains and Waters Sūtra, The; Sansui kyō | 29 | – | hi.2.3 | H.14 |
| Muchū setsumu; Talking of a Dream within a Dream | 27 | 60.27 | – | H.38 |
| Mujō seppō; The Insentient Preach the Dharma | 46 | 60.46 | – | H.53 |
| Needle of Seated Meditation; Zazen shin | 12 | – | – | H.27 |
| Nyorai zenshin; The Complete Body of the Tathāgata | 65 | 60.55 | – | H.71 |

## Appendix 4: Index of chapter titles

| | | | | |
|---|---|---|---|---|
| Ō saku sendaba; The King Requests Saindhava | 74 | – | – | H.81 |
| Ocean Seal Samadhi, The; Kaiin zanmai | 13 | 60.13 | – | H.31 |
| Offerings to the Buddhas; Kuyō shobutsu | T5 | 60.59 | – | H.87 |
| Old Buddha Mind, The; Kobutsushin | 9 | 60.09 | – | H.44 |
| Old Mirror, The; Kokyō | 19 | 60.19 | – | H.20 |
| One Bright Pearl; Ikka myōju | 7 | 60.07 | – | H.4 |
| One Hundred Gateways to the Illumination of the Dharma | T11 | – | – | – |
| Only Buddhas with Buddhas; Yui butsu yo butsu | S7 | – | hi.3.7 | H.91 |
| Painted Cake; Gabyō | 24 | 60.24 | – | H.40 |
| Pātra Bowl, The; Hou | 71 | 60.42 | – | H.78 |
| Plum Blossoms; Baika | 53 | – | – | H.59 |
| Prediction; Juki | 21 | 60.21 | – | H.32 |
| Principles of Seated Meditation; *Zazen gi* | 11 | 60.11 | – | H.58 |
| Procedures for the Hall of Gathered Clouds; Jū undo shiki | S2 | – | – | H.5 |
| Radiance; Kōmyō | 15 | 60.15 | – | H.36 |
| Raihai tokuzui; Making a Bow and Getting the Marrow | 28 | – | hi.1.8 | H.8 |
| Reading Other Minds; Tajintsū | 73 | – | – | H.80 |
| Real Marks of the Dharmas, The; Shohō jissō | 43 | – | hi.1.6 | H.50 |
| Realized Kōan, The; Genjō kōan | 1 | 60.01 | – | H.3 |
| Receiving the Precepts; Jukai | T2 | – | hi.2.10 | H.94 |
| Refuge in the Treasures of Buddha, Dharma, and Saṃgha | T6 | 60.60 | – | H.88 |
| Retreat, The; Ango | 72 | 60.57 | – | H.79 |
| Ryūgin; Song of the Dragon | 61 | 60.51 | – | H.65 |
| Samādhi of Self Verification, The; Jishō zanmai | 69 | – | hi.2.6 | H.75 |
| Sangai yui shin; The Three Realms Are Only Mind | 41 | 60.32 | – | H.47 |
| Sanjigō; Karma of the Three Times | T8 | – | – | – |
| Sanjigō; Karma of the Three Times | V7 | 60.08 | – | H.84 |
| Sanjūshichi hon bodai bunpō; The Thirty-seven Factors of Bodhi | 60 | – | hi.1.11 | H.73 |
| Sansui kyō; The Mountains and Waters Sūtra | 29 | – | hi.2.3 | H.14 |
| Sayings; Dōtoku | 33 | 60.33 | – | H.39 |
| Secret Words; Mitsugo | 45 | – | hi.2.4 | H.51 |
| Seeing Buddhas; Kenbutsu | 56 | 60.47 | – | H.61 |
| Senjō; Washing and Purifying | 54 | – | – | H.7 |

# 286 DŌGEN'S *SHŌBŌGENZŌ* VOLUME VIII

| | | | |
|---|---|---|---|
| Senmen; Washing the Face | 50 | – | – | H.56 |
| Senmen; Washing the Face | V4 | 60.50 | – | – |
| Sesshin sesshō; Talking of the Mind, Talking of the Nature | 42 | – | hi.3.6 | H.18 |
| Shime; Four Horses | T9 | 60.39 | – | H.85 |
| Shin fukatoku; The Mind Cannot Be Got | 8 | – | hi.1.4 | H.18 |
| Shin fukatoku; [Latter] the Mind Cannot Be Got | S4 | – | hi.1.3 | H.19 |
| Shinjin gakudō; Studying the Way with the Body and Mind | 4 | 60.04 | – | H.37 |
| Shisho; The Inheritance Certificate | 39 | – | hi.2.8 | H.16 |
| Shisho; The Inheritance Certificate | V2 | – | – | – |
| Shizen biku; The Bhikṣu of the Fourth Dhyāna | T10 | – | hi.3.2 | H.90 |
| Shoaku makusa; Do No Evils | 31 | 60.31 | – | H.10 |
| Shohō jissō; The Real Marks of the Dharmas | 43 | – | hi.1.6 | H.50 |
| Shōji; Birth and Death | S8 | – | hi.1.2 | H.92 |
| Shukke; Leaving Home | 75 | – | hi.3.3 | H.83 |
| Shukke kudoku; The Merit of Leaving Home | T1 | 60.58 | – | H.86 |
| Shunjū; Spring and Autumn | 37 | – | – | H.66 |
| Sky Flowers; Kūge | 14 | 60.14 | – | H.43 |
| Soku shin ze butsu; This Mind Itself Is the Buddha | 5 | 60.05 | – | H.6 |
| Sometimes; Uji | 20 | 60.20 | – | H.11 |
| Song of the Dragon; Ryūgin | 61 | 60.51 | – | H.65 |
| Soshi seirai i; The Intention of the Ancestral Master's | 62 | 60.52 | – | H.67 |
| Sound of the Stream, Form of the Mountain; Keisei sanshoku | 25 | 60.25 | – | H.9 |
| Space; Kokū | 70 | 60.56 | – | H.77 |
| Spiritual Powers; Jinzū | 35 | 60.35 | – | H.25 |
| Spring and Autumn; Shunjū | 37 | – | – | H.66 |
| Studying the Way with the Body and Mind; Shinjin gakudō | 4 | 60.04 | – | H.37 |
| Such; Inmo 17 | 60.29 | – | H.29 | |
| Sustained Practice, part 1; Gyōji | 16A | 60.16 | – | H.30 |
| Sustained Practice, part 2; Gyōji | 16B | 60.17 | – | H.30 |
| Sūtra Reading; Kankin | 30 | 60.30 | – | H.21 |
| Sūtras of the Buddhas; Bukkyō | 47 | – | hi.3.4 | H.52 |
| Tajintsū; Reading Other Minds | 73 | – | – | H.80 |
| Talk on Pursuing the Way; Bendōwa | S1 | – | – | H.1 |
| Talk on Pursuing the Way; Bendōwa | V1 | – | – | – |

*Appendix 4: Index of chapter titles*  287

| | | | | |
|---|---|---|---|---|
| Talking of a Dream within a Dream; | | | | |
| Muchū setsumu | 27 | 60.27 | – | H.38 |
| Talking of the Mind, Talking of the Nature; | | | | |
| Sesshin sesshō | 42 | – | hi.3.6 | H.48 |
| Teachings of the Buddhas, The; Bukkyō | 34 | – | hi.2.2 | H.24 |
| Ten Directions, The; Jippō | 55 | 60.45 | – | H.60 |
| Ten hōrin; Turning the Dharma Wheel | 67 | – | hi.2.5 | H.74 |
| Thirty-seven Factors of Bodhi, The; | | | | |
| Sanjūshichi hon bodai bunpō | 60 | – | hi.1.11 | H.73 |
| Three Realms Are Only Mind, The; | | | | |
| Sangai yui shin | 41 | 60.32 | – | H.47 |
| Transmitting the Robe; Den'e | 32 | – | hi.2.1 | H.13 |
| Tsuki; The Moon | 23 | 60.23 | – | H.42 |
| Turning the Dharma Wheel; Ten hōrin | 67 | – | hi.2.5 | H.74 |
| Twining Vines; Kattō | 38 | 60.38 | – | H.46 |
| Udonge; The Udumbara Blossom | 64 | 60.54 | – | H.68 |
| Udumbara Blossom, The; Udonge | 64 | 60.54 | – | H.68 |
| Uji; Sometimes | 20 | 60.20 | – | H.11 |
| Washing and Purifying; Senjō | 54 | – | – | H.7 |
| Washing the Face; Senmen | 50 | – | – | H.56 |
| Washing the Face; Senmen | V4 | 60.50 | – | – |
| Way of the Buddhas, The; Butsudō | 44 | – | hi.1.9 | H.49 |
| Way of the Buddhas, The; Butsudō (Dōshin) | S9 | – | hi.1.7 | H.93 |
| Yui butsu yo butsu; Only Buddhas | | | | |
| with Buddhas | S7 | – | hi.3.7 | H.91 |
| Zanmai ō zanmai; The King of Samādhis | | | | |
| Samādhi 66 | – | hi.1.10 | H.72 | |
| Zazen gi; Principles of Seated Meditation | 11 | 60.11 | – | H.58 |
| Zazen shin; Needle of Seated Meditation | 12 | – | – | H.27 |
| Zenki; Full Function | 22 | 60.22 | – | H.41 |

## Supplementary Notes to the Translation

The following supplementary notes treat certain items appearing multiple times in the *Shōbōgenzō*, collected here simply in order (a) to avoid repetition in the footnotes, and (b) to provide material too extensive for inclusion in the footnotes. Cross reference to entries in these notes is indicated by **bold type**.

**a blade within the laugh** (*shōri u tō* 笑裏有刀, or *shōchū u tō* 笑中有刀): An idiom deriving from a dialogue between Shushan Kuangren 疏山匡仁 (837-909) and Weishan Lingyou 潙山靈祐 (771–853). The dialogue is quoted in Dōgen's *Shōbōgenzō* in Chinese script (*shinji Shōbōgenzō* 眞字正法眼藏, DZZ.5:208, case 157) and appears as case 87 in the *Congrong Hermitage Record* (*Congrong lu* 從容録, T.2004.48:283b14-24):

> 舉。疏山到潙山便問。承師有言。有句無句如藤倚樹。忽然樹倒藤枯、句歸何處。潙山呵呵大笑。疏山云。某甲四千里賣布單來。和尚何得相弄。潙喚侍者取錢。還這上座。遂囑云。向後有獨眼龍。爲子點破。後到明昭舉前話。昭云。潙山可謂頭正尾正。只是不遇知音。疏復問。樹倒藤枯句歸何處。昭云。更使潙山笑轉新。疏於言下有省。乃云。潙山元來笑裏有刀。

Raised:

When Shushan arrived at [Mount] Weishan, he immediately asked [the abbot, Weishan Lingyou], "I've heard that the Master has a saying, 'Affirmative statements and negative statements are **like vines relying on a tree**.' If the tree suddenly falls, and the vines wither, where do the statements return?"

Weishan gave a big laugh, "Ha ha."

Shushan said, "I came four thousand *li*, selling cloth carpets [used as a "seat" for spirits in ritual]. How can you toy with me, Reverend?"

Weishan summoned his acolyte, saying, "Get some coins to repay this senior seat." Then he allowed that, "In the future, there will be a one-eyed dragon who will reveal it to you."

Later, [Shushan] went to Mingzhao and recounted the preceding story.

Mingzhao said, "Weishan can be called correct from head to tail; it is just that he didn't encounter one who '**knows the music.**'"

Shushan again asked, "If the tree falls, and the vines wither, where do the statements return?"

Mingzhao said, "You make Weishan laugh all over again."

Upon hearing those words, Shushan had a realization and said, "Weishan, from the beginning, had a blade within his laugh."

The point of this story is that Weishan's laugh in response to Shushan's initial question was, not rude or dismissive, but rather something like a sword, or "blade" (*tō* 刀), of insight that was intended to cut off Shushan's deluded thinking.

**a flower opens, and the world arises** (*ke kai sekai ki* 華開世界起): A line from the well-known "dharma transmission verse" (*denbō ge* 傳法偈) that the Twenty-seventh Ancestor of the Zen Lineage in India, Prajñātāra, is said to have spoken when he recognized his disciple Bodhidharma as his spiritual heir. The account found in the *Jingde Era Record of the Transmission of the Flame* (*Jingde chuandeng lu* 景德傳燈録, T.2076.51:216b12-16) reads:

尊者告曰、如來以正法眼付大迦葉。如是展轉乃至於我。我今囑汝。聽吾偈曰。心地生諸種、因事復生理、果滿菩提圓、華開世界起。

Venerable [Prajñātāra] addressed [Bodhidharma] saying, "The Tathāgata passed the true dharma eye to Great Kāśyapa. In this way, it has developed down to me. I now bequeath it to you. Hear my *gāthā*:

> From the mind ground, grow the seeds;
> From phenomena, emerges the principle.
> The fruit ripens, and bodhi is complete;
> A flower opens, and the world arises."

Also see "**a single flower opens five petals**."

**a head of three feet and a neck of two inches** (*zuchō sanjaku keichō nisun* 頭長三尺頸長二寸): A saying attributed to Dongshan Liangjie 洞山良价 (807–869) in a number of Chan texts, including his biography in the *Jingde Era Record of the Transmission of the Flame* (*Jingde chuandeng lu* 景德傳燈録, T.2076.51:323a2-9):

僧來舉。問茱萸如何是沙門行。茱萸曰、行即不無人覺即乖。師令彼僧去。進語曰、未審是什麼行。茱萸曰、佛行佛行。僧迴舉似師。師曰、幽州猶似可。最苦是新羅。僧却問師、如何是沙門行。師曰、頭長三尺頸長二寸。

A monk arrived and recounted [to Dongshan] that when he had asked Zhuyu, "What is the practice of a *śramaṇa*?" Zhuyu had answered, "It's not that he lacks practice; but, if people are aware of it, he deviates from it."

The Master [Dongshan] ordered that monk to go to Zhuyu and convey the response, "What kind of 'practice' is that, exactly?"

Zhuyu said, "Buddha practice, buddha practice." The monk returned and reported that to the Master.

The Master said, "Youzhou [Prefecture] seems all right; what is insufferable is [the Korean kingdom of] Silla."

The monk then asked the Master, "What is the practice of a *śramaṇa*?"

The Master said, "A head of three feet and a neck of two inches."

According to the *Discourse Record of Chan Master Yuanzheng of Mount Cao in Muzhou* (*Muzhou Caoshan Yuanzheng chanshi yulu* 撫州曹山元證禪師語錄, T.47.1987A:534b28-c8), the expression "a head three feet long and a neck two inches short" refers to a **water buffalo**:

三者沙門異類。謂先知有本分事了。喪盡今時一切凡聖因果德行。始得就體一般。名爲獨立底人。亦名沙門稱斷事。始得表裡情忘三世事盡。得無遺漏、得名佛邊事。亦云一手指天地。亦云具大沙門。轉却沙門稱斷邊事、不入諸勝報位。始得名爲沙門行。亦云沙門轉身。亦云披毛戴角。亦喚作水牯牛。恁麼時節始得入異類。亦云色類邊事。所以古人道頭長三尺頸短二寸。祇是這箇道理、不得別會。

Third is the "different types of the *śramaṇa*." To wit, when one has first gained knowledge of the matter of one's original disposition, and one entirely annihilates at that time all cause and effect and karmic results pertaining to what is ordinary or sagely, only then does one gain identity with the essence. This is called being an "independent person." It is also called "the *śramaṇa*'s judgment of affairs." Only then are internal and external passions forgotten, and affairs of the three times exhausted. When one is free from residual defilements, that is called "what is within the vicinity of the buddha." It is also said to be "one hand pointing to heaven and [one to] earth." It is also said to be "the completion of the great *śramaṇa*." Upon transitioning [from this life], the *śramaṇa* judges peripheral affairs and does not enter into the various ranks of karmic rewards. Only then can it be called the "practice of a *śramaṇa*." It is also said to be "the *śramaṇa*'s change of body." It is also said to be "clad in fur and crowned by horns." It is also named "becoming a water buffalo." At such a time, one [i.e., the *śramaṇa*] is first able to enter different types. This is also said to be "various appearances and peripheral affairs." That is why a man of old said, "A head three feet long and a neck two inches short." This alone is "this principle"; no other understanding will do.

The context of this passage is a discussion by Caoshan Benji 曹山本寂 (840–890) of "four kinds of different types" (*shishi irui* 四種異類), i.e., other species of living beings. For an explanation of that formula, see "**move among different types**."

The meaning of the term *śramaṇa* (*shamon* 沙門) in the two passages quoted above goes beyond its ordinary Buddhist sense of "renunciant" —

i.e., a person who cuts worldly ties by becoming a monk or nun and seeks liberation from the round of rebirth by means of austerities and various other modes of religious cultivation. Here and in other Zen texts, the *śramaṇa* is described as someone with great spiritual attainments, comparable to those of an arhat, who has entirely broken free from defilements, attachment, and karmic retribution in the round of rebirth. The expression "change of body" (*tenshin* 轉身), which usually refers to rebirth in one of the **six paths**, is used here in a novel way to refer to a spiritual breakthrough that frees the *śramaṇa* from the round of rebirth. This is called, by antiphrasis, "becoming a water buffalo," or "having a head three feet long and a neck two inches short."

In other contexts, of course, Zen masters employ terms such as "clad in fur and crowned by horns" (*himō taikaku* 披毛戴角) or "beast" (*chikushō* 畜生) as metaphors for the stupidity or amorality of certain people, especially monks. In his "Deportment of the Practicing Buddha" ("Shōbōgenzō gyōbutsu iigi" 正法眼藏行佛威儀, DZZ.1:64), for example, Dōgen says:

> わづかに無生の言句をききてあきらむることなく、身心の功夫をさしおくがごとくするものあり。これ愚鈍のはなはだしきなり。信・法・頓・漸の論にもおよばざる畜類といひぬべし。

There are those who have barely heard the term "no birth" and, without clarifying it, seem to set aside the concentrated effort of **body and mind**. This is stupidity in the extreme. They should be called a type of beast that does not reach the level of discussions even of faith or dharma, sudden or gradual.

He goes on to say that such people "pointlessly 'think only of water and grass'" (*itazura ni sui sō no tan nen naru* いたづらに水草の但念なる), alluding to a description of animals such as camels and donkeys in the *Lotus Sūtra* (*Miaofa lianhua jing* 妙法蓮華經, T.262.9:15c7-8):

> 但念水草、餘無所知。

They think only of water and grass and know of nothing else.

**a hundred fragments** (*hyaku zassui* 百雜碎): A common expression in Zen literature, referring literally to hundreds of "little pieces (*zassui* 雜碎)," or "bits." In some contexts, such as when there is reference to "hitting" with a **staff**, the implied meaning is "shattered into bits." When used metaphorically, according to ZGDJ (s.v. ひゃくざっすい), the idiom has two meanings: 1) the great awakening (*daigo* 大悟) that one experiences when one's discriminating deluded thinking (*funbetsu mōsō* 分別妄想) is stripped away, and 2) a multiplicity that is "incalculable" or "unquantifiable" (*muryō* 無量). There are other meanings, as well. In his *Blue Cliff Record* (*Biyan lu* 碧巖錄, e.g., T.2003.48:154b17), Yuanwu Keqin 圜悟克勤 (1063-1135) uses the expression "[I break this into] a hundred fragments" as an interlinear comment to indicate his disapproval of a phrase in a dialogue he is quoting. The expression is

Supplementary notes to the translation          293

similar in force to his frequently used critical comment, "thirty blows" (*sanjū bō* 三十棒). In the *Extensive Record of Chan Master Yunmen Kuangzhen* (*Yunmen Kuangzhen chanshi guanglu* 雲門匡眞禪師廣錄, T.1988.47:553c27-29), Yunmen Wenyan 雲門文偃 (864-949) is quoted as follows:

師示衆云、盡十方世界乾坤大地、以拄杖一畫百雜碎。三乘十二分教達磨西來、放過即不可。若不放過、不消一喝。

The master [Yunmen] addressed the congregation, saying: "The entire world in the ten directions, and the great earth with its yin and yang, with a single stroke of my **staff**, is [broken into] a hundred fragments. The **three vehicles and twelvefold teachings**, and Bodhidharma's '**coming from the west**': it will not do to overlook them. But if you do not overlook them, you are not worth a single shout."

The glyph 畫 (*ga*), rendered here as "stroke" [of a staff], usually refers to the stroke of an ink brush when writing, not the kind of "blow" (*bō* 棒) with a staff that might break something into pieces; so, Yunmen's remark is somewhat more ambiguous in Chinese than the English translation suggests. Another representative example of how the idiom "a hundred fragments" is used is found in the *Outline of the Linked Flames* (*Liandeng huiyao* 聯燈會要, ZZ.136:784a8-11; X.1557.79:185b11-14), where it is attributed to Xuansha Shibei 玄沙師備 (835-908), a dharma heir of Xuefeng Yicun 雪峰義存 (822-908):

時有僧出問。忽遇明鏡來時如何。師云。胡漢俱隱。玄沙云。我即不然。時有僧問。忽遇明鏡來時如何。沙云。百雜碎。明招云。當與麼時。莫道胡漢俱隱。別作麼生道。沙云破。招云喪也。

At that time there was a monk who came forward and asked, "How about when all of a sudden a bright mirror comes?"

The master [Xuefeng] said, "Foreigner and Han [Chinese] would both disappear."

[Commenting on this dialogue] Xuansha said, "I'm not like that."

At the time, there was a monk who asked, "How about when all of a sudden a bright mirror comes?"

Xuansha said, "[Shattered into] a hundred fragments."

Mingzhao said, "At just such a moment, what would you say instead of saying, 'Foreigner and Han both disappear'?"

Xuansha said, "Defeated."

Mingzhao said, "Dead."

Dōgen comments at length on this dialogue in his "The Old Mirror" ("Shōbōgenzō kokyō" 正法眼藏古鏡). Also see "**bright mirror**."

294 DŌGEN'S *SHŌBŌGENZŌ* VOLUME VIII

**a painted cake can't satisfy hunger** (*gabyō fu ka jū ki* 畫餅不可充飢; *e ni kakeru mochii, ue o yamuru ni atawazu* 畫にかけるもちひ、うゑをやむるにあたはず). A well-known Zen proverb that contrasts the value of a real thing with its representation, or description in texts — the latter being likened to "a painted cake." The saying derives from the biography of Xiangyan Zhixian 香嚴智閑 (d. 898), who is said to have suddenly attained awakening one day when, cutting grass with a sickle, he heard a bit of debris that he had accidentally sent flying go "clunk" as it hit a stalk of bamboo. That story appears, among other places, in the *Jingde Era Record of the Transmission of the Flame* (*Jingde chuandeng lu* 景德傳燈錄, T.2076.51:283c27–284a13):

鄧州香嚴智閑禪師青州人也。厭俗辭親觀方慕道。依溈山禪會。祐和尚知其法器。欲激發智光。一日謂之曰。吾不問汝平生學解及經卷冊子上記得者、汝未出胞胎未辨東西時。本分事試道一句來。吾要記汝。師懵然無對。沈吟久之、進數語陳其所解。祐皆不許。師曰、却請和尚爲説。祐曰、吾説得是吾之見解、於汝眼目何有益乎。師遂歸堂、遍檢所集諸方語句無一言可將酬對。乃自歎曰、畫餅不可充飢。於是盡焚之曰、此生不學佛法也。且作箇長行粥飯僧免役心神。遂泣辭溈山而去。抵南陽覩忠國師遺迹遂憩止焉。一日因山中芟除草木、以瓦礫擊竹作聲。俄失笑間廓然惺悟。遽歸沐浴焚香遙禮溈山。贊云、和尚大悲恩逾父母。當時若爲我説却、何有今日事也。

Chan Master Zhixian of Xiangyan in Dengzhou was a man from Qingzhou. Abhorring secular life, he left his parents and looked in every direction, searching for the way. He took refuge in the Chan assembly at Weishan [Mount Wei], where Reverend [Weishan] Lingyou recognized him as a vessel of the dharma.

Wanting to arouse in him the light of wisdom, one day [Lingyou] said to him: "I do not ask you about what you have learned by studying throughout your life, or what you remember from sūtras and books, but about the time before you emerged from the womb, and before you could tell east from west. Please try to say a single phrase about the matter of your original disposition. I want to give you a prediction."

The master [Zhixian] was stupefied and had no response. Caught up in doubt for a long time, he offered numerous words to express his understanding, but Lingyou did not approve any of them. The master said, "Please, Reverend, explain it for me."

Lingyou said, "What you would get from my explanation is my view; what benefit would it be to your **eyes**?"

The master returned to the hall and searched through all the sayings [of abbots] everywhere that he had collected, but there was not a single word that he could use as a suitable reply. Sighing, he said to himself, "A painted

*Supplementary notes to the translation*     295

cake can't satisfy hunger." With this, he burned all of them and said: "In this life, I will not study the buddha dharma. From now on, I will just be a meal-serving monk and will avoid straining my brain."

Shedding tears, he bid adieu to Weishan and left. Arriving at the former residence of the late National Teacher Nanyang Duzhong, he rested there. One day, when he was in the mountains removing grass and underbrush with a sickle, a bit of debris hit a bamboo stalk and made a noise. In the instant it took him to unconsciously laugh, he had an expansive awakening. Rushing back, he bathed, burned incense, and made prostrations to Weishan from afar. Praising him, he said, "Reverend, your great compassionate blessings exceed those of my father and mother. If at that time you had explained it for me, how could this day have ever come?"

The point of this story is that representations of awakening cannot assuage one's spiritual hunger: only awakening itself can. Xiangyan Zhixian attained awakening only after he gave up trying to grasp it conceptually. His breakthrough was made possible, however, by the extended effort that his teacher Weishan Lingyou 潙山靈祐 (771-853) instigated in him, and by Weishan's steadfast refusal to either approve a single phrase from him or supply him one to cling to. The saying "a painted cake can't satisfy hunger" was subsequently quoted by other Chan masters, such as Yuanwu Keqin 圜悟克勤 (1063-1135), who used it as an interlinear comment in his *Blue Cliff Record* (*Biyan lu* 碧巖錄, T.2003.48:178a3-5), but its appearance in Zen literature always alludes to Xiangyan's frustration with the textual tradition of Zen. In his "Painted Cake" ("Shōbōgenzō gabyō" 正法眼藏畫餅), Dōgen gives a novel interpretation of this saying, arguing that our spiritual hunger is itself "painted" and, therefore, can only be assuaged by a painted cake.

**a separate transmission outside the teachings** (*kyōge betsuden* 教外別傳): A famous slogan used to characterize the mode of dharma transmission employed by the Zen lineage. The "teachings" (*kyō* 教) referred to in this context are the discourses preached by Buddha Śākyamuni, which were handed down in the form of sūtras and subsequently explicated by scholarly monks in the śāstras, or commentarial literature. Zen masters are said to transmit Śākyamuni's buddha mind (*busshin* 佛心) — the very awakening that made him a buddha in the first place — as opposed to the teachings that he subsequently gave voice to.

The notion that Bodhidharma founded the Zen lineage in China by transmitting the Buddha's "mind dharma" (*shinbō* 心法), as opposed to his verbal teachings, first gained currency in texts dating from the eighth and ninth centuries. The Chan historian Guifeng Zongmi 圭峰宗密 (780-841), for example, echoed the understanding of his day when he wrote the following in his *Chart of the Master-Disciple Succession of the Chan Gate that Transmits the Mind Ground in China* (*Zhonghua chuanxindi chanmen shizi chengxi tu* 中華傳心地禪門師資承襲圖, ZZ.110:870a5-6; X.1225.63:33a5-6):

然達磨西來、唯傳心法。故自云、我法以心傳心、不立文字。

Bodhidharma, **coming from the west**, only transmitted the mind dharma. Thus, he himself said, "My method is to use mind to transmit mind; I do not depend on words and letters."

Zongmi was at pains, however, to refute the view of some of his contemporaries that "not depending on words and letters" meant any kind of literal rejection, or complete ignoring, of Buddhist sūtras on the part of Bodhidharma. In his *Preface to the Collected Writings on the Source of Chan* (*Chanyuan zhuquan ji douxu* 禪源諸詮集都序, T.2015:48.400b17-22) he wrote:

達摩受法天竺躬至中華、見此方學人多未得法、唯以名數爲解事相爲行。欲令知月不在指法是我心。故但以心傳心不立文字。顯宗破執。故有斯言。非離文字説解脱也。故教授得意之者、即頻讚金剛楞伽云、此二經是我心要。

When Bodhidharma received the dharma and brought it personally from Sindh to China, he saw that most of the practitioners in this land had not yet obtained the dharma, and that they merely took names and numbered lists for understanding and took formal affairs as practice. He wanted to make them understand that the moon does not consist in the pointing finger and that the dharma is one's own mind. Thus he simply used mind to transmit mind and did not depend on words and letters. He disclosed the axiom and destroyed attachments. It is for this reason that he spoke as he did. It was not that he preached liberation entirely apart from words and letters. Thus, those whom he instructed, who understood what he meant, always praised the *Diamond* and the *Entry into Laṅka*, saying, "These two sūtras are the essence of one's own mind."

Zongmi's view on this matter was subsequently echoed by Yongming Yanshou 永明延壽 (904–975), compiler of the *Records that Mirror the Axiom* (*Zongjing lu* 宗鏡錄, T.2016), and by others (mentioned below).

The expression "a separate transmission outside the teachings" first appears in the *Ancestors Hall Collection* (*Zutang ji* 祖堂集, CBETA.B.144.25:428b10-13), compiled in 952, in the biography of Shishuang Qingzhu 石霜慶諸 (807-888):

師問僧、從什摩處來。對云、雪峯來。師云、有什摩佛法因緣、你擧看。其僧便擧、和尚示衆云、三世諸佛不能唱、十二分教載不起、三乘教外別傳。十方老僧口到這裏百雜碎。

The Master [Shishuang] asked a monk, "Where have you come from?" [The monk] replied, "From Xuefeng."

*Supplementary notes to the translation* 297

The Master said, "If there is some episode that shows what his [teaching of the] buddha dharma is like, you should raise it for us to see."

The monk thereupon raised: "The Reverend [Xuefeng], addressing the assembly, said, 'There is a separate transmission outside the teachings of the **three vehicles**, which the buddhas of the three times cannot explain and which does not appear in the twelvefold teachings. When the words of old monks of the ten directions reach therein, they are [broken into] **a hundred fragments**.'"

The "old monks of the ten directions" referred to here are members of the Chan lineage, specifically those who are the abbots of "ten directions" (i.e., state-sponsored) monasteries. The point seems to be that Chan abbots have a way of speaking that distinguishes them from monks who lecture on sūtras, but that their words, too, are ultimately deficient. In the view of the eminent Zen historian Yanagida Seizan 柳田聖山 (1967, 472-473), the expression "a separate transmission outside the teachings" came into use in the tenth century as a polemic against the ecumenical interpretation of the Chan dharma promoted by Zongmi. Yanagida observes that the expression does not really differ in meaning from the older saying attributed to Bodhidharma, "not depending on words and letters," but because Zongmi had argued against a literal interpretation of that saying, it became necessary to reassert the Chan school's rejection of sūtras by coining a new slogan.

During the Song dynasty, influential texts such as the *Jingde Era Record of the Transmission of the Flame* (*Jingde chuandeng lu* 景德傳燈錄, T.2076), completed in 1004, and the *Tiansheng Era Extended Record of the Flame* (*Tiansheng guangdeng lu* 天聖廣燈錄, ZZ.135; X.1553), compiled in 1036, stressed the separateness and superiority of the Chan "mind dharma" vis-à-vis the sūtra tradition. The slogan "a separate transmission outside the teachings" was most often cited in connection with Bodhidharma; but, in texts dating from the end of the twelfth century, it also came to be attributed to Buddha Śākyamuni, who was supposed to have uttered it on the occasion of transmitting the dharma to Mahākāśyapa. The *Outline of the Linked Flames* (*Liandeng huiyao* 聯燈會要, ZZ.136:440b18-441a2; X.1557.79:14a6-8), compiled in 1183, says:

世尊在靈山會上、拈花示衆。衆皆默然。唯迦葉破顏微笑。世尊云、吾有正法眼藏、涅槃妙心、實相無相、微妙法門。不立文字、教外別傳、付囑摩訶迦葉。

The World-Honored One, at a gathering on Vulture Peak, **held up a flower** to address the congregation. In the congregation, all were silent. Only Kāśyapa **broke into a smile**. The World-Honored One said, "I have the **treasury of the true dharma eye**, the wondrous mind of nirvāṇa, the subtle dharma gate, the true sign of which is signless. Not depending on words and letters, as a separate transmission outside the teachings, I entrust it to Mahākāśyapa."

The idea is that, by holding up a flower, the Buddha preached a wordless sermon that was fundamentally different from and superior to his "teachings," which were first presented orally and then transmitted in the form of written sūtras.

There was, however, some pushback in the Song against that prevailing view. Fori Qisong 佛日契嵩 (1007-1072), for example, sympathized with the position taken earlier by Zongmi and Yanshou, which held that the dharma transmitted in the Zen lineage and the dharma preached by the Buddha in the sūtras were essentially the same. In his *Treatise on the True Lineage of Dharma Transmission* (*Chuanfa zhengzong lun* 傳法正宗論, T.2078.2080:782a28-b14), he writes:

其所謂教外別傳者、非果別於佛教也、正其教迹所不到者也。猶大論曰、言似言及、而玄旨幽邃。尋之雖深、而失之愈遠、其此謂也。昔隋之智者顗公、最爲知教者也。豈不曰。佛法至理、不可以言宣。。。。又經云、修多羅教如標月指。若復見月了知所標畢竟非月。是豈使人執其教迹耶。又經曰、始從鹿野苑終至跋提河、中間五十年、未曾説一字。斯固其教外之謂也。然此極此奧密。雖載於經亦但説耳。聖人驗此、故命以心相傳。而禪者所謂教外別傳乃此也。

The so-called "separate transmission outside the teachings" is not, in the final analysis, something apart from the teachings of the Buddha. Properly speaking, it is what is not reached by his teachings' traces. This is what the *Treatise on the Great Perfection of Wisdom*, for example, means when it says, "Even if the words are fitting and reach right up to it, still the mysterious meaning is profound; one may go very deep in seeking it and still miss it by far." Long ago, in the Sui dynasty, the sage Zhiyi was supreme in his knowledge of the teachings, but did he not say [in his *Profound Commentary on the Vimalakīrti Sūtra*], "The final principle of the buddha dharma cannot be expressed in words"? [portion elided]

Moreover, the *Sūtra* [*of Perfect Awakening*] says, "The teachings of the sūtras are like a finger that points at the moon; when you have turned and seen the moon, you will know that the indication is not the moon." Why is it that people become attached to the teachings' traces ? Again, in a sūtra [the Buddha] says, "For fifty years, from the Deer Park [the place of the Buddha's first sermon] up to the river Ajitavatī [the place of his death], I have yet to preach a single word." This is what the phrase "outside the teachings" is talking about. However, although these profound secrets are contained in the sūtras, they are still just talk. The sages verify it, and thus they decree a face-to-face transmission by means of mind. That is what is called in Chan "a separate transmission outside the teachings."

*Supplementary notes to the translation* 299

In Qisong's view, the Chan lineage was distinguished, not by its literal rejection of scriptures from the outset, but by its superior ability to penetrate to the very deepest meaning of the sūtras, a penetration that follows words as far as they can go and then, at the extreme limit of conceptualization, leaves them behind.

The expression "a separate transmission outside the teachings" eventually came to be incorporated in a famous formula said to characterize the Zen tradition:

A separate transmission outside the teachings (*kyōge betsuden* 教外別傳),
Not depending on words and letters (*furyū monji* 不立文字),
Pointing directly at the person's mind (*jikishi ninshin* 直指人心),
Seeing the nature and attaining buddhahood (*kenshō jōbutsu* 見性成佛).

The oldest source in which all four phrases of this formula are juxtaposed is the *Chrestomathy from the Ancestors Hall* (*Zuting shiyuan* 祖庭事苑, ZZ.113:132a10-13; X.1261.64:379a1-4), compiled in 1108 by Muan Shanqing 睦菴善卿 (dates unknown) and published in 1154:

傳法諸祖初以三藏教乘兼行、後達摩祖師單傳心印、破執顯宗。所謂教外別傳、不立文字、直指人心、見性成佛。然不立文字、失意者多。往往謂屏去文字、以默坐爲禪。斯實吾門之啞羊爾。

In transmitting the dharma, the ancestors initially carried it out in conjunction with the teaching vehicle of the tripiṭaka, but later the Ancestral Master Bodhidharma uniquely transmitted the mind seal, destroying attachments and disclosing the axiom. This is what is called "a separate transmission outside the teachings, not depending on words and letters, **pointing directly at the person's mind, seeing the nature and attaining buddhahood.**" However, those who mistake the meaning of "not depending on words and letters" are many. They constantly speak of abandoning words and letters and regard silent sitting as Chan. These are truly the dumb sheep of our school.

In writing this passage, Muan borrowed language from Zongmi's *Preface to the Collected Writings on the Source of Chan*, quoted above. He interpreted the slogans "a separate transmission outside the teachings" and "not depending on words and letters" as meaning that one should study words and letters and realize their purport without becoming attached to the literal meaning. He rejected the notion, exemplified by the passage from the *Outline of the Linked Flames of Our Lineage* quoted above, that the Buddha himself had engaged in a "separate transmission." In Muan's view, the Indian ancestral masters in the Zen lineage all transmitted the dharma in conjunction with the tripiṭaka, and it was Bodhidharma who first "uniquely transmitted the mind seal" as an expedient fitting the circumstances in China. For more on the provenence of the slogan in four phrases, see "**Pointing directly at the person's mind, seeing the nature and attaining buddhahood**."

Dōgen, in his "The Teachings of the Buddhas" ("Shōbōgenzō bukkyō" 正法眼藏佛教), clearly aligns himself with the position taken earlier by Zongmi, Yanshou, Qisong, and Muan:

> ある漢いはく、釋迦老漢、かつて一代の教典を宣説するほかに、さ らに上乗一心の法を摩訶迦葉に正傳す、嫡嫡相承しきたれり。しか あれば、教は赴機の戯論なり、心は理性の眞實なり。この正傳せる 一心を、教外別傳といふ。三乗十二分教の所談にひとしかるべきに あらず。一心上乗なるゆゑに、直指人心、見性成佛なり、といふ。

> この道取、いまだ佛法の家業にあらず、出身の活路なし、通身の威 儀にあらず。かくのごとくの漢、たとひ數百千年のさきに先達と稱 すとも、恁麼の説話あらば、佛法・佛道はあきらめず、通せざりけ る、としるべし。

Some fellows say that old man Śākya, besides preaching the scriptures throughout his lifetime, also directly transmitted to Mahākāśyapa the dharma of the one mind of the higher vehicle, which has been inherited by successor after successor. Therefore, the teachings are frivolous discourse directed at capacities, while the mind is the true reality of the essential nature. They call this one mind directly transmitted "a separate transmission outside the teachings." It should not be equated with what is talked about in the **three vehicles and twelvefold teachings**. Because it is the higher vehicle of the one mind, they say it is "pointing directly at the person's mind, seeing the nature and attaining buddhahood."

These words are not in the family occupation of the buddha dharma; they lack the survival route for leaving the body; they are not the **deportment** of the body throughout. We should realize that fellows like this, if they have such talk, have not clarified, have not penetrated, the buddha dharma or the way of the buddhas, even though they were calling themselves guides hundreds or thousands of years ago.

In this chapter and his "Sūtras of the Buddhas" ("Shōbōgenzō bukkyō" 正 法眼藏佛經), Dōgen argues that the sūtras and Zen masters convey the same teachings, and that the activities of the Zen master are the enactment of the sūtras.

**a single flower opens five petals** (*ikke kai goyō* 一華開五葉). A line from the well-known "dharma transmission verse" (*denbō ge* 傳法偈) that the Twenty-eighth Ancestor of the Zen Lineage in India, Bodhidharma (also known as the First Ancestor in China), is said to have spoken when he recognized his disciple Huike 慧可 as his spiritual heir. The verse, as found in the *Jingde*

*Era Record of the Transmission of the Flame* (*Jingde chuandeng lu* 景德傳燈録, T.2076.51:219c17-18), reads:

吾本來茲土、傳法救迷情。一華開五葉、結果自然成。

I originally came to this land
To transmit the dharma and save deluded beings.
A single flower opens five petals;
The fruit forms, ripening naturally of itself.

The earliest text in which this verse is attested is the *Ancestors Hall Collection* (*Zutang ji* 祖堂集, CBETA.B.144.25:335b13-14), first compiled in 952. The *Records that Mirror the Axiom* (*Zongjing lu* 宗鏡録, T.2016.48:939c28-940b15) by Yongming Yanshou 永明延壽 (904–975) attributes the verse to "the First Ancestor in this land [China], Bodhidharmatara," and then, immediately afterwards, gives the dharma transmission verses spoken by the "Second Ancestor, Great Master Ke"; the "Third Ancestor, Great Master Can"; the "Fourth Ancestor, Great Master Daoxin"; the "Fifth Ancestor, Great Master Hongren"; and the "Sixth Ancestor, Great Master Huineng." It appears from this arrangement that Yanshou took the "single flower" as a reference to Bodhidharma and the "five petals" as an indication of the five generations of main successors to the Chan lineage that followed him. The idea that the lineage split into five main branches following the Sixth Ancestor, Huineng, had not yet taken shape when the *Records that Mirror the Axiom* was compiled in 961: the oldest extant text to explicitly formulate that scheme of "five houses" (*wujia* 五家) of Chan was *The Eye of Humans and Devas* (*Rentian yanmu* 人天眼目, T.2006.48:333b21-22), compiled in 1188. From the thirteenth century on, however, the formula of "five houses" became accepted as orthodox history, and Bodhidharma's mention of "five petals" was often interpreted as his prediction of that branching of the lineage. Also see "**a flower opens, and the world arises**."

**all living beings in their entirety have buddha nature** (*issai shujō, shitsu u busshō* 一切衆生、悉有佛性): A doctrinal position accepted by most schools of East Asian Buddhism, including Zen. The *locus classicus* is the Northern text of the *Nirvāṇa Sūtra* (*Da banniepan jing* 大般涅槃經), which repeats this statement in thirteen different contexts. In his "Shōbōgenzō busshō" 正法眼藏佛性, Dōgen quotes the following two lines from the *Nirvāṇa Sūtra* (T.374.12:522c24):

釋迦牟尼佛言、一切衆生、悉有佛性。如來常住、無有變易。

Śākyamuni Buddha said, "All living beings in their entirety have buddha nature. The Tathāgata always abides, without any change."

A parable in the *Nirvāṇa Sūtra* (T.12.374:405b9-28) explains that all living beings have buddha nature, but most beings fail to realize that because it is obscured by mental "afflictions" (*bonnō* 煩惱; S. *kleśa*):

佛言、善男子、我者即是如來藏義。一切衆生悉有佛性、即是我義。如是我義、從本已來常爲無量煩惱所覆、是故衆生不能得見。善男子、如貧女人舍内多有眞金之藏。家人大小無有知者。時有異人善知方便語貧女人、我今雇汝。汝可爲我藝除草穢。女即答言、我不能也。汝若能示我子金藏、然後乃當速爲汝作。是人復言、我知方便能示汝子。女人答言、我家大小尚自不知、況汝能知。是人復言、我今審能。女人答言、我亦欲見并可示我。是人即於其家掘出眞金之藏。女人見已心生歡喜、生奇特想宗仰是人。善男子、衆生佛性亦復如是。一切衆生不能得見、如彼寶藏貧人不知。善男子、我今普示一切衆生所有佛性、爲諸煩惱之所覆蔽、如彼貧人有眞金藏不能得見。如來今日普示衆生諸覺寶藏、所謂佛性。而諸衆生見是事已、心生歡喜歸仰如來。善方便者即是如來。貧女人者即是一切無量衆生。眞金藏者即佛性也。

Buddha said, "Good sons! The word 'self' here refers to the womb of the tathāgata. All living beings in their entirety have buddha nature. This is the meaning of 'self.' This is the meaning of 'self,' but from the beginning it has always been obscured by countless mental afflictions, on account of which living beings are unable to see it. Good sons! It is like a poor woman who had a vast store of pure gold in her house, but the family members, young and old, did not know [where it was].

At the time there was a stranger who well understood skillful means, and he said to the poor woman, 'I'll hire you. You can do gardening and remove weeds for me.'

The woman replied, 'I can't do it. But if you can show me where my store of gold is, then I'll go to work for you right away.'

That person said, 'I have skillful means that will be able to show you.'

The woman replied, 'My family, young and old do not know. How could you know?'

That person said, 'I have the ability to investigate.'

The woman replied, 'I also want to see, so I'll join you, and you can show me.'

That person thereupon dug up the store of pure gold. When the woman saw it, her heart was filled with joy and amazement, and she deeply respected that person. Good sons! The buddha nature of living beings is also like this. That all living beings are unable to see it is just like the treasure store that poor people do not know of. Good sons! I now broadly show that all living beings have buddha nature, which has been concealed by mental afflictions. This is like the poor woman who had a store of pure

*Supplementary notes to the translation* 303

gold but was not able to see it. The Tathāgata today broadly instructs living beings to all awaken to their treasure store, which is called the buddha nature. And, when living beings have seen that, their hearts will fill with joy, and they will take refuge in the Tathāgata. The person with a good command of skillful means represents the Tathāgata. The poor woman represents all innumerable living beings. The store of pure gold represents the buddha nature."

At the opening of his Shōbōgenzō busshō" 正法眼藏佛性, Dōgen quotes the *Nirvāṇa Sūtra* line, *issai shujō, shitsu u busshō* 一切衆生、悉有佛性; in his commentary on the line, rather than read it "all living beings in their entirety have buddha nature," he famously recasts the sentence, treating the predicate "in their entirety have" (*shitsu u* 悉有) as the nominative "entirety of beings." Thus, he explains,

悉有の言は、衆生なり、群有なり。すなはち悉有は佛性なり、悉有 の一悉を衆生といふ。

The words "in their entirety have" refer to living beings, the multitude of beings. That is, the "entirety of beings" is buddha nature; one entirety of the "entirety of beings" is called "living beings."

Thus, on this reading, rather than all living (or sentient) beings *having* buddha nature, all beings (or entities) *are* buddha nature. The concept of buddha nature was one of the most widely discussed topics in East Asian Buddhism, subject to a wide range of interpretations. In his subsequent remarks in the "Shōbōgenzō busshō," Dōgen dismisses several of the most common views: that buddha nature is the potential to become a buddha, that it is the activity of cognition within us, or that it is a universal self pervading the world. Rather, in keeping with his novel reading of the *Nirvāṇa Sūtra* line, he prefers to treat buddha nature as existence itself — not an abstract principle of being, but the actual occurrence of things — or, as he puts it simply at the end of his essay, "fences, walls, tiles, and pebbles."

**all the worlds in the ten directions are the single eye of the *śramaṇa*** (*jin jippō kai ze shamon isseki gen* 盡十方界是沙門一隻眼; also read *isseki gan*): A saying attributed to the Tang-dynasty monk Changsha Jingcen 長沙景岑 (dates unknown), a dharma heir of Nanquan Puyuan 南泉普願 (748-835), in the former's biography in the *Jingde Era Record of the Transmission of the Flame* (*Jingde chuandeng lu* 景德傳燈録, T.2076.51:274a10-20):

上堂日、我若一向舉揚宗教、法堂裏須草深一丈。我事不獲已、所以 向汝諸人道、盡十方世界是沙門眼、盡十方世界是沙門全身、盡十方 世界是自己光明、盡十方世界在自己光明裏、盡十方世界無一人不是 自己。我常向汝諸人道、三世諸佛共盡法界衆生是摩訶般若光。光未 發時、汝等諸人、向什麼處委。光未發時尚無佛無衆生消息。何處得

304 DŌGEN'S *SHŌBŌGENZŌ* VOLUME VIII

山河國土來。時有僧問、如何是沙門眼。師云、長長出不得。又云、成佛成祖出不得。六道輪迴出不得。

At a convocation in the dharma hall [Changsha] said, "If I were to raise our essential teaching in full, within the dharma hall there would surely be grass one foot deep. But I myself am indeed deficient, so I say to you all that all the worlds in the ten directions are the eye of the *śramaṇa*; all the worlds in the ten directions are the entire body of the *śramaṇa*; all the worlds in the ten directions are the radiance of the self; all the worlds in the ten directions are within the radiance of the self; in all the worlds in the ten directions, there is no one that is not the self. I always say to all of you that the buddhas of the three times, together with living beings of all the worlds, are the light of *mahā-prajñā*. When the light has yet to shine forth, where do all of you place your trust? When the light has yet to shine forth, moreover, there are no buddhas and no living beings to give respite. How is it possible to get any mountains, rivers, or lands?"

At the time there was a monk who asked, "What is the eye of the *śramaṇa*?"

The Master said, "You can't get it out for a long, long time." Again, he said, "You can't get it out by attaining buddhahood or becoming an ancestor; you can't get it out by rebirth in the **six paths**."

A slightly variant version of this passage is found in the *Outline of the Linked Flames* (*Liandeng huiyao* 聯燈會要, ZZ.136:536a5-14; X.1557.79:61c12-21). In it, Changsha uses the expression "single eye of the *śramaṇa*" (*shamon isseki gen* 沙門一隻眼), not simply "eye of the *śramaṇa*" (*shamon gen* 沙門眼).

The term "*śramaṇa*" (*shamon* 沙門), meaning "ascetic," is used generically for religious renunciants and specifically for Buddhist monks. In the colophons to several chapters of his *Shōbōgenzō*, Dōgen calls himself a *śramaṇa*, which in those contexts simply means "monk" and is perfectly modest. There are numerous places in Zen literature, however, where *śramaṇa* are presented as heroic figures who, like the arhats, have overcome all defilements and attachments and thereby attained nirvāṇa. Such depictions are not always unambiguously positive, for they can contain some criticism, either explicit or implicit, that the *śramaṇa* lacks the bodhisattva's vow to remain in saṃsāra to save all living beings; see "**a head of three feet and a neck of two inches**." The expression "to lose one eye" (*shikkyaku isseki gen* 失却一隻眼), in Zen texts, can mean to be disabused of a deluded point of view or to transcend normal vision; see "**eye**."

Dōgen quotes the saying "all the worlds in the ten directions are the single eye of the *śramaṇa*" in three chapters of the *Shōbōgenzō*: "The Three Realms are Only Mind" ("Shōbōgenzō sangai yui shin" 正法眼藏三界唯心, DZZ.1:444), "The Insentient Preach the Dharma" ("Shōbōgenzō mujō seppō" 正法眼藏無情説法, DZZ.2:11), and "The Ten Directions"

*Supplementary notes to the translation*     305

("Shōbōgenzō jippō" 正法眼藏十方, DZZ.2:94). In the last of those chapters, he identifies this eye as one of the many eyes of the Śramaṇa Gautama.

**await awakening** (*taigo* 待悟): According to Dōgen, the "expectation" (*ki* 期, or *kitai* 期待) of an "awakening" (*go* 悟, *satori*) that, once attained, will obviate the need for any further Buddhist practice. The deluded conception of awakening as an ultimate, perfected state of being in which no further study of the way (*gakudō* 學道) is called for, he says, is an obstacle to liberation (*dodatsu* 度脱). In his "Great Awakening" ("Shōbōgenzō daigo" 正法眼藏大悟, Variant Text 6), Dōgen writes:

> もし待悟爲則せば、すでに大悟現成せむよりのちは、學道すべから
> ざるか。恁麼の見解は、佛道の行履なり、恁麼の行履＜は＞、佛頭
> の關捩、諸佛の大道にあらず。

> If we "take awaiting awakening as the norm," after great awakening has appeared, should we no longer study the way? Such a view is not conduct on the way of the buddhas; such conduct is not the **pivot** at the head of the buddhas, not the great way of the buddhas.

The point here is that buddhas, who are fully awakened beings, never cease studying the way. In the *Extensive Record of Reverend Dōgen* (*Dōgen oshō kōroku* 道元和尚廣錄, DZZ.4:164, no. 11), Dōgen applies this argument to the practice of seated meditation (*zazen* 坐禪):

> 諸宗坐禪、待悟爲則。譬如假船筏而度大海、將謂度海而可抛船矣。
> 吾佛祖坐禪不然、是乃佛行也。

> The seated meditation of the various schools makes awaiting awakening the norm. Like availing oneself of a raft to cross a great ocean, once one has crossed the ocean, one should let go of the boat. The seated meditation of our **buddhas and ancestors** is not like this: it is the practice of a buddha.

Again, the point is that buddhas never give up the practice of seated meditation, even after they realize great awakening. The error of "awaiting awakening," as Dōgen uses the term in both of these passages, is that it embraces a false conception of the goal of Buddhist practice.

In modern times, Dōgen's criticism of "awaiting awakening" is sometimes invoked in a contrast between Sōtō and Rinzai attitudes toward seated meditation — the former, in which the practitioner is said to engage in seated meditation for its own sake, with "nothing to be gained" (*mushotoku* 無所得), "just sitting" (*shikan taza* 祇管打坐), with "body and mind sloughed off" (*shinjin datsuraku* 身心脱落); the latter, sometimes dismissed as "the Zen of awaiting awakening" (*taigo zen* 待悟禪), which is said to treat meditation as a means to a spiritual awakening (*satori* 悟), brought about by the cultivation of a "great doubt" (*daigi* 大疑), or intense inquiry, into a kōan. This modern interpretation, however, is not well founded in what Dōgen actually says about "awaiting awakening." In a passage from "Great Awakening" ("Shōbōgenzō daigo" 正法眼藏大悟), the only other place where he employs the expression, he writes:

還假悟否。この道をしづかに參究して、胸襟にも換却すべし、頂顙にも換却すべし。近日大宋國禿子等いはく、悟道是本期。かくのごとくいひて、いたづらに待悟す。しかあれども、佛祖の光明にてらされざるがごとし。ただ眞善知識に參取すべきを、懶墮にして蹉過するなり、古佛の出世にも度脱せざりぬべし。

"Do they also avail themselves of awakening?" Quietly investigating these words, you should switch them for your breast; you should switch them for the crown of your head. Recently, shavelings in the Land of the Great Song say, "Awakening to the way is the basic expectation." So saying, they vainly await awakening. Nevertheless, they seem not to be illumined by the radiance of the buddhas and ancestors. Given over to laziness, they miss the fact that they should just study with a true wise friend. Even during the appearance in the world of the **old buddhas**, they would probably not have been liberated.

The "words" that Dōgen says students should earnestly and persistently investigate (*sankyū* 參究) — "Do they also avail themselves of awakening?" — come from a kōan involving Reverend Mihu of Jingzhao 京兆米胡和尚 (dates unknown) and Yangshan Huiji 仰山慧寂 (803-887), in his *Shōbōgenzō* in Chinese script (*shinji Shōbōgenzō* 眞字正法眼藏, DZZ.5:128, case 7), which Dōgen has just quoted in its entirety. Thus, when he criticizes Chinese monks who "vainly await awakening" (*itazura ni taigo su* いたづらに待悟す), he is obviously not blaming them for studying kōans, or for "contemplating the sayings" (*kanna* 看話) of ancestral teachers in an attempt to gain awakening. On the contrary, he takes them to task for their "laziness" (*randa* 懶墮) and their failure to study with, or "inquire of" (*sanshu* 參取), good teachers. If anything, what Dōgen seems to mean by "awaiting awakening" in this context is the failure on the part of some monks to make an effort to gain liberation by rigorously investigating kōans under the guidance of a true Zen master. Earlier in the same chapter, he says:

しかあればすなはち、三界を拈じて大悟す、百草を拈じて大悟す、四大を拈じて大悟す、佛祖を拈じて大悟す、公案を拈じて大悟す。みなともに大悟を拈來して、さらに大悟するなり。その正當恁麼時は而今なり。

Therefore, they take up the **three realms** and greatly awaken; they take up the hundred grasses and greatly awaken; they take up the **four elements** and greatly awaken; they take up the buddhas and ancestors and greatly awaken; they take up a kōan and greatly awaken. In every case, they are

*Supplementary notes to the translation* 307

taking up the great awakening and further awakening greatly. This very moment that they do so is the present.

In this passage, Dōgen does not single out kōan study as the *sine qua non* of Buddhist practice, but he certainly allows it as one of the circumstances in which people greatly awaken.

It is possible that some of the "shavelings in the Land of the Great Song" whom Dōgen criticized for "vainly awaiting awakening" were dharma heirs of Dahui Zonggao in the Linji (Rinzai) lineage, but there is no way to be certain of that. Dahui himself, it is worth noting, frequently criticized "waiting for awakening." In the *Discourse Record of Chan Master Dahui Pujue* (*Dahui Pujue chanshi yulu* 大慧普覺禪師語錄, T.1998A.47:921a23-25), for example, we find his response to a lay follower who had written that, "In my later years, blocked by knowledge, I have not had a single experience of awakening." Dahui replied:

顛倒有三。自言爲知解所障是一。自言未悟甘作迷人是一。更在迷中將心待悟是一。

You have three inverted views. You yourself say it is on account of knowledge that you are blocked; that is one. You yourself say you are not yet awakened and are fine with being a deluded person; that is [the second] one. Moreover, in the midst of delusion, you set your mind on awaiting awakening; that is [the third] one.

The claim that someone is "awaiting awakening" has always been a criticism directed against others; it has never been endorsed by any Zen masters as a legitimate approach.

**bag of skin** (*shu hitai* 臭皮袋): A bag made of animal skin; i.e., leather. In Buddhist and especially Zen literature, a common term for the body of a living being, usually (but not always) human, conveying some disgust for its fundamental impurity; by extension, a "person." In his "Buddha Nature" ("Shōbōgenzō busshō" 正法眼藏佛性), Dōgen quotes two external sources that use the term. The first is a kōan that appears as case 18 of the *Congrong Hermitage Record* (*Congrong lu* 從容錄, T.2004.48:238b25-c1):

舉。僧問趙州、狗子還有佛性也無。州云、有。僧云、既有、爲甚麼却撞入這箇皮袋。州云、爲他知而故犯。又有僧問、狗子還有佛性也無。州曰、無。僧云、一切衆生皆有佛性。狗子爲什麼却無。州云、爲伊有業識在。

Raised:

A monk asked Zhaozhou, "Does even a dog have buddha nature?"

Zhou said, "Yes."

The monk said, "So, if it [i.e., the dog] has it, then why did it [i.e., the buddha nature] force entry into this bag of skin?

308     DŌGEN'S *SHŌBŌGENZŌ* VOLUME VIII

Zhou said, "Because it knowingly committed an intentional crime."

There was another monk who asked, "Does even a dog have buddha nature?"

Zhou said, "No."

The monk said, "**All living beings have buddha nature**. Why doesn't the dog have it?"

Zhou said, "Because it has **karmic consciousness**."

The second is a line from *Reverend Shitou's Song of the Thatched Hut*:

欲識庵中不死人、豈離只今這皮袋

If you wish to know the undying person in the hermitage, how could it be apart from this present bag of skin?

Dōgen also uses "bag of skin" when referring in a critical way to Buddhist monks, especially Zen monks, sometimes in the form "stinking skin bag" (*shū hitai* 臭皮袋).

**bare mind in pieces** (*sekishin henpen* 赤心片片): A common expression in Zen literature, the precise sense of which is difficult to determine from the contexts in which it appears and thus remains a matter of conjecture based on its etymology. In ordinary Chinese and Japanese, the term "bare mind" (*sekishin* 赤心) is short for "mind of a newborn baby" (*sekishi no shin* 赤子之心), which means "pure-minded" in several senses: "kind-hearted"; "without artifice"; and "sincere." In Zen texts, "bare mind" is sometimes a metaphor for the buddha mind, which is said to operate in a similarly spontaneous and compassionate manner. In ordinary language, the expression "in pieces" (*henpen* 片片) has two meanings: 1) "piecemeal," or "partial"; and 2) to "flutter" or to "float lightly." Modern dictionary definitions of the expression "bare mind in pieces" vary. According to BGDJ (s.v. しゃくしんへんへん), it means "to be full to the brim with sincerity" (*shinjin ni michimichiteiru koto* 真心に満ち満ちていること). According to *Zengo jiten* 禅語辞典 (Koga Hidehiko [1991, 248]), it refers to a "meticulous sincerity" (*ikitodoita magokoro* 行き届いたまごころ). According to ZGDJ (s.v. せきしんへんぺん), "bare mind" refers to the exercise of "utmost compassion" (*hanahadashii jihi* はなはだしい慈悲), and "in pieces" means "here and there" (*tokorodokoro* 処処). We (the translators and editor of the present work) have speculated that it means either "the lively operation of the buddha mind in daily life" or "a sincere mind in every matter." Problems remain, however, with all of these interpretations. In particular, it is hard to see how the expression "in pieces" (*henpen* 片片) — which in ordinary usage indicates something "piecemeal," "partial," or "fluttering" — could come to mean "full to the brim," "meticulous," or "in every matter" when it is used in Zen texts to describe the "bare mind." Two examples of actual usage follow.

In his "Such" ("Shōbōgenzō inmo" 正法眼藏恁麼) chapter, Dōgen says:

赤心もとどまらず、片片として往來す。たとひまことありといふと
も、吾我のほとりにとどこほるものにあらず。

The bare mind also does not stand still but comes and goes in pieces; though there may be truth in it, it is not something that lingers in the vicinity of the self.

What Dōgen seems to mean here is that the buddha mind, despite being characterized by "truth," or "sincerity" (*makoto* まこと), is not something that is "stagnant," or "stuck" (*todokōru* 滯る) nearby, within our sense of "self" (*goga* 吾我); it is rather, something that comes and goes "in pieces" (*henpen toshite* 片片として), which is to say, in an inconstant, fragmented, or flitting manner.

In the *Discourse Record of Chan Master Yuanwu Foguo* (*Yuanwu Foguo chanshi yulu* 圓悟佛果禪師語錄, T.1997.47:790c7-13), Yuanwu Keqin 圜悟克勤 (1063-1135) employs the expression in his comment on a kōan involving Xuefeng Yicun 雪峰義存 (822-908) and the latter's disciple Xuansha Shibei 玄沙師備 (835-908):

舉。雪峯示衆云、世界闊一丈、古鏡闊一丈。世界闊一尺、古鏡闊一尺。玄沙指火爐云、且道、火爐闊多少。峯云、如古鏡闊。沙云、老和尚腳跟未點地在。師云、現成公案。古鏡本非火爐。打破籠羅。火爐即是古鏡。若非父子投機、爭見赤心片片。諸人作麼生會他道、這老漢腳跟未點地在。如來寶杖親蹤跡。

Raised:

Xuefeng addressed the assembly, saying, "If the breadth of the world is ten feet, the breadth of the **old mirror** is ten feet; if the breadth of the world is one foot, the breadth of the old mirror is one foot."

Xuansha pointed at the brazier and said, "Tell me, is the breadth of the brazier large or small?"

Feng said, "It's like the breadth of the old mirror."

Sha said, "This old reverend's heels haven't touched the earth."

[Comment]

The Master [Yuanwu] said, "A clear-cut case. The old mirror, fundamentally, is not a brazier: I smash the **cages and nets**. A brazier, however, is the old mirror. If this is not 'father and son in accord,' then competing views are 'the bare mind in pieces.' People, how do you understand his saying, 'This old reverend's heels haven't touched the earth'? The Tathāgata's jewelled staff is close by these traces."

Yuanwu's point seems to be that, although Xuansha, having asked a tricky question, appears to reject the response given by his teacher Xuefeng, neither

310 DŌGEN'S *SHŌBŌGENZŌ* VOLUME VIII

the "father" (teacher) nor the "son" (disciple) are in error. In this context, both men channel the "bare mind" of awakening by speaking spontaneously and unaffectedly, but that mind is "in pieces" because (on the surface, at least) their sayings do not agree.

**bearing the load coming, bearing the load going, bearing the load coming again** (*tanrai tanko yū tanrai* 擔來擔去又擔來): A saying attributed to Dōgen's teacher in China, Rujing 如淨 (1162–1227), in the context of his comment on a kōan, as reported in the *Discourse Record of Reverend Rujing* (*Rujing heshang yulu* 如淨和尚語錄, T.2002A.48:126b9-14):

復舉記得。古來有兩人尊宿。一人云、我逢人則不出、出則便爲人。一人云、我逢人則便出。出則不爲人。淨慈借兩人尊宿、作箇擔子、擔在肩上、要令四海五湖衲子遞代相傳也。恁麼擔謂之荷擔佛祖。且道、淨慈只今作麼生。擔來擔去又擔來、撼動風光透九垓。

Further raised, to bear in mind.

In the past there were two honored elders. One said, "When I happen to meet people, I do not show myself; but when I show myself, I benefit people."

The other one said, "When I happen to meet people, I show myself; but when I show myself, it doesn't benefit people."

[Rujing's comment]

"Here at Jingci [Monastery], I borrow [the kōan featuring] these two honored elders and make it into a load to bear on the shoulders. Then I order patch-robed monks of the four seas and five lakes [i.e., the entire world] to take turns [in bearing the load], transmitting it in succession. Bearing like this is what I call bearing the load that is the **buddhas and ancestors**. Tell me, what is Jingci [i.e., I, the abbot] up to right now? Bearing the load coming, bearing the load going, and bearing the load coming again, I shake the landscape, penetrating the far reaches of heaven and earth."

The glyph 擔 (*tan*), which may be translated as "to carry," "to shoulder," or "to bear," has the same metaphorical meanings in Chinese as the foregoing English renderings of it — namely, "to take upon oneself," or "to take responsibility for"; and "to suffer," or "to endure." The "load" that Rujing expects monks to bear (i.e., to take personal responsibility for) is the dharma of the buddhas and ancestors, which they should both embody in their own lives and teach to others.

**before and after cut off** (*zengo saidan* 前後際斷): An idiom that appears frequently in the "perfection of wisdom" (*hannya haramitsu* 般若波羅蜜; S. *prajñā-pāramitā*) genre of sūtras, where it indicates the emptiness (*kū* 空) of dharmas. For example, the *Great Perfection of Wisdom Sūtra* (*Mohe boruo boluomi jing* 摩訶般若波羅蜜經, T.223.8:332b25-c1) says:

## Supplementary notes to the translation
311

須菩提、譬如江河大海四邊水斷是名爲洲。須菩提、色亦如是前後際斷。受想行識前後際斷、乃至一切種智前後際斷。以是前後際斷故、一切法亦斷。須菩提、是一切法前後際斷故，即是寂滅，即是妙寶，所謂空、無所得、愛盡、無餘、離欲、涅槃。

Subhūti, if, for example, [a piece of land] is cut off on all four sides by the waters of a great river or ocean, we call it an island. Subhūti, form is also like this: its before and after are cut off. The before and after of sensation, conception, formations, and consciousness are cut off, and so on up to, the before and after of [a buddha's] omniscience are cut off. Because before and after are cut off in this way, all dharmas are also cut off. Because all dharmas are cut off, this is quiescence; this is the marvelous treasure that is called "emptiness," "nothing to be gained," "elimination of craving," "no remainder," "freedom from desire," and "nirvāṇa."

The "cutting off" (*dan* 斷) of "all dharmas" (*issai hō* 一切法) spoken of here refers to the fundamental "non-arising" (*fushō* 不生), or emptiness, of dharmas. The unspoken premises here are that dharmas do not arise without a cause, and that dharmas cut off from what precedes and follows them cannot be caused themselves or be the cause of anything else.

In some Zen texts, "before and after cut off" is a name for the insight that results when "not a single thought arises" (*ichinen fushō* 一念不生) and the "essence of mind" (*shin'yō* 心要), or "mind source" (*shingen* 心源) comes into view. The *locus classicus* of that usage is found in a short work by Chengguan 澄觀 (738-839), a patriarch of the Huayan school, that is included in the *Jingde Era Record of the Transmission of the Flame* (*Jingde chuandeng lu* 景德傳燈錄, T.2076.51:459b22-c22); it begins as follows:

五臺山鎭國大師澄觀答皇太子問心要

至道本乎其心。心法本乎無住。無住心體靈知。不昧性相寂然。包含德用該攝內外。能深能廣非有非空。不生不滅無終無始。求之而不得。棄之而不離。迷現量則惑苦紛然。寤眞性則空明廓徹。雖即心即佛、唯證者方知。然有證有知、則慧日沈沒於有地。若無照無悟、則昏雲掩蔽於空門。若一念不生、則前後際斷。照體獨立、物我皆如。直造心源、無智無得。

"Great Master Zhenguo of Mount Wutai, Chengguan's Reply to a Question of the Crown Prince Concerning the Essence of Mind"

The ultimate Way is fundamentally this mind. The mind-dharma is fundamentally nonabiding. The essence of the nonabiding mind is numinous awareness. Unobscured, its nature and characteristics are quiescent, but it contains virtuous functions that are fully included inside and out. It is capable of depth and capable of breadth, but it is neither existing nor empty. It does not arise and does not cease; it has no end and has no beginning. Seek it, and it is not attained. Discard it, and it is not removed. When there

312 DŌGEN'S *SHŌBŌGENZŌ* VOLUME VIII

is deluded perception, there is confusion and suffering, trouble and disorder. When one awakens to the true nature, the illumination of emptiness reaches everywhere. Although this mind is in itself buddha, only those who realize it thereby know it. But even when there is realization and there is knowing, still the sun of wisdom sinks below the earth of existence [i.e., the belief in really existing dharmas]. If there is no illumination and no awakening, then clouds of darkness conceal the gate of emptiness. If not a single thought arises, before and after are cut off. The body of illumination stands alone; things and self are all alike. One arrives directly at the mind-source, with no knowledge and no attainment.

In this context, "before and after are cut off" refers to ceasing, or at least seeing through, the mental discrimination (*funbetsu* 分別) that ordinarily conceals the "essence of mind." Chengguan's short treatise was reproduced in a number of other Chan texts, as well, including Yongming Yanshou's 永明延壽 (904–975) *Records that Mirror the Axiom* (*Zongjing lu* 宗鏡錄, T.2016.48:657c11), where it is referred to as the "Memorial to the Throne on the Essence of Mind" (*Xinyao qian* 心要牋); and Dahui Zonggao's 大慧宗杲 (1089–1163) *Treasury of the True Dharma Eye* (*Zhengfayanzang* 正法眼藏, ZZ.118:22b9-23a15; X.1309.67:567a3-b3).

**before King Majestic Voice** (*Ion'ō izen* 威音王以前; *Ion'ō yori saki* 威音王より さき): In Zen texts, an expression that points to the original state of things: the buddha mind itself, prior to the arising of any discriminating thought or dualistic understanding.

"King Majestic Voice" is the name of a buddha (actually, a succession of twenty billion buddhas with the same name) who appears in chapter 20 of the *Lotus Sūtra* (*Miaofa lianhua jing* 妙法蓮華經, T.262.9:50c2-14), entitled "The Bodhisattva 'Never Belittling'" (*Chang Buqing Pusa pin* 常不輕菩薩品). He is said to have lived "immeasurable, limitless, inconceivable kalpas ago," in a kalpa named "free from decay" (*risui* 離衰; S. *vinirbhoga*). In the Sanskrit text of the *Lotus Sūtra*, this buddha's name is given as Bhīṣmagarjitasvararāja, or "King Whose Voice is a Terrible Roar."

In the Zen tradition, King Majestic Voice somehow came to represent the most ancient, primal buddha, before whom none existed. Evidence of that understanding (which, contrary to ZGDJ s.v. いおん 威音, has no basis in the *Lotus Sūtra*) is found in the *Dharma Treasure Platform Sūtra of the Sixth Ancestor* (*Liuzu dashi fabaotan jing* 六祖大師法寶壇經, T.2008.48:357b29-c6), the thirteen-century edition of the *Platform Sūtra*:

永嘉玄覺禪師、溫州戴氏子。少習經論、精天台止觀法門。因看維摩經發明心地。偶師弟子玄策相訪、與其劇談。出言暗合諸祖、策云、仁者得法師誰。曰、我聽方等經論、各有師承。後於維摩經悟佛心

*Supplementary notes to the translation*        313

宗、未有證明者。策云、威音王已前即得、威音王已後、無師自悟、
盡是天然外道。

Chan Master Yongjia Xuanjue was a child of the Dai clan in Wenzhou. As a youth he trained in sūtras and śāstras and was well versed in the Tiantai dharma gate of calming and contemplation. By reading the *Vimalakīrti Sūtra*, he awakened to the mind ground. Chancing to meet a disciple of the Master [Huineng] by the name of Xuance who came to visit, he had a vigorous discussion with him. Because the words he spoke subtly matched those of the ancestors, Ce asked him, "Who was the master from whom you received the dharma?"

He replied, "When I listened to Mahāyāna sūtras and śāstras [being peached], in each case I had a teacher from whom I received instruction. Later, however, I awakened to the axiom of the buddha mind via the *Vimalakīrti Sūtra*, and I haven't had anybody verify [my understanding] yet."

Ce said, "Before King Majestic Voice, that is allowable; but, after King Majestic Voice, to awaken by oneself without a teacher is the other [i.e., non-Buddhist] path of natural occurrence."

This story ends with Yongjia Xuanjue staying at the monastery of the Sixth Ancestor, Huineng, for just one night and gaining the latter's approval as his dharma heir. Xuance's remark about "before" or "after" King Majestic Voice takes for granted the idea that that buddha, because he had no predecessor, could not have his awakening verified by a teacher. The same understanding underlies the following exchange involving Gushan Shenyen 鼓山神晏 (862–938) and Shushan Kuangren 疎山匡仁 (837–909), found in the *Ancestors Hall Collection* (*Zutang ji* 祖堂集, CBETA.B.144.25:465b14-466a2), compiled in 952:

因鼓山説著威音王佛次。師問鼓山、作摩生是威音王佛師。鼓山云、
莫無慚愧好。

Gushan was commenting on the successors of King Majestic Voice.

The Master [Shushan] asked Gushan, "What about the teacher of Buddha King Majestic Voice?"

Gushan said, "Do not be so entirely without shame!"

The unspoken premise of this dialogue, too, is that King Majestic Voice, being the first buddha, had no earlier buddha to be his teacher.

The expression "before King Majestic Voice" points to a state prior to all differentiated existence, when no buddhas (or any other things) have come into being, but the mind ground (*shinchi* 心地) abides nevertheless. In some texts, the phrasing used is "that side of King Majestic Voice" (*Ion'ō nahan* 威音王那畔), but the meaning is the same. As the Korean Seon (Zen) master Chinul 知訥 (1158-1210) explains in his *Straight Talk on the True Mind* (*Chinsim Chiksŏl* 眞心直説, T.2019A.48:1000a15-21):

據此經論眞心本體。超出因果通貫古今。不立凡聖無諸對待。如太虛空遍一切處。妙體凝寂絶諸戲論。不生不滅非有非無。不動不搖湛然常住。喚作舊日主人翁。名曰威音那畔人。又名空劫前自己。一種平懷無纖毫瑕翳。一切山河大地草木叢林萬象森羅、染淨諸法皆從中出。

This [i.e., the preceding set of quotations] is what sūtras and śāstras say about the root substance of the true mind. It transcends cause and effect and penetrates past and present. It does not depend on common or sagely and is without any of the opposites. Its sublime substance is quiet, and in it all conceptualization is cut off. It does not arise and does not cease; it is neither existent nor nonexistent. It does not move and does not shake; it is still and eternally abiding. To give it a name, it is the "old master of the house from days of yore." It is also called "the person on that side of Majestic Voice," and "one's self **before the kalpa of emptiness**." Uniform and equanimous, it has not a hair of error or distortion. Everything — the thicket of **myriad forms** that includes the mountains, rivers, whole earth, grasses, trees, and groves — all dharmas, whether defiled or pure, emerge from within it.

In twelfth-century China, sayings about King Majestic Voice became especially associated with the Caodong lineage and the method of "silent illumination" (*mokushō* 默照) that it taught. According to Dahui Zonggao 大慧宗杲 (1089–1163), a Chan master in the Linji lineage who was subsequently known as the father of the "Chan of contemplating sayings" (*kanna zen* 看話禪), the expression "that side of King Majestic Voice" was a hallmark of the Caodong tradition. In his letters to lay followers found in the *Discourse Record of Chan Master Dahui Pujue* (*Dahui Pujue chanshi yulu* 大慧普覺禪師語錄, T.1998A.47:941c2-7 and 933c6-10), Dahui criticized the expression:

爲禪者、或以無言無説、坐在黑山下鬼窟裏、閉眉合眼。謂之威音王那畔、父母未生時消息。亦謂之默而常照。爲禪者如此等輩不求妙悟。以悟爲落在第二頭。以悟爲誑謼人。以悟爲建立。自既不曾悟、亦不信有悟底。

Some take Chan to mean "no speaking, no explaining," sitting in the **ghost cave** beneath the Black Mountains with furrowed eyebrows and closed eyes. They call this "that side of King Majestic Voice," or the "state of repose **before your father and mother were born**." They also call it "being silent and constantly illuminating." The bunch who regard Chan like this do not seek sublime awakening. They take awakening as falling into a "second head." They take awakening as a deception played on people. They take awakening as a construct. Never having awakened themselves, they do not believe there is such a thing as awakening.

*Supplementary notes to the translation*  315

Also:

而今默照邪師輩、只以無言無説爲極則。喚作威音那畔事。亦喚作空劫已前事。不信有悟門。以悟爲誑。以悟爲第二頭。以悟爲方便語。以悟爲接引之辭。

Now the bunch of false teachers of silent illumination only take "no speaking, no explaining" as the highest principle, and this they call "that side of Majestic Voice," or **before the kalpa of emptiness**." They do not believe there is the gate of awakening. They regard awakening as madness. They regard awakening as a "second head." They regard "awakening" as an expression used as skillful means. They regard "awakening" as a word used to guide people.

Dahui's polemical assertion that Caodong masters do not believe in awakening is certainly not corroborated by their writings. Moreover, Dahui's own teacher, Yuanwu Keqin 圜悟克勤 (1063-1135), used the expression "before Majestic Voice" (*Ion izen* 威音已前) in much the same way as the Caodong masters, as is evident in the following lines from the *Discourse Record of Chan Master Yuanwu Foguo* (*Yuanwu Foguo chanshi yulu* 圓悟佛果禪師語錄, T.1997.47:725a27-28):

諸佛不出世、四十九年説。威音已前沒交涉。祖師不西來、少林有妙訣。

Buddhas do not appear in the world or preach for forty-nine years: before Majestic Voice, there are no such dealings. The ancestral teacher [Bodhidharma] has no **coming from the west**, and Shaolin has a profound secret.

In this context, "before Majestic Voice" means "from the standpoint of ultimate truth." From that standpoint, Yuanwu, too, would say that there is no such "thing" as awakening: it is just an expression used as skillful means.

In his "The Retreat" ("Shōbōgenzō ango" 正法眼藏安居), Dōgen refers to "Majestic Voice, King of Emptiness" (Ion Kūō 威音空王), perhaps identifying the buddha named King Majestic Voice with a buddha named King of Emptiness (Kūō 空王), who appears in chapter 9 of the *Lotus Sūtra*. No precedent for that identification is found in earlier Zen or broader Buddhist literature. There is, however, a saying that is quoted by Hongzhi Zhengjue 宏智正覺 (1091–1157) in the *Extensive Record of Chan Master Hongzhi* (*Hongzhi chanshi guanglu* 宏智禪師廣錄, T.2001.48:43c23-24) and various other Zen texts:

所以道、空劫威音前、別有一壺天。

Thus, there is the saying, "**Before the kalpa of emptiness** and Majestic Voice, there was a separate world in a jug."

316    DŌGEN'S *SHŌBŌGENZŌ* VOLUME VIII

The translation here takes the "kalpa of emptiness" (*kūgō* 空劫) and the time when Buddha Majestic Voice appeared in the world as two separate things, in accordance with the general understanding that the former period has no buddhas and that Majestic Voice is the first buddha to appear after it ends and the universe is regenerated. Nevertheless, it is grammatically possible to parse the Chinese here as meaning "before Majestic Voice of the kalpa of emptiness" (taking the two as contiguous), and that may have been how some people in Dōgen's day interpreted it. Because the phrase "King of Emptiness" (Kūō 空王) is an epithet used in connection with buddhas in general, it is also possible that when Dōgen spoke of "Majestic Voice, King of Emptiness" (Ion Kūō 威音空王), he did not intend to identify the buddha named King Majestic Voice with any particular buddha named King of Emptiness.

**before the kalpa of emptiness** (*kūgō izen* 空劫已前): In Buddhist scholasticism, world systems are said to progress through four kinds of eons, or kalpas: 1) kalpas of formation (*jōkō* 成劫), in which the universe takes shape; 2) kalpas of abiding (*jūkō* 住劫), in which the world of differentiation (the one in which humans live now) persists for a period of time; 3) kalpas of destruction (*egō* 壊劫), in which the universe gradually disintegrates and ends in total annihilation; and 4) kalpas of emptiness (*kūgō* 空劫, or *kūkō*), a period in which nothing whatseover exists, after which the whole process starts over again. Note that the term "emptiness" (*kū* 空), in this context, renders the Sanskrit *saṃvarta-siddha* ("utter dissolution"), not *śunyatā*. By this cyclical model, what comes "before" (*izen* 已前) a kalpa of emptiness would be a kalpa of destruction, but the Zen expression "before the kalpa of emptiness" is obviously not based on that model. What it points to, rather, is a state that is prior not only to the emergence of the universe but "before" even the distinction between existence (*u* 有) and nothingness (*kū* 空) and "before" any calculation of time whatsoever. According to Dahui Zonggao 大慧宗杲 (1089–1163), the expression "before the kalpa of emptiness" has the same meaning as "**before King Majestic Voice**" and "**before your father and mother were born.**" As the Korean Seon (Zen) master Chinul 知訥 (1158-1210) explains in his *Straight Talk on the True Mind* (*Chinsim Chiksŏl* 眞心直説, T.2019A.48:1000a15-21), all such expressions are names for the "root substance of the true mind" (*shinjin hontai* 眞心本體), or mind ground (*shinchi* 心地), which abides throughout the coming and going of kalpas:

> 據此經論眞心本體。超出因果通貫古今。不立凡聖無諸對待。如太虛空遍一切處。妙體凝寂絶諸戲論。不生不滅非有非無。不動不搖湛然常住。喚作舊日主人翁。名曰威音那畔人。又名空劫前自己。一種平懷無纖毫瑕翳。一切山河大地草木叢林萬象森羅。染淨諸法皆從中出。

This [i.e., the preceding set of quotations] is what sūtras and śāstras say about the root substance of the true mind. It transcends cause and effect

*Supplementary notes to the translation* 317

and penetrates past and present. It does not depend on common or sagely and is without any of the opposites. Its sublime substance is quiet, and in it all conceptualization is cut off. It does not arise and does not cease; it is neither existent nor nonexistent. It does not move and does not shake; it is still and eternally abiding. To give it a name, it is the "old master of the house from days of yore." It is also called "the person on that side of Majestic Voice," and "one's self before the kalpa of emptiness." Uniform and equanimous, it has not a hair of error or distortion. Everything — the thicket of **myriad forms** that includes the mountains, rivers, whole earth, grasses, trees, and groves — all dharmas, whether defiled or pure, emerge from within it.

The preface to the *Empty Hall Collection* (*Xutang ji* 虛堂集, ZZ.124:514a2-4; X.1304.67:322c8-10), written in 1295 by government official Jiang Duanli 姜端禮 in praise of the compiler Linquan Conglin 林泉從倫 (1223-1281), whose sobriquet was "Empty Hall," employs the trope of a "time before the kalpa of emptiness" (*kūgō zenji* 空劫前時):

空劫前時、有無手人、入無影林、採無根樹。向圓覺伽藍、依光明藏。布戒定慧之柱礎、架體相用之棟梁。以解脫爲門、運法空爲座。號曰虛堂。

In the time before the kalpa of emptiness, there was a person with no hands who entered the grove of no shadows and felled trees with no roots. Establishing the monastery of perfect awakening, he lived in the storehouse of radiance [a common name for an abbot's quarters]. He used giving, morality, concentration, and meditation as pedestals for the pillars, and set up the substance and attributes [of ultimate reality] as ridgepole and beams. For the gate, he used liberation; and, for the [abbot's] seat, he carried in the emptiness of dharmas. He took the sobriquet of "Empty Hall."

To call Lingquan Conglin a man who lived "before the kalpa of emptiness" amounts to saying that he had awakened to the mind ground, or buddha mind. The expression "your self before the kalpa of emptiness" (*kūgō izen jiko* 空劫以前自己) is raised as a kōan in several Chan records. In the *Discourse Record of Chan Master Wuben of Mount Dong in Junzhou* (*Dongshan Wuben chanshi yulu* 筠州洞山悟本禪師語錄, T.1986A.47:511c14-15), for example, a monk asks Dongshan Liangjie 洞山良价 (807–869) to comment on it:

僧問、如何是空劫已前自己。師曰、白馬入蘆華。

A monk asked, "What about 'your self before the kalpa of emptiness'?"

The Master [Dongshan] said, "A white horse enters the [white] flowering reeds."

In the *Extensive Record of Chan Master Hongzhi* (*Hongzhi chanshi guanglu* 宏智禪師廣錄, T.2001.48:119c27-29), it is raised by Danxia Zichun 丹霞子

淳 (1064–1117) and commented on by Hongzhi Zhengjue 宏智正覺 (1091–1157):

> 丹霞淳禪師、道價方盛。師乃造焉。霞問、如何是空劫已前自己。師曰、井底蝦蟆吞却月、三更不借夜明簾。

Chan Master Danxia Chun's way was flourishing. The Master [Hongzhi] arrived at his place. Danxia asked, "What about 'your self before the kalpa of emptiness'?"

The Master said, "If a frog at the bottom of a well swallows up the moon, at the third watch [i.e., midnight] you won't need a night-brightness screen."

In these cases, the question, "what about 'your self before the kalpa of emptiness'?" is asking, in effect, "Please demonstrate your awakening to the root substance of the true mind."

**before King of Emptiness** (*Kūō izen* 空王以前): An unusual expression that is employed by Dōgen (with variations in wording) in four different chapters of the *Shōbōgenzō*, but which finds only a single precedent in the entire Chinese Buddhist canon: the expression "the matter before Buddha King of Emptiness" (*Kūō butsu izen shi ji* 空王佛已前之事), attributed to a "Chan Master An of Taipin Monastery in Yongzhou" (Yongzhou Taipin An chanshi 永州太平安禪師) in the *Jianzhong Jingguo Era Continued Record of the Flame* (*Jianzhong jingguo xudeng lu* 建中靖國續燈錄, ZZ.136:323b3-4; X.1304.67:322c8-10), compiled in 1101, and in the *Jiatai Era Widespread Record of the Flame* (*Jiatai pudeng lu* 嘉泰普燈錄; ZZ.137:123b11; X.1559.79:330c11), compiled in 1204. Chan Master An's expression seems to be an idiosyncratic variation of the common Zen saying, "**before the kalpa of emptiness**" (*kūgō izen* 空劫已前).

"King of Emptiness" (Kūō 空王) is the name of a buddha who appears in chapter 9 of the *Lotus Sūtra* (*Miaofa lianhua jing* 妙法蓮華經, T.262:9.30a2-6), entitled "Prophecies Conferred on Learners and Adepts" (*Shou xuepuxueren ji* 授學無學人記), where it is said that Śākyamuni and Ānanda simultaneously made bodhisattva vows in his presence:

> 諸善男子、我與阿難等於空王佛所、同時發阿耨多羅三藐三菩提心。阿難常樂多聞。我常勤精進。是故我已得成阿耨多羅三藐三菩提。而阿難護持我法。

[The World-Honored One said,] "Good sons! I and Ānanda and others, in the presence of Buddha King of Emptiness, simultaneously aroused the thought of *anuttarā-samyak-saṃbodhi*, but Ānanda delighted in hearing much, while I always strove with vigor. For this reason, I have already attained *anuttarā-samyak-saṃbodhi*, while Ānanda has protected and memorized my dharma."

## Supplementary notes to the translation 319

In the Sanskrit text of the *Lotus Sūtra*, this buddha's name is given as Dharma-gahanābhyudgata-rāja ("King with a Hold on Countless Dharmas"). The *Lotus Sūtra* does not say that King of Emptiness has anything to do with the kalpa of emptiness (*kūgō* 空劫), nor does it associate him with King Majestic Voice (*Ion'ō* 威音王), a buddha whom it treats in chapter 20.

Dōgen, however, refers to a "Majestic Voice, King of Emptiness" (Ion Kūō 威音空王), in his "The Retreat" ("Shōbōgenzō ango" 正法眼藏安居), possibly identifying Buddha King of Emptiness with Buddha King Majestic Voice. In his "Reading Other Minds" ("Shōbōgenzō tashin tsū" 正法眼藏他心通), Dōgen speaks of "before King of Emptiness" (*Kūō no saki ni* 空王のさきに) and "after King of Emptiness" (*Kūō no nochi ni* 空王ののちに) in a way that parallels a saying from the *Platform Sūtra* comparing matters **"before King Majestic Voice"** (威音王已前) with those "after King Majestic Voice" (威音王已後). Because Dōgen also cites that *Platform Sūtra* passage elsewhere in the *Shōbōgenzō*, it appears that he may consider the names "King Majestic Voice" and "King of Emptiness" to be interchangeable. When he speaks in his "Seeing Buddha" ("Shōbōgenzō kenbutsu" 正法眼藏見佛) of seeing Buddha Śākyamuni "before King of Emptiness," moreover, he uses that expression as if it were synonymous with "before King Majestic Voice." Finally, in "Bringing Forth the Mind of Bodhi" ("Shōbōgenzō hotsu bodaishin" 正法眼藏發菩提心), Dōgen says that "the 'old buddha mind' is not on 'that side of King of Emptiness'" (*kobusshin, to iu wa, Kūō nahan ni arazu* 古佛心、といふは、空王那畔にあらず), mirroring the common saying "that side of King Majestic Voice" (*Ion'ō nahan* 威音王那畔). According to ZGDJ (s.v. くうおうぶつ), Buddha King of Emptiness was "the first buddha to arise in the kalpa of emptiness" and is identical with Buddha King Majestic Voice. That understanding, however, is based solely on the aforementioned chapters of the *Shōbōgenzō*; no precedent for it is found in earlier Zen or broader Buddhist literature.

**before your father and mother were born** (*bumo mishō zen* 父母未生前): Also *bumo mishō* 父母未生 and *bumo mishō izen* 父母未生以前. The grammar of the Chinese also supports the reading "before your father and mother gave birth [to you]." An expression widely used in Zen literature to point to the original state of affairs — the innate buddha mind (*busshin* 佛心) — that exists prior to the arising of discriminating thought. Dualistic thinking tends to obscure it, but that original state is always present even in the midst of delusion. The expression is often found in somewhat longer sayings such as "your original face before your father and mother were born" (*bumo mishō ji honrai menmoku* 父母未生時本來面目) and "your **nose** before your father and mother were born" (*bumo mishō zen bikū* 父母未生前鼻孔). According to Dahui Zonggao 大慧宗杲 (1089–1163), the expression "before your father and mother were born" has the same meaning as **"before King Majestic Voice"** and **"before the kalpa of emptiness."** As the Korean Seon (Zen)

320 DŌGEN'S *SHŌBŌGENZŌ* VOLUME VIII

master Chinul 知訥 (1158-1210) explains in his *Straight Talk on the True Mind* (*Chinsim Chiksŏl* 眞心直説, T.2019A.48:1000a15-21), all such expressions are names for the "root substance of the true mind" (*shinjin hontai* 眞心本體), or mind ground (*shinchi* 心地), which abides throughout the coming and going of kalpas.

**beginner's mind** (*shoshin* 初心): Or "initial thought." In ordinary Chinese, a state of innocence, or inexperience; the frame of mind of a "beginner" in anything. In Buddhist usage, the term may refer to a bodhisattva's "initial thought" of awakening (*hosshin* 發心; S. *cittotpāda*) or to a beginner or beginning stage in a practice. The latter is the meaning in an expression that appears often in Dōgen's writings (but not elsewhere): "the beginner and/or the latecomer" (*shoshin bangaku* 初心晚學). The term *bangaku* 晚學 (literally, "one who is late to study"), has two different meanings, depending on context. When juxtaposed with "beginner's mind," it refers to a person who begins Buddhist practice later in life, not as a youth or young adult. All latecomers are beginners but not all beginners are latecomers; so, *shoshin bangaku* 初心晚學 may also convey the sense of "a beginner [who is a] latecomer." A similar expression that appears fairly often in Chinese Buddhist texts is "latecomer students with beginners' abilities" (*shoki kōgaku* 初機後學). The other meaning of *bangaku* 晚學, also well attested in the *Shōbōgenzō*, is "latter-day students," or "students nowadays," who have come on the scene much "later" than the ancestral masters whose teachings are authoritative.

**beyond the buddha** (*butsu kōjō* 佛向上): An expression attributed to Dongshan Liangjie 洞山良价 (807–869) in his biography in the *Jingde Era Record of the Transmission of the Flame* (*Jingde chuandeng lu* 景德傳燈錄, T.2076.51:322b29-c3):

師有時云、體得佛向上事、方有些子語話分。僧便問、如何是語話。師曰、語話時闍梨不聞。曰、和尚還聞否。師曰、待我不語話時即聞。

On one occasion, the Master [Dongshan] said, "When you've experienced what's beyond the buddha, then you're in a position to talk a bit."

A monk asked, "What is this talk?"

The Master said, "When talking, the Ācārya [i.e., you] doesn't hear it."

The monk said, "Then does the Reverend hear it?"

The Master said, "Once I'm not talking, then I hear it."

Dōgen includes this anecdote in his *Shōbōgenzō* in Chinese script (*shinji Shōbōgenzō* 眞字正法眼藏, DZZ.5:132, case 12) and quotes it in his "Beyond the Buddha" ("Shōbōgenzō butsu kōjō ji" 正法眼藏佛向上事). There he states that Dongshan originated the saying "what's beyond the buddha" (*butsu kōjō ji* 佛向上事), also translatable as "the matter beyond the

*Supplementary notes to the translation*      321

buddha." The term "beyond" (*kōjō* 向上) in this context may mean "beyond the linguistic designation, or concept," of the thing called "buddha." If so, then Dongshan's point is that only people who can use language without becoming attached to names (i.e., mistaking them for really existing things) are qualified to speak about Buddhism.

Dongshan's saying was often raised as a kōan, as for example in the biography of Chan master Dinghui 定慧 (dates unknown) of Xiangzhou 襄州 found in the *Collated Essentials of the Five Flame Records* (*Wudeng huiyuan* 五燈會元, ZZ.138:295b5-6; X.1565.80:175b3-4):

僧問、如何是佛向上事。師曰、無人不驚。曰、學人未委在。師曰、不妨難向。

A monk asked, "What's 'the matter beyond the buddha'?"

The Master [Dinghui] said, "There's nobody who is not alarmed."

The monk said, "Your student has yet to abandon it."

The Master said, "It's really hard to approach."

Another example of Dongshan's saying being raised as a kōan is found in the *Extensive Record of Chan Master Yunmen Kuangzhen* (*Yunmen Kuangzhen chanshi guanglu* 雲門匡眞禪師廣錄, T.1988.47:558a8-10):

舉。洞山云、須知有佛向上事。僧問、如何是佛向上事。山云、非佛。師云、名不得、狀不得、所以言非。

Raised:

"Dongshan said, "You should know that there's a matter beyond the buddha." A monk asked, "What's the matter beyond the buddha?"

Dongshan said, "It's not buddha."

The Master [Yunmen] said [as a comment on the kōan], "It can't be named and can't be characterized, so he said,'It's not.'"

In the *Discourse Record of Chan Master Wuben of Mount Dong in Junzhou* (*Junzhou Dongshan Wuben chanshi yulu* 筠州洞山悟本禪師語錄, T.1986A.47:510b16-19), the wording of the preceding kōan changes, with the expression "matter beyond the buddha" replaced by "person beyond the buddha" (*butsu kōjō nin* 佛向上人). Yunmen Wenyan's 雲門文偃 (864-949) comment is appended, as are ones by Baofu Congzhan 保福從展 (d. 928) and Fayan Wenyi 法眼文益 (885–958):

示衆曰、知有佛向上人、方有語話分。時有僧問、如何是佛向上人。師曰、非佛。保福別云、佛非。雲門云、名不得、狀不得、所以言非。法眼別云、方便呼爲佛。

[Dongshan] addressed the assembly saying, "[You should] know that there is a person beyond the buddha. Only then will you be in a position to talk."

322 DŌGEN'S *SHŌBŌGENZŌ* VOLUME VIII

At the time there was a monk who asked, "What's 'the person beyond the buddha'?"

The Master [Dongshan] said, "It's not buddha."

Baofu [commenting on the preceding kōan] separately said, "Buddha is not."

Yunmen [commenting on the preceding kōan] said, "It can't be named and can't be characterized, so he [Dongshan] said, 'It's not.'"

Fayan [commenting on the preceding kōan] separately said, "It's an expedient to call [anything] 'buddha.'"

Dōgen quotes the latter version of the kōan (together with the comments by Yunmen, Baofu, and Fayan) in his "Beyond the Buddha," referring to Dongshan by his posthumous honorific title of "Great Master Wuben." In Zen texts, "person beyond the buddha" (*butsu kōjō nin* 佛向上人) is a term for one who, like the awakened Zen master, has transcended the distinction between the human and the buddha.

"What lies beyond the buddha" (*butsu kōjō ji* 佛向上事) has an antonym in the expression "what is within the confines [or vicinity] of the buddha" (*buppen ji* 佛邊事). The former alludes to the state of liberation, while the latter implies involvement in discriminating thought (*funbetsu* 分別) or deluded attachment to the concept of "buddha." A saying attributed to Jiashan Shanhui 夾山善會 (805–881) in the *Jingde Era Record of the Transmission of the Flame* (*Jingde chuandeng lu* 景德傳燈錄, T.2076.51:324a10-11) seems to confirm this interpretation:

若向佛祖邊學、此人未有眼目。

If one studies looking in the vicinity of the **buddhas and ancestors**, that person does not yet have the **eye**.

**Bian's jade disc** (*Benpeki* 卞璧): Reference to the legend of a jade annulus, discovered by a certain Bian He 卞和, who offered it to the kings of Chu 楚 (a feudal state that existed 740-330 B.C.E.) on three separate occasions, at great personal cost. The disc, better known as the "jade disk of Mister He" (*Heshi zhi bi* 和氏之璧), was supposed to have been used by Qin Shihuang 秦始皇, founder of the Qin dynasty, to create the signet of imperial succession that was the token of the "mandate of heaven" for emperors down through the Tang. Dōgen, relying on what was common knowledge in the China of his day (albeit erroneous from the standpoint of modern historians), associated Bian's jade with the imperial signet of state succession (*denkokuji* 傳國璽) of later dynasties. What Dōgen meant by "Bian's jade disc" is the most precious of worldly things: the ultimate in material wealth and political power.

*Supplementary notes to the translation* 323

The *Han Feizi* 韓非子, a Chinese classic of political philosophy written by the Legalist philosopher Han Fei at the end of the Warring States period (475-221 B.C.E.), describes the origins of the jade disk of Mister He as follows:

楚人和氏得玉璞楚山中。奉而獻之厲王。厲王使玉人相之。玉人曰、石也。王以和爲誑、而刖其左足。及厲王薨、武王即位、和又奉其璞而獻之武王。武王使玉人相之、又曰、石也。王又以和爲誑、而刖其右足。武王薨、文王即位、和乃抱其璞而哭於楚山之下。三日三夜、泣盡而繼之以血。王聞之、使人問其故。曰、天下之刖者多矣、子奚哭之悲也。和曰、吾非悲刖也。悲夫寶玉而題之以石、貞士而名之以誑。此吾所以悲也。王乃使玉人理其璞而得寶焉。遂命曰和氏之璧。(KR.3c0005.004.12b-13a)

Mister He, a person of Chu, obtained an unpolished block [of jade] from the mountains of Chu. He presented it as tribute to King Li. King Li had his jeweler examine it. The jeweler said, "It is stone." The king regarded He as deceitful and had his left foot amputated as punishment. When King Li died [ca. 740 BCE] and King Wu assumed the throne, He again presented the unpolished block as tribute to King Wu. King Wu had his jeweler examine it, and he too said, "It is stone." The king likewise regarded He as deceitful and had his right foot amputated as punishment. When King Wu died [ca. 690 BCE] and King Wen assumed the throne, He embraced the unpolished block and cried beneath the mountains of Chu. For three days and three nights he cried until his tears dried up and became blood. The king heard of this and sent a man to inquire. The man asked, "Throughout the realm many people have had their feet amputated as punishment. Why do you wail in grief?" He said, "I do not grieve at being punished by amputation. I grieve because precious jade is labeled as stone, and a man of integrity is deemed to be deceitful. That is what makes me grieve." The king thereupon had his jeweler polish [He's] unpolished block, and a precious [jade] was obtained from it. Subsequently it was designated the "jade disk of Mister He."

The expression "Bian He's three offerings" (*Benka sankan* 卞和三獻) appears in various Chan texts dating from the Song, including case 2 of the kōan collection *Congrong Hermitage Record* (*Congronglu* 從容録, T.2004.48:228b7-8).

A modern scholarly study of "Mr. He's jade disc" (*Heshi bi* 和氏璧) explains the item as follows:

In the more than 2,700 years ever since its first discovery, particularly in the Spring and Autumn period as well as in the Warring States period, Heshi Bi has been regarded as a gem that symbolizes control of a state, so was contested vehemently by the vassal state leaders at that time. At the time when Qin Shihuang unified China, Heshi Bi was even regarded as a

324     DŌGEN'S *SHŌBŌGENZŌ* VOLUME VIII

symbol of the imperial power and a sign of unification of the Qin Empire. However, Heshi Bi has been confused with Chuan Guo Xi (State-transferring Seal), which was transferred from one dynasty to another and became a symbol of transferring of state power, in the 1,143 years period from the end of Qin Dynasty (221BC-207BC) to Posterior Tang Dynasty (AD 923-936). For this reason, Heshi Bi has deeply affected the spirit and soul of the Chinese people in generations after generations. Therefore, Heshi Bi can be honored as the stone of kings and the stone of soul for the Chinese nation. (Chunyun Wang [2010, 196-199 "English abstract"]).

**body and mind** (*shinjin* 身心): All the phenomena that constitute a living being: loosely speaking, "external," or "physical," phenomena, and "internal," or "mental," phenomena. In terms of the five aggregates (*goun* 五蘊 or 五陰), "body" (*shin* 身) is the aggregate of materiality or "form," while "mind" (*shin* 心) consists of the aggregates of sensation, perception, formations, and consciousness. In terms of the twelve sense fields (*jūni sho* 十二處) "mind" corresponds to the the six sense faculties (*rokkon* 六根), while "body" corresponds to the six sense objects (*rokkyō* 六境 or *rokujin* 六塵). In the literature of Zen, the expression "body and mind" sometimes functions as a synonym for other binomial expressions that refer to the fusion of inner and outer realities, such as "sense faculties and dust." Dōgen uses "body and mind" in much the same way that he uses "**four elements and five aggregates**": to refer to what we might call the psychophysical organism. He also uses the expression "**body and mind sloughed off**" to refer to spiritual awakening.

**body and mind sloughed off** (*shinjin datsuraku* 身心脱落): One of Dōgen's favorite expressions for spiritual liberation. He occasionally reverses the word order of the original Chinese, resulting in "slough off body and mind" (*datsuraku shinjin* 脱落身心), which he also puts into Japanese syntax: *shinjin o datsuraku su* 身心を脱落す. In his "Face-to-Face Conferral" ("Shōbōgenzō menju" 正法眼藏面授, DZZ.2:60), Dōgen uses the latter expression to refer to his own awakening:

> 道元、大宋寶慶元年乙酉五月一日、はじめて先師天童古佛を禮拜面授す。やや堂奥を聽許せらる、わづかに身心を脱落するに、面授を保任することありて、日本國に本來せり。

On the first day of the fifth month of the junior wood year of the rooster, the first year of Baoqing in the Great Song, I, Dōgen, first paid obeisance to and had a face-to-face conferral from my former master, the **Old Buddha** of Tiantong. I was granted a certain access to the interior of the hall; when I somewhat sloughed off body and mind, having been entrusted with a face-to-face conferral, I came back to the Land of Japan.

*Supplementary notes to the translation* 325

According to Sōtō tradition, Dōgen gained awakening when he heard his master, Tiantong Rujing 天童如淨 (1162-1227), speak of "body and mind sloughed off." The root case (*honsoku* 本則) of chapter 51 of the *Record of the Transmission of Illumination* (*Denkōroku*, p. 519) by Keizan Jōkin 瑩山紹瑾 (1264-1325) reads:

第五十一祖、永平元和尚、參天童淨和尚。淨一日、後夜坐禪示衆曰、參禪者身心脱落也。師聞忽然大悟。直上方丈燒香。淨問曰、燒香事作麼生。師曰、身心脱落來。

The Fifty-first Ancestor, Reverend Eihei Gen, sought instruction from Reverend Tiantong Jing. One day, during late night seated meditation, Jing addressed the congregation, saying, "Studying Chan is body and mind sloughed off." Hearing this, the Master [Dōgen] suddenly had a great awakening. He went straight to the abbot's quarters and burned incense. Jing asked, "Why are you burning incense?" The Master [Dōgen] said, "Body and mind have been sloughed off."

This account gains credence from a sermon that Dōgen gave at his Daibutsu Monastery on the eighth day of the twelfth month (*rōhatsu* 臘八) in the year 1245, on the occasion of the [Buddha's] attainment of the way assembly (*jōdō e* 成道會), as recorded in the *Extensive Record of Reverend Dōgen* (*Dōgen oshō kōroku* 道元和尚廣錄, DZZ.3:82, no. 136):

汝等諸上座、要知瞿曇比丘因由麼。一由聞得天童脱落話而成佛道。二由大佛拳頭力得入諸人眼睛裏。神通智慧、化度衆生、忽見明星。

All you senior monks, do you want to know the causes of Gautama Bhikṣu's [attainment of the way]? The first was [my] being able to hear Tiantong's talk about "sloughed off" and then attain the way of the buddhas. The second is the power of Daibutsu's [i.e., my] **fist,** which can enter within all of your **eyes.** Its **spiritual powers** and wisdom convert and save living beings, who suddenly see the dawn star.

The implication here is that the Buddha's awakening was (figuratively speaking) enabled by Dōgen's own attainment of the way, which was in turn triggered by Rujing's saying, "Studying Chan is body and mind sloughed off."

Because the expression "body and mind sloughed off" has no known precedent in extant Chinese texts, it is generally assumed to be Dōgen's private recollection of Rujing's words, which he attributed to his teacher in many contexts but also used frequently, without attribution, as his own. Although we only know what Rujing meant by those words via Dōgen's quotations of him, there is one source that suggests the two men may have held somewhat different interpretations. That source is the *Record of the Baoqing Era* (*Hōkyō ki* 寶慶記, DZZ.7:18-20), where Dōgen relates a

326 DŌGEN'S *SHŌBŌGENZŌ* VOLUME VIII

conversation in which he asked Rujing, "What is 'body and mind sloughed off'?" and further questioned his teacher's reply:

堂頭和尚示曰、參禪者身心脱落也。不用燒香・禮拜・念佛・修懺・看經、祗管打坐而已。拜問、身心脱者何。堂頭和尚示曰、身心脱落者、坐禪也。祗管坐禪時、離五欲、除五蓋也。拜問、若離五欲、除五蓋者、乃同教家之所談也。即爲大小兩乘之行人者乎。堂頭和尚示曰、祖師兒孫、不可強嫌大兩乘之所説也。學者若背如來之聖教、何敢佛祖之兒孫者歟。拜問、近代疑者云、三毒即佛法、欲即祖道。若除彼等、即是取捨、還同小乘。堂頭和尚示曰、若不除三毒五欲等者、一如瓶沙王國阿闍世國之諸外道輩。佛祖之兒孫、若除一蓋一欲、則巨益也。與佛祖相見之時節也。

The Reverend Abbot said, "Studying Chan is body and mind sloughed off. There is no need to burn incense, make bows, recollect the buddha, practice repentance, or read the sūtras. **Just sit** and that is all."

I [Dōgen] respectfully enquired, "What is 'body and mind sloughed off'?"

The Reverend Abbot said, "Body and mind sloughed off is seated meditation. When one just sits in meditation, one is separated from the five desires and avoids the five obstructions."

I respectfully enquired, "If one separates from the five desires and avoids the five obstructions, then that's the same as what the Teachings schools talk about. Isn't that [what is taught] for the sake of practitioners of the two vehicles, great and small?"

The Reverend Abbot said, "Descendants of the ancestral masters cannot stubbornly reject what is taught by the two vehicles, great and small. If practitioners turn their backs on the sagely teachings of the Tathāgata, how could they possibly claim to be descendants of the ancestral masters?"

I respectfully enquired, "Doubters these days say that the three poisons are the buddha dharma and the five desires are the way of the ancestors. If you avoid those things, then that is selecting and rejecting, which is reverting to the same position as the Hīnayāna."

The Reverend Abbot said, "If you don't avoid the three poisons, five desires, and the like, then you're the same as the followers of other paths in the land of King Bimbisāra and the land of Ajātaśatru. As for us descendants of the **buddhas and ancestors**, if we avoid even one obstruction or one desire, then we benefit greatly. That's the time when we meet the buddhas and ancestors."

Here Rujing describes "body and mind sloughed off" as a state of concentration, achieved in seated meditation, in which the practitioner is free from desires associated with objects of the five senses and rid of the "five obstacles" (*gogai* 五蓋) to entering into the four dhyānas: desire, anger,

*Supplementary notes to the translation*          327

torpor, agitation, and doubt. As Dōgen notes in his follow-up question, those are traditional formulae found in both "Hīnayāna" and Mahāyāna sūtras, and the idea that practitioners should try to suppress such mental afflictions was often criticized in the Zen tradition as a "Hīnayāna" approach. Rujing chastised his disciple for doubting the value of any Buddhist sūtras and emphatically affirmed the value of suppressing harmful states of mind by means of meditation.

In remarks preserved in the *Extensive Record of Reverend Dōgen* (*Dōgen oshō kōroku* 道元和尚廣錄, DZZ.4:10, no. 424), Dōgen juxtaposes Rujing's saying with a famous one that also employs the trope of "sloughing off" (*datsuraku* 脱落):

> 上堂。古德云、皮膚脱落盡。先師云、身心脱落也。既到這裏且作麼生。良久云、誰道即心即佛、非心非仏非道。若人欲識祖師意、老兎巢寒鶴夢覺。

> At a convocation in the dharma hall, [Dōgen said,] "A virtuous one of old said, 'Skin sloughed off entirely.' My former master [Rujing] said, 'Body and mind sloughed off.' Having already arrived within this, how is it?" After a while, he [Dōgen] said, "Who says, '**This mind itself is the buddha**,' or 'No mind, no buddha, no way'? If people want to understand the **intention of the Ancestral Master**, it's a cold crane awaking from a dream in the den of an old hare."

The "virtuous one of old" quoted here is Yaoshan Weiyan 藥山惟儼 (751-834), who compared his own awakened state of mind to an ancient tree trunk whose superficial "bark and sapwood, branches and leaves have all sloughed off" (*hifu shiyō shitsukai datsuraku* 皮膚枝葉悉皆脱落), leaving "just a single reality" (*yui yū ichi shinjitsu* 唯有一眞實). Yaoshan's saying, which alludes to a passage in the *Nirvāṇa Sūtra* (*Da banniepan jing* 大般涅槃經 T.374.12:597a23-27), occurs in a conversation with Mazu Daoyi 馬祖道一 (709–788), who is well known for his sayings "this mind itself is the buddha" and "no mind, no buddha"; for more details, see "**slough off**."

As the preceding quotation suggests, Dōgen's own characterizations of "body and mind sloughed off," presented when he himself was an abbot, are more poetic than Rujing's rather doctrinal description of it as a meditative state free from the five desires and five obstructions. Elsewhere in the *Extensive Record of Reverend Dōgen* (*Dōgen oshō kōroku* 道元和尚廣錄, DZZ.3:192, no. 294), we read:

> 上堂。身心脱落也、不妨人認爲本源。法離斷常也、猶有自錯説虛實。所以道、塵塵見佛不謗佛、刹刹聞經不離經。要得靈山親授記。石頭大小點頭來。

> At a convocation in the dharma hall, [Dōgen said,] "As for body and mind sloughed off, it does not prevent people from recognizing what is the true

328 DŌGEN'S *SHŌBŌGENZŌ* VOLUME VIII

source. Dharmas are apart from nihilism and eternalism, yet we mistakenly, of ourselves, speak of them as vacuous or real. Hence it is said, 'Seeing buddha in every speck of dust does not belittle buddha; hearing sūtras in every instant is not apart from sūtras.' Do you want to get a personal prediction on Vulture Peak? Stones large and small are bowing their heads in assent."

Also in the *Extensive Record of Reverend Dōgen* (*Dōgen oshō kōroku* 道元和尚廣錄, DZZ.3:201, no. 306), we find:

上堂。身心脱落好參禪。猛作功夫鼻孔穿。業識茫茫無本可據。非他非自非衆生非因緣。雖然如是、喫粥爲先。

At a convocation in the dharma hall, [Dōgen said,] "Body and mind sloughed off is the excellent study of Zen. If you bravely make a concentrated effort, your **nose** will be pierced. **Karmic consciousness** is busy, busy, with no foundation on which to rely. It is not other, not self, not living beings, and not causes and conditions. Although matters are like this, eating rice gruel [i.e., the morning meal in a monastery] takes priority."

Again, in the *Extensive Record of Reverend Dōgen* (*Dōgen oshō kōroku* 道元和尚廣錄, DZZ.3:206, no. 318), we read:

上堂。先師示衆云、參禪者身心脱落也。大衆、還要委悉恁麼道理麼。良久云、端坐身心脱落、祖師鼻孔空華。正傳壁觀三昧、後代兒孫説邪。

At a convocation in the dharma hall, [Dōgen said,] "My former master addressed the assembly and said, 'Studying Chan is body and mind sloughed off.' Great assembly, do you want to fully understand this kind of principle?" After a while, he [Dōgen] said, "Sitting upright is body and mind sloughed off; the Ancestral Master's **nose** is sky flowers. He [Bodhidharma] directly transmitted the samādhi of wall-contemplation, but his descendants in later generations preached falsehoods."

Moreover, in the *Extensive Record of Reverend Dōgen* (*Dōgen oshō kōroku* 道元和尚廣錄, DZZ.3:212, no. 325), we find:

五月初一上堂。牛皮鞔露柱、露柱叫啾啾。人從橋上過、橋流水不流。古德雖恁麼道、今人還會麼。衲子身心脱落、無明業識拳頭。山家五月降梅雨、天下如今新麦秋。

At a convocation in the dharma hall on the first day of the fifth month, [Dōgen said,] "If an ox skin is stretched around a bare pillar, the pillar will sob, 'Boo-hoo.' When people cross over a bridge, the bridge flows and the water does not flow. The ancient worthies spoke like this, but can people of today also understand them? The patch-robed one's body and mind sloughed off is the **fist** of deluded karmic consciousness. At this mountain

*Supplementary notes to the translation*     329

house [i.e. monastery] in the fifth month, there is the falling of seasonal rains; all under heaven now enjoy a harvest of new barley."

In these remarks, Dōgen does at one point (echoing Rujing) equate "body and mind sloughed off" with "sitting upright" (*tanza* 端坐), and he also says that to realize it takes a "concentrated effort" (*kufū* 功夫), but he does not say that a person only experiences it while engaged in seated meditation. The overall suggestion, rather, is that "body and mind sloughed off" is a state in which one is free from the strictures of conventional language and logic even while immersed in ordinary, everyday life.

Rujing's opening dictum in the passage from the *Record of the Hōkyō Era*, where he admonishes his disciples to "**just sit**" (*shikan taza* 祇管打坐), is repeated by Dōgen (with minor variations) in a number of other contexts, including his "Continuous Practice, Part 2" ("Shōbōgenzō gyōji ge" 正法眼藏行持下, DZZ.1:198):

又いはく、參禪者身心脱落也、不用燒香・禮拜・念佛・修懺・看經、祇管打坐始得。

Again, he [Rujing] said, "Studying Chan is body and mind sloughed off. There is no need to burn incense, make bows, recollect the buddha, practice repentance, or read the sūtras. You'll only get it when you just sit."

For Rujing, evidently, the state of "body and mind sloughed off" is something gained only in seated meditation. Dōgen does not directly contradict that assertion anywhere in his writings, but he does problematize it by treating Rujing's dictum as a kōan, the deep meaning of which, he says, is hidden to most people. See "**just sit**" for Dōgen's interpretation of Rujing's admonition, which ostensibly rejects a number of devotional practices that all Buddhist monks (including those training under Rujing at Tiantong Monastery) routinely engaged in, and that Dōgen himself actively promoted.

**body stripped** (*dattai* 脱體): In ordinary language, to "cast off" (*datsu* 脱) the "body" (*tai* 體) means to "die." In some Daoist contexts, "stripping off the body" (which is subject to decay) implies the attainment of spiritual immortality. In Zen texts, the expression "body stripped" can indicate a state of liberation, synonymous with "**body and mind sloughed off**." Often, it carries the sense "to reveal all," or, as we might say, "to say it as it is" — hence, "the very thing itself," "the 'naked' thing." Dōgen speaks of "buddha nature with body stripped" (*dattai busshō* 脱體佛性), meaning the "fully exposed buddha nature." The glyphs 脱體 (*dattai*) are also translated herein as "expose the essence."

330 DŌGEN'S *SHŌBŌGENZŌ* VOLUME VIII

Jingqing Daofu 鏡清道怤 (868-937), a dharma heir of Xuefeng Yicun 雪峰義存 (822-908), uses the expression "body stripped" in case 46 of the *Blue Cliff Record* (*Biyan lu* 碧巖錄, T.2003.48:182b19-26):

鏡清問僧、門外是什麼聲。僧云、雨滴聲。清云、衆生顛倒迷己逐物。僧云、和尚作麼生。清云、洎不迷己。僧云、洎不迷己意旨如何。清云、出身猶可易、脫體道應難。洎。

Jingqing asked a monk, "Outside the gate, what sound is that?"

The monk said, "The sound of raindrops."

[Jing] Qing said, "Living beings are perverse: losing sight of themselves, they pursue things."

The monk said, "What about you, Reverend?"

Qing said, "I almost didn't lose sight of myself."

The monk said, "What's the meaning of 'I almost didn't lose sight of myself'?"

Qing said, "Even if leaving the body [i.e., attaining liberation] seems easy, it is surely difficult to speak of the body stripped [i.e., of the exposed essence]. I almost can."

This kōan is also found in Dōgen's *Shōbōgenzō* in Chinese script (*shinji Shōbōgenzō* 眞字正法眼藏, DZZ.5:270, case 286).

**break into a smile** (*hagan mishō* 破顏微笑): Literally, "to break one's face into a slight smile." A reference to the famous story of Śākyamuni's transmission of the "**treasury of the true dharma eye**" to Mahākāśyapa on Vulture Peak, thereby founding the Zen lineage. The earliest extant account in which Śākyamuni is said to have **held up a flower** in a wordless sermon, thereby eliciting a "slight smile" (*mishō* 微笑) of understanding from Mahākāśyapa, appears in the latter's biography in the *Tiansheng Era Extended Record of the Flame* (*Tiansheng guangdeng lu* 天聖廣燈錄, ZZ.135:612a1-4; X.1553.78:428c2-5), compiled in 1036:

如來在靈山説法、諸天献華。世尊持華示衆、迦葉微笑。世尊告衆曰、吾有正法眼藏、涅槃妙心、付囑摩訶迦葉。流布將來、勿令斷絕。仍以金縷僧伽梨衣付迦葉、以俟慈氏。

When the Tathāgata was on Vulture Peak preaching the dharma, the gods made an offering of flowers to him. The World-Honored One held up a flower to address the congregation, and Kāśyapa smiled slightly. The World-Honored One announced to the assembly, "I have the treasury of the true dharma eye, the wondrous mind of nirvāṇa, which I entrust to Mahākāśyapa. He should spread it and not allow it to be cut off in the future. I also give to Kāśyapa this *saṃghāṭī* robe sewn with gold thread, to keep until Maitreya comes."

*Supplementary notes to the translation*   331

The expression "break into a smile" does not appear in Chan literature until somewhat later. An early example is found in the *Outline of the Linked Flames* (*Liandeng huiyao* 聯燈會要, ZZ.136:440b18-441a2; X.1557.79:14a6-8), compiled in 1183:

世尊在靈山會上、拈花示衆。衆皆默然。唯迦葉破顏微笑。世尊云、吾有正法眼藏、涅槃妙心、實相無相、微妙法門。不立文字、教外別傳、付囑摩訶迦葉。

The World-Honored One, at a gathering on Vulture Peak, **held up a flower** to address the congregation. In the congregation all were silent. Only Kāśyapa broke into a smile. The World-Honored One said, "I have the treasury of the true dharma eye, the wondrous mind of nirvāṇa, the subtle dharma gate, the true sign of which is signless. Not relying on scriptures, as **a separate transmission outside the teachings**, I entrust it to Mahākāśyapa."

Other early occurrences of the expression "break into a smile" are found in the *Blue Cliff Record* (*Biyan lu* 碧巖錄, T.2003.48:155c21-22) by Yuanwu Keqin 圜悟克勤 (1063-1135); *The Eye of Humans and Devas* (*Rentian yanmu* 人天眼目, T.2006.48:325b12), published in 1188; and the *Discourse Record of Chan Master Dahui Pujue* (*Dahui Pujue chanshi yulu* 大慧普覺禪師語錄, T.1998A.47:813a29; 881b24-25), which contains the sayings of Dahui Zonggao 大慧宗杲 (1089–1163). By Dōgen's day, the expression had come to be used as a stand-alone emblem of the transmission to Mahākāśyapa.

Dōgen's *Shōbōgenzō* in Chinese script (*shinji Shōbōgenzō* 眞字正法眼藏, DZZ.5:258, case 253) contains the following version of the transmission story:

昔日靈山百萬衆前、世尊拈華瞬目。時迦葉一人、破顏微笑。世尊云、我有正法眼藏、付属摩訶大迦葉。

Once upon a time, before an assembly of a million on Vulture Peak, the World-Honored One held up a flower and blinked his eyes. At that time, Kāśyapa alone broke into a smile. The World-Honored One said, "I have the treasury of the true dharma eye; I bequeath it to Mahā, the Great, Kāśyapa."

This version of the story does not perfectly match any extant Chan text.

**bright mirror** (*myōkyō* 明鏡): A metaphor for the "mind" (*shin* 心), "buddha mind" (*busshin* 佛心), or "buddha nature" (*busshō* 佛性), which is said to "reflect" (*shō* 照) — to contain within itself without being disturbed — the "**myriad forms**" of all existence. In medieval China, mirrors (*kyō* 鏡) were made of bronze plates with one flat side that, if sufficiently polished, provided a reflective surface. Thus, in ordinary language, a mirror that is "bright" (*myō* 明), or "clear," is one that has been recently cleaned to remove any dirt or tarnish that may have built up on its surface. The "mind" that is compared to a mirror in many Chinese Buddhist texts is said to be "unproduced" (*musa* 無作) and inherently pure, but nevertheless covered and obscured by the adventitious "dust" (*jin* 塵) of sense objects (*kyō* 境) and mental afflictions (*bonnō* 煩惱). A common understanding evinced in those texts is that, in order to "gain the way and clarify the mind" (*tokudō myōshin* 得道明心), also known as "seeing the nature" (*kenshō* 見性), it is necessary to first calm the mind by practicing meditation, or dhyāna (*zen* 禪). The mind calming down is likened to waves dying down, such that a body of water becomes utterly placid and mirror-like in its reflectiveness. Tiantai Zhiyi 天台智顗 (538–597), for example, uses the metaphor of a "bright mirror" to explain the "factor of unified mind" (*isshin shi* 一心支) in his *Sequenced Introduction to the Dharma Realm* (*Fajie cidi chumen* 法界次第初門, T.1925.46:672a22-25):

四一心支。心與定法一、名一心支。行者既得四禪捨俱之定、捨念將息。則心無所依、泯然凝寂。一心在定、猶如明鏡。不動淨水、無波湛然、而照萬像皆現。

Fourth is the factor of unified mind: When the mind is unified in the act of concentration, that is called the "factor of unified mind." When practitioners have attained the concentration that accompanies equanimity in the fourth dhyāna, they relinquish thought and take a rest. Thus, the mind has nothing on which it relies: it is oblivious, frozen in tranquility. When the unified mind resides in concentration, it is just like a bright mirror. It is unmoving and insensate, without waves and utterly placid, and yet it reflects the myriad phenomena such that all are manifest.

The process of calming the mind in meditation is also compared to the act of polishing a mirror to remove the "dust" that obscures it. A famous example of that trope is found in the verse attributed to Shenxiu 神秀 (606?-706) in the Dunhuang manuscript of the *Platform Sūtra* (*Nanzong dunjiao zuishang Dasheng mohe boruo boluomi jing Liuzu Huineng Dashi yu Shaozhou Dafansi shifa tan jing* 南宗頓教最上大乘摩訶般若波羅蜜經六祖慧能大師於韶州大梵寺施法壇經, T.2007.48:337c1-2):

身是菩提樹、心如明鏡臺、時時勤拂拭、莫使有塵埃。

The body is the bodhi tree;
The mind, like a bright mirror [on a] stand.
Always strive to polish it;
And do not let there be any dust.

A slightly different version of the same verse, found in the *Tiansheng Era Extended Record of the Flame* (*Tiansheng guangdeng lu* 天聖廣燈錄, ZZ.135:644b17-18; X.1553.78:445a19-20) and the Yuan-dynasty edition of the *Dharma Treasure Platform Sūtra of the Sixth Ancestor* (*Liuzu dashi fabaotan jing* 六祖大師法寶壇經, T.2008.48:348b24-25), reads:

身是菩提樹、心如明鏡臺、時時勤拂拭、莫遣惹塵埃。

The body is the bodhi tree;
The mind, like a bright mirror [on a] stand.
Always strive to polish it;
And do not let the dust collect.

The verse that the Sixth Ancestor, Huineng 慧能, famously composed in response to Shenxiu's is quoted by Dōgen in his "The Old Mirror" ("Shōbōgenzō kokyō" 正法眼藏古鏡, DZZ.1:224); the version is the same as that found in the *Tiansheng Era Extended Record of the Flame* (*Tiansheng guangdeng lu* 天聖廣燈錄, ZZ.135:645a6-7; X.1553.78:445b2-4):

菩提本無樹、明鏡亦非臺、本來無一物、何處有塵埃。

Bodhi originally has no tree,
The bright mirror, no stand.
From the beginning, not one thing;
Where is there any dust?

Huineng's point is that, from the standpoint of the emptiness (*kū* 空) of dharmas, there is "not a single thing" (*mu ichi motsu* 無一物), i.e., no "dust" that needs to be polished off the "bright mirror" of the mind; so, the traditional **dhyāna practice** of calming the mind is unnecessary. In the Dunhuang manuscript version of the *Platform Sūtra* (*Nanzong dunjiao zuishang Dasheng mohe boruo boluomi jing Liuzu Huineng Dashi yu Shaozhou Dafansi shifa tan jing* 南宗頓教最上大乘摩訶般若波羅蜜經六祖慧能大師於韶州大梵寺施法壇經, T.2007.48:339a3-5), accordingly, Huineng redefines meditation (*zen* 禪) as "seeing the original nature" (*ken honshō* 見本性) in the midst of the "dust" of sense objects.

A famous exchange between Xuefeng Yicun 雪峰義存 (822-908) and his disciple Xuansha Shibei 玄沙師備 (835-908) involving a "bright mirror" appears in the biography of "Great Master Xuansha Zongyi of Fuzhou" in the *Jingde Era Record of the Transmission of the Flame* (*Jingde chuandeng lu* 景德傳燈錄, T.2076.51:344a13-16):

一日雪峯上堂曰、要會此事、猶如古鏡當臺。胡來胡現、漢來漢現。師曰、忽遇明鏡來時如何。雪峯曰、胡漢俱隱。師曰、老和尚脚跟猶未點地。

One day, at a convocation in the dharma hall, Xuefeng said, "If you wish to understand this matter, it is as if there were an **old mirror** on a stand: a foreigner comes, a foreigner appears; a Han [Chinese] comes, a Han appears."

The Master [Xuansha] said, "How about when all of a sudden a bright mirror comes?"

Xuefeng said, "Foreigner and Han would both disappear."

The Master said, "Your heels, Old Reverend, have yet to touch the ground."

A version of the same episode that features a different final comment by Xuansha is quoted by Dōgen in his "The Old Mirror" ("Shōbōgenzō kokyō" 正法眼藏古鏡, DZZ.1:226):

雪峰眞覺大師、あるとき衆にしめすにいはく、要會此事、我這裏如一面古鏡相似。胡來胡現、漢來漢現。時玄沙出問、忽遇明鏡來時如何。師云、胡漢俱隱。玄沙曰、某甲即不然。峰云、儞作麼生。玄沙曰、請和尚問。峰云、忽遇明鏡來時如何。玄沙曰、百雜碎。

Great Master Zhenjue of Xuefeng once addressed the assembly, saying, "If you wish to understand this matter, I'm here like one old mirror: a foreigner comes, a foreigner appears; a Han comes, a Han appears."

At that time, Xuansha came forth and asked, "How about when all of a sudden a bright mirror comes?"

The Master said, "Foreigner and Han would both disappear."

Xuansha replied, "I'm not like that."

Feng said, "How about you?"

Xuansha replied, "Ask me, Reverend."

Feng said, "How about when all of a sudden a bright mirror comes?"

Xuansha replied, "**A hundred fragments**."

The Chinese source that Dōgen quotes is uncertain, but a similar passage appears in the biography of "Chan Master Xuefeng Yicun of Fuzhou" in the *Outline of the Linked Flames* (*Liandeng huiyao* 聯燈會要, ZZ.136:784a7-10; X.1557.79:185b10-13):

示衆云、我這裏如一面古鏡相似。胡來胡現、漢來漢現。時有僧出問、忽遇明鏡來時如何。師云、胡漢俱隱。玄沙云、我即不然。時有僧問、忽遇明鏡來時如何。沙云、百雜碎。

[Xuefeng] addressed the congregation, "I'm here like one old mirror: a foreigner comes, a foreigner appears; a Han comes, a Han appears."

At that time there was monk who came forth and asked, "How about when all of a sudden a bright mirror comes?"

The Master [Xuefeng] said, "Foreigner and Han would both disappear."

Xuansha said, "I'm not like that."

At that time there was monk who asked, "How about when all of a sudden a bright mirror comes?"

[Xuan]sha replied, "A hundred fragments."

*Supplementary notes to the translation*     335

A different version of the same episode appears in the *Extensive Record of Chan Master Xuansha Shibei* (*Xuansha Shibei chanshi guanglu* 玄沙師備禪師廣錄, ZZ.126:353a7-12; X.1445.73:2a14-19):

師因新到相看、乃問、闍梨、近離什麼處。僧云、離雪峰。師云、雪峰近日有何句示人。僧云、和尚近日向僧道、我者裏如一面古鏡相似。胡來胡現。漢來漢現。時有僧問、忽遇明鏡來時如何。峰云、胡漢俱隱。師云、我不與麼道。其僧便問、彥相咨和尚、忽遇明鏡來時如何。師云、百雜碎。

The Master [Xuansha], when interviewing a newly arrived monk, asked him, "Ācārya, where have you come from?"

The monk said, "I just left [Mount] Xuefeng."

The Master asked, "These days, what saying does [Chan Master] Xuefeng use to instruct people?"

The monk said, "Recently, the Reverend [Xuefeng] addressed the saṃgha and said, 'I'm here like one old mirror: a foreigner comes, a foreigner appears; a Han comes, a Han appears.'

At that time there was monk who asked, 'How about when all of a sudden a bright mirror comes?'

Xuefeng said, 'Foreigner and Han would both disappear.'"

The Master [Xuansha] said, "I would not speak like that."

The monk asked, "If Yan Xiang [I] may inquire, Reverend, how about when all of a sudden a bright mirror comes?"

The Master said, "A hundred fragments."

In all of these episodes, after Xuefeng makes his point about the "**old mirror**," which stands for a type of consciousness that perfectly reflects its object, he is challenged with the question, "How about when all of a sudden a bright mirror comes?" The point here, which Xuefeng's response acknowledges, is that the "bright mirror," being in its essence empty of any objects of perception (and free from discriminations such as "foreigner" versus "Han Chinese"), would give the "old mirror" nothing to reflect. In all versions of the episode, Xuefeng's disciple Xuansha (either directly or indirectly) refutes his teacher's response. His comment, "A hundred fragments," implies that he is figuratively smashing the two mirrors of the metaphor, which has become too complicated to be of much use as a teaching device.

**bright windows** (*meisō* 明窓; also read *myōsō*): Wall openings or skylights that provide light for reading in the common quarters (*shuryō* 衆寮), sūtra reading halls (*kankindō* 看經堂), and other facilities in Buddhist monasteries where monks study scriptures. In Zen texts, references to "bright windows," sometimes coupled with the expression "illumine the mind," generally allude to the study of sūtras — the words of Buddha Śākyamuni — and of the discourse records (*goroku* 語録) of ancestral masters (*soshi* 祖師) in the Zen lineage. The *Imperial Edition of Baizhang's Rules of Purity* (*Chixiu Baizhang qinggui* 勅修百丈清規, T.2025.48:1146c3:) says:

明窓淨案古教照心。

At the clean desk by the bright window, illumine the mind with the old teachings.

**bring forth the mind** (*hosshin* 發心): Or "produce the thought." The initial resolve of the bodhisattva to achieve perfect awakening, or *anuttara-samyak-saṃbodhi*, for the sake of all living beings; an abbreviated form of "to bring forth the mind of bodhi" (*hotsu bodai shin* 發菩提心; S. *bodhi-cittotpāda*).

The expression "bringing forth the mind at the same time" (*dōji hosshin* 同時發心) is used in Mahāyāna literature to express the simultaneous aspiration of multiple bodhisattvas, but the point is sometimes made that no real gap exists between the initial "bringing forth the mind" and the ultimate goal. The *Nirvāṇa Sūtra* (*Da banniepan jing* 大般涅槃經, T.374.12:590a21-24) has a verse that Dōgen quotes in the T4 variant edition of "Bringing Forth the Mind of Bodhi" ("Shōbōgenzō hotsu bodai shin" 正法眼藏發菩提心, DZZ.2:334):

> 發心畢竟二不別、如是二心先心難、自未得度先度他、是故我禮初發心。初發已爲人天師、勝出聲聞及緣覺、如是發心過三界、是故得名最無上。

> Bringing forth the mind and the ultimate — the two are without distinction;
> But of these two minds, the former mind is more difficult.
> One delivers others before one is delivered oneself;
> Therefore, I pay obeisance to the initial bringing forth of the mind.
> Once it is brought forth, one is a teacher to devas and humans,
> Surpassing the *śrāvakas* and *pratyeka-buddhas*.

In the version of "Bringing Forth the Mind of Bodhi" ("Shōbōgenzō hotsu bodai shin" 正法眼藏發菩提心, DZZ.2:163) that appears in the seventy-five-chapter compilation of the *Shōbōgenzō*, Dōgen says:

> しかあれば、發心修行菩提涅槃は、同時の發心修行菩提涅槃なるべし。佛道の身心は、草木瓦礫なり、風雨水火なり。これをめぐらして佛道ならしむる、すなはち發心なり . . . . 修證もまたかくのごとし。

Hence, bringing forth the mind, practice, bodhi, and nirvāṇa must be a "simultaneous" bringing forth of the mind, practice, bodhi, and nirvāṇa. The **body and mind** on the way of the buddhas is grasses and trees, tiles and pebbles; is wind and rain, water and fire. To turn these into the way of the

*Supplementary notes to the translation* 337

buddhas — this is bringing forth the mind. . . . **Practice and verification** are also like this.

This might be read in two ways: (1) that, at the time we arouse such an aspiration, the things of this world simultaneously arouse the aspiration; or (2) that the aspiration is simultaneous with "practicing" and "attaining the way" in the following sentence.

There is no doubt that Dōgen regards "bringing forth the mind" as a momentous turning point in the spiritual life, no matter how or when it occurs. Earlier in the same chapter, "Bringing Forth the Mind of Bodhi" ("Shōbōgenzō hotsu bodai shin" 正法眼藏發菩提心, DZZ.2:162), he says:

あるいは夢中に發心するもの、得道せるあり、あるいは酔中に發心 するもの、得道せるあり。

There are those who gained the way having brought forth the mind in a dream; there are those who gained the way having brought forth the mind while drunk.

The idea of "bringing forth the mind in a dream" (*muchū ni hosshin su* 夢 中に發心す) may derive from a passage in the *Lotus Sūtra* (*Miaofa lianhua jing* 妙法蓮華經, T.262.9:39b20-c15), quoted in "Talking of a Dream within a Dream" ("Shōbōgenzō muchū setsumu" 正法眼藏夢中説夢, DZZ.1:300), that offers the dream of a bodhisattva career as one of the benefits promised devotees of the scripture:

又夢作國王、捨宮殿眷屬、及上妙五欲。行詣於道場、在菩提樹下、 而處師子座、求道過七日、得諸佛之智。

They also dream of becoming the king of a country,
Who abandons his palace and his entourage,
And the most marvelous pleasures of the five senses;
And, going to the place of awakening,
There, beneath the bodhi tree,
Then sits upon the lion throne
And, seeking the way for seven days,
Attains the wisdom of the buddhas.

The notion of "bringing forth the mind while drunk" (*suichū ni hosshin su* 酔中に發心す) may allude to a story, retold in "Leaving Home" ("Shōbōgenzō shukke kudoku" 正法眼藏出家功德, DZZ.2:268), that is found in the *Treatise on the Great Perfection of Wisdom* (*Dazhidu lun* 大智度 論, T.1509.25:161b17-23):

復次如佛在祇洹、有一醉婆羅門。來到佛所求作比丘。佛勅阿難與剃 頭著法衣。醉酒既醒驚怪己身忽爲比丘即便走去。諸比丘問佛、何以聽此醉婆羅門作比丘。佛言、此婆羅門無量劫中初無出家心。今因醉故暫發微心。以是因緣故後當出家得道。

Again, when the Buddha was at Jetavana, there was a drunken brahman who came to the Buddha seeking to become a bhikṣu. The Buddha encouraged Ānanda to shave his head and dress him in a dharma robe. When the intoxication had worn off, [the brahman] was startled to find that he had suddenly become a bhikṣu and immediately ran away. The bhikṣus asked the Buddha why he had permitted the drunken brahman to become a bhikṣu. The Buddha said, "For innumerable kalpas, this brahman has never had the thought of leaving home. Now, because of his drunkenness, he has briefly brought forth this subtle thought. As a result of this, he will in the future leave home and gain the way."

**brisk and lively** (*kappatsupatsu* 活鱍鱍; also written 活潑潑): A loose translation of a Chinese idiom expressing vitality, through the quick, powerful movements of a jumping fish. Usually described as a reference to a fish flapping its tail in a lively manner, as when swimming up a waterfall. Or, because the glyphs *patsupatsu* 鱍鱍 (C. *popo*) may be onomatopoeic, the concrete image here may be the "flap-flapping" sound that the rapidly flapping tail of a landed fish makes as it struggles desperately to save its life (*katsu* 活) by getting back into the water. In any case, in the literature of Zen, "brisk and lively" refers metaphorically to the spontaneous workings of the buddha mind, which in an awakened individual gives rise to lively repartee and vigorous action.

**buddha faces, ancestor faces** (*butsumen somen* 佛面祖面): A reference to the "**buddhas and ancestors**" (*busso* 佛祖) that comprise the Zen lineage, including: the **seven buddhas** of antiquity, ending with Buddha Śākyamuni; the twenty-eight ancestral masters (*soshi* 祖師) in India, ending with Bodhidharma; the six ancestral masters in China, ending with Huineng; and all of their dharma heirs. While not particularly common in Zen texts, the expression "buddha faces, ancestor faces" occurs quite frequently in Dōgen's writings. The addition of the word "face" (*men* 面) adds little to the meaning, except perhaps to emphasize the fact that members of the Zen lineage appear in the world, one after another, as individuals with different faces and characteristics, despite their underlying commonality.

**buddhas and ancestors** (*busso* 佛祖): In the Zen tradition at large, a name for the Zen lineage (Zenshū 禪宗) itself, conceived as comprising: the **seven buddhas** of antiquity, ending with Buddha Śākyamuni; the twenty-eight ancestral masters (*soshi* 祖師) in India, ending with Bodhidharma (Bodaidaruma 菩提達磨 or 菩提達摩); the six ancestral masters in China, extending from the First Ancestor (*shoso* 初祖), Bodhidhama, through the

## Supplementary notes to the translation

Sixth Ancestor, Huineng 六祖慧能; and all of the Zen masters (*zenji* 禪師) who were dharma heirs in the five houses (*goke* 五家) of Zen that stemmed from the "main lineage" (*shōshū* 正宗) of Huineng, as well as those who were dharma heirs in several "collateral offshoots" (*bōshutsu* 旁出) of the Zen lineage that branched off from one of the first five ancestral masters in China.

When Dōgen uses the term "buddhas and ancestors" in his *Shōbōgenzō*, he often has in mind this conception of the Zen lineage as a whole, which was first definitively articulated in the *Jingde Era Record of the Transmission of the Flame* (*Jingde chuandeng lu* 景德傳燈錄), a massive collection of biographies of Zen masters that was organized along genealogical lines and completed in 1004.

However, in his "Buddhas and Ancestors" ("Shōbōgenzō busso" 正法眼藏佛祖), Dōgen merely lists fifty-seven names in the Zen lineage as it extends down to him personally. The list is divided into three sections: the seven buddhas of antiquity, ending with Buddha Śākyamuni; the twenty-eight Indian ancestors, ending with Bodhidharma; and twenty-three generations of Chan masters in China, beginning with Bodhidharma and ending with Rujing 如淨 (1162–1227), from whom Dōgen himself received dharma transmission.

The figure named by Dōgen in the eleventh generation in China, "Most Reverend Liangjie" (*Ryōkai dai oshō* 良价大和尚), is Dongshan Liangjie 洞山良价 (807-869), renowned as the founder of the Caodong lineage (Sōtōshū 曹洞宗). The lineage that Dōgen traces from Dongshan down to Rujing comprises, in their respective generations: (12th) Yunju Daoying 雲居道膺 (d. 902); (13th) Tongan Daopi 同安道丕 (dates unknown); (14th) Tongan Guanzhi 同安觀志 (dates unknown); (15th) Liangshan Yuanguan 梁山緣觀 (dates unknown); (16th) Dayang Jingxuan 大陽警玄 (941-1027); (17th) Touzi Yiqing 投子義青 (1032-1083); (18th) Furong Daokai 芙蓉道楷 (1043-1118); (19th) Danxia Zichun 丹霞子淳 (1064-1117); (20th) Zhenxie Qingliao 眞歇清了 (1089-1151); (21st) Tiantong Zongjue 天童宗珏 (1091-1162); (22nd) Xuedou Zhijian 雪竇智鑑 (1105-1192); and (23rd) Tiantong Rujing 天童如淨 (1162-1227).

There is no doubt that Dōgen regards Rujing, whom he calls "my former master, the Old Buddha," as the greatest ancestral master of his day in China. However, Dōgen also uses the epithet "**old buddha**" with regard to Hongzhi Zhengjue 宏智正覺 (1091–1157), a.k.a. Tiantong Zhengjue 天童正覺. Hongzhi was a dharma heir of Danxia Zichun, the nineteenth generation in Dōgen's list of Zen masters in China, and a dharma brother of Zhenxie Qingliao, who alone occupies the twentieth generation in Dōgen's list. Hongzhi revived the monastery on Mount Tiantong (Tiantongshan 天童山) and served as its abbot from 1129 until his death in 1157. He also produced a number of influential texts, including the *Extensive Record of Chan Master*

*Hongzhi* (*Hongzhi chanshi guanglu* 宏智禪師廣錄) and two major kōan collections. One of the latter, known as "Reverend Tiantong Jue's Verses on Old Cases" (*Tiantong Jue heshang songgu* 天童覺和尚頌古) became the basis for the *Congrong Hermitage Record* (*Congrong lu* 從容錄, T.2004); the other "Reverend Tiantong Jue's Investigation of Old Cases" (*Tiantong Jue heshang niangu* 天童覺和尚拈古) was the basis for the *Qingyi Record* (*Qingyi lu* 請益錄, ZZ.117; X.1307). The list in Dōgen's "Buddhas and Ancestors" gives the impression that the line of ancestors leading from Zichun to Rujing were the most important members of the Caodong lineage, but the sub-branch of the lineage stemming from Hongzhi, known in Japan as the "Wanshi branch" (Wanshiha 宏智派), was more prominent in both China and Japan in the thirteenth century. Dōgen himself was heavily influenced in his choice of Zen stories and themes to comment on by the *Extensive Record of Chan Master Hongzhi*.

To summarize, what Dōgen meant by "buddhas and ancestors" was, depending on context, either (a) the seven buddhas of antiquity and all the ancestral masters in the Zen lineage founded by Buddha Śākyamuni; (b) the Sōtō lineage in general; or (c) his own particular branch of that lineage, culminating in his teacher Rujing and himself. He also used the terms "buddha" (*butsu* 佛) and "ancestor" (*so* 祖) interchangeably to refer to anyone who had attained the way (*jōdō* 成道).

**buddhas of the three times, I don't know they exist; cats and white oxen, on the other hand, I know they exist** (*sanze shobutsu fuchi u, rinu byakko kyaku chi u* 三世諸佛不知有、狸奴白牯却知有): A saying attributed to Nanquan Puyuan 南泉普願 (748-835) in numerous Zen texts and often raised as a kōan — as, for example, in the biography of National Teacher Deshao 德韶國師 (891-972) in the *Jingde Era Record of the Transmission of the Flame* (*Jingde chuandeng lu* 景德傳燈錄, T.2076.51:408c15-17); and in the *Congrong Hermitage Record* (*Congrong lu* 從容錄, T.2004.48:270b2-8), where it is case 69. Dōgen includes this kōan in his *Shōbōgenzō* in Chinese script (*shinji Shōbōgenzō* 眞字正法眼藏, DZZ.5:272, case 293) and quotes it in "The Thirty-seven Factors of Bodhi" ("Shōbōgenzō sanjūshichi hon bodai bunpō" 正法眼藏三十七品菩提分法). The *Ancestors Hall Collection* (*Zutang ji* 祖堂集), first compiled in 952, contains two versions of Nanquan's saying: the standard one (CBETA.B.144.25:554a13-14) found in the aforementioned works, and a variant (CBETA.B.144.25:532a12-b1) that reads:

南泉云、祖佛不知有、狸奴白牯卻知有。

Nanquan said, "[Chan] ancestors and buddhas, I don't know they exist; cats and white oxen, on the other hand, I know they exist."

According to *Zengo jiten* 禅語辞典 (471b), the expression "cats and white oxen" (*rinu byakko* 狸奴白牯) refers literally to wild cats (*yama neko* 山猫) and castrated plow oxen (*kyosei shita kōgyū* 去勢した耕牛).

*Supplementary notes to the translation* 341

It might seem to modern readers that Nanquan was contrasting buddhas — mythological beings who are only witnessed in literature, iconography, and dreams — with real, clearly visible life forms. Was he, then, a kind of positivist who denied the existence of the supernatural? That was the take of many twentieth-century scholars who claimed that the Chan school arose in Tang-dynasty China as a sectarian movement that rejected the "superstitious" beliefs, merit-making rituals, and abstruse philosophical doctrines that characterized the mainstream Buddhism of the day. The meaning of Nanquan's saying becomes clearer, however, when we understand that the expression "cats and white oxen" was not some randomly selected example of really existing beings, but (as Koga and Iriya point out) a fixed idiom in Zen texts that refers metaphorically to crude, ignorant people. The following account of "Postulant Ganzhi of Chizhou," who is included in the *Jingde Era Record of the Transmission of the Flame* (*Jingde chuandeng lu* 景德傳燈錄, T.2076.51:279b7-12) as a dharma heir of Nanquan Puyuan, shows what the latter meant by "cats and white oxen":

池州甘贄行者、將錢參貫文入僧堂。於第一坐面前云、請上座施財。
上坐云、財施無盡法施無窮。甘云、恁麼道爭得某甲錢。却將出去。
上坐無語。又於南泉設粥云、請和尚念誦。南泉云、甘贄行者設粥。
請大衆爲狸奴白牯念摩訶般若波羅蜜。甘乃禮拜便出去。

Postulant Ganzhi of Chizhou, who handled the [kitchen's] cash, entered the saṃgha hall seeking a string of coins. In front of the number-one seat he said, "Please, may the senior seat make a donation."

The senior seat said, "Gifts of material things are limitless; gifts of the dharma are inexhaustible."

Gan said, "If that is how you speak, how about my cash?" He then turned to leave.

The senior seat was speechless.

Then, when he [Ganzhi] was setting out the rice gruel [for breakfast] at [the monastery on Mount] Nanquan, he said, "Reverend, please initiate the recitation."

[The abbot] Nanquan said, "Postulant Ganzhi is setting out the rice gruel. May the great assembly please recite the *Great Perfection of Wisdom* for the benefit of cats and white oxen."

Gan thereupon bowed and left.

To understand his story, some detailed knowledge of Buddhist monastic life in Tang- and Song-dynasty China is needed. Postulants (*anja* 行者) were lay people who aspired to be monks but had to wait in line (often for years) to get one of a limited number of government-approved ordinations. In the meantime, they resided in a monastery, where they had their own quarters and engaged in some Buddhist practices, such as meditation and sūtra study but spent most of their time as assistants to monks who held official positions, such as comptroller and head cook. One of the main duties of postulants was to serve meals, which were provided to the "great assembly" (*daishu* 大眾) of monks at their seating places on the platforms (also used for communal meditation and sleep) in the saṃgha hall. At times there was a "lead donor" (*seshu* 施主), generally a lay supporter but sometimes another monk, who would pay for a special meal. It was the job of a postulant to escort the donor into the saṃgha hall for a rite in which the merit produced by his gift, and by the associated chanting of sūtras, would be dedicated to whatever ends he specified (e.g., recovery from illness or help for ancestral spirits). In the preceding story, Postulant Ganzhi cheekily asks the senior seat (the monk with the most seniority in the great assembly) to volunteer as the "lead donor" for the meal that is about to be served. The senior seat gives a pompous answer that Ganzhi rejects, leaving him speechless. Then Ganzhi asks the abbot, Naquan, who has joined the great assembly for the meal, to initiate the group recitation of the mealtime verses. Nanquan, who has heard the exchange between Ganzhi and the senior seat, facetiously asks the assembly to recite the *Great Perfection of Wisdom* (a vast sūtra in 600 fascicles) and dedicate the resulting merit "for the benefit of cats and white oxen." On the face of it, such a dedication could simply be an act of compassion comparable to praying for the salvation of "all living beings," but there is a double meaning: because the senior seat has been identified by Ganzhi as the "lead donor," *he* is the rightful beneficiary of the dedication, and Nanquan is in effect calling him a dumb beast.

So, the contrast drawn in the dialogue is between "buddhas" and "ignoramuses." What did Nanquan mean when he said he knew of the existence of the latter, but did not know of the existence of the former? Perhaps his remark was self-referential, and he meant that he had first-hand knowledge of delusion but not of buddhahood as that is ordinarily imagined: a state completely free from delusion.

**buddhas, the world-honored ones, appear in the world for the reason of one great matter alone** (*shobutsu seson yuii ichi daiji innen ko shutsugen o se* 諸佛世尊唯以一大事因緣故出現於世): A line from a passage in chapter 2 of the *Lotus Sūtra* (*Miaofa lianhua jing* 妙法蓮華經, T.262.9:7a22-27), in which Śākyamuni announces that the purpose of Buddhism is to lead beings to buddhahood:

> 舍利弗、云何名諸佛世尊唯以一大事因緣故出現於世。諸佛世尊、欲令眾生開佛知見使得清淨故出現於世。欲示眾生佛之知見故出現於世。欲令眾生悟佛知見故出現於世。欲令眾生入佛知見道故出現於世。

Śāriputra, why do we say that the buddhas, the world-honored ones, appear in the world for the reason of one great matter alone? The buddhas,

Supplementary notes to the translation

the world-honored ones, appear in the world because they wish to cause living beings to open the knowledge and insight of a buddha and attain purification. They appear in the world because they wish to show to living beings the knowledge and insight of a buddha. They appear in the world because they wish to cause living beings to awaken to the knowledge and insight of a buddha. They appear in the world because they wish to cause living beings to enter the way of the knowledge and insight of a buddha.

**burning house** (*kataku* 火宅): Reference to a famous parable found in chapter 3, "Parables" (*Piyu* 譬喩), of the *Lotus Sūtra* (*Miaofa lianhua jing* 妙法蓮華 經), in which a father lures his heedless children from a burning house with the offer of goat, deer, and ox carts, and then, once they are safely outside, presents them with great carts pulled by swift white oxen. The burning house is said to represent saṃsāra, or more specifically, the **three realms** of rebirth. The children represent ordinary living beings caught up in saṃsāra, who do not realize the gravity of their situation. The father, a wealthy man whose vast mansion is on fire, represents the Buddha, who must rely on expedient means (*hōben* 方便; S. *upāya*) to induce living beings to seek liberation. In the section of the parable of the burning house quoted below (T.262.9:12b13-13a26), the seven phrases underlined in the translation are ones that Dōgen directly quotes or indirectly alludes to in the *Shōbōgenzō*.

舍利弗、若國邑聚落、有大長邑聚落者、其年衰邁、財富無量 、多有田宅及諸僮僕。其家廣大、唯有一門。多諸人衆、一百、二百乃至五百人、止住其中。堂閣朽故、牆壁隤落、柱根腐敗、梁棟傾危。周匝俱時欻然火起、焚燒舍宅。長者諸子、若十、二十、或至三十、在此宅中。長者見是大火從四面起、即大驚怖、而作是念、我雖能於此所燒之門安隱得出、而諸子等、於火宅内、樂著嬉戲、不覺不知、不驚不怖。火來逼身、苦痛切己，心不厭患，無求出意。

舍利弗、是長者作是思惟。我身手有力、當以衣裓、若以机案、從舍出之。復更思惟、是舍唯有一門、而復狹小。諸子幼稚、未有所識、戀著戲處、或當墮落、爲火所燒。我當爲説怖畏之事，此舍已燒、宜時疾出、無令爲火之所燒害。作是念已、如所思惟、具告諸子、汝等速出。父雖憐愍、善言誘喩、而諸子等樂著嬉戲、不肯信受。不驚不畏、了無出心。亦復不知何者是火、何者爲舍、云何爲失。但東西走戲、視父而已。

爾時長者即作是念。此舍已爲大火所燒。我及諸子若不時出、必爲所焚。我今當設方便、令諸子等得免斯害。父知諸子先心。各有所好種種珍玩奇異之物、情必樂著、而告之言、汝等所可玩好、希有難得、汝若不取、後必憂悔。如此種種、羊車、鹿車、牛車、今在門外、可以遊戲。汝等於此火宅、宜速出來、隨汝所欲、皆當與汝。

爾時諸子聞父所説珍玩之物、適其願故、心各勇鋭。互相推排、競共馳走、爭出火宅。是時長者見諸子等安隱得出、皆於四衢道中露地而坐、無復障礙、其心泰然、歡喜踊躍。時諸子等各白父言、父先所許玩好之具，羊車、鹿車、牛車、願時賜與。

舍利弗、爾時長者各賜諸子等一大車。其車高廣、衆寶莊校、周匝欄楯、四面懸鈴。又於其上張設幰蓋、亦以珍奇雜寶而嚴飾之。寶繩絞絡、垂諸華纓、重敷綩綖、安置丹枕。駕以白牛、膚色充潔、形體姝好、有大筋力、行步平正、其疾如風、又多僕從而侍衛之。

所以者何。是大長者財富無量、種種諸藏悉皆充溢、而作是念、我財物無極、不應以下劣小車與諸子等。今此幼童、皆是吾子、愛無偏黨。我有如是七寶大車、其數無量、應當等心各各與之、不宜差別。所以者何。以我此物、周給一國猶尚不匱、何況諸子。

是時諸子各乘大車、得未曾有、非本所望。舍利弗、於汝意云何。是長者等與諸子珍寶大車、寧有虛妄不。

舍利弗言、不也，世尊。是長者但令諸子得免火難、全其軀命。非爲虛妄。何以故。若全身命、便爲已得玩好之具、況復方便於彼火宅而拔濟之。世尊、若是長者、乃至不與最小一車、猶不虛妄。何以故。是長者先作是意、我以方便令子得出。以是因緣，無虛妄也。何況長者自知財富無量、欲饒益諸子、等與大車。

佛告舍利弗、善哉、善哉。如汝所言。舍利弗、如來亦復如是。則爲一切世間之父、於諸怖畏、衰惱、憂患、無明闇蔽、永盡無餘。而悉成就無量知見、力、無所畏、有大神力及智慧力。具足方便、智慧波羅蜜、大慈大悲。常無懈倦、恒求善事、利益一切。而生三界朽故火宅、爲度衆生生老病死、憂悲、苦惱、愚癡、闇蔽、三毒之火。教化令得阿耨多羅三藐三菩提。見諸衆生爲生老病死、憂悲苦惱之所燒煮、亦以五欲財利故、受種種苦。又以貪著追求故、現受衆苦、後受地獄、畜生、餓鬼之苦。若生天上、及在人間、貧窮困苦、愛別離苦、怨憎會苦、如是等種種諸苦。衆生沒在其中、歡喜遊戲、不覺不知、不驚不怖、亦不生厭、不求解脫。於此三界火宅東西馳走、雖遭大苦、不以爲患。

[The Buddha said,] "Śāriputra, suppose that in some city or town there was a wealthy man who was advanced in years, rich beyond measure, and possessed of many estate lands and vassals. His house was vast but had only one gate. A community of many people resided within: as many as one hundred, two hundred, or even five hundred people. The halls and towers were decaying; the walls were collapsing; the bases of the pillars were rotting; and the beams and ridgepoles were tilting precariously.

All at once, fires suddenly broke out, setting the dwelling ablaze throughout. The wealthy man's children, perhaps ten, twenty, or as many as thirty of them, were inside that house. When the wealthy man saw the big flames arising on all four sides, he was greatly alarmed and thought to himself, 'I can get out to safety through this gate that is ablaze. But my children, enjoying themselves in play within the burning house, do not perceive it, do not know it, are not alarmed, are not afraid. The fire is closing in on

*Supplementary notes to the translation* 345

them, they are close to experiencing pain and suffering, but their minds feel no aversion, and they have no idea of trying to get out.'

Śāriputra, that wealthy man had the following thought: 'My body and arms have strength. I could use my robes, or perhaps use a table, to carry them out from the house.' But then he reconsidered: 'The house has only one gate, and that is narrow. The children are young, they still have no comprehension, they are attached to their places of play, and if they should jump off [the robe or table], they will be burned by the fire. I must explain to them the fearfulness of the situation: that this house is already burning, and that now is the time to make an urgent escape. I must not let them be burned and injured by the fire.' Having entertained these thoughts and considered matters in this way, he announced to the children, 'You all must get out at once!' But though the father was compassionate and used good words to advise them, the children were caught up in the enjoyment of their play and refused to heed him. They were not alarmed, not afraid, and had no mind to get out. Moreover, they did not even know what a fire is, what a house is, or what it is that is called 'loss.' They just ran about playing, this way and that, looking at their father, and that is all.

At that time, the wealthy man had this thought: 'This house is already engulfed in a great fire. If I and my children do not get out now, we will certainly be burned up. I must now devise some expedient means to make the children able to escape this injury.' The father knew his children's preferences. Each had some kind of costly toy or extraordinary item that they liked and that would be sure to delight them. He spoke to them, saying, 'The toys you like are rare and hard to obtain. If you don't take them [now], you'll surely regret it later. These kinds of goat carts, deer carts, and ox carts are now outside the gate, where you can play with them. If you just quickly go out from this burning house, I will give each of you whichever you want.'

When the children heard about the costly toys spoken of by their father, because those corresponded to their wishes, they became eager in mind and, pushing each other out of the way, competed in a mad dash to exit the burning house first. At that time, the wealthy man, seeing his children safely out and seated out of harm's way on open ground at a crossroad, was calmed and rejoiced. Then, the children each spoke to the father, saying, 'Father, the toys we like, which you said earlier we could have — the goat carts, deer carts, and ox carts — please give them to us now.'

Śāriputra, at that time, the wealthy man bestowed identical great carts on each of his children. These carts were high and wide, adorned with jewels and surrounded by railings with bells suspended on the four sides. Stretched over the top was a canopy, which was also decorated with sundry treasures, rare and precious. [Each cart] was interlaced with ropes

346 DŌGEN'S *SHŌBŌGENZŌ* VOLUME VIII

of jewels, with tassels of flowers hanging from them; it was spread with layers of fine carpet, upon which rested vermilion pillows. [Each cart] was yoked to a white ox that had an immaculate hide, a beautiful physique, and great muscular strength, its gait even, its speed like the wind. In addition, [each cart] had many servants to wait on and guard it.

What was the reason for this? That great, wealthy man's financial resources were incalculable; he had various kinds of storehouses that were all full to overflowing; and he had this thought: 'My money and goods are limitless; it would not be fitting for me to present my sons with inferior, small carts. These youths are all my children, and my love for them is without bias or partiality. I possess an immeasurable number of seven-jeweled great carts such as these, so I should, even-mindedly, give one to each of them; it would be inappropriate to discriminate. Why? Because even if I distributed these things throughout the country, they would not be exhausted. How much less so [would they be exhausted] if it is just my children?'

At that time, each of the children rode in their cart, getting something they had never had before, which was not what they had originally expected. Śāriputra, what do you think about this? When that wealthy man impartially gave his sons great carts with rare gems, did he engage in falsehood or not?"

Śāriputra said, "No, World-Honored One. That wealthy man only enabled his children to escape the disaster of the fire and preserve their lives. That was not a falsehood. Why? Because the preservation of their lives was in itself a prerequisite of gaining any playthings, not to mention the fact that it [i.e., his promise of various playthings] was an expedient means that rescued them from that burning house. World-Honored One, if that wealthy man had not bestowed on them even the smallest of carts [after they came out of the house], there still would have been no falsehood. Why? Because that wealthy man from the start had the idea, 'I will use expedient means to enable the children to get out.' Under those circumstances, there is no falsehood. How much less so when the wealthy man, knowing of himself that he was rich beyond measure and desiring to confer benefits on his children, equally gave them large carts."

The Buddha said to Śāriputra, "Very good, very good. It is just as you say. And, Śāriputra, the World-Honored One is also like this. To wit, he is a father to all worlds, in whom all fear, distress, anxiety, ignorance and darkness are exhausted, with no remainder. Also, he brings to realization incalculable knowledge and insight, strength, fearlessness, and great spiritual powers, as well as the power of wisdom. He is fully equipped with expedient means, the *pāramitā* of wisdom, and great mercy and great compassion. He is ever free from fatigue and always seeks to do good, benefiting all. Moreover, he is born in the three realms — the rotted, old, burning house — for the sake of delivering living beings from the fires of birth, old age, sickness, and death, [and from] grief, suffering, ignorance, darkness, and the three poisons. His teaching enables them to attain *anuttara-samyak-saṃbodhi*. He sees living beings burned by the fires of birth, old age, sickness, and death, of grief and suffering, and sees them experiencing all kinds of pain due to the five desires and [the desire for] money. Also, because of their desirous attachments and pursuits, they experience a heap of pain in the present and later undergo the pain of [rebirths as] hell beings, animals, or hungry ghosts. Even if they are reborn as devas or humans, they have all kinds of suffering, such as the pain of poverty and destitution, the pain of being separated from what one loves, and the pain of encountering what one hates. Living beings, although sunk in a multitude of such sorrows, rejoice and play; they do not perceive it, do not know it, are not alarmed, are not afraid; unrepulsed, they do not seek liberation. Dashing about madly this way and that in the burning house that is the three realms, they meet with great pain but are not troubled on that account."

The text of the *Lotus Sūtra* goes on to explain that the three types of cart offered by the father to his children as enticements to get them out of the burning house represent the "**three vehicles**" taught by the Buddha. The children who came out of the house hoping for goat carts (*yōsha* 羊車) are said to be like followers of the *śrāvaka* vehicle (*shōmonjō* 聲聞乘), who "wish to quickly leave the three realms and individually seek nirvāṇa." Those who came out of the house for deer carts (*rokusha* 鹿車) are said to be like followers of the *pratyeka-buddha* vehicle (*byakushibutsujō* 辟支佛乘), who "seek self-originating wisdom, delight in solitary tranquility, and profoundly understand the conditioned nature of all dharmas." Those who come out for the ox carts (*gosha* 牛車) are said to be like followers of the buddha vehicle (*butsujō* 佛乘), also called the great vehicle (*daijō* 大乘), or Mahāyāna. They are bodhisattvas who "seek omniscience, buddha wisdom, the happiness of all living beings, and the liberation of all."

The *Lotus Sūtra* states explicitly that the Tathāgata's offering of all three vehicles — not just the *śrāvaka* vehicle and the *pratyeka-buddha* vehicle, but the buddha vehicle as well — was an expedient means intended to motivate living beings to seek liberation. Some interpreters of the text have taken that to mean that the ox carts initially offered to the children by the father as a lure were not the same as the splendid "white ox carts" (*byakugosha* 白牛車) that he actually bestowed on them after they emerged from the house. That distinction rests on the Mahāyāna doctrine of two truths, which holds that all conceptual constructs (including that of the "buddha vehicle") are at best true only on the conventional level but false (or rather, "empty") from the standpoint of ultimate truth. In other words, the "ox cart" — i.e., the

348    DŌGEN'S *SHŌBŌGENZŌ* VOLUME VIII

"buddhahood" — that deluded beings hear about and seek is qualitatively different from what they experience when they actually attain liberation, which cannot be verbalized without reification and distortion.

This interpretation is found in "The *Lotus* Turns the *Lotus*" ("Shōbōgenzō *Hokke* ten *Hokke*" 正法眼藏法華轉法華, S3:4-5), where the Sixth Ancestor, Huineng 慧能, instructs the monk Fada 法達 on the meaning of the "Expedient Means" (*Fangbian* 方便) chapter of the *Lotus Sūtra*:

なんぢいままさに信すべし、佛知見者、只汝自心なり。かさねてし めす偈にいはく、心迷法華轉、心悟轉法華、誦久不明己、與義作讐 家、無念念即正、有念念成邪、有無俱不計、長御白牛車。

"Now you should believe that the knowledge and insight of a buddha is just your own mind." In a gāthā repeating this, he said,

> If your mind is deluded, the *Lotus* turns you;
> If your mind is awakened, you turn the *Lotus*.
> Long recitation without clarifying oneself,
> Turns the meaning into your foe.
> The thinking of no-thought is correct;
> The thinking with thoughts yields the false.
> When not concerned with either one,
> We drive forever the white ox cart.

It is clear from this that the "white ox cart" stands for the "knowledge and insight of a buddha," which is "just your own mind." Fada, after hearing the verse, asks Huineng a couple of questions, the second of which is:

又、經に三車をとくに、大牛車と白牛車と、いかなる區別かあらん。

"Also, in the [*Lotus*] sūtra, in its explanation of the three vehicles, what is the distinction between the great ox cart and the white ox cart?"

Huineng replies that the "one vehicle" (a.k.a. the buddha vehicle, i.e., "one's own mind") is "real" (*jitsu* 實) — the "ultimate truth," whereas the "three carts" (i.e., the three vehicles) are "provisional" (*ke* 假) — merely "conventional truth."

**cages and nets** (*rōra* 籠羅): See "nets and cages."

**chairs, bamboo, and wood** (*isu chiku boku* 椅子竹木): An allusion to a dialogue between Luohan Guichen 羅漢桂琛 (867-928) and his teacher Xuansha Shibei 玄沙師備 (835-908), found in the *Jingde Era Record of the Transmission of the Flame* (*Jingde chuandeng lu* 景德傳燈録, T.2076.51:371a9-13) and other sources. The version recorded in Dōgen's *Shōbōgenzō* in Chinese script (*shinji Shōbōgenzō* 眞字正法眼藏, DZZ.5:186, case 112) reads as follows:

## Supplementary notes to the translation

地藏院眞應大師、因玄沙問、三界唯一心、汝作麼生會。師指椅子
曰、和尚、喚這箇作什麼。沙曰、椅子。師云、和尚不會三界唯心。
沙云、我喚這箇作竹木。汝喚作什麼。師云、某甲亦喚作竹木。沙
曰、盡大地覓一箇會佛法人不可得。

Great Master Zhenying of Dizang Cloister was once asked by Xuansha,
"'The **three realms** are but one mind.' How do you understand this?"

The Master pointed to a chair and said, "Reverend, what do you call this?"

Xuansha said, "A chair."

The Master said, "Reverend, you don't understand '**the three realms are
only mind**.'"

Xuansha said, "I call this bamboo and wood. What do you call it?"

The Master said, "I also call it bamboo and wood."

Xuansha said, "I can't find a single person anywhere on all the whole
earth who understands the buddha dharma."

**clarify the meaning apart from the sense; don't take the norm from within
the words** (*jikishu shigai myō shū, maku kō gonchū shu soku* 直須旨外明宗、
莫向言中取則): A saying attributed to Luopu Yuan'an 洛浦元安 (834–898)
in Wansong Xingxiu's 萬松行秀 (1166–1246) commentary on case 41 of
the *Congrong Hermitage Record* (*Congrong lu* 從容錄, T.2004.48:254a20-29),
which is entitled "Luopu About to Die" (*Luopu linzhong* 洛浦臨終):

師云、洛浦臨終、婆心太切。首座盡情吐露、返責非時。彥從不出脣
皮、許伊合會。直得再三撈漉、可憐一向沈埋。克賓甘罰饙飯錢。瞎驢故滅正
法眼。玄覺云、且道、從上座實不會。爲復怕鉢袋子沾著伊。故燈錄收從、入
法嗣之列。浦嘗示衆云、直須旨外明宗。莫向言中取則。僧問、行不思議處如
何。浦云、青山常擧足、白日不移輪。以斯驗之、首座從公皎然可見。洛浦分
上還有人收後也無。百年之後却有天童。

The Master [Hongzhi Zhengjue 宏智正覺 (1091–1157), a.ka. Tiantong 天
童] said, "When Luopu was about to die, his grandmotherly heart [i.e.,
kindness] was extreme. The head seat [i.e., the first of Luopu's interlocutors in the kōan] fully bared his heart and exposed himself but was up-
braided [by Luopu] for the inappropriate timing [of his remark]. Yancong
[i.e., the second of Luopu's interlocutors] did not show the skin of his lips
[i.e., did not open his mouth and speak in a way that revealed anything],
but [Luopu] commended him, saying, 'You should understand.' Although
he [Luopu] **scooped** him [Yancong] **up two or three times**, lamentably he
[Yancong] could only sink into oblivion."

Kebin [a Linji lineage monk of the Tang dynasty] willingly paid the fine
of cash for the rice casserole [offered to the assembly of monks by the
loser in "dharma combat"]. The blind ass [i.e., Linji's disciple, Sansheng]
intentionally extinguished [Linji's] true dharma eye.

350 DŌGEN'S *SHŌBŌGENZŌ* VOLUME VIII

[Yongjia] Xuanjue said, "Tell me, did Senior Seat [Yan] Cong really not understand? Or did he fear that the bowl bag would get him wet?" As it happens, the records [of the transmission] of the flame include [Yan] Cong in the ranks of dharma heirs.

[Luo] Pu once addressed the assembly saying, "Clarify the meaning apart from the sense; don't take the norm from within the words." A monk asked, "What is it like to course in that which is inconceivable?" [Luo] Pu said, "The blue mountains are always raising their feet; the bright sun doesn't revolve on high."

Using this [saying] to test them, the head seat and Mister [Yan] Cong can be seen clearly. As for Luopu, does he have a worthy successor, or not? A hundred years later, there was Tiantong.

**clouded eyes and sky flowers** (*eigen kūge* 翳眼空華). The four glyphs are also translateable as "the sky flowers of clouded eyes." The term "clouded eyes" (*eigen* 翳眼) refers to a medical condition in which the vision is blurred or spots are seen before the eyes. The glyph 翳 (ei) can refer to any kind of "film" or "screen" that obscures things, but when used in connection with "eyes" (*gen* 眼), it is used interchangeably with the glyph 瞖 (*ei*), meaning "cataracts." Several sūtras refer to what is seen by "clouded eyes" as "sky flowers" (*kūge* 空華; S. *khapuṣpa*): a kind of optical illusion in which a person thinks they see flowers floating in the sky. "Flowers in the sky" is a common Buddhist metaphor for things (dharmas) that appear to exist independently in the external world but are actually the product of one's own mind, arising from faulty cognition or reasoning. The metaphor of "clouded eyes" and the "sky flowers" that result is explained, for example, in the *Sūtra Explaining Dharmas via the Mahāyāna Doctrine of Accompanying Factors* (*Dasheng suizhuan xuanshuo zhufa jing* 大乘隨轉宣説諸法經, T.652.15:774b29-c11):

時佛告師子遊戲菩薩摩訶薩言、善哉善哉、善男子。世間一切衆生妙明元心、本來清淨無諸垢染。圓滿十方湛然寂靜。猶如虛空本無塵翳寂然清淨。衆生眼病空華發生。華生華滅病眼所見。眼翳既消空華亦滅。清淨虛空本來不動。妙明元心亦復如是。本來清淨無諸垢染。衆生顛倒背覺合塵。於諸塵境分別心生。眼見於色、耳聞於聲、鼻嗅諸香、舌甞於味、身受諸觸、意了法塵。此六根識各各自偶諸塵境界。於諸塵境妄想執著。便生愛染造種種業。業成受報墮諸苦海。生死輪迴受大苦惱。

At that time the Buddha addressed the Bodhisattva-mahāsattva Siṃha-vikrīḍita, saying:

Splendid, splendid, good son. The wondrously clear fundamental mind of all living beings in the world is originally pure and free from all defilements. It is complete and full through the ten directions, deeply calm and tranquil. It is like empty space, which is originally free from dust and cloudiness, calm and pure. But when the eyes of living beings

Supplementary notes to the translation 351

are diseased, sky flowers appear in it. Flowers appearing and flowers disappearing are what diseased eyes see. Once the cloudiness of the eyes has been removed, the sky flowers also disappear. Pure empty space is originally unmoving. The wondrously clear fundamental mind is also like this. It is originally pure and free from all defilements. Living beings, however, have inverted views, which oppose awakening and conform with the dust [of sense objects]. With regard to sense objects, they give rise to a mind that discriminates. Their eyes see forms; their ears hear sounds; their noses smell fragrances; their tongues taste flavors; their bodies receive feelings of touch; and their minds cognize mental objects. The six sense faculties and modes of consciousness each couple with their own sense objects and spheres of cognition, and with regard to those objects and spheres there is deluded conceptualizing and attachment. That gives rise to the taint of desire, and it produces every sort of karma. Karma makes [beings] receive retribution and fall into oceans of suffering. Revolving through birth and death, they experience great suffering and distress.

The *Heroic March Sūtra* (*Shoulengyan jing* 首楞嚴經, T.945.19:120b17–c8) contains the following passage, which Dōgen evidently had in mind when he wrote "Sky Flowers" ("Shōbōgenzō kūge" 正法眼藏空華):

富樓那言、若此妙覺本妙覺明與如來心不增不減、無狀忽生山河大地諸有爲相。如來今得妙空明覺、山河大地有爲習漏何當復生。佛告富樓那、譬如迷人於一聚落惑南爲北、此迷爲復因迷而有、因悟所出。富樓那言、如是迷人、亦不因迷、又不因悟。何以故。迷本無根、云何因迷。悟非生迷、云何因悟。佛言、彼之迷人正在迷時、倏有悟人指示令悟。富樓那、於意云何。此人縱迷、於此聚落更生迷不。不也、世尊。富樓那、十方如來亦復如是。此迷無本、性畢竟空。昔本無迷。似有迷覺、覺迷迷滅，覺不生迷。亦如瞖人見空中花。瞖病若除華於空滅。忽有愚人、於彼空花所滅空地待花更生。汝觀是人爲愚、爲慧。富樓那言、空元無花、妄見生滅。見花滅空、已是顛倒。勅令更出、斯實狂癡。云何更名如是狂人爲愚、爲慧。佛言、如汝所解。云何問言、諸佛如來妙覺明空、何當更出山河大地。又如金鑛雜於精金。其金一純更不成雜。如木成灰不重爲木。諸佛如來菩提涅槃亦復如是。

Pūrṇa said, "I suppose that this wondrous awakening, which at root is a wondrous awakening whose illumination shares in the mind of the tathāgatas and has neither increase nor decrease, suddenly and for no reason gives rise to mountains, rivers, the whole earth, and all other conditioned forms. If so, then how could the tathāgatas, who have now attained the awakening that illuminates marvelous emptiness, again give rise to the conditioned, contaminated [perception of] mountains, rivers, and the whole earth?"

The Buddha informed Pūrṇa, "It is, for example, like a bewildered person who, in a certain village, becomes confused and takes south for north. Is their bewilderment something that comes into existence on the basis of some other delusion, or is it something that arises from [clear] understanding?"

Pūrṇa said, "A person bewildered like that does not become so on the basis of either delusion or understanding. Why is that? Because bewilderment fundamentally has no root: why say the cause is delusion? Understanding does not give rise to bewilderment: why say the cause is understanding?"

The Buddha said, "What if that bewildered person, while still caught up in delusion, were suddenly to meet a person of clear understanding who pointed out [north] to them and made them understand. Pūrṇa, tell me what you think. Would that person lapse into delusion and again become bewildered [about north and south] in that village?"

[Pūrṇa said,] "They would not, World-Honored One."

[The Buddha said,] "Pūrṇa, the tathāgatas of the ten directions are also like this. The delusion [we are speaking of] has no basis: its nature, in the final analysis, is empty. From the start, fundamentally, there is no delusion. It may seem as if there are delusion and awakening, but when one awakens to delusion that delusion is extinguished, and awakening does not give rise to delusion. Again, it is like a person with cataracts who sees flowers in the sky. If the disease of cataracts is removed, the flowers disappear from the sky. But what if there was a foolish person who waited for the flowers to again arise at the same place in the sky where the sky flowers had disappeared? Would you regard that person as foolish, or as wise?"

Pūrṇa said, "The sky originally has no flowers; they are falsely seen as arising and disappearing. To see flowers as vanishing from the sky is already an inverted view; to will them to reappear is real lunacy. How could we call a person who is deranged like that either foolish or wise?"

The Buddha said, "It is, indeed, as you have explained. So how can you ask, 'When will the buddhas, the tathāgatas whose wondrous awakening illuminates emptiness, again produce [deluded perceptions of] mountains, rivers, and the whole earth?' It is like gold ore that has pure gold mixed in with it. Once that gold has been purified, it cannot again become mixed. It is like wood which, having [burnt and] become ashes, cannot again be wood. The bodhi and nirvāṇa of the buddhas, the tathāgatas, are also like this."

**coming from the west** (*seirai* 西來): An abbreviation of the fixed saying, "the Ancestral Master's coming from the west." A reference to the story of the transmission of the Zen lineage to China by the First Ancestor, Bodhidharma, who is said to have been the Twenty-eighth Ancestor of the

Supplementary notes to the translation    353

lineage in India, in the "Western regions" (*saiiki* 西域). Bodhidharma is celebrated in Zen texts for his transmission of the "mind dharma" (*shinbō* 心法), or awakened "buddha mind" (*busshin* 佛心), that Buddha Śākyamuni purportedly vouchsafed to the First Ancestor of the Zen lineage in India, Mahākāśyapa, as **"a separate transmission outside the teachings."** The phrase "coming from the west" thus stands for the establishment of the "mind dharma" as the highest form of Buddhism in China. It also serves as shorthand for all of Bodhidharma's legendary exploits in the "Eastern Earth" (*tōchi* 東地), China, which include such episodes as: his meeting with Emperor Wu of the Liang dynasty, in which he declared  that the latter's conventional promotion of Buddhism had produced "no merit" (*mu kudoku* 無功德); the nine years he spent "facing a wall" (*menpeki* 面壁) at the Shaolin Monastery on Mount Song; and his pronouncement that his four disciples had, respectively, gained his **"skin, flesh, bones, and marrow."** See also **"intention of the Ancestral Master's coming from the west."**

**counting sand** (*sansha* 算沙; also written 算砂): A common pejorative for those who merely study the details of doctrine; what we might call "spiritual bean counters." From *Great Master Yongjia Zhenjue's Song of Realizing the Way* (*Yongjia Zhenjue dashi zhengdao ge* 永嘉眞覺大師證道歌, T.2076.51:461a11-12):

吾早年來積學問、亦曾討疏尋經論。分別名相不知休、入海算沙徒自困。却被如來苦訶責、數他珍寶有何益。從來蹭蹬覺虛行、多年枉作風塵客。

From my early years I piled up scholastic learning;
Oh, how I searched for commentaries and investigated the sūtras and śāstras!
Discriminating names and forms, I knew no rest;
Counting sand in the ocean, uselessly stressing myself.
Then I pulled back, having been painfully criticized by the Tathāgata:
"What benefit is there in calculating the treasure of others?"
My frustrated struggles up to then, I realized, had been futile;
So many years spent vainly stirring up adventitious dust.

**crown of the head** (*chōnei* 頂顆): The top of the human head. In Zen texts, the true person or the true identity of someone or something: "who they really are" or "what it really is." Dōgen regularly uses "crown of the head," like **"eye"** and **"nose"** as (a) synecdoche for the person, and (b) the "pinnacle" or best of someone (or something). When used in reference to **buddhas and ancestors** in general or particular Zen masters, these body parts stand for their wisdom or essential message. In some contexts, "crown of the head" may refer to a buddha's *uṣṇīṣa*, the protuberance on the top of his head that is one of his thirty-two marks, sometimes taken as symbolic of his wisdom.

**crystal clear on all eight sides** (*reirō hachimen* 玲瓏八面): A variant of "the eight sides are crystal clear" (*hachimen reirō* 八面玲瓏), a common term for perfect clarity. The root image is the tinkling sound of crystal [or jewel] pendants (*reirō* 玲瓏) as they hit each other, which can be heard throughout the eight points of the compass. Metaphorically, *reirō* 玲瓏 refers to a gem, a sound, or anything else, that is "beautifully clear." The expression "clear as tinkling crystal" (*reirei rōrō* 玲玲瓏瓏) is used by Hongzhi Zhengjue 宏智正覺 (1091–1157) as a metaphor for spiritual insight; it appears, for example, in the *Extensive Record of Chan Master Hongzhi* (*Hongzhi chanshi guanglu* 宏智禪師廣錄, T.2001.48:13a15-18):

> 上堂云、同中有異、功亡就位。異中有同。在位借功。一步密移玄路轉。全身放下劫壺空。隱隱密密、玲玲瓏瓏。記取深雲須變豹。自然死水不藏龍。(T.2001.48.13a15-18)

At a convocation in the dharma hall, [Hongzhi] said: "Within sameness there is difference: non-duality is lost, and the consequence is the [five] positions. Within difference there is sameness: while in the [five] positions, we avail ourselves of non-duality. With a single step, what is secret shifts, and the hidden path takes a turn. The entire body is thrown away, and one plunders the jar of emptiness. Mysteriously secret, clear as tinkling crystal. To remember deep clouds, one must bring the dead [pieces in a board game] back to life in a single move. Water that is naturally stagnant does not hide dragons."

**cut off an arm** (*danpi* 斷臂): In Zen literature, this expression refers to the story of how Huike 慧可, who later became the Second Ancestor of the Chan lineage in China, was accepted as a disciple of the First Ancestor, the Indian monk Bodhidharma. Prior to that, Huike was a monk named Shenguang 神光, who had trained in meditation for eight years under Chan Master Baojing 寶靜禪師 of Mount Xiang 香山 in Longmen 龍門. He traveled to the Shaolin Monastery on Mount Song to study with Bodhidharma but was initially spurned by that master, who always sat upright facing a wall and ignored all who came to enquire of him. Shenguang stood all night in the snow to demonstrate his earnestness as a would-be disciple; and, when that did not work, he cut off his own left arm and presented it to the master. Bodhidharma accepted him as a disciple and had him change his name to Huike. The following account from the *Jingde Era Record of the Transmission of the Flame* (*Jingde chuandeng lu* 景德傳燈錄, T.2076.51:219b9-20) picks up at the point where Shenguang's initial appeal for instruction has been rejected by Bodhidharma:

> 光自惟曰、昔人求道敲骨取髓、刺血濟饑、布髮掩泥、投崖飼虎。古尚若此、我又何人。其年十二月九日夜天大雨雪。光堅立不動。遲明積雪過膝。師憫而問曰、汝久立雪中。當求何事。光悲淚曰、惟願和尚慈悲開甘露門廣度群品。師曰、諸佛無上妙道曠劫精勤、難行能

## Supplementary notes to the translation

行、非忍而忍。豈以小德小智、輕心慢心、欲冀眞乘、徒勞勤苦。光
聞師誨勵、潛取利刀自斷左臂、置于師前。師知是法器、乃曰、諸佛
最初求道、爲法忘形。汝今斷臂吾前。求亦可在。師遂因與易名曰慧
可。

[Shen]guang thought to himself, "The people of old, in seeking the way, smashed their bones and extracted the marrow; drew their blood to save the starving; let down their hair to cover the mud [for the Buddha to walk across]; and threw themselves from cliffs to feed tigers. If people of old were like this, then what person am I?" On the ninth day of the twelfth month of that year [2nd year of the Datong era, or 528 C.E.], in the evening there was great rain and snow, but Guang stood firm and did not move. By morning the snow had piled up past his knees.

The Master [Bodhidharma] took pity and inquired of him, saying: "You have long stood in the snow. You must be seeking something."

Guang shed pitiful tears and said, "I only request, Reverend, that out of compassion you open the ambrosia gate and broadly deliver every kind of living being."

The Master said, "The unsurpassed marvelous way of the buddhas is to vigorously strive for vast kalpas, practicing that which is difficult to practice and enduring that which is difficult to endure. How can you, with inferior virtue and inferior wisdom, a shallow mind and an arrogant mind, wish for the true vehicle and pointlessly labor in austerities?"

When Guang heard the Master's admonition, he stealthily took a sharp knife, cut off his own left arm, and placed it in front of the Master.

The Master, knowing that he was a vessel of the dharma, said, "When buddhas first seek the way, they forget their physical form for the sake of the dharma. You now cut off an arm in front of me; that which you seek is something you are capable of." The Master, on that account, had him change his name to Huike ["Capable of Wisdom"].

**cypress tree at the front of the garden** (*teizen hakujushi* 庭前柏樹子): A saying attributed to Zhaozhou Congshen 趙州從諗 (778-897). It is found, among numerous other Zen texts, as case 47 of the *Congrong Hermitage Record* (*Congrong lu* 從容錄, T.2004.48.256c14-16) and case 37 of the *Gateless Barrier* (*Wumen guan* 無門關, T.2005.48.297c5-6), which reads as follows:

趙州因僧問、如何是祖師西來意。州云、庭前柏樹子。

Zhaozhou was once asked by a monk, "What is the **intention of the Ancestral Master's coming from the west**?"

Zhaozhou said, "The cypress tree at the front of the garden."

356 DŌGEN'S *SHŌBŌGENZŌ* VOLUME VIII

A longer version of the exchange appears in the *Outline of the Linked Flames* (*Liandeng huiyao* 聯燈會要, ZZ.136:528a17-b2; X.1557.79:57c24-58a3 and 666b12-14; X.1557.79:127a24-b2); in Dōgen's *Shōbōgenzō* in Chinese script (*shinji Shōbōgenzō* 眞字正法眼藏, DZZ.5:190, case 119); and in his "The Cypress Tree" ("Shōbōgenzō hakujushi" 正法眼藏柏樹子), where it reads as follows:

大師、因有僧問、如何是祖師西來意。師云、庭前柏樹子。僧曰、和尚莫以境示人。師云、吾不以境示人。僧云〔曰〕、如何是祖師西來意。師云、庭前柏樹子。

The Great Master was once asked by a monk, "What is the intention of the Ancestral Master's coming from the west?"

The Master said, "The cypress tree at the front of the garden."

The monk said, "Reverend, don't show a person with an object."

The Master said, "I don't show a person with an object."

The monk said, "What is the intention of the Ancestral Master's coming from the west?"

The Master said, "The cypress tree at the front of the garden."

The literature of Zen is filled with countless instances of disciples asking masters, "What is the intention (or meaning) of the Ancestral Master's coming from the west?"; for examples, see "**intention of the Ancestral Master's coming from the west**." Zhaozhou's response became so famous in the later Zen tradition that the mere mention of a "cypress tree (*hakujushi* 柏樹子 or 栢樹子) was enough to evoke the aforementioned kōan. Apart from that Buddhist context, the cypress, an evergreen native to China used in decorative planting, was traditionally thought of as a symbol of constancy and long life.

Dahui Zonggao's 大慧宗杲 (1089–1163) *Treasury of the True Dharma Eye* (*Zhengfayanzang* 正法眼藏, ZZ.118:61b2-8; X.1309.67:586b7-14) contains a conversation attributed to Zhaozhou in which his interlocutor is depicted as already familiar with and expecting his famous "cypress tree" response:

趙州和尚示衆云、法本不生、今則無滅。更不要道、纔語是生不語是滅。諸人、且作麼生是不生不滅底道理。僧問、艸是不生不滅麼。曰、遮漢只認得箇死語。問、如何是丈六金身。曰、袖頭打領、腋下剜襟。僧云、學人不會。曰、不會、倩人裁。問、如何是西來意。曰、版齒生毛。問、栢樹子還有佛性也無。曰、有。云、幾時成佛。曰、待虛空落地時。云、虛空幾時落地。曰、待栢樹子成佛時。

Reverend Zhaozhou addressed the assembly saying, "Dharmas originally have no arising, so right now they have no disappearing. It's not necessary to speak any further. At the very moment we say, 'This arises,' we don't say, 'This disappears.' People, what do you make of this principle of not arising and not disappearing?"

Supplementary notes to the translation

A monk asked, "Does grass not arise and not disappear?"

[Zhaozhou] said, "This guy is only able to understand these dead words."

[The monk] asked, "What about the sixteen-foot golden body [said to be made of one blade of grass]?"

[Zhaozhou] said, "His sleeve ends strike his neck; his breast scoops out his collar."

[The monk] said, "Your student doesn't understand."

[Zhaozhou] said, "If you don't understand, you rely on people to judge for you."

[The monk] asked, "What is the intention of the Ancestral Master's coming from the west?"

[Zhaozhou] said, "Front teeth grow moldy [from never opening the mouth to speak]."

[The monk] asked, "Does even a cypress tree have buddha nature?"

[Zhaozhou] said, "It has."

[The monk] said, "How long before it attains buddhahood?"

[Zhaozhou] said, "It waits for when empty space falls to the earth."

[The monk] said, "When will empty space fall to the earth?"

[Zhaozhou] said, "It waits for when the cypress tree attains buddhahood."

The question, "Does even a cypress tree have buddha nature?" echoes another famous kōan involving Zhaozhou, in which he is asked, "Does even a dog have buddha nature?" and answers, "No."

**deportment** (*iigi* 威儀, also read *igi*; S. *īryāpatha*): In ordinary parlance, a "dignified demeanor" associated with adherence to proper decorum, etiquette, and ritual propriety. In Buddhist texts, a reference to the "four deportments" (*shi iigi* 四威儀; S. *īryāpatha*) of walking, standing, sitting, and reclining (*gyōjūzaga* 行住坐臥), which is also a set phrase used to indicate "at all times, whatever one is doing." In Buddhist vinaya texts such as the *Sūtra of the Three Thousand Rules of Deportment* (*Sanqian weiyi jing* 三千威儀經, T.1470.24), which Dōgen sometimes quotes, "deportment" refers to proper conduct for monks and nuns, including following moral precepts, norms of personal etiquette, modes of dress, and various other ritual procedures (*sahō* 作法). In the Zen tradition, the expression "original deportment" (*hon iigi* 本威儀) indicates a monk's most formal robes and accoutrements.

The expression "deportment of the practicing buddha" (*gyōbutsu iigi* 行佛威儀), which Dōgen uses as the title of a chapter of his *Shōbōgenzō*, could well be parsed as "to practice (*gyō* 行) the deportment (*iigi* 威儀) of a buddha (*butsu* 佛)." That could mean either "to act like a buddha" or "to follow the etiquette established by the Buddha." It is clear from the opening words

358 DŌGEN'S *SHŌBŌGENZŌ* VOLUME VIII

of the chapter, however, that Dōgen wants us to take *gyōbutsu* 行佛 as a "practicing buddha," in contrast to other notions of "buddha."

In his "Needle of Seated Meditation" ("Shōbōgenzō zazen shin" 正法眼藏坐禪箴, DZZ.1.113), Dōgen speaks of "deportment beyond sound and form," (*shōshiki kōjō iigi* 聲色向上威儀). That abstract concept is a variation on a phrase best known from a verse by Xiangyan Zhixian 香嚴智閑 (d. 898) recorded in Dōgen's *Shōbōgenzō* in Chinese script (*shinji Shōbōgenzō* 眞字正法眼藏, DZZ.5:134, case 17) and invoked elsewhere in Dōgen's writings:

處處無蹤跡、聲色外威儀。

No traces wherever I go;
Deportment beyond sound and form.

This verse also appears in the *Outline of the Linked Flames* (*Liandeng huiyao* 聯燈會要, ZZ.136:566a8; X.1557.79:76c19-20).

**dharma rain** (*hō'u* 法雨; S. *dharma-varṣa*): A metaphor that compares the free and indiscriminate dispensing of Buddhist teachings to all living beings to rain, which falls indiscriminately on and sustains all forms of plant life. In the "Introduction" (*Xupin* 序品) chapter of the *Lotus Sūtra* (*Miaofa lianhua jing* 妙法蓮華經, T.262.9:3c11-14), for example, we find:

爾時文殊師利語彌勒菩薩摩訶薩及諸大士、善男子等、如我惟忖、今佛世尊欲説大法、雨大法雨，吹大法螺，擊大法鼓，演大法義。

At that time, Mañjuśrī said to the bodhisattva-mahāsattva Maitreya and the great beings, "Good sons, I presume that the Buddha, the World-Honored One, wishes to preach a great dharma, to rain down a great dharma rain, to blow the conch-shell horn of a great dharma, to beat the drum of a great dharma, and to expound the meaning of a great dharma."     L a t e r in the same chapter, Mañjuśrī predicts that the Buddha is about to preach the sūtra (T.262.9:5b19-21):

今佛放光明、助發實相義。諸人今當知、合掌一心待。佛當雨法雨、充足求道者。

Now, the Buddha has emitted this light,
To help express the meaning of the real marks.
All should now know this,
And wait single-mindedly.
The Buddha will rain down the dharma rain,
Satisfying those who seek the way.

See "**roots, stalks, branches, and leaves, flowers and fruit, lustrous and colored**" for a subsequent passage in the *Lotus Sūtra* (T.262.9:19c24-27) that uses the trope of varied plants of the world all being watered by the same rain to make the point that "dharma rain," while uniform in flavor and

*Supplementary notes to the translation*   359

universal in distribution, is nevertheless received by various living beings in a manner that is suited to their own particular needs and capacities.

Japanese Zen monks engaged in alms gathering (*takuhatsu* 托鉢) in public places (e.g. while walking down a shopping street) announce their presence by shouting "*hō'u*" ("dharma rain"). The idea behind this is that, by giving anyone and everyone they meet an opportunity to make a donation and earn merit, they are freely and indiscriminately spreading the dharma.

**dharmas abide in their dharma positions** (*hō jū hōi* 法住法位; *hō wa hōi ni jū shi* 法は法位に住し). An expression that derives from the "Expedient Means" (*Fangbian* 方便) chapter of Kumārajīva's translation of the *Lotus Sūtra* (*Miaofa lianhua jing* 妙法蓮華經, T.262.9:9b6-11):

未來世諸佛、雖説百千億、無數諸法門、其實爲一乘、諸佛兩足尊、知法常無性、佛種從緣起、是故説一乘、是法住法位、世間相常住、於道場知已、導師方便説。

Buddhas of future ages,
Although they preach hundreds, thousands, millions
Of innumerable dharma gates,
In truth do so for the sake of the one vehicle.
Buddhas, honored among bipeds,
Know that dharmas always lack intrinsic nature,
And that the seeds of buddhahood sprout through causal conditions,
Which is why they preach the one vehicle.
The dharmas abide in their dharma positions;
The marks of the world constantly abide.
Having already learned this in the place of practice,
The guiding teachers explain it through skillful means.

The corresponding passage from the extant Sanskrit of the *Lotus Sūtra* reads: "The abiding of the dharma, the fixedness of the dharma, permanently abiding in the world (S. *dharma-sthitiṃ dharma-niyāmatāṃ ca nitya-sthitāṃ loki*)." Thus, the glyphs 法住法位 (*hō jū hōi*), translated here as "dharmas abide in their dharma positions," may have been intended by Kumārajīva to refer to the "teachings" (*hō* 法) of the buddhas, or buddha dharma (*buppō* 佛法), which "abides" (*jū* 住) and is "positioned" (*i* 位) in the world. Our English translation, however, follows the traditional East Asian interpretation of Kumārajīva's Chinese, which takes the glyph 法 (*hō*) as referring to the "things" (dharmas) that, while impermanent and causally conditioned, are the really existing, irreducible constituent elements that make up the phenomenal world of human experience. Each dharma is said to exist with its own characteristic "mark" (*sō* 相; S. *lakṣaṇa*) and in its own

360 DŌGEN'S *SHŌBŌGENZŌ* VOLUME VIII

place and moment — its unique spatial and temporal "dharma position" (*hōi* 法位), without changing into anything else.

**divulging the matter and achieving accord** (*tenji tōki* 展事投機): A fixed idiom in Zen texts, used especially for the relationship between master and disciple. Our translation here follows BGDJ (s.v. てんじとうき) and ZGD (s.v. てんじとうき), which both explain that "divulge the matter" (*tenji* 展事) means to speak one's mind, or reveal to another what one really thinks, and that "achieve accord" (*tōki* 投機) means to match the understanding of one's interlocutor, often a Zen master, and to reach a mutual agreement. *The Eye of Humans and Devas* (*Rentian yanmu* 人天眼目, T.2006.48:322a8-11) contains the following account, which seems to bear out that interpretation:

> 仰山親於耽源處、受九十七種圓相。後於溈山處、因此〇相頓悟。後有語云、諸佛密印豈容言乎。又曰、我於耽源處得體、溈山處得用。謂之父子投機。故有此圓相。

When Yangshan [Huiji (803-877)] was an intimate disciple at Danyuan's [Yingzhen] place, he learned about ninety-seven kinds of circular signs. Later, at Weishan's place, he was suddenly awakened by this "O" sign. After that he had a saying, "The secret seal of the buddhas — how could it possibly be put in words?" He also said, "At Danyuan's place I got the substance; at Weishan's place I got the function." This is what we call "father and son achieving accord." Thus, there are these circular signs.

The "circular sign" (*ensō* 圓相), or "sign of completeness," discussed here is a circle drawn with brush and ink on paper, or in the air with a gesture of the arm and hand.

However, scholars are not in agreement on the meaning of *tenji tōki* 展事投機. According to Urs App (1989, 50), in his *The Eye of Humans and Devas* (*Rentian yanmu* 人天眼目, T.2006.48:14-15), Fenyang Shanzhao 汾陽善昭 (947-1024) explains eighteen types of question that students ask Chan masters. One type is *tōki* 投機, or "questions that take advantage of an occasion." That is, questions "in which the questioner shows that he still has a doubt as to his attainment and expresses his desire for confirmation." According to this interpretation, which App made in consultation with Iriya Yoshitaka 入矢義高 (1910-1998), *tenji tōki* 展事投機 should be translated as "[a student] divulging the matter [of their own uncertainty] and taking advantage of the opportunity [to learn from the teacher]."

In their translation of *The Blue Cliff Record* (Cleary and Cleary 1992, 82-83), Thomas Cleary and J.C. Cleary render *tenji tōki* 展事投機 as "laying out facts in accordance with the situation" (*Biyan lu* 碧巖錄, T.2003.48:153a11-13):

> 金烏急、玉兔速。善應何曾有輕觸。展事投機見洞山、跛鱉盲龜入空谷。

The Golden Raven hurries;

The Jade Rabbit is swift.

Has there ever been carelessness in a good response?

To see Tung Shan as laying out the facts in accordance with the situation

Is like a lame tortoise and a blind turtle entering an empty valley.

In modern Japanese, *tōki* 投機 means "to venture" something, "to speculate" (in the sense of risking money in an investment), or "to gamble."

**dominate the market** (*zandatsu kōshi* 攙奪行市): To control prices, as in the saying of Xuansha Shibei 玄沙師備 (835–908), recorded in Dōgen's *Shōbōgenzō* in Chinese script (*shinji Shōbōgenzō* 眞字正法眼藏, DZZ.5:146, case 38):

福州雪峰山眞覺大師〈嗣德山、諱義存〉指火炉謂玄沙云、三世諸佛、盡在裡許、轉大法輪。沙云、近日王令稍嚴。師云、作麼生。沙曰、不許人攙奪行市。

Great Master Zhenjue of Mount Xuefeng, Fuzhou (succeeded Deshan, named Yicun), pointed to the stove and said to Xuansha, "The buddhas of the three times are all inside here turning the great dharma wheel." Sha said, "These days the king's orders are rather strict."

The Master said, "How so?"

Sha said, "They don't permit people to dominate the market."

**Dongshan's three roads** (*Tōzan sanro* 洞山三路): Three phrases attributed to Dongshan Liangjie 洞山良价 (807–869), a.k.a. Chan Master Wuben 悟本禪師, indicating three modes of guiding students. The formula appears in the *Discourse Record of Chan Master Wuben of Mount Dong in Junzhou* (*Junzhou Dongshan Wuben chanshi yulu* 筠州洞山悟本禪師語錄, T.1986A.47:511a26-b3):

師示衆曰、我有三路接人、鳥道、玄路、展手。僧問、師尋常教學人行鳥道、未審如何是鳥道。師曰、不逢一人。云、如何行。師曰、直須足下無絲去。云、祇如行鳥道、莫便是本來面目否。師曰、闍黎因甚顛倒。云、甚麼處是學人顛倒。師曰、若不顛倒、因甚麼却認奴作郎。云、如何是本來面目。師曰、不行鳥道。

The Master [Dongshan] addressed the assembly, saying, "I have three roads for engaging people: the path of the bird, the dark road, and the open hand."

A monk asked, "The Master always has the student follow the path of the bird. I don't understand. What is the path of the bird?"

The Master said, "You don't meet a single person."

[The monk] said, "How do you follow it?"

The Master said, "You should go without a string at your feet."

[The monk] said, "If you just follow the path of the bird, then isn't this your original face?"

The Master said, "How could the Ācārya get it so wrong?"

[The monk] said, "Where did this student get it wrong?"

The Master said, "If you didn't get it wrong, how could you take the servant as the master?"

[The monk] said, "What is the original face?"

The Master said, "It doesn't follow the path of the bird."

A nearly identical passage, beginning at the point where a monk asks, "What is the path of the bird?" is also found in the *Jingde Era Record of the Transmission of the Flame* (*Jingde chuandeng lu* 景德傳燈錄, T.51.2076:322c21-27).

In this context, Dongshan only elaborates on the first of his "three roads" — the "path of the bird" — which he says entails "going without a string at your feet" (*sokka mu shi ko* 足下無絲去). This is probably an allusion to the practice of tying a string to the leg of a falcon when training it to return to its handler. Because the "path of the bird" is presented here as a method by which Dongshan guides students, the metaphor of "no string on the foot" likely means not holding them back in any way and compelling them to proceed on their own. In any case, the "path of the bird" is generally taken to imply "a way that follows no route and leaves no traces." ZGDJ (866d, s.v. ちょうどう) gives two meanings: 1) "a narrow, steep path that is impassable to all but birds"; 2) "one of 'Dongshan's three paths': the path that birds fly through the air; because birds leave no tracks in the sky, a metaphor for leaving no traces or cutting off all contact with others."

What the two remaining paths signify is not explained in the preceding passage. However, in the *Extensive Record of Chan Master Hongzhi* (*Hongzhi chanshi guanglu* 宏智禪師廣錄, T.2001.48:64a29-b4), we do find a comment by Hongzhi Zhengjue 宏智正覺 (1091–1157) on all "three roads," which sheds some light on how they were understood in the Caodong tradition:

小參僧問記得、洞山和尚、有三路學、鳥道、玄路、展手。如何是鳥道。師云、應處無蹤跡、絲毫不礙身。僧云、如何是玄路。師云、圓同太虛。無欠無餘。僧云、如何是展手。師云、當機的的用、的的用當機。

At a small convocation a monk asked, "I recall that Reverend Dongshan said, 'I have three roads for engaging people: the path of the bird, the dark road, and the open hand.' What is the 'path of the bird'?"

The Master [Hongzhi] said, "It must be a place that has no footprints, where one's body is not obstructed by the slightest string."

Supplementary notes to the translation 363

The monk said, "What is the 'dark road'?"

The Master said, "Complete sameness and great vacuity, with no deficiency and no excess."

The monk said, "What is the 'open hand'?"

The Master said, "One's according with abilities functions clearly and simply; one's clear and simple functioning accords with abilities."

Hongzhi's comment suggests that the "path of the bird" is an approach where there are no footprints to follow, because birds leave no tracks when they fly through the air, and one where there is no hindrance to movement in any direction, as in the open sky. His comment on the "dark road" does little to explain what sort of approach it is or how a teacher could lead a student on it. The meaning of "open hand," according to Hongzhi, refers to the skillful means employed by a bodhisattva to help living beings. Hongzhi's take on "Dongshan's three paths," however, seems to regard them not as three methods of training, but rather as three stages on a single path: 1) to get free from restrictions, 2) to gain an understanding of emptiness, and 3) to reach out to help others.

**doubting your head and accepting its reflection** (*meitō nin'yō* 迷頭認影): An allusion to the story of Yajñadatta that appears the *Heroic March Sūtra* (*Shoulengyan jing* 首楞嚴經, T.945.19:121b9-14):

室羅城中演若達多、忽於晨朝以鏡照面。愛鏡中頭眉目可見、瞋責己頭不見。面目以爲魑魅無狀狂走。於意云何、此人何因無故狂走 。富樓那言、是人心狂更無他故。

[The Buddha said,] "In the City of Śrāvastī, there was one Yajñadatta, who suddenly one morning took a mirror and looked at the reflection of his face. He wanted to be able to see his head, eyebrows, and eyes in the mirror, but was outraged that his own head was not visible. He took the face [that he saw] as that of a trickster spirit and, although that had no basis in fact, he ran around insanely. What do you think? Why did that person run around insanely for no reason?" Pūrṇa [Buddha's interlocutor] said, "That person was mentally deranged; there was no other reason."

The basic story here is that Yajñadatta did not recognize the face that he saw in the mirror as his own, mistaking it for the face of a trickster spirit (*chimi* 魑魅) — a "goblin" with a human head and beast-like body that likes to deceive people. He jumped to the conclusion that his own head was missing and ran around insanely looking for it. Thus, the meaning of the saying "doubting your head and accepting its reflection" is that Yajñadatta became "confused about," or "doubted" (*mei* 迷) his own head (*tō* 頭), but "accepted as real," or "believed in" (*nin* 認) the "reflection" (*yō* 影) that he took to be the face of a trickster spirit. In the *Heroic March Sūtra* itself, the

364 DŌGEN'S *SHŌBŌGENZŌ* VOLUME VIII

point of the Yajñadatta story seems to be that "delusion, fundamentally, has no cause" (*mō gen muin* 妄元無因).

In the literature of Zen, the story of Yajñadatta is often used as a metaphor for the inability to see one's own original face, or innate buddha nature, which is always there whether one recognizes that fact or not. To "run about insanely" looking for one's own head is to seek some "awakening," or "satori," that one imagines has been lost.

In his "Deportment of the Practicing Buddha" ("Shōbōgenzō gyōbutsu iigi" 正法眼藏行佛威儀, DZZ.1:67), Dōgen writes:

行盡・明盡、これ強爲の爲にあらず、迷頭認影に大似なり、回光返照に一如なり。

Fully practicing it [i.e., the deportment of the practicing buddha], fully clarifying it — this is not a forced act: it is "just like doubting your head and accepting its reflection"; it is the same as turning the light around and shining it back.

The sentence likely reflects the words of the eleventh-century figure Dayu Shouzhi 大愚守芝 (dates unknown) found in the *Outline of the Linked Flames* (*Liandeng huiyao* 聯燈會要, ZZ.136:634a8; X.1557.79:111a3):

若向言中取則、句裏明機、大似迷頭認影。

If you take the norm from within the words and clarify the point inside the text, it is just like doubting your head and accepting its reflection.

Although, in Dayu's use, the phrase is a simile for a misguided reliance on texts, Dōgen seems here to be giving it a positive valance.

**dragged through the mud and drenched with water** (*dadei taisui* 拖泥帶水): Also written 拕泥帶水. A fixed expression, with a colloquial Chinese sense something like "bumbling." In Buddhist texts, it evokes the image of the pristine lotus flower, which is rooted in the muck but rises above the muddy water: a standard metaphor for the bodhisattva, who remains in saṃsāra out of compassion for living beings but is detached from it by dint of insight into the emptiness of dharmas. In Zen texts, "dragged through the mud and drenched with water" is a metaphor for being "sullied" by words and concepts. It is used both in a pejorative sense, for deluded thinking, and in a positive sense, in ironic praise of the Zen master who "gets his hands dirty," so to speak, in the teaching of his students.

An example of the former usage is found in Yuanwu Keqin's 圜悟克勤 (1063-1135) commentary on case 37 of the *Blue Cliff Record* (*Biyan lu* 碧巖錄, T.2003.48:175a13-15):

舉。盤山垂語云、三界無法何處求心。

Raised:

Panshan gave instruction, saying, "In the **three realms**, there are no dharmas; where would you seek mind?"

Yuanwu's commentary (*Biyan lu* 碧巖錄, T.2003.48:175a25-b2) includes the following:

古人道、聞稱聲外句、莫向意中求。且道他意作麼生。直得奔流度刃、電轉星飛。若擬議尋思、千佛出世、也摸索他不著。若是深入閫奧、徹骨徹髓、見得透底。盤山一場敗缺。若承言會宗左轉右轉底。盤山只得一橛。若是拕泥帶水、聲色堆裏轉、未夢見盤山在。

An ancient said, "If you hear mention of a phrase that is outside of language, do not seek it within thought." But tell me, what did he mean? Get it instantly, like a raging torrent, the sharpness of a blade, the flash of lightning, or a shooting star. If you deliberate and seek it through reasoning, even if a thousand buddhas appear in the world, you will grope for it in vain. If, however, you deeply enter the inner sanctum, penetrating the bone and penetrating the marrow, you will be able to see through the matter. From that perspective, Panshan has made one huge blunder. If you hear the words and understand the import, you may turn left or turn right [as you please]. From that perspective, Panshan is only half right. But if you are dragged through the mud and drenched with water, turning about in an accumulation of sound and form, then even in your dreams you have yet to see where Panshan is.

In this context, it is clear that to be "dragged through the mud and drenched with water" is to be caught up in deluded thinking.

The latter, positive usage is attributed, for example, to Xuedou Zhongxian 雪竇重顯 (980–1052) in his *Discourse Record of Chan Master Mingjue* (*Mingjue chanshi yulu* 明覺禪師語錄, T.1996.47:673c16-20):

師開堂日、於法座前顧謂大眾云、若論本分相見、不必高陞寶座。乃以手指一劃云、諸人隨山僧手看、無量諸佛國土一時現前。各各子細觀瞻、其或涯際未知。不免拖泥帶水、即便陞座。僧正宣疏了。

On the day that the Master [Xuedou] opened the dharma hall [upon being installed as abbot], he turned to address the great assembly from in front of the dharma seat, saying, "If I think about having an audience with the original lot, it's not necessary to be promoted to this jeweled seat." Then he pointed once with his hand and said, "If you people follow this mountain monk's hand and look, limitless buddha lands will appear simultaneously. If you carefully examine each of them, its boundary is yet to be known. I cannot avoid being dragged through the mud and drenched with water, so I will mount the seat. Superintendent of the saṃgha, read aloud the document [of appointment to the abbacy]."

366 DŌGEN'S *SHŌBŌGENZŌ* VOLUME VIII

In this case, to be "dragged through the mud and drenched with water" is to assume the duties of the abbot of a Zen monastery, who is expected to take the high seat in the dharma hall on a regular basis to teach and debate the assembled monks and lay supporters. Xuedou's point is that every person's "original lot" (*honbun* 本分) — their buddha nature — is both innate to them and fundamentally incommunicable through language, so there is something absurd, and even defiling, about the very act of one person trying to lead another to awakening. Such expedient means are necessary, Xuedou acknowledges, but should always be seen as problematic.

**dried-up tree** (*koboku* 枯木): Or "dead wood," "dead tree," "withered tree," etc.; the somewhat infelicitous translation "dried-up" seeks to preserve lexical continuity with Dōgen's other uses of *ko* 枯 ("to dry out," "to be dried out"). In some contexts, a tree that is standing but dead and withered, without any leaves, buds, sap, or hint of life. In other contexts, a piece of wood. In ordinary Chinese, a metaphor for a decrepit old person.

In Buddhist texts, a metaphor for the trance of cessation (*metsujin jō* 滅盡定; S. *nirodha-samāpatti*) or any state of profound mental calm attained through the prolonged practice of seated meditation. Also, an epithet for an ascetic monk who constantly sits in meditation and never lies down to sleep. "Dried-up-tree hall" (*kobokudō* 枯木堂) is a common name for a meditation hall (*zendō* 禪堂), written on a plaque over the front door.

In the literature of Zen, a metaphor (often pejorative) for the seemingly lifeless thing or person, especially the mind in trance or otherwise free from thoughts. Also, a name for a **practitioner of dhyāna** who attains deep mental calm and, though lacking true insight into the buddha mind, mistakes that state of trance for awakening. The expression often appears in the compound "dried-up trees and dead ashes" (*koboku shikai* 枯木死灰), in reference to a lifeless thing or mistaken kind of meditation practice. The source for the latter is likely a Daoist text like the *Zhuangzi* 莊子. The second book (Qiwu lun 齊物論, KR.5c0126.002.1a) of that classic opens with Jiqi of Nanguo 南郭子綦 leaning on his armrest and gazing at the heavens. His companion Yancheng Ziyou 顔成子遊 exclaims,

何居乎、形固可使如槁木、而心固可使如死灰乎。

"What's this? Can you actually make the body like a dried-up tree and the mind like dead ashes?"

In his "The Way of the Buddhas" ("Shōbōgenzō butsudō" 正法眼藏佛道), Dōgen quotes a passage in *Shimen's Grove Record* (*Shimen linjian lu* 林間錄, ZZ.148:590b7-12; X.1624.87:247c21-248a1), by Juefan Huihong 覺範慧洪 (1071-1128), alias Shimen 石門, that criticizes the classification of Bodhidharma as a **practitioner of dhyāna**:

## Supplementary notes to the translation

菩提達磨初自梁之魏、經行於嵩山之下、倚杖於少林。面壁燕坐而
已。非習禪也。久之、人莫測其故、因以達磨爲習禪。夫禪那、諸行
之一耳。何足以盡聖人。而當時之人以之爲。史者又從而傳茲習禪之
列。使與枯木死灰之徒爲伍。雖然聖人非止於禪那、而亦不違禪那。

When Bodhidharma first went from Liang to Wei, he proceeded to the foot
of Mount Song, where he rested his **staff** at Shaolin [Monastery]. There he
just sat facing a wall. It was not the practice of dhyāna, but after a while,
others, unable to fathom what he was doing, made [Bodhi]dharma a practitioner of dhyāna. Now, dhyāna is but one among various practices; how
could it suffice to exhaust [the practice of] the sage? Nevertheless, people
of the time took it in this way; and those who wrote histories followed
this and recorded him among practitioners of dhyāna, thus making him a
confederate of the partisans of "dried-up trees and dead ashes." Although
the sage does not stop [his mind] in dhyāna, he does not oppose dhyāna.

The historians criticized here for their failure to understand Bodhidharma
are Daoxuan 道宣 (596–667) and Zanning 贊寧 (919-1002), who classified
Bodhidharma as a practitioner of dhyāna in their *Additional Biographies
of Eminent Monks* (*Xu gaoseng zhuan* 續高僧傳, T.260.50:551b27ff)
and *Song Biographies of Eminent Monks* (*Song gaoseng zhuan* 宋高僧傳,
T.2061.50:756a2ff), respectively. Huihong believed that Bodhidharma had
transmitted the buddha mind (*busshin* 佛心) to China and founded the Chan
lineage there; he was irate that Daoxuan failed to mention those facts and
lumped Bodhidharma together with partisans of trance meditation: "dried-
up trees and dead ashes" (*koboku shikai* 枯木死灰).

**dust** (*jin* 塵): In ordinary language, infinitesimal motes of dust; minute
particles. In Buddhist texts, 1) dirt, pollution, or defilement; in particular,
the afflictions such as greed, anger, and delusion that stain the mind; or 2)
an object of any of the six senses.

**eight or nine tenths complete** (*hakku jō* 八九成): An expression used by Zen
masters to judge an interpretation offered by an interlocutor in a debate. The
usual meaning is "not bad," "almost there," or "good but not the whole story,"
but it is occasionally used as ironic high praise. The biography of Shishuang
Qingzhu 石霜慶諸 (807-888) in the *Jingde Era Record of the Transmission of
the Flame* (*Jingde chuandeng lu* 景德傳燈錄; T.2076.51:321a8-12) contains
the following exchange between that Chan master and his eventual dharma
heir, Yungai Zhian 雲蓋志安 (dates unknown):

雲蓋問、萬戶俱閉即不問、萬戶俱開時如何。師曰、堂中事作麼生。
曰、無人接得渠。師曰、道也大殺道也。只道得八九成。曰、未審和
尚作麼生道。師曰、無人識得渠。

368    DŌGEN'S *SHŌBŌGENZŌ* VOLUME VIII

Yungai asked, "I don't ask about the myriad doors being all shut; what's it like when the myriad doors are all open?"

The Master [Shishuang] said, "What about inside the hall?"

[Yungai] said, "There's no one able to engage him."

The Master said, "You talk big talk, but your saying is only eight or nine tenths complete."

[Yungai] said, "I wonder, Reverend, what would you say?"

The Master said, "There's no one who's aware of him."

A variation of this dialogue appears in Dōgen's *Shōbōgenzō* in Chinese script (*shinji Shōbōgenzō* 眞字正法眼藏, DZZ.5:216, case 179):

雲蓋山志安禪師〈嗣石霜〉在石霜會時、有僧問石霜、萬戸俱閉時如何。霜云、堂中事作麼生。僧經半年方始道得云、無人接渠。霜曰、道也太煞道、只道得八九成。時師聞却、禮請石霜、爲道。霜不道。師乃抱霜、從方丈後去坐曰、和尚若不道、須打和尚去。霜曰、得在。師乃禮拜不住。霜云、無人識渠。師於言下大悟。

When Chan Master Zhian of Mount Yungai (heir to Shishuang) was staying in Shishuang's assembly, a monk asked Shishuang, "What's it like when the myriad doors are all shut?"

Shuang said, "What about inside the hall?"

The monk spent half a year before he was finally able to reply, saying, "There's no one who engages him."

Shuang said, "You talk big talk, but your saying is only eight or nine tenths complete."

At the time, the Master [Yungai] heard this and begged Shishuang to say something. Shuang did not say anything. The Master then wrapped his arms around Shuang, took him behind the abbot's quarters, and sat him down, saying, "Reverend, if you don't say something, I'll have to hit you."

Shuang said, "Fine."

The Master then made bows without stopping.

Shuang said, "There's no one who's aware of him."

Hearing these words, the Master had a great awakening.

For an example of the expression being used by Caoshan Benji 曹山本寂 (840-901), see **"like the well looking at the donkey."**

**employ the twelve times** (*shitoku jūni ji* 使得十二時): In medieval China, the day was divided into twelve "hours," or "times" (*ji* 時), that were labeled using the twelve astrological branches (*jūni shi* 十二支). Each Chinese "hour" corresponds to two hours on the modern Western clock. The notion of "employing the twelve times" occurs frequently in the *Shōbōgenzō*; it comes

*Supplementary notes to the translation*      369

from a popular saying attributed to the famous Tang-dynasty Chan master Zhaozhou Congshen 趙州從諗 (778-897). The *Outline of the Linked Flames* (*Liandeng huiyao* 聯燈會要, ZZ.136:533b18-534a1; X.1557.79:60c7-9), for example, reads:

問、十二時中、如何用心。師云、汝被十二時使。老僧使得十二時。

[A monk] asked, "How does one use the mind throughout the twelve times [of the day]?"

The Master [Zhaozhou] said, "You are employed by the twelve times. This old monk employs the twelve times."

**everyday tea and rice** (*kajō sahan* 家常茶飯): In ordinary Chinese, a reference to the "daily fare" of the home, or what may be called "homestyle cooking." In the literature of Zen, an expression that is used metaphorically to refer to "normal, essential matters": something akin to what in English is said to be one's "bread and butter."

For example, the expression was used by Furong Daokai 芙蓉道楷 (1043–1118) in a dialogue with Touzi Yiqing 投子義青 (1032-1083), from whom he later inherited the dharma, as reported in Dōgen's *Shōbōgenzō* in Chinese script (*shinji Shōbōgenzō* 眞字正法眼藏, DZZ.5:202, case 143) and the *Outline of the Linked Flames* (*Liandeng huiyao* 聯燈會要, ZZ.136:917a6-10; X.1557.79:252a12-16):

師問投子、佛祖意句、如家常茶飯。離此之餘、還別有爲人言句也無。子云、汝道、寰中天子勅、還假禹湯堯舜也無。師擬開口、子拈拂子驀口打云、儞發意來時、早有二十棒分。師於此契悟。

The Master [Daokai] asked Touzi, "The intention and phrases of the **buddhas and ancestors** are like everyday tea and rice. Other than those, are there separate words and phrases to help people, or not?"

[Tou] Zi said, "You tell me: when 'within the imperial domain, the son of heaven' issues a command, does he turn back and avail himself of [the emperors of antiquity] Yu, Tang, Yao, and Shun, or not?"

When the Master hesitated and opened his mouth, Zi took his **whisk** and instantly hit him, saying, "If you bring forth intention, you already deserve thirty blows."

With this, the Master tallied and awakened.

In this dialogue, Daokai evidently used the expression "everyday tea and rice" in a somewhat disparaging manner to suggest that the very ubiquity and commonplace nature of the "intention and phrases of the buddhas and ancestors" renders them somehow deficient. He was, however, chastised for that by his teacher, Touzi Yiqing, who compared those words and sayings to imperial commands.

370 DŌGEN'S *SHŌBŌGENZŌ* VOLUME VIII

Dōgen clearly uses the expression "everyday tea and rice" in a positive sense, to indicate that "talking about and asking about the buddha-nature" is a good thing that Zen monks should do. For example, in his "Buddha-Nature" chapter ("Shōbōgenzō busshō" 正法眼藏佛性), Dōgen says:

しかあれば、佛性の道取問取は、佛祖の家常茶飯なり。

Thus, talking about and asking about the buddha-nature is the "everyday tea and rice" of the buddhas and ancestors.

**eye** (*ganzei* 眼睛, *ganmoku* 眼目, or *gan* 眼): The glyphs 眼睛 (*ganzei*) can refer specifically to the "pupil of the eye" or the "eyeball(s)," and the glyphs 眼目 can indicate the "eyeball(s)," but all of the glyphs given here are regularly used to refer to the "eye(s)" in general, both as a physical body part and in the metonymical sense of "vision."

In Buddhist texts generally, the word "eye" is a metaphor for spiritual insight. More specifically, there is a standard list of "five eyes" (*gogen* 五眼), or levels of vision, which is variously interpreted in the Buddhist literature but most commonly understood as: (1) *nikugen* 肉眼 (S. *māṃsa-cakṣus*), the "physical eye" of ordinary sight; (2) *tengen* 天眼 (S. *divya-cakṣus*), the "deva eye" of **spiritual powers** (*jinzū* 神通); (3) *egen* 慧眼 (S. *prajñā-cakṣus*), the "wisdom eye" that sees emptiness; (4) *hōgen* 法眼 (S. *dharma-cakṣus*), the "dharma eye" of the bodhisattva that seeks the welfare of others; and (5) *butsugen* 佛眼 (S. *buddha-cakṣus*), the omniscient "buddha eye."

In Zen texts, the word "eye" is also used as (a) synecdoche for the person, (b) the best feature of someone (or something), and (c) that which is most important, or essential. The term occurs often in the *Shōbōgenzō* in all of these senses, as well as in the two particular metaphors that are explained below.

The expression "eyes [or eyeballs] in the skull" (*dokuro ri ganzei* 髑髏裏眼睛), attributed to Xiangyan Zhixian 香嚴智閑 (d. 898), evokes the image of a dried-out skull-bone that is nevertheless equipped with glaring eyes. In Zen texts, a "skull" (*dokuro* 髑髏) is someone who is "dead" in the metaphorical sense of having detached from mental discrimination (*funbetsu* 分別); the "eye in the skull," therefore, represents a kind of direct, intuitive insight that does not involve the deluded discrimination of "things" (dharmas). The expression was raised as a kōan and commented on by various masters, including Shishuang Qingzhu 石霜慶諸 (807–888) and Caoshan Benji 曹山本寂 (840–890), as evidenced by the following account that appears in the *Discourse Record of Chan Master Yuanzheng of Mount Cao in Muzhou* (*Muzhou Caoshan Yuanzheng chanshi yulu* 撫州曹山元證禪師語錄, T.1987A.47:529b25-c7):

僧問香嚴、如何是道。香嚴曰、枯木裏龍吟。僧云、如何是道中人。香嚴曰、髑髏裏眼睛。僧不領、乃問石霜、如何是枯木裏龍吟。石霜

## Supplementary notes to the translation

曰、猶帶喜在。僧云、如何是髑髏裏眼睛。石霜曰、猶帶識在。又不
領、乃舉似師。師曰、石霜老聲聞作這裏見解。因示頌曰、枯木龍吟
眞見道、髑髏無識眼初明、喜識盡時消息盡、當人那辨濁中清。僧遂
又問師、如何是枯木裏龍吟。師曰、血脈不斷。云、如何是髑髏裏眼
睛。師曰、乾不盡。云、未審還有得聞者麼。師曰、盡大地人未有一
人不聞。云、未審枯木裏龍吟是何章句。師曰、不知是何章句。聞者
皆喪。

A monk asked Xiangyan, "What is the way?"

Xiangyan said, "The dragon song in the **dried-up tree**."

A monk said, "What about the person on the way?"

Xiangyan said, "The eyeball in the skull."

The monk did not understand, so he asked Shishuang, "What's [the meaning of] 'the dragon song in the dried-up tree'?"

Shishuang said, "Still harboring joy."

The monk said, "What's [the meaning of] 'the eyeball in the skull'?"

Shishuang said, "Still harboring consciousness."

[The monk] still did not understand, so he raised [Xiangyan's sayings] with the Master [Caoshan].

The Master [Caoshan] said, "That old *śrāvaka* Xiangyan has set up a viewpoint here [in his sayings]."

He then made a verse comment [on the kōan] that went:

The dragon song in the dried-up tree is the true path of seeing [S. *darśana-mārga*];

When the skull has no consciousness, the eye is first clear.

At the time when joy and consciousness are exhausted, vicissitudes are exhausted;

How could the person themself discriminate this? It's pure water in the mud.

A monk then again asked the Master [Caoshan], "What's 'the dragon song in the dried-up tree'?"

The Master said, "The blood vessel not severed."

[The monk] said, "What's 'the eyeball in the skull'?"

The Master said, "Not entirely dry."

[The monk] said, "Well, can anyone hear it?"

The Master said, "Among all the people on earth, there isn't one who can't hear it."

[The monk] said, "I wonder, what verse does the dragon sing in the dried-up tree?"

The Master said, "I don't know what verse it is. Everyone who hears it loses their life."

In this context, to "to lose one's life" (*sō* 喪, literally "to be mourned") means to gain awakening. This discussion of the dragon song and the eyeball in the skull is referenced by Dōgen in his "Song of the Dragon" ("Shōbōgenzō ryūgin" 正法眼藏龍吟) and included in his *Shōbōgenzō* in Chinese script (*shinji Shōbōgenzō* 眞字正法眼藏, DZZ.5:142, case 28).

Elsewhere in Zen literature, the expression "losing the eye(s)" (*tashitsu ganzei* 打失眼睛) is a metaphor for gaining awakening. An example of this usage is found in the *Discourse Record of Reverend Rujing* (*Rujing heshang yulu* 如淨和尚語錄, T.2002A.48:122b14-15), in a formal verse that Tiantong Rujing 天童如淨 (1162–1227) presented at a convocation in the dharma hall on the 8th day of the 12th month (*rōhatsu* 臘八) — the day on which the Buddha's attainment of the way (*jōdō* 成道) is celebrated in East Asia:

六年落草野狐精、跳出渾身是葛藤。打失眼睛無覓處、誑人剛道悟明星。

For six years, a fox spirit, lurking in the grass;
The whole body that sprang out was **tangled vines**.
When he lost his eye and had nothing to seek,
He fooled people by saying he awakened to the dawn star.

In "The Eye" ("Shōbōgenzō ganzei" 正法眼藏眼睛), Dōgen comments on this verse as well as another by Rujing that begins:

瞿曇打失眼睛時、雪裏梅華只一枝。

At the time that Gautama lost his eye,
It was just one branch of plum blossoms in the snow.

Related expressions include "gouging out the eyes" (*kesshutsu ganzei* 抉出眼睛, or *ganzei kesshutsu* 眼睛抉出) and "poking out the eyes" (*tosshutsu ganzei* 突出眼睛). In all of these cases, "eye" evidently stands for the ordinary, deluded way of viewing the world through the lens of mental discrimination; to "lose the eye" thus indicates the transcendence of normal vision.

The expression "lose one eye" (*shikkyaku isseki gen* 失却一隻眼) is attributed to Jiashan Shanhui 夾山善慧 (805–881), as a retrospective comment on an exchange involving him when he was a young monk in training, a fellow trainee named Dingshan Shenying 定山神英 (dates unknown), and Chan master Damei Fachang 大梅法常 (752-839), to whom they turned to resolve a disagreement between them. The exchange, as it appears in the *Jianzhong Jingguo Era Continued Record of the Flame* (*Jianzhong jingguo xudeng lu* 建中靖國續燈錄, ZZ.136:362b14-363a4; X.1556.78:803a24-b6), is raised as a

## Supplementary notes to the translation

kōan and coupled with a comment by Chan Master Xuedou Zhongxian 雪竇重顯 (980–1052):

舉。夾山與定山同行言話次。定山云、生死中無佛、則無生死。夾
山云、生死中有佛、則不迷生死。互相不肯、同上大梅。相見了、具
説前事。夾山問、未審那箇是親、那箇是疎。梅云、一親一疎。山又
問、那箇親。梅云、且去、明日來。夾山至來日又問、未審那箇親。
梅云、親者不問、問者不親。夾山後住云、我當時在大梅失却一隻眼。
師云。夾山不知換得一隻眼。大梅老漢當時聞舉。若以棒一時打出、
豈止畫斷兩人葛藤、亦乃爲天下宗匠。

Raised:

When Jiashan and Dingshan were training together they had the following discussion.

Dingshan said, "Within birth and death there are no buddhas; therefore, there is no birth and death."

Jiashan said, "Within birth and death there are buddhas; therefore, one is not deluded about birth and death."

Disagreeing with one another, they went together to see Damei. Having exchanged greetings with him, they fully explained the preceding matter.

Jiashan asked, "I wonder, which one of us is close [to the truth], and which is distant?"

Damei said, "One is close; one is distant."

[Jia]shan again asked, "Which one is close?"

Damei said, "Go away for now; come back tomorrow."

When the next day came, Jiashan again asked, "I wonder, which one is close?"

Damei said, "The one who is close does not ask; the one who asks is not close."

Later, when Jiashan was abbot [of the Jiashan Monastery] he said, "At the time, when I was at [Mount] Damei, I lost an eye."

The Master [Xuedou] commented:

"Jiashan, not knowing, got an eye back in exchange. Old guy Damei, at the time, listened and spoke up. Suppose he had used his **staff** in that moment to drive them off: how could that possibly have stopped their calculating, cut off the vines that entangled the two of them, and resulted in [Jiashan] becoming one of the world's great masters?"

Xuedou's comment makes it clear that what Jiashan meant by "losing an eye" was being disabused of a deluded point of view; "getting an eye back in exchange," conversely, means gaining in wisdom.

## 374 DŌGEN'S *SHŌBŌGENZŌ* VOLUME VIII

**Fences, walls, tiles, and pebbles** (*shō heki ga ryaku* 牆壁瓦礫): A fixed expression, appearing frequently in Dōgen's writing, for the world of insentient objects, which is nevertheless spiritually "alive" with significance — as, for example, the phenomenal manifestation of the buddha mind (*busshin* 佛心). In his "The Old Buddha Mind" ("Shōbōgenzō kobutsushin" 正法眼藏古佛心), Dōgen quotes an exchange said to have taken place between National Teacher Dazheng (Dazheng guoshi 大證國師), i.e., Nanyang Huizhong 南陽慧忠 (d. 775), and an unnamed monk:

國師、因僧問、如何是古佛心。師云、牆壁瓦礫。

The National Teacher was once asked by a monk, "What is the old buddha mind?"

The Teacher said, "Fences, walls, tiles, and pebbles."

Variants of this conversation occur in several texts. The extant passage closest to Dōgen's version seems to be that of the *Collection of Verse Comments on Old Cases of the Seon [i.e., Zen] Gate* (*Sŏnmun yŏmsong chip* 禪門拈頌集, K.1505.46:66b). The *Collection of the Essential Teachings of Our Lineage* (*Zongmen tongyao ji* 宗門統要集, ZTS.1:31c5) has the question put, not by "a monk," but by Dongshan Liangjie 洞山良价 (807-869). The best-known variant is found in the *Jingde Era Record of the Transmission of the Flame* (*Jingde chuandeng lu* 景德傳燈錄, T.2076.51:438a9-12):

僧又問、阿那箇是佛心。師曰、牆壁瓦礫。是僧曰、與經大相違也。涅槃云、離牆壁無情之物故名佛性。今云是佛心。未審心之與性爲別不別。師曰、迷即別悟即不別。

A monk asked further, "What is the buddha mind?"

The Master answered, "Fences, walls, tiles, and pebbles."

The monk said, "That greatly contradicts the sūtras. The *Nirvāṇa [Sūtra]* says, 'It is called buddha nature because it is apart from insentient things such as fences and walls.' Yet you now say those are the buddha mind. I wonder, is this 'mind' distinguishable or not distinguishable from the [buddha] nature?"

The Master said, "When deluded, they're distinguishable; when awakened, they're not distinguishable."

**fill the ditches and clog the gullies** (*tenkō sokugaku* 塡溝塞壑): A Zen expression that means something is ubiquitous, or "extends or pervades everywhere." Dōgen's use of the expression likely reflects the words of Yuanwu Keqin 圜悟克勤 (1063-1135), as found, for example, in the Blue Cliff Record (*Biyan lu* 碧巖錄, T.2003.48:156c10):

千古萬古、黑漫漫。塡溝塞壑、無人會。

From a thousand ages past, ten thousand ages past;

*Supplementary notes to the translation* 375

The blackness is everywhere.
It fills the ditches and clogs the gullies;
No one understands it.

In his "Needle of Seated Meditation" ("Shōbōgenzō zazen shin" 正法眼藏坐禪箴), Dōgen gives the expression "fills the ditches and fills the gullies" (*mizo ni michi, tani ni mitsu* 溝にみち、壑にみつ) in Japanese translation. In another context, this is said of the bodies of those who have died of starvation along the roadside. The expression also occurs in the text of Dōgen's "Beyond the Buddha" ("Shōbōgenzō butsu kōjō ji" 正法眼藏佛向上事) preserved in the twenty-eight-text *Shōbōgenzō* collection (DZZ.2:572), where it serves to describe what Dōgen calls there "studying with the body":

佛道をならふに、しばらく二の様子あり。いはゆる、こころしてならひ、身してならふなり。身してならふ、といふは、坐禪辦道するところに、作佛をもとめざる行佛あり。公案見成するに、身佛もとより作仏にあらず。羅籠ひさしくやぶれぬれば、坐佛さらに作佛をさへず。かくのごとく、身してならふとき、千古萬古、とこしなへにほとけにいり、魔にいるちからあり。進歩退歩に、溝にみち壑にみつ、ひかりをあらしむる、これを父母未生以前の面目といはざらめやは。

In studying the way of the buddhas, there are provisionally two types: studying with the mind and studying with the body. "Studying with the body" means that, where the way is pursued in seated meditation, there is the practice of a buddha that does not seek to make a buddha. In the realization of the kōan, from the beginning, the embodied buddha is not making a buddha. When the "**nets and cages**" are long broken, a seated buddha does not interfere with making a buddha. When we study with the body like this, "from a thousand ages, ten thousand ages past," from eternity, we have the power to "enter into buddha and enter into Māra." In **stepping forward and stepping back**, we display a light that "fills the ditches, fills the gullies." How could this not be called our "**face before our our father and mother were born**"?

Interestingly, it is "blackness" (*koku manman* 黑漫漫) that Yuanwu says "fills the ditches and clogs the gullies," whereas Dōgen uses the expression with reference to "light" (*hikari* ひかり). Both are metaphors for something — perhaps the buddha nature or buddha mind — that is inconceivable (*fukashigi* 不可思議) but nevertheless immanent.

**fist** (*kentō* 拳頭): In Zen literature, "raising a fist" (*juki kentō* 竪起拳頭, *nen kentō* 拈拳頭, *ju kentō* 豎拳頭, or *kentō o koki su* 拳頭を擧起す) is a gesture that a master makes to express what is beyond language and discrimination. It is similar in this respect to the gesture of silently raising an implement such as a **whisk** or a **staff**: all are depicted as responses to direct questions or substitutes for verbal remarks in ritual settings where instruction by the abbot is expected. Zen masters are also said, in some stories, to "beat with the fist" (*kentō da* 拳頭打 or *ken da* 拳打) as a means of startling disciples out of their deluded attachments to conceptual constructs. For both of these reasons, the term "fist" came to refer, by synecdoche, to the person of a Zen master. Thus, an "old fist" (*rō kentō* 老拳頭) is an experienced master; a "stinking fist" (*shū kentō* 臭拳頭) is a Zen master who is not worthy of his position or title, although the adjective "stinking" may also be used as a kind of back-handed praise. "Fist" can also indicate a "true master" or, by extension, the "true self" (*shinjitsu ga* 眞實我), which is the buddha mind, or buddha-nature. To "taste the fist" (*kitsu kentō* 喫拳頭 or *kentō wo kissu* 拳頭を喫す) means to deeply experience the teachings (if not the actual blows) of a true Zen master or to awaken to one's true self.

Case 11 in the kōan collection *Gateless Barrier* (*Wumen guan* 無門關, T.2005.48:294b6-15), entitled "Zhaozhou Compares the Hermitage Masters" (*Zhou kan anzhu* 州勘庵主), deals with the gesture of raising a fist:

趙州到一庵主處問、有麼有麼。主堅起拳頭。州云、水淺不是泊舡處。便行。又到一庵主處云、有麼有麼。主亦堅起拳頭。州云、能縱能奪能殺能活。便作禮。

無門曰、一般堅起拳頭、爲甚麼肯一箇不肯一箇。且道、諸訛在甚處。若向者裏、下得一轉語、便見趙州舌頭無骨。扶起放倒得大自在。雖然如是、爭奈趙州却被二庵主勘破。若道二庵主有優劣、未具參學眼。若道無優劣、亦未具參學眼。

Zhaozhou, arriving at the place of one hermitage master, asked, "Anything here? Anything here?"

The master raised a fist.

Zhou said, "Where the water's too shallow is no place to moor a boat." He then left.

Arriving at the place of another hermitage master, he again asked, "Anything here? Anything here?"

That hermitage master also raised a fist.

Zhou said, "Able to let go, able to snatch up. Able to kill; able to give life." He then made a bow.

[Commenting,] Wumen says:

> They were identical in raising a fist, so why did he assent to one and not assent to the other? Tell me, where does the mistake lie? If you look herein and are able to utter a turning word, you will see that Zhaozhou's tongue is unrestrained. In helping [others] up or knocking [them] down, he has great autonomy. Even so, how is Zhaozhou, on the contrary, seen through by the two hermitage masters? If you say that there is some superiority or inferiority with regard to the two

*Supplementary notes to the translation*   377

hermitage masters, you aren't equipped yet with the **eye** for study. If you say that there is no superiority or inferiority, you also aren't equipped with the eye for study.

The premise of this story is that the gesture of raising a fist, while it may signal a master's profound appreciation of the ineluctable deficiency of language as a means for describing reality or communicating the ultimate truth, can also be aped by people who have no real understanding of what it signifies. The root case indicates that the famous Chan master Zhaozhou Congshen 趙州從諗 (778–897), whose true insight it takes as a given, was able to distinguish a phony gesture from a real one. In his comment, however, the compiler of the *Gateless Barrier*, Wumen Huikai 無門慧開 (1183-1260), raises the questions of what criteria Zhaozhou could have used in judging the two hermitage masters, and whether he actually saw any difference between them or merely said whatever popped into his head at the time.

In his "Sūtras of the Buddhas" ("Shōbōgenzō bukkyō" 正法眼藏佛經), Dōgen criticizes Chan masters who employ such gestures in ignorance:

有空のむねあきらめざれば、人もし問取するとき、みだりに拳頭を
たつ、しかあれども、たつる宗旨にくらし。正・邪のみちあきらめ
ざれば、人もし問取すれば、拂子をあぐ、しかあれども、あぐる宗
旨にあきらかならず。

Since they have not clarified the import of being and emptiness, when someone puts a question to them, they arbitrarily raise their fist, even though they are in the dark about what it means to raise it. Since they have not clarified the ways of the true and the false, when someone puts a question to them, they raise their whisk, even though they are not clear what it means to raise it.

Dōgen evidently felt confident that he could tell the difference between a phony gesture and one that was grounded in genuine understanding.

In several chapters of the *Shōbōgenzō*, Dōgen quotes or alludes to a verse by his teacher Rujing 如淨 (1162–1227) that appears in the *Discourse Record of Reverend Rujing* (*Rujing heshang yulu* 如淨和尚語錄, T.2002A.48:131b28-29):

無明業識幢。竪起漫天黑。一句不相當。拳頭飛霹靂咦。老婆心切血
滴滴。

A banner of ignorant **karmic consciousness**;
When raised up, all the heavens are black.
A single line will not suffice;
A fist and flying thunderbolts.
Grandma's mind is kind; the blood drips.

In this context, the word "fist" refers to both the person and the actions of the Zen master, whose teaching is motivated by "grandmotherly" compassion even when it appears violent.

**five ranks** (*goi* 五位): Also translateable as "five positions." In the *Shōbōgenzō*, the reference is to the "five ranks of upright and inclined" (*shōhen goi* 正偏五位), also known as "Dongshan's five ranks" (*Tōzan goi* 洞山五位). For various meanings of the pairing of the glyphs 正 (*shō*) and 偏 (*hen*) as opposites, see "**upright or inclined**." Several different versions of the "five ranks" formula appear in texts associated with the Sōtō lineage, as explained below.

Dongshan Liangjie 洞山良价 (807–869), founder of the lineage, is said to have listed the "five ranks" as: 1) the "inclined within the upright" (*shō chū hen* 正中偏), 2) the "upright within the inclined" (*hen chū shō* 偏中正), 3) "coming from within the upright" (*shō chū rai* 正中來), 4) "proceeding within both conjoined" (*ken chū shi* 兼中至), and 5) "arriving within both conjoined" (*ken chū tō* 兼中到). In his *Discourse Record of Chan Master Liangjie of Mount Dong in Ruizhou* (*Ruizhou Dongshan Liangjie chanshi yulu* 瑞州洞山良价禪師語錄, T.1986B.47:525c1-8), Dongshan comments on these as follows:

師、作五位君臣頌云。正中偏。三更初夜月明前、莫怪相逢不相識、隱隱猶懷舊日嫌。偏中正。失曉老婆逢古鏡、分明覷面別無眞、休更迷頭猶認影。正中來。無中有路隔塵埃、但能不觸當今諱、也勝前朝斷舌才。兼中至。兩刃交鋒不須避、好手猶如火裏蓮、宛然自有冲天志。兼中到。不落有無誰敢和、人人盡欲出常流、折合還歸炭裏坐

The Master [Dongshan] made verse comments on the "five ranks of lord and minister," saying:

"Inclined Within the Upright":

In the third watch, the early evening, before there is moonlight,

Do not find it strange to meet something you are not acquainted with.

It is indistinct, like some resentment still harbored from a past dislike.

"Upright Within the Inclined":

At dawn a grandmother encounters the **old mirror**;

What she clearly sees in front of her is nothing other than her own likeness.

Do not again "doubt one's own head yet believe in its reflected image."

"Coming from Within the Upright":

Within nothingness there is a road separate from the dust [of the world or senses];

If you can avoid infringing on the taboo name of the present [emperor],
You will surpass in genius those of former dynasties with cut-off tongues.

"Proceeding within Both Conjoined":
When two swords cross tips, it is not possible to retreat;
Their expertise is just like the lotus in the fire.
Likewise, there is naturally a will to soar into the heavens.

"Arriving within Both Conjoined":
Not falling into being or nothingness, who would presume to interfuse them?
Individual people all desire to leave the constant flow,
But join together when they return to sit within the embers.

The first rank in this scheme, it would seem, represents the state of karmically conditioned delusion, which one experiences gratuitously in the midst of an inherently "upright" (originally perfect) state of affairs. The second rank represents awakening: the "grandmother" who sees herself clearly in the mirror is contrasted with the deluded person who "doubts one's own head yet believes in its reflected image" (*mei tō yu nin yō* 迷頭猶認影); that saying alludes to the *Heroic March Sūtra* (*Shoulengyan jing* 首楞嚴經, T.945.19:121b9-14) story of Yajñadatta who, when he looked in a mirror for the first time in his life, believed that what he saw there was a trickster spirit who had stolen his head. The third rank seems to refer to a state in which one avoids speaking about and thereby sullying or misrepresenting one's awakening. The fourth rank, perhaps, represents a move to re-enter the "fire" of the ordinary world without being burnt up by it, in the manner of the compassionate bodhisattva who does speak to help others. The fifth rank, finally, seems to indicate a state in which the very discrimination of "upright" and "inclined" is abandoned.

*The Eye of Humans and Devas* (*Rentian yanmu* 人天眼目, T.2006.48:313c 16-24) contains a somewhat different interpretation that is attributed to Dongshan's disciple Caoshan Benji 曹山本寂 (840–890) under the heading "Five Ranks of Lord and Minister" (*goi kunshin* 五位君臣):

> 僧問曹山五位君臣旨訣。山云、正位即屬空界、本來無物。偏位即色界、有萬形像。偏中正者、舍事入理。正中來者、背理就事。兼帶者、冥應衆緣、不隨諸有、非染非淨、非正非偏。故曰虛玄大道。無著眞宗。從上先德、推此一位、最妙最玄。要當詳審辨明。君爲正位。臣爲偏位。臣向君是偏中正。君視臣是正中偏。君臣道合、是兼帶語。

A monk asked Caoshan the meaning of the five ranks of lord and minister. Shan said,

The rank of "upright" belongs to the realm of emptiness: from the origin there is not a thing. The rank of "inclined" is the realm of form: there are myriad images. "Upright within the inclined" is to abandon phenomena and enter principle. "Coming from within the upright" is to turn one's back on principle and approach phenomena. "Both conjoined" is the profound response to conditions, without following things: it is neither stained nor pure, neither upright nor inclined. Thus, it is called "the great way that is vacant and profound." It is the true axiom of no attachment. From ancient times, the previous worthies have extolled this one rank as the most sublime and most profound. You should, with careful attention to detail, distinguish and clarify it as follows. The lord represents the rank of "upright"; the minister represents the rank of "inclined." The minister facing the lord is "the upright within the inclined"; the lord seeing the minister is "the inclined within the upright." The lord and minister talking together is the term "both conjoined."

In this passage, the "five ranks" are: 1) "upright" (*shō* 正), 2) "inclined" (*hen* 偏), 3) "upright within the inclined" (*hen chū shō* 偏中正), 4) "coming from within the upright" (*shō chū rai* 正中來), and 5) "both conjoined" (*kentai* 兼帶).

The preceding passage also appears, with only slight variation, in the *Discourse Record of Chan Master Yuanzheng of Mount Cao in Muzhou* (*Muzhou Caoshan Yuanzheng chanshi yulu* 撫州曹山元證禪師語錄, T.1987A.47:527a 5-12). Later in that text (T.1987A.47:533b18-24), another explanation attributed to Caoshan appears under the heading "Meaning of the Five Ranks" (*goi shiketsu* 五位旨訣):

> 正中來者、太過也。全身獨露、萬法根源、無咎無譽。偏中至者、中孚也。隨物不礙、木舟中虛、虛通自在。正中偏者、巽也。虛空破片、處處圓通、根塵寂爾。偏中正者、兌也。水月鏡像、本無生滅、豈有蹤跡。兼中到者、重離也。正不必虛、偏不必實、無背無向。

"Coming from within the upright" is [*Yijing* hexagram 28] "great excess": the entire body is solitary and exposed; the root source of the myriad dharmas is without blame and without praise.

"Proceeding within the inclined" is [*Yijing* hexagram 61] "inner truth": according with things without obstruction; empty space within a wooden boat, unimpeded and autonomous.

"Inclined within the upright" is [*Yijing* hexagram 57] "the gentle": a broken splinter in empty space; everywhere perfectly penetrating, the sense faculties and their objects are quiescent.

"Upright within the inclined" is [*Yijing* hexagram 58] "joyous": the moon in the water is an image in a mirror; fundamentally there is no arising or ceasing, so how could there be any footprints?

Supplementary notes to the translation  381

"Arriving within both conjoined" is [*Yijing* hexagram 30] "harmonizing with all things": the "upright" is not necessarily empty, the "inclined" is not necessarily real; there is no turning the back and there is no facing.

In this passage, four of the five ranks are the same as those listed in the *Discourse Record of Chan Master Liangjie of Mount Dong in Ruizhou*, but the order in which they appear is different in the two texts. Also, the rank called "proceeding within both conjoined" in the *Discourse Record of Chan Master Liangjie* is replaced in this passage with "proceeding within the inclined." In a comment attributed to Jiyin 寂音 — better known as Huihong Juefan 慧洪覺範 (1071-1128) — in *The Eye of Humans and Devas* (*Rentian yanmu* 人天眼目, T.2006.48:314b12), the phrase "proceeding within both conjoined" (*ken chū shi* 兼中至) is said to have resulted from an orthographic error that should be corrected to read "proceeding within the inclined" (*hen chū shi* 偏中至).

The *Discourse Record of Chan Master Yuanzheng of Mount Cao in Muzhou* (*Muzhou Caoshan Yuanzheng chanshi yulu* 撫州曹山元證禪師語錄, T.1987A.47: 533b24-c4), still under the heading "Meaning of the Five Ranks" (*goi shiketsu* 五位旨訣), contains yet a third explanation attributed to Caoshan:

又曰。心機泯絶、色空俱忘(是云正)。到頭無諱、曾無變動(是云中)。更無覆藏、全體露現(是云偏)。是曰正中偏。山是山、水是水、無人安名字、無物堪比倫、是曰偏中正。淨裸裸赤洒洒、面目堂堂、盡天盡地、獨尊無二、是曰正中來。宛如寰中天子、不借禹湯堯舜令。眼見耳聞、終不借他力、耳之不入聲中。聲之不塞耳根。裏頭才轉身。塵中未帶名、是曰偏中至。不是心、不是境、不是事、不是理。從來離名狀、天眞忘性相。是曰兼中到。

He [Caoshan] also said:

When the functioning of mind is extinguished, form and emptiness are both forgotten (this is called "upright"); when, in the end, there is no avoiding, then there is no change (this is called "within"); when there is no concealing, the entire substance is exposed (this is called "inclined"): [altogether] this is called "inclined within the upright."

Mountains are mountains, waters are waters, and there is no person to assign a name and no things to compare or classify: this is called "upright within the inclined."

Pure and stripped bare, naked and washed clean, the original face is magnificent, uniquely honored and nondual: this is called "coming from within the upright."

It is just like within the imperial domain, [where] the son of heaven does not borrow [the authority of] Yu, Tang, Yao, and Shun to give orders; the eyes see and the ears hear, and they will never borrow the powers of another's [eyes and ears]; the ear does not enter into sound, and sound

382    DŌGEN'S *SHŌBŌGENZŌ* VOLUME VIII

does not fill up the faculty of hearing; amidst the dust [of the senses], not attaching names: this is called "proceeding within the inclined."

No mind, no objects [of mind], no phenomena, and nor principle; originally detached from description, reality in itself, forgetting nature and signs: this is called "arriving within both conjoined."

In addition to the four interpretations of the "five ranks" formula outlined above, the Sōtō tradition also attributes "five stages of meritorious work" (*kōkun goi* 功勳五位) to Dongshan Liangjie. For details, see ZGDJ (s.v. こうくんごい).

Dōgen does not seem to have had much patience with the complex intellectual machinations associated with interpretations of the "five ranks." In his "Spring and Autumn" ("Shōbōgenzō shunjū" 正法眼藏春秋), he mentions the "five ranks of the upright or inclined, etc." (*shōhen nado no goi* 正偏等の五位) and says that people should stop using that formula to characterize "the buddha dharma of the Eminent Ancestor" (*Kōso no buppō* 高祖の佛法), Dongshan. He also voices criticism of people who misuse the "five ranks" formula in his "The Way of the Buddhas" ("Shōbōgenzō butsudō" 正法眼藏佛道; 44:23) and "Sūtras of the Buddhas" ("Shōbōgenzō bukkyō 正法眼藏佛經; 47:16). The issue is complicated, however, by his remark in the latter chapter (47:20):

> また、高祖の三路・五位は節目にて、杜撰のしるべき境界にあらず。宗旨正傳し、佛業直指せり、あへて餘門にひとしからざるなり。

Furthermore, the "three paths" and "five ranks" of the Eminent Ancestor are the crux, not in the realm known to illiterates. Their essential point has been correctly transmitted, and the work of the buddha directly indicated; they are by no means equivalent to the other traditions.

**for a lifetime not leaving the grove** (*isshō furi sōrin* 一生不離叢林): From a saying attributed to Zhaozhou Congshen 趙州從諗 (778-897) in a number of Chan texts, including the *Discourse Record of Reverend Zhaozhou* (*Zhaozhou zhenji chanshi yulu bing xingzhuang* 趙州真際禪師語錄并行狀, *Guzunsu lu* 古尊宿錄, ZZ.118:308a5-6; X.1315.68:77c24-78a2) and the *Outline of the Linked Flames* (*Liandeng huiyao* 聯燈會要, ZZ.136:528b7-9; X.1315.68:77c24-78a2):

> 示衆云、儞若一生不離叢林、不語十年五載、無人喚儞作啞漢、已後佛也不奈儞何。

[Zhaozhou] addressed the assembly, saying, "If for a lifetime you don't leave the grove and don't talk for ten years or five years, no one will call you a mute; after that, even the Buddha won't know what to make of you."

The term "grove" (*sōrin* 叢林) is a common idiom for a Buddhist monastery, deriving from the Sanskrit *saṃghārāma* (*sōgyaran* 僧伽藍),

Supplementary notes to the translation 383

meaning a "garden," or "grove" (S. *ārāma*) in which members of the saṃgha congregate. Dōgen quotes this passage accurately in "Sustained Practice, Part 1" ("Shōbōgenzō gyōji jō" 正法眼藏行持上). In "Sayings" ("Shōbōgenzō dōtoku" 正法眼藏道得), however, he gives a somewhat different version:

趙州眞際大師、示衆云、若一生不離叢林、兀坐不道十年五載、無人喚作啞漢。已後諸佛也不及哉。

Great Master Zhenji of Zhaozhou addressed the assembly, saying, "If for a lifetime you don't leave the grove, **sitting fixedly** without saying anything for ten years or five years, no one will call you a mute; after that, even the buddhas won't reach you."

Dōgen's version of Zhaozhou's words here, which is also found (with slight variation) in his *Extensive Record of Reverend Dōgen* (*Dōgen oshō kōroku* 道元和尚廣錄, DZZ.4:190, no. 13), has no known source.

**forfeit one's body and lose one's life** (*sōshin shitsumyō* 喪身失命): A fixed expression for dying; also used metaphorically in Zen for some other kind of "death," with (depending on the context) either a negative or a positive connotation. The expression is perhaps best known from the famous problem, posed by Xiangyan Zhixian 香嚴智閑 (d. 898), of the man hanging by his teeth over a thousand-foot cliff who is asked the meaning of Bodhidharma's **coming from the west**. As found in Dōgen's *Shōbōgenzō* in Chinese script (*shinji Shōbōgenzō* 眞字正法眼藏, DZZ.5:254, case 243), the kōan reads:

香嚴寺襲燈大師＜嗣大溈諱智閑＞示衆云、如人千尺懸崖上樹。口嚙樹枝、脚不踏樹、手不攀枝。樹下忽有人問、如何是祖師西來意。當恁麼時、若開口答佗、即喪身失命。若不答佗、又違佗所問。當恁麼時、且道、作麼生即得。

Great Master Xideng of Xiangyan Monastery (succeeded Dagui; known as Zhixian) addressed the congregation, saying:

> It is like a person who is up a tree on the edge of a thousand-foot precipice. His mouth bites onto a tree branch, but his feet have no place to stand on the tree, and his hands have no hold on a branch. All of a sudden, a person beneath the tree asks him, "What is the **intention of the Ancestral Master's coming from the west**?" At such a time, if he opens his mouth to answer the other person, he forfeits his body and loses his life. If he does not answer the other person, he disregards what the other has asked. Now tell me, at such a time, what would you do to resolve [this dilemma]?

The preposterous scenario that Xiangyan posits makes it clear that the expression to "forfeit one's body and lose one's life" is not to be taken literally. In this context, to open one's mouth and speak represents the "fatal error" of engaging in conceptual thinking or verbalization, which can never

384  DŌGEN'S *SHŌBŌGENZŌ* VOLUME VIII

convey the ultimate truth without distortion. To keep one's mouth shut and save oneself from such error, however, is to break the bodhisattva's vow to save others.

The above kōan is found in many Zen texts, including the biography of "Chan Master Zhixian of Xiangyan in Dengzhou" in the *Jingde Era Record of the Transmission of the Flame* (*Jingde chuandeng lu* 景德傳燈錄, T.2076.51:284b21-24). Dōgen commented on it in his "The Intention of the Ancestral Master's Coming from the West" ("Shōbōgenzō soshi seirai i" 正法眼藏祖師西來意). He also appended a verse comment to it, which is found in Volume 9, case 87, of the *Extensive Record of Reverend Dōgen* (*Dōgen oshō kōroku* 道元和尚廣錄, DZZ.4:242):

喪身失命死中活、猶惜孃生兩片皮、擬欲答他言滿口、問來也是口銜枝。

"Forfeiting his body and losing his life" but alive in death,
He is still sparing of the two lips born of his mother.
Hesitant, but wanting to answer the other, words fill his mouth;
The questioner, too, holds a branch in his mouth like a [horse's] bit.

According to ZGDJ (s.v. そうしんしつみょう), Dōgen took the saying "forfeit one's body and lose one's life" here as a synonym of "**body and mind sloughed off**." If so, he interpreted the "death" that it refers to not as any kind of defeat, but rather as a symbol of awakening.

**form is itself emptiness; emptiness is itself form** (*shiki soku ze kū, kū soku ze shiki* 色即是空、空即是色): A famous line from the *Heart Sūtra* (*Bore boluomiduo xin jing* 般若波羅蜜多心經, T.251.8:848c7-9):

舍利子、色不異空、空不異色。色即是空、空即是色。受想行識亦復如是。

Śāriputra, form is not different from emptiness; emptiness is not different from form. Form is itself emptiness; emptiness is itself form. Sensation, conception, formations, and consciousness are also like this.

"Form" (*shiki* 色; S. *rūpa*), the first of the "five aggregates" (*goun* 五蘊 or 五陰; S. *pañca-skandha*), refers to the outward appearance (shape, color, quality, feature, sign, mark, distinguishing characteristic, etc.) of any nameable or identifiable thing or phenomenon. According to the Buddhist doctrine of "emptiness" (*kū* 空, S. *śūnyatā*), all such things are, in the final analysis, mental constructs. The names we use to identify forms do not correspond to any discrete entities that actually exist, in and of themselves (prior to our discrimination of them), in the way that we imagine them to. In other words, whatever "form" we may perceive is essentially a mental construct, not a really existing thing. By the same token, the naming of things as "empty" (*kū* 空, S. *śūnya*), or "marked by emptiness" (*kūsō* 空相; S. *śūnyatā-lakṣaṇa*), is itself a mental construct: an imputation of "form."

Supplementary notes to the translation                    385

Thus, all forms are empty, and "emptiness" is nothing but a form. The *Heart Sūtra* suggests that the other four aggregates — sensation, conception, formations, and consciousness — are also conceptual constructs that lack the "own being" (*jishō* 自性; S. *svabhāva*), or independent existence, we habitually assign to them.

**four births** (*shishō* 四生): The four ways in which sentient beings are born in saṃsāra: (1) "womb born" (*taishō* 胎生; S. *jarāyujā*) as mammals; (2) "transformation born" (*keshō* 化生; S. *upapādukā*) as those in the heavens and hells, as well as the incarnations of buddhas and advanced bodhisattvas; (3) "moisture born" (*shisshō* 濕生; S. *saṃsveda*) as lower forms of animal life, such as insects; and (4) "egg born" (*ranshō* 卵生; S. *aṇḍaja*) as birds, fish, and reptiles.

**four continents** (*shishū* 四州): Also referred to as the "four continents under heaven" (*shi tenka* 四天下). In traditional Buddhist cosmology, four great land masses (S. *catur-dvīpa*), or islands, said to surround Mount Sumeru (*Shumisen* 須彌山), which is at the center of the world system. They are: 1) the Northern Continent (*Hokushū* 北洲) of Uttarakuru (*Kurushū* 倶盧洲, a.k.a. *Hokkuro* 北倶盧), whose inhabitants live a thousand years and, because they scarcely experience the first sacred truth of suffering, have no aptitude for Buddhism; 2) the Southern Continent (*Nanshū* 南洲) of Jambudvīpa (*Enbudai* 閻浮提, or "Rose Apple Island," a.k.a. *Nan Senbushū* 南贍部州), where our "human path" (*nindō* 人道; S. *mānuṣya-gati*) is located (see **six paths**) and where buddhas are born as human beings in the *kṣatriya* class; 3) the Eastern Continent of Pūrva-videha (*Tō Shōshinshū* 東勝身洲); and 4) the Western Continent of Avara-godānīya (*Sai Gokeshū* 西牛貨洲).

**four elements and five aggregates** (*shidai goun* 四大五蘊 or 四大五陰): Two standard Buddhist formulae for analyzing what is regarded by most people, deludedly, as their "self" (*ga* 我; S. *ātman*) — the totality of their person and its experience of the world — into a set of constituent elements (dharmas) that are claimed to be all that actually exists.

The "four elements" (*shidai* 四大; S. *catvāri-mahā-būtāni*) are 1) earth (*chi* 地), 2) water (*sui* 水), 3) fire (*ka* 火), and 4) wind (*fū* 風). These are conceived as the primary forms of matter (S. *mahābhūta*) of which the physical world is composed. Another formula adds space (*kū* 空) to this list, resulting in the "five elements" (*godai* 五大; S. *pañca-mahā-būtāni*); the further addition of consciousness (*shiki* 識) gives the six elements (*rokudai* 六大).

Buddhist texts often describe the living human body as being comprised of the four elements: 1) earth represents a person's solid flesh and bones; 2) water represents their blood and other bodily fluids; 3) fire represents bodily heat; and 4) wind represents breathing. When a person is alive the four elements are conjoined, but upon death they disperse. Indeed, death is explained as a loss of one or more of the elements: "water" if a person loses blood; "wind" if they stop breathing; "fire" when the body stops moving and becomes cold; and "earth" when, sooner or later, it falls apart. Meditation on the four elements is presented in early Buddhist texts as a means of counteracting attachment to the body as anything permanent, attractive, or worthy of identifying as "self."

The formula of "five aggregates" (*goun* 五蘊 or 五陰; S. *pañca-skandha*) is somewhat more sophisticated, in that it analyzes the person, or "self," into five groups (S. *skandha*, literally "heaps") of phenomena (dharmas) that are mental and psychological as well as physical. The five are: 1) form (*shiki* 色; S. *rūpa*), which is the stuff of the material world as analyzed, for example, into the "four elements"; 2) sensation (*ju* 受; S. *vedanā*), or raw sensory input, which may be pleasant, unpleasant, or neutral; 3) perception (*sō* 想; S. *samjñā*), in which raw sensory data is distinguished, named, and correlated according to conceptual criteria; 4) formations (*gyō* 行; S. *saṃskāra*), which are karmically "formed," or conditioned, predilections that manifest themselves as intentional or habitual actions and reactions; and 5) consciousness (*shiki* 識; S. *vijñāna*), which includes the functions of memory, imagination, abstract thinking, etc. Meditation on the five aggregates, which are to be viewed as causally conditioned and impermanent, is also designed to counteract the deluded attachment to "self."

Dōgen's use of the expression "four elements and five aggregates" in some contexts seems to be informed by a saying attributed to the Tang-dynasty Chan master Zhaozhou Congshen 趙州從諗 (778–897), which Dōgen quotes in his *Shōbōgenzō* in Chinese script (*shinji Shōbōgenzō* 眞字正法眼藏, DZZ.5:270, case 88) and elsewhere:

趙州、因僧問、未有世界、早有此性。世界壞時、此性不壞。如何是不壞之性。師曰、四大五蘊。僧曰、此猶是壞底。如何是不壞之性。師曰、四大五蘊。

Once, a monk asked Zhaozhou, "Before the world existed, there was already this nature. When the world is destroyed, this nature won't be destroyed. What is this nature that won't be destroyed?"

The Master said, "The four elements and the five aggregates."

The monk said, "These are still something destroyed. What is this nature that won't be destroyed?"

The Master said, "The four elements and five aggregates."

**ghost cave** (*kikutsu* 鬼窟): A term that derives from a longer expression: "ghost cave at the Black Mountains" (*Kokusan kikutsu* 黑山鬼窟) or "ghost cave beneath the Black Mountains" (*Kokusan ge kikutsu* 黑山下鬼窟), based on the Buddhist tradition that there are mountain ranges to the north of

Jambudvīpa inhabited by phantoms. To "make one's living inside the ghost cave" is a metaphor for spiritual delusion and, in particular, for the tendency to parrot other people's words without comprehending them. The latter sense derives from the popular understanding that ghosts, being disembodied spirits, need to cling to other life forms (e.g., grasses and trees) for support.

In the *Discourse Record of Chan Master Fayan* (*Fayan chanshi yulu* 法演禪師語錄, T.1995.47:657a13-18), for example, the following remarks are attributed to Wuzu Fayan 五祖法演 (d. 1104):

上堂云、佛祖生冤家、悟道染泥土。無爲無事人、聲色如聾瞽。且道如何即是、恁麼也不得、不恁麼也不得、恁麼不恁麼總不得。忽有箇漢出來道、恁麼也得、不恁麼也得、恁麼不恁麼總得。則向伊道、我也知、儞向鬼窟裏作活計。

At a convocation in the dharma hall, [Fayan] said, "[To speak of] **buddhas and ancestors** is to create enemies; to awaken to the way is to wallow in the mud. A person with no purpose and no concerns is as if deaf and blind to sound and form. So, tell me, what exactly is this 'such is not got; not-such is not got; and such and not-such are both not got'? [Suppose that] instantly there is a guy who comes forth and says, 'Such is got; not-such is got; and such and not-such are both got'? I would respond to him immediately and say, 'Now I know that you make your living inside the ghost cave.'"

Here, the error of the hypothetical interlocutor is that he challenges the master by merely flipping the master's words from negative ("not got") to positive ("got"), a rhetorical move that can be done mechanically, without any true understanding.

In some instances, the metaphor of the "ghost cave" also alludes to the philosophical nihilism that can result from a misapprehension of the doctrine of emptiness. The biography of Xuansha Shibei 玄沙師備 (835-908) in the *Jingde Era Record of the Transmission of the Flame* (*Jingde chuandeng lu* 景德傳燈錄, T.2076.51:346c16-21), for example, reads:

僧問、承和尚有言、盡十方世界是一顆明珠。學人如何得會。師曰、盡十方世界是一顆明珠、用會作麼。師來日却問其僧、盡十方世界是一顆明珠、汝作麼生會。對曰、盡十方世界是一顆明珠、用會作麼。師曰、知汝向山鬼窟裏作活計。

A monk asked, "I have heard, Reverend, that you have a saying: 'All the worlds in the ten directions are **one bright pearl**.' How am I, your student, to understand that?"

The Master [Xuansha] said, "All the worlds in the ten directions are one bright pearl. What's the use of understanding?"

The next day, the Master turned the tables and asked that monk, "All the worlds in the ten directions are one bright pearl. How do you understand that?"

[The monk] replied, "All the worlds in the ten directions are one pearl. What's the use of understanding?"

The Master said, "Now I know that you make your living in the ghost cave under the mountains."

The "understanding" that Xuansha initially deems "useless" here is evidently the conceptual, intellectual sort of understanding, not the true awakening that is the goal of Zen practice. The monk who repeats Xuansha's words, "What's the use of understanding?" is called a "ghost" because he parrots them without any real understanding of their deeper meaning.

In some contexts, the metaphor of the "ghost cave" indicates an approach to seated meditation practice that wrongly stresses quietism: a forced calming of the mind in trance. That meaning is found in Dahui Zonggao's 大慧宗杲 (1089–1163) criticism of so-called "silent illumination" (*mokushō* 默照), in the *Discourse Record of Chan Master Dahui Pujue* (*Dahui Pujue chanshi yulu* 大慧普覺禪師語錄, T.1998A.47:941c2-7):

> 爲禪者、或以無言無説、坐在黑山下鬼窟裏、閉眉合眼。謂之威音王那畔、父母未生時消息。亦謂之默而常照。爲禪者如此等輩不求妙悟。以悟爲落在第二頭。以悟爲誑謼人。以悟爲建立。自既不曾悟、亦不信有悟底。

Some take Chan to mean "no speaking, no explaining," sitting in the ghost cave beneath the Black Mountains with furrowed eyebrows and closed eyes. They call this "beyond King Majestic Voice," or the "state of repose before your father and mother were born." They also call it "being silent and constantly illuminating." The bunch who regard Chan like this do not seek sublime awakening. They take awakening as falling into a "second head." They take awakening as a deception played on people. They take awakening as a construct. Never having awakened themselves, they do not believe there is such a thing as awakening.

**goes along with it** (*zui ta ko* 隨他去): These three glyphs can also be translated literally as "in accord with that, go," or "go along with it," in the imperative voice. They come from a dialogue involving Dasui Fazhen 大隋法眞 (834-919), quoted in Dōgen's *Shōbōgenzō* in Chinese script (*shinji Shōbōgenzō* 眞字正法眼藏, DZZ.5:138, case 24):

> 益州大隋山神照大師〈嗣長慶大安、諱法眞〉因僧問、劫火洞然、大千俱壞。未審這箇還壞也無。師曰、壞。僧曰、恁麼則隨他去也。師曰、隨他去。

*Supplementary notes to the translation* 389

Great Master Shenzhao of Mount Dasui in Yizhou (succeeded Changqing Daan, called Fazhen) was once asked by a monk, "When the conflagration at the end of the kalpa rages, the chiliocosm will all be destroyed. I don't understand. Will this also be destroyed?"

The Master [Dasui] said, "It will be destroyed."

The monk said, "If so, then it goes along with it."

The Master said, "It goes along with it."

Because the demonstrative pronoun "this" (*shako* 這箇) in the monk's initial question has no antecedent in the dialogue, we are left to surmise what he is talking about. There is, however, ample precedent in Zen literature for the use of the word "this," in the absence of an antecedent, to point to that which is ultimately real and immediate but beyond accurate verbal description or conceptualization. The word "this" is similar to the noun "thusness" (S. *tathatā*, variously rendered as *shinnyo* 眞如, *nyonyo* 如如, *nyoze* 如是, or *nyo* 如) in that it points to "reality as it is" without delimiting it in any specific way. Its referent is the same as the shout (*katsu* 喝) for which Linji Yixuan 臨濟義玄 (d. 866) is famous.

In Dōgen's "The Thirty-seven Factors of Bodhi" ("Shōbōgenzō sanjū-shichi hon bodai bunpō" 正法眼藏三十七品菩提分法), he says, "From birth to old age, it's just *this*" (*jū shō shi rō, shi ze shako* 從生至老、只是這箇), thereby repeating a remark made by Mazu Daoyi 馬祖道一 (709–788) to his student Prelate Liang 亮座主 (dates unknown) in a kōan that Dōgen includes in his *Shōbōgenzō* in Chinese script (*shinji Shōbōgenzō* 眞字正法眼藏, DZZ.5:126, case 4):

師拂袖而去。祖召曰、座主。師回首。祖曰、從生至老、只是這箇。

The Master [Liang] shook his sleeves and went to leave. [Ma] Zu called to him, "Prelate!"

The Master turned his head. Zu said, "From birth to old age, it's just *this*."

A similar saying is attributed to Shitou Xiqian 石頭希遷 (710–790) in the biography of Wuxie Lingmo 五洩靈黙 (747-818) in the *Jinge Era Record of the Transmission of the Flame* (*Jingde chuandeng lu* 景德傳燈錄, T.2076.51:254b9-12):

師不領其旨。告辭而去至門、石頭呼之云、闍梨。師迴顧。石頭云、從生至老只是遮箇。漢更莫別求。

The Master [Wuxie] did not understand his [Shitou's] teaching. He bid farewell and was just going out the door when Shitou called to him, "Ācārya!"

The Master [Wuxie] turned and looked back. Shitou said, "From birth to old age, it's just *this*. A man shouldn't look for anything else."

390     DŌGEN'S *SHŌBŌGENZŌ* VOLUME VIII

In his "Painted Cake" ("Shōbōgenzō gabyō" 正法眼藏畫餅), Dōgen says, "We should study for a while the fact that *this* is a painted cake" (*shibaraku shako wa gabyō naru koto o sankyū subeshi* しばらく這箇は畫餅なること を參學すべし). In all these examples, because "this" has no delimiting antecedent, it refers to "everything," or "our situation right here and now." An awareness of what "this" is, moreover, is tantamount to awakening.

Elsewhere in Zen literature, the expression "this matter" (*shako no koto* 這 箇の事) refers to the "matter of birth and death" (*shōji no koto* 生死の事), or the "single great matter" (*ichi daiji* 一大事) that all Zen monks should strive to resolve through awakening. Likewise, "this standpoint" (*shako no denchi* 這箇の田地) refers to the point of view of an awakened person, who sees what is real.

Thus, when the monk asked Dasui whether "this" will also be destroyed in the conflagration at the end of the kalpa, he was asking whether ultimate reality itself (perhaps meaning the awakened "buddha mind") is a conditioned phenomenon that disappears with the destruction of the chiliocosm, or whether it is something eternal and beyond the reach of karmic conditioning. Dasui states clearly that the former is the case. The monk reasons, "If so, then it [i.e., "this"] goes along with it [i.e., the destruction]." Dasui's final statement, "It goes along with it," can be construed either as a simple affirmation of the monk's understanding, or as an admonition that "[You should] go along with it," or as both (a double meaning, which is probably what is intended here).

**good in the beginning, middle, and end** (*sho chū go zen* 初中後善): Also commonly phrased "good in the beginning, good in the middle, and good in the end" (*shozen chūzen gozen* 初善中善後善). A description of the buddha dharma, found in various sūtras. The *Āgama of Combined Discourses* (*Za ahan jing* 雜阿含經, T.99.2:86c24-26), for example, says:

爾時、世尊告諸比丘、我今當爲汝等説法、初中後善、善義善味、純 一滿淨、梵行清白。

At that time, the World-Honored One addressed the bhikṣus: "I now, for all of you, preach the dharma. It is good in the beginning, middle, and end; good in meaning and good in flavor; unadulterated and completely pure; noble in practice and clearly intelligible."

The *Sūtra of the Past Activities of the Buddha* (*Fo benxing ji jing* 佛本行集經, T.190.3:857b1-3) says:

而彼世尊説法、初善中善後善。其義微妙、唯獨具足、畢竟清淨。

That dharma preached by the World-Honored One is good in the beginning, good in the middle, and good in the end. Its meaning is subtle, uniquely complete, and ultimately pure.

*Supplementary notes to the translation*    391

The *Great Perfection of Wisdom Sūtra* (*Mohe boruo boluomi jing* 摩訶般若波羅蜜經, T.223.8:257c25-27) says:

佛言、菩薩若佛現在、若佛滅度後、爲衆生説法。初中後善、妙義好語、淨潔純具。

The Buddha said, "Bodhisattvas, whether the Buddha is present or after the Buddha has passed away, preach the dharma for the sake of living beings. It is good in the beginning, middle, and end; subtle in meaning and well spoken; pure and unadulterated.

Chapter 1 of the *Lotus Sūtra* (*Miaofa lianhua jing* 妙法蓮華經, T.262.9:3c17-26) says:

諸善男子。如過去無量無邊不可思議阿僧祇劫、爾時有佛號日月燈明、如來、應供、正遍知、明行足、善逝、世間解、無上士、調御丈夫、天人師、佛世尊。演説正法、初善中善後善。其義深遠、其語巧妙。純一無雜、具足清白、梵行之相。爲求聲聞者説應四諦法、度生老病死、究竟涅槃。爲求辟支佛者説應十二因緣法。爲諸菩薩説應六波羅蜜、令得阿耨多羅三藐三菩提、成一切種智。

Good sons! In the past, an immeasurable, infinite, inconceivable number of *asaṃkhya* kalpas ago, there was a buddha named Sun Moon Lamplight, a Tathāgata, Worthy of Offerings, Perfectly Knowing, Perfected in Wisdom and Conduct, Well-Gone, Knower of the World, Unsurpassed, Tamer of Persons, Teacher of Devas and Humans, World-Honored Buddha. He preached the true dharma, which was good in the beginning, good in the middle, and good in the end. Its meaning was profound; its wording was wonderfully suitable. It was pure and unadulterated, complete and clearly intelligible, and marked by the practice of purity. For those who sought the *śrāvaka* [vehicle], he preached according to the dharma of the four truths; salvation from birth, old age, sickness, and death; and final nirvāṇa. For those who sought the *pratyeka-buddha* [vehicle], he preached according to the dharma of the twelve links of dependent arising. For bodhisattvas, he preached according to the six perfections, causing them to gain *anuttarā-samyak-saṃbodhi* and attain knowledge of all forms [*sarvākāra-jñāna*, the omniscience of a buddha].

Later in the same chapter of the *Lotus Sūtra* (T.262.9:4a1) it is again said that the dharma preached by the buddha named Sun Moon Lamplight (Riyuedengming 日月燈明; S. Candrasūryapradīpa) was "good in the beginning, middle, and end" (*shochūgo zen* 初中後善). The *Lotus Sūtra* passage quoted above suggests that the **three vehicles** — those of the *śrāvaka*, *pratyeka-buddha*, and bodhisattva — may correspond to the dharma preached in the "beginning, middle, and end," respectively, of a buddha's teaching career.

**gouge out Bodhidharma's eye** (*kesshutsu Daruma ganzei* 抉出達磨眼睛): The expression "gouge out the eye" (*kesshutsu ganzei* 抉出眼睛, or *ganzei kesshutsu* 眼睛抉出), is used, like the more common "poke out the eye" (*tosshutsu ganzei* 突出眼睛), for getting the point of Zen. Dōgen's use of the trope of "gouging out Bodhidharma's eye" reflects a remark by his late teacher, Tiantong Rujing 天童如淨 (1162-1227), found in the *Discourse Record of Reverend Rujing* (*Rujing heshang yulu* 如淨和尚語錄, T.2002A.48:121c12-13):

抉出達磨眼睛、作泥彈子打人。高聲云、看。海枯徹過底、波浪拍天高。

"I gouge out [Bodhi-] Dharma's eye, make a ball of mud, and hit people." Raising his voice, he said, "Look! The ocean, dried up right through to the bottom; the waves, so high they pound the heavens."

**high places are high and level, low places are low and level** (*kōsho kōhei, teisho teihei* 高處高平、低處低平): A well-known saying by Yangshan Huiji 仰山慧寂 (803-887) in a conversation with his teacher Weishan Lingyou 溈山靈祐 (771–853); see, e.g., the *Jingde Era Record of the Transmission of the Flame* (*Jingde chuandeng lu* 景德傳燈錄, T.2076.51:282b18-21). The version in Dōgen's *Shōbōgenzō* in Chinese script (*shinji Shōbōgenzō* 眞字正法眼藏, DZZ.5:138, case 23) reads as follows:

袁州仰山通智大師〈嗣溈山、諱慧寂〉師一日隨溈山開田。師問曰、遮頭得恁麼低、那頭得恁麼高。溈山云、水能平物。但以水平。師曰、水也無憑。和尚、但高處高平、低處低平。溈山然之。

Great Master Tongzhi, of Mount Yang in Yuanzhou (succeeded Weishan, named Huiji). One day, the Master [Yangshan] was preparing a [rice] paddy with Weishan. The Master said, "This side is this low, and that side is that high."

Weishan said, "Water can level things. Just use water to level it."

The Master said, "Water's no good. Reverend, it's just that the high places are high and level, and the low places are low and level."

Weishan approved this.

This dialogue assumes familiarity with wet-field rice agriculture, in which a paddy must be level to hold water when it is flooded, after which the seedlings are transplanted in neat rows. Yangshan's final remark clearly jumps from the arena of practicality, in which it is obviously necessary to level the paddy, to a metaphysical plane where his point seems to be that all things in the universe, despite their manifest differences of "high" versus "low," etc., are in some sense already "level," or "equal" (*byō* 平). That would be the case when apparently discrete, differentiated phenomena are viewed through a philosophical lens such as the doctrines of the "emptiness of dharmas" or "consciousness only."

*Supplementary notes to the translation*          393

As is witnessed in Volume 9, case 66, of his *Extensive Record of Reverend Dōgen* (*Dōgen oshō kōroku* 道元和尚廣錄, DZZ.4:226-228), Dōgen raised this kōan and composed the following verse comment on it:

山前一片閑田地、上下高低任草料、欲算方圓料曲直、東西南北一青苗。

In front of the mountain, a piece of fallow land;

Up and down, high and low, grass for fodder has been allowed to grow.

We may want to calculate square and round, or to measure crooked and straight;

But from east and west and south and north, it's one green [rice] seedling.

Here, the expression "one green seedling" stands in stark contrast to the multiple rows of seedlings that would ordinarily be planted in a rice paddy. This is a literary device that Dōgen uses to point to the ultimate "equality" (*byō* 平), or metaphysical uniformity, of all things, despite the human tendency to calculate differences.

At a convocation in the dharma hall (*jōdō* 上堂) recorded in Volume 4, no. 273, of his *Extensive Record of Reverend Dōgen* (*Dōgen oshō kōroku* 道元和尚廣錄, DZZ.3.182), Dōgen also quoted and commented on the lines "high places are high and level" and "low places are low and level":

遮裏是什麼處在。說著不得、行著不得、入室不得、上堂不得、下語不得、入門不得、解脱不得。何階級之有。修證即不無。高處高平、是九山之與須彌山。低處低平、其八海之與大海。向上不名道膺、直下無第二人。

Where are we here? It can't be talked about; it can't be practiced; the [abbot's] room can't be entered; the dharma hall can't be convened in; words [commenting on kōans] can't be appended; the gate can't be entered; and liberation can't be gained. What stages are there? [As Nanyue Huairang said in a famous dialogue with the Sixth Ancestor, Huineng], "It's not that it lacks **practice and verification**, ...." [As Yangshan Juiji said,] "High places are high and level": this is comparing the nine mountains with Mount Sumeru. "Low places are low and level": that is comparing the eight seas with the great ocean. [Yunju Daoying said, "If I say something] beyond that, I'm not named Daoying." Right here, there is no second person.

Here, too, Dōgen seems to take the saying "high places are high and level, low places are low and level" as the expression of a deep sameness that underlies surface differences.

Dōgen also quotes Yangshan's remark about "high and low places" in his *Rules of Purity for Stewards* (*Chiji shingi* 知事規, DZZ.6:160) and in a nearly identical passage that appears in his *Admonitions for the Chef* (*Tenzo kyōkun* 典座教訓, DZZ.6:6):

394 DŌGEN'S *SHŌBŌGENZŌ* VOLUME VIII

調粥時菜、次打併今日齋時所用飯羹等盤桶并什物調度、精誠淨潔洗
灌、彼此可安高處安于高處、可安低處安于低處。高處高平、低處低
平。㮇杓等類、一切物色、一等打併、眞心鑑物、輕手取放。

When cooking the vegetable side dishes for the morning gruel, also pre-
pare the platters and tubs used for rice, soup, etc., as well as the various
utensils and supplies that will be used for the day's midday meal. Wash
them so that they are completely pure and clean, placing up high those
that belong in high places and putting down low those that belong in low
places. "High places are high and level; low places are low and level."
Treat utensils such as tongs and ladles, and all other implements and in-
gredients, with equal respect; handle all things with sincerity, picking
them up and putting them down with courtesy.

In this context, the point of quoting Yangshan is simply to emphasize the
principle that all the implements and foodstuffs in the kitchen, in addition
to having their own particular places and uses that must be recognized and
honored, are to be handled with equal care and respect.

**his body throughout is hands and eyes** (*tsūshin ze shugen* 通身是手眼): A
remark attributed to Daowu Yuanzhi 道吾圓智 (769-835) in a conversation
with fellow disciple Yunyan Tansheng 雲巖曇晟 (782-841), both dharma
heirs of Yaoshan Weiyan 藥山惟儼 (751-834), regarding the thousand-armed,
thousand-eyed Bodhisattva Avalokiteśvara (*senju sengen Kannon* 千手千眼觀
音). Dōgen's *Shōbōgenzō* in Chinese script (*shinji Shōbōgenzō* 眞字正法眼藏,
DZZ.5:182, case 105) has the following exchange:

雲巖問道吾、大悲菩薩、用許多手眼作什麼。吾曰、如人夜間背手摸
枕子。師曰、我會也、我會也。吾云、儞作麼生會。師曰、遍身是手
眼。吾曰、道即太煞道、祗道得八九成。師曰、師兄作麼生。吾曰、
通身是手眼。

Yunyan asked Daowu, "How does the bodhisattva of great compassion
use so many hands and **eyes**?"

Wu said, "Like a person searching behind for his pillow in the night."

The Master [Yunyan] said, "I understand. I understand."

Wu said, "How do you understand it?"

The Master said, "His body everywhere is hands and eyes."

Wu said, "You talk big talk, but what you say is only **eight or nine tenths
complete**."

The Master said, "What would you say, elder brother?"

Wu said, "His body throughout is hands and eyes."

This dialogue appears in many Chan sources, including the *Discourse
Record of Chan Master Yuanwu Foguo* (*Yuanwu Foguo chanshi yulu* 圓悟

*Supplementary notes to the translation*  395

佛果禪師語錄; T.1997.47:799b23-27), *Extensive Record of Chan Master Hongzhi* (*Hongzhi chanshi guanglu* 宏智禪師廣錄, T.2001.48:23b19-24), and the kōan collection *Congrong Hermitage Record* (*Congrong lu* 從容錄; T.2004.48:261b28-c4), where it is raised as case 54. Dōgen discusses a slightly different version of the conversation in his "Avalokiteśvara" chapter ("Shōbōgenzō kannon" 正法眼藏觀音).

**hitting and banging** (*chikujaku katsujaku* 築著磕著; also read *chikujaku kaijaku*): A common expression in Zen texts, comprised of two verbs that mean (1) to "beat," or "hit" (*chiku* 築), as with a **fist** or **staff**, and (2) to "crash together" (*katsu* 磕), as when one boulder impacts another, or (onomatopoeically) to "make a crashing sound." The glyph 著 (*jaku*) that is appended to both verbs is an auxiliary particle that intensifies the action or signals its successful completion. Thus, the expression as a whole is taken to mean either (1) "hitting with a whacking sound," or "striking a resounding blow," or (2) "banging together," or "hitting one another."

The expression "I hit with a whack" (*chikujaku katsujaku* 築著磕著) is a common interlinear remark used in kōan collections to signal the commentator's disapproval of a line in the dialogue; its meaning in that context is the same as the expression "[I give you] thirty blows" (*sanjū bō* 三十棒).

In the *Discourse Record of Chan Master Fayan* (*Fayan chanshi yulu* 法演禪師語錄, T.1995.47:650a7-9), the expression is attributed to Wuzu Fayan 五祖法演 (d. 1104):

若有一人發眞歸源、十方虛空築著磕著。

When someone reveals the truth and returns to the source, empty space throughout the ten directions hits and bangs.

Dōgen quotes this line in his "Turning the Dharma Wheel" ("Shōbōgenzō ten hōrin" 正法眼藏轉法輪; DZZ.2:182). In this instance, the image that Fayan conjures up is one of different areas of "empty space" (*kokū* 虛空) "banging together," perhaps with a great roar. That momentous occurrence is a metaphor for a person's awakening, but consider this: when empty space hits empty space, there is actually no collision at all. Perhaps the meaning of Fayan's trope is that awakening makes all the difference in an individual's outlook but does not really change anything in the phenomenal world.

In the context of Dōgen's "Sūtra Reading" ("Shōbōgenzō kankin" 正法眼藏看經, DZZ.1:332), the meaning of the term "hitting and banging" is even less clear:

不隨は渾隨なり、このゆゑに築著磕著なり。

"Not to follow along" is completely to follow along. It is, therefore, hitting and banging.

The context here is Venerable Prajñātāra's response to the king of eastern India, who asked why he did not turn (i.e., read) the sūtras (*tengyō* 轉經). Prajñātāra said that when he breathes out, "he does not follow along with conditions" (*fuzui shuen* 不隨衆緣).

**hold up a flower** (*nenge* 拈華 or 拈花): A reference to the famous story of Śākyamuni's transmission of the **"treasury of the true dharma eye"** to Mahākāśyapa on Vulture Peak, thereby founding the Zen lineage. The earliest extant account in which Śākyamuni is said to have held up a flower in a wordless sermon, thereby eliciting a "slight smile" (*mishō* 微笑) of understanding from Mahākāśyapa, appears in the latter's biography in the *Tiansheng Era Extended Record of the Flame* (*Tiansheng guangdeng lu* 天聖廣燈錄, ZZ.135.612a1-4; X.1553.78:428c2-5), compiled in 1036:

> 如來在靈山説法、諸天献華。世尊持華示衆、迦葉微笑。世尊告衆曰、吾有正法眼藏、涅槃妙心、付囑摩訶迦葉。流布將來、勿令斷絶。仍以金縷僧伽梨衣付迦葉、以俟慈氏。

> When the Tathāgata was on Vulture Peak preaching the dharma the gods made an offering of flowers to him. The World-Honored One held up a flower to address the congregation, and Kāśyapa smiled slightly. The World-Honored One announced to the assembly, "I have the treasury of the true dharma eye, the wondrous mind of nirvāṇa, which I entrust to Mahākāśyapa. He should spread it and not allow it to be cut off in the future. I also give to Kāśyapa this *saṃghāṭī* robe sewn with gold thread, to keep until Maitreya comes."

Most subsequent versions of this story do not include the added detail, frequently mentioned by Dōgen, that Śākyamuni also "blinked his eyes" (*shunmoku* 瞬目) when he held up a flower. For the story with that variation, see "**holding up a flower and blinking the eyes**."

**holding up a flower and blinking the eyes** (*nenge shunmoku* 拈華瞬目): Most accounts of the founding of the Zen lineage at an assembly on Vulture Peak say that Śākyamuni "held up a flower" (*nenge* 拈華 or 拈花) in a wordless sermon, eliciting a "slight smile" (*mishō* 微笑) of understanding from Mahākāśyapa, who was then publicly entrusted by the Buddha with the **"treasury of the true dharma eye"**; see "**hold up a flower**."

A variant account of the transmission to Mahākāśyapa on Vulture Peak claims that the wordless sermon preached by the Buddha took place when he merely blinked his eyes. This is reported in *The Eye of Humans and Devas* (*Rentian yanmu* 人天眼目, T.2006.48:308b6-9), a collection of Chan lore edited by Huiyan Zhizhao 晦巖智昭 (dates unknown) and published in 1188:

*Supplementary notes to the translation* 397

昔靈山會上、世尊以青蓮目瞬示大衆。無能領其密意。惟大迦葉獨領解佛旨。經云、佛告大迦葉云、吾有正法眼藏涅槃妙心、付囑與汝。汝當流布勿令斷絕。

Long ago, at an assembly on Vulture Peak, the World-Honored One used a blink of his blue lotus eyes to instruct the great assembly. None could apprehend his secret meaning. Only Mahākāśyapa alone grasped the Buddha's purport. A sūtra says, "The Buddha said to Mahākāśyapa, 'I have the treasury of the true dharma eye, the wondrous mind of nirvāṇa, which I entrust to you. You should spread it and not allow it to be cut off.'"

This account mentions a flower, but it does not say that the Buddha held one up. Rather, it says that he instructed the assembly by "winking" or "blinking" (*shun* 瞬) his "blue lotus eyes" (*seiren moku* 青蓮目). The blue lotus (*shōren* 青蓮; S. *utpala*) is a variety of water lily (*suiren* 睡蓮) that has petals with clearly distinguished blue and white parts. Because the shape and coloration of the petals are suggestive of a large human eye, the term *utpala* was used in Indian scriptures to describe the eyes of impressive people, especially the Buddha; the flower was sometimes referred to poetically as a "buddha eye."

In a few Chan texts, the two versions of Buddha's wordless sermon to the assembly on Vulture Peak were combined, resulting in the unusual assertion that Śākyamuni "held up a flower and blinked his eyes." The earliest example of this is found in the *Discourse Record of Chan Master Huihui of Jingci* [Monastery] (*Jingci Huihui chanshi yulu* 淨慈慧暉禪師語錄, ZZ.124:941b1-2; X.1428.72:142c8-9), which contains the sayings of Zide Huihui 自得慧暉 (1097–1183), a disciple of Hongzhi Zhengjue 宏智正覺 (1091–1157) in the Caodong lineage:

上堂因日、記得靈山會上百億衆前、當時世尊拈華瞬目。衆皆無措。只有金色頭陀破顏微笑。

At a convocation in the dharma hall, [Huihui] said, "I recall that at the time of the assembly on Vulture Peak, before a gathering of billions, the World-Honored One held up a flower and blinked his eyes. All in the assembly were at a loss. Only the Golden-Hued Ascetic [Mahākāśyapa] broke into a slight smile."

Dōgen's *Shōbōgenzō* in Chinese script (*shinji Shōbōgenzō* 眞字正法眼藏, DZZ.5:258, case 253) contains the following version of the transmision story:

昔日靈山百萬衆前、世尊拈華瞬目。時迦葉一人、破顏微笑。世尊云、我有正法眼藏、付属摩訶大迦葉。

Once upon a time, before an assembly of a million on Vulture Peak, the World-Honored One held up a flower and blinked his eyes. At that time, Kāśyapa alone broke into a slight smile. The World-Honored One said, "I

398    DŌGEN'S *SHŌBŌGENZŌ* VOLUME VIII

have the treasury of the true dharma eye; I bequeath it to Mahā, the Great, Kāśyapa."

This version of the story does not perfectly match any extant Chan text, but it is the one that Dōgen seems to have accepted as historically accurate. He rarely spoke of the Buddha's "holding up a flower" in isolation, without immediately mentioning his "blinking the eyes."

**I alone am honored** (*yui ga doku son* 唯我獨尊): Words attributed to the baby Śākyamuni, the bodhisattva (soon-to-be the Buddha), in various accounts of his birth found in Chinese Buddhist texts.

The *Sūtra of the Collected Past Activities of the Buddha* (*Fo benxing ji jing* 佛本行集經, T.190.2:699a10-15), translated by Jñānagupta (Shenajueduo 闍那崛多, 523-600/605), gives the following account of the Buddha's birth:

童子初生、無人扶持、住立於地。各行七步、凡所履處、皆生蓮花。顧視四方、目不曾瞬。不畏不驚、住於東面、不似孩童呱然啼叫、言音周正、巧妙辭章、而説是言。一切世間、唯我獨尊、唯我最勝。我今當斷生老死根。

When the boy was first born, without anybody's support, he stood in place on the ground. A lotus flower grew from each of the places where his feet had trod when he walked seven steps. Looking around in the four directions, his eyes had not yet blinked. Unafraid and unsurprised, he stayed facing east. Then, with an exclamation unlike the wail of a baby, the sound of his voice entirely proper, with skillful language, he spoke these words: "I alone am honored in all worlds, and I alone am supreme. I will now cut off the root of birth, old age, and death."

A slightly different account is found in the *Great Tang Record of Travels to Western Lands* (*Datang xiyu ji* 大唐西域記, T.2087.51:902a26-b2) by the famous pilgrim monk Xuanzang 玄奘 (602–664), who made the following remarks in his account of his visit to the Lumbinī Grove 臘伐尼林 in India, renowned as the Buddha's birthplace:

菩薩生已、不扶而行、於四方各七步、而自言曰、天上天下唯我獨尊。今茲而往、生分已盡。隨足所蹈，出大蓮花。二龍踊出、住虛空中。而各吐水、一冷一煖，以浴太子。

After the bodhisattva was born, he walked without assistance, taking seven steps in each of the four directions and speaking by himself, saying, "I alone am honored in heaven and beneath heaven. Now [i.e., in this life] I shall depart, my karmic endowment having been exhausted." From the places where his feet had stepped, great lotus flowers sprang forth. Two dragons emerged and hovered in empty space, each spitting water, one cool and one warm, to bathe the prince.

## Supplementary notes to the translation

"In heaven" (*tenjō* 天上) means among all the devas; "beneath heaven" (*tenka* 天下) means among all human beings throughout the world. The glyphs 唯我獨尊 (*yui ga doku son*) can also be rendered more literally as "I alone am the exclusively honored one" or "Only I am exclusively honored."

Yet another account appears in the *Various Aspects of the Mūlasarvāstivāda Vinaya* (*Genben shuo yiqie youbu pinaiye zashi* 根本説一切有部毘奈耶雜事, T.1451.24:298a8-11), translated by Yijing 義淨 (635-713):

> 菩薩生時、帝釋親自手承置蓮花上、不假扶侍。足蹈七花、行七步已、遍觀四方。手指上下、作如是語、此即是我最後生身、天上天下唯我獨尊。

At the time when the bodhisattva was born, Indra himself, with his own hand, offered up lotus flowers and continuously waited on him. His [i.e., the bodhisattva's] feet stepping on seven flowers, he walked seven steps, then looked around in the four directions. His hands pointed up and down, and he spoke as follows: "This is my final birth body; I alone am honored in heaven and beneath heaven."

The Buddha's birthday assembly (*Butsu tanjō e* 佛誕生會) in East Asia, also known in Japan as the "flower festival" (*hana matsuri* 花祭), centers on an image of the baby Buddha with his right hand pointing up to heaven and his left hand pointing down to earth, enshrined under a canopy of flowers representing the Lumbinī Grove.

From the Song dynasty on, virtually all Chinese Buddhist texts had come to agree on the date of the Buddha's birth and the content of his first words. Those are found, for example, in a work completed in 1269 by the Tiantai school monk Zhipan 志磐 (dates unknown), the *Complete Chronicle of the Buddhas and Ancestors* (*Fozu tongji* 佛祖統紀, T.2035.49:469c22-24):

> 四月八日、佛從母夫人右脇而出。自行七步、舉右手而言曰、天上天下唯我獨尊。

On the 8th day of the 4th month, the Buddha emerged from his mother's right side. Walking seven steps by himself, he raised his right hand and said, "I alone am honored in heaven and beneath heaven."

Texts associated with the Zen tradition do not differ in their presentation of this basic information. For example, the *Outline of the Linked Flames* (*Liandeng huiyao* 聯燈會要, ZZ.136:439a5-7; X.1557.79:13a11-12), a work compiled by Huiweng Wuming 晦翁悟明 (dates unknown) and printed in 1189 reads:

> 世尊初生下、一手指天、一手指地。周行七步、目顧四方云、天上天下、唯我獨尊。

As soon as the World-Honored One was born, with one hand he pointed to the heavens, and with one hand he pointed to the earth. Walking around for seven paces, he gazed in the four directions and said, "I alone am honored in heaven and beneath heaven."

Zen texts, however, interpret the baby Buddha's saying in ways that are unique to the Zen tradition. The *Records that Mirror the Axiom* (*Zongjing lu* 宗鏡錄, T.2016.48.417c19-23), compiled in 961 by Yongming Yanshou 永明延壽 (904–975), contains the following explanation:

二空無我所顯、眞如爲其自性。諸聖分證、諸佛圓證、此清淨法界、即眞如妙心。爲諸佛果海之源、作群生實際之地。此皆是立宗之異名、非別有體。或言宗者、尊也。以心爲宗。故云、天上天下唯我獨尊。

When the two kinds of emptiness, or no self, are revealed, suchness is their [i.e., all dharmas'] own nature. What sages partially realize and buddhas fully realize is this pure dharma realm, which is the wondrous mind of suchness. We regard this [mind] as the source of the ocean of the fruit of the buddhas; we construe it as the ground of living beings' reality. These are all different names for the axiom, not separately existing substances. Some say that the axiom is the "honored." [The Chan tradition] takes mind as the axiom. Thus [the Buddha] said, "I alone am honored in heaven and beneath heaven."

Yanshou's point here is that what is "exclusively honored" (*doku son* 獨尊) is the "wondrous mind of suchness" (*shinnyo myōshin* 眞如妙心), which is the awakened mind of a buddha.

There are also a number of instances in Zen literature where the words of the baby Buddha are raised as a kōan for comment. In the *Extensive Record of Chan Master Yunmen Kuangzhen* (*Yunmen Kuangzhen chanshi guanglu* 雲門匡眞禪師廣錄, T.1988.47:560b16-19), for example, Yunmen Wenyan 雲門文偃 (864-949) comments:

舉。世尊初生下、一手指天、一手指地。周行七步、目顧四方云、天上天下唯我獨尊。師云、我當時若見、一棒打殺與狗子喫却。貴圖天下太平。

Raised:

As soon as the World-Honored One was born, with one hand he pointed to the heavens, and with one hand he pointed to the earth. Walking around for seven paces, he gazed in the four directions and said, "I alone am honored in heaven and beneath heaven."

[comment]

The Master [Yunmen] said, "If I'd witnessed this at the time, I'd have killed him with a single blow of my **staff** and fed him to the dogs, so that great peace would prevail beneath heaven."

Supplementary notes to the translation 401

In the biography of Chan Master Luoshan Yicong of Fuzhou 福州羅山義聰 禪師 (dates unknown) included in the *Jingde Era Record of the Transmission of the Flame* (*Jingde chuandeng lu* 景德傳燈錄, T.2076.51:381a17-19), we find a similar exchange:

問、手指天地唯我獨尊。爲什麼却被傍者責。師曰、謂言胡鬚赤。

[Someone] asked, "When [the Buddha] pointed his hands to heaven and earth [and said], 'I alone am honored in heaven and beneath heaven,' why wasn't he scolded afterwards by those at his side?"

The Master [Luoshan] said, "That is called 'saying that the barbarian's beard is red.'"

What Luoshan means is that it is not necessary to point out the absurdity of the baby Buddha's speech, for that is as obvious as the barbarian's (i.e., Bodhidharma's) famously red beard.

**if you wish to know the meaning of "buddha nature," you should observe the conditions of the time** (*yoku chi busshō gi, tō kan jisetsu innen* 欲知佛性義、當觀時節因緣). The initial phrase may also be translated, "If you wish to know what [real thing] the term 'buddha nature' refers to." The glyphs 時節因緣 (*jisetsu innen*) may be read either as "conditions of the time" or as "time and conditions." In his "Shōbōgenzō busshō" 正法眼藏佛性 (DZZ.1:17), Dōgen attributes the saying to Buddha Śākyamuni, as if he were quoting the Chinese of an existing sūtra:

佛言、欲知佛性義、當觀時節因緣。時節若至、佛性現前。

The Buddha said, "If you wish to know the meaning of 'buddha nature,' you should observe the conditions of the time." If the time arrives, buddha nature appears.

The saying that Dōgen attributes to the Buddha is not a direct quotation of any extant sūtra, nor does the following remark ("if the time arrives, buddha nature appears") correspond perfectly to any extant source. The closest precedent is found in *Grouped Sayings from the Chan Tradition* (*Chanlin leiju* 禪林類聚, ZZ.117:176a16-b2; X.1299.67:89a10-14), where a similar set of words is attributed to Baizhang Huaihai 百丈懷海 (749-814):

潙山祐禪師在百丈時、夜侍立次。丈云、看爐内有火也無。師看了來報云無。丈躬自至爐、深撥忽得少火。乃挾起云、儞道無這箇聻。師因而契悟。丈云、欲知佛性義、當觀時節因緣。時節若至、其理自彰。便知己物、不從外得。汝善護持。

When Chan Master Weishan You was at [Mount] Baizhang and serving as attendant [to the abbot, Baizhang Huaihai] at night, Zhang said, "See if there is fire in the brazier or not."

The Master [Weishan] looked and reported back, saying, "There is none."

402 DŌGEN'S *SHŌBŌGENZŌ* VOLUME VIII

Zhang went to look in the brazier himself. He stirred deep within it and soon found a small ember. Raising it up with pincers he declared, "You say there is none, but look at this!"

The Master, due to this, tallied [with Baizhang's meaning] and awakened.

Zhang said, "If you wish to know the meaning of 'buddha nature,' you should observe the conditions of the time. If the time arrives, its principle will appear of itself. Just know your own things: it does not come from outside. You should guard this well."

A nearly identical quote is also attributed to Baizhang in the *Collection of the Essential Teachings of Our Lineage* (*Zongmen tongyao ji* 宗門統要集, ZTS.1:83c7-d1):

丈云、欲知佛性義、當觀時節因緣。時節若至、其理自契。

Zhang said, "'If you wish to know the meaning of buddha nature, you should observe the conditions of the time.' If the time arrives, you will naturally tally with its principle."

Other sources, however, state that Baizhang was quoting a sūtra when he said, "If you wish to see buddha nature, you should observe the conditions of the time." In its biography of Baizhang's dharma heir Weishan Lingyou 溈山靈祐 (771–853), the *Jingde Era Record of the Transmission of the Flame* (*Jingde chuandeng lu* 景德傳燈錄, T.2076.51:264b19-27) says:

一日侍立百丈問誰。師曰、靈祐。百丈云、汝撥鑪中有火否。師撥云、無火。百丈躬起深撥得少火。舉以示之云、此不是火。師發悟禮謝陳其所解。百丈曰、此乃暫時岐路耳。經云、欲見佛性當觀時節因緣。時節既至、如迷忽悟、如忘勿憶。方省己物不從他得。故祖師云、悟了同未悟、無心得無法。只是無虛妄凡聖等心。本來心法元自備足。汝今既爾善自護持。

One day when he [Weishan] was serving as attendant, Baizhang asked him, "Who are you?"

The Master said, "Lingyou."

Baizhang said, "You should stir inside the brazier to see if there is any fire or not."

The Master stirred and said, "There is no fire."

Baizhang himself got up, stirred deeply, and found a small ember. Raising it up to show, he said, "Is this not fire?"

The Master had an awakening, bowed in thanks, and explained what he had understood.

Baizhang said, "This, however, is only a temporary fork in the road. The sūtra says, 'If you wish to see the buddha nature, you should observe the conditions of the time.' When the time has arrived, it will be as if suddenly

*Supplementary notes to the translation*　　　403

awakening from delusion, as if suddenly* remembering what had been forgotten. Just reflect on your own things: it does not come from outside. That is why the ancestral master [Dhītika, the Fifth Ancestor of the Zen Lineage in India] said, 'To be awakened is the same as not yet being awakened; no mind attains no dharmas.' It is simply the mind of equanimity that has no false notions of ordinary [delusion] or sagely [awakening]. The fundamental mind-dharma is originally complete unto itself. You are now already like this. Guard it well!"
[* reading 忽 for 勿]

In his *Eihei Monastery Rules of Purity for Stewards* (*Eiheiji chiji shingi* 永平寺知事清規, DZZ.6:108), Dōgen quotes a dialogue that is virtually identical to the preceding one from *Jingde Era Record of the Transmission of the Flame*; the only difference is that, according to Dōgen, Weishan was serving as head cook (*tenzo* 典座) when the exchange between him and Baizhang took place. Baizhang's reference to a sūtra in that dialogue was perhaps the basis for Dōgen's attribution of the saying "if you wish to know the meaning of 'buddha nature'... etc." to the Buddha. The *Discourse Record of Chan Master Lingyou of Mount Wei in Tanzhou* (*Tanzhou Weishan Lingyou chanshi yulu* 潭州潙山靈祐禪師語錄, T.1989.47:577a14-16) also states that Baizhang quoted a sūtra:

百丈云、此乃暫時岐路耳。經云、欲識佛性義、當觀時節因緣。時節既至、如迷忽悟、如忘忽憶。

Baizhang said, "This, however, is only a temporary fork in the road. The sūtra says, 'If you wish to experience the meaning of buddha nature, you should observe the conditions of the time.' When the time has arrived, it will be as if suddenly awakening from delusion, as if suddenly remembering what had been forgotten."

This raises the question of what sūtra Baizhang was quoting. The *Tiansheng Era Extended Record of the Flame* (*Tiansheng guangdeng lu* 天聖廣燈錄, ZZ.135:749b11-14) depicts Chan Master Fenyang Shanzhao 汾陽善昭 (947-1024) quoting the same passage as Baizhang and attributing it to the *Heroic March Sūtra* (*Shoulengyan jing* 首楞嚴經):

師上堂云、夫説法看疑者。須及時節。觀根投機。應病用藥。不及時節。總喚作非時語。所以楞嚴會上云、欲知佛性義、當觀時節因緣。若明君臣父子。邪正觸淨。顯然自分。喚作野老謳歌。皇道坦然、佛法現前。

At a convocation in the dharma hall the Master [Shanzhao] said,
Now, when preaching the dharma and attending to doubts, one must reach [i.e., wait for] the [proper] time. Observing the capacities [of the audience], one seizes the opportunity. To respond to illness, one uses medicines. If one does not reach the time, in general that is called

404    DŌGEN'S *SHŌBŌGENZŌ* VOLUME VIII

speaking at the wrong time. That is why, in the *Śuraṅgama* assembly, [Buddha] said, "If you wish to know the meaning of buddha nature, you should observe the conditions of the time." If there are wise rulers and vassals, fathers and sons, then evil and good, polluted and pure, will be evident to oneself. [In the *Record of Linji* (*Linji lu* 臨濟錄)] this is called "aged rustics sing songs." The way of the emperor will be stable, and the dharma of the Buddha will be manifest.

Extant recensions of the *Heroic March Sūtra*, however, do not contain the saying quoted by Baizhang and Shanzhao. Modern Sōtō scholarship holds that Baizhang was restating a line from the *Nirvāṇa Sūtra* (*Da banniepan jing* 大般涅槃經, T.374.12:532a18-19), which reads:

欲見佛性、應當觀察時節形色。是故我説一切衆生悉有佛性、實不虛妄。

If you wish to see the buddha nature, you should observe the forms at the time. Therefore, my teaching that all living beings in their entirety have the buddha nature is true, not false.

The saying "if you wish to know the meaning of 'buddha nature,' you should observe the conditions of the time" became a fixed idiom that was raised, in the manner of a kōan, by numerous Chan masters in Song- and Yuan-dynasty China. The words that follow the saying vary considerably in the records of different masters and may often be read as commentaries on that "old case." Some comments appear to have been produced spontaneously, such as the one by Baizhang who purportedly said, "If the time arrives, its [buddha nature's] principle will appear of itself." Other commentaries begin by quoting already established comments, as in the following example from the *Discourse Record of Chan Master Yuanwu Foguo* (*Yuanwu Foguo chanshi yulu* 圓悟佛果禪師語錄, T.1997.47:749c19-25), where Yuanwu Keqin 圓悟克勤 (1063-1135) first quotes Baizhang and then adds his own remark:

僧問、世尊久默斯要及至末後、爲什麼獨召飲光密傳法眼。師云、正是龍頭蛇尾。進云、一點水墨兩處成龍。師云、帶累山僧。進云、苦瓠連根苦。甜瓜徹蒂甜。師云灼然。進云、也是烏龜喫生菜。師云、取性。乃云、欲知佛性義、當觀時節因緣。時節若至其理自彰。苟或時節未至。理地未明。

A monk asked, "The World-Honored One was silent for a long time about this essential thing before he reached the end of his life. How come only Kāśyapa got the secret transmission of the dharma eye?"

The Master [Yuanwu] said, "This [monk questioning me] is precisely a dragon's head with a snake's tail."

[The monk] added, "With a single dab of India ink, it becomes a dragon in both places."

*Supplementary notes to the translation*  405

The Master said, "You're annoying this mountain monk [i.e., me]."

[The monk] added, "The bitter gourd is bitter to its roots. The sweet melon is sweet through to its stem."

The Master said, "Obvious."

[The monk] added, "Still, this is a blind turtle eating raw vegetables."

The Master said, "Grasping at the nature." Then he said, [quoting a sūtra] "If you wish to know the meaning of 'buddha nature,' you should observe the conditions of the time. [quoting Baizhang] If the time arrives, its principle will appear of itself. [speaking for himself] If, on the other hand, the time has yet to arrive, the ground of principle is still unclear."

A number of Chan masters also use the saying "if you wish to know the meaning of 'buddha nature,' you should observe the conditions of the time" as "attached words" (*jakugo* 著語) to comment on other kōans. In his *Blue Cliff Record* (*Biyan lu* 碧巖錄, T.2003.48:154c2-6), for example, Yuanwu Keqin employs it in his prose comment on Case 14, which involves Yunmen Wenyan 雲門文偃 (864-949):

舉。僧問雲門、如何是一代時教。雲門云、對一説。禪家流、欲知佛性義、當觀時節因緣。謂之教外別傳、單傳心印、直指人心、見性成佛。釋迦老子、四十九年住世。。。。

Raised.

A monk asked Yunmen, "What about the [Buddha's] teachings of an entire lifetime?"

Yunmen said, "To each, an appropriate explanation."

[Yuanwu's comment]

Followers of the Chan house, "If you wish to know the meaning of 'buddha nature,' you should observe the conditions of the time." We call this, "**A separate transmission outside the teachings**, individually transmitting the mind-seal, **pointing directly at the person's mind, seeing the nature and attaining buddhahood**." Old Śākya stayed in the world for forty-nine years....

The phrase "conditions of the time" (*jisetsu innen* 時節因緣) (or "time and conditions") took on a life of its own in Chan literature, being often raised as a topic for comment, in the manner of a kōan. In the biography of Chan Master Tanying Daguan 曇穎達觀 (989-1060) found in the *Additional Records of the Transmission of the Flame* (*Xu chuandeng lu* 續傳燈錄, T.2077.51:489b24-26), for example, a monk asks about the meaning of the phrase:

上堂大眾集定、有僧纔出禮拜。師曰、欲識佛性義、當觀時節因緣。僧便問、如何是時節因緣。師便下座。

406     DŌGEN'S *SHŌBŌGENZŌ* VOLUME VIII

At a convocation in the dharma hall, the great assembly had just gathered and settled in their places when a monk came out of the ranks prematurely and made a bow.

The Master said, "If you wish to experience the meaning of 'buddha nature,' you should observe the conditions of the time."

The monk then asked, "What are 'the conditions of the time'?"

The Master got down from the [abbot's high] seat [thus ending the convocation].

In the *Discourse Record of Chan Master Mingjue* (*Mingjue chanshi yulu* 明覺禪師語錄, T.1996.47:683c18-19), to cite but one other example, the phrase is raised for the master, Xuedou Zhongxian 雪竇重顯 (980–1052), to comment on:

上堂、僧問、如何是時節因緣。師云、瞌睡漢。僧便喝。師云、詐惺惺。

At a convocation in the dharma hall a monk asked, "What about 'the conditions of the time'?"

The Master said, "A dozing guy."

The monk gave a shout.

The Master said, "Pretending to be alert."

**in the realms everywhere, it has never been hidden** (*henkai fu zō zō* 徧界不曾藏 or 遍界不曾藏): A saying attributed, in two different contexts, to Chan Master Shishuang Qingzhu 石霜慶諸 (807-888). Dōgen's *Shōbōgenzō* in Chinese script (*shinji Shōbōgenzō* 眞字正法眼藏, DZZ.5:156-158, case 58) has the following exchange:

潭州石霜山普會大師（嗣道吾、諱慶諸）、因僧問、三千里外、遠聞石霜。有箇不顧。師曰、是。僧云、只如萬象歷然、是顧不顧。師曰、我道不驚衆。僧曰、不驚衆是不與萬象合。如何是不顧。師曰、徧界不曾藏。

Great Master Puhui of Mount Shishuang in Tanzhou (heir to Daowu, styled Qingzhu) was asked by a monk, "I've heard of Shishuang from afar, three thousand miles away. Is there anything you're unconcerned about?"

The Master said, "Yes."

The monk said, "Suppose the **myriad forms** were distinctly arrayed; would you be concerned with them or unconcerned?"

The Master said, "I would say, 'Don't alarm the multitude.'"

The monk said, "Not alarming the multitude is not uniting with the myriad forms. How is that unconcerned?"

*Supplementary notes to the translation* 407

The Master said, "In the realms everywhere, it has never been hidden."

Dōgen is here quoting the *Collection of the Essential Teachings of Our Lineage* (*Zongmen tongyao ji* 宗門統要集; ZTS.1:155d1-2); nearly identical versions of this exchange appear in the *Outline of the Linked Flames* (*Liandeng huiyao* 聯燈會要; ZZ.136:762b11-14), the *Collated Essentials of the Five Flame Records* (*Wudeng huiyuan* 五燈會元; ZZ.138.182b16-18), and various other Chan texts. Often the exchange is treated as a kōan, with an attached comment by Xuedou Zhongxian 雪竇重顯 (980–1052): "Who is it that is unconcerned?"

The other context in which the saying is attributed to Shishuang appears in his biography in the *Jingde Era Record of the Transmission of the Flame* (*Jingde chuandeng lu* 景德傳燈錄; T.2076.51:321a2-7):

師居方丈。有僧在明窗外問、咫尺之間爲什麼不覩師顏。師曰、我道遍界不曾藏。僧舉問雪峯、遍界不曾藏意旨如何。雪峯曰、什麼處不是石霜。僧迴舉雪峯之語呈師。師曰、老大漢有什麼死急。

The Master [Shishuang] was in the abbot's quarters. There was a monk outside a lighting window [located above eye level] who asked, "I'm very close to you, Master; how come I can't see your face?"

The Master said, "I would say, 'In the realms everywhere, it has never been hidden.'"

The monk brought this up with Xuefeng and asked, "What's the meaning of 'in the realms everywhere, it has never been hidden'?"

Xuefeng said, "Where isn't it Shishuang?"

The monk returned and reported what Xuefeng had said to the Master. The Master said, "That old bigshot, having such an outcry!"

Here, Shishuang's saying, "in the realms everywhere, it has never been hidden," is raised as a topic that Xuefeng Yicun 雪峰義存 (822-908) comments on. Xuefeng's comment on Shishuang's saying, in turn, becomes a topic for Shishuang himself to comment on.

The entire exchange, down through Shishuang's criticism of Xuefeng for "having such an outcry," became a kōan that was commented on subsequently by numerous Zen masters. Dahui Zonggao 大慧宗杲 (1089-1163), for example, includes it in his *Treasury of the True Dharma Eye* (*Zhengfayanzang* 正法眼藏; ZZ.118:86b2-5) and reports a comment on it made by Xuansha Shibei 玄沙師備 (835-908), a dharma heir of Xuefeng.

The *Collection of the Essential Teachings of Our Lineage* (*Zongmen tongyao ji* 宗門統要集; ZTS.1:155b4-c3) repeats this kōan and then quotes comments on it by Xuansha and four other eminent Chan masters, including the Caodong founder Dongshan Liangjie 洞山良价 (807-869); the Yuan-dynasty expansion of this text, *Extended Collection of the Essential Teachings of Our Lineage*

(*Zongmen tongyao zhengxu ji* 宗門統要正續集; CBETA.P.1519.154:861a4-862a2) adds three more comments, including that of the celebrated Caodong master Hongzhi Zhengjue 宏智正覺 (1091–1157).

**intention of the Ancestral Master's coming from the west** (*soshi seirai i* 祖師西來意): A reference to Bodhidharma, the Indian monk who is said to have transmitted the "mind dharma" (*shinbō* 心法), or awakening, of Buddha Śākyamuni from the west to China, where he became the first ancestor of the Zen lineage; see **"coming from the west."** The Chinese term *yi* 意, translated here as "intention," can indicate either (a) "intent," or "purpose," or (b) "meaning, or "significance"; hence the phrase can be (and perhaps more often is) read "the meaning of the Ancestral Master's coming from the west." However it is interpreted, the literature of Zen is filled with countless instances of disciples asking masters, "What is the intention/meaning of the Ancestral Master's coming from the west?" The question, in effect, asks for a comment on the essence of the Zen tradition, which is awakening, and it elicits a wide variety of striking responses, many of which appear on the surface to be *non sequiturs*. The following examples are all dialogues that Dōgen quotes or alludes to somewhere in the *Shōbōgenzō*.

A famous response by Zhaozhou Congshen 趙州從諗 (778-897) is found in case 47 of the *Congrong Hermitage Record* (*Congrong lu* 從容錄, T.2004.48.256c14-16) and case 37 of the *Gateless Barrier* (*Wumen guan* 無門關, T.2005.48.297c5-6), which reads as follows:

趙州因僧問、如何是祖師西來意。州云、庭前柏樹子。

Zhaozhou was once asked by a monk, "What is the intention of the Ancestral Master's coming from the west?"

Zhaozhou said, "The **cypress tree at the front of the garden.**"

The *Extensive Record of Chan Master Yunmen Kuangzhen* (*Yunmen Kuangzhen chanshi guanglu* 雲門匡眞禪師廣錄, T.1988.47:545b29-c1) contains the response of Yunmen Wenyen 雲門文偃 (864-949):

問如何是祖師西來意。師云、日裏看山。

[Someone] asked, "What is the intention of the Ancestral Master's coming from the west?"

The Master [Yunmen] said, "**Seeing the mountain in the daylight**."

In the biography of a dharma heir of Fayan Wenyi 法眼文益 (885–958) named Chan Master Daochang of Dazhi Cloister 大智院道常 (dates unknown), which appears in the *Jingde Era Record of the Transmission of the Flame* (*Jingde chuandeng lu* 景德傳燈錄, T.2076.51:416c9-14), Daochang is asked to comment on an exchange involving Xuansha Shibei 玄沙師備 (835-908):

*Supplementary notes to the translation* 409

僧舉人問玄沙曰、三乘十二分教即不問。如何是祖師西來意。玄沙曰、三乘十二分教不要。其僧不會、請師爲説。師曰、汝實不會。曰、實不會。師示偈曰、不要三乘要祖宗、三乘不要與君同、君今欲會通宗旨、後夜猿啼在亂峯。

A monk raised [the story], "A person queried Xuansha saying, 'I'm not asking about the **three vehicles and twelvefold teachings**, but what is the intention of the Ancestral Master's coming from the west?'

Xuansha said, 'The three vehicles and twelvefold teachings are unnecessary.'"

The monk did not understand [the story], so he asked the Master [Daochang] to explain it. The Master said, "You really don't understand?"

[The monk] replied, "I don't understand."

The Master recited a verse for him:

> Not to need the **three vehicles** is to need the ancestral teaching;
>
> The three vehicles being "unnecessary" applies, likewise, to you.
>
> Your present desire to understand and penetrate the essential point [is like]
>
> A monkey crying among the wild peaks late at night.

In his "Sayings" ("Shōbōgenzō dōtoku" 正法眼藏道得), Dōgen discusses the response given by a hermit who drank from a stream. The version recorded in his *Shōbōgenzō* in Chinese script (*shinji Shōbōgenzō* 眞字正法眼藏, DZZ.5:218, case 183) reads as follows:

雪峰山畔、有一僧卓庵。多年不剃頭。自作一柄木杓、去溪邊舀水喫。時有僧問、如何是祖師西來意。庵主云、溪深杓柄長。僧歸舉似雪峰。峰曰、也甚奇怪。雖然如是、須是老僧勘過始得。峰一日、同侍者將剃刀去訪他。纔相見便問、道得即不剃汝頭。庵主便將水洗頭、師便與他剃却。

On the edge of Mount Yuefeng, there was a monk who set up a hermitage. For many years, he did not shave his head. He made himself a wooden ladle and went to a stream to scoop up water to drink.

On one such occasion, a monk asked him, "What is the intention of the Ancestral Master's coming from the west?"

The hermit said, "The stream is deep, the ladle long."

The monk returned [to the monastery on the mountain] and raised this with Yuefeng.

Feng said, "Very strange. It may be so, but this old monk will have to investigate it."

One day, Feng and his acolyte, carrying a razor, went to visit him. As soon as they met, he asked, "If you've attained the way, why not shave your head?"

The hermit brought some water and washed his head; the Master shaved him.

In many cases, the full saying ("intention of the Ancestral Master's coming from the west") is abbreviated to: "intention of coming from the west" (*seirai i* 西来意). For example, the biography of Shishuang Qingzhu 石霜慶諸 (807–888) in the *Jingde Era Record of the Transmission of the Flame* (*Jingde chuandeng lu* 景德傳燈錄, T.2076.51:320c25-28) contains this exchange:

僧問、如何是西來意。師曰、空中一片石。僧禮拜。師曰、會麼。曰、不會。師曰、賴汝不會。若會即打破爾頭。

A monk asked, "What is the intention of coming from the west?"

The Master said, "A single stone in space."

The monk bowed. The Master [Shishuang] said, "Do you understand?"

He said, "I don't understand."

The Master said, "I trust you don't understand. If you understood, it [or, perhaps, I] would bust your head."

Another common abbreviation is: "intention of the Ancestral Master" (*soshi i* 祖師意). For example, in the *Extensive Record of Chan Master Hongzhi* (*Hongzhi chanshi guanglu* 宏智禪師廣錄, T.48.2001:2c3), we find:

上堂云、明明百草頭、明明祖師意。

At a convocation in the dharma hall, [Hongzhi] said, "**Perfectly clear, the tips of the hundred grasses**; perfectly clear, the intention of the Ancestral Master."

**iron bull** (*tetsugyū* 鐵牛): In Chinese culture at large, a metaphor for anything (including a person) that is "strong," "steadfast," or "immovable." That association derives from a story about the legendary Emperor Yu 禹, putative founder of the Xia dynasty, circa 2000 BCE, who is said to have made and worshiped a gigantic iron bull in order to keep the Yellow River (Huanghe 黄河) from flooding. Known as the "iron bull of the Shan region" (*Senpu tetsugyū* 陝府鐵牛), the image is said to have represented the tutelary deity of the river. Legend has it that the head of the statue was in Henan (河南, literally "south of the river"), while its tail was in Hebei ("north of the river"), so it is imagined to have been large enough to reach from one bank to the other.

*Supplementary notes to the translation*          411

In the *Tiansheng Era Extended Record of the Flame* (*Tiansheng guangdeng lu* 天聖廣燈錄, ZZ.135:837b3-7), the Song-dynasty Chan Master Yaoshan Liyu 藥山利昱 (dates unknown), a disciple of Liangshan Yuanguan 梁山緣觀 (dates unknown) in the Caodong lineage, uses the expression "the iron bull of Shan vomits up heaven and earth" to refer to a certain kind of realization:

師上堂云、山河大地日月星辰與諸上座同生。三世諸佛與諸上座同
參。三藏聖教與諸上座同時。還信得及麼。若也信得及、陝府鐵牛吞
却乾坤。雖然如是被法身礙却、轉身不得。順知有出身之路。作麼生
是諸上座出身之路。道。道。良久。云、若道不得、永沈苦海。珍
重。

At a convocation in the dharma hall, the Master [Yaoshan Liyu] said, "Mountains, rivers, and the whole earth, the **sun, moon, and stars**, are born together with you senior seats; the buddhas of the three times study together with you senior seats; the sacred teachings of the three baskets are simultaneous with you senior seats. Do you believe it? If you believe it, the iron bull of Shan vomits up heaven and earth. But even so, if we're obstructed by the dharma body, we can't turn our bodies. We know there's a road out of the body. What is the senior seats' road out of the body? Speak! Speak!"

After a while, he said, "If you can't speak, you'll be sunk forever in the sea of suffering. Take care of yourselves."

A kōan known as "Fengxue's Iron Bull" (*Fūketsu tetsugyū* 風穴鐵牛), featuring Chan Master Fengxue Yanzhao 風穴延沼 (896–973), is case 38 in the *Blue Cliff Record* (*Biyan lu* 碧巖錄, T.2003.48:175c9-24) and case 29 in the *Congrong Hermitage Record* (*Congrong lu* 從容錄, T.2004.48:246a17-28), which reads as follows:

舉。風穴在郢州衙內、上堂云、祖師心印狀似鐵牛之機。去即印住。
住即印破。只如不去不住。印即是、不印即是。時有盧陂長老出問
云、某甲有鐵牛之機。請師不搭印。穴云、慣釣鯨鯢澄巨浸、却嗟蛙
步驟泥沙。陂佇思。穴喝云、長老何不進語。陂擬議。穴打一拂子
云、還記得話頭麼。試舉看。陂擬開口、穴又打一拂子。牧主云、佛
法與王法一般。穴云、見箇什麼。牧云、當斷不斷返招其亂。穴便下
座。

Raised:

When Fengxue was residing in the government office of Yingzhou prefecture, at a convocation in the dharma hall, he said, "The mind seal of the ancestral masters is like the working of the iron bull. When removed, the impression remains. When left in place, the impression is ruined. But suppose it is neither removed nor left in place: is sealing then right, or not right?"

412 DŌGEN'S *SHŌBŌGENZŌ* VOLUME VIII

At the time, there was one Elder Lu Pi who came forward and said, "I have the working of the iron bull. Please, Reverend, do not impress the seal."

[Feng]xue said, "Accustomed to angling for big fish on a limpid sea, I regret to find instead a frog crawling in the muddy sand."

[Lu] Pi paused to think [what to say].

[Feng]xue shouted and said, "Elder, why don't you speak further?"

[Lu] Pi hesitated.

[Feng]xue hit him once with his **whisk** and said, "Can you remember my saying? See if you can quote it."

[Lu] Pi was about to open his mouth when [Feng]xue hit him once again with the whisk.

The Governor said, "The law of the Buddha and the law of the king are the same."

[Feng]xue said, "What have you seen?"

The Governor said, "When what should be cut off is not cut off, that allows for uprisings [i.e., disturbances, both spiritual and political].

[Feng]xue thereupon got down from the [high] seat [in the dharma hall].

The iron bull appears regularly in the trope, "like a mosquito on an iron bull" (*nyo bunsu jō tetsugyū* 如蚊子上鐵牛), which likens the Zen student's attempt to attain awakening by intellectual means to a mosquito trying to bite and draw nourishment from the impenetrable hide of an animal that has no blood. The meaning of "futility" or "impossibility" is clear from the comment made by Xiangshan Yunliang 香山蘊良 (dates unknown) on the story that, when Mazu Daoyi 馬祖道一 (709–788) entered the buddha hall, his disciple Baizhang Huaihai 百丈懷海 (720–814) rolled up the prostration mat (*haiseki* 拜席) on which Mazu, as abbot, was to make bows; the comment is found in the *Jianzhong Jingguo Era Continued Record of the Flame* (*Jianzhong jingguo xudeng lu* 建中靖國續燈錄, ZZ.136:120b11-13):

明州香山蘊良禪師。問、馬祖陞堂、百丈捲席、意旨如何。師云、蚊子上鐵牛。僧曰、畢竟如何。師云、烏龜倒上樹。

Chan Master Yunliang of Xiangshan in Minzhou was asked, "Mazu ascended to the hall, and Baizhang rolled up the mat: what does it mean?"

The Master said, "A mosquito on an iron bull."

The monk said, "So, after all, what does it mean?"

The Master said, "A turtle climbing backward up a tree."

In this case, Yunliang was probably commenting on the futility of the monk's question, "What does it mean?" rather than the futility of Baizhang's action of rolling up the prostration mat. All Buddhist monks would have

*Supplementary notes to the translation* 413

understood that, in a ritual setting where the abbot was supposed to lead the congregation in making prostrations to the buddha enshrined on the altar (probably Śākyamuni), what Baizhang did was an extremely inappropriate action. What the monk was asking was what Baizhang might have meant by that symbolic action. One possible interpretation is that he was signalling Mazu's lack of qualifications to serve as abbot, a gesture that would surely have been ironic in intent, given that Mazu's was his own revered teacher and an indisputably great Chan master. Another possibility is that Baizhang was signalling Mazu's spiritual superiority to the Buddha, which would make it inappropriate for him to humble himself in prostrations.

**it would surely take ten thousand years** (*jikishu bannen* 直須萬年): From a saying by Shishuang Chingzhu 石霜慶諸 (807-888) found in the *Jingde Era Record of the Transmission of the Flame* (*Jingde chuandeng lu* 景德傳燈錄, T.2076.51:284c26):

> 許州全明上坐先問石霜、一毫穿衆穴時如何。石霜云、直須萬年後。

Senior Seat Quanming of Xuzhou first asked Shishuang, "What about when 'a single hair pierces multiple holes'?"

Shishuang said, "It would surely take ten thousand years."

This conversation is also recorded in Dōgen's *Shōbōgenzō* in Chinese script (*shinji Shōbōgenzō* 眞字正法眼藏, DZZ.5:166-188, case 85):

> 石霜、因許州全明上座問、一毫穿衆穴時如何。師曰、直須萬年後。曰、萬年後如何。師曰、登科任汝登科、拔萃任汝拔萃。明次問径山諲。諲曰、光靴任汝光靴、結果任汝結果。

Shishuang was once asked by Senior Seat Quanming of Xuzhou, "What about when 'a single hair pierces multiple holes'?"

The Master [Shishuang] said, "It would surely take ten thousand years."

[Quanming] said, "What about after ten thousand years?"

The Master said, "Passing the examinations is up to your passing the examinations; excelling at them is up to your excelling at them."

[Quan] Ming subsequently asked Yin of Jingshan.

Yin said, "Shiny shoes are up to your shiny shoes; the fruit forming is up to your fruit forming."

A version found in the kōan collection entitled *Comments on the "Collection of Gems of Wisdom from All Quarters"* (*Nian bafang zhuyu ji* 拈八方珠玉集, ZZ.119:277b15-278a3; X.1310.67:671b19-c1) attributes the saying "it would surely take ten thousand years" to Jingshan Hongyin 徑山洪諲 (d. 901):

# 414 DŌGEN'S *SHŌBŌGENZŌ* VOLUME VIII

舉。潭州石霜和尚、僧問云、一毫穿衆穴時如何。霜云、直須老去。
僧云、老後如何。霜云、登科任你登科。拔萃任你拔萃。又問、如何
是長。霜云、不屈曲。僧云、如何是短。霜云、雙陸盆邊不喝彩。其
僧又問徑山、一毫穿衆穴時如何。山云、直須萬年去。僧云、萬年後
如何。山云、光靴任你光靴、結裹任你結裹。又問、如何是長。山
云、千聖不能量。僧云、如何是短。山云、蟭螟眼裏著不滿。

Raised.

Reverend Shishuang of Tanzhou was asked by a monk, "What about when 'a single hair pierces multiple holes'?"

[Shi] Shuang said, "It would surely take until one is elderly."

The monk said, "What about after one is elderly?"

Shuang said, "Passing the examination depends on your passing the examinations; excelling at them is up to your excelling at them."

The monk also asked, "What about 'long'?"

Shuang said, "It is not twisted."

The monk said, "What about 'short'?"

Shuang said, "The sides of a basin between two hills do not cheer."

That monk also asked Jingshan, "What about when 'a single hair pierces multiple holes'?"

[Jing] Shan said, "It would surely take ten thousand years."

The monk said, "What about after thousand years?"

Shan said, "Shiny shoes are up to your shiny shoes; the fruit forming is up to your fruit forming."

The monk also asked, "What about 'long'?"

Shan said, "A thousand sages cannot measure it."

The monk said, "What about 'short'?"

Shan said, "It doesn't fill the eye of a mite."

The saying "a single hair pierces multiple holes" (*ichigō sen shuketsu* 一毫穿衆穴) may have been in use before it was raised as a kōan by Senior Seat Quanming and commented on by Shishuang. It appears in Zen literature, in any case, independently of the comment, "It would surely take ten thousand years." The *Jianzhong Jingguo Era Continued Record of the Flame* (*Jianzhong jingguo xudeng lu* 建中靖國續燈錄, ZZ.136:404b14-16), for example, records a verse that Chan Master Zuxin Baojue 祖心寶覺 (1025-11) wrote on the "great treasury of sūtras" (*daizōkyō* 大藏經):

一毫穿衆穴、衆穴一毫收。雲自帝鄉去、水歸江漢流。

A single hair pierces multiple holes;

Multiple holes are included in a single hair.

Clouds depart from the imperial capital;

Water returns to the [Yangzi] River, flowing through the Han [River, the watershed of which is the Han Chinese homeland].

What "a single hair pierces multiple holes" is supposed to mean in Zen discourse is unclear. The verb *sen* 穿, rendered here as "pierce," may also be translated as "open up" or "dig." Because the tip of a very fine "hair" (*gō* 毫) is scarcely a suitable tool for excavating anything, the saying may refer to an accomplishment that is nigh on impossible, or, as Shishuang says, something that "would surely take ten thousand years."

**jewel in the robe** (*eju* 衣珠): A reference to a parable found in chapter 8 of the *Lotus Sūtra* (*Miaofa lianhua* jing 妙法蓮華經, T.262.9:29a5-16), in which an "intimate friend" sews a "precious jewel" (*hōju* 寶珠) into his inebriated friend's robe prior to the latter's departure on a journey, so that he will not lack resources. The traveler, however, does not know he carries the jewel in his robe and thus becomes destitute in foreign lands. Later the two chance to meet again, and the "intimate friend" reveals the existence of the jewel.

> 譬如有人至親友家、醉酒而臥。是時親友官事當行、以無價寶珠繫其衣裏、與之而去。其人醉臥、都不覺知。起已遊行、到於他國。爲衣食故、勤力求索、甚大艱難。若少有所得、便以爲足。於後親友會遇見之、而作是言、咄哉丈夫、何爲衣食乃至如是。我昔欲令汝得安樂、五欲自恣、於某年日月、以無價寶珠繫汝衣裏。今故現在、而汝不知。勤苦憂惱、以求自活、甚爲癡也。汝今可以此寶貿易所須、常可如意，無所乏短。佛亦如是。

Suppose there is a man who goes to an intimate friend's house, becomes drunk on alcohol, and falls asleep. At the time, the intimate friend has to attend to official business, so he takes a priceless jewel, sews it into the lining of the man's robe as a gift, and then departs. Because the man is in a drunken sleep, he perceives and knows nothing of this. After he gets up, he sets out on a journey and arrives in a foreign land. He searches vigorously to find clothing and food but suffers great difficulties; and, if what he receives is scanty, he has to be satisfied with that. Later, the intimate friend happens to meet him, and this is what he says: "My good man, this is ridiculous! Why do you go to these lengths for clothing and food? Long ago I wanted to ensure that you would gain ease and joy, and indulge the five desires. On such-and–such a year, month, and day, I sewed a priceless jewel into the lining of your robe. It must be there now, but you don't know about it. It is absurd in the extreme that you have worked so hard, suffering and miserable, seeking a livelihood. You should now take the jewel and exchange it for whatever you need, so that things will always go as you wish, and you will never be in want of anything." The Buddha is also like this [intimate friend].

416    DŌGEN'S *SHŌBŌGENZŌ* VOLUME VIII

In the Sūtra, the "jewel in the robe" represents the fact that, without realizing it, the arhats are actually on the bodhisattva path leading to buddhahood; in later usage, it can represent the innate buddha nature, which all living beings possess but do not avail themselves of because they are not aware of it. The inebriated man of this parable is also referred to in Zen literature as the "impoverished guest" (*hinkyaku* 貧客).

**jewel in the topknot** (*keiju* 髻珠): In Indian Buddhist literature, the "bright jewel in the topknot" (*keichū myōju* 髻中明珠) is sometimes treated as the insignia of kingship, or what in Western societies is called "the crown." The *Āgama of Combined Discourses* (*Za ahan jing* 雜阿含經; S. *Saṃyuktāgama*, T.99.2:177c27-29), for example, contains the following passage:

即捨位與子、以髻中明珠冠其子首、集諸大臣，香水灌頂。

[The king] then relinquished his position to his son: he took the bright jewel in his topknot and capped his son with it, gathering his grand ministers and consecrating his [son's] head with perfumed water.

The "jewel in the topknot," by extension, also came to refer to the highest or finest example of anything, as in the English expression "crowning achievement." That is the meaning of the metaphor found in chapter 14 of the *Lotus Sūtra* (*Miaofa lianhua jing* 妙法蓮華經, T.262.9:38c19-39a17), where the Buddha's preaching of the sūtra itself (saving the best for last) is compared to a wheel-turning king (*tenrin'ō* 轉輪王; S. *cakravartin*) who does not readily give away the "bright jewel in his topknot" as a reward for his troops's victory in battle but finally does bestow it on one outstanding hero:

文殊師利、是法華經、於無量國中、乃至名字不可得聞、何況得見受持讀誦。文殊師利、譬如強力轉輪聖王、欲以威勢降伏諸國、而諸小王不順其命、時轉輪王起種種兵而往討罰。王見兵衆戰有功者、即大歡喜、隨功賞賜、或與田宅、聚落、城邑。或與衣服、嚴身之具。或與種種珍寶、金、銀、琉璃、車渠、馬腦、珊瑚、虎珀、象馬車乘、奴婢人民。唯髻中明珠、不以與之。所以者何。獨王頂上有此一珠、若以與之、王諸眷屬必大驚怪。文殊師利、如來亦復如是、以禪定智慧力得法國土、王於三界、而諸魔王不肯順伏。如來賢聖諸將與之共戰，其有功者、心亦歡喜，於四衆中爲説諸經，令其心悅，賜以禪定、解脱、無漏根力、諸法之財，又復賜與涅槃之城、言得滅度，引導其心、令皆歡喜，而不爲説是法華經。文殊師利、如轉輪王、見諸兵衆有大功者、心甚歡喜、以此難信之珠、久在髻中不妄與人、而今與之。如來亦復如是。。。。文殊師利、此法華經、是諸如來第一之説、於諸説中最爲甚深，末後賜與，如彼強力之王久護明珠，今乃與之。

Mañjuśrī, as for this *Lotus Sūtra*, throughout innumerable countries, people cannot even hear its name, much less be able to see, receive, uphold, read, or recite it.

Mañjuśrī, suppose, for example, that there is a strong wheel-turning king who wants to use his power to dominate other countries, but the lesser kings [of those lands] do not follow his commands. At that time, the wheel-turning king assembles troops of all sorts who go to make them submit. If the king sees men in his army who are effective in battle, he is greatly pleased and bestows awards that correspond to their deeds. He may give land for farming and housing, or villages, or cities. Or he may give clothing and accessories to adorn the body. Or he may give all kinds of rare gems, gold, silver, beryl, cornelian, agate, coral, or amber; or elephants, horses, carts, or vehicles; or male and female servants, or common people. The only thing he does not give to them is the bright jewel in his topknot. Why? Because only on the head of the king is this jewel found. Should he give it away, the attendants of the king would inevitably be alarmed and bewildered.

Mañjuśrī, the Tathāgata is also like this. Using the strength of dhyāna concentration and wisdom he gains dharma lands and becomes king in the **three realms**, but the Māra King does not agree to submit. Leaders among the Tathāgata's worthies and sages engage him [Māra] in battle; and, when some of those prove effective, his [the Tathāgata's] mind is also pleased. To the fourfold assembly he preaches various sūtras, making their minds happy. He bestows on them dhyāna concentration, liberation, the power of uncontaminated faculties, and a wealth of teachings. Furthermore, he bestows on them the citadel of nirvāṇa, speaks to them about attaining cessation, guides their minds, and makes all of them joyful; but he does not preach this *Lotus Sūtra* for them.

Mañjuśrī, if the wheel-turning king sees that there is in his army a man who is greatly effective, his mind is extremely joyful. He takes this unbelievably fine jewel, which has long been in his topknot, and which he has never recklessly given to any person and gives now to that man. The Tathāgata is also like this....

Mañjuśrī, this *Lotus Sūtra* is the number-one preaching of the tathāgatas; among all the preachings it is the most profound. That it is bestowed at the very end is like that powerful king who long guarded the bright pearl, and now finally gave it.

A Song-dynasty text entitled *Explanation of Phrases from the Lotus Sūtra* (*Lianhua jing jujie* 法華經句解) refers to the "bright jewel in the topknot" that the king does not readily give away as "**one bright pearl**" (*ikka myōju* 一顆明珠, ZZ.48:128a15-16; X.604.30:564b22-23). Dōgen uses the latter expression as the title of a chapter in *Shōbōgenzō*.

**just sit** (*shikan taza* 祇管打坐; also written 只管打坐): An admonition deriving from a Chinese saying that Dōgen attributes to his master, Tiantong Rujing 天童如淨 (1162-1227), in several different contexts. In the *Extensive Record of Reverend Dōgen* (*Dōgen oshō kōroku* 道元和尚廣錄, DZZ.4:18, no. 432), for example, we find:

> 上堂。佛佛祖祖家風、坐禪辦道也。先師天童云、跏趺坐乃古佛法也。參禪者身心脫落也。不要燒香・禮拜・念佛・修懺・看經、祇管打坐始得。

At a convocation in the dharma hall, [Dōgen said,] "The house style of the **buddhas and ancestors** is to pursue the way in seated meditation. My former master, Tiantong, said, 'Cross-legged sitting is indeed the method of the **old buddhas**. Studying Chan is **body and mind sloughed off**. There is no need to burn incense, make bows, recollect the buddha, practice repentance, or read the sūtras. You'll only get it when you just sit.'"

For translations of two nearly identical sayings attributed to Rujing by Dōgen in the latter's *Record of the Baoqing Era* (*Hōkyō ki* 寶慶記, DZZ.7:18-20) and his "Continuous Practice, Part 2" ("Shōbōgenzō gyōji ge" 正法眼藏行持下, DZZ.1:198), see "**body and mind sloughed off**." Variations of the Chinese saying also appear in three other contexts: in the *Extensive Record of Reverend Dōgen* (*Dōgen oshō kōroku* 道元和尚廣錄, DZZ.4:240, case 85), where Rujing's saying is held up as a kōan to which Dōgen attaches a verse comment; in the "Sūtras of the Buddhas" ("Shōbōgenzō bukkyō" 正法眼藏佛經, DZZ.2:17-18); and in "The King of Samādhis Samādhi" ("Shōbōgenzō zanmai ō zanmai" 正法眼藏三昧王三昧, DZZ.2:178). The latter two are analyzed below.

A seventh occurrence of Rujing's saying, albeit one that is not attributed to him, appears in Japanese translation in Dōgen's "Talk on Pursuing the Way" ("Bendō wa" 辨道話, DZZ.2:462):

> 參見知識のはじめより、さらに燒香・禮拜・念佛・修懺・看經をもちいず、ただし打坐して身心脫落することをえよ。

From the start of your consultation with a wise friend, without further need of burning incense, making bows, recollecting the buddha, practicing repentance or reading sūtras, just sit and attain the sloughing off of body and mind.

Dōgen's Japanese translation here, using a construction that accurately reflects the grammar of the original Chinese, renders Rujing's admonition to "just sit" (*qiguan dazuo* 祇管打坐, J. *shikan taza*) with the adverb "just" (*tadashi* ただし) and the verb "sit" (*taza shite* 打坐して). The function of the adverb "just" is to exclude practices other than sitting in meditation, not to exclude any particular approach to seated meditation, such as one that

# Supplementary notes to the translation 419

might involve "contemplating the saying" (*kan watō* 看話頭) of an ancestral master.

Given the fact that the practices of burning incense (*shōkō* 燒香), making bows (*raihai* 禮拜), recollecting the buddha (*nenbutsu* 念佛), practicing repentance (*shusan* 修懺), and sūtra reading (*kankin* 看經) were an integral part of the etiquette and training at all major Buddhist monasteries in Song-dynasty China, including the Tiantong Monastery where Rujing served as abbot for a couple of years, we may wonder how literally he expected his disciples to take his admonition to "just sit." It is certain, in any case, that Dōgen did not understand his teacher to be proscribing the aforementioned practices in any literal sense, for he actively promoted all of them in his *Shōbōgenzō*. Dōgen brought up Rujing's dictum frequently, but when he did so it was not as any kind of practical advice, but rather as a kōan: a profound yet abstruse saying of an ancestral master that is hard to understand and needs to be meditated on.

Dōgen's citation and discussion of Rujing's saying in his "Sūtras of the Buddhas" ("Shōbōgenzō bukkyō" 正法眼藏佛經, DZZ.2:17-18) makes a good case in point:

> 先師尋常道、我箇裏、不用燒香・禮拜・念佛・修懺・看經、祇管打坐、辦道功夫、身心脱落。かくのとくの道取、あきらむるともがら、まれなり。ゆゑはいかん。看經をよんで看經とすれば、觸す、よんで看經とせざれば、そむく。不得有語、不得無語、速道速道。この道理、參學すべし、この宗旨あるゆえに、古人云、看經須具看經眼。まさにしるべし、古今にもし經なくば、かくのごときの道取あるべらず。脱落の看經あり。不用の看經あること、參學すべきなり。

My former master always said, "Here, there is no need to burn incense, make bows, recollect the buddha, practice repentance, or read the sūtras; just sitting, making concentrated effort to pursue the way, body and mind are sloughed off." Those who clarify such words are rare. Why? If we take "read the sūtras" as "read the sūtras," we violate them; if we take them not as "read the sūtras," we oppose them. "You can't say anything; you can't say nothing. Speak! Speak!" We should study this principle. Because of this essential point, a person of old said, "To read the sūtras, you must possess the eye for reading the sūtras." We should realize that, if there were no sūtras in past and present, there would be no such words. We should study that there is a reading of the sūtras that is "**sloughed off**"; there is a reading of the sūtras that is "no need."

Dōgen explicitly states here that Rujing's dictum, "Just sit, etc." is a saying that few people can comprehend, and that it should be rigorously investigated (*sangaku* 參學). In short, he urges contemplation (*kan* 看) of this saying (*wa* 話), up to the point when the practitioner can understand it and "speak quickly" (*hayaku iu* 速道) to demonstrate that understanding.

420    DŌGEN'S *SHŌBŌGENZŌ* VOLUME VIII

In this commentary, Dōgen makes it clear that he does not take Rujing's admonition to "make no use" (*fuyō* 不用) of sūtra reading as a literal rejection of that practice but rather as advice concerning the proper outlook, or "**eye**," with which sūtras should be read. "Sloughed off sūtra reading" (*datsuraku no kankin* 脱落の看經), presumably, takes place when one understands the words but "makes no use" of them — i.e., does not reify the names and concepts found in them and cling to those as really existing things. For Dōgen, it would seem, "just sit" was actually a name for the proper state of non-attachment — the state of "body and mind sloughed off" (*shinjin datsuraku* 身心脱落) — in which one should engage in sūtra reading and all other practices.

In "The King of Samādhis Samādhi" ("Shōbōgenzō zanmai ō zanmai" 正法眼藏三昧王三昧, DZZ.2:178), we read:

先師古佛云、參禪者、身心脱落也、祇管打坐始得。不要燒香・禮拜・念佛・修懺・看經。あきらかに佛祖の眼睛を挟出しきたり、佛祖の眼睛裏に打坐すること、四五百年よりこのかたは、ただ先師ひとりなり、震旦國に齊肩すくなし。打坐の佛法なること、佛法は打坐なることをあきらめたる、まれなり。たとひ打坐を佛法と體解すといふとも、打坐を打坐としれる、いまだあらず。いはんや佛法を佛法と保任するあらんや。しかあれべすなはち、心の打坐あり、身の打坐とおなじからず。身の打坐あり、心の打坐とおなじからず。身心脱落の打坐あり、身心脱落の打坐とおなじからず。既得恁麼ならん、佛祖の行解相應なり。この念想觀を保任すべし。この心意識を參究すべし。

My former master [Rujing], the **Old Buddha**, said, "Studying Chan is body and mind sloughed off. You'll only get it when you just sit; you don't need to burn incense, make bows, recollect the buddha, practice repentance, or read the sūtras."

For the last four or five hundred years, clearly my former master is the only one who has plucked out the **eye** of the buddhas and ancestors, who sits within the eye of the buddhas and ancestors. There are few of equal stature in the Land of Cīnasthāna. It is rare to have clarified that sitting is the buddha dharma, that the buddha dharma is sitting. Even if [some] realize sitting as the buddha dharma, they have not understood sitting as sitting — let alone maintained the buddha dharma as the buddha dharma.

This being the case, there is the sitting of the mind, which is not the same as the sitting of the body. There is the sitting of the body, which is not the same as the sitting of the mind. There is the sitting of "body and mind sloughed off," which is not the same as the sitting of "body and mind sloughed off." To have got such is the accordance of practice and understanding of the buddhas and ancestors. We should maintain this thought,

*Supplementary notes to the translation*          421

idea, and perception; we should investigate this mind, mentation, and consciousness.

In this commentary, Dōgen indicates that "sitting" (*taza* 打坐) is an expression that has a number of different meanings. What he calls the "sitting of the body" (*mi no taza* 身の打坐), presumably, is the physical posture of zazen. In contrast to that, we may infer, "mental sitting" (*kokoro no taza* 心の打坐) is a kind of concentration or state of mind that can be cultivated in any posture, whatever the practitioner is doing. When "body and mind are sloughed off" (*shinjin datsuraku* 身心脱落), the practitioner is no longer attached to any physical or mental phenomena, and that liberated, or awakened, state is also referred to — metaphorically, of course — as "sitting" (*taza* 打坐). This "sitting of the body and mind sloughed off" (*shinjin datsuraku no taza* 身心脱落の打坐), however, is "not the same" (*onajikarazu* おなじからず) as the identically named "sitting of the body and mind sloughed off" (*shinjin datsuraku no taza* 身心脱落の打坐); for, in the latter and highest kind of "sitting," all such designations are cast aside as ultimately false. In this context, therefore, it would seem that Dōgen does not take Rujing's "just sit" literally as an admonition to dedicate oneself exclusively to the practice of zazen but interprets it rather as advice to "just attain awakening." Rujing's dictum, interpreted in this manner, could be restated as follows: "In studying Zen, the essential thing is awakening, not dedication to any particular practices such as burning incense, making prostrations, recollecting buddhas, practicing repentances, or reading sūtras." Indeed, insofar as Dōgen equates the highest form of "sitting" (*taza* 打坐) with liberation itself, which transcends any and all practices, he might just as well have added meditation — i.e. physical (*shin* 身) and mental (*shin* 心) "sitting" (*taza* 打坐) — to the list of conventional Buddhist practices that Rujing deemed "unnecessary" (*fuyō* 不用).

Dōgen almost never treats the compound *shikan taza* 祇管打坐 as a verbal noun, which is to say, as the name of a particular practice that might be translated "just sitting" in English. One exception is found in "The Old Mirror" ("Shōbōgenzō kokyō" 正法眼藏古鏡, DZZ.1:238):

> あるとき馬祖の菴にいたるに、馬祖侍立す。南嶽とふ、なんぢ近日作什麼。馬祖いはく、近日道一祇管打坐するのみなり。

One time, when Nanyue went to Mazu's hermitage, Mazu stood to attend him. Nanyue asked, "What are you doing these days?"
Mazu said, "These days, Daoyi just sits."

The Japanese here, *Dōitsu shikan taza suru nomi* 道一祇管打坐するのみ, could be translated "Daoyi only does just sitting." The grammar suggests, in other words, that "just sitting" (*shikan taza* 祇管打坐) is a discrete practice that Mazu Daoyi "engages in exclusively" (*suru nomi* するのみ). Another instance in which Dōgen seems to treat *shikan taza* as a noun is in his "Extensive Study" ("Shōbōgenzō henzan" 正法眼藏遍參, DZZ.2:117):

遍參は、ただ祇管打坐、身心脱落なり。

Extensive study is simply "just sitting" with "body and mind sloughed off."

If Dōgen had intended the word "just" (*shikan* 祇管) to serve as an adverb here, he could have said "extensive study is to simply 'just sit'" (*henzan wa, tada shikan ni taza nari* 偏參は、ただ祇管に打坐なり).

These two passages open the door to the idea, widely promoted in the later tradition, that "just sitting" was a distinctive mode of seated meditation practice taught by Dōgen. If that were the case, however, we might also expect to find "just sitting" featured prominently in his meditation manuals, which include: the "Principles of Zazen" ("Shōbōgenzō zazen gi" 正法眼藏坐禪儀, DZZ.1:100-102) and "Needle of Seated Meditation" ("Shōbōgenzō zazen shin" 正法眼藏坐禪箴, DZZ.1:103-113); two recensions of *Universally Recommended Instructions for Zazen* (*Fukan zazengi* 普勸坐禪儀, DZZ.5:4-12); and the section of *Procedures for Cultivating the Way* (*Bendōhō* 辨道法, DZZ.6:38-40) in which Dōgen explains procedures for zazen. The words *shikan taza*, however, do not appear in any of those texts.

In chapter 50 of his *Record of the Transmission of Illumination* (*Denkōroku* 傳光録, p. 510), Keizan Jōkin 瑩山紹瑾 (1264-1325) says that when Dōgen's teacher Rujing 如淨 (1162–1227) was a monk in training, "all he did was just sitting" (*shikan taza suru nomi nari* 只管打坐するのみなり). Keizan does not spell out very clearly what the practice of "just sitting" entails, but we do get a hint from his *Pointers for Regulating the Mind in Seated Meditation* (*Zazen yōjin ki* 坐禪用心記; T.2586.82:413b8-10), where he says:

念誓斷煩悩、誓證菩提。只管打坐、一切不爲。是參禪要術也。

Recall your vows to eliminate mental afflictions and vows to authenticate bodhi. Just sit, with no purpose whatsoever. This is the essential technique for studying Zen.

In the subsequent Sōtō Zen tradition, "just sitting" came to be explained as seated meditation that is engaged in for its own sake, with "nothing to be gained" (*mushotoku* 無所得) — i.e., without any intention of gaining awakening — and without any object of contemplation other than the mind-ground itself. Seated meditation in modern Sōtō Zen is not coupled with the contemplation of a kōan, as it is in Rinzai Zen. The practice of "just sitting" is said to be based on the doctrine of the "identity of **practice and realization**" (*shushō ittō* 修證一等), according to which, "practice" (*shugyō* 修行) is not a means of attaining awakening, but rather a way of "attesting to" (*shō* 證) the buddha-nature that is innate in all living beings.

*Supplementary notes to the translation*        423

**karmic consciousness** (*gosshiki* 業識; also read *gōshiki*): Synonymous with "consciousness that accords with karma" (*zuigosshiki* 隨業識; also read *zuigōshiki*). Consciousness that arises as a result of one's prior deeds (karma) or consciousness that results in future actions (karma) and states of being.

In the Yogācāra school of Buddhist philosophy with its doctrine of "consciousness only" (*yuishiki* 唯識), "karmic consciousness" is a technical term. Basically, it refers to transformations that take place in the eighth consciousness, or "storehouse-consciousness" (*araya shiki* 阿賴耶識; S. *ālaya-vijñāna*), in accord with karmic conditions. Those transformations are the diverse phenomena of ordinary experience that manifest themselves through the first six consciousnesses — visual, auditory, olfactory, gustatory, physical (touch), and mental (ideas) — and are filtered through the lens of the seventh consciousness, which is "self-consciousness" (*manashiki* 末那識; S. *kliṣṭa-manas*). Such deluded mental activity is said to continue until one has a kind of direct insight, or awakening, that reveals all phenomena to be "only mind" (*yui shin* 唯心). The term "karmic consciousness" appears, for example, in a work attributed to Maitreya (the celestial bodhisattva said to have instructed Asaṅga in Yogācāra philosophy) entitled *Treatise on the Stages of Yoga Practitioners* (*Yuqie shidi lun* 瑜伽師地論, T.1579.30:321a17-23):

云何緣起體。若略説由三種相建立緣起。謂從前際中際生、從中際後際生、中際生已、若趣流轉、若趣清淨究竟。云何從前際中際生、中際生已、復趣流轉。謂如有一不了前際無明所攝。無明爲緣、於福非福及與不動身語意業。若作若增長、由此隨業識、乃至命終流轉不絶。

[Question:] What are the karmic conditions that give rise to the body? [Answer] To give an explanation in brief, there are three kinds of causal attributes that underlie karmic conditioning. Those are: things that arise in the present in accordance with past [karma]; things that arise in the future in accordance with present [karma]; and things that arise in the present but stop there, whether one is destined for rebirth in saṃsāra or destined for ultimate purity.

[Question:] How, when things arise in the present due to past [karma], but stop after arising in the present, can there still be rebirth in saṃsāra?

[Answer] Because there is still a bit of incomprehension, which is ignorance stored up from the past. With ignorance as a condition, one engages in actions of body, speech, and mind that are good, bad, or morally neutral. Whether they have just been generated or already reached fruition, these [actions] give rise to karmic consciousness, which extends until the end of the present life and throughout rebirth in saṃsāra, with no break.

As this passage shows, "karmic consciousness" in the Yogācāra system is a device for explaining, in the absence of an underlying "self" (*ga* 我; S. *ātman*), the continuity of karmic conditioning over multiple lifetimes.

The *Mahāyāna Awakening of Faith* (*Dasheng qixin lun* 大乘起信論, T.1666.32:577b6-7), an influential text that claims to be authored by Aśvaghoṣa and translated from Sanskrit but was probably compiled in China, explains that "karmic consciousness" is one of five different names for the "storehouse-consciousness" (*ariya shiki* 阿梨耶識; S. *ālaya-vijñāna*), which contains the seeds of karmic recompense in its aspect of "arising and ceasing" (*shōmetsu* 生滅):

一者名爲業識、謂無明力不覺心動故。

The first name is "karmic consciousness," because through the power of ignorance the unawakened mind is activated [in the storehouse-consciousness].

In the literature of Zen, the expression "karmic consciousness," like many other Buddhist technical terms, is used in a rather loose way, with little of the philosophical precision that informs its discussion in contexts such as the *Treatise on the Stages of Yoga Practitioners* and the *Mahāyāna Awakening of Faith*. Nevertheless, the gist remains. For example, the topic is raised by Weishan Lingyou 潙山靈祐 (771–853) — a.k.a. Daweishan 大潙山 — in a conversation with his student Yangshan Huiji 仰山慧寂 (803–887) that is found in several Chinese sources. Dōgen records one version in his *Shōbōgenzō* in Chinese script (*shinji Shōbōgenzō* 眞字正法眼藏, DZZ.5:196, case 130):

大潙問仰山、忽有人問、一切衆生、但有業識、茫茫無本可據。子作麼生驗。仰曰、慧寂有驗處。時有僧面前過。寂召曰、闍梨。僧廻頭。寂云、和尚、這箇便是業識、茫茫無本可據。師云、此是獅子一滴乳、迸散六斛驢乳。

Dawei asked Yangshan, "What if someone asks, 'In all living beings, the karmic consciousness is vague and confused, without a basis to rely on.' How would you test it?"

Yang[shan] said, "Huiji [i.e., I] has a way to test it."

At that moment, a monk passed in front of them. [Hui] Ji called him, saying, "Ācārya."

The monk turned his head. Ji said [to Dawei], "Reverend, this [i.e., the monk's turning his head when called] is 'the karmic consciousness is vague and confused, without a basis to rely on.'"

The Master [Dawei] said, "Now, this is scattering a drop of lion's milk into six measures of donkey milk."

Here, Yangshan Huiji's point seems to be that the working of deluded karmic consciousness is not really "vague and confused" (*mōmō* 茫茫), but rather a process of stimulus and automatic response within a causal nexus.

The *Discourse Record of Chan Master Yuanwu Foguo* (*Yuanwu Foguo chanshi yulu* 圓悟佛果禪師語錄,T.1997.47:744b3-8), to cite another example, contains the following discussion between Yuanwu Keqin 圜悟克勤 (1063-1135) and a monk who kept pestering him with questions at a convocation in the dharma hall:

進云、雲巖道、和尚有也未、又作麼生。師云、挖泥涉水兩三重。進云、未審雲巖會了恁麼道、不會了恁麼道。師云、與闍黎一般。進云、忽有人問、和尚併却咽喉唇吻、作麼生道。師云、合取。進云、恁麼則與雲巖一般去也。師云、直截根源人不識。忙忙業識幾時休。

[The monk] further asked, "Yunyan said, 'Reverend, do you have it, or not yet?' What about that?"

The Master [Yuanwu] said, "**Dragged through the mud** and crossing over water two or three times."

[The monk] further asked, "I wonder, did Yunyan understand such talk, or not understand such talk?"

The Master said, "Same as you, Ācārya."

[The monk] further asked, "What if someone asks, 'Reverend, have you shut your wind-pipe and mouth?' what would you say?"

The Master said, "Closed up."

[The monk] further asked, "If so, you're the same as Yunyan."

The Master said, "The root source is directly cut, but people have not noticed; the busy, busy karmic consciousness, when will it rest?"

In this case, Yuanwu seems to be using the phrase "busy, busy karmic consciousness" (*bōbō gosshiki* 忙忙業識) as a comment on the deluded mental state of his pesky interlocutor.

In the *Discourse Record of Reverend Rujing* (*Rujing heshang yulu* 如淨和尚語錄, T.2002A.48:131b28-29), to cite a final example, we find the following verse:

無明業識幢、豎起漫天黑。一句不相當、拳頭飛霹靂咦。老婆心切血滴滴。

A banner of ignorant karmic consciousness;
When raised up, all the heavens are black.
A single line will not suffice;
A **fist** and flying thunderbolts.
Grandma's mind is kind; the blood drips.

Here "karmic consciousness" is used in a loose poetic sense, its function compared to the raising of a banner.

426 DŌGEN'S *SHŌBŌGENZŌ* VOLUME VIII

**kill the buddha** (*setsubutsu* 殺佛): An expression best known from words attributed to Linji Yixuan 臨濟義玄 (d. 866) in the *Discourse Record of Chan Master Linji Huizhao of Zhenzhou* (*Zhenzhou Linji Huizhao chanshi yulu* 鎮州 臨濟慧照禪師語錄, T.1985.47:500b21-25):

> 道流、爾欲得如法見解、但莫受人惑。向裏向外、逢著便殺。逢佛殺 佛、逢祖殺祖、逢羅漢殺羅漢、逢父母殺父母、逢親眷殺親眷、始得 解脫、不與物拘、透脫自在。

Followers of the way, if you want a view that accords with the dharma, just don't accept [other] people's confusion. Whatever you encounter, either within or without, kill it. If you meet a buddha, kill the buddha. If you meet an ancestor, kill the ancestor. If you meet an arhat, kill the arhat. If you meet your father and mother, kill your father and mother. If you meet your relatives, kill your relatives. Only then will you attain liberation. If you do not grasp "things," you will pass beyond and be autonomous.

Because Linji was obviously not advocating homicide in any literal sense, a metaphorical interpretation of the verbs "meet" (*hō* 逢) and "kill" (*setsu* 殺; also read *satsu*) is called for here. To "meet" something means to conceive of it and name it. To "kill" it, Linji explains, means to "not grasp" (*fuku* 不 拘) that conceptual entity in a way that reifies it as a really existing "thing" (*motsu* 物). "Killing," in other words, is Linji's colorful way of referring to what in Buddhist technical terminology is called realizing the emptiness (*kū* 空) of all dharmas (*issai hō* 一切法).

**know the music** (*chi in* 知音): Literally, a person who "understands" (*chi* 知) the "tone," or "music" (*in* or *on* 音). Metaphorically, the expression refers to a friend who fully understands one's thoughts and feelings even when one does not articulate them verbally: an "intimate friend," or "soul mate." This meaning comes from a story about Bo Ya 伯牙, a famous lute (*kin* 琴) player, and his friend Zhong Ziqi 鍾子期, which appears in fascicle five ("The Questions of Tang"; Tang wen 湯問) of the *Book of Liezi* (*Liezi* 列子, KR5c0124.005.12a):

> 伯牙善鼓琴、鍾子期善聽。伯牙鼓琴、志在登高山。鍾子期曰、善 哉、峨峨分若泰山。志在流水、鍾子期曰、善哉、洋洋分若江河。伯 牙所念、鍾子期必得之。伯牙游於泰山之陰、卒逢暴雨，止於巖下。 心悲、乃援琴而鼓之。初爲霖雨之操、更造崩山之音。曲每奏、鍾子 期輒窮其趣。伯牙乃舍琴而嘆曰、善哉、善哉、子之聽夫。志想象猶 吾心也。吾於何逃聲哉。

Bo Ya was good at playing the lute, and Zhong Ziqi was a good listener. When Bo Ya played his lute with his mind on climbing high mountains, Zhong Ziqi said: "Excellent! That is lofty, like Mount Tai." When [Bo Ya played] with his mind on flowing waters, Zhong Ziqi said: "Excellent! That is broadly flowing, like the great [Yangtze and Yellow] rivers."

*Supplementary notes to the translation* 427

Whatever was thought by Bo Ya, Zhong Ziqi was sure to get it. When Bo Ya was roaming on the north side of Mount Tai, there was a sudden torrential rainstorm, so he took shelter under a cliff. His mind melancholy, he took up his lute and played it. First, he made the noise of persistent rain, and then he produced the sound of a mountain landslide. Whatever melody he played, Zhong Ziqi easily intuited his meaning. Bo Ya then set aside his lute and said with a sigh: "Excellent! Excellent! How well you listen! What your thoughts imagine is exactly what is in my mind. How can I possibly escape being heard?"

Because Zhong Ziqi could understand whatever Bo Ya was thinking or feeling just by listening to him play his lute, he is said to have "known the music" of Bo Ya.

In the literature of Zen, the expression "know the music" is a metaphor for the intuitive understanding of a Zen master's intended meaning, whether or not the message is couched in language, also known as the "transmission of mind by means of mind" (*ishin denshin* 以心傳心).

**knowledge at birth** (*shōchi* 生知): An expression, also translated herein as "innate knowledge," that derives from the *Analects of Confucius* (*Lunyu* 論語, 16:9; KR.1h0005.008.16b-17a). Dōgen quotes a slight variant in his "The Bhikṣu of the Fourth Dhyāna" ("Shōbōgenzō shizen biku" 正法眼藏四禪比丘, DZZ.2:432-433) and then criticizes it:

論語云、生而知之上、學而知之者次、困而學之又其次也。困而不學、民斯爲下矣。もし生知あらば、無因のとがあり、佛法には無因の説なし。

In the *Analects*, it is said,

> Those born with knowledge are the highest; those who gain knowledge through learning are next; those who learn with difficulty are next; those who do not learn even with difficulty — of the people, these are the lowest.

If you posit innate knowledge, you commit the error of denying causality; in the buddha dharma, there is no teaching that denies causality.

Despite criticizing the concept of "innate knowledge" (*shōchi* 生知) in this way and prefacing his quotation of the *Analects* with the statement that "in the teachings of the buddhas, there is no innate knowledge" (*bukkyō, mu shōchi* 佛教、無生知), Dōgen briefly explains a list of four types of human faculties in his "Great Awakening" ("Shōbōgenzō daigo" 正法眼藏大悟, DZZ.1:92), beginning with 1) "those who know at birth" (*shōchi* 生知); the remaining items are 2) "those who know from study" (*gaku ni chi* 學而知), 3) those with buddha knowledge (*butchisha* 佛知者), and 4) those who know without a teacher (*mushichisha* 無師知者). Because this list does not appear elsewhere in Buddhist literature, it seems to be of Dōgen's own design. In his "Empty Space" ("Shōbōgenzō kokū" 正法眼藏虚空, DZZ.2:211), he gives a slightly different list of four types of wisdom or knowledge: 1) "wisdom gained with a teacher" (*ushichi* 有師智), 2) "wisdom gained without a teacher" (*mushichi* 無師智), 3) "innate knowledge" (*shōchi* 生知), and 4) "knowledge gained from study" (*gaku ni chi* 學而知).

**lacquer bucket** (*shittsū* 漆桶): Synonymous with "black lacquer bucket" (*koku shittsū* 黑漆桶). A metaphor for the darkness of ignorance, or a deluded state of mind. In Dōgen's day, the expression "as black as lacquer" (*kuroki koto urushi no gotoshi* 黒きこと漆の如し) was used in much the same way as the English "pitch black." Some interpreters assume that the material object on which the figure of speech is based is a bucket full of black-tinted liquid lacquer (for use by craftsmen), but it is more likely an empty wooden bucket with an interior sealed by (dry) black lacquer. The *Discourse Record of Reverend Longmen Foyan of Shuzhou* (*Shuzhou Longmen Foyan heshang yulu* 舒州龍門佛眼和尚語錄, *Guzunsu lu* 古尊宿錄, ZZ.118:503a12-13; X.1315.68:175b13-14) contains the following dialogue:

上堂、僧問、劫火洞然、大千俱壞。未審此箇壞不壞。師云、黑漆桶裏黃金色。進云、請師答話。師云、閑言語。

At a convocation in the dharma hall, a monk asked, "When the conflagration at the end of the kalpa rages, the chiliocosm will all be destroyed. I wonder: will *this* be destroyed, or not destroyed?"

The Master said, "Within the black lacquer bucket, the color of gold."

[The monk] went on to say, "Please, Master, answer the question."

The Master said, "Useless chatter."

In this context, the expression "black lacquer bucket" cannot mean a bucket containing black lacquer in liquid form, for there is said to be a glint of gold within it. The force of the metaphor, presumably, is that the buddha nature may be glimpsed even in the midst of delusion, and that it is always present, even after the destruction of the cosmos. In the *Encouragement to Pass Through Chan Barriers* (*Changuan cejin* 禪關策進, T.2024.48:1104a7), Chan master Chushi Fanqi 楚石梵琦 (1296–1370) is quoted as saying:

參狗子無佛性話、忽然打破漆桶。

If you investigate the saying "the dog has no buddha nature," you will suddenly break through the lacquer bucket.

In this case, "breaking through the lacquer bucket" (*taha shittsū* 打破漆桶) is a metaphor for attaining awakening. In other Zen texts, a sudden awakening is referred to as "removing the black lacquer bucket" (*nenkyaku koku shittsū* 拈却黑漆桶) or "the bottom of the bucket dropping out" (*tsūtei datsu* 桶底脱). These expressions suggest that to be deluded is like having

*Supplementary notes to the translation* 429

a bucket covering one's head and obscuring one's vision, or like looking down into a bucket at close range and seeing nothing but black. There are also instances where "lacquer bucket" (or "bucket of lacquer") is used as a derogatory epithet to refer to ignorant monks or deluded people in general, as in the expression "wooden ladles and lacquer buckets" (*mokushaku shittsū* 木杓漆桶).

**lanterns and pillars** (*tōrō rochū* 燈籠露柱): See "**pillars and lanterns**."

**like the well looking at the donkey** (*nyo i so ro* 如井覷驢): The punch line of a dialogue featuring Caoshan Benji 曹山本寂 (840-901) and Senior Seat De 德上座 (dates unknown). The version found in Dōgen's *Shōbōgenzō* in Chinese script (*shinji Shōbōgenzō* 眞字正法眼藏, DZZ.5:194, case 125) reads:

曹山本寂禪師、問德上座云、佛眞法身、猶若虛空。應物現形、如水中月。作麼生説簡應底道理。德云、如驢覷井。師曰、道即太煞道、只道得八九成。德曰、和尚又如何。師曰、如井覷驢。

Chan Master Benji of Caoshan questioned Senior Seat De, saying,

"'The true dharma body of a buddha
Is just like empty space.
It manifests its shape in response to beings,
Like the moon in the water.'
How do you explain the principle of this response?"

De said, "Like a donkey looking in a well."

The Master said, "You talk big talk, but what you say is only **eight or nine tenths complete**."

De said, "Reverend, what would you say?"

The Master said, "Like the well looking at the donkey."

This dialogue is raised as a kōan and commented on in the discourse records of numerous Zen masters, including the *Extensive Record of Chan Master Hongzhi* (*Hongzhi chanshi guanglu* 宏智禪師廣錄; T.2001.48:23b2-9). The verse that Caoshan challenges Senior Seat De to interpret is from the *Sūtra of Golden Light* (*Jin guangming jing* 金光明經; T.663.16:344b3-4); it is also quoted by Dōgen in "The Moon" ("Shōbōgenzō tsuki" 正法眼藏都機).

**like vines relying on a tree** (*nyo tō i ju* 如藤倚樹): A saying attributed to Weishan Lingyou 潙山靈祐 (771-853) and brought up again in a conversation he had with Shushan Kuangren 疏山匡仁 (837-909), which was frequently raised as a topic for comment by later Chan masters. For example, in the biography of Chan Master Chaoxin Haiyin 超信海印禪師 (Song-dynasty, dates unknown) that is included in the *Jianzhong Jingguo Era Continued Record of the Flame* (*Jianzhong jingguo xudeng lu* 建中靖國續燈錄, ZZ.136:381b8-11), we find:

舉。潙山示衆云、有句無句。如藤倚樹。後疎山問云、樹倒藤枯時如
何。山呵呵大笑、歸方丈。

樹倒藤枯伸一問。呵呵大笑有來由。羫羊掛角無尋處。直到如今笑未休。

Raised:

Weishan addressed the assembly saying, "Affirmative statements and
negative statements are like vines relying on a tree."

Later, Shushan asked him, "What about when the tree falls, and the vines
wither?"

[Wei]shan gave a big laugh, "Ha, ha," and returned to the abbot's quarters.

[Chaoxin Haiyin's comment:]

He lays out a single question. The big laugh, "Ha, ha," has a reason. When
mountain goats lock horns, there is nothing to investigate. Until you have
a laugh like this, you will get no rest.

A slightly different version of the kōan is found in Dōgen's *Shōbōgenzō* in
Chinese script (*shinji Shōbōgenzō* 眞字正法眼藏, DZZ.5:208, case 157):

疏山到潙山便問、承師有言、有句無句、如藤倚樹。忽然樹倒藤枯、
句歸何處。潙山呵呵大笑。

When Shushan arrived at Mount Wei, he immediately asked [the abbot,
Weishan Lingyou], "I've heard that the Master has a saying, 'Affirmative
statements and negative statements are like vines relying on a tree.' If the
tree suddenly falls, and the vines wither, where do the statements return?"

Weishan gave a big laugh, "Ha, ha."

For an extended dialogue between Shushan and Weishan that begins with
this conversation, and a comment on it by a Chan master named Mingzhao
明昭 (dates unknown), see "**a blade within the laugh**."

The *Jiatai Era Widespread Record of the Flame* (*Jiatai pudeng lu* 嘉泰普燈
錄, ZZ.137:394b15-16) quotes a comment by Foxing Fatai 佛性法泰 (dates
unknown):

樹倒藤枯意若何。潙山開口笑呵呵。
可怜三尺龍泉劍。喚作陶家壁上梭。

[Case:]

[Someone asked,] What's the meaning of [the saying], "When the tree
falls, the vines wither"?

Weishan laughed out loud, "Ha, ha."

[Comment:]

How sad the three-foot Longquan sword;

To be called a shuttle on the Tao family's wall.

## Supplementary notes to the translation

"The Longquan sword" (*Ryūsen ken* 龍泉劍) refers to a weapon reputed to be of the highest quality, produced in the Longquan 龍泉 ("Dragon Spring") district of what is now Zhejiang Province. "The shuttle" (*sa* 梭) recalls a tale about the general Taokan 陶侃 recorded in the *Jinshu* 晉書 (66, Taokan juan 陶侃傳):

> 侃少時漁于雷澤、網得一織梭、以掛於壁。有頃雷雨、自化爲龍而去。

> When Kan was small, he was fishing in Leize ("Thunder Marsh") and netted a weaver's shuttle. He hung it on the wall. Sometime later, there was a thunderstorm; it transformed itself into a dragon and departed.

**make a mistake of a mistake** (*shōshaku jushaku* 將錯就錯): An idiom that often has the somewhat positive sense of "recognizing one's mistake as such," "turning a mistake to one's advantage," or "making the best of a bad situation." In some contexts, however, the same four glyphs have the entirely negative meaning of "making mistake after mistake," or "adding one mistake to another."

An example of the first, positive meaning is found in the words of Hongzhi Zhengjue 宏智正覺 (1091–1157), also known as Tiantong Zhengjue 天童正覺, found in the *Extensive Record of Chan Master Hongzhi* (*Hongzhi chanshi guanglu* 宏智禪師廣錄, T.2001.48:49b1-13):

> 開爐上堂僧問、丹霞燒木佛意旨如何。師云、天寒宜向火。擁毳任堆堆。僧云、夜冷更深更爇一軀去也。師云、也須照管眉毛始得。僧云、通身紅爛去、方始是知音。師云、爲它閑事長無明。僧云、只如院主、爲甚麼眉鬚墮落。師云、也與上座病痛一般。僧云、不解作客、勞煩主人。師云、還它本色漢手段始得。師乃云、十月朔風雨肇寒天。意作叢席地爐今日開。免燒木佛無斟酌。大衆、丹霞無斟酌。何似院主無斟酌。師復云、本合便恁麼休却。天童忍俊不禁。爲爾諸人下箇注脚。丹霞將錯就錯。院主眉鬚墮落。如聾如盲大家翁。攪擾殺爾不要惡。

> At a convocation in the dharma hall on the occasion of opening the braziers [on the 1st day of the 10th month], a monk asked, "What did Danxia mean to indicate by burning a wooden buddha?"

> The Master [Hongzhi] said, "When the weather is cold, you should face a fire, wrap yourself in a wool shawl, and just sit there."

> The monk said, "When the freezing cold of the night is intense, instead one burns a single body."

> The Master said, "Even so, one must protect the eyebrows; one only gets it then."

> The monk said, "When the entire body is glowing red, only then does one '**know the music**.'"

The Master said, "For the sake of those trifling matters, one remains long in ignorance."

The monk said, "What about the cloister chief [who criticized Danxia for burning the wooden buddha]; for the sake of what did his eyebrows fall off?"

The Master said, "Well, it's the same disease as yours, Senior Seat."

The monk said, "When one who doesn't understand is the guest, it's hardship for the host."

The Master said, "You'll only get it when you turn to the devices of that genuine fellow."

The Master thereupon said, "On the first day of the tenth month, it's windy and rainy, and the cold weather begins. For that reason, on this day we open the monastery's braziers. If we overlook the burning of wooden buddhas, we lack the ability to act as the circumstances demand. Great assembly, Danxia did not lack appropriate action in accordance with the circumstances. How was it that the cloister chief lacked appropriate action?"

The Master, replying [to his own question], said, "Fundamentally, such rejection [of burning buddhas] is fitting, but I, Tiantong, smile knowingly and don't prohibit it. For you people here, I will append a comment [on the episode]: Danxia made a mistake of a mistake; the cloister chief's eyebrows fell off. For an old man of a great family who is as if deaf and blind, he doesn't have to be immoral to make a big disturbance like this."

An example of the negative meaning — "making mistake after mistake" — is found in the *Discourse Record of Chan Master Huanglong Huinan* (*Huanglong Huinan chanshi yulu* 黃龍慧南禪師語錄, T.2019.47:638b3-10):

上堂、舉。馬祖因僧問如何是祖師西來意。祖云、近前來、向汝道。僧近前。祖攔腮一掌云、六耳不同謀。師云、古人尚乃不同謀。如今無端聚集一百五六十人欲漏洩其大事。如今忽有明眼人覷見、是一場禍事。雖然如是、如今既到這裡。將錯就錯。鬼神茶飯也少不得。良久云、十字街頭吹尺八。酸酒冷茶愁殺人。以拂子擊禪床。

Raised at a convocation in the dharma hall:

Mazu was once asked by a monk, "What is the **intention of the Ancestral Master's coming from the west**?"

[Ma]zu said, "Come forward, close to me, and I'll tell you."

The monk came face to face with him. [Ma] Zu grabbed his jaw, gave him a slap, and said, "Six ears [i.e., three people] can't keep a secret."

[Commenting on the kōan]:

The Master [Huinan] said, "The ancient one, after all, couldn't keep a secret. Nowadays, with no end, the accumulated desires of one hundred and fifty or sixty people taint this great matter. Nowadays, there's a clear-eyed person who looks upon us and sees a great danger! Although it's like

*Supplementary notes to the translation* 433

this, nowadays we've already reached this point, making mistake after mistake! When it comes to tea and rice for the ancestral spirits, deficiencies won't do."

After a while, he said, "Where two streets cross, blowing a shakuhachi. Sour wine and cold tea afflict people." Taking his **whisk**, he hit the meditation seat.

Another example of the negative meaning — "making mistake after mistake"— is found in the *Discourse Record of Chan Master Dahui Pujue* (*Dahui Pujue chanshi yulu* 大慧普覺禪師語錄, T.1998A.47:824a22-23):

上堂。即念離念、覺與非覺、有心無心、若善若惡。攪成一塊、將錯就錯。

At a convocation in the dharma hall, [Dahui said], "'This very thought and freedom from thoughts,' 'being aware and being unaware,' 'having mind and having no mind,' 'whether good or whether evil' — to mix these [opposites] together to make one lump is making a mistake of a mistake."

The meaning here seems to be that, while discriminating (*funbetsu* 分別) such opposites represents a kind of mistake (because the distinctions are merely conventional designations which, while having a certain usefulness, are ultimately false), that fundamental error is aggravated by the claim that there is no difference between the things so distinguished.

In his kōan collection entitled *Blue Cliff Record* (*Biyan lu* 碧巖錄), Yuanwu Keqin 圜悟克勤 (1063-1135) uses the phrase as "attached words" (*jakugo* 著語), or interlinear comments, in eight different "root cases" (*honsoku* 本則). Root case 32, for example, says that one Senior Seat Ting 定上座 was "suddenly awakened" (*kotsunen daigo* 忽然大悟) just as he was about to bow to the Chan Master Linji Yixuan 臨濟義玄 (-866). After those words (*Biyan lu* 碧巖錄, 2003.48:171c1-2), Yuanwu inserts the comment:

如暗得燈。如貧得寶。將錯就錯。

Like getting lamplight when its dark. Like a poor man getting treasure. Making a mistake of a mistake.

"Making a mistake of a mistake" may be interpreted as something positive here, since Senior Seat Ting's bewilderment turned into awakening. However, we might just as well interepret Yuanwu's comment as "adding one mistake to another," on the gounds that he meant to point out the ultimate emptiness of the categories "delusion" and "awakening," which are employed in the root case.

**man of iron** (*tekkan* 鐵漢): A term that occurs frequently in Dōgen's writings. According to ZGDJ (s.v. てっかん), it refers to "a strong-willed practitioner" (*ishi no tsuyoi shugyōsha* 意志の強い修行者). However, it can also be interpreted as a reference to bodhi, or the awakened "buddha mind" (*busshin* 佛心), itself.

In the literature of Zen, the term occurs most frequently in a verse attributed to Li Zunxu 李遵勗 (988-1038), a lay practitioner who interacted with several Chan masters and is best known as the compiler of the *Tiansheng Era Extended Record of the Flame* (*Tiansheng guangdeng lu* 天聖廣燈錄), preface dated 1036. Li is often referred to by the honorific title Commandant Escort (*fuma duwei* 駙馬都尉), conferred on him because he was married to a daughter of the Song Emperor Taizong 宋太宗 (927-997). His verse, as it appears in the *Jiatai Era Widespread Record of the Flame* (*Jiatai pudeng lu* 嘉泰普燈錄; ZZ.137:309a13-14; X.1559.79:423c24-424a1), reads as follows:

參禪須是鐵漢。著手心頭便判。直趣無上菩提。一切是非莫管。

To study Chan, one should be a man of iron.
Lay your hand on the mind and decide.
Proceed directly to unsurpassed bodhi.
Do not deal with any right or wrong.

The verse, with a slight variant in the opening line, also appears in the *Collected Records of Chan Master Fozhao Deguang* (*Fuzhao Deguang chanshi zouduilu* 佛照德光禪師奏對錄, *Records of Past Venerables* (*Guzunsu lu* 古尊宿錄, ZZ.118.830b7-11; X.1315.68:338c18-22). There it is quoted by Chan Master Fozhao 佛照禪師 (a.k.a. Fayun Gao 法雲杲, dates unknown) in an exchange with Emperor Xiaozong 孝宗 (1127-1194) of the Song, said to have taken place 1176:

上曰、祖師也是性燥、俗人中還有如此者麼。師云、有。如本朝李附馬問石門聰和尚云、弟子欲學禪、得否。門云、此是大丈夫事。非將相之所能爲。李於是契悟。乃述頌云、學道須是鐵漢、著手心頭便判、直趣無上菩提、一切是非莫管。

The Emperor said, "The ancestral masters were geniuses, but are there also ones like that among the laity?"

The Master [Fozhao] said, "There are. For example, Commandant Escort Li of this court asked Reverend Shimen Cong, 'Your disciple wishes to study Chan; can I do so, or not?' [Shi]men said, 'This is a matter for great men. It is not something than can be accomplished by generals and high-ranking officials.' Li, with this, tallied and awakened. He then produced a verse that went:

To study the way, one should be a man of iron.
Lay your hand on the mind and decide.

*Supplementary notes to the translation* 435

Proceed directly to unsurpassed bodhi.
Do not deal with any right or wrong.

Shimen Yuncong 石門蘊聰 (965-1032), whose words are said to have awakened Li Zunxu, was a Chan master in the Linji lineage. This version of Li's verse is quoted and commented on as a kōan by Dahui Zonggao 大慧宗杲 (1089–1163) in his *Discourse Record of Chan Master Dahui Pujue* (*Dahui Pujue chanshi yulu* 大慧普覺禪師語錄; T.1998A.47:890c14-17). Both versions of the verse appear in a number of other collections of Zen lore as well.

**manifestation of the full function** (*zenki gen* 全機現): The glyph 機 (*ki*), translated here as "function," has the basic meanings of 1) "pivot," "spring," "device," or "mechanism." Its extended meanings include: 2) the "impulse" or "motive power" that drives some activity; 3) an initial movement or action that signals or portends some future development; 4) a "suitable occasion" or "opportunity" to act; 5) the "pivotal issue," "key," or "main point" to something; and 6) the "capacities" or "talents" of a person, or the "capabilities" of a device. In Buddhist literature, the glyph 機 (*ki*) can refer to the varying "abilities" of students, meaning their karmically determined level of perspicacity and potential for awakening. Zen literature refers to the "Zen function" (*Zenki* 禪機) of an awakened master, who can respond spontaneously and appropriately when asked questions and when confronted with students caught up in deluded thinking. The sayings and other teaching methods (e.g., shouts and blows) employed by Zen masters are also referred to as "devices" (*kikan* 機關).

As used by Dōgen, the glyphs 全機 (*zenki*) have at least two possible interpretations. When 全 (*zen*) is taken as an adjective with the meaning "full" or "complete," it indicates that a person (a Zen master) is fully equipped with every sort of ability. ZGDJ (s.v. ぜんき) explains this kind of "full function" (*zenki* 全機) as follows:

Ki 機 means "function" (*kiyō* 機用), or "workings" (*hataraki* はたらき). "Full function" refers to the Zen person's (*Zensha* 禪者) great activities (*dai katsudō* 大活動), which are free and unimpeded (*jizai muge* 自在無礙).

If, on the other hand, the glyph 全 (*zen*) is taken as a noun meaning "the whole," or "everything," then the glyphs 全機 (*zenki*) can be interpreted as "the function of the whole [of existence]," or perhaps as "the workings of the mind ground (*shinji* 心地), or buddha mind (*busshin* 佛心), or buddha nature (*busshō* 佛性)," which is conceived as underlying all of phenomenal existence.

The expression "manifestation of the full function" comes from the *Discourse Record of Chan Master Yuanwu Foguo* (*Yuanwu foguo chanshi yulu* 圜悟佛果禪師語錄, T.1997.47:793b29-c8), where it appears in a verse comment that Yuanwu Keqin 圜悟克勤 (1063–1135) attaches to a kōan

436 DŌGEN'S *SHŌBŌGENZŌ* VOLUME VIII

involving Daowu Yuanzhi 道悟圓智 (769–835) and the latter's dharma heir Jianyuan Zhongxing 漸源仲興 (dates unknown):

舉。道吾漸源至一家弔慰。源撫棺木云。生耶死耶。吾云。生也不道死也不道。源云。爲什麼不道。吾云。不道不道。行至中路。源云。請和尚爲某甲道。若不道則打和尚去也。吾云。打即任打。道即不道。師拈云。銀山鐵壁有什麼階昇處。山僧今夜錦上鋪華。八字打開。商量這公案去也。生也全機現。死也全機現。不道復不道。箇中無背面。直下便承當。不隔一條線。逼塞大虛空。赤心常片片。

Raised [for comment]:

Daowu and Jianyuan went to a house for a funeral. Yuan put his hand on the coffin and said, "Alive or dead?"

Wu said, "I don't say alive; I don't say dead."

Yuan said, "Why don't you say?"

Wu said, "I don't say, I don't say."

On their way back, Yuan said, "Please, Reverend, say it for me. If you don't say it, I'll hit you."

Wu said, "Hit me if you will, but I won't say."

The Master [Yuanwu] raised this, saying, "A silver mountain, an iron wall: what stairs are there to climb them? Tonight, this mountain monk will spread out flowers on brocade: fully exposing myself, I interpret the [key] eight glyphs of this kōan:

> Alive, the manifestation of the full function; dead, the manifestation of the full function.
>
> Not saying and again not saying; right here, he doesn't turn away or face it.
>
> Directly acceding to it, without the gap of a single thread.
>
> Secluded in great empty space; the bare mind always in pieces."

The "eight glyphs" of the kōan that Yuanwu Keqin refers to are evidently those of Daowu's initial utterance, "I don't say alive; I don't say dead" (*shō ya fu dō shi ya fu dō* 生也不道死也不道). The translation here reflects a double entendre that Yuanwu employs, for the glyphs 八字打開 (*hachiji takai*), which literally mean "eight glyphs opened up," is also an idiom that means "to expose oneself" by fully opening one's robes. The two halves of a robe, which cross at the neck in a "V" shape when one is properly dressed, take the shape of the glyph "eight" (*hachi* 八) when they are opened up.

**manifestation of the great function** (*daiyū genzen* 大用現前): A term in Zen literature that has two complementary referents: 1) the workings of the buddha mind (*busshin* 佛心), which is innate in all people but typically obscured by discursive thinking; and 2) the teaching methods of the awakened master, who is said to freely employ expedient means (*hōben* 方便; S. *upāya*), without premeditation, in a manner that perfectly responds to the needs of the student in each particular situation.

The term "great function" (*daiyū* 大用; also read *daiyō*) has its roots in the Daoist tradition, where it refers to the workings of the *dao* 道, or "way," which functions spontaneously and perfectly "without acting" (*wu wei* 無爲) in an intentional way. There is also the idea that "great usefulness" (*dayong* 大用), paradoxically, consists in "having no possible use" (*wu suo keyong* 無所可用). In the first chapter of the *Zhuangzi* 莊子, entitled "Free and Easy Wandering" (Xiaoyaoyou 逍遙遊; KR.5c0126.001.16a), we find:

惠子謂莊子曰、吾有大樹、人謂之樗。其大本擁腫而不中繩墨、其小枝卷曲而不中規矩。立之塗、匠者不顧。今子之言、大而無用，衆所同去也。莊子曰、子獨不見狸狌乎。卑身而伏、以候敖者。東西跳梁、不避高下、中於機辟、死於罔罟。今夫斄牛、其大若垂天之雲。此能爲大矣、而不能執鼠。今子有大樹、患其無用。何不樹之於無何有之鄉、廣莫之野、彷徨乎無爲其側、逍遙乎寢臥其下。不夭斤斧、物無害者。無所可用、安所困苦哉。

Said Hui Shih to Chuang-tzŭ

"I have a great tree, people call it the tree-of-heaven. Its trunk is too knobby and bumpy to measure with the inked line, its branches are too curly and crooked to fit compasses or L-square. Stand it up in the road and a carpenter wouldn't give it a glance. Now this talk of yours is big but useless, dismissed by everyone alike."

"Haven't you ever seen a wild cat or a weasel? It lurks crouching low in wait for strays, makes a pounce east or west as nimble uphill or down, and drops plumb into the snare and dies in the net. But the yak now, which is as big as a cloud hanging from the sky, this by being able to be so big is unable to catch as much as a mouse. Now if you have a great tree and think it's a pity it's so useless, why not plant it in the realm of Nothing-whatever, in the wilds which spread out into nowhere, and go roaming away to do nothing at its side, ramble around and fall asleep in its shade?

> Spared by the axe
> No thing will harm it.
> If you're no use at all,
> Who'll come to bother you?"

(Translation by A.C. Graham; Graham 2001, 47.)

Later in the same text, in the chapter entitled "The World of Human Beings" (Renjianshi 人間世; KR.5c0126.004.12a), another gnarled and twisted tree (this one a huge, ancient oak) that a carpenter complained was "useless" (*mu sho kayō* 無所可用) appeared to the carpenter in a dream and said:

且予求無所可用久矣、幾死，乃今得之。爲予大用。使予也而有用、且得有此大也邪。

I would add that this quest of mine to become of no possible use to anyone has been going on for a long time: only now, on the verge of death, have I achieved it, and to me it is supremely useful. Supposing that I had been useful too, would I have had the opportunity to grow so big? (Translation by A.C. Graham; Graham 2001, 48.)

That which is of "great use" (*daiyong* 大用), or "great function," to the tree is precisely its uselessness as timber. The glyphs 規矩 (*guiju*), translated literally above (in the passage from "Free and Easy Wandering") as "compass and square," which are carpenter's tools, later came to refer to any rules, procedures, or established standards of human behavior.

In Chinese Buddhist texts, the term "great function" refers to the expedient means of a buddha or bodhisattva. The *Great Calming and Insight* (*Mohe zhiguan* 摩訶止觀, T.1911.46:81b15-18) by Tiantai Zhiyi 天台智顗 (538–597), for example, says:

四學大方便者。即是如來無謀善權、無方大用。住首楞嚴種種示現、不可思議巧方便力、示諸衆生虚空中風。

Fourth [in a list of five bodhisattva practices] is the study of great expedient means. This is a tathāgata's skillful teaching that is without plan, his great function that is without predisposition. Abiding in the *śūraṅgama* [samādhi], he gives every kind of instruction and, by the power of inconceivably ingenious expedient means, teaches living beings [freely like] wind in empty space.

In this passage, "great function" clearly refers to the teaching methods of a tathāgata, but it retains the Daoist sense of spontaneity and effortlessness.

In the Zen tradition, the expression "manifestation of the great function" is best known from its occurrence in the *Extensive Record of Chan Master Yunmen Kuangzhen* (*Yunmen Kuangzhen chanshi guanglu* 雲門匡眞廣錄, T.1988.47:554c2-4):

師有時云、大用現前不存軌則。僧便問、如何是大用現前。師乃拈拄杖高聲唱云、釋迦老子來也。

The Master [Yunmen] once said, "The manifestation of the great function does not abide in rules."

*Supplementary notes to the translation* 439

A monk then asked, "What is the manifestation of the great function?"

The Master thereupon raised his **staff** and called out in a loud voice, "Old Master Śākya has come."

Later in the same text (T.1988.47:571b21-24), we find:

因僧隨師出三門。師問、古人道、大用現前不存軌則。作麼生是不存軌則。無對。復云、儞問我、與儞道。僧便問。師引聲云、釋迦老子來也。僧又無對。

A monk was following the Master [Yunmen] out through the triple gate [i.e. the main gate of the monastery].

The Master asked him, "An ancient said, 'The manifestation of the great function does not abide in rules.' What is this not abiding in rules?"

The monk had no response.

The Master further said, "You ask me. I'll say something for you."

The monk asked.

The Master said in a drawn-out voice, "Old Master Śākya has come."

The monk again had no response.

It is not clear who the "ancient" (*kojin* 古人) was that Yunmen Wenyan 雲門文偃 (864-949) said he was quoting, but the saying could well be a paraphrase of the two *Zhuangzi* stories involving twisted trees, whose "great function" was their refusal to be measured by the carpenter's "compass and square."

In the biography of Chan Master Daan of Fuzhou 福州大安禪師 (793-883) in the *Jingde Era Record of the Transmission of the Flame* (*Jingde chuandeng lu* 景德傳燈錄, T.2076.51:267c23-26), the saying that Yunmen quotes is raised as a topic:

問、大用現前不存軌則時如何。師云、汝用得但用。僧乃脫膊遶師三匝。師云、向上事何不道取。僧擬開口、師便打云、遮野狐精出去。

[A monk] asked, "What about when 'the manifestation of the great function does not abide in rules'?"

The Master [Daan] said, "Your [idea of] function grasps only function."

The monk thereupon bared his arm and circumambulated the Master three times.

The Master said, "The matter that is beyond: why don't you speak of that?"

When the monk was about to open his mouth, the Master hit him and said, "This fox spirit! Get out!"

In Yuanwu Keqin's 圜悟克勤 (1063-1135) "pointer" (*suiji* 垂示) to case 3 of the *Blue Cliff Record* (*Biyan lu* 碧巖錄, T.2003.48:142c4-9), he says:

440 DŌGEN'S *SHŌBŌGENZŌ* VOLUME VIII

一機一境、一言一句、且圖有箇入處。好肉上剜瘡、成窠成窟。大用現前不存軌則。且圖知有向上事。蓋天蓋地又摸索不著。恁麼也得、不恁麼也得、太廉纖生。恁麼也不得、不恁麼也不得、太孤危生。不涉二塗、如何即是。請試舉看

One device or one object, one word or one phrase: these provisionally aim at having a place of entrance. However, this is gouging a wound in healthy flesh; it is creating a nest or creating a burrow. The manifestation of the great function does not abide in rules. The provisional aim is to [make you] know of the matter that is beyond; that covers the heavens and covers the earth, but when you grope for it, you don't attain it. "Such" is got; "not-such" is got: these [phrases] entail an extreme of subtle defilement. "Such" is not got; "not-such" is not got: these [phrases] entail an extreme of isolated peril. Without walking on either of those two paths, what is correct? Please give it a try. I raise [the following kōan] for you to contemplate.

Here, it is the main case (*honsoku* 本則), or kōan, which Yuanwu quotes immediately after these remarks, that he refers to as a provisional teaching device: a "manifestation of the great function."

**manifesting a body to preach the dharma** (*genshin seppō* 現身説法): An allusion to a famous passage in the "Universal Gate" (*Pumen* 普門) chapter of the *Lotus Sūtra* (*Miaofa lianhua jing* 妙法蓮華經, T.262.9:57a20-26), in which the Buddha describes the thirty-three manifestations of the Bodhisattva Avalokiteśvara; the passage begins:

無盡意菩薩白佛言、世尊、觀世音菩薩、云何遊此娑婆世界。云何而為衆生説法。方便之力、其事云何。佛告無盡意菩薩、善男子、若有國土衆生應以佛身得度者、觀世音菩薩、即現佛身而爲説法。應以辟支佛身得度者、即現辟支佛身而爲説法、應以聲聞身得度者、即現聲聞身而爲説法。

The Bodhisattva Akṣayamati addressed the Buddha, saying, "World-Honored One, how does the Bodhisattva Avalokiteśvara disport himself in this Sahā world? How does he preach the dharma for living beings? What are his powers of expedient means?"

The Buddha said to the Bodhisattva Akṣayamati, "Good man, if there are in the land living beings who ought to attain deliverance by a buddha body, the Bodhisattva Avalokiteśvara manifests a buddha body and preaches the dharma to them. If there are those who ought to attain deliverance by a *pratyeka-buddha*, then he manifests the body of a *pratyeka-buddha* and preaches the dharma to them. If there are those who ought to attain deliverance by a *śrāvaka*, then he manifests the body of a *śrāvaka* and preaches the dharma to them."

*Supplementary notes to the translation* 441

**measure of the buddha** (*butsuryō* 佛量): This is a term that Dōgen employs in six chapters of the *Shōbōgenzō*, but it does not appear in any other Zen texts and is rare even in Buddhist literature at large. The precedents found in the latter may have been known to Dōgen, but they do not provide any definitive basis for determining what he meant by the term.

In more than half of the three dozen instances that the glyphs 佛量 (*butsuryō*) appear in Chinese Buddhist canons (those digitized by CBETA), the meaning is simply "number of buddhas." The *Sūtra on the Entry into Laṅka* (*Lengqie abaduoluo bao jing* 楞伽阿跋多羅寶經, T.670.16:511c5), for example, says:

三世諸佛量、非如恒河沙。

The number of buddhas in the three times is not like the sands of the Ganges.

Similarly, in the *Treatise on the New [translation of the] Flower Garland Sūtra* (*Xin huayanjing lun* 新華嚴經論, T.1739.36:990a13-14), the author Li Tongxuan 李通玄 (635–730 or 646–740) says:

此須彌山微塵爲佛量也。

I take this [saying] "atoms comprising Mount Sumeru" as a reference to the number of buddhas.

Another attested meaning of the glyphs 佛量 is the "size (i.e., height) of the Buddha," which tradition sets at "sixteen feet" (*jōroku* 丈六), or twice the height of an ordinary person. The *Commentary on the Procedures of the Four-Part Vinaya* (*Sifen lü xingshi chao* 四分律行事鈔, T.1804.40:89c10-11) by Daoxuan 道宣 (596-667), for example, says:

多論云。佛量丈六。常人半之、衣廣長皆應半也。

According to the *Sarvāstivāda-vinaya-vibhāṣā* [*Sapoduolun* 薩婆多論], "The measure of the Buddha is sixteen feet. The ordinary person is half of that, so the dimensions of the [monk's] robe should all be half [of the Buddha's robe.]"

In the *Commentary on the Vinaya Pratimokṣa* (*Lü jieben shu* 律戒本疏, T.2788.85:638b12-14), similarly, the "measure of the Buddha" (*butsuryō* 佛量) is explained with the statement that "the Buddha's body is sixteen feet" (*busshin jōroku* 佛身丈六).

Two additional, closely related meanings of the glyphs 佛量 that can be inferred from a few sūtra commentaries are, as ZGDJ (s.v. ぶつりょう) puts it: 1) "the capacity of a buddha" (*butsu no rikiryō* 佛の力量); and 2) "the thinking of a buddha" (*butsu no shiryō* 佛の思量). The *Treatise on the Great Amitābha Sūtra* (*Mohe Amituo jing zhonglun* 摩訶阿彌陀經衷論, ZZ.32:581a2-4; X.401.22:153b18-19) says:

所謂心量奈何。虚空無盡、世界無盡、則衆生之心量亦無盡。心量
者、心所能至之分量也。諸佛量周法界。既通法界之事理。

What about that which is called "mental scope"? Empty space is inexhaustible, and worlds are inexhaustible, so the mental scope of living
beings is also inexhaustible. What we mean by "mental scope" is the extent to which the mind can reach. The buddhas' [mental] scope reaches
throughout the dharma realm. It completely penetrates the phenomena
and principle of the dharma realm.

Because this passage directly compares the "buddhas' scope" (*shobutsuryō*
諸佛量) with the "mental scope of living beings" (*shujō shi shinryō* 衆生之心
量), it is clear that the former term refers to the mental capacity of a buddha.
The *Record of Seeking the Profound [Meaning] of the Flower Garland Sūtra*
(*Huayan jing tanxuan ji* 華嚴經探玄記, T.1733.35:457c17-19) says:

次二證理心。一正證、二後得。後三赴佛心。一見佛身、二順佛量
智、三究佛理智。

Next, there are two ways of realizing the mind as principle. The first is
direct realization, and the second is subsequent attainment. In the case of
subsequent [attainment], there are three approaches to the buddha mind:
first, seeing the Buddha's body; second, according with the Buddha's discriminating wisdom; and third, attaining the Buddha's non-discriminating
wisdom.

In this passage, "discriminating wisdom" (*ryōchi* 量智), meaning wisdom
that involves "measuring," or "weighing" (*ryō* 量) in the sense of "thinking
about" (*shiryō* 思量) things, is distinguished from "non-discriminating
wisdom," which is direct insight into the "principle" (*ri* 理) of emptiness.
Thus, the term "measure of the buddha" (*butsuryō* 佛量) could be interpreted
as an abbreviation of "a buddha's discriminating wisdom" (*butsu ryōchi* 佛
量智).

According to BGDJ (1198d), 佛量 renders the Sanskrit *buddha-pramāṇatā*
and refers to "the Buddha being an authoritative basis of knowledge" (*butsu
ga chishiki konkyo to naru koto* 佛が知識根拠となること). This definition
interprets the glyph 量 (*ryō*) as a translation of the Sanskrit *pramāṇa*, which
in Buddhist texts refers to the "standard" of correct cognition. Traditionally,
there are said to be "three means of valid cognition" (*sanryō* 三量; S.
*pramāṇa-traya*): 1) direct perception (*genryō* 現量; S. *pratyakṣa-pramāṇa*),
2) inference (*hiryō* 比量; S. *anumāna-pramāṇa*), and 3) scriptural authority
(*shōgyōryō* 聖教量 or 正教量; S. *āgama-pramāṇa*). If the term *buddha-
pramāṇatā* does indeed appear in Sanskrit literature, it is not clear how "the
authority of the Buddha" would differ from "scriptural authority." In any
case, there are no instances in Chinese Buddhist canons of the glyphs 佛

量 being used in the sense of *buddha-pramāṇa*, so it is unlikely that Dōgen would have had such a meaning in mind.

The *Flower Garland Sūtra* (*Huayan jing* 華嚴經, T.279.10:275a11-17), while it does not employ the two glyphs 佛量 as a discrete technical term, nevertheless juxtaposes them in the course of listing of things that are "equal in number / measure" (*ryōtō* 量等) to the bodies of the Tathāgata:

佛子、如來應正等覺成正覺時、得一切衆生量等身、得一切法量等身、得一切刹量等身、得一切三世量等身、得一切佛量等身、得一切語言量等身、得眞如量等身、得法界量等身、得虚空界量等身、得無礙界量等身、得一切願量等身、得一切行量等身、得寂滅涅槃界量等身。

Children of the Buddha, when the Tathāgata is on the point of perfect awakening and attains right awakening, he gets bodies equal in measure [i.e., number] to all living beings; he gets bodies equal in measure to all dharmas; he gets bodies equal in measure to all lands; he gets bodies equal in measure to all of the three times; he gets bodies equal in measure to all buddhas; he gets bodies equal in measure to all words; he gets bodies equal in measure to suchness; he gets bodies equal in measure to the dharma realm; he gets bodies equal in measure to the realm of empty space; he gets bodies equal in measure to the realm of non-obstruction; he gets bodies equal in measure to all vows; he gets bodies equal in measure to all activities; and he gets bodies equal in measure to the realm of extinction, which is nirvāṇa.

This passage, with its exuberant play on the concept of "measure" (*ryō* 量), bears some similarity to the *Shōbōgenzō* passages in which Dōgen speaks of the "measure of the buddha." Dōgen conjoins that expression, which he may or may not have borrowed from any external source, with a bunch of similar terms: the "measure of the mind" (*shin ryō* 心量); the "measure of the one mind" (*isshin ryō* 一心量); the "measure of the body" (*shin ryō* 身量); the "measure of the dharma" (*hō ryō* 法量), the "measure of the dharma realm" (*hokkai ryō* 法界量), the "measure of the flower" (*ka ryō* 華量); the "measure of an ancestor" (*soryō* 祖量); the "measure of the mind of the **buddhas and ancestors**" (*busso shin ryō* 佛祖心量); the "measure of **one blade of grass**" (*ikkyōsō ryō* 一莖草量); the "measure of awakening" (*go ryō* 悟量); the "measure of understanding" (*e ryō* 會量); and the "measure of all the worlds" (*jinkai ryō* 盡界量). Of these, the first six expressions are found in Chinese Buddhist literature at large; the last six are neologisms that Dōgen himself made up.

**move among different types** (*irui chū gyō* 異類中行): In ordinary language, the expression "different types" (*irui* 異類) can refer to: 1) different kinds, or varieties, of anything; 2) ethnic groups that differ from one's own;

and 3) individual people who vary in constitution or aptitude. In contexts influenced by Buddhist ideas, it can also refer to: 4) any of the **six paths**, a.k.a. six destinies of rebirth, other than the human.

In the Sōtō Zen tradition, the expression "move among different types" is associated especially with remarks attributed to Nanquan Puyuan 南泉普願 (748-835) in the *Discourse Record of Chan Master Benji of Mount Cao in Muzhou* (*Muzhou Caoshan Benji chanshi yulu* 撫州曹山本寂禪師語錄, T.1987B.47:543b24-c22). The context is a formula known as the "four kinds of different types" (*shishu irui* 四種異類), which is expounded by Caoshan Benji 曹山本寂 (840–890). In brief, the first kind is "different types in our goings and comings" (*ōrai irui* 往來異類), which refers to rebirth as a deva, denizen of hell, hungry ghost, animal, or *asura*. The second kind is "different types of the bodhisattva's identification [with living beings]" (*bosatsu dō irui* 菩薩同異類), which refers to the various identities, practices, and skillful means that bodhisattvas embrace in carrying out their vows to save all livings beings, having "already realized the fruit of nirvāṇa" (*ishō nehan shi ka* 已證涅槃之果) themselves but "not abandoning the types who remain in saṃsāra" (*fusha shōji rui* 不捨生死類). The third kind is "different types of the *śramaṇa*" (*shamon irui* 沙門異類), a trope that involves ascribing rebirth as beasts "clad in fur and crowned by horns" to *śramaṇas* as an ironic, antiphrastic way of signifying their complete liberation from karmic retribution; for details, see "**a head of three feet and a neck of two inches**." The fourth kind is "different types within our school" (*shūmon chū irui* 宗門中異類). Because it includes Nanquan's explanation of "moving among different types," Caoshan's exposition of it is given here in full (T.1987B.47:543c14-22):

四者宗門中異類者。如南泉曰、智不到處、切忌道著。道著則頭角生。喚作如如、早是變也、直須向異類中行。道取異類中事。洞山曰、此事直須妙會。事在其妙、體在妙處。余自道、此事直須虛。一位全無的的也。覷面兼帶始得。若是作家語不偏不正、不有不無、呼爲異類中虛。 此事直須作家橫身。逢木著木。逢竹著竹。須護觸犯。囑囑囑囑。

Fourth is "different types within our school." As Nanquan said, "Of the place that knowledge doesn't reach, it's strictly forbidden to speak; if you speak, horns will grow on your head. If you name anything as such-and-such, you have already undergone this transformation, and you necessarily move among different types." Speaking is a matter among different types. Dongshan said, "This matter is surely the mysterious understanding. Matters consist in this mystery; the body consists in a mysterious place." Speaking for myself [Caoshan], this matter is surely vacuous. Any one position is entirely without clarity. You only get it when you hold two positions at once. If the author's words are neither inclined nor upright, neither positing existence nor denying it, that is called "vacuity among

## Supplementary notes to the translation

different types." This matter is surely the author's risking their life. If you encounter wood, you attach to [the name] "wood." If you encounter bamboo, you attach to "bamboo." You must guard against violations. Please! Please! Please! Please!

As this explanation makes clear, to "move among different types," in Nanquan's usage, is a metaphor for speaking and "naming" (*kansa* 喚作). Language, of course, can scarcely function without using nouns, but naming necessarily involves mental discrimination (*funbetsu* 分別): drawing more or less arbitrary lines around the "things" named in ways that serve our own purposes. This, Caoshan says, is what one does as the "author" (*sakke* 作家) of one's own reality. The problem, according to the Buddhist doctrine of emptiness, is that we not only name things such as "wood" or "bamboo," we attach (*jaku* 著) to the things named as if they actually existed as discrete entities (S. *dharmas*) in the external world, in and of themselves (S. *svabhāva*), entirely apart from our discrimination of them. Laboring under that fundamental delusion, according to Nanquan and Caoshan, is what it means to be involved in saṃsāra, i.e., to "move among different types."

Another important context for understanding Dōgen's use of the expression "move among different types" is an extended dialogue said to have taken place between Nanquan, Yunyan Tansheng 雲巖曇晟 (782-841), and the latter's older brother disciple, Daowu Zongzhi 道吾宗智 (769–835), who is also named in some texts as Daowu Yuanzhi 道吾圓智. Both Daowu and Yunyan are said to be dharma heirs of Yaoshan Weiyan 藥山惟儼 (751-834), who also figures in the dialogue. As quoted by Dōgen in his *Shōbōgenzō* in Chinese script (*shinji Shōbōgenzō* 眞字正法眼藏, DZZ.5:154-156, case 57), the story reads:

道吾山宗智禪師、〈嗣藥山〉離藥山到南泉。泉問、闍梨、名什麼。
師曰、宗智。泉曰、智不到處、作麼生宗。師曰、切忌道著。泉云、
灼然、道著即頭角生。至三日後、師與雲巖在後架把針次、泉過見
乃再問、前日道、智不到處、切忌道著、道著即頭角生。合作麼生
行履。師便抽身入僧堂。泉便去、師却來坐。巖乃問、師兄、適來、
爲甚不祇對和尚。師曰、儞得與麼靈利。巖不薦却去問泉云、適來因
緣、智頭陀作麼生不祇對和尚。泉云、他却是異類中行。巖曰、如何
是異類中行。泉云、不見道、智不到處、切忌道著。道著即頭角生、
直須向異類中行。巖亦不會。師知巖不薦乃曰、此人因緣不在此。
便與廻藥山。山觀二人廻乃問巖、汝到甚處去來。巖曰、到南泉。山
曰、泉有何言句。巖遂舉前話。山曰、子作麼生會他這箇時節、便廻
來。巖無対。山乃大笑。巖便問、如何是異類中行。山曰、吾今日
困。別時來。巖曰、某甲特爲此事歸來。山曰、且去。巖便出。師在
方丈外聞巖不薦、不覺咬得指頭血出。師却來問巖曰、師弟、去問和
尚那因緣作麼生。巖曰、和尚不爲某甲說。師便低頭。師與雲巖同時
到藥山次、山云、智不到處、切忌道著、道著即頭角生。師便珍重出
去。巖遂問、智師兄爲什麼不祇対和尚。山曰、我今日背痛。是他却

會。汝去問取。巖遂問、師兄、適來、爲甚不祇対和尚。師曰、我今日頭痛。儞去問取和尚。後雲巖遷化、遣人馳辭書。師覽後曰、雲巖不知有。悔當時不向伊道。然雖如是、要且不違藥山之子。

Chan Master Zongzhi of Mount Daowu (dharma heir of Yaoshan) left Yaoshan and reached Nanquan.

Nanquan asked, "Ācārya, what's your name?"

The Master [Daowu] said, "Zongzhi [literally, 'Knowledge of the Axiom']."

[Nan] Quan said [punning on the name], "What's the Axiom where Knowledge doesn't reach?"

The Master said, "It's strictly forbidden to speak of it."

Quan said, "Clearly, if you speak, horns will grow on your head."

Three days later, when the Master was engaged in needlework at the washstand together with Yunyan, Nanquan saw him and asked again, "The saying of the other day — 'Of the place that knowledge doesn't reach, it's strictly forbidden to speak; if you speak, horns will grow on your head' — what is your conduct [i.e., mode of being — dumb beast or human] with regard to that?"

The Master extracted himself and entered the saṃgha hall. When Quan was gone, the Master came back and sat. [Yun] Yan asked him, "Elder brother, just now, why didn't you interact with the Reverend [Nanquan]?"

The Master said, "You have such perspicacity."

Yan was utterly confused. He withdrew and asked Quan, "In the incident just now, why didn't Ascetic [Zong] Zhi interact with you, Reverend?"

Quan said, "He was avoiding this 'moving among different types.'"

Yan said, "What is 'moving among different types'?"

Quan said, "Didn't you hear the saying, 'Of the place that knowledge doesn't reach, it's strictly forbidden to speak; if you speak, horns will grow on your head, and you necessarily move among different types'?"

Yan still did not understand.

The Master [Daowu], knowing that Yan was utterly confused, said [to himself], "This person's karmic affiliation does not reside here [with Nanquan]." He returned together with him [i.e., with Yunyan] to Yaoshan.

When [Yao] Shan saw the two men returning, he asked Yan, "Where have you come from?"

Yan said, "I've been to Nanquan."

Shan said, "What words does Nanquan have?"

Yan thereupon brought up the preceding saying.

Shan said, "Son, what did you understand of him, that now you return?"

*Supplementary notes to the translation* 447

Yan had no reply.

Shan gave a big laugh.

Yan asked, "What is 'moving among different types'?"

Shan said, "I'm tired today. Come back some other time."

Yan said, "I came back especially on account of this matter."

Shan said, "Just go, for now."

Yan left.

The Master [Daowu], was outside the abbot's quarters. When he heard Yan's utter confusion, he unconsciously bit down on his fingertip and drew blood. The Master withdrew. [Later] he came to Yan and inquired, "Younger brother, when you asked the Reverend [Yaoshan] about that incident, how did it go?"

Yan said, "The Reverend would not explain it for me."

The Master bowed his head.

When the Master and Yunyan together went to Yaoshan, [Yao] Shan said, "Of the place that knowledge doesn't reach, it's strictly forbidden to speak; if you speak, horns will grow on your head."

The Master bid him farewell and left.

Yan thereupon asked, "Why didn't elder brother [Zong] Zhi interact with you, Reverend?"

Shan said, "I have back pain today. The other understands; you should go ask him."

Yan thereupon asked, "Elder brother, just now, why didn't you interact with the Reverend?"

The Master said, "I have a headache today. You should go ask the Reverend."

Later, when Yunyan died, a messenger hurried [to Daowu] with a notifying letter. After reading it, the Master said, "Yunyan didn't know anything. How regrettable that, at that time, he did not come to grips with the saying. Although he was like that, in the end he was none other than a son of Yaoshan."

Dōgen apparently drew on two separate sources to create this account. One source was the biography of "Chan Master Daowu Zongzhi of Tanzhou" 潭州道吾宗智禪師 that appears in the *Outline of the Linked Flames* (*Liandeng huiyao* 聯燈會要, ZZ.136:374a14-b12). That work, which was printed in 1189, contains the entire story of Daowu, Nanquan, Yunyan, and Yaoshan down through the line "the Master [Daowu] bowed his head." The second source that Dōgen quoted was the biography of "Chan Master Daowu Yuanzhi of Tanzhou" 潭州道吾圓智禪師 that appears in the *Jingde Era*

448 DŌGEN'S *SHŌBŌGENZŌ* VOLUME VIII

*Record of the Transmission of the Flame* (*Jingde chuandeng lu* 景德傳燈錄, T.2076.51:314a15-24), which was completed in 1004:

師與雲巖侍立次、藥山曰、智不到處切忌道著。道著即頭角生。智頭陀怎麼生。師便出去。雲巖問藥山曰、智師兄爲什麼不祇對和尚。藥山曰、我今日背痛。是他却會。汝去問取。雲巖即來問師曰、師兄適來爲什麼不祇對和尚。師曰、汝却去問取和尚。雲巖臨遷化時、遣人送辭書到。師展書覽之曰、雲巖不知有。悔當時不向伊道。然雖如是、要且不違藥山之子。

When the Master [Daowu], together with Yunyan, was serving as an acolyte [to Yaoshan], Yaoshan said, "Of the place that knowledge doesn't reach, it's strictly forbidden to speak; if you speak, horns will grow on your head. What about you, Ascetic [Yuan] Zhi?"

The Master left.

Yunyan asked Yaoshan, "Why didn't elder brother [Yuan] Zhi interact with you, Reverend?"

Yaoshan said, "I have back pain today. The other understands; you should go ask him."

Yunyan returned and asked the Master, "Elder brother, just now, why didn't you interact with the Reverend?" The Master said, "You should go ask the Reverend."

When Yunyan was about to die, he sent a messenger to deliver a notifying letter [to Daowu].

When he had opened and read it, the Master said, "Yunyan didn't know anything. How regrettable that, at that time, he did not come to grips with the saying. Although he was like that, in the end he was none other than a son of Yaoshan."

This passage, which corresponds to the final section of Dōgen's account (beginning with the line, "When the Master [Daowu] and Yunyan together went to Yaoshan..."), indicates that it was Yaoshan who first said, "Of the place that knowledge doesn't reach, it's strictly forbidden to speak; if you speak, horns will grow on your head." It would seem, then, that when Daowu first spoke to Nanquan and the latter punned on the second glyph of his name (Zhi 智, or "Knowledge"), they both had prior knowledge of Yaoshan's saying. However, if we read only the account of Daowu's exchange with Nanquan that is found in the *Outline of the Linked Flames of Our Lineage*, we get the impression that it was Nanquan who first pieced the saying together, starting with his pun ("There is a place that Knowledge does not reach"), then incorporating Daowu's reply ("It's strictly forbidden to speak"), and finally adding his own concluding remark ("If you speak, horns will grow on your head"). Yaoshan, in this reading, only learns of the saying when he asks Yunyan, "What words does Nanquan have?" As noted above, the

*Discourse Record of Chan Master Benji of Mount Cao in Muzhou* attributes the saying to Nanquan. The one thing that is certain, no matter how we read these conflicting accounts, is that none of them attributes the words "move among different types" to anyone but Nanquan.

Nanquan's words are often raised as a topic of discussion in Zen literature. They appear, for example, as case 10 in the kōan collection known as the *Empty Hall Collection* (*Xutang ji* 虛堂集, ZZ.124:526b5-11), under the heading "Nanquan's Different Types" (*Nansen irui* 南泉異類):

舉。雲巖道吾自南泉回藥山。巖問藥山、如何是異類中行。山云、吾今困倦。且待別時來。巖云、某甲特爲此事來。山云、且去。巖便出。道吾在方丈外。聞雲巖不薦、不覺咬得指頭血出。吾却下來問巖。兄云、問和尚那因緣作麼生。巖云、不爲某甲説。吾便低頭。

Raised:

Yunyan and Daoyu returned to Yaoshan from Nanquan. [Yun] Yan asked Yaoshan, "What is 'moving among different types'?"

[Yao] Shan said, "I'm tired now. Wait for some other time and come back."

Yan said, "I came especially for this matter."

Shan said, "Just go, for now."

Yan left.

Daowu was outside the abbot's quarters. When he heard Yan's utter confusion, he unconsciously bit down on his fingertip and drew blood. [Dao] Wu withdrew and later inquired of Yan. The elder brother [Daowu] said, "When you asked the Reverend [Yaoshan] about that incident, how did it go?"

Yan said, "The Reverend would not explain it for me."

Wu bowed his head.

In the Sōtō Zen tradition, the figure of Yunyan Tansheng 雲巖曇成 (782-841) is crucial because he is recognized as the teacher of Dongshan Liangjie 洞山良价 (807–869), founder of the Caodong (Sōtō) lineage. In the biographies of his elder brother disciple Daowu Zongzhi (or Yuanzhi), however, Yunyan is cast as a dimwit who, try as he might, cannot understand Nanquan's saying, "moving among different types." It is true that, at the end of the account in *Outline of the Linked Flames of Our Lineage*, Daowu bows his head (*teitō* 低頭) when Yunyan says, "The Reverend [Yaoshan] would not explain it for me"; that could be a gesture of respect, but from the context it seems more like a sign of disappointed resignation on the part of the elder brother. The account in the *Jingde Era Record of the Transmission of the Flame* ends with Daowu saying of Yunyan, "Although he was like that [i.e., unable to comprehend Nanquan's saying], in the end he was none other than a son of Yaoshan." This statement sounds suspiciously like an interpolation by some later editor (perhaps the compiler of the *Jingde Era Record*) designed

450     DŌGEN'S *SHŌBŌGENZŌ* VOLUME VIII

to support the claim — hardly justified by the depiction of him in Daowu's biography — that Yunyan was a dharma heir of Yaoshan. There are other anomalies in the tradition surrounding Yunyan, as well. Biographical data pertaining to him has led modern scholars to determine his dates as 782-841, while his elder brother disciple Daowu is reckoned to have lived from 769–835. In the *Jingde Era Record* biography of Daowu, however, Yunyan dies before Daowu. The biography of Yunyan that appears in the *Record of the Transmission of Illumination* (*Denkōroku* 傳光録, p. 375) by Keizan Jōkin 瑩山紹瑾 (1264-1325) says that Yunyan first trained as an acolyte under Baizhang for twenty years, after which he sought instruction from Yaoshan. Yunyan is said to have attained a great awakening when Yaoshan, having asked him what teaching Baizhang expounded, commented on the story of Baizhang using a **staff** to chase the great assembly out of the dharma hall. This hardly comports with the two accounts of Yunyan's interactions with Yaoshan that Dōgen combines in case 57 of his *Shōbōgenzō* in Chinese script (*shinji Shōbōgenzō* 眞字正法眼藏, op. cit).

**myriad forms** (*manzō* 萬象; also read *banzō*): A term that is used interchangeably with "myriad images" (*banshō* 萬像; also read *manzō*). Both terms can also be translated as "the myriad phenomena" and are synonymous in that sense with the expression "myriad things" (*manmotsu* 萬物). In these contexts, "myriad" (*man* or *ban* 萬, literally "ten thousand") means "a vast number" or "all." The "myriad forms" are all the things that exist in the universe, in all of their infinite diversity and mutability: the totality of existence. Also found in the expression "thicket of myriad forms" (*manzō shinra* 萬象森羅), based on the image of a dense stand of trees; the expression "myriad forms of the thicket" (*shinra manzō* 森羅萬象) is a common variant with the same sense.

In the Daoist classic, *The Book of the Way and its Virtue* (*Daode jing* 道德經, KR.5c0046.000.001a), the Way (*dō* 道), which itself is formless and ineffable, is said to be the "mother of the myriad things" (*manmotsu shi mo* 萬物之母): a kind of primal "nothingness" from which all existence arises and unfolds in orderly fashion. The Daoist understanding had some influence on the Chinese Buddhist use of the term "myriad forms," which is often mentioned in opposition to or conjunction with "emptiness" (*kū* 空).

In the *Discourse Record of Chan Master Yuanzheng of Mount Cao in Muzhou* (*Muzhou Caoshan Yuanzheng chanshi yulu* 撫州曹山元證禪師語録, T.1987A.47:527a5-6), for example, we read:

> 因有僧問五位君臣旨訣。師曰、正位即空界、本來無物。偏位即色界、有萬象形

> On one occasion there was a monk who asked about the "deep meaning of the five positions of ruler and ministers."

*Supplementary notes to the translation* 451

The Master [Caoshan] said: "The position of 'upright' is the realm of emptiness: from the start, there are no things. The position of 'inclined' is the form realm: there exist myriad forms and shapes."

For the full context of this passage, see "**five ranks**."

A famous verse concerning the "myriad forms" is attributed to Chan Master Changqing Huileng 長慶慧稜 (854–932) in his biography in the *Jingde Era Record of the Transmission of the Flame* (*Jingde chuandeng lu* 景德傳燈錄, T.2076.51:347b27-28):

萬象之中獨露身、唯人自肯乃方親、昔時謬向途中覓、今日看如火裏冰。

Amidst the myriad forms there is a solitary exposed body;
Only when people have affirmed themselves can they be intimate with it.
In ancient times they deludedly sought it along the path;
In the present day they regard it like ice within fire.

A debate over the meaning of the opening line of this verse, featuring two of Changqing's former students — Fayan Wenyi 法眼文益 (885–958) and Head Seat Zhizhao 子昭首座 (dates unknown) — is presented as Case #64 of the *Congrong Hermitage Record* (*Congrong lu* 從容錄, T.2004.48:267a4-13):

子昭首座問法眼、和尚開堂承嗣何人。眼云、地藏。昭云、太辜負長慶先師。眼云、某甲不會長慶一轉語。昭云、何不問。眼云、萬象之中獨露身意作麼生。昭乃堅起拂子。眼云、此是長慶處學得底、首座分上作麼生。昭無語。眼云、只如萬象之中獨露身、是撥萬象不撥萬象。昭云、不撥。眼云、兩箇。參隨左右皆云、撥萬象。眼云、萬象之中獨露身聻。

Head Seat Zizhao asked Fayan, "You, Reverend, have opened the hall. Who did you receive [dharma] inheritance from?"

[Fa]Yan said, "Dizang."

[Zi]Zhao said, "You're very ungrateful to our late master, Changqing."

Yan said, "I don't understand Changqing's single turning word."

Zhao said, "Why don't you ask me?"

Yan said, "What's the meaning of, 'Amidst the myriad forms there is a solitary exposed body'?"

Zhao raised his **whisk**.

Yan said, "That's something you got studying at Changqing's place. What do make of it on your own, Head Seat?"

Zhao was speechless.

Yan said, "If it were the case that 'amidst the myriad forms there is a solitary exposed body,' would that expunge the myriad forms, or not expunge the myriad forms?"

Zhao said, "Not expunge."

Yan said, "[That leaves] a duality."

Everyone in attendance [in the dharma hall] said, "It would expunge the myriad forms."

Yan said, "Then what about, 'Amidst the myriad forms there is a solitary exposed body'?"

Fayan and Zhizhao had been fellow students under Changqing Huileng. When the latter died, Fayan moved on to attain dharma inheritance from Dizang Guichen 地藏桂琛 (867-928). Then he returned to assume the abbacy of Changqing's former monastery, an event that was marked by a ceremonial "opening of the [dharma] hall" (*kaidō* 開堂), with him presiding. Zhizhao, who held the position of head seat in the monastery, challenged Fayan by asking him from whom he had inherited the dharma. In the course of the exchange that followed, Fayan raised the famous saying attributed to Changqing — "Amidst the myriad forms there is a solitary exposed body" — and challenged Zhizhao to respond to whether that "would expunge the myriad phenomena, or not expunge the myriad phenomena" (*ze hatsu banshō, fuhatsu banshō* 是撥萬象、不撥萬象). The "solitary exposed body" refers to one's own nature, or buddha nature, so what Fayan's question amounts to is, "When a person sees the buddha nature (i.e., is awakened), do they still experience all the myriad forms of the world in the same way as before, or not?" From Fayan's point of view, both the "yes" and the "no" answer are mistaken.

**Nanyue polishes a tile** (*Nangaku ma sen* 南嶽磨甎): The name of a famous episode involving Mazu Daoyi 馬祖道一 (709-788) and his teacher, Nanyue Huairang 南嶽懷讓 (677-744). The version found in Dōgen's *Shōbōgenzō* in Chinese script (*shinji Shōbōgenzō* 眞字正法眼藏, DZZ.5:128-130, case 8) reads as follows:

洪州江西馬祖大寂禪師〈嗣南嶽、諱道一〉參侍南嶽、密受心印、蓋拔同參。住傳法院、常日坐禪。南嶽知是法器、往師所問曰、大德、坐禪圖箇什麼。師曰、圖作佛。南嶽乃取一甎、於師庵前石上磨。師遂間、師作什麼。南嶽曰、磨作鏡。師曰、磨甎豈得成鏡耶。南嶽曰、坐禪豈得作佛耶。師曰、如何即是。南嶽曰、如人駕車、車若不行、打車即是、打牛即是。師無對。南嶽又示曰、汝爲學坐禪、爲學坐佛。若學坐禪、禪非坐臥。若學坐佛、佛非定相。於無住法、不應取捨。汝若坐佛、即是殺佛。若執坐相、非達其理。師聞示誨、如飲醍醐。

## Supplementary notes to the translation

Chan Master Daji, Mazu of Jiangxi in Hongzhou (descendant of Nanyue, named Daoyi), while attending Nanyue, secretly received the mind seal, for he stood out from his fellow students. He stayed at the Chuanfa Cloister, where he always practiced seated meditation.

Nanyue, recognizing that he was a vessel of the dharma, went to the Master's place and asked, "Most Virtuous One, what are you figuring to do, sitting there in meditation?"

The Master said, "I'm figuring to make a buddha."

Nanyue thereupon took up a tile and began to rub it on a stone in front of the Master's hermitage. At length, the Master asked, "Master, what are you making?"

Nanyue said, "I'm polishing this to make a mirror."

The Master said, "How can you produce a mirror by polishing a tile?"

Nanyue replied, "How can you make a buddha by sitting in meditation?"

The Master said, "So, what is right?"

Nanyue replied, "When someone's driving a cart, if the cart doesn't go, is beating the cart right, or is beating the ox right?"

The Master had no reply. Nanyue went on: "Are you studying seated meditation, or are you studying seated buddha? If you're studying seated meditation, meditation is not sitting or reclining. If you're studying seated buddha, buddha is no fixed mark. In a nonabiding dharma, there should be no grasping or rejecting. If you're a seated buddha, this is **killing the buddha**. If you grasp the mark of sitting, this is not reaching its principle."

When the Master heard this teaching, it was as if he drank ghee.

Dōgen often refers to this story and comments on it at length in his "Needle of Seated Meditation" ("Shōbōgenzō zazen shin" 正法眼藏坐禪箴).

Nanyue's allegory of "beating the ox" (*dagyū* 打牛) versus "beating the cart" (*dasha* 打車) reflects a story found in the *Great Adornment Discourse Sūtra* (*Da zhuangyan lun jing* 大莊嚴論經, T.201.4:266a15-b2), in which a *bhikṣuṇī*, coming upon a brahmanical ascetic engaged in the *pañca-tapas*, or "five fires" (*gonetsu* 五熱; the yogic ordeal of sitting in the sun surrounded by four fires), criticizes him for broiling the wrong thing. When the ascetic asks in anger, "What should I broil?" the *bhikṣuṇī* replies,

汝若欲知可炙處者、汝但炙汝瞋恚之心。若能炙心是名眞炙。如牛駕車、車若不行乃須策牛不須打車。身猶如車、心如彼牛。

If you wish to know what you should broil, you should broil your mind of anger. If you can broil the mind, this is called true broiling. It is like the ox that pulls the cart: if the cart doesn't go, you should whip the ox, not beat the cart. The body is like the cart; the mind is like the ox.

454     DŌGEN'S *SHŌBŌGENZŌ* VOLUME VIII

Chan master Yongming Yanshou 永明延壽 (904–975) in his *Records that Mirror the Axiom* (*Zongjing lu* 宗鏡錄, T.2016.48:787b12-15), paraphrases an unnamed sūtra in which the same allegory is explicitly explained:

> 如西天尼乾子、五熱炙身、生大邪見。佛弟子謂之言曰、善男子、如世人駕牛車於路。欲速有所至、打牛即是、打車即是。尼乾聞之、勃然作色。佛弟子曰、善男子。牛喻於心、車喻於身。何得苦身而不修心。不用炙身、應當炙心。

It is like the *nirgrantha* [non-Buddhist ascetic] of Sindh in the West who broiled his body with the five fires, bringing forth a hugely false view. Disciples of the Buddha spoke to him, saying, "Good son, it is like a worldly person who drives an ox cart on the road. If he wants to quickly get to where he is going, is beating the ox right, or is beating the cart right?" When the *nirgrantha* heard that, he was furious, and his face turned red with anger. The disciples of the Buddha said, "Good son, the 'ox' in this allegory stands for the mind, and the 'cart' stands for the body. How can you torture your body and not discipline your mind? It is not necessary to broil your body; you should 'broil' your mind."

**nets and cages** (*rarō* 籮籠; also written 羅籠): Also found in reverse order: "cages and nets" (*rōra* 籠羅). "Nets" (*mōra* 網羅) for catching fish or birds, and woven bamboo "cages" (*hanrō* 樊籠) used to cage birds or coop up animals. By extension, a term indicating "restraints" (*sokubaku* 束縛) such as fetters or shackles used to hold prisoners. Metaphorically, any kind of entrapment or bondage that human beings may find themselves in. Used in Zen texts for mental afflictions (*bonnō* 煩惱) and deluded conceptualizing (*mōsō* 妄想), which are likened to spiritual and cognitive "snares" or "traps," albeit ones that are gratuitously self-imposed.

**nose** (*bikū* 鼻孔): In Zen texts, there are two main sets of metaphorical meanings. In the first place, "nose" refers by synecdoche to (a) the person, especially (b) that which is essential to the person, or (c) the very essence or identity of someone or something. The latter connotations derive, perhaps, from the notion that the innate buddha nature (like one's own nose) is something intimate that one constantly makes use of, while not seeing it or even being aware of its presence most of the time. A second constellation of meanings derive from the concrete image of a **water buffalo** being led by the nose. Because the buffalo is a large, powerful, headstrong beast, the way to control it (to pull a plow or cart) is by a rope attached to a ring that has been passed through a hole drilled through its nostrils: if the rope pulls too hard on the ring, the animal experiences pain, so it learns to move when led and not to try to escape. To "pierce the nostrils" (*senkyaku bikū* 穿却鼻孔 or *senka bikū* 穿過鼻孔) and "grasp by the nose" (*habi* 巴鼻) are metaphors for (a) the devices that a Zen master uses to guide his students or (b) the individual's

# Supplementary notes to the translation    455

ability to get a "hold" or "handle" on the central problem of Zen, variously construed as gaining control over own's mind or "seeing the [buddha] nature" (*kenshō* 見性). The expression "pull a person by the nose" (*ei jin bikū* 拽人鼻孔) is an example of the former usage; to "drill one's own nostrils oneself" (*jike bikū jike sen* 自家鼻孔自家穿) is an example of the latter. There are a number of other variations on this theme. The expression "no nose hold" (*mu habi* 無巴鼻) refers to that which is conceptually "ungraspable," or "unattainable." The expressions "tweak the nose" (*nenshō bikū* 拈將鼻孔 or *nenkyaku bikū* 拈却鼻孔) and "strike the nose" (*chikujaku bikū* 築著鼻孔) also appear in the literature of Zen, either as descriptions of something that masters literally do to disciples to startle them out of their usual patterns of deluded conceptualizing, or as metaphors for the ways that masters use language to make disciples awaken to what is essential: their innate buddha nature. "To lose the nose" (*shitsukyaku bikū* 失却鼻孔), according to *Zengo jiten* 禅語辞典 (185), means to completely lose face or reputation; according to ZGDJ (1042c), it means to miss the main point of something.

In his "Empty Space" ("Shōbōgenzō kokū" 正法眼藏虛空), Dōgen quotes an exchange between two dharma heirs of Mazu Daoyi 馬祖道一 (709–788), Shigong Huizang 石鞏慧藏 (dates unknown) and Xitang Zhizang 西堂智藏 (735-814 or 738-817), where the former "grabs the nose" (*ha bikū* 把鼻孔) of the latter and "pulls" (*ei* 拽) it. A slightly different version of the story appears in his *Shōbōgenzō* in Chinese script (*shinji Shōbōgenzō* 眞字正法眼藏, DZZ.5:256, case 248):

撫州石鞏慧藏禪師〈嗣馬祖〉問西堂、汝還解捉得虛空麼。西堂曰、解捉得。師曰、汝作麼生捉。西堂以手撮虛空。師曰、儞不解捉虛空。西堂云、師兄作麼生捉。師把西堂鼻孔拽。西堂作忍痛聲云、大殺人、拽人鼻孔、直得脫去。師曰、直得恁麼把捉始得。

Chan Master Huizang of Shigong in Fuzhou (heir of Mazu) asked Xitang, "Can you grab hold of empty space?"

Xitang said, "I can."

The Master said, "How do you do it?"

Xitang pinched the air with his fingers.

The Master said, "You can't grab empty space."

Xitang said, "How do you do it, elder brother?"

The Master grabbed Xitang's nose and pulled it.

Xitang gave a cry of pain and said, "What a brute! Pulling a person's nose, you could take it right off!"

The Master said, "That's how you have to grab hold of it."

456 DŌGEN'S *SHŌBŌGENZŌ* VOLUME VIII

**not an inch of grass for ten thousand miles** (*banri musun sō* 萬里無寸草): A saying attributed to Dongshan Liangjie 洞山良价 (807-869) that is traditionally linked with a comment on it by Shishuang Qingzhu 石霜慶諸 (807-888), forming a well-known kōan. The version included in Dōgen's *Shōbōgenzō* in Chinese script (*shinji Shōbōgenzō* 眞字正法眼藏, DZZ.5:166, case 82) reads as follows:

> 洞山夏末示衆曰、初秋夏末。直須向萬里無寸草處去。衆無語。僧擧似石霜。霜曰、何不道、出門便是草。

> At the end of the summer [retreat], Dongshan addressed the assembly saying, "It's the beginning of autumn, and the summer retreat is at its end. You should head for the place where there's not an inch of grass for ten thousand miles." The assembly was silent.

> A monk raised this with Shishuang. Shuang said, "Why not say that, once you go out the gate, it's grass."

A longer version of the same anecdote appears in the biography of Shishuang in the *Jingde Era Record of the Transmission of the Flame* (*Jingde chuandeng lu* 景德傳燈録, T.2076.51:321a17-21):

> 因僧擧洞山參次示衆曰、兄弟秋初夏末。或東去西去、直須向萬里無寸草處去始得。又曰、只如萬里無寸草處、且作麼生去。師聞之乃曰、出門便是草。僧擧似洞山。洞山曰、大唐國内能有幾人。

> Once a monk brought up [to Shishuang] the case of Dongshan, who had addressed an assembly on a formal occasion saying, "Brothers, it's the beginning of autumn, and the summer retreat is at its end. You may go off to the east or off to the west, but you should head for the place where there's not an inch of grass for ten thousand miles; only then will you get it." The monk then asked, "How do we go to such a place where there's not an inch of grass for ten thousand miles?"

> The Master [Shishuang] listened to this and said, "Once you go out the gate, it's grass."

> The monk brought that [i.e., Shishuang's comment] up with Dongshan. Dongshan said, "In this Land of the Great Tang, how many people can there be?"

The story also appears in slightly garbled form as case 89 of the *Congrong Hermitage Record* (*Congrong lu* 從容録, T.2004.48:285a4-12), entitled "Dongshan's 'No Grass'":

> 擧。洞山示衆云、秋初夏末。兄弟或東或西、直須向萬里無寸草處去。又云、只如萬里無寸草處、作麼生去。石霜云、出門便是草。大陽云、直道、不出門亦是草漫漫地。

*Supplementary notes to the translation* 457

Raised:

Dongshan addressed the assembly saying, "It's the beginning of autumn, and the summer retreat is at its end. Brothers, whether it is east or west, you should head for the place where there's not an inch of grass for ten thousand miles."

It was also said, "How do we go to such a place where there is not an inch of grass for ten thousand miles?"

Shishuang said, "Once you go out the gate, it's grass."

Taiyang said, "Even not going out the gate, it's grass spread everywhere over the earth."

Other versions of the story make it clear that a monk reported Dongshan's words to Shishuang and asked, "How do we go to such a place?" The wording here, however, is open to the possibility that Dongshan himself raised that question, which was answered by Shishuang. The second comment attached here is perhaps by Taiyang Huijian 大陽慧堅 (dates unknown), a dharma heir of Lingquan Guiren 靈泉歸仁 (dates unknown) in the lineage following Dongshan.

In one version or another, the kōan known as "Dongshan's 'No Grass'" was raised and commented on by many Chinese Chan masters throughout the Song and Yuan dynasties. It appears, among other places, in the *Extensive Record of Chan Master Hongzhi* (*Hongzhi chanshi guanglu* 宏智禪師廣録, T.2001.48:26b24-26), the *Discourse Record of Chan Master Dahui Pujue* (*Dahui Pujue chanshi yulu* 大慧普覺禪師語録, T.1998A.47:834c3-9), and the *Discourse Record of Reverend Rujing* (*Rujing heshang yulu* 如淨和尚語録, T.2002A.48:129a1-5). A number of Chan masters also used Dongshan's saying, "Not an inch of grass for ten thousand miles," as "attached words" (*jakugo* 著語) to comment on other kōans.

An item that appears in a collection of random quotations found in fascicle 27 of the *Jingde Era Record of the Transmission of the Flame* (*Jingde chuandeng lu* 景德傳燈録, T.2076.51:435b25-26) provides some crucial context for understanding Dongshan's reference to "grass":

江南國主問老宿、予有一頭水牯牛萬里無寸草。未審、向什麼處放。

The Head of State of Jiangnan asked an elder [monk of abbot rank], "I have a **water buffalo**, and there is not an inch of grass for ten thousand miles; I don't understand, in what place should I release it [to graze]?"

No reply is given in the text. The question alone, nevertheless, suggests that the "grass" of Dongshan's saying is wild grass that domesticated water buffalo can be released to seek out and feed on.

Given that context, we might suppose that Dongshan used "grass" as a metaphor for some kind of spiritual nourishment that monks could seek

458 DŌGEN'S *SHŌBŌGENZŌ* VOLUME VIII

("going east or west") following their release from the summer retreat (*ge ango* 夏安居) spent within the confines of the monastery, when it was customary to go out the gate on pilgrimage (*angya* 行脚). However, Dongshan enjoins his monk followers to "head for the place where there's not an inch of grass for ten thousand miles," so what he evidently means by "grass" is something that is naturally appealing (either to the senses or the intellect) but best avoided. The "place where there's not an inch of grass" seems to be a metaphor for a spiritual standpoint that precludes all attachments.

The expression "hundred grasses" (*hyakusō* 百草) is used as a metaphor for "the infinite variety of things in the world" or, in Buddhist texts, for "all living things"; see "**perfectly clear, the tips of the hundred grasses**." Given that context, Dongshan's admonition can also be read as saying something like, "Wherever you go, make sure you remember that none of the things you encounter really exists."

**not defiled** (*fuzenna* 不染汚): In ordinary language, to be clean, pure, unsoiled, etc. In Buddhist texts, the glyphs 不染 (*fuzen*) translate the Sanskrit *akliṣṭā*, which means "without mental afflictions." The *locus classicus* of the term "not defiled" in the literature of Zen is a dialogue featuring the Sixth Ancestor, Huineng 慧能, and his disciple Nanyue Huairang 南嶽懷讓 (677-744), to which Dōgen often makes reference. Here is the version of the story given in his *Shōbōgenzō* in Chinese script (*shinji Shōbōgenzō* 眞字正法眼藏, DZZ.5:178, case 101):

南嶽山大慧禪師〈嗣曹谿、諱懷讓〉參六祖。祖曰、從什麼處來。師曰、嵩山安國師處來。祖曰、是什麼物恁麼來。師罔措。於是執侍八年、方省前話。乃告祖云、懷讓會得、當初來時、和尚接某甲、是什麼物恁麼來。祖云、爾作麼生會。師曰、説似一物即不中。祖曰、還假修證否。師曰、修證即不無、染汚即不得。祖曰、祇此不染汚、是諸佛之所護念。汝亦如是、吾亦如是、乃至西天諸祖亦如是。

Chan Master Dahui of Mount Nanyue (descendant of Caoxi, named Huairang) visited the Sixth Ancestor. The Ancestor asked him, "Where do you come from?"

The Master said, "I come from the National Teacher An on Mount Song."

The Ancestor said, "What thing is it that comes like this?"

The Master was without means [to answer]. After attending [the Ancestor] for eight years, he finally understood the previous conversation. Thereupon, he announced to the Ancestor, "I've understood what you put to me when I first came: '**What thing is it that comes like this**?'"

The Ancestor asked, "How do you understand it?"

The Master replied, "To say it's like any thing wouldn't hit it." The Ancestor said, "Does it nevertheless depend on **practice and verification**?"

*Supplementary notes to the translation*          459

The Master answered, "It's not that it lacks practice and verification, but it can't be defiled by them."

The Ancestor said, "Just this 'not defiled' is what the buddhas bear in mind. **You're also like this, I'm also like this**, and all the ancestors of Sindh in the West [i. e., India] are also like this."

For another version of this dialogue and a discussion of its overall meaning, see "**what thing is it that comes like this?**"

In his "Principles of Seated Meditation" (Shōbōgenzō zazengi" 正法眼藏 坐禪儀, DZZ.1:89), Dōgen says:

兀兀と坐定して、思量箇不思量底なり、不思量底如何思量、これ非 思量なり。これすなはち坐禪の法術なり。坐禪は習禪にはあらず、 大安樂の法門なり、不染汚の修證なり。

Sitting fixedly, think of not thinking. How do you think of not thinking? Non-thinking. This is the art of seated meditation. Seated meditation is not the **practice of dhyāna**. It is the dharma gate of great ease and joy. It is non-defiling **practice and verification**.

Dōgen indicates here that, in some cases, "practice and verification" can be defiling, but that buddhas are "not defiled" by them. The difference between "defiled" and "undefiled," therefore, must have something to do with the attitude or understanding of the person who is engaged with them.

**obstructed by the eye** (*higen ge* 被眼礙): A line from a saying of Fayan Wenyi 法眼文益 (885-958) that appears in a number of Zen texts, such as the *Outline of the Linked Flames* (*Liandeng huiyao* 聯燈會要, ZZ.136:878a5-6). Dōgen quotes it in his *Shōbōgenzō* in Chinese script (*shinji Shōbōgenzō* 眞字 正法眼藏, DZZ.5:186, case 111):

因開井被砂塞却泉眼、乃問僧、泉眼不通、被砂塞却。道眼不通、被 什麼物礙。僧無対。師自代云、被眼礙。

Once, [Fayan] was digging out a well blocked by sand to open the "eye of the spring" (*sengen* 泉眼). He asked a monk, "When the eye of the spring doesn't flow (*tsū* 通), it's the sand that blocks it. When the eye of the way doesn't penetrate (*tsū* 通), what is it that obstructs it?"

The monk had no reply.

The Master answered for him, "It's obstructed by the eye."

The implication here is that the "eye of the way" (*dōgen* 道眼), which sees the "subtle true dharma, the true sign of which is signless" (*jissō musō, mimyō shōbō* 實相無相、微妙正法), is "obstructed by the eye" (*higen ge* 被眼 礙) of ordinary vision, which sees signs (*sō* 相, S. *nimitta*) and forms (*shiki* 色, S. *rūpa*).

460 DŌGEN'S *SHŌBŌGENZŌ* VOLUME VIII

**old buddha** (*kobutsu* 古佛): In the East Asian Buddhist tradition at large, a *pratyeka-buddha* (*byakushika budda* 辟支迦佛陀). Also, a generic name for the "**seven buddhas of the past**" (*kako shichi butsu* 過去七佛), the last of whom was Buddha Śākyamuni. In his "Buddha Nature" ("Shōbōgenzō busshō" 正法眼藏佛性), Dōgen refers to Śākyamuni as "the Old Buddha."

In the Zen tradition, an honorific epithet for revered ancestral masters (*soshi* 祖師). In his "Needle of Seated Meditation" ("Shōbōgenzō zazen shin" 正法眼藏坐禪箴), for example, Dōgen says that his teacher, Tiantong Rujing 天童如淨 (1162-1227), referred to the Caodong 曹洞 master Hongzhi Zhengjue 宏智正覺 (1091-1157) as "Old Buddha Hongzhi" (*Wanshi kobutsu* 宏智古佛). Those words appear in the *Discourse Record of Reverend Rujing* (*Rujing heshang yulu* 如淨和尚語錄, T.2002A.48:127a25-26):

正當恁麼、且與宏智古佛相見。擧拂子云、相見已了。

"At just such a time, we meet the Old Buddha Hongzhi." He raised his **whisk** and said, "Have you met him?"

In "The Old Buddha Mind" ("Shōbōgenzō kobutsushin" 正法眼藏古佛心), Dōgen quotes Xuefeng Yicun 雪峰義存 (822-908), who called Zhaozhou Congshen 趙州從諗 (778-897) an "old buddha," and comments that Xuefeng himself must also have been one. Xuefeng's remark is found in the *Discourse Record of Xuefeng* (*Xuefeng yulu* 雪峰語錄, ZZ.119:964b16; X.1333.69:81c7-10) and other texts; Dōgen includes it in his *Shōbōgenzō* in Chinese script (*shinji Shōbōgenzō* 眞字正法眼藏, DZZ.5:268, case 283):

雪峰、因僧問、古澗寒泉時如何。師曰、瞪目不見底。僧曰、飲者如何。師曰、不從口入。後有僧擧似趙州。州曰、不可從鼻孔裏入。僧却問、古澗寒泉時如何。州曰、苦。僧曰、飲者如何。州曰、死。師聞之云、趙州古佛。師從此不答話。

Once, a monk asked Xuefeng, "How about when it's the cold spring of the old stream?"

The Master said, "Though you stare at it, you can't see to the bottom."

[The monk] said, "How about the one who drinks from it?"

The Master said, "It won't go in from his mouth."

Later, there was a monk who raised this with Zhaozhou. Zhou said, "It can't be that it goes in through his **nose**."

The monk asked again, "How about when it's the cold spring of the old stream?"

Zhou said, "Bitter."

The monk said, "How about the one who drinks from it?"

Zhou said, "He dies."

*Supplementary notes to the translation*                    461

The Master, hearing this, said, "Zhaozhou is an old buddha." After this, the Master did not give answers [to this question].

Dōgen frequently refers to his own teacher, Rujing, as "my former master, the Old Buddha" (*senshi kobutsu* 先師古佛). He occasionally quotes "an old buddha" without naming the master in question, and he speaks of "old buddhas" in the plural as a kind of general reference to all the ancestral masters in the Zen lineage. Such usages are common to Zen literature at large and are grounded in the claim that all dharma heirs in the Zen lineage are buddhas because the dharma that the Zen lineage transmits is the buddha mind (*busshin* 佛心). In his "Making a Bow and Getting the Marrow" ("Shōbōgenzō raihai tokuzui" 正法眼藏禮拜得髓) (DZZ.1:307), Dōgen says:

得法せらんはすなはち一箇の眞箇なる古佛。

Anyone who has gained the dharma is one true old buddha.

**old mirror** (*kokyō* 古鏡): In common parlance, a reference to the ancient bronze mirrors of China, often thought of as somehow magical for their reflective power. In the Buddhist context, a metaphor for consciousness, especially for the type or feature of consciousness that perfectly reflects its object — the "mirror wisdom," often said to be inherent in all consciousness and fully realized in the awakened mind. For details of that metaphor, and the famous exchange between Xuefeng Yicun 雪峰義存 (822-908) and his disciple Xuansha Shibei 玄沙師備 (835-908) in which the former speaks of an "old mirror" that simply reflects whoever comes before it, whether a foreigner or a Han Chinese, see "**bright mirror**."

Another episode involving those two monks that also features an "old mirror" is found in Dōgen's *Shōbōgenzō* in Chinese script (*shinji Shōbōgenzō* 眞字正法眼藏, DZZ.5:184, case 109). The version given in his "The Old Mirror" ("Shōbōgenzō kokyō" 正法眼藏古鏡, DZZ.1:234) reads:

雪峰示衆云、世界闊一丈、古鏡闊一丈。世界闊一尺、古鏡闊一尺。
時玄沙指火爐云、且道、火爐闊多少。雪峰云、似古鏡闊。玄沙云、
老和尚、脚跟未點地在。

Xuefeng addressed the assembly, saying, "If the breadth of the world is ten feet, the breadth of the old mirror is ten feet; if the breadth of the world is one inch, the breadth of the old mirror is one inch."

At that point, Xuansha pointed at the brazier and said, "Tell me the size of the brazier."

Xuefeng said, "It's like the breadth of the old mirror."

Xuansha said, "The Old Reverend's heels haven't touched the earth."

A slightly different version of this exchange, raised as a kōan and commented on by Yuanwu Keqin 圜悟克勤 (1063-1135), also appears in the

462    DŌGEN'S *SHŌBŌGENZŌ* VOLUME VIII

*Discourse Record of Chan Master Yuanwu Foguo*; for a translation, see "**bare mind in pieces**."

Yet another episode involving an "old mirror," one that features the Tang-dynasty monk Chan Master Huiran of Sansheng Cloister 三聖院慧然禪師 (dates unknown), who studied with Linji Yixuan 臨濟義玄 (died 866) and other masters, is recorded in Dōgen's *Shōbōgenzō* in Chinese script (*shinji Shōbōgenzō* 眞字正法眼藏, DZZ.5:272, case 294):

> 雪峰與三聖行次、見一隊猢猻。師曰、祇這猢猻、各各背一面古鏡。聖曰、歷劫無名、何以彰爲古鏡。師曰、瑕生也。聖云、一千五百人善知識、話頭也不識。師曰、老僧住持事繁。

Once, when Xuefeng and Sansheng were traveling, they saw a group of monkeys. The Master [Xuefeng] said, "Each of these monkeys is bearing an old mirror on its back."

[San] Sheng said, "It's been nameless across the kalpas. Why do you express it as 'an old mirror'?"

The Master said, "A flaw's developed."

Sheng said, "Fifteen hundred wise friends wouldn't even know what you're talking about."

The Master said, "This old monk's abbot's business is complicated."

**one blade of grass** (*ikkyō sō* 一莖草): In Zen texts, "one blade of grass" is emblematic of a very simple, common thing that is said to be, from an awakened point of view, equal in value and significance to something that is ordinarily taken to be far grander, such as the "sixteen-foot body" (*jōroku shin* 丈六身) of the Buddha, an entire monastery (*bonsetsu* 梵刹), or the "way" (*dō* 道) of the buddhas. Examples of these comparisons follow.

In the *Discourse Record of Chan Master Yuanwu Foguo* (*Yuanwu Foguo chanshi yulu* 圓悟佛果禪師語錄, T.1997.47:731b3-4), Yuanwu Keqin 圜悟克勤 (1063-1135) says:

> 拈一莖草現丈六身、吹一布毛傳正法眼。離無離有絶聖絶凡、八字打開分明顯示了也。

Holding up one blade of grass manifests the sixteen-foot body; blowing on one piece of lint transmits the true dharma eye.

In his prose commentary on case 47 of the *Congrong Hermitage Record* (*Congrong lu* 從容錄; T.2004.48:257a19-21), entitled "Zhaozhou's Cypress" (*Jōshū hakujushi* 趙州柏樹), the compiler of the text, Wansong Xingxiu 萬松行秀 (1166–1246), quotes Zhaozhou Congshen 趙州從諗 (778–897) as follows:

> 州嘗云、有時將一莖草作丈六金身用。有時將丈六金身作一莖草用。

*Supplementary notes to the translation* 463

[Zhao]zhou once said, "Sometimes I take one blade of grass and use it as a sixteen-foot golden body; sometimes I take a sixteen-foot golden body and use it as one blade of grass."

"Sixteen-foot golden body" (*jōroku konjin* 丈六金身) is another way of referring to the body of the Buddha, whose golden color is one of his thirty-two marks. The same saying, albeit not attributed to Zhaozhou, also appears in the prose commentary on case 4 in the *Blue Cliff Record* (*Biyan lu* 碧巖錄, T.2003.48:143b21-23).

Case 4 of the *Congrong Hermitage Record* (T.2004.48:230a4-6), entitled "The World-Honored One Pointed to the Ground" (*Seson shichi* 世尊指地), compares planting a blade of grass to building a monastery:

舉。世尊與衆行次以手指地云、此處宜建梵刹。帝釋將一莖草插於地上云、建梵刹已竟。世尊微笑。

Raised.

When the World-Honored One was walking with the assembly, he pointed to the ground with his hand and said, "This place is suitable for constructing a monastery."

Lord Śakra [Indra] took one blade of grass, stuck it in the ground, and said, "The construction of the monastery has been completed."

The World-Honored One smiled slightly.

Tiantong Jue's (Hongzhi Zhengjue 宏智正覺, 1091–1157) verse commentary on this kōan in the *Congrong Hermitage Record* (T.2004.48:230a13-16) reads:

百草頭上無邊春、信手拈來用得親、丈六金身功德聚。等閑携手入紅塵、塵中能作主、化外自來賓。觸處生涯隨分足、未嫌伎倆不如人。

On the tips of the hundred grasses, a limitless spring;

Randomly picking one up and using it, he was able to come close to

The accumulation of merit of the sixteen-foot golden body.

Casually cooperating, he entered the red dust [of the mundane world],

And within the dust was able to reign supreme,

A guest arriving from outside the [Buddha's] realm of teaching.

Whatever he touched in this world, in accordance with his capacity, was sufficient;

He did not dislike playing tricks and was not comparable to humans.

In this verse, Tiantong Jue may be comparing the merit (*kudoku* 功德) accumulated by building a gilded or metal image of the Buddha that is 16 feet tall to that of using one blade of grass as an offering to the Buddha. Also see "**perfectly clear, the tips of the hundred grasses**."

464 DŌGEN'S *SHŌBŌGENZŌ* VOLUME VIII

Finally in the biography of Chan Master Zhengqin Yuanyun (dates unknown) that appears in the *Jingde Era Record of the Transmission of the Flame* (*Jingde chuandeng lu* 景德傳燈錄, T.2076.51:368c4), we read:

曰、如何是道。師曰、楞伽峯頂一莖草。

[Someone] said, "What is the way?"

The Master said, "One blade of grass on top of Laṅkā Peak."

**one bright pearl** (*ikka myōju* 一顆明珠): Literally, a "single kernel" (*ikka* 一顆) of "bright," or "luminous" (*myō* 明), "pearl" (*ju* 珠). In Chinese mythology, a "bright pearl" is a magical jewel that is said to give off light. The *Collection of Tales of Gods* (*Soushen ji* 搜神記), an Eastern Jin-dynasty (266–420) compilation of tales concerning gods and ghosts attributed to Gan Bao 干寶 (d. 336), tells of the "pearl of the Marquis of Sui," also called the "pearl of the numinous serpent," which was one inch in diameter, pure white, and glowed in the dark. After the Marquis gave medical treatment to a large, wounded serpent that he chanced to encounter on a hillside, the serpent came to him carrying the bright pearl in its mouth as a thank-you gift. In Chinese lore, the "pearl of the numinous serpent," together with the "jade of Mount Jing," came to be owned by the First Emperor of the Qin Dynasty (221-206 BCE) and were the two most precious and powerful items in existence at the time. They were symbols, not only of priceless value, but also of the wisdom of the sage rulers of antiquity.

In the literature of Zen, the expression "one bright pearl" is attributed both to Dongshan Liangjie 洞山良价 (807–869) and, more commonly, to Xuansha Shibei 玄沙師備 (835-908). The *Discourse Record of Chan Master Wuben of Mount Dong in Junzhou* (*Junzhou Dongshan Wuben chanshi yulu* 筠州洞山悟本禪師語錄, T.1986A.47:507c14-17) contains the following discussion between Dongshan and his teacher, Yunyan Tansheng 雲巖曇成 (782-841):

師問雲巖、某甲有餘習未盡。巖曰、汝曾作甚麼來。師曰、聖諦亦不為。巖曰、還歡喜也未。師曰、歡喜則不無。如糞掃堆頭拾得一顆明珠。

The Master [Dongshan] inquired of Yunyan, "I have residual afflictions that are not yet exhausted."

Yan said, "What have you been doing?"

The Master said, "I don't do even the [four] sacred truths."

Yan said, "Have you reverted from joy [the first of the ten stages on the bodhisattva path]?"

The Master said, "It's not that I lack joy, but it's like finding one bright pearl in a pile of filth."

*Supplementary notes to the translation*  465

The biography of Xuansha, as it appears in the *Jingde Era Record of the Transmission of the Flame* (*Jingde chuandeng lu* 景德傳燈錄, T.2076.51:346c16-21), includes the following exchange:

僧問、承和尚有言、盡十方世界是一顆明珠。學人如何得會。師曰、盡十方世界是一顆明珠、用會作麼。師來日却問其僧、盡十方世界是一顆明珠、汝作麼生會。對曰、盡十方世界是一顆明珠、用會作麼。師曰、知汝向山鬼窟裏作活計。

A monk asked, "I've heard, Reverend, that you have a saying: 'All worlds in the ten directions are one bright pearl.' How is your student to understand it?"

The Master [Xuansha] said, "All worlds in the ten directions are one bright pearl. What's the use of understanding?"

The next day, the Master turned the tables and asked that monk, "All worlds in the ten directions are one bright pearl. How do you understand it?"

[The monk] replied, "All worlds in the ten directions are one bright pearl. What's the use of understanding?" The Master said, "Now I know that you make your living inside the mountain **ghost cave**."

This kōan is included in Dōgen's *Shōbōgenzō* in Chinese script (*shinji Shōbōgenzō* 眞字正法眼藏, DZZ.5:132, case 15). It is also quoted and commented on by Dōgen in his "One Bright Pearl" ("Shōbōgenzō ikka myōju" 正法眼藏一顆明珠). There, Dōgen associates Xuansha's "one bright pearl" with other jewels that appear as well-known metaphors in Buddhist literature, including two from the *Lotus Sūtra*: the "bright **jewel in the topknot**" that a king reserves as his supreme reward to only the most worthy follower; and the "precious jewel" (*hōju* 寶珠), or "**jewel in the robe**," that a friend attaches inside a drunken man's robe so that the latter will have resources on his upcoming journey. The latter comes to symbolize the buddha nature that is innate in all living beings, whether they are aware of it or not. Perhaps that is what Xuansha meant by the "one bright pearl," which he says is not to be "understood" as an object of discursive thinking. According to ZGDJ (s.v. いっかみょうじゅ), the metaphor of "one bright pearl" expresses the "true mark" (*shinjissō* 眞實相) of this world, which is perfect and complete as it is, and not divided into internal "mind" and external "form." That interpretation is consistent with a somewhat different version of Xuansha's exchange with the unnamed monk. The biography of Chan Master Ciyun Yanlong 慈雲彥隆 (dates unknown) that appears in the *Jianzhong Jingguo Era Continued Record of the Flame* (*Jianzhong jingguo xudeng lu* 建中靖國續燈錄, ZZ.136:306b8-14), for example, contains the following record of that kōan being raised and commented on:

# DŌGEN'S *SHŌBŌGENZŌ* VOLUME VIII

上堂。舉。玄沙示衆云、盡大地都來是一顆明珠。時有僧便問曰、既是一顆明珠、學人爲什麼不識。沙云、全體是珠。更教誰識。僧曰、雖然全體是、爭奈學人不識。沙云、問取儞眼。

師云、諸禪德、遮箇公案喚作嚼飯餧小兒。把手更與杖。還會麼。若未會、須是扣己而參、直要眞實。不得信口掠虛。徒自虛生浪死。參。

Raised at a convocation in the dharma hall:

Xuansha addressed the congregation, saying, "The whole earth in its entirety is one bright pearl."

At the time, there was a monk who asked, "If this is one bright pearl, how come your student is not conscious of it?"

Sha said, "The entire body is the pearl; who [apart from it] would be made conscious of it?"

The monk, "Granted it's the entire body, still, why is your student not conscious of it?"

Sha said, "Ask your **eyes**."

[Comment]

The Master [Yanlong] said, "Chan worthies, I call this kōan chewing rice to feed an infant or expressing affection by giving someone [a blow with] one's **staff**. Have you understood? If you have yet to understand, you must question yourself and investigate directly what is real. Do not speak loosely and vacuously, because what follows are vain births and waves of death. Investigate!"

In the *Congrong Hermitage Record* (*Congrong lu* 從容錄, T.2004.48:287b3-c29), a kōan collection compiled by Chan Master Wansong Xingxiu 萬松行秀 (1166–1246), case 93, entitled "Luzu Does Not Understand" (*Roso fue* 魯祖不會), features a dialogue between Luzu Baoyun 魯祖寶雲 (dates unknown) and Nanquan Puyuan 南泉普願 (748-835):

舉。魯祖問南泉、摩尼珠人不識、如來藏裏親收得。如何是藏。泉云、王老師與汝往來者是。祖云、不往來者。泉云、亦是藏。祖云、如何是珠。泉召云、師祖。祖應諾。泉云、去。汝不會我語。

Raised:

Luzu asked Nanquan, "'The *maṇi* jewel, something that people aren't conscious of, is personally obtained within the womb of the tathāgata,' but what is that womb?"

Quan said [using a self-referential sobriquet], "It's that which goes and comes with Old Master Wang and you."

Zu said, "And that which doesn't go or come?"

Quan said, "That, too, is the womb."

*Supplementary notes to the translation*   467

Zu said, "What about the jewel?"

Quan called him [by name], "Mister Zu!"

Zu responded, "Yes?"

Quan said, "Go. You don't understand what I'm saying."

In his prose commentary on this root case, Wansong points out that Luzu's initial question contains a quotation from the *Song of Realizing the Way* (*Zhengdao ge* 證道歌, T.2014.48:395c22-23) by Chan Master Yongjia Xuanjue 永嘉玄覺 (675–713), the relevant part of which reads:

摩尼珠人不識、如來藏裏親收得。六般神用空不空、一顆圓光色非色。

The *maṇi* jewel, something that people are not conscious of,

Is personally obtained within the womb of the tathāgata.

The spiritual action of the six senses is emptiness that is not empty;

The single sphere of perfect luminosity has a form that is not form.

Wansong goes on to note that, "The Sanskrit word *maṇi* (*mani* 摩尼), translated here [in China] as 'wish-fulfilling' (*nyoi* 如意), also means 'unblemished luminosity' (*muku kō* 無垢光)." He then quotes a line from the *Laṅkāvatāra Sūtra* (*Ru Lengqie jing* 入楞伽經, T.671.16:519a1-2) that reads:

寂滅者名爲一心、一心者名爲如來藏。

That which is quiescent is called the "one mind." The "one mind" is called the "womb of the tathāgata."

Later, in his prose commentary on the verse by Tiantong Jue (Hongzhi Zhengjue 宏智正覺, 1091–1157), Wansong quotes a passage from the *Lotus Sūtra* (*Miaofa lianhua jing* 妙法蓮華經, T.262.9:39a7-9) in which the Buddha explains how a wheel-turning king, with a "mind most joyful," finally bestows the jewel from his topknot on a worthy warrior. He concludes by commenting on the kōan in which Dongshan speaks of "one bright pearl":

洞山云、歡喜即不無、如糞掃堆頭拾得一顆明珠相似。萬松道、我不似洞山、乞兒見小利。歡喜則不歡喜。如來藏中擊碎一顆明珠相似。

Dongshan said, "It's not that I lack joy, but it's like finding one bright pearl in a pile of filth."

Wangsong says, "I'm not like Dongshan, a beggar who has his eye on small profit. My joy is not being joyful. It's like hitting and pulverizing the one bright pearl in the womb of the tathāgata."

In this way, Wansong associates the *maṇi* jewel of unblemished luminosity, Chan Master Yongjia's "single sphere of perfect luminosity" (*ikka enkō* 一顆圓光), the **"bright jewel in the topknot"** (*keichū myōju* 髻中明珠) of the *Lotus Sūtra* parable, and Dongshan's "one bright pearl" (*ikka myōju* 一顆明

珠). What he suggests is that all of these are different names for the "one mind" (*isshin* 一心), as that is explained in the *Laṅkāvatāra Sūtra*.

**one great treasury of the teachings** (*ichi daizō kyō* 一大藏教): All of the teachings of Śākyamuni that eventually came to be written down and compiled in the Buddhist canon (*daizōkyō* 大藏經; S. *tripiṭaka*). An example of this usage is found in the *Blue Cliff Record* (*Biyan lu* 碧巖錄, T.2003.48:204a25-26), where the compiler Yuanwu Keqin 圜悟克勤 (1063-1135) refers to the "one great treasury of the teachings that Old Śākya preached for forty-nine years" (*Shaka rōshi, shijūku nen, setsu ichi daizō kyō* 釋迦老子、四十九年、説一大藏教). In the literature of Zen, the verbal "teachings" (*kyō* 教) of the Buddha that comprise the canon are often contrasted with the "mind of Buddha" (*busshin* 佛心), conceived as the awakening that Śākyamuni had before he ever tried to share it with others through the medium of language. Proponents of the Zen lineage claim that it is superior to the so-called "teachings lineages" (*kyōshū* 教宗) — e.g., the Huayan and Tiantai schools of Buddhism — because the former conveys the buddha mind directly from master to disciple as "**a separate transmission outside the teachings**," while the latter rely on scriptures (*monji* 文字). Sūtra reading (*kankin* 看經), whether done quietly and individually for meaning, or aloud and collectively as a merit-generating rite, was a routine feature of Zen monastic life in Dōgen's day. The literature of Zen, however, contains many instances of masters cautioning their disciples not to become attached to verbal constructs as if they conveyed ultimate truth but to regard them as merely skillful devices (*hōben* 方便). The *Extensive Record of Chan Master Yunmen Kuangzhen* (*Yunmen Kuangzhen chanshi guanglu* 雲門匡眞禪師廣錄, T.1988.47:572c3-5), for example, contains the following passage:

師因見僧看經乃云、看經須具看經眼。燈籠露柱一大藏教無欠少。拈起拄杖云、一大藏教總在拄杖頭上。

When the Master [Yunmen] saw a monk reading a sūtra, he said, "To read the sūtras you must possess the **eye** for reading sūtras. The **lanterns and pillars**: [these are] one great treasury of the teachings, with nothing lacking." Raising his **staff** he said, "The one great treasury of the teachings, in its entirety, resides here on the tip of my staff."

What Yunmen Wenyan 雲門文偃 (864-949) evidently means here by "one great treasury of the teachings" is no longer the mass of sūtra and vinaya literature attributed to Śākyamuni Buddha, but rather the ineffable essence of those teachings. In case 14 of the *Blue Cliff Record* (T.2003.48:154c2-7), Yuanwu Keqin praises Yunmen's ability to "take the one great treasury of the teachings and boil it down to just three words," namely, "To each, an appropriate explanation" (*tai issetsu* 對一説):

## Supplementary notes to the translation

舉。僧問雲門、如何是一代時教。雲門云、對一説。

禪家流、欲知佛性義、當觀時節因緣。謂之教外別傳、單傳心印、直指人心、見性成佛。釋迦老子、四十九年住世、三百六十會、開談頓漸權實。謂之一代時教。這僧拈來問云。如何是一代時教。雲門何不與他紛紛解説。却向他道箇對一説。雲門尋常一句中。須具三句。謂之函蓋乾坤句、隨波逐浪句、截斷衆流句。放去收來、自然奇特、如斬釘截鐵。教人義解卜度他底不得。一大藏教、只消三箇字。

Raised:

A monk asked Yunmen, "What about the [Buddha's] teachings of an entire lifetime?"

Yunmen said, "To each, an appropriate explanation."

[Yuanwu's comment]

Followers of the Chan house, "**If you wish to know the meaning of 'buddha nature,' you should observe the conditions of the time**." We call this, "**A separate transmission outside the teachings**, individually transmitting the mind-seal, **pointing directly at the person's mind, seeing the nature and attaining buddhahood**." Old Śākya stayed in the world for forty-nine years, and in three-hundred-sixty assemblies he discoursed on sudden versus gradual, provisional and ultimate truth. That is called the "teachings of an entire lifetime." It is what the monk raised as a topic when he asked, "What about the teachings of an entire lifetime?" Why didn't Yunmen give him a detailed explanation, instead of just saying to him, "To each, an appropriate explanation"? For Yunmen, as a matter of course, within each single phrase, three phrases should be at work. Those are: a phrase that boxes and covers heaven and earth; a phrase that follows the waves and goes with the tide; and a phrase that cuts off all flows. In letting things go and gathering them together, he is naturally extraordinary, as if he were severing spikes or slashing through iron. He incites people to interpret and conjecture about his meaning, but they don't get it. He takes the one great treasury of the teachings and boils it down to just three words.

**one strip of iron** (*ichijō tetsu* 一條鐵): Short for "one strip of iron for ten thousand miles" (*banri ichijō tetsu* 萬里一條鐵), a common Zen idiom for the ultimate unity of the myriad phenomena. The glyphs 一條 (*ichijō*), taken literally, mean "one piece," or "a single strip." However, they are also used metaphorically to refer to things that are unified, connected, or homogeneous, and to people who act or think alike. An early occurrence of the saying is found in the biography of "Chan Master Xian of Shimen Monastery on Mount Fenghuang in Xiangzhou" in the *Jingde Era Record of the Transmission of the Flame* (*Jingde chuandeng lu* 景德傳燈錄, T.51.2076:366b7-10):

日、如何是境中人。師曰、風射舊簾櫳、因般若寺遭焚。有人問曰、既是般若爲什麼被火燒。師曰、萬里一條鐵。

[Someone] asked, "What about the person in the midst of worldly affairs?"

The Master [Xian] said, "When the wind blows by an old bamboo cage, it makes the temple of wisdom (*prajñā*) burn down."

Someone else asked, "If it is indeed wisdom, how can it be subject to incineration?"

The Master said, "One strip of iron for ten thousand miles."

Chan Master Xian 獻禪師 (dates unknown) was a dharma heir of Chan Master Shiqian 師虔禪師 (d. 904), who was in turn an heir of Dongshan Liangjie 洞山良价 (807-869). Elsewhere in Zen literature, there is reference to "Dongshan's 'one strip of iron for ten thousand miles,'" as if the saying originated with him or was associated with his lineage.

**only buddhas with buddhas can exhaustively investigate the real marks of the dharmas** (*yui butsu yo butsu nai nō gūjin shohō jissō* 唯佛與佛乃能究盡諸法實相): A line in the "Expedient Means" (*Fangbian* 方便) chapter of Kumārajīva's translation of the *Lotus Sūtra* (*Miaofa lianhua jing* 妙法蓮華經, T.262.9:5c10-13), from which the Tiantai tradition derives its characteristic teaching of the "tenfold suchnesses" (*jū nyoze* 十如是):

唯佛與佛乃能究盡諸法實相。所謂諸法如是相、如是性、如是體、如是力、如是作、如是因、如是緣、如是果、如是報、如是本末究竟等。

Only buddhas with buddhas can exhaustively investigate the real marks of the dharmas: that the dharmas are of such a mark, such a nature, such a substance, such a power, such an action, such a cause, such a condition, such an effect, such a recompense, such an ultimate equivalence from beginning to end.

The extant Sanskrit for this passage is somewhat different from Kumārajīva's version and lists only five aspects of the dharmas known by the Tathāgata: which (S. *ya*) the dharmas are; how (S. *yathā*) they are; what they are like (S. *yādṛś*); what their marks (S. *lakṣaṇa*) are; and what their natures (S. *svabhāva*) are.

**ordinary mind is the way** (*byōjō shin ze dō* 平常心是道): Words spoken by Nanquan Puyuan 南泉普願 (748-835) to Zhaozhou Congshen 趙州從諗 (778-897). The version of the dialogue found in the latter's biography in the *Jingde Era Record of the Transmission of the Flame* (*Jingde chuandeng lu* 景德傳燈錄, T.2076.51:276c14-19) reads:

*Supplementary notes to the translation* 471

異日問南泉、如何是道。南泉曰、平常心是道。師曰、還可趣向否。南泉曰、擬向即乖。師曰、不擬時如何知是道。南泉曰、道不屬知不知。

Another day, he [i.e., Zhaozhou] asked Nanquan, "What is the way?"

Nanquan said, "The ordinary mind is the way."

The Master said, "Should we head for it?"

Nanquan said, "If we try to head toward it, we turn away from it."

The Master said, "When we don't try, how do we know it's the way?"

Nanquan said, "The way has nothing to do with knowing or not knowing."

A similar dialogue is also found in Dōgen's *Shōbōgenzō* in Chinese script (*shinji Shōbōgenzō* 眞字正法眼藏, DZZ.5:134, case 19).

In the *Discourse Record of Chan Master Yuanwu Foguo* (*Yuanwu Foguo chanshi yulu* 圓悟佛果禪師語錄, T.1997.47:750a16-19), we read:

趙州初參南泉、悟平常心是道後、來有問西來意。便對曰、庭前柏樹子。以至鎭州出大蘿蔔頭。我在青州作一領布衫重七斤。

After Zhaozhou had first studied under Nanquan and awakened to "ordinary mind is the way," someone came and asked him about the "**intention of [the Ancestral Master's] coming from the west**." He replied, "The **cypress tree at the front of the garden**." He went on to say [when approached by a monk who asked if he had seen Nanquan in person], "Zhenzhou [district] produces big radishes." [When challenged by a monk who asked, "The ten thousand things return to the one; what place does the one return to?"] he said, "When I was in Qingzhou I made a collared linen shirt that weighed seven catties [4.4 kilograms]."

Yuanwu's point here seems to be that all of these famous sayings attributed to Zhaozhou are demonstrations of the "ordinary mind" (*byōjō shin* 平常心), which thinks of ordinary things like cypress trees, radishes, and linen shirts. Realizing that awakening, or "buddha mind" (*busshin* 佛心), is not some special, exalted state of mind that is divorced from one's everyday consciousness, of course, is not an ordinary accomplishment.

**peach blossoms** (*tōka* 桃華): A common symbol of springtime in secular literature, the peach blossom appears often in the *Shōbōgenzō* in connection with the story of Lingyun Zhiqin 靈雲志勤 (dates unknown), who is said to have awakened to the way upon viewing peach trees in bloom. Lingyun's biography in the *Jingde Era Record of the Transmission of the Flame* (*Jingde chuandeng lu* 景德傳燈錄, T.2076.51:285a23-26) reads:

福州靈雲志勤禪師本州長溪人也。初在潙山因桃華悟道。有偈曰、三十來年尋劍客、幾逢落葉幾抽枝。自從一見桃華後、直至如今更不疑。

Chan Master Lingyun Zhiqin of Fuzhou prefecture was a man from Changxi in Benzhou. He first awakened to the way on Mount Weishan on account of peach blossoms. He has a verse that says:

> Thirty years a passenger seeking the sword;
> So many times I encountered falling leaves and budding branches.
> After once seeing the peach blossoms,
> I'm like this now, without further doubts.

The expression "passenger seeking the sword" (*jin ken kyaku* 尋劍客) is an allusion to the story, from *Master Lü's Spring and Autumn Annals* (*Lüshi chunqiu* 春秋, KR.3j0009.015-22a-b), of the stupid man of Chu 楚 who accidentally dropped his sword from a boat and marked the spot where he might recover it by notching the gunwale. What Lingyun means to say in the first two lines of his verse is that he witnessed falling leaves in the autumn and blossoms on trees in the spring for thirty years but was not awakened by those because he was seeking awakening in an entirely deluded way. The story of "Lingyun's peach blossoms" (*Reiun tōka* 靈雲桃花) is raised as a kōan and commented on in a number of Zen texts, including: the *Treasury of the True Dharma Eye* (*Zhengfayanzang* 正法眼藏, ZZ.118:36b14-17) by Dahui Zonggao 大慧宗杲 (1089-1163); the *Empty Hall Collection* (*Xutang ji* 虛堂集, ZZ.117:549b12-550b12, case 16); and Dōgen's own *Shōbōgenzō* in Chinese script (*shinji Shōbōgenzō* 眞字正法眼藏, DZZ.5:206, case 155). Dōgen also treats the story of Lingyun's awakening in his "Sound of the Stream, Form of the Mountain" ("Shōbōgenzō keisei sanshoku" 正法眼藏谿聲山色), which gives a slightly different version of the famous verse:

> 又、靈雲志勤禪師は、三十年の辦道なり。あるとき遊山するに、山脚に休息して、はるかに人里を望見す。ときに春なり。桃華のさかりなるをみて、忽然として悟道す。偈をつくりて大潙に呈するにいはく、三十年來尋劍客、幾回葉落又抽枝、自從一見桃華後、直至如今更不疑。大潙いはく、從緣入者、永不退失。すなはち許可するなり。

Again, Chan Master Lingyun Zhiqin pursued the way for thirty years. Once, while traveling in the mountains, resting at the foot of a mountain, he looked out at a village in the distance. The time was spring, and, seeing the peach blossoms in bloom, he suddenly awakened to the way. Composing a gāthā, he presented it to Dawei.

> Thirty years a passenger seeking the sword.
> How many times have the leaves fallen and the branches budded?
> After once seeing the peach blossoms,
> I'm like this now, without further doubts.

Dawei said, "Those who enter from objects never regress or lose it." This was his acknowledgement.

*Supplementary notes to the translation* 473

"Dawei" 大潙 is another name for Chan master Weishan Lingyou 潙山靈祐 (771-853), who is said to have approved Lingyun as a dharma heir upon hearing his verse.

**perfectly clear, the tips of the hundred grasses** (*meimei hyaku sōtō* 明明百草頭): A saying best known from a conversation between Layman Pang Yun 龐蘊居士 (740?-808) and his daughter, Lingzhao 靈照, found in the *Discourse Record of Layman Pang* (*Pang jushi yulu* 龐居士語錄, ZZ.120:61b3-5):

> 居士一日坐次、問靈照曰、古人道、明明百草頭、明明祖師意。如何會。照曰、老老大大、作這箇語話。士曰、你作麼生。照曰、明明百草頭、明明祖師意。士乃笑。

> One day when Layman Pang was sitting, he asked [his daughter] Lingzhao: "An ancient said, 'Perfectly clear, the tips of the hundred grasses; perfectly clear, the intention of the Ancestral Master.' How do you understand it?"

> Lingzhao said, "An old man like you still makes such talk?"

> The Layman said, "What do you make of it?"

> Lingzhao said, "Perfectly clear, the tips of the hundred grasses; perfectly clear, the intention of the Ancestral Master."

> The Layman laughed.

In this text, the two-phrase saying is raised as a kōan (attributed to an unnamed "ancient") that is already in circulation; elsewhere in Zen literature it is treated independently of any mention of Layman Pang. For example, in the *Extensive Record of Chan Master Hongzhi* (*Hongzhi chanshi guanglu* 宏智禪師廣錄, T.48.2001:2c3):

> 上堂云、明明百草頭、明明祖師意。

> At a convocation in the dharma hall, [Hongzhi] said, "Perfectly clear, the tips of the hundred grasses; perfectly clear, the intention of the Ancestral Master."

In his *Shōbōgenzō* in Chinese script (*shinji Shōbōgenzō* 眞字正法眼藏, DZZ.5:168, case 88), Dōgen quotes the common version of the exchange that appears in the *Discourse Record of Layman Pang*; but in the *Shōbōgenzō*, where the saying occurs several times, he consistently uses an unusual variant: "perfectly clear, the intention of the **buddhas and ancestors**" (*meimei busso i* 明明佛祖意). His use of what is most likely the plural "buddhas and ancestors" (*busso* 佛祖) suggests that Dōgen may have understood the original *soshi* 祖師 as a plural ("ancestral masters"); but the latter is better understood as an abbreviation of the well-known saying, "**intention of the Ancestral Master's coming from the west**," which refers to the first ancestor

474 DŌGEN'S *SHŌBŌGENZŌ* VOLUME VIII

of Zen in China, Bodhidharma, who is said to have come from India in the sixth century.

The expression "hundred grasses" (*hyakusō* 百草) is used as a metaphor for "the infinite variety of things in the world" or, in Buddhist texts, for "all living things." According to *Hanyu da cidian* 漢語大詞典, s.v. 草, when the glyph 頭 (*tou*) follows the glyph for "grass" (*cao* 草), the resulting compound refers to "grass sprouts" (*caoduan* 草端), or "tips of grass" that are just beginning to protrude from the soil. However, the glyph 頭 can also serve as a suffix that does not change the meaning of a noun but has a kind of particularizing force similar to the definite article "the" (as opposed to the indefinite "a" or "some") in English. If that is how it is used here, then 百草頭 (*baicaotou*) simply means "the hundred [particular types of] grasses."

**pillars and lanterns** (*rochū tōrō* 露柱燈籠): Also found in reverse order: "lanterns and pillars" (*tōrō rochū* 燈籠露柱). The free-standing pillars and the lanterns of monastic buildings; regularly used in Zen texts for the immediate surroundings of the inanimate phenomenal world (or of the monks' environment).

The buddha halls (*butsuden* 佛殿) and dharma halls (*hattō* 法堂) at major Zen monasteries are built using a traditional Chinese style of post-and-beam construction. The posts or "pillars" (*chū* 柱) that support the roof are solid wood and round like the tree trunks they are made from. They stand in a regular geometrical pattern — e.g., six pillars across by six pillars deep, with a set "space" (*ken* 間), often two meters wide, between them. The spaces between the pillars on the perimeter of the building are filled by walls (with or without windows) or doors, but the pillars that stand in the interior of the building are "bare" (*ro* 露), in the sense that they are entirely exposed all the way around, with no adjoining walls. When the great assembly (*daishu* 大衆) of monks gathers in the dharma hall to receive formal instruction from the abbot, it lines up on the east and west sides of the hall in regular rows that align with and resemble the rows of bare pillars. Perhaps for that reason, the expression "bare pillars" came to indicate insentient things that stand in contrast to human beings. In the literature of Zen, ignorant monks who remain mute and unmoving when questioned by a Zen master are sometimes called "bare pillars" or "blockheads" (*mokutō* 木頭).

The glyphs translated here as "lantern" refer literally to a "hamper," or "cover" (*rō* 籠) that shields the "flame of a lamp" (*tō* 燈). In East Asia, portable lanterns are typically made of a bamboo framework, covered on the sides with paper to block the wind (which might blow out the candle) but open at the bottom and top (to allow in air and prevent the device from catching on fire). In Buddhist monasteries, there are also large, stationary lanterns that are made of stone, or occasionally metal. Those are located both outside and within major buildings such as buddha halls, dharma halls, and

*Supplementary notes to the translation*　　　475

mortuary halls, where they are arranged in pairs adjacent to the main altars. One practical function of such stationary lanterns was (before electricity) to provide light at night, but the burning of oil within them is also conceived as an offering of light to whatever beings (buddhas, bodhisattvas, ancestors, etc.) are enshrined on the altar. Because the lanterns found inside a buddha hall or dharma hall often have dimensions (height and circumference) that are similar to those of a person, and because they stand beside the altars in roughly the same position as attendant monks who serve the abbot in various rituals, Zen masters like to use them (along with the "bare pillars"), as examples of insentient things that stand in contrast to human beings.

In Zen literature, abbots are sometimes depicted referring to "pillars" or "pillars and lanterns" in unconventional ways, as if they were people. The biography of Shitou Xiqian 石頭希遷 (700-790) that appears in the *Jingde Era Record of the Transmission of the Flame* (*Jingde chuandeng lu* 景德傳燈録, T.2076.51:309b27-29) and the *Outline of the Linked Flames* (*Liandeng huiyao* 聯燈會要, ZZ.136:738a3-4), for example, contains an exchange that Dōgen repeats in his *Shōbōgenzō* in Chinese script (*shinji Shōbōgenzō* 眞字正法眼藏, DZZ.5:148, case 41):

石頭無際大師〈嗣青原諱希遷〉因僧問、如何是祖師西來意。師曰、問取露柱。僧曰、某甲不會。師曰、我更不會也。

Great Master Wuji of Shitou (succeeded Qingyuan; called Xiqian) was once asked by a monk, "What is the **intention of the Ancestral Master's coming from the west**?"
The Master said, "Ask the pillars."
The monk said, "I don't understand."
The Master said, "I don't understand either."

Shitou's remark about "asking the pillars" is open to various interpretations, but there are at least two ways of reading the symbolism of the bare pillar itself. If we regard the pillar as something insentient and dumb, then to ask it a question is utterly pointless; so, perhaps what Shitou means is that the question about "coming from the west" is unanswerable in words and foolish to even ask. On the other hand, if we take the pillar as a symbol of reality itself — something that clearly and obviously exists right in front of us — then perhaps what Shitou means is that the pillar, in the very muteness of its presence, can answer the question more directly and eloquently than he himself can using words. Dōgen alludes to Shitou's words in his "Buddha Nature" ("Shōbōgenzō busshō" 正法眼藏佛性, DZZ.1:21), in a comment on the Fourth Ancestor's remark to a disciple that "you have no buddha-nature" (*nyo mu busshō* 汝無佛性):

# 476 DŌGEN'S *SHŌBŌGENZŌ* VOLUME VIII

佛性成佛のとき、無佛性なるか、佛性發心のとき、無佛性なるかと
問取すべし、道取すべし。露柱をしても問取せしむべし、露柱にも
問取すべし、佛性をしても問取せしむべし。

When buddha nature attains buddhahood, is this "no buddha nature"?
When buddha nature brings forth the mind [of bodhi], is this "no buddha
nature"? We should ask this; we should say it. We should make the pillars
ask it; we should ask it to the pillars. We should make buddha nature ask
it.

In this context, Dōgen juxtaposes "pillars" and "buddha nature" in a way
that seems to equate them: neither can ask or answer questions in any literal
sense, but both, he says, should be made to.

Another classic example of "lanterns and pillars" (*tōrō rochū* 燈籠
露柱) in Zen literature appears in the *Extensive Record of Chan Master
Yunmen Kuangzhen* (*Yunmen Kuangzhen chanshi guanglu* 雲門匡眞禪師廣錄,
T.1988.47:572c3-5), where Yunmen Wenyan 雲門文偃 (864-949) is quoted
as follows:

師因見僧看經乃云、看經須具看經眼。燈籠露柱一大藏教無欠少。拈
起拄杖云、一大藏教總在拄杖頭上。

When the Master [Yunmen] saw a monk reading a sūtra he said, "To read
the sūtras, you must possess the **eye** for reading the sūtras. The lanterns
and pillars: the **one great treasury of the teachings**, with nothing lacking."

Raising his **staff** he said, "The one great treasury of the teachings resides
here on the tip of my staff."

**pivot** (*kanreisu* 關棙子, also written 關捩子): Also translateable as "mechanism." The pivots at the top and bottom of a door frame on which the door
turns. Also, a device (such as a spring) that causes movement. In Buddhist
texts, by extension: 1) the pivotal point of something: the fundamental
principle on which an argument or insight turns; or 2) a teaching device, or
"skillful means" (*hōben* 方便; S. *upāya*).

**pointing directly at the person's mind, seeing the nature and attaining
buddhahood** (*jikishi ninshin, kenshō jōbutsu* 直指人心、見性成佛): Two
phrases that are best known from their inclusion in a famous formula said to
characterize the Zen tradition:

A separate transmission outside the teachings (*kyōge betsuden* 教外別傳),

Not depending on words and letters (*furyū monji* 不立文字),

Pointing directly at the person's mind (*jikishi ninshin* 直指人心),

Seeing the nature and attaining buddhahood (*kenshō jōbutsu* 見性成佛).

For the provenance of this formula, see "**a separate transmission outside
the teachings**."

*Supplementary notes to the translation* 477

The oldest source in which the expressions "pointing directly at the person's mind" and "seeing the nature and attaining buddhahood" are conjoined is the *Essentials of the Transmission of Mind* (*Chuanxin fayao* 傳心法要, T.2012A.48:384a3-6), a discourse record of Huangbo Xiyun 黃檗希運 (751-850). In that text, Huangbo discusses the following dialogue between Senior Seat Ming 明上座 and the Sixth Ancestor, Huineng 慧能, who had just been recognized as successor by the Fifth Ancestor and fled the latter's monastery with the indignant Ming in pursuit. After being awakened by Huineng's admonition "not to think of good or evil" (*fushi zen aku* 不思善惡) but "return to your face **before your father and mother were born**," Ming bowed and said,

> 如人飲水冷煖自知。某甲在五祖會中、枉用三十年工夫。今日方省前非。六祖云、如是。到此之時方知、祖師西來、直指人心、見性成佛、不在言説.

"It's like a person who drinks water and knows for themself whether it is cool or warm. I have spent thirty years in the assembly of the Fifth Ancestor, exerting myself in vain. Today, for the first time, I have realized my previous error."

The Sixth Ancestor said, "Just so. Having reached this moment, for the first time, you understand that the 'Ancestral Master's **coming from the west**, pointing directly at the person's mind, seeing the nature and attaining buddhahood' does not consist in verbal expression."

In this context, the teaching method of "pointing directly at the person's mind" is attributed by Huineng to the First Ancestor of the Zen lineage in China, Bodhidharma, who was said to have transmitted the Buddha's "mind dharma" (*shinbō* 心法), as opposed to his verbal teachings that were embodied in sūtras.

The expression "pointing directly at the person's mind" is not found in Chinese Buddhist literature in any source older than Huangbo's *Essentials of the Transmission of Mind*; in subsequent works, it is associated almost exclusively with Bodhidharma. However, the Tiantai school monk Youyan Tanwu 有嚴曇武 (died 1101) used the expression in a preface he wrote to Tiantai Zhiyi's 天台智顗 (538–597) *One Hundred Records of Guoqing [Monastery]* (*Guoqing bailu* 國清百錄, T.1934.46:793b6-9):

> 昔我祖智者禪師。本靈山聖衆之一人也。陳隋朝出現世間、代佛宣祕爲人天眼目。六十餘州直指人心。

In ancient times, our ancestor, Dhyāna Master Zhizhe [i.e., Zhiyi], was originally one of the people in the sacred assembly on Vulture Peak [when the Buddha preached the *Lotus Sūtra*]. Much later, during the Sui dynasty [581-618], he appeared in the world and explained the hidden [meaning of the *Lotus Sūtra*] on the Buddha's behalf, becoming known as the "eye

478     DŌGEN'S *SHŌBŌGENZŌ* VOLUME VIII

of humans and devas." In more than sixty regions [of China], he pointed directly at the person's mind.

This passage suggests that the expression "pointing directly at the person's mind" may have been used independently of the Chan school and its Bodhidharma story, but it is also possible that Youyan borrowed the phrase to argue that Zhiyi had been just as intuitive and spontaneous a teacher as Bodhidharma.

The glyphs rendered here as "seeing the nature and attaining buddhahood" (*kenshō jōbutsu* 見性成佛) can also be translated as "seeing the nature is attaining buddhahood." Long before the rise of the Chan school, that expression was attributed to the fourth-century monk Sengliang 僧亮, in the *Anthology of Commentaries on the Nirvāṇa Sūtra* (*Da banniepan jing jijie* 大般涅槃經集解), a work compiled by Baoliang 寶亮 (444–509). Sengliang was commenting on the following passage (attributed to Buddha Śākyamuni) in the *Nirvāṇa Sūtra* (*Niepan jing* 涅槃經, T.374.12:445c4-9):

> 善男子、佛性即是如來、如來即是法、法即是常。善男子、常者即是如來、如來即是僧、僧即是常。以是義故從因生法不名爲常。是諸外道無有一法不從因生。善男子、是諸外道不見佛性如來及法。是故外道所可言説悉是妄語無有眞諦。

Good sons! Buddha-nature is itself tathāgata; tathāgata is itself the dharma; and the dharma is itself permanent. Good sons! Permanence is itself tathāgata; tathāgata is itself saṃgha; and the saṃgha is itself permanent. According to this principle, dharmas that arise from causes are not called permanent. Now, the various other paths do not have a single dharma that does not arise from causes. Good sons! The various other paths do not see Buddha nature, tathāgata, or dharma. Therefore, what can be taught by followers of other paths consists entirely of falsehood, with nothing of ultimate truth.

Sengliang's commentary on the preceding passage from the *Nirvāṇa Sūtra*, as quoted by Baoliang (T.1763.37:490c26-28), reads:

> 僧亮曰、見性成佛。即性爲佛也。如來即法者、法即性空、性空即法、法即佛性也。佛性是有、性空是無。佛見有無名覺也。

Sengliang says, "Seeing the nature is attaining buddhahood. To wit, the nature itself is buddha. In the [*Nirvāṇa Sūtra*'s] words, 'tathāgata is itself the dharma,' the dharma referred to is the emptiness of own-nature, and the emptiness of own-nature is the dharma, so the dharma is the buddha nature. Buddha nature is existence, but the emptiness of own-nature is non-existence. When a buddha sees existence and non-existence, that is called awakening."

*Supplementary notes to the translation*  479

Even after the expression "see the nature and attain buddhahood" became associated with Bodhidharma, Baoliang's citation of Sengliang continued to be used in the literature of Zen.

Within the Zen tradition, the expression "see the nature and attain buddhahood" is best known from its occurrence in the *Platform Sūtra of the Sixth Ancestor* (*Liuzu tanjing* 六祖壇經). The Dunhuang mansucript of that text (*Nanzong dunjiao zuishang Dasheng mohe boruo boluomi jing Liuzu Huineng Dashi yu Shaozhou Dafansi shifa tan jing* 南宗頓教最上大乘摩訶般若波羅蜜經六祖慧能大師於韶州大梵寺施法壇經, T.2007.48:340a23-26) quotes Huineng as saying:

悟此法者，即是無念、無憶、無著。莫去誑妄，即自是眞如性。用智慧觀照於一切法、不取不捨、即見性成佛道。

When you awaken to this dharma, you have no thoughts, no memories, and no attachments. Do not drive away deceptive falsehoods, for of themselves they have the nature of true suchness. When you use wisdom to illuminate all dharmas, neither grasping nor discarding them, then you see the nature and attain the way of the buddhas.

The expression "see the nature" (*kenshō* 見性) appears many other times throughout that text.

In his "The Bhikṣu of the Fourth Dhyāna" ("Shōbōgenzō shizen biku" 正法眼藏四禪比丘, DZZ.2:426), however, Dōgen strongly criticizes the idea that one can simply "see one's nature and attain buddhahood":

佛法、いまだその要、見性にあらず。西天二十八祖・七佛、いづれの處にか佛法の、ただ見性のみなりとある。六祖壇經に、見性の言あり、かの書、これ僞書なり、附法藏の書にあらず、曹溪の言句にあらず、佛祖の兒孫、またく依用せざる書なり。

In the buddha dharma, the essence has never been "seeing one's nature." Where have the twenty-eight ancestors of Sindh in the West or the **seven buddhas** said that the buddha dharma was just "seeing one's nature"? The words "seeing one's nature" are found in the *Platform Sūtra of the Sixth Ancestor*, but that book is a spurious text — not a text of the transmitted dharma treasury, not the words of Caoxi, a book absolutely not relied on by the descendants of the **buddhas and ancestors**.

"Caoxi" 曹溪 here refers to the Sixth Ancestor, Huineng of Caoxi 曹溪慧能.

**practice and verification** (*shushō* 修證): Usually understood as an abbreviation of two terms when those are used in combination: "practice" (*shugyō* 修行) and "verification of awakening" (*shōgo* 證悟). The *locus classicus* of the term "practice and verification" in the literature of Zen is a dialogue featuring the Sixth Ancestor, Huineng 慧能 (638-713) and his disciple Nanyue Huairang 南嶽懷讓 (677-744), to which Dōgen often makes reference. Here is the version of the story given in his *Shōbōgenzō* in Chinese script (*shinji Shōbōgenzō* 眞字正法眼藏, DZZ.5:178, case 101):

南嶽山大慧禪師〈嗣曹谿、諱懷讓〉參六祖。祖曰、從什麼處來。師曰、嵩山安國師處來。祖曰、是什麼物恁麼來。師罔措。於是執侍八年、方省前話。乃告祖云、懷讓會得、當初來時、和尚接某甲、是什麼物恁麼來。祖云、爾作麼生會。師曰、説似一物即不中。祖曰、還假修證否。師曰、修證即不無、染汚即不得。祖曰、祗此不染汚、是諸佛之所護念。汝亦如是、吾亦如是、乃至西天諸祖亦如是。

Chan Master Dahui of Mount Nanyue (descendant of Caoxi, named Huairang) visited the Sixth Ancestor. The Ancestor asked him, "Where do you come from?"

The Master said, "I come from the National Teacher An on Mount Song."

The Ancestor said, "What thing is it that comes like this?"

The Master was without means [to answer]. After attending [the Ancestor] for eight years, he finally understood the previous conversation. Thereupon, he announced to the Ancestor, "I've understood what you put to me when I first came: '**What thing is it that comes like this**?'"

The Ancestor asked, "How do you understand it?"

The Master replied, "To say it's like any thing wouldn't hit it." The Ancestor said, "Does it nevertheless depend on practice and verification?"

The Master answered, "It's not that it lacks practice and verification, but it can't be defiled by them."

The Ancestor said, "Just this '**not defiled**' is what the buddhas bear in mind. **You're also like this, I'm also like this**, and all the ancestors of Sindh in the West [i. e., India] are also like this."

In the context of this exchange between Huineng and Huairang, the "practice" of Buddhism and the "verification," or realization, of the "thing that comes in such a way" (i.e., the innate buddha nature, which as Huairang indicates is "not like any thing") appear to be two separate actions. "Practice" and "verification," in other words, are normally understood to stand in relation as cause and effect. The Sōtō tradition (e.g., ZGDJ 505c, s.v. しゅしょういっとう), however, points out that Dōgen taught the "sameness of practice and verification" (*shushō ittō* 修證一等), meaning that cultivation (practice) is itself authentication, or verification (awakening). Some interpret the two glyphs for "practicing" (*shū* 修) and "verifying" (*shō* 證) as a verb-object compound, translatable as "cultivate authentication." For another version of the dialogue and a discussion of its overall meaning, see "**what thing is it that comes like this?**"

In his "Principles of Seated Meditation" ("Shōbōgenzō zazengi" 坐禪儀, DZZ.1:89) Dōgen says:

## Supplementary notes to the translation 481

兀兀と坐定して、思量箇不思量底なり、不思量底如何思量、これ非
思量なり。これすなはち坐禪の法術なり。坐禪は習禪にはあらず、
大安樂の法門なり、不染汚の修證なり。

Sitting fixedly, think of not thinking. How do you think of not thinking?
Non-thinking. This is the art of seated meditation. Seated meditation is
not the **practice of dhyāna**. It is the dharma gate of great ease and joy. It is
non-defiling practice and verification.

Here we find the idea that seated meditation is not a "practice" that leads
to "verification" and may be dispensed with after attaining awakening. It is,
rather, something that embodies both "practice and verification."

**practice of dhyāna** (*shūzen* 習禪): See "**practitioner of dhyāna.**"

**practitioner of dhyāna** (*shūzen* 習禪): One of the ten categories of Chinese
Buddhist monk employed in the "biographies of eminent monks" (*kōsō den*
高僧傳) literature. There, the term denotes a monk who specializes in the
practice of meditation (*zen* 禪; S. *dhyāna*) or the explication of so-called
"dhyāna sūtras" (*zenkyō* 禪經), as the latter were understood in early Chinese
Buddhism. Other categories include sūtra translators (*yakkyō* 譯經), exegetes
(*gige* 義解), vinaya experts (*myōritsu* 明律), and so on.

The glyphs 習禪 (*shūzen*) are an abbreviation of the expression "to
practice dhyāna" (*shujū zenna* 修習禪那) and are also translated herein as
"the practice of dhyāna." In both the Indian and the East Asian contexts, the
term "dhyāna" is used in two ways: 1) A narrower sense, in which it refers
specifically to successive stages of mental absorption, or trance, known as
the four dhyānas (*shizen* 四禪); and (2) a broader sense, in which it includes
*both* the inducement of mental calm (*shi* 止; S. *śamatha*) and the cultivation
of insight (*kan* 觀; S. *vipaśyanā*).

In the literature of Zen, "practitioner of dhyāna" is a term of disparagement
for monks who specialize in various forms of meditation theory and practice
but do not understand that what Bodhidharma transmitted to China was not
merely dhyāna concentration (*zenjō* 禪定), i.e., the fifth of the six perfections
(*roku haramitsu* 六波羅蜜; S. *ṣaḍ-pāramitā*), but rather the awakening of
Buddha Śākyamuni — the buddha mind (*busshin* 佛心) — itself. One of the
most explicit expressions of the idea that the Zen lineage is not characterized
by dhyāna in the sense of "meditation" is found in *Shimen's Grove Record*
(*Shimen linjian lu* 石門林間錄, ZZ.148:590b7-12; X.1624.87:247c21-248a1),
a work completed in 1107 by Huihong Juefan 慧洪覺範 (1071-1128), alias
Shimen:

菩提達磨初自梁之魏。經行於嵩山之下、倚杖於少林。面壁燕坐而
已。非習禪也。久之、人莫測其故、因以達磨爲習禪。夫禪那、諸行

# 482 DŌGEN'S *SHŌBŌGENZŌ* VOLUME VIII

之一耳。何足以盡聖人。而當時之人以之爲。史者又從而傳茲習禪之
列。使與枯木死灰之徒爲伍。雖然聖人非止於禪那、而亦不違禪那。

When Bodhidharma first went from Liang to Wei, he proceeded to the foot of Mount Song, where he rested his staff at Shaolin. There he just sat facing a wall. It was not the practice of dhyāna; but, after a while, others, unable to fathom what he was doing, made Bodhidharma a practitioner of dhyāna. Now, dhyāna is but one among various practices; how could it suffice to exhaust [the practice of] the sage? Nevertheless, people of the time took it in this way; and those who wrote histories followed this and recorded him among practitioners of dhyāna, thus making him a confederate of the partisans of **dried-up trees** and dead ashes. Although the sage does not stop at dhyāna, he does not oppose dhyāna.

The "historians" referred to here are Daoxuan 道宣 (596–667) and Zanning 贊寧 (920-1001), who classified Bodhidharma as a practitioner of dhyāna in their *Additional Biographies of Eminent Monks* (*Xu gaoseng zhuan* 續高僧傳) and *Song Biographies of Eminent Monks* (*Song gaoseng zhuan* 宋高僧傳), respectively. The source of Huihong's ire was the fact that Daoxuan did not distinguish Bodhidharma in any fundamental way from the other eminent dhyāna masters that he treated in his *Additional Biographies*.

In his "Principles of Seated Meditation" ("Shōbōgenzō zazengi" 正法眼藏坐禪儀, DZZ.1:89), Dōgen echoes Huihong's *Shimen's Grove Record*, which was recommended to him by his teacher, Tiantong Rujing 天童如淨 (1162–1227), when he says that seated meditation (*zazen* 坐禪) is not the practice of dhyāna (*shūzen* 習禪):

兀兀と坐定して、思量箇不思量底なり、不思量底如何思量、これ非
思量なり。これすなはち坐禪の法術なり。坐禪は習禪にはあらず、
大安樂の法門なり、不染汚の修證なり。

Sitting fixedly, it is "thinking of not thinking." "How do you think of not thinking?" It is "nonthinking." "This is the art of seated meditation." Seated meditation is not the practice of dhyāna. It is the dharma gate of great ease and joy. It is nondefiling **practice and verification**.

Dōgen's statement goes a bit further than Huihong's, however, for he redefines seated meditation as "nonthinking" (*hi shiryō* 非思量), which presumably is not limited to a sitting posture.

**Prelate Liang** (*Ryō zasu* 亮座主): Dates unknown; also referred to in the *Shōbōgenzō* as "Prelate Liang of Xishan in Hongzhou" (*Kōshū Seizan Ryō zasu* 洪州西山亮座主); Xishan 西山 ("Mount Xi") is located in present-day Jiangxi province. Liang was a monk who is said to have become prominent as a lecturer on sūtras, but to have given that up after encountering Chan

*Supplementary notes to the translation* 483

Master Mazu Daoyi 馬祖道一 (709-788), gaining some insight, and becoming the latter's dharma heir.

In texts dating from the Tang dynasty, the term "prelate" (*zasu* 座主, literally "holder of the [lecture] seat") refers to the "abbot," or spiritual leader, of a Buddhist monastery. In Song-dynasty Chan texts, it refers to the scholarly abbot of a "Teachings monastery" (*kyōji* 教寺 or *kyōin* 教院) — an institution where the abbacy is restricted to members of the Tiantai school — who lectures on doctrinal matters from the high seat (*kōza* 高座) in the dharma hall (*hattō* 法堂); it is thus a term of disparagement, implying a knowledge of Buddhist scriptures that is intellectually comprehensive but lacks genuine spiritual insight.

Dōgen mentions or alludes to Prelate Liang several times in the *Shōbōgenzō*. In his "Empty Space" ("Shōbōgenzō kokū" 正法眼藏虚空, DZZ.2:211), he quotes the following dialogue, which is found in various Chan sources, as well as his own *Shōbōgenzō* in Chinese script (*shinji Shōbōgenzō* 眞字正法眼藏, DZZ.5:126, case 4):

洪州西山亮座主、因參馬祖。祖問、講什麼經。師曰、心經。祖曰、將什麼講。師曰、將心講。祖曰、心如工伎兒、意如和伎者、六識爲伴侶、爭解講得經。師曰、心既講不得、莫是虚空講得麼。祖曰、却是虚空講得。師拂袖而退。祖召云、座主。師回首。祖曰、從生至老、只是這箇。師因而有省。遂隱西山、更無消息。

Prelate Liang of Xishan in Hongzhou once went to consult with Mazu. Mazu asked him, "What sūtra are you lecturing on?"

The Master [Liang] said, "The *Heart Sūtra*."

Mazu said, "With what do you lecture?"

The Master said, "I lecture with the mind."

Mazu said, "'The mind is like the lead actor; the intellect, like a supporting actor; the six consciousnesses make up the cast.' How can they lecture on the sūtra?"

The Master said, "Since the mind can't lecture, isn't it empty space that can lecture?"

Mazu said, "In fact, it's empty space that can lecture."

The Master shook out his sleeves and withdrew. Mazu called after him, "Prelate!"

The Master turned. Mazu said, "From birth to old age, it's just this."

The Master thereupon had an insight. He subsequently hid himself in Mount Xi and was not heard of again.

**public realm** (*kugai* 公界): 1) A reference to the world at large; any place that is frequented by ordinary people. 2) In Buddhist texts, "all the worlds in the ten directions" (*jin jippō sekai* 盡十方世界), throughout which the buddha nature is manifested (*busshō genjō* 佛性現成). 3) In Song- and Yuan-dynasty Buddhist monastic rules, the areas that were shared by the great assembly of monks (*daishu* 大衆) in training: the saṃgha hall (*sōdō* 僧堂), common quarters (*shuryō* 衆寮), sūtra library (*kyōzō* 經藏), washstands (*goka* 後架), toilets (*tōsu* 東司), etc. That was in contradistinction to the private quarters that the abbot, retired abbots, and a few other high-ranking officers held, which only they or their servants could enter freely; those officers could, of course, entertain guests in their private quarters. The "public realm" of a monastery was, in principle, off limits to anyone other than duly registered monk residents. The only truly public places in a monastery were the buddha hall (*butsuden* 佛殿) and dharma hall (*hattō* 法堂), where lay people and visiting government officials were, on occasion, welcomed to attend major religious services presided over by the abbot. 4) The "expressions common property of the cloister" (*inmon no kugai* 院門の公界) and "implements in the public realm" (*kugai no chōdo* 公界の調度), both of which occur in the *Shōbōgenzō*, refer to furnishings, works of art, scriptures, and ritual implements that are the permanent possessions of a monastic community at large and not to be appropriated as private property by any individual, especially the abbot when he leaves office and transfers to another institution.

**putting a head on top of your head** (*zujō an zu* 頭上安頭; also read *tōjō an tō*): A common expression in Zen texts for the mistake of adding something superfluous, of saying something unnecessary, or imagining or seeking something one already has. The *Discourse Record of Chan Master Linji Huizhao of Zhenzhou* (*Zhenzhou Linji Huizhao chanshi yulu* 鎮州臨濟慧照禪師語錄, T.1985.47:500c4-8), for example, says:

向爾道、無佛、無法、無修、無證。祇與麼傍家擬求什麼物。瞎漢、頭上安頭。是爾欠少什麼。道流、是爾目前用底與祖佛不別、祇麼不信、便向外求。莫錯、向外無法、內亦不可得。

"I say to you there is no buddha, no dharma, no practice, and no realization. What are you seeking on such a side path? Blind men! Putting a head on top of your head! What do you lack? Followers of the way, the functioning that is before your very eyes does not differ from that of the ancestors and buddhas. It is just that you don't believe it and seek something external. Make no mistake! Outside there are no dharmas, and inside, too, there is nothing that can be obtained."

The *Extensive Record of Chan Master Yunmen Kuangzhen* (*Yunmen Kuangzhen chanshi guanglu* 雲門匡眞禪師廣錄, T.1988.47:552a4-5) says:

Supplementary notes to the translation 485

上堂云、和尚子直饒爾道、有什麼事。猶是頭上安頭、雪上加霜。棺木裏眨眼。

At a convocation in the dharma hall [Yunmen] said, "Even if this Reverend speaks like this, what matter is there? It's like putting a head on top of your head; like adding frost on top of snow; like winking your eye inside a wooden coffin.

**raise the eyebrows and blink the eyes** (*yōbi shunmoku* 揚眉瞬目): In Zen texts, these are examples of ordinary everyday actions that people generally perform without thinking or special effort, mentioned to indicate the spontaneous workings of the buddha mind. Zen masters are also depicted using such non-verbal gestures intentionally as teaching devices, in which case they are clearly meant to signify something. The *Extensive Record of Chan Master Yunmen Kuangzhen* (*Yunmen Kuangzhen chanshi guanglu* 雲門匡眞禪師廣錄, T.1998.47:556a24-26) contains the following discussion of the use of such devices:

師有時云、彈指謦欬揚眉瞬目拈槌竪拂、或即圓相、盡是撩鉤搭索。佛法兩字未曾道著。道著即撒屎撒尿。

Once the Master [Yunmen] said, "Snapping the fingers, clearing the throat, raising the eyebrows, blinking the eyes, lifting the mallet [to sound a signal by striking a block], holding up the **whisk**, or drawing a circle [in the air] — all of these are hooked devices for catching people. I have never yet uttered the two words 'buddha dharma.' If I did utter them, it would be like sprinkling piss and spreading shit."

The expression "raise the eyebrows and blink the eyes" is probably best known from the saying of Mazu Daoyi 馬祖道一 (709-788), in a conversation with Yaoshan Weiyan 藥山惟儼 (745-828) that Dōgen repeats in his *Shōbōgenzō* in Chinese script (*shinji Shōbōgenzō* 眞字正法眼藏, DZZ.5:204, case 150):

江西大寂禪師、示藥山云、我有時教伊揚眉瞬目、有時不教伊揚眉瞬目。有時教伊揚眉瞬目者是、有時教伊揚眉瞬目者不是。藥山忽然大悟。

Chan Master Daji of Jiangxi [i.e., Mazu] addressed Yaoshan saying, "Sometimes, I have him raise his eyebrows and blink his eyes; sometimes, I don't have him raise his eyebrows and blink his eyes. Sometimes, having him raise his eyebrows and blink his eyes is it; sometimes, having him raise his eyebrows and blink his eyes is not it."
Yaoshan immediately had a great awakening.

For the full context of this conversation, see Yaoshan's biography in the *Collated Essentials of the Five Flame Records* (*Wudeng huiyuan* 五燈會元,

486    DŌGEN'S *SHŌBŌGENZŌ* VOLUME VIII

ZZ.138:163a9-b10), translated in the entry **"skin and dermis sloughed off."** Dōgen discusses Mazu's words in his "Sometimes" ("Shōbōgenzō uji" 正法眼藏有時). In his "Buddha Nature" ("Shōbōgenzō busshō" 正法眼藏佛性), Dōgen juxtaposes the expression "raising the eyebrows and blinking the eyes" with **"break into a smile,"** which is an allusion to the famous story of Śākyamuni's transmission of the **"treasury of the true dharma eye"** to Mahākāśyapa on Vulture Peak. It would seem from this that Dōgen may have equated "raising the eyebrows and blinking the eyes" with Śākyamuni's action of **"holding up a flower and blinking the eyes."** The association of these two instances of "blinking the eyes" is fairly common in the Japanese Sōtō tradition following Dōgen, but it does not have a clear precedent in Chinese Chan texts.

**realized kōan** (*genjō kōan* 現成公案, also written 見成公案): a) The title of the first text in the seventy-five- and sixty-chapter compilations of the *Shōbōgenzō* (and the third text in the Honzan edition); originally composed in the autumn of 1233, probably at Dōgen's Kōshō Monastery 興聖寺 near the imperial capital of Heiankyō (modern Kyoto), it seems to have been revised in 1252, at the Eihei Monastery 永平寺 in the province of Echizen, as one of its author's final works. A relatively brief essay, the "Shōbōgenzō genjō kōan" is among the best-known, most closely studied works by Dōgen, sometimes described as encapsulating the entire message of his *Shōbōgenzō*. The theme of the essay is Buddhist spiritual practice, famously described here as the study of the self, in which one forgets the self, sloughs off body and mind, and is verified by all things. Such practice, we are told, has no end: it is the practitioner's natural environment, like water to a fish or the sky to a bird; it is like the wind that is always blowing, even as we fan ourselves.

b) A fixed phrase found frequently in Zen literature and used (in varied iterations) throughout the *Shōbōgenzō*. The phrase originally carried the juridical sense of a legal matter, or case (*kōan* 公案), in which the finding, or verdict, has been completed (*genjō* 現成); in Dōgen's writings and in subsequent Sōtō usage, it often takes on a rich semantic life of its own, in which the sense is greatly expanded to suggest something like "the ultimate truth of Buddhism made manifest."

The *locus classicus* of the expression *genjō kōan* 現成公案 (C. *xiancheng gongan*) is a dialogue found in the *Jingde Era Record of the Transmission of the Flame* (*Jingde chuandeng lu* 景德傳燈錄, T.2076.51:291b17-19), in the biography of the ninth-century figure Muzhou Daoming 睦州道明 (dates unknown), also known as Muzhou Daozong 睦州道蹤, and as Venerable Chen 陳尊宿 and Chen Puxie 陳蒲鞋 ("Straw Sandal Chen"):

師見僧來云、見成公案、放汝三十棒。僧云、某甲如是。師云、三門金剛爲什麼舉拳。僧云、金剛尚乃如是。師便打。

*Supplementary notes to the translation* 487

Seeing a monk coming, the Master [Muzhou] said, "It's a settled case, but I spare you the thirty blows."

The monk said, "I'm just like this."

The Master said, "Why do the Vajra Wielders in the triple gate raise their **fists**?"

The monk said, "The Vajra Wielders are also just like this."

The Master hit him.

Here, the Chan master assumes the role of a magistrate pardoning a defendant found guilty in a court case. The monk's crime, apparently, was entering the master's monastery through the triple gate at the main entrance. When the monk seems complacent in his guilt, the master challenges his understanding of the crime by asking how he views the icons of the two protective deities installed in that gate (and, hence, the meaning of entering a monastery). When the monk identifies his state with that of the deities, the master punishes him.

Muzhou's remark was well known in Chan circles and came to be included in lists of what we might call "gate-entering" encounters, in which a master challenges a newly arrived student. So, for example, we find this list by the prominent Linji master Dahui Zonggao 大慧宗杲 (1089-1163), in the *Discourse Record of Chan Master Dahui Pujue* (*Dahui Pujue chanshi yulu* 大慧普覺禪師語錄, T.1998A.47:914a21-24):

德山見僧入門、便棒。臨濟見僧入門、便喝。雪峯見僧入門、便道是甚麼。睦州見僧入門、便道現成公、案放爾三十棒。

Deshan saw a monk entering the gate and struck him with a staff. Linji saw a monk entering the gate and shouted at him. Xuefeng saw a monk entering the gate and said, "What is this?" Muzhou saw a monk entering the gate and said, "It's a settled case, but I spare you the thirty blows."

Dahui's list here is a variant of gate-entering episodes celebrated by his teacher, Yuanwu Keqin 圜悟克勤 (1063-1135) in the *Discourse Record of Chan Master Yuanwu Foguo* (*Yuanwu Foguo chanshi yulu* 圓悟佛果禪師語錄, T.1997.47:750 a19-21). Yuanwu was particularly fond of Muzhou's saying, often borrowing the latter's expression in his own teaching. Thus, we find him beginning a lecture with the following (T.1997.47:769a28-29):

師云、現成公案。不隔一絲毫。普天匝地。是一箇大解脱門、與日月同明、與虛空等量。

The Master said, "A settled case: Without a hair's breadth of separation, the whole of heaven, all of earth, are but a single gate of the great liberation, bright as the sun and moon, vast as empty space."

488 DŌGEN'S *SHŌBŌGENZŌ* VOLUME VIII

Here, and in other examples from Yuanwu's day (the twelfth century), it is clear that the phrase "a settled case" had escaped its original context to become a term of art in the vocabulary of the Chinese Chan masters. In the process, the "case" (*kōan* 公案) here had transcended its narrowly juridical connotation and assumed a broader sense of law, or truth, applicable to "the whole of heaven and all of earth." Such is the sense of "the realized kōan" that Dōgen encountered in his reading of the literature of Song-dynasty Chan; such is the sense he adopted and adapted in his own writing.

Explanations of this broader sense of *genjō kōan* typically take the term *kōan* 公案 as indicating the established norm, or fixed principle, of things, while the term *genjō* 現成 is explained as "presently accomplished" (*genzen jōju* 現前成就); together, the two terms are said to express the ultimate truth already present, or realized, in things — in the technical language of Dōgen's Buddhism, "the real marks of the dharmas" (*shohō jissō* 諸法實相); or, more simply, the things around us as manifestations of ultimate reality.

Whatever the value of such explanations of *genjō kōan*, they will be difficult to apply to all the many appearances of this expression in the *Shōbōgenzō*, in which, as is quite common in his writing, Dōgen plays with its component glyphs. Variations on the four glyphs 現成公案 (or 見成公案) occur some twenty times in the work, sometimes used in reverse order (公案現成), sometimes treated as Japanese nouns (現成の公案), sometimes taken together as a Japanese verb (現成公案す), sometimes taken apart in parallel phrases (到は現成するなり、到は公案なり), and so on. In addition, Dōgen uses the term *kōan* 公案 in its familiar meaning of an edifying Zen anecdote and uses the term *genjō* 現成 (or 見成) in hundreds of contexts other than *genjō kōan*. Although, in this translation, we have chosen, with considerable hesitation, to translate *genjō kōan* as "realized kōan," in many of these contexts, we have found it preferable to render *genjō* with English such as "appear," "occur," "manifest," "express," etc.

As is clear from his many uses of it, as well as his choice of it as the title of an important essay, the expression *genjō kōan* represents a key term in Dōgen's Buddhism; yet nowhere in the *Shōbōgenzō* does its author offer a statement of how exactly he understands the expression. Perhaps the closest we have to such a statement is found in one of his lectures recorded in the *Extensive Record of Reverend Dōgen* (*Dōgen oshō kōroku* 道元和尚廣錄, DZZ.3:40, no. 60):

上堂。云。諸人直須辦肯箇見成公案。作麼生是見成公案。便是十方諸佛古今諸祖是矣。而今現成。諸人見也麼。而今揭簾放簾、上牀下牀是矣。好箇見成公案、諸人爲甚不會不參。山僧今日、不惜性命、不惜眉毛、爲諸人再説、爲諸人重説。卓拄杖一下便下座。

In a convocation address, he said,

*Supplementary notes to the translation*      489

All of you should confirm this realized kōan. What is the realized kōan? It is the buddhas of the ten directions, the ancestors of past and present. They are realized right now. Do you see them? Right now, our lifting the screen and lowering the screen [at the entrance to the saṃgha hall], our getting up on and getting down from the [meditation] platform is it. This fine realized kōan — why don't you understand it, why don't you study it? Today, this mountain monk without begrudging my life, without begrudging my eyebrows, tells you this again, repeats this for you.

Standing up his staff, he got down from the seat.

Here, at least, it seems that Dōgen is treating the "realized kōan," not as an abstract metaphysical expression, but as a term for the instantiation of Zen tradition through its practice: the everyday acts of the monks in his audience are realizing the kōan of the precedents set by the buddhas and ancestors. Here, Dōgen may be reimagining, now in his own terms, what Muzhou may have meant by his calling the act of the monk's entering his monastery a "settled case."

***Reverend Shitou's Song of the Thatched Hut*** (*Shitou heshang caoan ge* 石頭和尚草庵歌): A poem, attributed to Shitou Xiqian 石頭希遷 (710–790), that Dōgen quoted or alluded to in several chapters of the *Shōbōgenzō*. It is included in fascicle 30 of the *Jingde Era Record of the Transmission of the Flame* (*Jingde chuandeng lu* 景德傳燈錄, T.2076.51:461c8-21):

吾結草庵無寶貝。飯了從容圖睡快。成時初見茆草新。破後還將茆草蓋。住庵人鎮常在。不屬中間與內外。世人住處我不住。世人愛處我不愛。庵雖小含法界。方丈老人相體解。上乘菩薩信無疑。中下聞之必生怪。問此庵壞不壞。壞與不壞主元在。不居南北與東西。基址堅牢以爲最。青松下明窗內。玉殿朱樓未爲對。衲帔幪頭萬事休。此時山僧都不會。住此庵休作解。誰誇鋪席圖人買。迴光返照便歸來。廓達靈根非向背。遇祖師親訓誨。結草爲庵莫生退。百年抛却任縱橫。擺手便行且無罪。千種言萬般解。只要教君長不昧。欲識庵中不死人。豈離而今遮皮袋。

I built this thatched hut that has nothing of worth;
After a meal, I relaxed, figuring on a quick nap.
When it was done, the thatch looked new at first;
Once it falls apart, the place will be strewn with the grass.
The person dwelling in the hermitage resides at ease,
Not belonging to the middle, or inner or outer.
Where the worldly dwell, I don't dwell;
What the worldly love, I don't love.
Though small, my hut holds the dharma realm;
Its ten square feet and this old man have come to a deep understanding.

The bodhisattva of the higher vehicle has a faith free from doubt;
When middle and lower types hear of it, they surely find it strange.
You ask if this hut is destructible or not;
Whether it is or not, its owner is here from the start.
He isn't in the south or the north, the east or the west;
But he prizes a strong foundation.
Beneath green pines; within the hut illuminated by windows;
Jewelled halls and vermilion towers can't compare.
A patched robe and a head covering; he's put to rest the myriad affairs;
Now, the mountain monk meets no one at all.
He stays in this hut, retired from the work of liberation;
Who would proudly arrange a seat [for an abbot's sermon] in anticipation of people buying in?
Turning the light and shining it back, he immediately comes back home;
The all-pervading spiritual root turns neither toward nor away.
Once you meet the ancestral masters and get familiar with their instructions,
Bind some grass to make a hut and don't turn back.
Casting one hundred years aside, abandon yourself to freedom;
Wave your hand and leave. May you be blameless!
The thousand words and myriad explanations
Are only to keep the lord from getting confused.
If you wish to know the undying person in the hermitage,
How could it be apart from this present **bag of skin**?

**rice, hemp, bamboo, and reeds** (*tō ma chiku i* 稲麻竹葦): Plants — both cultivated and wild — that grow in dense profusion. In ordinary Chinese, the expression "rice, hemp, bamboo, and reeds" is a simile for things (including people) standing closely together in large number, with no intervening spaces. The expression was used by Kumārajīva to translate the Sanskrit *naḍa*, or "reeds," in a verse from the "Expedient Means" (*Fangbian* 方便) chapter of the *Lotus Sūtra* (*Miaofa lianhua jing* 妙法蓮華經, T.262.9:6a11-13):

新發意菩薩、供養無數佛、了達諸義趣、又能善説法、如稲麻竹葦、充滿十方利。

Bodhisattvas who have newly produced the thought of awakening,
Who make offerings to countless buddhas,
Who have thoroughly understood the gist of the teachings,
And are well able to preach the dharma,
Are like rice, hemp, bamboo, and reeds
That fill the *kṣetras* of the ten directions.

Supplementary notes to the translation 491

In this context, "like rice, hemp, bamboo, and reeds" (*nyo tō ma chiku i* 如稻麻竹葦) is a figure of speech meant to illustrate the large number of bodhisattvas in all the buddha lands (*bussetsu* 佛利; S. *buddha-kṣetra*) of the ten directions.

**robe of the Tathāgata** (*nyorai e* 如來衣): The monastic robe, or *kāṣāya* (*kesa* 袈裟), worn by Buddha Śākyamuni. By extension, the robes worn by all Buddhist monks and nuns, which are emblematic of their status as "home leavers" (*shukke* 出家; S. *pravrājaka*) who belong to the monastic saṃgha.

The expression "robe of the Tathāgata" is closely associated in East Asia with a verse that appears in the "Dharma Master" (*Fashi* 法師) chapter of the *Lotus Sūtra* (*Miaofa lianhua jing* 妙法蓮華經, T.262.9:32a18-22):

若人説此經、應入如來室、著於如來衣、而坐如來座、處衆無所畏、廣爲分別説。大慈悲爲室、柔和忍辱衣、諸法空爲座、處此爲説法。

One who is to preach this sūtra,
Should enter the room of the Tathāgata,
Don the robe of the Tathāgata,
Sit in the seat of the Tathāgata,
In the assembly, fearlessly
Preaching broadly with discrimination.
Great compassion is the room;
Harmony and forbearance are the robe;
The emptiness of dharmas is the seat;
In these, he preaches the dharma.

The expression "robe of forbearance" (*ninniku e* 忍辱衣), which Dōgen uses in "Transmitting the Robe" ("Shōbōgenzō den'e" 正法眼藏傳衣, DZZ.1:365), reflects the line of this verse that reads "harmony and forbearance are the robe" (*nyūwa ninniku e* 柔和忍辱衣).

In East Asia, the *kāṣāya* is a formal, outer vestment that is handled with the utmost respect and donned on ceremonial occasions, often after reciting the "Verse for Donning the *Kāṣāya*" (*Takkesa ge* 搭袈裟偈). The version of that verse found in the *Rules of Purity for the Chan Park* (*Chanyuan qinggui* 禪苑清規, ZZ.111:924b11-12; X.1245.63:547a17-18) reads:

大哉解脱服、無相福田衣、披奉如來戒、廣度諸衆生。

How great the vestment of liberation,
Robe that is a signless field of merit.
Wrapped in the precepts of the Tathāgata,
We deliver living beings everywhere.

492          DŌGEN'S *SHŌBŌGENZŌ* VOLUME VIII

The terms "vestment of liberation" (*gedappuku* 解脱服), "robe that is a field of merit" (*fukuden e* 福田衣), and "signless robe" (*musō e* 無相衣), which Dōgen uses in "Transmitting the Robe," all derive from this verse.

The expression "robe of great mercy and great compassion" (*daiji daihi e* 大慈大悲衣), which Dōgen also uses in "Transmitting the Robe," finds some precedent in a Song text entitled *Diagrams of Six Items Prescribed by the Buddha* (*Fozhi biqiu liuwu tu* 佛制比丘六物圖, T.1900.45:897d18-28) by Yuanzhao 元照 (1048–1116), who is known primarily as a vinaya scholar:

有二。初通名者、總括經律。或名袈裟、或名道服、或名出世服、或名法衣、或名離塵服、或名消瘦服、或名蓮華服、或名間色服、或名慈悲衣、或名福田衣、或名臥具、亦云敷具。次別名者。一梵云僧伽梨、此云雜碎衣。從用則名入王宮聚落衣。二欝多羅僧、名中價衣。從用名入衆衣。三安陀會、名下衣。從用名院内道行雜作衣。若從相者、即五條、七條、九條、乃至二十五條等。義翻多別且提一二。

There are two [classes of names for monastic robes]. First are the common names found throughout the sūtras and vinaya. One such name is "*kāṣāya*"; another is "vestment of the way"; another is "vestment of appearing in the world"; another is "dharma robe"; another is "vestment free of [worldly] dust"; another is "vestment of emaciation"; another is "lotus blossom vestment"; another is "vestment of neutral color"; another is "robe of compassion"; another is "robe that is a field of merit"; another is "reclining implement," also called "sitting implement." Next are the names for different types [of robes]. 1) In Sanskrit, the *saṃghāṭī* ["assembly robe"]; this is known as the "robe of various numbers of panels." From its use, it is called the "robe for entering royal palaces and towns [for alms-gathering or preaching]." 2) The *uttarāsaṃghā* ["upper robe"], known as the "robe of middling value." From its use, it is called the "robe for entering the [monastic] congregation." 3) The *antarvāsa* ["inner robe"], known as the "under robe." From its use, it is called the "robe for practice of the way and miscellaneous work within the cloister." When we accord with the forms [established for robes], there are those with five panels, seven panels, nine panels, and so on, up to twenty-five panels, etc. There are many differences in the translated meanings [of the Sanskrit terms], so I have only presented one or two.

This passage is based on Indian vinaya texts translated into Chinese; it does not reflect actual practice in East Asia. In the colder climates of Central Asia and China, the Indian mode of dress was often insufficient, so monks from those regions wore their native clothing and draped the Indian "assembly robe" or "upper robe" on top of that. In Chinese Buddhism in general, and in the Japanese Zen tradition that imported Chinese monastic practices during the Kamakura period, the notion of "three robes" named (in transliteration) *antarvāsa*, *uttarāsaṃgha*, and *saṃghāṭī* remained, but

*Supplementary notes to the translation* 493

all three evolved into formal ceremonial garments, known generically as *kāṣāya*, that are worn over native Chinese or Japanese undergarments and Chinese-style robes (*koromo* 衣). The *antarvāsa* (*andae* 安陀會) became the "five-panel robe" (*gojōe* 五條衣), or "five-panel *kāṣāya*" (*gojō kesa* 五條袈裟); the *uttarāsaṃgha* (*uttarasō* 欝多羅僧) became the "seven-panel robe" (*shichijōe* 七條衣), or "seven-panel *kāṣāya*" (*shichijō kesa* 七條袈裟); and the *saṃghāṭī* (*sōgyari* 僧伽梨) became the "nine-panel robe" (*kujōe* 九條衣), or "nine-panel *kāṣāya*" (*kujō kesa* 九條袈裟). Worn over a Chinese-style full-length sleeved robe that was tied at the waist with a belt or sash, the *kāṣāya* lost its function as a practical piece of clothing to cover and protect the body but retained its meaning as an emblem of membership in the monastic order.

**roots, stalks, branches, and leaves, flowers and fruit, lustrous and colored** (*kon kyō shi yō ke ka kō shiki* 根莖枝葉・華果光色): A line from a verse in chapter 5 the *Lotus Sūtra* (*Miaofa lianhua jing* 妙法蓮華經, T.262.9:19c24-27) describing the varied plants of the world being watered by the same rain:

其雲所出、一味之水、草木叢林、隨分受潤。一切諸樹、上中下等、
稱其大小、各得生長、根莖枝葉華菓光色、一雨所及、皆得鮮澤。

What issues from that cloud is water of a single flavor, but the grasses, trees, and groves each receive moisture in accordance with their lot. All the various trees, whether superior, middling, or inferior, whether large or small, are each enabled to grow. Roots, stalks, branches, and leaves, flowers and fruit, lustrous and colored — all are reached by the one rain and enabled to be fresh and well watered.

The "rain" in this verse represents the teachings of the Buddha, or "**dharma rain**," that is said to be uniform in flavor and universal in distribution but nevertheless received by various forms of vegetation (representing all living beings) in a manner that is suited to their own particular needs and capacities.

**saṃgha hall, buddha hall, kitchen, and mountain gate** (*sōdō butsuden zuku sanmon* 僧堂・佛殿・廚庫・山門): Four major buildings in the layout of a Zen monastery. Recalling a saying attributed to Yunmen Wenyan 雲門文偃 (864-949) in various sources, including the *Discourse Record of Chan Master Yuanwu Foguo* (*Yuanwu Foguo chanshi yulu* 圓悟佛果禪師語錄, T.1997.47:803a25-27) and Dōgen's *Shōbōgenzō* in Chinese script (*shinji Shōbōgenzō* 眞字正法眼藏, DZZ.5:166, case 81):

雲門示衆云、人人盡有光明在、看時不見暗昏昏。作麼生是光明。衆
無對。自代云、僧堂佛殿厨庫三門。

Yunmen addressed the assembly saying, "People all have a radiance, but when they look for it, they can't see it in the darkness. What is this radiance?"

The assembly had no response, so he himself said for them, "Saṃgha hall, buddha hall, kitchen, and triple gate."

The "saṃgha hall" (*sōdō* 僧堂) is the facility in which the registered monks normally meditate, eat, and sleep. The "buddha hall" (*butsuden* 佛殿) houses the main object of worship (*honzon* 本尊), generally an image of Buddha Śākyamuni. The "kitchen" (*zuku* 廚庫) is a large building that includes storage areas and administrative offices as well as a cooking area where meals for the whole community are prepared. The "triple gate" (*sanmon* 三門), so called for its three bays, is a two-story hall that symbolizes the entrance to the monastery; it is more commonly referred to as the homophonous "mountain gate" (*sanmon* 山門). In the standard monastic layout, three of the four buildings that Yunmen mentions would be immediately adjacent to the dharma hall (*hattō* 法堂), where he is speaking: the saṃgha hall to its west; the kitchen to its east, and the buddha hall to its south. The triple gate is just south of the buddha hall. The thrust of his remark may thus be to imply that the members of his audience are mistakenly seeking the "radiance" of awakening somewhere outside the place where they are presently standing.

**scoop up two or three times** (*saisan rōroku* 再三撈摝): The term *rōroku* 撈摝 (also written 撈漉) means "to fish out" something from the water with a scoop or wicker basket, or to "dredge" for something. The expression "scoop up two or three times" reflects a line from the eighth of the ten verses that comprise the *Ten Discourses on the Profound* (*Shi xuantan* 十玄談), a short work by Tong'an Changcha 同安常察 (dates unknown) that is included in the *Jingde Era Record of the Transmission of the Flame* (*Jingde chuandeng lu* 景德傳燈録, T.2076.51:455c5-8). The verse in question, entitled "The Trigger of Conversion" (*kaiki* 迴機), reads:

涅槃城裏尚猶危、陌路相逢沒定期。權挂垢衣云是佛、却裝珍御復名誰。木人夜半穿靴去、石女天明戴帽歸。萬古碧潭空界月、再三撈漉始應知。

To be within the walled city of Nirvāṇa is, after all, like being in peril;

Encountering others on its narrow lanes has no fixed time.

When we provisionally don dirty [monk's] robes, [people] say, "This is a buddha";

When we dress up in exquisite clothing, on the other hand, we are called "Who's that?"

The wooden man, in the middle of the night, puts on his shoes and leaves;

The stone woman, at the break of dawn, puts on her hat and returns.

Blue depths ten thousand ages old, the moon in an empty realm;

You'll only know it when you scoop it up two or three times.

Supplementary notes to the translation          495

The final two lines of this verse are quoted by Dōgen in his "The Old Mirror" ("Shōbōgenzō kokyō" 正法眼藏古鏡, DZZ.1:231). They allude to the trope of the "moon in the water" (*suichū getsu* 水中月), which, like the word "awakening," is a mere reflection of the real thing. Just as the moon in the water cannot be "scooped up" with a net, awakening cannot be grasped through conceptual thinking.

**secondary and primary recompense** (*eshō* 依正): An abbreviation of "secondary recompense and primary recompense" (*ehō shōhō* 依報正報). Two kinds of "karmic recompense" (*kahō* 果報, *gōhō* 業報, or *hō* 報), or fruits of past actions. "Primary recompense" (*shōhō* 正報) refers to the physical and mental makeup that a person is born with. "Secondary recompense" (*ehō* 依報), which can also be translated as "circumstantial recompense," refers to the environment that one is born into, and to the things that happen to one (as if through good or bad luck) during one's lifetime.

**seeing the mountain in the daylight** (*nichiri kanzan* 日裏看山): Perhaps meaning "as clear as seeing a mountain in broad daylight." Likely reflecting the words of Yunmen Wenyen 雲門文偃 (864-949) in the *Extensive Record of Chan Master Yunmen Kuangzhen* (*Yunmen Kuangzhen chanshi guanglu* 雲門匡眞禪師廣錄, T.1988.47:545b29-c1):

問如何是祖師西來意。師云、日裏看山。

[Someone] asked, "What is the **intention of the Ancestral Master's coming from the west**?"
The Master [Yunmen] said, "Seeing the mountain in the daylight."

The saying came to be used as a kōan. The *Tiansheng Era Extended Record of the Flame* (*Tiansheng guangdeng lu* 天聖廣燈錄, ZZ.135:792a5-6), a work compiled in 1036, records the following exchange under the heading of "Chan Master Zhao Hengshan of Yingzhou" 郢州趙橫山禪師:

上堂、有僧問、先師道、日裏看山。意旨如何。師云、老僧今日困。

At a convocation in the dharma hall there was a monk who asked, "An ancient master said, 'Seeing the mountain in the daylight.' What did he mean?"
The Master [Hengshan] said, "This old monk is tired today."

The *Empty Valley Collection* (*Konggu ji* 空谷集, ZZ.117:582b2-6), a collection of one hundred verses on old cases originally compiled by Touzi Yiqing 投子義青 (1032-1083), includes "Seeing the Mountain in the Daylight" as case 46, prefaced by an "address to the assembly" (*jishu* 示衆) by the editor, Danxia Zichun 丹霞子淳 (1064–1117):

496 DŌGEN'S *SHŌBŌGENZŌ* VOLUME VIII

示衆云。説不眞、擧不似。一則一、二則二。失却口、摸著鼻。莫有
知下落的麼。

擧。僧問雲門、如何是祖師西來意。門云、日裏看山。

The address to the assembly says, "Speaking of it is not true; raising it [as a topic] bears no resemblance. One case is one; two cases are two. He [Yunmen] inadvertently blurted it out; I grab his **nose**. Didn't he know the case was closed?"

Raised.

> A monk asked Yunmen, "What is the intention of the Ancestral Master's coming from the west?"
>
> [Yun] Men said, "Seeing the mountain in the daylight."

**seven buddhas** (*shichi butsu* 七佛; S. *sapta-tathāgata*): Also known as the "seven buddhas of the past" (*kako shichi butsu* 過去七佛). A list that includes Śākyamuni and six buddhas who are said to have preceded him, lined up in quasi-genealogical order. A number of Zen texts claim that the Zen lineage began with the seven buddhas, culminating with Buddha Śākyamuni, who was followed by the twenty-eight Indian ancestral masters (*soshi* 祖師). The influential *Jingde Era Record of the Transmission of the Flame* (*Jingde chuandeng lu* 景德傳燈錄, T.2076.51:204b5-9), for example, draws on the *Longer Āgama Sūtra* (*Chang ahan jing* 長阿含經; S. *Dīrghāgama*; T.1.1:1c16ff) to give one standard list: (1) Vipaśyin (Piposhi 毘婆尸); (2) Śikhin (Shiqi 尸棄); (3) Viśvabhū (Pishepo 毘舍浮); (4) Krakucchandha (Juliusun 拘留孫); (5) Kanakamuni (Junahanmouni 拘那含牟尼); (6) Kāśyapa (Jiashe 迦葉), and (7) Śākyamuni (Shijiamouni 釋迦牟尼).

The list of seven buddhas has Indian origins, but there is much uncertainty about some of the Sanskrit reconstructions, and the vagaries of transliteration into Chinese resulted in a number of variant names. According to the *Sūtra of the Names of the Thousand Buddhas of the Past Adornment Kalpa* (*Guoqu zhuangyanjie qian foming jing* 過去莊嚴劫千佛名經, T.446.14:375c27-28), Vipaśyin, Śikhin, and Viśvabhū are the final three buddhas of the past, Adornment Kalpa (*shōgon kō* 莊嚴劫; S. *vyūha-kalpa*). A companion text, the *Sūtra of the Names of the Thousand Buddhas of the Present Worthy Kalpa* (*Xianzai xianjie qian foming jing* 現在賢劫千佛名經, T.447.14:376a22-23), says that the first four buddhas of the present, Worthy Kalpa (*kengō* 賢劫; S. *bhadra-kalpa*) are Kanadī, Kanakamuni, Kāśyapa, and Śākyamuni.

The idea that the first three of the seven buddhas lived in the past, Adornment Kalpa and the next four buddhas lived in the present, Worthy Kalpa is attested in several Chinese Buddhist sources, including Zen texts such as the *Dharma Treasure Platform Sūtra of the Sixth Ancestor* (*Liuzu Dashi fabao tan jing* 六祖大師法寶壇經, T.2008.48:361b26-29), and texts that have no connection to the Zen tradition, such as the *Complete Chronicle of the Buddhas and Ancestors* (*Fozu tongji* 佛祖統紀; J. *Busso tōki*, T.2035.49:298a16). The *Great Compassion Sūtra* (*Dabei jing* 大悲經, T.380.12:958a21-22) states that Śākyamuni is the fourth buddha of the present kalpa; he is to be succeeded in the future by 966 buddhas, beginning with Maitreya.

In the *Extensive Record of Reverend Dōgen* (*Dōgen oshō kōroku* 道元和尚廣錄, DZZ.6:33, no. 446), Dōgen names the three buddhas of the Adornment Kalpa as (1) Bibashi 毘婆尸, (2) Shiki 尸棄, and (3) Bishafu 毘舍浮, and the four buddhas of the Worthy Kalpa as (4) Kuruson 拘樓孫, (5) Kunagonmuni 拘那含牟尼, (6) Kashō 迦葉, and (7) Shakamuni 釋迦牟尼; this list, with the exception of one variant glyph in the name of the fourth buddha, is identical to that found in the *Jingde Era Record of the Transmission of the Flame*.

Several Zen texts contain the fixed expression "thing prior to the seven buddhas" (*shichi butsu izen ji* 七佛已前事), which seems to assume that because the Zen lineage began with the seven buddhas, what existed before them was some kind of primal nothingness. The expression is similar in that respect to the saying "**before King Majestic Voice.**" In the *Discourse Record of Chan Master Yuanwu Foguo* (*Yuanwu Foguo chanshi yulu* 圓悟佛果禪師語錄, T.47.1997:739b14), the two sayings appear in apposition:

七佛已前威音那畔。

Before the seven buddhas, on that side of Majestic Voice.

In Chinese Buddhism at large, however, what comes "prior to the seven buddhas" are the first 997 buddhas named in the *Sūtra of the Names of the Thousand Buddhas of the Past Adornment Kalpa*.

A famous verse found widely throughout Buddhist literature is referred to in the Zen and Tendai traditions as the "Gāthā of the Common Precepts of the Seven Buddhas" (*shichi butsu tsūkai ge* 七佛通戒偈). The earliest occurrence of this usage is found in a work by Tiantai Zhiyi 天台智顗 (538-597), the founder of the Tiantai school in China, which is entitled *Hidden Meaning of the Lotus Sūtra* (*Miaofa lianhua jing xuanyi* 妙法蓮華經玄義, T.1716.33: 695c26-27):

又七佛通戒偈云、諸惡莫作、衆善奉行、自淨其意、是諸佛教。

Moreover, the Gāthā of the Common Precepts of the Seven Buddhas," says:
> Do no evil,
> Practice the good,
> And purify one's own mind:
> This is the teaching of the buddhas.

The influential Tiantai school monk Zhanran 湛然 (711-782) explains the meaning of the title of the verse in his *Explanation of the Profound Meaning of the Lotus* (*Fahua xuanyi shiqian* 法華玄義釋籤, T.1717.33:843c10-11):

七佛通戒偈者、皆用此偈以爲略戒、遍攝諸戒故名爲通。

In the "Gāthā of the Common Precepts of the Seven Buddhas," the term "common" is used because all [the buddhas] use this gāthā to summarize the precepts and [the verse] encompasses the various precepts.

This remark treats the term "seven buddhas" as a virtual synonym of "the buddhas of past and present" (*kagen shobutsu* 過現諸佛). The verse itself, without the title that refers to "seven buddhas," appears in early Buddhist scriptures such as the *Increased by One Āgama Sūtra* (*Zhengyi ahan jing* 增一阿含經; S. *Ekōttarāgama-sūtra*, T.125.2:551a13-14) and the *Dharma Phrase Sūtra* (Pāli, *Dhammapada*) and its Chinese equivalent (*Faju jing* 法句經, T.210.4:567b1-2). It also appears in Mahāyāna scriptures such as the *Nirvāṇa Sūtra* (*Da banniepan jing* 大般涅槃經, T.375.12:693c12-13).

**seven feet or eight feet** (*shichi shaku hachi shaku* 七尺八尺): A phrase from a conversation between Xuefeng Yicun 雪峰義存 (822-908) and his dharma heir Xuansha Shibei 玄沙師備 (835-908), on which Dōgen comments in his "Prediction" chapter ("Shōbōgenzō juki" 正法眼藏授記, DZZ.1:249ff). The version recorded in Dōgen's *Shōbōgenzō* in Chinese script (*shinji Shōbōgenzō* 眞字正法眼藏, DZZ.5:158, case 60) reads:

玄沙、因侍雪峰行次、峰指面前地云、這一片田地、好造箇無縫塔。師曰、高多少。峰乃上下顧視。師曰、人天福報、即不無和尚、靈山授記、未夢見在。峰云、儞作麼生。師曰、七尺八尺。

Once, when Xuansha was traveling with Xuefeng as his attendant, [Xue]Feng pointed at the ground in front of them and said, "This piece of land would be a good place to build a seamless stūpa [as my memorial]."

The Master [Xuansha] said, "How tall would it be?"

Feng looked up and down.

The Master said, "Reverend, you are not lacking in the fortunate recompense of humans and devas, but you have not seen the conferral [of the **treasury of the true dharma eye**] on Vulture Peak even in your dreams."

Feng said, "How about you?"

The Master said, "Seven feet or eight feet."

A "seamless stūpa" (*muhōtō* 無縫塔), also known as an "egg-shaped stūpa" (*rantō* 卵塔), is a posthumous memorial for a deceased eminent monk made of several pieces of carved stone, including a flat base, sometimes a vertical stand, and a single large egg-shaped piece that gives the stūpa its name as "seamless." Some feature a capstone shaped like the roof of a wooden pagoda. Either the base or the egg-shaped piece itself may be inscribed with the name of the deceased monk whose ashes are interred within.

*Supplementary notes to the translation*          499

The use of the measurement "seven feet or eight feet" occurs regularly in the *Shōbōgenzō*, generally in ironic reference to something immeasurable.

**sit fixedly** (*gotsuza* 兀坐): Also translated herein as "fixed sitting." A reference to the assiduous, prolonged practice of seated meditation (*zazen* 坐禪). The term sometimes has a positive connotation in Zen literature, as in the phrase "the blue-eyed barbarian [Bodhidharma] sat fixedly [facing a wall (*menpeki* 面壁)] for nine years" (*Hekiganko gotsuza kunen* 碧眼胡兀坐九年). More often, however, it is used in a pejorative sense, as in the expressions: "always sit fixedly like wood or stone" (*jō gotsuza nyo bokuseki* 常兀坐如木石); "sit fixedly like a rotten stump" (*gotsuza nyo koshu* 兀坐如枯株); "sit fixedly like a squatting monkey" (*gotsuza nyo zon'en* 兀坐如蹲猿); and "foolish Zen of sitting fixedly" (*chizen gotsuza* 癡禪兀坐).

The Zen tradition has a long history of redefining dhyāna (*zen* 禪) as the wisdom that is associated with seeing the buddha-nature, or as the "true calm" that comes from insight into the emptiness of dharmas, both of which it presents as "Mahāyāna" approaches, as opposed to the "Hīnayāna" style **practice of dhyāna** (*shūzen* 習禪) that it characterizes as sitting in meditation to bring the mind to a stop in "frozen concentration" (*teigyō* 定凝). Such redefinitions are evident in early Zen texts like the *Treatise Determining the Truth About the Southern Lineage of Bodhidharma* (*Putidamo Nanzong ding shifei lun* 菩提達摩南宗定是非論, CBETA.B.142.25:69a10-70a3) by Heze Shenhui 荷澤神會 (670-762):

何名坐禪。和上答、若教人坐、凝心入定、住心看淨、起心外照、攝心內證者、此是障菩提。今言坐者、念不起爲坐。今言禪者、見本性爲禪。所以不教人坐身住心入定。若指彼教門爲是者、維摩詰不應訶舍利弗宴坐。

[Question] "What do you call 'seated meditation'?"
The Reverend [Shenhui] replied: "If one instructs people to sit, to freeze the mind and enter into concentration, to settle the mind and observe its purity, to rouse the mind and illuminate what is outside, or to concentrate the mind and verify what is inside, those are obstructions of bodhi. When I speak of 'seated' now, what I mean by 'seated' is thought not being aroused. When I speak of 'meditation' now, what I mean by 'meditation' is seeing the original nature. If their [Northern Lineage] method of teaching were correct, then Vimalakīrti would not have been justified when he reproached Śāriputra for sitting at ease."

A similar argument is found in the Dunhuang manuscript of the *Platform Sūtra* (*Nanzong dunjiao zuishang Dasheng mohe boruo boluomi jing Liuzu Huineng Dashi yu Shaozhou Dafansi shifa tan jing* 南宗頓教最上大乘摩訶般若波羅蜜經六祖慧能大師於韶州大梵寺施法壇經, T.2007.48:338b19-23):

迷人著法相、執一行三昧、眞心座不動、除妄不起心、即是一行三昧。若如是、此法同無情、却是障道因緣。道須通流、何以却滯。心不住法、道即通流。住即被縛。若坐不動是、維摩詰不合呵舍利弗宴坐林中。

Deluded people attach to the marks of dharmas and cling to "single practice samādhi." [They think that] true mind is sitting without moving, clearing away delusion and not giving rise to thoughts. They take that as "single practice samādhi." If that were so, then this dharma [of true mind] would be the same as insentience and would instead be the cause of obstructing the way. The way should flow freely; why obstruct it? When the mind does not dwell on dharmas, the way flows freely. When it dwells, that is being bound. If sitting without moving is good, why did Vimalakīrti rebuke Śāriputra for sitting at ease in the forest?

Both of these early Zen texts refer to a passage in the *Vimalakīrti Sūtra* (*Weimojie suoshuo jing* 維摩詰所説經, T.475.14:539c18-22) where Śāriputra says to the Buddha:

憶念我昔、曾於林中宴坐樹下、時維摩詰來謂我言。唯、舍利弗。不必是坐、爲宴坐也。夫宴坐者、不於三界現身意、是爲宴坐。不起滅定而現諸威儀、是爲宴坐。

I recall that once in the past, when I was sitting at ease beneath a tree in the forest, Vimalakīrti came to me and said: "Ah, Śāriputra, this sitting [you are doing] is not necessarily [true] sitting at ease. What is sitting at ease? Not manifesting **body or mind** in the **three realms**: this is sitting at ease. Not arising from the concentration of extinction and yet properly deporting oneself in various activities: this is sitting at ease."

The *Commentary on the Vimalakīrti Sūtra* (*Weimojing chao* 維摩經抄; T.2773.85:426a11-19), another text found among the Dunhuang manuscripts, uses the term "sitting fixedly" (*gotsuza* 兀坐) as a synonym of "sitting at ease" (*enza* 宴坐):

經曰、夫宴坐者、不於三界現身意相、是爲宴坐。述曰、此淨名居士以大呵小也。小乘見定散之二相、所以捨散而取定。既有定可取著相分別還成非定。或閑林淨處、結跏趺坐、閉目合口、心識不行、出入息斷、此是小乘禪定之相。大乘菩薩則不如是。定散俱泯。出入雙如眞心湛然、是爲眞定。豈可以閉目合口兀坐林中而眞定邪。不妨散。走三界以利生散。不妨定凝。一如而不動是故。

The [*Vimalakīrti*] *Sūtra* says, "What is sitting at ease? Not manifesting body or mind in the three realms: this is sitting at ease."

Explanation:

The lay practitioner Vimalakīrti uses the great [vehicle] to criticize the small [vehicle]. The Hīnayāna views concentration and distraction as two

*Supplementary notes to the translation* 501

opposites, such that one obtains concentration by getting rid of distraction. [However,] given that when one obtains concentration one attaches to its characteristics, that discrimination results, after all, in non-concentration. Moreover, when one secludes oneself in a quiet place like a forest, sits with legs crossed, shuts the eyes and closes the mouth, has no movement of mind or consciousness, and ceases breathing out or in, these are the marks of Hīnayāna dhyāna concentration. Mahāyāna bodhisattvas are not like this. They deny both concentration and distraction. They regard the profound stillness of the true mind, which is the same whether one is in or out [of dhyāna as understood in the Hīnayāna], as true concentration. How could they possibly take sitting fixedly in the forest with eyes shut and mouth closed as true concentration? There is no harm in distraction, and [in any case] to flee the three realms to gain some benefit produces distraction. There is also no harm in frozen concentration. That is because they [the bodhisattvas] see the sameness [of concentration and distraction] and remain imperturbable.

In the kōan known as "**Yaoshan's not thinking**," which appears several times in Dōgen's writings, a monk asks Yaoshan Weiyan 藥山惟儼 (751-834), "What are you thinking [sitting there so] fixedly?" Dōgen approves and makes much of Yaoshan's answer, "I'm thinking of not thinking," but the subtext of the dialogue is the monk's implied criticism (à la Vimalakīrti) of "fixed sitting." In his "Needle of Seated Meditation" ("Shōbōgenzō zazen shin" 正法眼藏坐禪箴) and elsewhere, however, Dōgen reframes "sitting fixedly" as something positive.

**six paths** (*rokudō* 六道; S. *ṣad-gati*): Also called the "six destinies" (*rokushu* 六趣). The six stations of rebirth in saṃsāra that are experienced by sentient beings in accordance with their karma, or actions: (1) hell-beings (*jigoku* 地獄道; S. *naraka*); (2) hungry ghosts (*gaki* 餓鬼; S. *preta*); (3) animals (*chikushō* 畜生; S. *tiryagyoni*); (4) titans, or demigods (*ashura* 阿修羅, *shura* 修羅; S. *asura*); (5) humans (*ningen* 人間; S. *manuṣya*); and heavenly beings (*tenjō* 天上, *ten* 天; S. *deva*), or gods. Among these, the first three are called the "three evil paths" (*san akudō* 三惡道) or "three lower paths" (*ge sanzu* 下三塗); they are also referred to simply as the "evil paths" (*akudō* 惡道), "evil destinies" (*akushu* 惡趣), or "three roads" (*sanzu* 三途). The second three are known as the "three good paths" (*san zendō* 三善道).

There is also an account of saṃsāra, common enough but somewhat less frequent in Buddhist literature, that posits "five paths" (*godō* 五道; S. *pañca-gati*). The latter formula is identical to the "six paths" in every respect, except that it omits the path of the *asura*. It was, perhaps, an earlier version of the "six paths" model, to which *asura* was later added.

**skin, flesh, bones, and marrow** (*hi niku kotsu zui* 皮肉骨髓): An allusion to a famous story in which Bodhidharma tests and evaluates his disciples, likening the depth of their respective understandings of his teaching to "skin" (the shallowest insight), "flesh," "bones," and "marrow" (the deepest insight). As it appears in the biography of Bodhidharma in the *Jingde Era Record of the Transmission of the Flame* (*Jingde chuandeng lu* 景德傳燈錄, T.2076.51:219b27-c5), the story reads as follows:

迄九年已欲西返天竺、乃命門人曰、時將至矣。汝等蓋各言所得乎。時門人道副對曰、如我所見、不執文字、不離文字、而爲道用。師曰、汝得吾皮。尼總持曰、我今所解、如慶喜見阿閦佛國、一見更不再見。師曰、汝得吾肉。道育曰、四大本空、五陰非有、而我見處、無一法可得。師曰、汝得吾骨。最後慧可、禮拜後、依位而立。師曰、汝得吾髓。

After nine years had passed [since Bodhidharma's arrival in China], he wished to return to the west, to India, so he commanded his followers saying, "The time is coming. Why don't each of you say what you have attained?"

At the time, the follower Daofu said, "My present view is, without being attached to the written word or being detached from the written word, one still engages in the function of the way."

The Master [Bodhidharma] said, "You've gotten my skin."

The nun Zongchi said, "My present understanding is, it's like Ānanda's seeing the land of Buddha Akṣobhya: seen once, it isn't seen again."

The Master said, "You've gotten my flesh."

Daoyu said, "The **four elements** are originally empty; the **five aggregates** are nonexistent. My view is that there's not a single dharma to attain."

The Master said, "You've gotten my bones."

Finally, Huike, after making a prostration, stood in his place.

The Master said, "You've gotten my marrow."

In his "Tangled Vines" ("Shōbōgenzō kattō" 正法眼藏葛藤), Dōgen quotes a slightly different version of this story in which Huike is said to have "made three prostrations and stood in place" (*sanpai e i ni ryū* 三拜依位而立); that expression is used by Dōgen in his "Studying the Way with Body and Mind" ("Shōbōgenzō shinjin gakudō" 正法眼藏身心學道) as a stand-alone allusion to Bodhidharma's selection of Huike as his leading dharma heir. Throughout the *Shōbōgenzō*, Dōgen regularly uses the expression "skin, flesh, bones, and marrow" to indicate the essence or truth or entirety of something or someone, as handed down in the ancestral tradition of Zen.

## Supplementary notes to the translation 503

**slough off** (*datsuraku* 脱落): A compound verb that literally means to "disrobe" or "take off" (*datsu* 脱) and "drop" or "let fall" (*raku* 落). The concrete image is one of a person undressing, a snake shedding its skin, or a tree trunk losing its leaves, branches, and bark. When employed metaphorically in Buddhist texts, the idea is that when superficial coverings fall away, the bare essence of a thing is revealed. For example, in the *Āgama of Combined Discourses* (*Za ahan jing* 雜阿含經, T.99.2:246a11-16), we read:

> 婆蹉白佛、瞿曇、譬如近城邑聚落、有好淨地、生堅固林、有一大堅固樹、其生已來經數千際。日夜既久、枝葉零落、皮膚枯朽、唯幹獨立。如是、瞿曇、如來法律離諸枝條柯葉、唯空幹堅固獨立。

Vatsagotra said to the Buddha, "Gautama, suppose, for example, that nearby a city or village there was a nice pure place which produced a grove of *śāla* trees, and that [in it] there was one great *śāla* tree that had passed several thousand years since arising. Being already very old, its branches and leaves have dropped off, its bark and sapwood have rotted and peeled away, and only its trunk stands alone. In this way, Gautama, the Tathāgata's dharma and vinaya dispense with the various twigs and branches, stems and leaves, and stand alone [like] the bare trunk of the *śāla* tree."

The glyphs translated here as "bark and sapwood" (*hifu* 皮膚) are, in many other contexts, better rendered simply as "skin."

In the literature of Zen, the expression "skin sloughed off" (*hifu datsuraku* 皮膚脱落) is used as a metaphor for spiritual liberation, or awakening. In his *Records that Mirror the Axiom* (*Zongjing lu* 宗鏡錄, T.48.2016:488b14-23), Yongming Yanshou 永明延壽 (904–975) cites a passage from the *Nirvāṇa Sūtra* (*Da banniepan jing* 大般涅槃經, T.374.12:597a23-27) to argue for the fundamental purity of the mind-nature (*shinshō* 心性):

> 只爲衆生無智不修、而墮愚闇、不照心性、枉陷輪迴。若不得宗鏡之智光、何由顯於心寶。且衆生無漏智性、本自具足、以客塵所蔽。似鏡昏塵。但能知鏡本明、塵即慚盡。客塵盡處、眞性朗然。如大涅槃經云、如大村外有娑羅林。中有一樹、先林而生、足一百年。是時林主、灌之以水、隨時修治。其樹陳朽。皮膚枝葉、悉皆脱落、唯貞實在。如來亦爾所有陳故。悉已除盡、唯有一切眞實法在。

It is just due to living beings' lack of knowledge and failure to practice that they fall into stupidity, fail to illuminate the mind-nature, and get trapped revolving in rebirth. If one does not attain the light of wisdom that mirrors the axiom, how can one manifest the mind-jewel? Now, living beings are from the start fully equipped in themselves with uncontaminated wisdom, but that is covered by adventitious dust. It is like a mirror obscured by dust. If one can just know the mirror's original luminosity, the dust immediately becomes ashamed and disappears, and in that place

504 DŌGEN'S *SHŌBŌGENZŌ* VOLUME VIII

where the adventitious dust has disappeared, the real nature is clear. It is as said in the *Great Nirvāṇa Sūtra*:

> "It is as if there were a grove of *śāla* trees outside a large village. Within the grove there is one tree older than the others, which has been growing for one hundred years. The master of the grove irrigates the grove with water at appropriate times to maintain it. However, that tree is dehydrated and withered. Its bark and sapwood [i.e., skin], branches and leaves have all sloughed off, and only its core remains. The Tathāgata is also like that in what he explains, for he has entirely removed all else, and only the whole of the real dharma remains."

This passage from the *Nirvāṇa Sūtra* is alluded to in a famous saying that is attributed to Yaoshan Weiyan 藥山惟儼 (751-834) in many sources, including the *Discourse Record of Chan Master Mazu Daoyi of Jiangxi* (*Jiangxi Mazu Daoyi chanshi yulu* 江西馬祖道一禪師語錄, ZZ.119:816b5-6):

侍奉三年。一日祖問之曰、子近日見處作麼生。山曰、皮膚脱落盡、唯有一眞實。

[Yaoshan] attended [Mazu] for three years. One day, [Ma]zu asked him, "Son, these days, what is your viewpoint?"

[Yao]shan said, "Skin sloughed off entirely, there's just a single reality."

Yaoshan's saying came to be raised as a kōan and commented on in numerous Zen texts, including: the *Discourse Record of Chan Master Yuanwu Foguo* (*Yuanwu Foguo chanshi yulu* 圓悟佛果禪師語錄, T.1997.47:721a19-b4); the *Treasury of the True Dharma Eye* (*Zhengfayanzang* 正法眼藏, ZZ.118: 82a15-b16) by Dahui Zonggao 大慧宗杲 (1089–1163); the *Pearl String Collection of Verses on Old Cases from the Chan Lineage* (*Chanzong songgu lianzhu tongji* 禪宗頌古聯珠通集, ZZ.115:164b16-165a6); and the *Discourse Record of Reverend Xutang* (*Xutang heshang yulu* 虛堂和尚語錄, T.2000.47:1011a25-b4).

Yaoshan Weiyan is an important figure in the Sōtō tradition, for he is identified as a dharma heir of Shitou Xiqian 石頭希遷 (710–790) in the second generation after the Sixth Ancestor, Huineng 慧能; and his "dharma grandchild" (*hōson* 法孫), Dongshan Liangjie 洞山良价 (807–869), is revered as the founder of the Sōtō Zen lineage. The full context of Yaoshan's saying is given in his biography, which explains that he also trained under Mazu Daoyi 馬祖道一 (709–788), an ancestral master who is not included in the Sōtō lineage. Yaoshan's initial awakening is said to have occurred when he left Shitou, went to study with Mazu, and heard Mazu's comment on an instruction from Shitou that had previously dumbfounded him. After his awakening, Yaoshan is said to have remained with Mazu as an attendant for three years, at which point Mazu asked him about his viewpoint (*kenjo* 見處). Mazu approved Yaoshan's response, "Skin sloughed off entirely, there's

Supplementary notes to the translation 505

just a single reality," and sent him back to Shitou, who recognized him as a dharma heir. Yaoshan's biography, as found in the *Collated Essentials of the Five Flame Records* (*Wudeng huiyuan* 五燈會元, ZZ.138:163a9-b10), reads as follows:

澧州藥山惟儼禪師、絳州韓氏子。年十七、依朝陽西山慧照禪師出家。納戒于衡嶽希操律師、博通經論、嚴持戒律。一日、自歎曰、大丈夫當離法自淨。誰能屑屑事細行於布巾邪。首造石頭之室、便問、三乘十二分教某甲粗知、甞聞南方直指人心、見性成佛。實未明了。伏望和尚慈悲指示。頭曰、恁麼也不得、不恁麼也不得、恁麼不恁麼總不得。子作麼生。師罔措。頭曰、子因緣不在此。且往馬大師處去。師稟命恭禮馬祖、仍伸前問。祖曰、我有時教伊揚眉瞬目、有時不教伊揚眉瞬目、有時揚眉瞬目者是、有時揚眉瞬目者不是。子作麼生。師於言下契悟。便禮拜。祖曰、儞見甚麼道理便禮拜。師曰、某甲在石頭處、如蚊子上鐵牛。祖曰、汝既如是、善自護持。侍奉三年。一日、祖問、子近日見處作麼生。師曰、皮膚脫落盡、唯有一眞實。祖曰、子之所得、可謂協於心體、布於四肢。既然如是、將三條篾束取肚皮、隨處住山去。師曰、某甲又是何人、敢言住山。祖曰、不然、未有常行而不住、未有常住而不行。欲益無所益、欲爲無所爲。宜作舟航。無久住此。師乃辭祖返石頭。

Chan Master Weiyan of Yaoshan [i.e., Mount Yao] in Lizhou was a son of the Han Clan of Jiangzhou Prefecture. In his seventeenth year, he went forth from household life under Chan Master Xishan Huizhao of Chaoyang. He received the precepts from Vinaya Master Xicao in Hengyue, broadly mastered the sūtras and śāstras, and strictly observed the moral precepts. One day, he lamented to himself, saying, "A great person should detach from dharmas and purify himself. Who can, with every single crumb, make an issue of trivial [mealtime] rules about their napkin?"

When he first entered Shitou's room he asked, "The **three vehicles and twelvefold teachings**, I roughly know. I once heard that in the south [they say], '**pointing directly at the person's mind, seeing the nature and attaining buddhahood**' — this I haven't really understood yet. I humbly hope your reverence will compassionately instruct me about it."

[Shi]tou said, "Such can't be got; not such can't be got; both such and not such can't be got. What will you do?"

The Master was dumbfounded.

[Shi]tou said, "Your karmic connection is not here. For the time being, go to Great Master Ma[zu]'s place."

The Master obeyed this command and paid respects to Mazu, telling him of the aforementioned question [posed by Shitou].

[Ma]zu said, "Sometimes, I have him **raise his eyebrows and blink his eyes**; sometimes, I don't have him raise his eyebrows and blink his eyes.

Sometimes, having him raise his eyebrows and blink his eyes is it; sometimes, having him raise his eyebrows and blink his eyes is not it. What do you make of that?"

With these words, the Master tallied and awakened. He made bows.

[Ma]zu said, "What principle do you see that you make bows?"

The Master said, "When I was at Shitou's place, I was 'like a mosquito on an **iron bull**.'"

[Ma]zu said, "If you are like this, then guard it well."

He attended upon [Mazu] for three years. One day, [Ma]zu asked, "Son, these days, what is your viewpoint?"

The Master said, "Skin sloughed off entirely, there's just a single reality."

[Ma]zu said, "What you have attained, son, can be called the harmonizing of mind and body, and the stretching out of the four limbs. Since you are already like this, you should gird your belly with three strips of woven bamboo and go serve as abbot of a monastery somewhere."

The Master said, "Who am I, that you say I should presume to serve as abbot of a monastery?"

[Ma]zu said, "If you do not do so, then you will still lack 'constantly going without abiding,' and you will still lack 'constantly abiding without going.' Even if you wanted to benefit others, there would be none who are benefited; and even if you wanted to do something, there would be nothing that is done. You should make yourself into a ferry boat. You should not abide here for long."

The Master thereupon left [Ma]zu and returned to Shitou.

Another common object of the verb "slough off" in Zen texts is "mind and dust" (*shinjin* 心塵). "Mind" (*shin* 心) in this context refers to the "organ" (*kon* 根) that thinks, i.e. the faculty of thought, while "dust" (*jin* 塵) refers to dharmas in the sense of "objects of thought." "Mind," in short, is the last of the six sense faculties, and "dust" is the last of the six sense objects. An example of this usage appears in the *Extensive Record of Chan Master Hongzhi* (*Hongzhi chanshi guanglu* 宏智禪師廣錄, T.2001.48:63a5-10), where Hongzhi Zhengjue 宏智正覺 (1091–1157) is quoted as saying:

心是根、法是塵。兩種猶如鏡上痕。塵垢盡時光始現。心法雙忘性卽眞。到恁麼時、一切脱落去始得。正脱落時、彼我俱不著處所。所以道、周遍十方心、不在一切處。箇時不是一切心。箇時不是一切法。所以遍一切處。

Mind is the faculty; dharmas are the dust [i.e., sense objects]. Both classes are just like blemishes on a mirror. When the dusty filth is exhausted, the luminosity [of the mirror] first appears. When mind and dharmas are both forgotten, the nature is true. Arriving at such a time, when all is sloughed

Supplementary notes to the translation     507

off, one first attains it. Precisely when [all is] sloughed off, both other and self are not attached to any place. Accordingly, it is said, "Mind pervading the ten directions does not exist in any place." At that time there are no mental states whatsoever. At that time there are no dharmas whatsoever. Accordingly, it [i.e., the luminosity] pervades all places.

In the biography of Qingshan Puneng 慶善普能 (dates unknown) in the *Jianzhong Jingguo Era Continued Record of the Flame* (*Jianzhong jingguo xudeng lu* 建中靖國續燈錄, ZZ.136:320b2-3), that Chan master also speaks of dropping off both "mind and dust":

一切衆生只爲心塵未脱、情量不除、見色聞聲、隨波逐浪、流轉三界。

All living beings, simply because mind and dust are not yet dropped off, are not free from feelings and thoughts, see colors and listen to sounds, go with the waves and follow the billows, and transmigrate through the **three realms**.

Dōgen's teacher, Rujing 如淨 (1163–1228), in the *Discourse Record of Reverend Rujing* (*Rujing heshang yulu* 如淨和尚語錄, T.2002A.48:130c19), is said to have composed a verse that had the line:

心塵脱落開岩洞。

Mind and dust are sloughed off, opening a cave in a cliff.

In the Sōtō Zen tradition beginning with Dōgen, the saying "**body and mind sloughed off**" (attributed to Rujing) came to be used to refer both to awakening and to the practice of seated meditation. Dōgen speaks of "sloughing off" other things as well in his *Shōbōgenzō*, for example: "slough off defilement" (*zenna o datsuraku seri* 染汚を脱落せり); "slough off one's old nest" (*kyūka o datsuraku suru* 舊窠を脱落する); "slough off beginninglessness and endlessness" (*mushi mushū o datsuraku seru* 無始無終を脱落せる); and "a reading of the sūtras that is sloughed off" (*datsuraku no kankin* 脱落の看經). When the object of the verb in Dōgen's usage is an abstract concept, what "slough off" points to is a realization that the concept is merely a conventional designation, not an indicator of anything that is ultimately real. When the object is a concrete action, "sloughing off" could indicate a literal ceasing of it, but in those cases, too, Dōgen seems to be referring to a kind of cognitive detachment from the action, facilitated by insight into the emptiness of dharmas, even as one continues to engage in it. That is certainly the case in his "Sūtras of the Buddhas" ("Shōbōgenzō bukkyō" 正法眼藏佛經, DZZ.2:18), where he says, "To read the sūtras, you must possess the eye for reading the sūtras," and equates having that "**eye**" of wisdom with "sloughing off" sūtra reading; for details, see "**just sit**."

**spiritual powers** (*jinzū* 神通; S. *abhijñā*, *ṛddhi*): Paranormal powers ascribed to buddhas, bodhisattvas, and other adepts of meditative practice. Such powers were called "god-like" (*ten* 天) or "spiritual" (*jin* 神) because they were believed to be the natural abilities of devas, or gods. Buddhist texts, however, stress that human beings, too, can obtain spiritual powers through the **practice of dhyāna**.

A standard list of paranormal powers found throughout Buddhist literature is that of the "six spiritual powers" (*roku jinzū* 六神通). Those are given in the following order in a section of Tiantai Zhiyi's 天台智顗 (538–597) *Sequenced Introduction to the Dharma Realm* (*Fajie cidi chumen* 法界次第初門, T.1925.46:678b19-c19) entitled "Introduction to the Six Spiritual Powers" (*Roku jinzū shomon* 六神通初門):

1) "Deva eye" (*tengen* 天眼; S. *divya-cakṣus*): Paranormal vision, such as that of the devas, which can see all forms everywhere without obstruction and can discern the deaths and rebirths of all living beings throughout the six destinies.

2) "Deva ear" (*tenni* 天耳; S. *divya-śrotra*): Paranormal hearing, such as that of the devas, which can hear the words spoken by living beings throughout the six destinies and all other sounds in the universe.

3) "Knowing other minds" (*chi tashin tsū* 知他心通 or *tashintsū* 他心通; S. *para-citta-jñāna*): The ability to discern the state of mind and particular thoughts of other beings, especially a person's spiritual state — whether or not his or her mind is defiled, concentrated, liberated, and the like.

4) "Recollection of former lives" (*shukumyō chi* 宿命智 or *shukumyō tsū* 宿命通; S. *pūrva-nivāsānusmṛti* or *jāti-smara*): The ability to know one's own previous states of existence and what was done in each of them, through 80,000 great kalpas of prior lifetimes, and to know the prior existences and actions of other living beings throughout the six destinies.

5) "Spiritual bases" (*jinsoku* 神足, *nyoisoku* 如意足, *shin nyoi tsū* 身如意通, or *shintsū* 身通; S. *ṛddhi-pāda*): Paranormal physical powers. A standard list, found in many texts, gives the following: ability to manifest mentally produced images of one's body in any world with complete autonomy; to disappear; to pass through solid objects; to enter the earth; to walk on water; to fly; to touch the sun and moon; and to ascend to the heavens of Brahmā. The abilities to cause the earth to shake, and to produce fire and water from the sides of one's body are often included in the list.

6) "Knowledge of the exhaustion of the contaminants" (*rojin chi* 漏盡智; S. *āsrava-kṣaya-jñāna*): Knowledge of one's own purification; the recognition that one has been purged of the three kinds of contamination, which are desire, existence, and nescience. This power is achieved only by those who have had insight into the truth of the buddha dharma.

There is also a standard scheme of "five spiritual powers" (*go jinzū* 五神通) that contains all but the last item on this list of "six spiritual powers."

*Supplementary notes to the translation*          509

Indian Buddhist literature is not shy in asserting that Buddha Śākyamuni demonstrated his spiritual powers in front of wonderstruck audiences on various occasions. The ability to fly into the air, "emitting water from the upper body, emitting fire from the lower body" (*shinjō shussui, shinge shukka* 身上出水、身下出火), is one of the earliest examples of Buddhist powers in the literature, a feat said to have been demonstrated by Gautama himself in the famous "twin miracle" (S. *yamakaprātihārya*) at Śrāvastī. It became a standard motif in accounts of the "spiritual bases" (*jinsoku* 神足; S. *ṛddhi-pāda*), the fifth of the "six spiritual powers" as Zhiyi lists them. Chapter 27 of the *Lotus Sūtra* (*Miaofa lianhua jing* 妙法蓮華經, T.262.9:60a5-7) tells the story of the two sons of the king Śubhavyūha, who convert their father to the buddha dharma by impressing him with their powers:

踊在虛空高七多羅樹。現種種神變。於虛空中行住坐臥。身上出水身下出火。身下出水身上出火。

They leap into empty space to the height of seven *tāla* trees and show various spiritual transformations. They walk, stand, sit, and recline in empty space. They emit water from their upper bodies; they emit fire from their lower bodies. They emit water from their lower bodies; they emit fire from their upper bodies.

Texts authored by Chinese Buddhists, however, tend to be more circumspect in the claims they make about paranormal powers. In his account of the six spiritual powers, for example, Zhiyi suggests that each is obtained and utilized only "while in deep dhyāna concentration" (*shin zenjō chū* 深禪定中). With regard to the "deva eye" and "deva ear," he says that the adept, while absorbed in meditative trance, creates a new body in the form realm (*shikikai* 色界; S. *rūpa-dhātu*), where god-like beings have bodies made of subtle material, and uses the eyes and ears of that divine body for paranormal vision and hearing. Of the third item on the list, Zhiyi has the following to say (T.1925.46:678c6-8):

三、知他心通。修他心智者、若於深禪定中、發他心智、即能知六道衆生心及數法、種種所緣念事。是爲他心通。

Three: the paranormal power of cognizing other minds. The cultivation of knowing other minds is as follows: if, while in deep dhyāna concentration, one gives rise to knowledge of other minds, then one will be able to cognize the minds of living beings in the **six paths**, as well as their mental dharmas, i.e., every sort of thought that they have as an object [of the mental faculty]. That is reading other minds.

When the adept arises from deep dhyāna concentration, presumably, they are back in the desire realm (*yokukai* 欲界; S. *kāma-dhātu*) with their gross material body, which has no paranormal powers; see **three realms**. In this account, Zhiyi duly reports what Chinese translations of Indian Buddhist

510 DŌGEN'S *SHŌBŌGENZŌ* VOLUME VIII

texts say about the six spiritual powers, but he makes it seem as if the exercise of those powers is a purely subjective experience. The adept absorbed in trance might feel himself to be flying through the air or spewing fire and water from his body, but such feats would not be witnessed by other people: if they looked at him, they would just see a person sitting still in meditation.

The teaching concerning spiritual powers was widespread throughout both the technical and popular literature of Buddhism and represented one of the common assumptions of the Buddhist community in East Asia. Discussion of the powers also occurs with some frequency in the texts of the Chinese Chan masters, who tended in one way or another to redefine, dismiss, or make light of the traditional understandings of the teaching. In his "Spiritual Powers" ("Shōbōgenzō jinzū" 正法眼藏神通, DZZ.1:394), for example, Dōgen says that "the five powers or six powers are all small spiritual powers" (*gotsū rokutsū mina shōjinzū nari* 五通六通みな小神通なり). The "great spiritual powers" (*daijinzū* 大神通), he says, are the "spiritual powers of a buddha" (*butsu jinzū* 佛神通), which are manifested in "the ocean of this inexhaustible dharma realm, constant and unchanging" (*ima no mujin hokkaikai no jō fuhen naru* いまの無盡法界海の常不變なる). The idea here is that all of phenomenal existence, including matters that appear to be utterly mundane from the conventional point of view, is equally miraculous. It is in this spirit that Dōgen quotes the last two lines of a verse attributed to Layman Pang 龐居士 in the *Jingde Era Record of the Transmission of the Flame* (*Jingde chuandeng lu* 景德傳燈錄, T.2076.51:263b9-12):

日用事無別、唯吾自偶諧、頭頭非取捨、處處勿張乖、朱紫誰爲號、
丘山絶點埃、神通竝妙用、運水及般柴。

Everyday affairs, without discrimination,
Are only me, agreeing with myself.
Thing after thing, I have no grasping or rejecting;
Place after place, I do not proclaim or oppose.
Vermilion and purple robes: how could they be markers [of a person's true worth]?
In hills and mountains, I cut off the tiniest speck of dust [of worldly defilement].
The spiritual powers and the wondrous functions:
Bearing water and carrying firewood.

Layman Pang's saying, "bearing water and carrying firewood," may also have recalled, for Dōgen, a famous story in the *Lotus Sūtra* (*Miaofa lianhua jing* 妙法蓮華經, T.262.9:34c6) of the prior career of Buddha Śākyamuni, in which the latter "drew water and gathered firewood" (*kyūsui shūshin* 汲水拾薪) for his teacher, the future Devadatta. In Dōgen's time, when the Tendai school held a series of lectures on the *Lotus Sūtra*, on the day that the

*Supplementary notes to the translation* 511

Devadatta chapter was discussed, the audience brought offerings of water and firewood, thus ritually re-enacting the Buddha's service.

Valorizations of everyday activities as manifestations of profound spiritual attainment are found throughout the literature of Zen. The "Song of Reverend Nanyue Lanzan" (*Nanyue Lanzan heshang ge* 南嶽懶瓚和尚歌) found in the *Jingde Era Record of the Transmission of the Flame* (*Jingde chuandeng lu* 景德傳燈錄, T.2076.51:461b21), for example, says:

饑來喫飯、困來即眠。愚人笑我、智乃知焉。

When I get hungry, I have rice;
When I get tired, I sleep.
Fools may laugh at me,
But the wise understand.

In his "Everyday Matters" ("Shōbōgenzō kajō" 正法眼藏家常, DZZ.2:126), Dōgen quotes and comments on a saying of his teacher Rujing 天童如淨 (1162–1227) that incorporates the first two lines of this verse.

**staff** (*shujō* 拄杖): In ordinary language, a "stick," "cane," or "staff" (*jō* 杖) that is used as a "prop," or "support" (*shu* 拄) for standing or walking. When used as a verb, the glyph *jō* 杖 also means "to beat with a stick." In the context of a court of law, it refers more specifically to a set number of "blows" that are meted out on the spot to convicted criminals as punishment. The glyph *bō* 棒, which means "stick," "cane," or "staff" (but can also indicate a metal "rod" or "bar"), is used interchangeably with *jō* 杖 to refer to "blows."

In the Buddhist context, a "staff" (*shakujō* 錫杖; S. *khakkharaka*) was standard equipment for wandering monks; it was typically made of wood with metal rings fixed to the top, which when rattled might scare off wild animals. To "hang up the staff" (*kashaku* 掛錫) means to stop travelling and take up residence in a monastery, for the duration of at least one retreat.

In East Asia, a "staff" (*shujō* 拄杖), often missing the metal rings, was an item of regalia wielded by the abbots of monasteries during formal rituals as an emblem of their rank. In Zen literature, abbots are often depicted using their staffs as instructional devices, either holding them up to symbolize something or using them to hit or chase away disciples. The *Continued Transmission of the Flame* (*Xu chuandeng lu* 續傳燈錄, T.2077.51:479b12-16), for example, portrays the response of a Chan master named Rifang 日芳 (dates unknown) to a monk who asked about **Yunmen's three phrases**:

僧問、如何是函蓋乾坤句。師竪起拄杖。僧曰、如何是截斷衆流句。師橫按拄杖、僧曰、如何是隨波逐浪句。師擲下拄杖。僧曰、三句外請師道。師便起去。

A monk asked, "What about the phrase 'boxing and covering heaven and earth'?"

The Master [Rifang] raised up his staff.

The monk said, "What about the phrase 'cutting off all flows'?"

The Master held his staff horizontally.

The monk said, "What about the phrase 'chasing the waves and following the billows'?"

The Master threw down his staff.

The monk said, "Please, Master, speak about what is apart from the three phrases."

The Master immediately got up and left.

Zen masters also use expressions such as "thirty blows" (*sanjū bō* 三十棒 or *sanjū jō* 三十杖) metaphorically to indicate their authority to judge spiritual matters, comparing that to the authority of an imperially appointed magistrate in a court of law. The classic example of such usage is found in the *Extensive Record of Chan Master Yunmen Kuangzhen* (*Yunmen Kuangzhen chanshi guanglu* 雲門匡眞禪師廣錄, T.1988.47:547a11-13):

德山和尚纔見僧入門、拽拄杖便趁。睦州和尚見僧入門來便云、現成公案、放爾三十棒。

Reverend Deshan, when he first saw a monk enter the gate, brandished a staff, and chased him away. Reverend Muzhou, seeing a monk come in through the gate, said to him, "It [yours] is a settled case, but I release you from the thirty blows."

Such stories and locutions are so common that the word "staff" came, by metonymy, to represent the person of a Zen master.

**stepping forward and stepping back** (*shinpo taiho* 進步退步): In ordinary language, the expression "advance or retreat" (*shintai* 進退) is commonly used to indicate any sort of bodily movement forward vs. movement back; participation vs. disengagement; progress vs. regress; etc. It also has the meaning of "course of action" or "movement" in general. Buddhist texts speak of "advance or retreat" on the spiritual path, and monastic rules such as the *Imperial Edition of Baizhang's Rules of Purity* (*Chixiu Baizhang qinggui* 勅修百丈清規, T.2019.48:1112a13-14) contain detailed prescriptions for ritual procedures like "entering and exiting [a ceremony hall] by the two ranks [of monastic officers]" (*ryōjo shintai* 兩序進退) and "engagement and disengagement [with the abbot] by acolytes" (*jisha shintai* 侍者進退). The expression "approach and withdraw" (*shintai* 進退) is also used to refer to the movements of the abbot when he leaves the prostration mat (*haiseki* 拜席), advances to the altar to make offerings before an enshrined deity, and then returns to his original place.

*Supplementary notes to the translation* 513

The expression "stepping forward, stepping back" (*shinpo taiho* 進歩退步) occurs regularly in Dōgen's writings, but it is not found anywhere else in Zen texts or the Chinese Buddhist canon, so it may have been coined by him. ZGDJ (s.v. しんぽたいほ) gives three meanings, each illustrated by a passage from the *Shōbōgenzō*: 1) the everyday back and forth of sitting [i.e., *zazen* 坐禪] and manual labor [i.e., *samu* 作務] (*nichijō no zasa shintai no koto* 日常の坐作進退のこと); for example, in "One Bright Pearl" ("Shōbōgenzō ikka myōju" 正法眼藏一顆明珠): "stepping forward and stepping back in the **ghost cave** at the Black Mountains — this is nothing but **one bright pearl**" (*Kokusan kikutsu no shinpo taiho, kore ikka myōju naru nomi nari* 黑山鬼窟の進歩退步、これ一顆明珠なるのみなり); 2) going and coming, exiting and entering (*korai shutsunyu* 去來出入); for example, in "Buddha Nature" ("Shōbōgenzō busshō" 正法眼藏佛性): "'then vanished' and 'then manifest' are the stepping forward and stepping back of the form of the disk" (*soku on soku gen wa, rinsō no shinpo taiho nari* 即隱即現は、輪相の進歩退步なり); and 3) the meaning of "ascending or descending" [up toward buddhahood and down to save living beings]; also used in the sense of "rank of upright" and "rank of inclined" [in the **five ranks** formula] (*kōjō kōge no i. shōi hen'i ni mo mochiiru* 向上向下の意。正位偏位の意にも用いる); for example, in "Face-to-Face Conferral" ("Shōbōgenzō menju" 正法眼藏面授): "you should investigate the life-saving path on which we step forward and step back" (*shinpo taiho no katsuro o sankyū subeshi* 進歩退步の活路を參究すべし).

**such a person** (*inmo nin* 恁麼人): A phrase from a discourse attributed to Yunju Daoying 雲居道膺 (d. 902) in his biography in the *Jingde Era Record of the Transmission of the Flame* (*Jingde chuandeng lu* 景德傳燈録, T.2076.51:335c14-23):

言語如鉗夾鉤鎖相續不斷。始得頭頭上具物物上新、可不是精得妙底事。道汝、知有底人終不取次。十度擬發言九度却休去。爲什麼如此。恐怕無利益。體得底人心如臘月扇。口邊直得醭出。不是汝彊爲任運如此。欲得恁麼事、須是恁麼人。既是恁麼人、何愁恁麼事。學佛邊事是錯用心。假饒解千經萬論。講得天華落石點頭、亦不干自己事。況乎其餘有何用處。若將有限心識、作無限中用、如將方木逗圓孔。多少差訛。

Speaking words is like being yoked to a chain with links that continue without end. If you first attain it by placing a head atop your head or equipping things with new thingness, you will not be able to grasp the marvelous matter. I tell you, a person who knows this, in the end, will not engage in loose talk. For every ten times you consider spouting words, nine times you should desist. Why so? Because you will fear that there will be no benefit. The mind of a person with experience is like a fan in the twelfth month. On the sides of one's mouth, one soon has scum appear. It is not that one has to work at it: things are naturally like this.

> If you want to get such a thing,
> You should be such a person;
> Since you are such a person,
> Why worry about such a thing?

Studying Buddhist matters is a mistaken attentiveness. Even if you can understand a thousand sūtras and ten thousand *śāstras*, or lecture so well that heavenly flowers fall down on your head, still you have not cracked the matter of your own self. Of what use could it [studying] be in other affairs? If you want to limit mind and consciousness while doing limitless tasks, then that is like fitting a square peg into a round hole. It is big mistake.

The verse in four phrases of five glyphs each, which is set apart for emphasis in the preceding translation, was subsequently quoted and commented on in a great many Zen texts.

**sun face, moon face** (*nichimen gachimen* 日面月面): A poetic way of referring to the sun and moon, or to daytime and nighttime. In Buddhist texts, an allusion to two buddhas, Sun-faced (*Nichimen* 日面) and Moon-faced (*Gachimen* 月面), named in the *Sūtra on the Names of the Buddhas* (*Foming jing* 佛名經, T.440.14:154a21-23):

復有佛名月面。彼月面佛壽命一日一夜。過月面世尊。復有佛名日面。彼日面佛壽命滿足千八百歲。過日面世尊。

There is also a buddha named "Moon-faced." Moon-faced Buddha has a life span of one day and one night. In the past, [he was called] "Moon-faced World-Honored One." There is also a buddha named "Sun-faced." Sun-faced Buddha has a life span of a full one-thousand eight-hundred years. In the past, [he was called] "Sun-faced World-Honored One."

In the Zen tradition, the expression "sun face, moon face" is best known from a kōan involving Mazu Daoyi 馬祖道一 (709-788), which appears as case 3 of the *Blue Cliff Record* (*Biyan lu* 碧巖錄, T.2003.48:142c10-12):

馬大師不安。院主問、和尚近日尊候如何。大師云、日面佛月面佛。

Great Master Ma was unwell. The head of cloister asked, "Reverend, how is your condition these days?"

The Great Master said, "Sun-faced buddha, moon-faced buddha."

The same kōan also appears as case 36 of the *Congrong Hermitage Record* (*Congrong lu* 從容錄, T.2004.48:251b20-22), and in numerous other Zen records. The *Extensive Record of Chan Master Hongzhi* (*Hongzhi chanshi guanglu* 宏智禪師廣錄, T.2001.48:21c21-25), for example, gives Hongzhi Zhengjue's 宏智正覺 (1091–1157) verse comment on it:

舉。馬大師不安。院主問、和尚近日尊位如何。大師云、日面佛月面佛。頌曰、日面月面、星流電卷。鏡對像而無私。珠在盤而　　。君不見。鉗鎚前百鍊之金。刀尺下一機之絹。

Raised:

Great Master Ma was unwell. The head of cloister asked, "Reverend, how is your condition these days?"

The Great Master said, "Sun-faced buddha, moon-faced buddha."

Verse Comment:

Sun-faced, moon-faced; stars spread out, lightning rolls up. The mirror faces images without self-interest; the pearl revolves freely on a tray. Don't you see? In front of the pincers and hammer, gold refined by a hundred smeltings; beneath the knife and tape measure, silk cloth from a single loom.

It would seem from this verse comment that Hongzhi, at least, did not think Mazu was referring to the two buddhas referenced in *Sūtra on the Names of the Buddhas*, but rather to two different "faces," or appearances, that are reflected in the one mirror-like buddha mind.

**sun, moon, and stars** (*nichigetsu seishin* 日月星辰): A common generic expression in Buddhist texts for the "celestial bodies." It occurs often in Dōgen's writings, not infrequently together with the expression "the mountains, rivers, and the whole earth." The latter combination has a number of precedents in Zen literature. The best known is an exchange between Weishan Lingyou 溈山靈祐 (771–853), a.k.a. Dawei 大溈, and his student Yangshan Huiji 仰山慧寂 (803–887), found, for example, in the *Outline of the Linked Flames* (*Liandeng huiyao* 聯燈會要, ZZ.136:544a5-7). As quoted in Dōgen's *Shōbōgenzō* in Chinese script (*shinji Shōbōgenzō* 眞字正法眼藏, DZZ.5:212, case 168), it reads:

大溈問仰山、妙淨明心、汝作麼生會。仰曰、山河大地、日月星辰。

Dawei asked Yangshan, "The wondrous, pure, clear mind — how do you understand it?"

Yang said, "The mountains, rivers, and the whole earth, the sun, moon, and stars."

Another precedent is found in the *Tiansheng Era Extended Record of the Flame* (*Tiansheng guangdeng lu* 天聖廣燈錄, ZZ.135:837b3-4), in the biography of the Song-dynasty Chan Master Yaoshan Liyu 藥山利昱 (dates unknown), a disciple of Liangshan Yuanguan 梁山緣觀 (dates unknown) in the Caodong lineage:

516 DŌGEN'S *SHŌBŌGENZŌ* VOLUME VIII

師上堂云、山河大地日月星辰與諸上座同生。三世諸佛與諸上座同
參。三藏聖教與諸上座同時。

At a convocation in the dharma hall, the Master [Yaoshan Liyu] said, "Mountains, rivers, and the whole earth, the sun, moon, and stars, are born together with you senior seats; the buddhas of the three times study together with you senior seats; the sacred teachings of the three baskets are simultaneous with you senior seats."

Such imagery had its roots in Indian Buddhist cosmology. For example, the *Longer Āgama Sūtra* (*Chang ahan jing* 長阿含經; S. *Dīrghāgama*; T.1.1:37b27-c6), translated in 413, contains the following passage:

婆悉吒、今當爲汝説四姓本緣。天地始終終劫盡壞時、衆生命終、皆生
光音天。自然化生、以念爲食、光明自照、神足飛空。其後此地盡變
爲水、無不周遍。當於爾時、無復日月星辰、亦無晝夜年月歲數、唯
有大冥。其後此水變成大地。光音諸天福盡命終、來生此間。

Vasiṣṭha, I will now explain to you the origins of the four castes. When heaven and earth from beginning to end were destroyed at the end of the [previous] kalpa, living beings passed out of existence, and all were born [again] in the heaven of radiant sound. They were born through spontaneous transformation, and they took thoughts as food, shone with their own radiance, and used their paranormal physical powers to fly through space. When that [phase] was finished, the land was entirely transformed into water, with nowhere that it [i.e., the water] did not extend. At that time, there were no more sun, moon, or stars; also, there was no day or night, no years or months, and no counting of one's age in years: there was only a great darkness. When that [phase] was finished, the water transformed into the whole earth. The fortunate devas of [the heaven of] radiant sound all passed out of existence and were reborn among [beings of] this [earth].

After that, the *Longer Āgama Sūtra* continues, the beings who had once been devas devolved into insects and other lowly life forms and began to eat earthly food. The period of great darkness ended; the sun, moon, and stars appeared in the sky; day and night started alternating; and years and months began to be counted.

**tangled vines** (*kattō* 葛藤): Literally, "kudzu vine" (*katsu* or *kuzu* 葛), a climbing bean plant with large tuberous starch roots (called "arrowroot") used in cooking; and "wisteria" (*tō* or *fuji* 藤), a twining vine with long clusters of purple flowers, used in basket weaving and as an ornamental shrub. In ordinary language, the trope of "tangled vines" is used metaphorically to refer to any kind of "entanglement," "complication," "confusion," or "conflict." When Dōgen uses *kattō su* 葛藤す as a verb in the *Shōbōgenzō*, we

*Supplementary notes to the translation* 517

translate it as "becoming entangled." We also render it as "entanglement" in some contexts.

In the literature of Zen, a metaphor for either: 1) the "tangle," "complexity," or "complication" of discursive thinking in general; 2) a merely intellectual approach to understanding a Buddhist text, doctrine, or saying; or 3) the complicated language and structure of a kōan collection, in which there are "verse comments" (*ju* 頌) appended to "root cases" (*honsoku* 本則), as well as introductory "instructions" (*suiji* 垂示), prose "evaluations" (*hyōshō* 評唱), and interlinear "attached words" (*jakugo* 著語). Thus, the expression "tangled vines" sometimes refers to the deluded conceptualizing or deluded attachments of ordinary people, but it is also used to refer ironically to the verbal teaching devices of Zen masters, which run the risk of entangling students in even more delusion than they started with. Dōgen also uses the expression in the more positive sense of "intertwining," as for example the interactions between master and disciple.

**the bottle gourd vine entwines the bottle gourd** (*koro tō shuten koro* 胡[or 胡]蘆藤種纏胡蘆): A saying found in the *Discourse Record of Reverend Rujing* (*Rujing heshang yulu* 如淨和尚語錄, T.2002A.48:128b17-20):

佛成道上堂。瞿曇臘月八、夜半走出山。賊路羊腸曲。偷心虎背斑。鈍置人天者一番。天童恁麼撿舉。且道、該當也無。落賺兒孫頭盡禿。胡蘆藤種纏胡蘆。

At a convocation in the dharma hall celebrating the Buddha's attainment of the way, [Rujing said] "Gautama, on the eighth day of the month of offerings [i.e., the 12th month], ran out of the mountains in the middle of the night. On the criminal path, the sheep's entrails are twisted; in the thieving mind, the tiger's back is striped. Among those who fool humans and devas, he is number one. [I] Tiantong, in this way, denounce his misconduct. So, tell me: is this to the point, or not? As for the impostor's descendants, their heads are entirely bald. The bottle gourd vine entwines the bottle gourd."

In his "Tangled Vines" ("Shōbōgenzō kattō" 正法眼藏葛藤, DZZ.1:417), Dōgen attributes the saying to Rujing:

先師古佛云、胡蘆藤種纏胡蘆。

My former master, the **Old Buddha**, said, "The bottle gourd vine entwines the bottle gourd."

Dōgen also attributes the saying to Rujing in his "The Insentient Preach the Dharma" ("Shōbōgenzō mujō seppō" 正法眼藏無情説法, DZZ.2:12). The "vines" (*tō* 藤) in this trope, like the "**tangled vines**" (*kattō* 葛藤) often mentioned in Zen literature, represent the "complications" and "confusion"

518 DŌGEN'S *SHŌBŌGENZŌ* VOLUME VIII

of discursive thinking. The point of Rujing's saying seems to be that our very existence is itself a tangle.

**the one word "enter"** (*nyū shi ichiji* 入之一字): An allusion to a conversation between Yangshan Huiji 仰山慧寂 (803-887) and the magistrate Lu Xisheng 陸希聲 (d. 895), which appears in Dōgen's *Shōbōgenzō* in Chinese script (*shinji Shōbōgenzō* 眞字正法眼藏, DZZ.5:200, case 139):

> 仰山問陸郎中、承聞郎中看經得悟、是否。郎中曰、是。弟子看涅槃經、道不斷煩惱而入涅槃。師堅拂子云、只如這箇、作麼生入。郎中曰、入之一字、也不用得。師曰、入之一字、不爲郎中。郎中便起去。

Yangshan asked Magistrate Lu, "I've heard that the Magistrate had an understanding while looking at a sūtra. Is that so?"

The Magistrate said, "Yes. Your disciple was looking at the *Nirvāṇa Sūtra*, where it says, 'Enter nirvāṇa without eradicating the afflictions.'"

The Master [Yangshan] raised his **whisk** and said, "If it's this, how will you enter?"

The Magistrate said, "The one word 'enter' is of no use."

The Master said, "The one word 'enter' is not for the Magistrate."

Wherepon the Magistrate rose and left.

The line quoted by the magistrate does not, in fact, occur in the *Nirvāṇa Sūtra* but can be found in the *Vimalakīrti Sūtra* (*Weimojie suoshuo jing* 維摩詰所説經, T.475.14:539c25), where Vimalakīrti says to Śāriputra:

> 不斷煩惱而入涅槃、是爲宴坐。若能如是坐者、佛所印可。

To enter nirvāṇa without eliminating the afflictions: this is sitting at ease. Being able to sit like this is what is approved by the Buddha.

The same dialogue is also found in the *Outline of the Linked Flames* (*Liandeng huiyao* 聯燈會要, ZZ.136:565b5-8), printed in 1189.

The biography of Yangshan Huiji that appears in the *Jingde Era Record of the Transmission of the Flame* (*Jingde chuandeng lu* 景德傳燈錄, T.2076.51:283a23-26), completed in 1004, gives a rather different version:

> 鄭愚相公問、不斷煩惱而入涅槃時如何。師堅起拂子。公曰、入之一字不要亦得。師曰、入之一字不爲相公。

Minister Duke Zhengyu asked, "What's it like when you enter nirvāṇa without eradicating the afflictions?"

The Master [Yangshan] raised his whisk.

The Duke said, "[It would seem that] the one word 'enter' isn't necessary."

*Supplementary notes to the translation* 519

The Master said, "The one word 'enter' is not for the Minister Duke."

**the three realms are only mind** (*sangai yui shin* 三界唯心): A saying that expresses the Yogācāra doctrine of "consciousness only" (*yuishiki* 唯識; S. *vijñapti-mātra, citta-mātra*), which holds that nothing in the **three realms** exists apart from one of the "eight modes of consciousness" (*hasshiki* 八識; S. *aṣṭa-vijñānāni*): (1) visual consciousness (*genshiki* 眼識; S. *cakṣur-vijñāna*); (2) auditory consciousness (*nishiki* 耳識; S. *śrota-vijñāna*); (3) olfactory consciousness (*bishiki* 鼻識; S. *ghrāṇa-vijñāna*); (4) gustatory consciousness (*zesshiki* 舌識; S. *jihvā-vijñāna*); (5) tactile consciousness (*shinshiki* 身識; S. *kāya-vijñāna*); (6) mental consciousness (*ishiki* 意識; S. *mano-vijñāna*); (7) defiled consciousness (*manashiki* 末那識, or *zenma i* 染汚意; S. *kliṣṭa-manas*), which produces the "view of self" (*gaken* 我見); and 8) the "storehouse consciousness" (*zōshiki* 藏識; S. *ālaya-vijñāna*), or "root consciousness" (*honjiki* 本識).

The *locus classicus* of the saying "the three realms are only mind" is the *Sūtra on the Entry into Laṅka* (*Lengqie jing* 楞伽經, T.671.16:555c28-c1), a scripture that helped popularize Yogācāra doctrine in Chinese Buddhism and was associated with Bodhidharma in Zen lore:

> 以彼不能入菩薩行、未曾覺知三界唯心、未曾修行菩薩諸法、未曾修行諸波羅蜜十地之行。

> With this, one cannot enter bodhisattva practice, has never known that the three realms are only mind, has never practiced bodhisattva teachings, and has never practiced the ten stages of the various perfections.

The saying was subsequently cited by the Chan master Yongming Yanshou 永明延壽 (904–975) in his *Records that Mirror the Axiom* (*Zongjing lu* 宗鏡錄, T.2016.48:423c25-26):

> 經云、三界唯心、萬法唯識

> As the Sūtra says, "The three realms are only mind; the myriad dharmas are only consciousness."

It was often raised as a topic for comment by Chan teachers such as Yunmen Wenyan 雲門文偃 (864-949), whose sayings are preserved in the *Extensive Record of Chan Master Yunmen Kuangzhen* (*Yunmen Kuangzhen chanshi guanglu* 雲門匡眞禪師廣錄; T.1988.47:546a25-26):

> 問、如何是三界唯心萬法唯識。師云、我今日不答話。

> [Someone] asked, "What about, 'The three realms are only mind; the myriad dharmas are only consciousness'?"

> The Master [Yunmen] said, "Today I'm not saying anything in response."

520 DŌGEN'S *SHŌBŌGENZŌ* VOLUME VIII

**thinking and perceiving** (*ryo chi nen kaku* 慮知念覺): A loose translation of terms for cognitive functions not commonly found as a set in Buddhist literature but appearing several times in the *Shōbōgenzō*, where they seem to stand collectively for the "ordinary operations of consciousness." The translation takes them as two compound expressions (the first of which does occur elsewhere in the *Shōbōgenzō* in reference to the thinking mind); as individual terms, they might be rendered "considering, knowing, thinking, and perceiving or being aware."

The first of the two compounds, "thinking" (*ryochi* 慮知), did have a long history of usage as a Buddhist technical term prior to Dōgen. In his *Great Calming and Insight* (*Mohe zhiguan* 摩訶止觀, T.1911.46:19-21), for example, Tiantai Zhiyi 天台智顗 (538–597) used the term in the course of explaining the Sanskrit word *bodhicitta*, or "thought of bodhi" (*bodai shin* 菩提心):

菩提者天竺音也、此方稱道。質多者天竺音、此方言心。即慮知之心也。

*Puti* [i.e., S. *bodhi*] is the Sindhu pronunciation; over here [in China], we render it as "way" [*dao*]. *Zhiduo* [i.e., S. *citta*] is the Sindhu pronunciation; over here, we say "mind," which is to say, the mind of thinking.

A more literal translation of "thinking" (*ryochi* 慮知), which might pertain in other contexts, would be "knowing through deliberation" or "discriminative cognition." The term "mind of thinking" (*ryochi shi shin* 慮知之心) can also be rendered as "conceptualizing mind."

The *Sūtra of Adamantine Absorption* (*Jingang sanmei jing* 金剛三昧經; S. *Vajrasamādhi-sūtra*, T.273.9:366c15-20), an apocryphal scripture that was probably written in Korea around 685 but circulated widely in China, uses the glyphs 慮知 (*ryochi*) in the following way, translated in this context as "conceptualization":

解脫菩薩而白佛言、尊者、云何如來藏性寂不動。佛言、如來藏者、生滅慮知相隱理不顯。是如來藏性寂不動。解脫菩薩而白佛言、尊者、云何生滅慮知相。佛言、菩薩、理無可不。若有可不、即生諸念、千思萬慮、是生滅相。

Liberation Bodhisattva addressed the Buddha, saying, "World-Honored One, what does it mean to say that the essence of the *tathāgata-garbha* is calm and unmoving?"

The Buddha said, "The *tathāgata-garbha* is that characteristic of [constantly] arising and ceasing conceptualization which conceals the principle so it is not manifested. This is [the meaning of] 'the essence of the *tathāgata-garbha* is calm and unmoving.'"

Liberation Bodhisattva addressed the Buddha, saying, "World-Honored One, what do you mean by 'the characteristic of arising and ceasing conceptualization'?"

*Supplementary notes to the translation*  521

The Buddha said, "Bodhisattva, the principle has neither accepting or rejecting. When there is accepting or rejecting, there is the arising of various thoughts: the thousand ideas and myriad concepts that are marked by arising and ceasing."

In his *Records that Mirror the Axiom* (*Zongjing lu* 宗鏡錄, T.2016.48: 433a27-28), Chan master Yongming Yanshou 永明延壽 (904–975) paraphrased Zhiyi's *Great Calming and Insight* as follows (although the exact quote is not found in the extant text):

止觀云、起一念慮知之心、隨善惡而生十道。

The *Calming and Insight* says, "If one gives rise to a single thought with the conceptualizing mind, one is born in one of the ten destinies, in accordance with the good or evil [of that mental karma]."

It is clear from these contexts that the term "conceptualization" (*ryochi* 慮知), or "thinking," is virtually synonymous with the more common Buddhist technical term "discrimination" (*funbetsu* 分別). The Sōtō Zen master Keizan Jōkin 瑩山紹瑾 (1264–1325), in a short work entitled *Explanation of the Three Capacities for Seated Meditation* (*Sankon zazen setsu* 三根坐禪説, Kohō Chisan (1937, 251), says:

中根坐禪者、放捨萬事、休息諸緣。十二時中無暫怠隙、就出息入息、斷斷工夫。或提撕一則公案。注變眼於鼻端、自家本來面目、不涉生死去來。眞如佛性妙理、不墮慮知分別。不覺不知而無不覺。

Those of middling capacity for seated meditation "cast aside the myriad affairs and discontinue the various involvements." Throughout the twelve times [of the day], without a moment of idleness or interruption, they make a whole-hearted, concentrated effort to follow their outgoing breaths and incoming breaths. Or they stay focused on a single kōan. They fix their wandering eyes on the tips of their **noses**, stay within their own original faces, and do not cross over into the comings and goings of birth and death. The wondrous principle of the buddha nature of true suchness does not fall into conceptualization and discrimination. Although they "do not perceive and do not know," they are not unawakened.

Here, "conceptualization" (*ryochi* 慮知) and "discrimination" (*funbetsu* 分別) are explicitly identified. The first of the quotations in this passage comes from the genre of texts known as "principles of seated meditation" (*zazengi* 坐禪儀); the second comes from the *Lotus Sūtra* parable of the "**burning house.**"

The second compound expression, "perceiving" (*nenkaku* 念覺), is glossed by ZGDJ (s.v. ねんかく) as "the discriminating mind of living beings" (*shujō no funbetsu shin* 衆生の分別心), but the example given is from Dōgen's "This Mind Itself Is the Buddha" ("Shōbōgenzō soku shin ze butsu" 正法眼藏即

心是佛). The glyphs 念覺 (*nenkaku*) appear often in the Chinese Buddhist canon, but never with that meaning; in virtually every case, they occur in compounds that refer to the fifth of the "seven factors of awakening" (*shichi kakubun* 七覺分; S. *sapta-bodhyaṅga*), which is the "factor of mindfulness" (*nenkaku bun* 念覺分 or *nenkaku shi* 念覺支; S. *smṛti-saṃbodhyaṅga*).

There is, however, one instance in the canon where the glyphs 念覺 (*nenkaku*) seem to refer to ordinary (as opposed to awakened) operations of consciousness. That is a passage in the *Great Adornment Discourse Sūtra* (*Da zhauanyan lun jing* 大莊嚴論經, T.201.4:260b7-9), also quoted by Chan master Yongming Yanshou 永明延壽 (904–975) in his *Records that Mirror the Axiom* (*Zongjing lu* 宗鏡錄, T.2016.48:787b12-15), in which some brahmans question the Buddha about how memory can function if there is no self:

> 問、若無我者、先所作事、云何故憶而不忘失。答、以有念覺與心相應、便能憶念三世之事而不忘失。

Question: "If there is no self, how is it that what we did before is remembered and not forgotten?"

Answer: "Because there is perceiving together with [the dharmas] associated with mind, which enables us to remember matters of the three times and not forget them."

In this context, "perceiving" (*nenkaku* 念覺) refers to the aspect of ordinary consciousness that calls to mind past and future events.

**this mind itself is the buddha** (*soku shin ze butsu* 即心是佛): Or "this very mind is the buddha." A very common phrase in Zen literature, with slight variants such as *ze shin soku butsu* 是心即佛, *soku shin soku butsu* 即心即佛, *ze shin ze butsu* 是心是佛. Often associated especially with a saying of Mazu Daoyi 馬祖道一 (709-788), in response to a question by Damei Fachang 大梅法常 (752-839); the exchange appears in many Zen texts, including the *Jingde Era Record of the Transmission of the Flame* (*Jingde chuandeng lu* 景德傳燈錄, T.2076.51:254c3-4) and Dōgen's *Shōbōgenzō* in Chinese script (*shinji Shōbōgenzō* 眞字正法眼藏, DZZ.5:266, case 278):

> 問、如何是佛。大寂云、即心是佛。師即大悟。

[Damei Fachang] asked, "What is a buddha?"

Daji [i.e., Mazu] said, "This mind itself is the buddha."

The Master [Damei] immediately had a great awakening.

The particular phrase, "this mind itself is the buddha," seems to first occur in China, but there is an Indian precedent for the equation of the mind and the buddha — most famously, perhaps, in a verse in the *Flower Garland Sūtra* (*Huayan jing* 華嚴經; S. *Buddhāvataṃsaka-sūtra*, T.278.9:465c26-29):

*Supplementary notes to the translation* 523

心如工畫師、畫種種五陰、
一切世界中、無法而不造。
如心佛亦爾、如佛衆生然、
心佛及衆生、是三無差別。

Mind is like a master artist, painting the multifarious five aggregates;

Within all worlds, there are no dharmas not created by it.

As is mind, so also is buddha;

As is buddha, just so are living beings.

Mind, buddha, and living beings —

These three are without distinction.

Although its provenance is in fact uncertain, the Zen tradition sees an early precedent in a line from the *Mind-King Inscription* (*Xin wang ming* 心王銘), a short text attributed to the sixth-century figure Fu dashi 傅大士 (497-569) in the *Jingde Era Record of the Transmission of the Flame* (*Jingde chuandeng lu* 景德傳燈錄, T.2076.51:457a2-3):

是心是佛是佛是心。

The mind is the buddha; the buddha is this mind."

**three heads and eight arms** (*sanzu happi* 三頭八臂): Also written "three faces and eight arms" (*sanmen happi* 三面八臂). A form in which certain Buddhist divinities, especially those envisioned in the Tantric, or "esoteric teachings" (*mikkyō* 密教) pantheon, are said to manifest themselves. According to the *Commentary on the Sūtra of Humane Kings* (*Renwang huguo bore boluomiduo jing shu* 仁王護國般若波羅蜜多經疏, T.1709.33:515c27-28), for example, the wisdom king (*myōō* 明王) known as Trailokyavijaya (Gōsanze Kongō 降三世金剛) has three heads and eight arms. That is not an iconographically fixed or identifying feature of the deity, however, for he is also depicted with four faces and eight arms; with one face and four arms; and with one face and two arms. A Song-dynasty Chinese text entitled *Verses on the Sūtras of the Esoteric Strongmen [i.e., Vajra Holders] and Authoritative Deva Kings* (*Miji lishi daquan shenwang jing ji song* 密跡力士大權神王經偈頌, T.1688.32:777a25-26) says that the wisdom king Ucchuṣma (J. *Ejaku myōō* 穢跡明王, a.k.a. *Ususama myōō* 烏蒭瑟摩明王) has three heads and eight arms; but he is also depicted with a single head and two, four, or six arms. The same text (T.1688.32:777b3-7) explains how powerful deva kings (*daiken jinnō* 大權神王) can "provisionally manifest" (*kegen* 化現) themselves in a "wrathful form with three heads and eight arms" (*sanzu happi funnu sō* 三頭八臂忿怒相). In general, when Buddhist deities such as these take on a fearsome, wrathful form in which they brandish weapons as well as ritual implements in their multiple hands, the anger and threat of violence that they display is said to be directed at evildoers, troublesome demons, and non-Buddhist gods, for in essence they are protectors of the buddha dharma.

In the literature of Zen, the expression "three heads and eight arms," and the similar "three heads and six arms" (*sanzu roppi* 三頭六臂), are used somewhat whimsically to refer to the many ways in which the buddha nature (*busshō* 佛性) manifests itself. An example is found in the *Discourse Record of Chan Master Yuanwu Foguo* (*Yuanwu Foguo chanshi yulu* 圓悟佛果禪師語錄, T.1997.47:796c25-797a4):

舉。雪竇云、乾坤之內宇宙之間、中有一寶掛在壁上。達磨九年面壁、不敢正眼覷著。如今衲僧要見。劈脊便打。師拈云、雪竇妙中之妙奇中之奇。向佛祖頭上提持。衲僧頂門鑿竅。不妨自在。要且只見錐頭利、不見鑿頭方。若是蔣山則不然。乾坤之內宇宙之間、中有一寶。竪起拄杖子云、在拄杖頭上。拈起也天回地轉。放下也草偃風行。有時八臂三頭。有時壁立千仞。如今莫道衲僧要見。直饒。

Raised:

Xuedou said, "In heaven and earth, throughout the cosmos, there's a singular treasure, hanging on a wall. Bodhidharma faced the wall for nine years, but of course he did not adjust his eyes to try to see [anything]. Nowadays, when patch-robed monks try to see [some imagined "singular treasure"], I aim for their backs and strike!"

The master [Yuanwu] commented, saying, "Xuedou is the rarest among the most exquisite of the extraordinary. He grasps what is over the heads of the **buddhas and ancestors**, and he drills holes in the heads of patch-robed monks. He is unobstructed and autonomous. Even if you want to see the sharpness of the tip of an awl, you cannot see the tip when it is drilling. If this were Jiangshan, it would not be like that. 'In heaven and earth, throughout the cosmos, there's a singular treasure.'"

Holding up his **staff**, he [Yuanwu] said, "It's on the tip of the staff. Take it up, and the heavens revolve and the earth turns; let it go, and the grass bends as the wind moves. Sometimes, it's eight arms and three heads; sometimes, it's a wall rising a thousand fathoms. Nowadays, I do not say that patch-robed monks try to see; I immediately pardon them."

The "singular treasure" (*ippō* 一寶) that Yuanwu says sometimes manifests itself in the form of an eight-armed, three-headed deity is the buddha nature that is immanent in all living beings. The same may be said of the "master within the master" (*shu chū shu* 主中主) that is the topic of the following exchange, which appears in the biography of Fenzhou Shanzhao 汾州善昭 (947-1024) in the *Jingde Era Record of the Transmission of the Flame* (*Jingde chuandeng lu* 景德傳燈錄, T.2076.51:305a26-27):

曰如何是主中主。師曰、三頭六臂驚天地。忿怒那吒撲帝鍾。

[A monk] asked, "What is the master within the master?"

*Supplementary notes to the translation* 525

The master [Fenzhou] said, "His three heads and six arms startle heaven and earth. The wrathful Naṭa knocks down the imperial bell."

The name Naṭa, meaning "dancer" in Sanskrit, belongs to a dharma-protecting *asura* (*ashura* 阿修羅) king who is usually said to have three heads and eight arms.

**three realms** (*sangai* 三界; S. *traidhātuka, trailokya*): Three "worlds," or "realms" (*kai* 界; S. *dhātu*) where birth can occur. The three are: (1) the desire realm (*yokukai* 欲界; S. *kāma-dhātu*), where beings have gross material bodies and are preoccupied with sensuality; (2) the form realm (*shikikai* 色界; S. *rūpa-dhātu*), where beings are free from the afflictions of the desire realm but still have bodies of subtle material; and (3) the formless realm (*mushikikai* 無色界; S. *ārūpya-dhātu*), where beings exist as purely spiritual entities, free from all traces of physicality. The three realms are conceived as places where beings are born in accordance with their past actions (karma), and together they comprise all existence in saṃsāra. The human path (*ningen dō* 人間道; S. *manuṣya-gati*) — i.e., rebirth as a human — locates one in the desire realm, but people do not have to die and be reborn to experience the pure dharmas (mental and physical phenomena) associated with the form realm: those can be accessed temporarily through the practice of dhyāna. That practice is said to have the karmic result of rebirth in various heavens (*ten* 天) in either the form realm or the formless realm, depending on what level of dhyāna had been practiced in the previous lifetime.

The basic formula of "three realms" is sometimes juxtaposed with a similar model of "nine levels" (*kuji* 九地) of existence. The first level is the "desire realm with its five destinies" (*yokukai goshu chi* 欲界五趣地): devas, humans, hell beings, hungry ghosts, and animals. The next four levels are the "four dhyāna heavens" (*shizen ten* 四禪天), which are the abodes of devas in the form realm and correspond to the four stages of dhyāna (*shizen* 四禪; S. *catur-dhyāna*). The remaining four levels, all in the formless realm, are states of existence that correspond to the "four formless attainments" (*shi mushiki jō* 四無色定; S. *ārūpya-samāpatti*).

Another model that divides the "three realms" into sub-realms is known as the "twenty-five forms of existence" (*nijūgo u* 二十五有). The desire realm is said to have fourteen existences: the "four evil paths" (*shi akudō* 四惡道) of hell beings, hungry ghosts, animals, and *asuras*; the "**four continents**" inhabited by human beings; and the "six heavens of the desire realm" (*roku yokuten* 六欲天). The form realm is said to have seven existences: the "four dhyāna heavens" and three other heavens. The formless realm, finally, has four existences: the "four emptiness heavens" (*shi kūshoten* 四空處天), which correspond to the four "formless attainments."

526 DŌGEN'S *SHŌBŌGENZŌ* VOLUME VIII

**three vehicles** (*sanjō* 三乗): According to Mahāyāna scriptures, Buddha Śākyamuni taught three different "vehicles" (*jō* 乗; S. *yāna*), or paths to liberation, that suited the varying capacities of living beings: 1) the vehicle of the *śrāvakas* (*shōmonjō* 聲聞乗; S. *śrāvaka-yāna*), literally "voice-hearers" (direct disciples of the Buddha who heard him preach), which aims at arhatship and the individual attainment of nirvāṇa; used more broadly to reference all forms of Buddhism that do not accept the legitimacy of the Mahāyāna sūtras; 2) the vehicle of *pratyeka-buddhas* (*engakujō* 緣覺乗; S. *pratyekabuddha-yāna*) who "awaken on their own" (*dokkaku* 獨覺) and are also known as buddhas "awakened by conditions" (*engaku* 緣覺); and 3) the vehicle of bodhisattvas (*bosatsujō* 菩薩乗), which aims at attaining buddhahood for the sake of all living beings and begins with a vow not to enter nirvāṇa as long as other beings remain in saṃsāra. The first two vehicles are sometimes referred to collectively as the Small Vehicle (*shōjō* 小乗; S. *Hīnayāna*), while the third is called the Great Vehicle (*daijō* 大乗; S. *Mahāyāna*).

An early Mahāyāna claim, first presented in the perfection of wisdom genre of sūtras, is that the Buddha initially preached the inferior *śrāvaka* and *pratyeka-buddha* vehicles to disciples who did not have the capacity to understand or follow the superior bodhisattva vehicle, which he subsequently revealed when some were ready to receive it. The first two vehicles fall short of the highest truth, but they are not false because the Buddha used them as expedient means (*hōben* 方便; S. *upāya*) to convert beings in a manner that was accessible to them and effective.

Subsequent Mahāyāna sūtras, notably the *Lotus Sūtra*, argue that the three vehicles are all just skillful means and that Śākyamuni really taught only the "one buddha vehicle" (*ichi butsu jō* 一佛乗; S. *eka-buddhayāna*), also called the "one vehicle" (*ichijō* 一乗; S. *ekayāna*) or "buddha-vehicle" (*butsu jō* 佛乗; S. *buddhayāna*); see "**burning house**." There is a passage in chapter 2 of the *Lotus Sūtra* (*Miaofa lianhua jing* 妙法蓮華經, T.262.9:9c17-20) in which Śākyamuni explains why he decided to preach the three vehicles as an expedient device:

尋念過去佛、所行方便力。我今所得道、亦應説三乗。作是思惟時、十方佛皆現。梵音慰喩我、善哉釋迦文。

I recalled the buddhas of the past
And the power of the expedient devices they practiced.
Now that I have gained the way,
I too should preach the three vehicles.
When I had this thought,
The buddhas of the ten directions all appeared,
Their Brahmā voices consoling and instructing me,
"Excellent, Śākyamuni."

Supplementary notes to the translation

A verse at the conclusion of chapter 7 of the *Lotus Sūtra* (*Miaofa lianhua jing* 妙法蓮華經, T.262.9:27b1-2) reads:

諸佛方便力、分別説三乗。唯有一佛乗、息處故説二。

With the power of their expedient means, the buddhas
Discriminate and preach the three vehicles.
There is only the one buddha vehicle;
They preach the other two as a place of rest.

**three vehicles and twelvefold teachings** (*sanjō jūnibun kyō* 三乗十二分教): A standard expression for all the teachings of the Buddhist canon, categorized by intended audience and narrative genre. See "**three vehicles**" for details of the *śrāvaka*, *pratyeka-buddha*, and bodhisattva vehicles. The "twelvefold teachings" (*jūnibun kyō*; 十二分教; S. *dvādaśāṅga-dharma-pravacana*) are traditionally listed as:

1) discourses (*shūtara* 修多羅, or *kyō* 經; S. *sūtra*)
2) corresponding verses (*giya* 祇夜, or *ōju* 應頌; S. *geya*)
3) predictions (*wakarana* 和伽羅那, or *juki* 授記; S. *vyākaraṇa*)
4) verses (*gyada* 伽陀, or *fuju* 諷頌; S. *gāthā*)
5) sermons preached without prompting (*udana* 優陀那, or *jisetsu* 自説; S. *udāna*)
6) causal narratives (*nidana* 尼陀那, or *innen* 因縁; S. *nidāna*)
7) accounts of previous lives of Buddha's disciples (*itaimokutaka* 伊帝目多伽, or *honji* 本事; S. *itivṛttaka*)
8) accounts of previous lives of Buddha (*jataka* 闍多伽, or *honshō* 本生; S. *jātaka*)
9) expanded discourses (*hibutsuryak* 毘佛略, or *hōkō* 方廣; S. *vaipulya*)
10) miracles performed by Buddha (*abudatsuma* 阿浮達磨, or *kehō* 希法; S. *adbhuta-dharma*)
11) parables (*apadana* 阿波陀那, or *hiyu* 譬喩; S. *avadāna*)
12) instruction in doctrine (*yūbadaisha* 優婆提舎, or *rongi* 論議; S. *upadeśa*)

In Zen texts, the expression "three vehicles and twelvefold teachings" refers in a loose way to all the verbal "teachings" (*kyō* 教) of the Buddha, which are typically contrasted with his "mind dharma" (*shinbō* 心法): the awakened "buddha mind" (*busshin* 佛心) of Śākyamuni, from which all of the verbal teachings subsequently flowed in accordance with expedient means (*hōben* 方便; S. *upāya*). The Zen tradition (*zenke* 禪家) claims superiority to the "teaching houses" (*kyōke* 教家) such as Tendai and Kegon on the grounds that it alone transmits the mind dharma, while the latter transmit second- and third-hand verbiage. Dōgen mentions the "three vehicles and twelvefold teachings" throughout the *Shōbōgenzō* and discusses that formula in some detail in his "The Teachings of the Buddhas" ("Shōbōgenzō bukkyō" 正法眼藏佛教).

528     DŌGEN'S *SHŌBŌGENZŌ* VOLUME VIII

**three three in front, three three in back** (*zen sansan go sansan* 前三三後三三): This is the punchline of a kōan commonly referred to as "Mañjuśrī's 'three three in front and back'" (*Monju zengo sansan* 文殊前後三三). The version found in Dōgen's *Shōbōgenzō* in Chinese script (*shinji Shōbōgenzō* 眞字正法眼藏, DZZ.5:194-196, case 127) reads:

> 文殊問無著、近離甚處。著云、南方。殊云、南方佛法如何住持。著曰、末法比丘少奉戒律。殊曰、多少衆。著云、或三百或五百。著問文殊、此間佛法如何住持。殊曰、凡聖同居龍蛇混雜。著云、多少衆。殊曰、前三三後三三。

Mañjuśrī asked Asaṅga, "Where have you come from?"

Asaṅga said, "The south."

Mañjuśrī said, "How is the buddha dharma maintained in the south?"

Asaṅga said, "Few bhikṣus in [this age of] the final dharma keep the precepts."

Mañjuśrī said, "How big was the saṃgha?

Asaṅga said, "Maybe three hundred, maybe five hundred."

Asaṅga asked Mañjuśrī, "How is the buddha dharma maintained around here?"

Mañjuśrī said, "Common people and sages reside together, dragons and snakes intermingle."

Asaṅga said, "How big is the saṃgha?"

Mañjuśrī said, "Three three in front, three three in back."

This kōan also appears as case 35 of the *Blue Cliff Record* (*Biyan lu* 碧巖錄, T.2003.48:173b29-c8), where the prose commentary on it begins as follows (T.2003.48:173c9-21):

> 無著遊五臺、至中路荒僻處。文殊化一寺、接他宿。遂問、近離甚處。著云、南方。殊云、南方佛法、如何住持。著云、末法比丘、少奉戒律。殊云、多少衆。著云、或三百或五百。無著却問文殊、此間如何住持。殊云、凡聖同居、龍蛇混雜。著云、多少衆。殊云、前三三後三三。却喫茶、文殊舉起玻璃盞子云、南方還有這箇麼。著云、無。殊云、尋常將什麼喫茶。著無語。遂辭去、文殊令均提童子送出門首。無著問童子云、適來道前三三後三三、是多少。童子云、大德。著應喏。童子云、是多少。又問、此是何寺。童子指金剛後面。著回首、化寺童子。悉隱不見。只是空谷。

When Asaṅga was pilgrimaging about on [Mount] Wutai, he reached a place en route that was wild and desolate. Mañjuśrī magically produced a monastery, invited him to lodge there overnight, and then asked, "Where have you come from?"

Asaṅga said, "The south."

*Supplementary notes to the translation* 529

Mañjuśrī said, "How is the buddha dharma maintained in the south?"

Asaṅga said, "Few bhikṣus in [this age of] the final dharma keep the precepts."

Mañjuśrī said, "How big was the saṃgha?"

Asaṅga said, "Maybe three hundred, maybe five hundred."

Asaṅga in turn asked Mañjuśrī, "How is it [the buddha dharma] maintained around here?"

Mañjuśrī said, "Common people and sages reside together, dragons and snakes intermingle."

Asaṅga said, "How big is the saṃgha?"

Mañjuśrī said, "Three three in front, three three in back."

When they went to drink tea, Mañjuśrī raised a crystal cup and said, "Do they also have this in the south?"

Asaṅga said, "No."

Mañjuśrī said, "What do they ordinarily use to drink tea?"

Asaṅga was speechless. Then, when he took his leave, Mañjuśrī ordered his young postulant, Kunti, to escort him out to the front of the gate. Asaṅga asked the youth, "That saying from a while ago, 'three three in front, three three in back,' — how many is that?"

The youth said, "O, Great Worthy!"

Asaṅga said, "Yes?"

The youth said, "How many is that?"

[Asaṅga] also asked, "What monastery is this?"

The youth pointed at the eaves [of the main gate] behind the [statues of the two] Vajra Holders [where the monastery name plaque hung]. When Asaṅga turned his head, the phantom monastery and the youth were entirely hidden and could not be seen. There was only an empty valley.

Mount Wutai (Wutaishan 五臺山) is famous in East Asian Buddhist lore as the sacred abode of the bodhisattva Mañjuśrī (Monju 文殊), who is said to appear in miraculous ways to pilgrims who seek him there. Asaṅga (Mujaku 無著) was an Indian Buddhist monk who flourished in the fourth century and was well known in China as a founder of the Yogācāra school. In this fanciful story, he is depicted as a monk who has been at a monastery in southern China and then set out on a pilgrimage by foot (*angya* 行脚) to Mount Wutai in the north.

Given that the monastery where Asaṅga seeks lodging for the night is a magical display created by Mañjuśrī, it is obvious that the true answer to the question "how many monks are there in residence?" is "none." Mañjuśrī's answer, however, is "three three in front, three three in back," which, as

530 DŌGEN'S *SHŌBŌGENZŌ* VOLUME VIII

Asaṅga's subsequent question — "how many is that?" — makes clear, is an ambiguous number. The glyphs 三三 (*sansan*) can be read either as: 1) "three and three," or six; 2) "three threes," or nine; or 3) "three tens and three," or thirty-three. The gylphs 前後 (*zengo*) are also ambiguous, for they can be read either as: 1) "before and after"; 2) "former and latter" (referring to "common people and sages"); or 3) "front and back" (as in "dragon head, snake tail" [*ryūtō dabi* 龍頭蛇尾], a term for monks who put on a false front of being virtuous and wise). It may not be entirely coincidental that these ambiguities themselves comprise a set of "three and three."

In any case, the saying "three three in front, three three in back" was being treated in Zen literature as a kōan from at least as early as the tenth century. For example, the biography of Lingyun Zhiqin 靈雲志勤 (dates unknown) in the *Jingde Era Record of the Transmission of the Flame* (*Jingde chuandeng lu* 景德傳燈錄; T.2076.51:285b16-18) contains the following exchange with Xuefeng Yicun 雪峰義存 (822-908):

雪峯問云、古人道前三三後三三。意旨如何。師云、水中魚、山上鳥。

Xuefeng asked, "An ancient said, 'Three three in front, three three in back.' What did he mean?"

The master [Zhiqin] said, "In the water, fish; over the mountains, birds."

The *Discourse Record of Reverend Yangqi Fanghui* (*Yangqi Fanghui heshang yulu* 楊岐方會和尚語錄; T.1994A.47:645c10-12) contains a verse comment by Yangqi Fanghui 楊岐方會 (992–1049) on the kōan:

【前三三後三三】
前三後三是多少。大事光輝明皎皎。回頭不見解空人。滿目白雲臥荒草。

"Three Three in Front, Three Three in Back"

Front three and back three; how many is this?

The splendor of the great matter is clear and bright.

If you turn your head, you will not see the person who understands emptiness.

Filling my eyes with white clouds, I recline in wildly growing grass.

The traditional interpretation within the Sōtō school is that the expression "three three in front, three three in back" indicates something "innumerable" or "unlimited." SK.2:211, for example, says:

前三三、後三三とは、三と三で六というではない。これは無邊際ということである。

"Three three in front, three three in back" does not mean "three and three are six": it means "boundless."

*Supplementary notes to the translation* 531

Echoing this, ZGDJ (618b, s.v. ぜんごさんさん) says that the expression means "incalculable and innumerable" (*muryō musū* 無量無数).

Another possible interpretation is that Mañjuśrī, when asked about the size of the saṃgha at his monastery, ignored that question and continued to remark on the diverse virtue of its members. "Three three" might allude to a system of classifying violations of monastic rules that is found in Indian vinaya texts and Chinese commentaries on them. The *Ten Chapter Vinaya* (*Shisong lü* 十誦律; T.1435.23.399b18-20) contains the following passage:

問。如佛言、有一住處自恣時識事不識人、何者是事何者是人。答事名罪。罪因緣起。得罪者名爲人。

Question: When, as the Buddha says, "At the time of the repentance ceremony in one dwelling place [i.e., monastery], there may be awareness of an event but no awareness of the person," what is the "event" and what is the "person"?

Answer: "Event" refers to an offense. Offenses arise from causes and conditions. The one who incurs the offense is the "person."

A Chinese text entitled *Xingzong Record of the Commentary on the Annotated Pratimokṣa of the Four Part Vinaya* (*Sifen lü hanzhu jieben shu xingzong ji* 四分律含注戒本疏行宗記; ZZ.62:469a16-b3; X.714.39:786b11-16) elaborates on this distinction between the offense (a violation of monastic rules) and the offender who commits it by outlining "three classes of three" (*sansan hon* 三三品) situations that may occur:

【疏】初三句中、一識事識犯、二識事疑犯、三識事不識犯。【疏】中品三句、一疑事識犯、二疑事疑犯、三疑事不識犯。【疏】下品三句、一不識事識犯、二不識事疑犯、三不識事不識犯。

First three (*sho san* 初三):
    1) aware of the offense, aware of the offender
    2) aware of the offense, uncertain of the offender
    3) aware of the offense, not aware of the offender
Middle three (*chūbon san* 中品三):
    1) uncertain of the offense, aware of the offender
    2) uncertain of the offense, uncertain of the offender
    3) uncertain of the offense, not aware of the offender
Last three (*gebon san* 下品三):
    1) not aware of the offense, aware of the offender
    2) not aware of the offense, uncertain of the offender
    3) not aware of the offense, not aware of the offender

The idea here is that the saṃgha as a whole at the end of the retreat, after individual monks have either confessed to committing offenses themselves or claimed that offenses were committed by others, may have nine different degrees of awareness (or consciousness or certainty) concerning what actually happened. Thus, if what Mañjuśrī says is read as "three threes in front, three threes in back," what he might mean is that the criteria for gauging the purity of a monastic community is so complex, and the intermingling of "dragon and snake" individuals (or traits) so complicated, that any kind of definitive judgment would be a gross oversimplification.

**tossing out a tile and taking in a jade** (*hōsen ingyoku* 抛甎引玉): An idiom that, in literary usage, is a polite way to ask another person for a capping verse for one's poem and, by extension, to get back more than one offered. Also used in Zen texts for the repartee between interlocutors, as, for example, by Zhaozhou Congshen 趙州從諗 (778–897) in the *Jingde Era Record of the Transmission of the Flame* (*Jingde chuandeng lu* 景德傳燈錄, T.2076.51:277a29-b2):

> 大衆晚參師云、今夜答話去也、有解問者出來。時有一僧便出禮拜。師云、比來抛塼引玉却、引得箇墼子。

> At the evening convocation of the great assembly, the Master [Zhaozhou] said, "Tonight, I'll answer questions. Anyone who can put a question come forward."

> Thereupon, a monk came forward and bowed.

> The Master said, "Here, I toss out a tile to take in a jade, and what I get is this brick."

**treasury of the true dharma eye** (*shōbōgenzō* 正法眼藏): An expression found only in texts associated with the Zen tradition, with a meaning that changed over time.

In the *Baolin Biographies* (*Baolin zhuan* 寶林傳, compiled in 801), *Ancestors Hall Collection* (*Zutang ji* 祖堂集, compiled in 952), *Records that Mirror the Axiom* (*Zongjing lu* 宗鏡錄, compiled in 961), and *Jingde Era Record of the Transmission of the Flame* (*Jingde chuandeng lu* 景德傳燈錄, compiled in 1004), the expression "treasury of the true dharma eye" refers to the "treasury of sūtras" (*shutara zō* 修多羅藏; S. *sūtra-piṭaka*) that was compiled at the First Council, after the death of the Buddha. It is said that the compilation was organized by Mahākāśyapa and that the sūtras were recited from memory by Ānanda, each one beginning, "Thus have I heard...." In those early Zen texts, the non-verbal dharma that Śākyamuni is said to have entrusted to Mahākāśyapa when founding the Zen lineage is called the "clear dharma eye" (*shōjō hōgen* 清淨法眼). The *Jingde Era Record of the Transmission of the Flame* (T.2076.51:205b26-28), for example, says:

> 説法住世四十九年、後告弟子摩訶迦葉、吾以清淨法眼、涅槃妙心、實相無相、微妙正法、將付於汝。汝當護持。

*Supplementary notes to the translation*        533

After he had preached the dharma in the world for forty-nine years, he told his disciple Mahākāśyapa, "I entrust to you the clear dharma-eye, the wondrous mind of nirvāṇa, the subtle true dharma, the true sign of which is signless. You should protect and maintain it."

The "subtle true dharma, the true sign of which is signless" (*jissō musō, mimyō shōbō* 實相無相、微妙正法), which is synonymous here with the "wondrous mind of nirvāṇa" (*nehan myōshin* 涅槃妙心), refers to the very awakening (S. *bodhi*) of Śākyamuni — that which made him a buddha in the first place, before he preached any sermons. The Zen tradition claims to have transmitted that "buddha mind" (*busshin* 佛心) down through its lineage of ancestral masters (*soshi* 祖師), in what is called "**a separate transmission outside the teachings**."

The earliest attested referent of the expression "treasury of the true dharma eye" in Zen texts, as noted above, is the "treasury of sūtras" preached by the Buddha and compiled after his death at the First Council. Already in the *Jingde Era Record of the Transmission of the Flame*, however, there is evidence of a shift in meaning, whereby "treasury of the true dharma eye" became synonymous with the "wondrous mind of nirvāṇa," or "buddha mind," that the Zen lineage claimed to transmit. Beginning with the *Tiansheng Era Extended Record of the Flame* (*Tiansheng guangdeng lu* 天聖廣燈錄, ZZ.135:612a1-3), a text completed in 1036, the expression "clear dharma eye" was replaced by "treasury of the true dharma eye" in all accounts of the first transmission to Mahākāśyapa:

如來在靈山説法、諸天献華。世尊持華示衆、迦葉微笑。世尊告衆曰、吾有正法眼藏、涅槃妙心、付囑摩訶迦葉。流布將來、勿令斷絶。

When the Tathāgata was on Vulture Peak preaching the dharma, the gods made an offering of flowers to him. The World-Honored One **held up a flower** to address the congregation, and Kāśyapa smiled slightly. The World-Honored One announced to the assembly, "I have the treasury of the true dharma eye, the wondrous mind of nirvāṇa, which I entrust to Mahākāśyapa. He should spread it and not allow it to be cut off in the future."

Because "treasury of the true dharma eye" is substituted for the term "clear dharma eye" that appears in the same context in earlier texts, we know that the adjective "clear" (*shōjō* 清淨) and the adjective "true" (*shō* 正) both modify the noun "dharma eye" (*hōgen* 法眼). The references, in other words, are to a "clear eye of the dharma" and a "true eye of the dharma." The adjectives "true" and "clear" are virtual synonyms here: both refer to an "eye" (*gen* 眼) that sees the dharma in a manner that is clear-sighted and accurate, as opposed to vision that is clouded or distorted. That Dōgen parsed the expression "treasury of the true dharma eye" in this way is evident from

534 DŌGEN'S *SHŌBŌGENZŌ* VOLUME VIII

the following passage that appears in his "The Teachings of the Buddhas" ("Shōbōgenzō bukkyō" 正法眼藏佛教):

これを拈來せざらんもの、いかでか佛祖の正眼を單傳せん。正法眼藏を體達せざるは、七佛の法嗣にあらざるなり。

How could those who have not taken this up uniquely transmit the true eye of the **buddhas and ancestors**? Those who have not personally realized the treasury of the true dharma eye are not the dharma heirs of the **seven buddhas**.

The "true eye" (*shōgen* 正眼) mentioned here is short for "true eye of the dharma" (*shōbōgen* 正法眼).

Nevertheless, many Sōtō Zen monks and scholars in Japan have interpreted the grammar of the glyphs 正法眼藏 (*shōbōgenzō*) in a different way, taking the first two glyphs as a semantic unit that means "true dharma" (*shōbō* 正法) and treating that compound as an adjective that modifies "eye" (*gen* 眼). Based on that reading, the English translation of the four glyphs would be "treasury of the eye of the true dharma." Having taken "true dharma" as one semantic unit, many Sōtō monks also treat the final two glyphs, 眼藏 (*genzō*), as a second unit that means "eye collection," or "eye treasury." Based on that reading, the English translation of the four glyphs would be "eye treasury of the true dharma." Neither of these readings is gramatically incorrect, but the philological evidence adduced above shows that they were not the readings intended when the glyphs 正法眼藏 (*shōbōgenzō*) were used in Zen texts dating from the ninth, tenth, and eleventh centuries.

By the twelfth century, the expression "treasury of the true dharma eye" had also begun to be used as a name for a "treasury" (*zō* 藏), or "canon," that was made up entirely of written records of the sayings of numerous Zen masters, as opposed to the sayings of the Buddha preserved in the Tripiṭaka. Examples include a kōan collection compiled by Dahui Zonggao 大慧宗杲 (1089-1163) entitled *Treasury of the True Dharma Eye* (*Zhengfayanzang* 正法眼藏), and one by Dōgen popularly known as *Shōbōgenzō* in Chinese script (*shinji Shōbōgenzō* 眞字正法眼藏), a.k.a. *Shōbōgenzō Three Hundred Cases* (*Shōbōgenzō sanbyaku soku* 正法眼藏三百則).

*Treasury of the True Dharma Eye* is also the title, of course, of the famous collection of essays by Dōgen that is written in Japanese and translated into English in the present set of eight volumes. The work contains a great many quotations in classical Chinese taken from the records of various Chan masters and other Buddhist texts (especially the *Lotus Sūtra*), all of which Dōgen comments on in Japanese. Because he uses those quotes to illustrate a wide range of doctrines and practices common to the Buddhist tradition in East Asia, it is reasonable to conclude that he intended the title to refer in a general way to all the teachings of Śākyamuni Buddha, as those were interpreted within the Zen tradition down to his day.

*Supplementary notes to the translation*　　535

**true human body** (*shinjitsu nintai* 眞實人體): Or "body of the true human (or person)." This expression, found often in the *Shōbōgenzō*, is ambiguous and can be parsed in two ways. This translation adopts the former reading, common in interpretations of the *Shōbōgenzō*; but Dōgen may well have had both readings in mind. His use of the expression derives from two sources: a saying attributed to Xuansha Shibei 玄沙師備 (835-908), and another saying attributed to Yuanwu Keqin 圜悟克勤 (1063-1135).

The *Extensive Record of Chan Master Xuansha Shibei* (*Xuansha Shibei chanshi guanglu* 玄沙師備禪師廣錄, ZZ.126:374a9-13; X.1445.73:12c1-5) says:

上堂云、我今問儞諸人。我時時向儞道、盡十方世界是箇眞實人體。
更莫外求。何以故。只此四大五蘊。身田根識、用處無功。所以儞眼
有不見色。耳有不聞聲。意有不分別。會麼。眼、耳、意、用處無別
故。且作麼生。諸仁者、會麼。

At a convocation in the dharma hall, [Xuansha] said:

Now I pose a question to all of you people. From time to time, I say to you, 'All the worlds in the ten directions are this true human body.' Don't seek them externally. Why? Because they're simply the **four elements and five aggregates**. The root consciousness in the field of the physical body makes use of the sense bases effortlessly. Thus, your eyes have a form that you don't see, your ears have a sound that you don't hear, and your minds have discrimination that you don't distinguish. Do you understand? It's because the eye, ear, and mind make use of the sense bases without discrimination. So, what is this? Gentlemen, do you understand?"

Xuansha's saying was subsequently raised as a topic by his dharma heir, Huiqiu Jizhao 慧球寂照 (d. 913), in an exchange found in Dōgen's *Shōbōgenzō* in Chinese script (*shinji Shōbōgenzō* 眞字正法眼藏, DZZ.5:196, case 131); and reported in Jizhao's biography in the *Jingde Era Record of the Transmission of the Flame* (*Jingde chuandeng lu* 景德傳燈錄, T.2076.51:372c4-6):

師問了院主、只如先師道、盡十方世界是眞實人體。爾還見僧堂麼。
了曰、和尚莫眼華。師曰、先師遷化肉猶暖在。

The master [Huiqiu] asked Cloister Chief Liao, "Just as our late master [Xuansha] said: 'All the worlds in the ten directions are the true human body.' Do you see the saṃgha hall?"

Liao said, "Reverend, don't have eye flowers."

The master said, "Our late master has passed away, but his flesh remains warm."

The second saying using our expression is found in the *Discourse Record of Chan Master Yuanwu Foguo* (*Yuanwu Foguo chanshi yulu* 圜悟佛果禪師語錄, T.1997.47:740b19-26):

上堂云、法身無相應機現形。法眼無瑕隨照鑑物。安排不得處是天眞佛。受用不及處乃向上機。若能上絕攀仰下絕己躬、鼻孔摩觸家風、髑髏常千世界。則一爲無量無量爲一。小中現大大中現小。更討甚麼生死去來地水火風聲香味觸。都盧是箇眞實人體。還有人向箇裏承當得麼。識取摩尼無價珠、當來受用無窮極。

At a convocation in the dharma hall, [Yuanwu] said:

The dharma body is signless, but it takes shape and appears in response to the capacities [of living beings]. The dharma eye has no defect, but in accordance with illumination it observes things. That which cannot be arranged is the natural buddha. The place where its enjoyment cannot reach — that is the key to what is beyond. If upwardly you cut off climbing and seeking, and downwardly cut off your self and person, then your **nose** will rub against the house style [of Chan], and your skeleton will last through a thousand worlds. Accordingly, the one will be innumerable, and the innumerable will be one. The large will appear in the middle of the small, and the small will appear in the middle of the large. I ask you, what are coming and going, birth and death; earth, water, fire, and wind; sound, smell, taste, and touch? They're all this true human body. Again, is there anyone who can turn within here and accede to it? If you recognize the priceless *maṇi* jewel, in the future your enjoyment of it will have no limit."

Elsewhere in his recorded sayings, Yuanwu often uses the expression "true person (or true human)" (*shinjitsu nin* 眞實人). So, for example, two passages in the *Discourse Record of Chan Master Yuanwu Foguo* (*Yuanwu Foguo chanshi yulu* 圓悟佛果禪師語錄, T.1997.47:717a15-17; 757c2):

一念遍十方、盡大地是眞實人、總刹海爲大解脱。

When a single moment of thought pervades the ten directions, the whole earth in its entirety is the true person, and all the lands and seas become the great liberation.

淨裸裸赤灑灑、全體只是箇眞實人。

Pure, stripped bare, and stark naked, the whole body is just this true person.

Thus, it may well be that his use of *ko shinjitsu nintai* 箇眞實人體 in our passage is better parsed as "this body of the true person." In contrast, the term *shinjitsu nin* 眞實人 does not occur in the *Shōbōgenzō* apart from the expression *shinjitsu nintai* 眞實人體; rather, in his "Studying the Way with Body and Mind" ("Shōbōgenzō shinjin gakudō" 正法眼藏身心學道), Dōgen seems to take *nintai* as a compound: in explaining Xuansha's famous remark, he writes, "though 'the human body' may be obstructed by self and other, it is 'all the ten directions'" (*nintai wa tatoi jita ni keige seraru to iu tomo, jin jippō nari* 人體はたとひ自他に罣礙せらるといふとも、盡十方なり).

In the *Extensive Record of Reverend Dōgen* (*Dōgen oshō kōroku* 道元和尚廣錄, DZZ.3:48, no. 74), Dōgen cites several closely related expressions used to define rebirth in saṃsāra:

上堂舉、圜悟禪師道、生死去來眞實人體。南泉道、生死去來是眞實體。趙州道、生死去來是眞實人體。長沙道、生死去來是諸佛眞實體。師云、四員尊宿各展家風、俱端鼻孔。道也道得、只是未在。若是興聖又且不然、生死去來只是生死去來。

At a convocation in the dharma hall, [Dōgen] raised [the following sayings]:

Chan Master Yuanwu said, "Coming and going, birth and death, are the true human body." Nanquan said, "Coming and going, birth and death: these are the true body." Zhaozhou said, "Coming and going, birth and death: these are the true human body." Changsha said, "Coming and going, birth and death: these are the true body of the buddhas."

The master [Dōgen] said,

These four honored elders each expounded their house styles, and all straightened **noses**. They have said what they were able to say, but it is not sufficient. If it were Kōshō [i.e., Dōgen], moreover, I would not be like this. Coming and going, birth and death, are just coming and going, birth and death."

However Yuanwu and Dōgen may have understood the four glyphs of the expression *shinjitsu nintai* 眞實人體, subsequent Sōtō commentary has tended to parse them as the "true human body" (*shinjitsu no nintai* 眞實の人體). In chapter 19 of the *Record of the Transmission of Illumination* (*Denkōroku* 傳光錄) by Keizan Jōkin 瑩山紹瑾 (1264-1325), for example, Dōgen's quote of Yuanwu is rendered into Japanese as "the true human body of coming and going, birth and death" (*shōji korai shinjitsu no nintai* 生死去來眞實の人體).

**true person of no rank** (*mui shinnin* 無位眞人): The term "true person" (*shinnin* 眞人) first occurs in Chapter 6 of the Zhuangzi 莊子 (Dazongshi 大宗師, KR.5c0126.006.2a), describing the ideal sage of ancient times, who accords with the Dao by having no purpose (*mui* 無爲):

古之眞人、不知説生、不知惡死。其出不訢、其入不距。翛然而往、翛然而來而已矣。不忘其所始、不求其所終。受而喜之、忘而復之。是之謂不以心捐道、不以人助天。是之謂眞人。若然者、其心志、其容寂、其顙頯。

The True Men of old did not know how to be pleased that they were alive, did not know how to hate death, were neither glad to come forth nor reluctant to go in; they were content to leave as briskly as they came. They did not forget the source where they began, did not seek out the destination where they would end. They were pleased with the gift that they received, but forgot it as they gave it back. It is this that is called "not allowing the thinking of the heart to damage the Way, not using what is of man to do the work of Heaven." Such a one we call the True man. Such men as that had unremembering hearts, calm faces, clear brows. (Translation by A.C. Graham; Graham 2001, 85.)

Because the "true person" in this context is one who does not resist or obstruct the Dao, or "way," their actions are those of the great way (*daidō* 大道) itself, which is involved in birth and death but nevertheless transcends them. The term "true person" subsequently became a term of art in Daoism, as well as Buddhism, for the true nature of the person, and/or for one who has realized that nature. In Zen literature, a "true person" (*shinnin* 眞人, or *shinjitsunin* 眞實人) is one who has "attained the way" (*jōdō* 成道) by gaining awakening. The term "true person" also refers to the "mind ground" (*shinchi* 心地), "buddha mind" (*busshin* 佛心), or "buddha nature" (*busshō* 佛性) itself.

The expression "true person of no rank" was coined by Linji Yixuan 臨濟義玄 (d. 866). The *locus classicus* is the *Discourse Record of Chan Master Linji Huizhao of Zhenzhou* (*Zhenzhou Linji Huizhao chanshi yulu* 鎮州臨濟慧照禪師語錄, T.1985.47:496c10-11):

上堂云、赤肉團上有一無位眞人。常從汝等諸人面門出入。未證據者看看。

At a convocation in the dharma hall, [Linji] said, "In this lump of red meat, there's one true person of no rank, always going in and out of your faces. Those who haven't verified it, look, look!"

The expression "lump of red meat" (*shaku nikudan* 赤肉團) refers to the human body. The term translated here as "face" (*menmon* 面門) may be rendered more literally as "gates (*mon* 門) of the face (*men* 面)," which include the mouth and nostrils. That which is "always going in and out" of people's faces, provided they are alive and breathing, is "air" (*ki* 氣), a term that also has the more abstract meaning of "life force." It seems, therefore, that what Linji means by the "true person of no rank" is, in the first place, that which animates the physical body, without which it would be lifeless "meat" (*niku* 肉). The term "true person" (*shinnin* 眞人) is also used in Zen literature to refer to the "buddha nature" (*busshō* 佛性) that is immanent in all living beings. Linji describes it as being "without" (*mu* 無) any "location," "position," or "rank" (*i* 位) because it is a universal and transcendent principle, not a "thing" that can be singled out or grasped by discriminating thought. Those who "see the nature" (*kenshō* 見性) are awakened to the fact that they are already buddhas, by virtue of being alive. Those who do not yet see it are enjoined to "look, look!"

## Supplementary notes to the translation

**turn the light around and shine it back** (*ekō henshō* 回光返照; also written 迴光返照, 廻光返照): A common idiom used in reference to Buddhist practice as the investigation of one's own mind, as opposed to the external world. The saying occurs in many Zen texts; here, e.g., is a version found in the *Discourse Record of Chan Master Huanglong Huinan* (*Huanglong Huinan chanshi yulu* 黃龍慧南禪師語錄, T.1993.47:638a5-9):

> 人人盡握靈蛇之珠、箇箇自抱荊山之璞、不自回光返照、懷寶迷邦。不見道、應耳時若空谷、大小音聲無不足。應眼時如千日、萬像不能逃影質。擬議若從聲色求、達磨西來也大屈。

Every single person, without exception, grasps the pearl of the numinous serpent; every single one embraces the uncut jade of Mount Jing. But if you do not turn the light around and shine it back on yourself, you are one who [as in *Analects*, 17] "keeps his treasure hidden in his bosom and leaves his kingdom in confusion." Have you not read this saying? "When it accords with the ears, it is like [the echoing spirits of] an empty valley: the sounds great and small are never insufficient. When it accords with the eye, it is like a thousand suns: the myriad phenomena cannot outrun their shadows." But if you seek externally from sound and form, then Bodhidharma's "**coming from the west**" will be a big humiliation.

Huanglong is here invoking lines from a verse by Mazu's disciple Gaocheng Fazang 高城法藏, found in the *Verses of Ancestral Masters of the Chan Gate* (*Chanmen zhuzushi jirong* 禪門諸祖師偈頌, ZZ.116:929b18-930a5). In the *Extensive Record of Reverend Dōgen* (*Dōgen oshō kōroku* 道元和尚廣錄, DZZ.3:186-188, no. 282), Dōgen cites Huanglong's saying in a convocation address:

> 上堂、人人盡握夜光之珠、家家自抱荊山之璞、雖未廻光返照、若爲懷寶迷鄉。不見道、應耳時如空谷神、大小音聲無不足。應眼時如千日照、萬像不能逃影質。若從聲色外邊求、達磨西來也大屈。

At a convocation in the dharma hall, [Dōgen said]: "Every single person, without exception, grasps the night-illuminating pearl; house after house embraces the uncut jade of Mount Jing. But as long as you do not turn the light around and shine it back on yourself, you will be like one who [as in *Analects*, 17] 'keeps his treasure hidden in his bosom and leaves his kingdom in confusion.' Have you not read this saying? 'When the ears respond, it is like [the echoing spirits of] an empty valley: the sounds great and small are never insufficient. When the eyes respond, it is like the shining of a thousand suns: the myriad phenomena cannot outrun their shadows.' But if you seek externally from sound and form, then Bodhidharma's "coming from the west" will be a big humiliation."

540     DŌGEN'S *SHŌBŌGENZŌ* VOLUME VIII

Dōgen's rendition changes "pearl of the numinous serpent" to "night-illuminating jewel," and adds the word "shining" to the expression "thousand suns" (*senjitsu* 千日).

**turning the head and changing the face** (*kaitō kanmen* 回頭換面; also written 廻頭換面; also read *uitō kanmen*). Also found in reverse order: "changing the face and turning the head" (*kanmen kaitō* 換面回頭). Dōgen's version of the expression is unusual: it usually-takes the form 改頭換面. A multivalent expression that has two well attested meanings and a couple of other accepted scholarly interpretations. In the first place, it refers to the process of transmigration through birth and death in accordance with one's karma. The *Discourse Record of Chan Master Baojue Zuxin* (*Baojue Zuxin chanshi yulu* 寶覺祖心禪師語錄, ZZ.120:227b5-7; X.1343.69:218c17-18), for example, says:

生生死死、死死生生、隨業受報。六道四生、改頭換面、有形無形。

Birth after birth, death after death, you receive rewards in accordance with your karma. In the **six paths** and **four births**, you renew your head and change your face, either having form or having no form.

Secondly, it can indicate a surface change that occurs while the interior reality remains constant. For example, Keizan Jōkin 瑩山紹瑾 (1264–1325), in his *Record of the Transmission of Illumination* (*Denkōroku*, p. 474), says:

佛佛祖祖、換面回頭し來れども、必ず背面なく上下なく、邊表なく自他なく相授底あり。之を喚で不空の空と名く。即ち是れ諸人實歸の處なり。箇箇悉く具足圓滿せずといふことなし。

Although buddha after buddha and ancestor after ancestor have been "changing their faces and turning their heads," there is certainly something they transmit from one to another that has no back or front, has no up or down, has no borders or surface, and has no self or other. When this is named, it is called "emptiness that is not empty." This is the place of true refuge for all of you. Not a single one of you is not fully equipped, complete and full.

The gist of the expression "changing faces and turning their heads" here is that, while the Zen lineage of **buddhas and ancestors** is made up of individuals who are born and die in accordance with their own unique karma, the dharma that is transmitted through the lineage remains fundamentally the same. That also seems to be the thrust of the expression "turning the head and changing faces" in a passage that appears in Dōgen's "Needle of Seated Meditation" ("Shōbōgenzō zazen shin" 正法眼藏坐禪箴, DZZ.1:14):

先師無此語なり、この道理、これ祖祖なり。法傳・衣傳あり。おほよそ回頭換面の面面、これ佛佛の要機なり。換面回頭の頭頭、これ祖祖の機要なり。

Supplementary notes to the translation    541

[Guangxiao Huijue's saying,] "My former master had no such words" — this principle is "ancestor after ancestor." They have the transmission of the dharma, the transmission of the robe. In sum, face after face of "turning the head and changing the face" is the "essential function of buddha after buddha"; head after head of "changing the face and turning the head" is "the functioning essence of ancestor after ancestor."

In addition to these two meanings, *Zengo jiten* 禅語辞典 (54), gives a third one: "to be reborn as an entirely different human being." Some traditional commentaries on the *Shōbōgenzō*, moreover, take the expression to mean that "turning the head is changing the face," and that it indicates the inseparability or interdependence of two things (e.g., of master and disciple), like two sides of the same coin.

**upright or inclined** (*shōhen* 正偏): The glyphs translated here as "upright" (*shō* 正) and "inclined" (*hen* 偏) are also used in ordinary language to indicate: 1) "vertical" vs. "slanted"; 2) the "main" vs. "side" doors of a building; 3) the "center" vs. "flanking" spaces set up for a ritual, which are occupied by the "main" vs. "secondary" performers; 4) "fair" vs. "biased" judgments; and 5) "correct" vs. "deviant" behavior.

In the technical language of Chinese divination, the glyphs 正 (*shō*) and 偏 (*hen*) indicate the "one middle and two outer" lines of a trigram.

In Buddhist texts, the expression "upright or inclined" is used metaphorically to refer to 1) ultimate truth (*daiichi gitai* 第一義諦; S. *paramārtha-satya*) vs. conventional truth (*zokutai* 俗諦; S. *saṃvṛti-satya*) or 2) "true emptiness" (*shinkū* 眞空) vs. "marvelous existence" (*myōu* 妙有). Some English translations render the pair 正 (*shō*) and 偏 (*hen*) as "absolute and relative."

In the Zen tradition, a reference to the "five ranks of upright and inclined" (*shōhen goi* 正偏五位); see **"five ranks."**

**vastness beyond the line of ink** (*kōzen jōboku gai* 曠然繩墨外). An "ink line" (*jōboku* 繩墨, also written *bokujō* 墨繩) is a carpenter's plumb line, similar to a "chalk line." Metaphorically, the term "ink line" refers to any set of standards, rules, precepts, or behavioral "lines" that should be followed. The expression "vastness beyond the line of ink" appears a few times in the literature of Chan, always attributed to Yuanwu Keqin 圜悟克勤 (1063-1135). The *locus classicus* is found in the *Discourse Record of Chan Master Yuanwu Foguo* (*Yuanwu Foguo chanshi yulu* 圓悟佛果禪師語錄, T.1997.47:803a16-24), in the context of Yuanwu's comment on a kōan involving Shitou Xiqian 石頭希遷 (710–790) and the latter's dharma heir Yaoshan Weiyan 藥山惟儼 (751-834):

# 542 　DŌGEN'S *SHŌBŌGENZŌ* VOLUME VIII

舉。石頭見藥山坐次問。爾在此作什麼。山云。一物不爲。頭云。恁
麼則閑坐也。山云。閑坐則爲也。頭云。汝道不爲。不爲箇什麼。
山云。千聖亦不識。石頭以頌讚之。從來共住不知名。任運相將只麼
行。自古上賢猶不識。造次凡流豈可明。

擺撥佛祖縛、曠然繩墨外。一物亦不爲、縱橫得自在。古鑑臨臺明辨
去來。金鎚影動鐵樹華開。任運相將不可陪。法雲隨處作風雷。

Raised:

Shitou saw Yaoshan sitting [in meditation] and asked, "What are you doing here?"

Shan said, "I'm not doing a single thing."

Tou said, "If so, then you're just sitting idly."

Shan said, "Idle sitting is doing something."

Tou said, "You said you're not doing anything What is this 'not doing'?"

Shan said, "Even a thousand sages don't know."

Shitou praised him with a verse comment:

> We've dwelt together up to now, but I don't know his name.
>
> We've naturally, together, come to act like this.
>
> From ancient times, the wisest have 'not known' in just this way.
>
> How could a careless, ordinary person possibly be clear about it?

[Yuanwu's comment]

When you throw off the bonds of the **buddhas and ancestors**, there is a
vastness beyond the line of ink. When "not doing a single thing," you
gain autonomy in every situation. When the old mirror descends to its
stand, it clearly discriminates going and coming. When the shadow of the
golden mallet moves, flowers bloom on the iron tree. When they [Shitou
and Yaoshan] are "naturally together," there can be no further increase. In
all places where there are dharma clouds, they produce wind and thunder.

The term "bonds" (*baku* 縛), in most Buddhist contexts, refers to the
mental afflictions — greed, hatred, and delusion — that bind people to
suffering in the round of rebirth. In Yuanwu's comment, however, it is the
very teachings of the buddhas and ancestors who comprise the Zen lineage
that are deemed "bonds" to be thrown off if one is to obtain perfect freedom.
The expression "vastness beyond the line of ink" thus alludes to a liberation
that is not constrained by the norms of Buddhist practice (especially the
practice of sitting in meditation) and not bound by attachment to the sayings
of Zen masters that survive as ink on paper.

*Supplementary notes to the translation* 543

**water buffalo** (*suikogyū* 水牯牛): Water buffalo (*Bubalus bubalis*) often appear in Zen lore, with several different symbolic meanings. The creature in question is a domesticated animal, commonly employed in East Asia for pulling plows or carts; it is also used as a source of meat, milk, and leather. The males may be castrated to make them more manageable.

When the glyphs 牯 (*ko*) or 牛 (*gyū*) are used in Chinese translations of Indian Buddhist scriptures, it is possible that the animals referred to are some other kind of bovid. Thus, in the absence of the initial 水 (*sui*), meaning "water," translators of Chinese Buddhist texts often use the terms "ox" or "bull" to render those glyphs into English; see, for example, the "white ox" (*byakugyū* 白牛) that pulls an ox-cart (*gosha* 牛車) in the *Lotus Sūtra* parable of the "**burning house**"; also see "**iron bull**." In Zen texts where the context is clearly East Asian, however, even when translators say "ox" or "bull," the referent may be the water buffalo, for the glyph 牛 (*gyū*) is a generic label that includes water buffalo (*suigyū* 水牛) as a subset.

Dōgen mentions water buffalo three times in the *Shōbōgenzō*. One instance, found in "Sustained Practice, Part 1" ("Shōbōgenzō gyōji jō" 正法眼藏行持上, DZZ.1:153), is a quotation of Changqing Da'an 長慶大安 (793-883), who was given the nickname "Later Dawei" (Hou Dawei 後大潙) because he succeeded Weishan Lingyou 潙山靈祐 (771-853) as abbot of the Tongqing Monastery 同慶寺 on Mount Dawei 大潙山 in present-day Hunan Province:

後大潙和尚いはく、我二十年在潙山、喫潙山飯、屙潙山屙、不參潙山道。只牧得一頭水牯牛、終日露回回也。

Reverend Hou Dawei said, "For twenty years, I stayed at Weishan, eating Weishan's rice and shitting Weishan's shit; I didn't study [the abbot] Weishan's way; I just managed to herd a single water buffalo, everywhere exposed all day long."

This is an abbreviated, somewhat variant version of a passage quoted by Dōgen in his "Everyday Matters" ("Shōbōgenzō kajō" 正法眼藏家常, DZZ.2:128), also found in the biography of Chan Master Da'an in the *Jingde Era Record of the Transmission of the Flame* (*Jingde chuandeng lu* 景德傳燈錄, T.2076.51:267c6-10):

安在潙山三十來年、喫潙山飯、屙潙山屎、不學潙山禪、只看一頭水牯牛。若落路入草、便牽出。若犯人苗稼、即鞭撻。調伏既久。可憐生受人言語。如今變作箇露地白牛、常在面前、終日露迥迥地。趁亦不去也。

[At a convocation in the dharma hall, the Master (Da'an) said,] "An stayed at Weishan [Monastery] for some thirty years, eating Weishan's rice and shitting Weishan's shit. I didn't study [the abbot] Weishan's Chan; I just watched over a single water buffalo. If it strayed from the road into the

544 DŌGEN'S *SHŌBŌGENZŌ* VOLUME VIII

grass, I would drag it out; if it damaged someone's crops, I would whip it. The discipline went on for a long time; how sad for it, having to take orders from someone. Now, it's changed into this 'white ox on open ground,' always in front of me, everywhere exposed all day long. I can chase it off, and it still won't leave."

It is clear from this passage that the "single water buffalo" (*ittō suikogyū* 一頭水牯牛) Da'an is talking about is his own mind. The "road" of this allegory is the bodhisattva path to buddhahood, and the "grass" — what water buffalo forage on — represents whatever is naturally tempting, either to the senses or the intellect, but best avoided by the monk in training; see **"not an inch of grass for ten thousand miles."** The word translated here as "damage" (*han* 犯), in the Buddhist context, means to break the moral precepts (*kai* 戒). The expression "white ox on open ground" (*roji byakugo* 露地白牛) is an allusion to the scene in the *Lotus Sūtra* in which the father, having enticed his children from their burning house (of saṃsāra) and seeing them now safely seated "in the open" (*roji* 露地), presents them with carts (the buddha vehicle) pulled by great "white oxen (*byakugo* 白牛)"; see **"burning house."**

The third place in the *Shōbōgenzō* where herding "a single water buffalo" occurs is in "The Thirty-seven Factors of Bodhi" ("Shōbōgenzō sanjūshichi hon bodai bunpō" 正法眼蔵三十七品菩提分法, DZZ.2:140):

定覺支は、機先保護機先眼なり、自家鼻孔自家穿なり、自家把索自家牽なり。しかもかくのごとくなりといへども、さらに牧得一頭水牯牛なり。

"The concentration limb of awakening" is "what is before the function preserves the eye before the function"; it is "drilling one's own nostrils oneself"; it is "pulling oneself with one's own rope." Nevertheless, be that as it may, going further, it is "managing to herd a single water buffalo."

To "herd" (*boku* 牧) a water buffalo (literally, "set it out to pasture") means to domesticate it and train it to obey. Because the beast is large, powerful, and headstrong, the way to control it is by a rope attached to a ring that has been passed through a hole drilled through its nostrils: if the rope pulls too hard on the ring, the animal experiences pain, so it learns to move when led and not to try to escape. In this passage, the water buffalo stands for one's own mind, so the expressions "drill one's own nostrils oneself" and "pull oneself with one's own rope" refer to gaining control over one's own mind or "seeing [one's own true] nature" (*kenshō* 見性); see **"nose."**

The comparison of spiritual self-discipline (Zen practice) to catching and training a water buffalo that has escaped and run off into the wild is depicted graphically in several illustrated texts called "oxherding pictures." The one that is best known in Japan is the *Verses and Prefaces on the Ten Buffalo-herding Scenes by Reverend Kuo'an, Abbot of Mount Liang in Dongzhou* (*Zhu*

*Dingzhou Liangshan Kuo'an heshang Shiniutu song xu* 住鼎州梁山廓庵和尚十牛圖頌序, ZZ.113:917a1-920b6; X.1269.64:773c1-775a18), better known in English as the *Verses on the Ten Oxherding Pictures*. The work features ten ink paintings under the following headings: 1) Searching for the Buffalo (*jingyū* 尋牛); 2) Seeing the Traces (*kenshaku* 見跡); 3) Seeing the Buffalo (*kengyū* 見牛); 4) Catching the Buffalo (*tokugyū* 得牛); 5) Herding the Buffalo (*bokugyū* 牧牛); 6) Riding the Buffalo and Returning Home (*kigyū kika* 騎牛歸家); 7) Forgetting the Buffalo and Keeping the Person (*bōgyū sonjin* 忘牛存人); 8) Person and Buffalo both Forgotten (*nin gyū gubō* 人牛俱忘); 9) Returning to the Origin and Reverting to the Source (*henpon gengen* 返本還源); and 10) Entering the Marketplace with Helping Hands (*nitten suishu* 入鄽垂手). Kuo'an 廓庵 (dates unknown), a monk who is said to have lived in the twelfth century, prefaces the first scene with the words:

從來不失、何用追尋。由背覺以成疎。在向塵而遂失。

From the start, it [i.e., the buffalo] has never been lost, so why the chase and search? Because he [i.e., the herdsman] paid it no attention, it became estranged. He turned toward the dust [of worldly concerns], and it got lost as a consequence.

The "traces" (*shaku* 跡, also written *seki* 迹) that the herdsman sees in the second scene, which are the hoof tracks of the buffalo, stand for the sūtras and "teachings" (*kyō* 教) of Buddhism, which provide a merely intellectual understanding of the innate buddha mind (*busshin* 佛心) — the "buffalo" — that is always present, whether one realizes it or not. The description of the ninth scene, "Returning to the Origin and Reverting to the Source," was originally a Daoist expression meaning to realize the primary source of all existence, which is the great way (*daidō* 大道). The expression was subsequently borrowed by Buddhist theoreticians such as Tiantai Zhiyi 天台智顗 (538–597) and Guifeng Zongmi 圭峰宗密 (780-841), who used it to refer to gaining insight into the innate buddha nature, or "mind ground" (*shinchi* 心地).

Apart from the trope of "herding" a water buffalo as a metaphor for dealing with one's own mind, the animal also appears in Zen literature as a symbol of rebirth in a lower state of being. The biography of Nanquan Puyuan 南泉普願 (748-835) in the *Jingde Era Record of the Transmission of the Flame* (*Jingde chuandeng lu* 景德傳燈錄, T.2076.51:259a27-28), for example, contains the following famous exchange:

第一座問、和尚百年後向什麼處去。師云、山下作一頭水牯牛去。

The [monk in the position of] number-one-seat asked, "Reverend, where will you be a hundred years from now?"
The Master [Nanquan] said, "Down the mountain, I'll be a water buffalo."

The biography of Weishan Lingyou 溈山靈祐 (771-853) in the *Jingde Era Record of the Transmission of the Flame* (*Jingde chuandeng lu* 景德傳燈錄, T.2076.51:265c22-26) contains a similar anecdote:

師上堂示衆云、老僧百年後、向山下作一頭水牯牛。左脅書五字云、溈山僧某甲。此時喚作溈山僧、又是水牯牛、喚作水牯牛、又云溈山僧。喚作什麼即得。

At a convocation in the dharma hall, the Master [Weishan] addressed the assembly, saying, "In a hundred years, this old monk will have headed down the mountain and become a water buffalo. On my left flank will be written five glyphs that read, 'Monk So-and-so of Weishan [Monastery].' At that time the monk named 'Weishan' will also be a water buffalo, and the one named 'water buffalo' will also be called 'Monk Weishan.' Which name gets it?"

In Buddhist contexts such as these, the expression "down the mountain" or "at the foot of the mountain" (*sange* 山下) also has the meaning of "away from this monastery."

Yuanwu Keqin's 圜悟克勤 (1063-1135) commentary to case 24 of the *Blue Cliff Record* (*Biyan lu* 碧巖錄, T.2003.48:165a4-15), which involves Weishan and a nun named Liu Tiemo 劉鐵磨 (dates unknown), invokes the same saying:

舉。劉鐵磨到溈山。山云、老牸牛、汝來也。磨云、來日臺山大會齋。和尚還去麼。溈山放身臥。磨便出去。

劉鐵磨如擊石火、似閃電光。擬議則喪身失命。禪道若到緊要處、那裏有許多事。他作家相見、如隔牆見角便知是牛。隔山見煙便知是火。拶著便動。捺著便轉。溈山道、老僧百年後、向山下檀越家作一頭水牯牛。左脅下書五字云、溈山僧某甲。且正當恁麼時、喚作溈山僧即是、喚作水牯牛即是。如今人問著、管取分疎不下。劉鐵磨久參、機鋒峭峻。人號爲劉鐵磨。

Raised:

Liu Tiemo arrived at Mount Wei. [Wei] Shan said, "Old cow, you've come!"

Mo said, "Tomorrow there's a great maigre feast at Mount Tai. Will you go, Reverend?"

Weishan relaxed his body and lay down.

Mo immediately left.

[Comment:]

Liu Tiemo was like a spark from a flint, like a flash of lightening; take time to think [before responding], and one **forfeits one's body and loses one's life**. On the way of Chan, if you get to the most essential place, where is there tolerance for numerous affairs? This encounter between maestros is like seeing horns on the other side of a barrier and knowing there's a

Supplementary notes to the translation 547

buffalo; it's like seeing smoke on the other side of a mountain and knowing there's a fire. If pressed with a question, they move; if pushed down with the hands, they roll away. Weishan said, "In a hundred years, this old monk will have headed down the mountain and become a water buffalo at a lay patron's house. On my left flank will be written five glyphs that read, 'Monk So-and-so of Weishan [Monastery].' At just such a time, would naming me 'Monk Weishan' be right, or would naming me 'water buffalo' be right? When today's people are asked that, they are certainly unable to give a clear explanation." Liu Tiemo was a long-time practitioner who was mentally sharp and precipitous [i.e., of sublime character]. People called her "Grinding Iron [Tiemo 鐵磨] Liu."

In many contexts, Zen masters employ terms such as "clad in fur and crowned by horns" (*himō taikaku* 披毛戴角) or "beast" (*chikushō* 畜生) as metaphors for the stupidity or amorality of certain people, especially other monks. In the cases of Nanquan and Weishan, however, their self-deprecating remarks about being reborn as water buffalo, a destiny that would ordinarily be construed as resulting from some bad karma, is clearly a kind of false modesty. By the same token, when Weishan calls Liu Tiemo an "old cow" (*rō jigo* 老牸牛), that is not an insult but rather a form of backhanded praise. In the *Discourse Record of Chan Master Yuanzheng of Mount Cao in Muzhou* (*Muzhou Caoshan Yuanzheng chanshi yulu* 撫州曹山元證禪師語錄, T.47.1987A:534c3-6), Caoshan Benji 曹山本寂 (840–890) uses the example of rebirth as a water buffalo to describe the "different types of the *śramaṇa*" (*shamon irui* 沙門異類) in a positive way:

轉却沙門稱斷邊事、不入諸勝報位。始得名爲沙門行。亦云沙門轉身。亦云披毛戴角。亦喚作水牯牛。恁麼時節始得入異類。

Upon transitioning [from this life], the *śramaṇa* judges peripheral affairs and does not enter into the various ranks of karmic rewards. Only then can it be called the "practice of a *śramaṇa*." It is also said to be "the *śramaṇa*'s change of body." It is also said to be "clad in fur and crowned by horns." It is also named "becoming a water buffalo." At such a time, one [i.e., the *śramaṇa*] is first able to enter different types.

In this context, to say that the *śramaṇa* is reborn as a water buffalo is an ironic, antiphrastic way of signifying their complete liberation from karmic retribution; for more on this trope, see "**move among different types**" and "**a head of three feet and a neck of two inches**."

**water doesn't flow** (*sui furyū* 水不流): From a verse attributed to the layman Shanhui Dashi 善慧大士 (497-569), also known as Fu Dashi 傅大士, in his biography in the *Jingde Era Record of the Transmission of the Flame* (*Jingde chuandeng lu* 景德傳燈錄, T.2076.51:430b6-7):

空手把鋤頭、步行騎水牛、人從橋上過、橋流水不流。

548     DŌGEN'S *SHŌBŌGENZŌ* VOLUME VIII

Empty handed yet grasping a hoe,
Walking yet riding a **water buffalo**,
A person passes over the bridge;
The bridge flows, and the water doesn't.

**what thing is it that comes like this?** (*ze jūmo butsu inmo rai* 是什麼物恁
麼來): This is a question that the Sixth Ancestor, Huineng 慧能, poses to
his eventual dharma heir, the monk Nanyue Huairang 南嶽懷讓 (677-744),
when the latter first comes from Mount Song to seek instruction from him.
Lines from the dialogue between those two, which is one of Dōgen's favorite
episodes in all of Zen literature, are cited throughout the *Shōbōgenzō*. The
version recorded in Dōgen's *Shōbōgenzō* in Chinese script (*shinji Shōbōgenzō*
眞字正法眼藏, DZZ.5:178, case 101) reads as follows:

嶽山大慧禪師〈嗣曹溪、諱懷讓〉參六祖。祖曰、從什麼處來。師
曰、嵩山安國師處來。祖曰、是什麼物恁麼來。師罔措。於是執侍八
年、方省前話。乃告祖云、懷讓會得、當初來時、和尚接某甲、是什
麼物恁麼來。祖云、爾作麼生會。師曰、説似一物即不中。祖曰、還
假修證否。師曰、修證即不無、染汚即不得。祖曰、祇此不染汚、是
諸佛之所護念。汝亦如是、吾亦如是、乃至西天諸祖亦如是。

Chan Master Dahui of Mount Nanyue (descendant of Caoxi, named Huairang) visited the Sixth Ancestor. The Ancestor asked him, "Where do
you come from?"

The Master said, "I come from National Teacher An on Mount Song."

The Ancestor said, "What thing is it that comes like this?"

The Master was without means [to answer]. After attending [the Ancestor]
for eight years, he finally understood the previous conversation. Thereupon, he announced to the Ancestor, "Huairang has understood what the
Reverend put to me when I first came: 'What thing is it that comes like
this?'"

The Ancestor asked, "How do you understand it?"

The Master replied, "To say it's like any thing wouldn't hit it."
The Ancestor said, "Then does it depend on **practice and verification**?"

The Master answered, "It's not that it lacks practice and verification, but
it can't be defiled by them."

The Ancestor said, "Just this '**not defiled**' is what the buddhas bear in
mind. **You're also like this, I'm also like this**, and all the ancestors of
Sindh in the West [i. e., India] are also like this."

In this dialogue, the expression "comes like this" (*inmo rai* 恁麼來) is a
play on the term *nyorai* 如來, literally "thus come," which translates the
Sanskrit *tathāgata* and is used both as an epithet of the Buddha and as a

*Supplementary notes to the translation* 549

reference to buddhas in general. Thus, one reading of Huineng's question, "What thing is it that comes like this?" might take it as asking, "What is a buddha?" At the same time, however, it is clear that the "thing that comes like this," which Nanyue finally verifies in an immediate, intuitive way after eight years of assiduous practice under Huineng, is Nanyue's "own original nature" (*jiko honshō* 自己本性), or "original nature" (*honshō* 本性) for short. The Zen tradition also calls this "one's own original lot" (*jiko honbun* 自己本分), "unborn original nature" (*mushō honshō* 無生本性), "original face" (*honrai menmoku* 本來面目), "own self" (*jiko* 自己), "real self" (*shinjitsu ga* 眞實我), "lord master" (*shujinkō* 主人公), and so on. All such expressions are loosely synonymous in Zen texts with "buddha nature" (*busshō* 佛性), and it is said that the goal of Zen practice is to "see the [original / buddha] nature and attain buddhahood" (*kenshō jōbutsu* 見性成佛). When asked by Huineng to describe what he has finally seen, however, Nanyue demurs with the remark, "To say it's like any thing wouldn't hit it." That is because insight into the emptiness of dharmas (*hō* 法) — i.e., the unreality of "things" (*motsu* 物) as we conventionally conceive of them — is central to awakening, and all the names for that which is ultimately real misrepresent it by reifying it. Huineng's follow-up question, "Does it depend on practice and verification?" further probes Nanyue's insight. From one point of view, "one's own original lot" does not depend on anything at all: it utterly transcends karmic conditioning and thus provides escape from suffering in saṃsāra. However, without spiritual "practice" (*shu* 修) and the "verification" (*shō* 證) that comes with it, one will not "see the original nature" (*ken honshō* 見本性) or experience any relief from suffering. Thus, Nanyue says, "It's not that it [i.e., the "original nature"] lacks practice and verification, but it can't be defiled by them." In this context, to be **"not defiled"** means to be free from emotional and conceptual attachment to **"practice and verification,"** even as one earnestly engages in those. That, Huineng says approvingly, is what he himself, his disciple Nanyue, and all the awakened **buddhas and ancestors** of the Zen lineage are like. In any case, his words, **"You're also like this, I'm also like this"** are clearly an affirmation of Nanyue's awakening.

Throughout the literature of Zen, it is very common for dialogues to begin with the abbot of a monastery asking a newly arrived (*shintō* 新到) monk who has an audience (*shōken* 相見) with him a question such as "Where did you come from?" (*jū jūmosho rai* 從什麼處來 or *gonri jūmosho* 近離什麼處). On one level, these inquiries are about the newcomer's background: what monasteries he has trained in, and what teachers he has had. When another master is named in the reply, there is often a follow-up question that asks, "What are his teachings?" On another level, however, the question "Where do you come from?" is an implicit inquiry into the newcomer's present degree of understanding: his awakening or delusion. Thus, Huineng's follow-up question to Huairang — "What thing is it that comes like this?" — not only puns on the term "thus come," it doubles down on the implied

550 DŌGEN'S *SHŌBŌGENZŌ* VOLUME VIII

question, "What is your understanding?" The question is best known from this dialogue, but it is attributed to Chan masters other than Huineng, as well, in the context of interviews with newly arrived monks. In some of those instances, the masters may be consciously alluding to the famous dialogue between Huineng and Huairang.

The expression attributed to Huineng in the dialogue, "what the buddhas bear in mind" (*shobutsu shi sho gonen* 諸佛之所護念), which can also be translated as "what the buddhas guard and care for," has considerable precedent in Chinese sūtra literature. It appears, for example, in the *Great Perfection of Wisdom Sūtra* (*Da bore boluomiduo jing* 大般若波羅蜜多經, T.220.7:889c23-25):

若菩薩乘善男子等能書般若波羅蜜多、種種莊嚴、受持、讀誦、供養、恭敬、常爲諸佛之所護念。由此因緣獲大饒益。

If good sons in the bodhisattva vehicle can copy this *Perfection of Wisdom*, adorn it in various ways, receive and keep it, read and recite it, make offerings to it and revere it, they will always be borne in mind by the buddhas. By means of these causes and conditions, they will reap great benefits.

The expression also appears in the "Medicine King" (*Yaowang* 藥王) chapter of the *Lotus Sūtra* (*Miaofa lianhua jing* 妙法蓮華經, T.262.9:31b21-24):

藥王、當知如來滅後、其能書、持、讀誦、供養、爲他人説者、如來則爲以衣覆之、又爲他方現在諸佛之所護念。

Medicine King, you should know that after the extinction of the Tathāgata, if there are those who can copy, keep, read and recite [this sūtra], make offerings to it and expound it for others, the Tathāgata will use his robe to cover them, and they will also be borne in mind by the buddhas present in other regions.

In light of these passages, what Huineng's remark might mean is that people (in this case, Huairang) who are not defiled by practice and verification even as they engage in it are "borne in mind" (i.e., watched over and protected) by the buddhas.

There is another, slightly different version of the dialogue between Huineng and Huairang that is found in the latter's biography in the *Jingde Era Record of the Transmission of the Flame* (*Jingde chuandeng lu* 景德傳燈錄, T.2076.51:240c7-17):

南嶽懷讓禪師者姓杜氏。金州人也。年十五往荊州玉泉寺、依弘景律師出家。受具之後、習毘尼藏。一日自歎曰、夫出家者爲無爲法。時同學坦然知師志高邁、勸師謁嵩山安和尚。安啓發之、乃直詣曹谿參六祖。祖問、什麼處來。曰、嵩山來。祖曰、什麼物恁麼來。曰、説似一物即不中。祖曰、還可修證否。曰、修證即不無、汚染即不得。

祖曰、只此不汚染諸佛之所護念。汝既如是、吾亦如是。西天般若多羅讖、汝足下出一馬駒、蹋殺天下人。並在汝心不須速說。師豁然契會。執侍左右一十五載。

Chan Master Nanyue Huairang's family was the Du clan. He was a man of Jinzhou. At age fifteen he went to Yuquan Monastery in Jingzhou and left home [i.e., became a monk] under the tutelage of Vinaya Master Hongjing. After receiving the full precepts, he trained in the *Vinaya-piṭaka*. One day he sighed to himself, "Leaving home is for the sake of the unconditioned dharma." At the time, a fellow trainee, Tanran, knowing that the Master's [Huiarang's] resolution was exceptional, encouraged him to call on Reverend An of Mount Song. With An's advice, he went directly to [Mount] Caoxi and visited the Sixth Ancestor.

The Ancestor asked him, "Where do you come from?"

He said, "From Mount Song."

The Ancestor said, "What thing is it that comes like this?"

He said, "To say it's like any thing wouldn't hit it."

The Ancestor said, "Then does it depend on practice and verification?"

The Master answered, "It's not that it lacks practice and verification, but it can't be defiled by them."

The Ancestor said, "Just this 'not defiled' is what the buddhas bear in mind. According to the prophecy of Prajñātāra of Sindh in the West, there will emerge from beneath your feet a colt that will trample to death everyone in the world. Bear this in mind and don't speak of it too soon."

The Master clearly tallied with and understood [Huineng]. He waited on him closely for fifteen years.

The "colt" (*maku* 馬駒) mentioned in the prophecy is a thinly veiled reference to Nanyue Huairang's eminent dharma heir, Mazu Daoyi 馬祖道一 (709–788), whose name translates literally as "horse (*ma* 馬) ancestor (*zu* 祖)." The first glyph is his secular clan name, Ma, and the second glyph recognizes him as the founding ancestor of one of the two major branches of the Chan lineage in the generations following the Sixth Ancestor, Huineng.

The two versions of the dialogue presented above differ mainly in their accounts of its chronology. In the version that Dōgen includes in his *Shōbōgenzō* in Chinese script (*shinji Shōbōgenzō* 眞字正法眼藏), it takes Huairang eight years to finally understand and be able to respond to Huineng's question: "What thing is it that comes like this?" In the version that appears in the *Jingde Era Record of the Transmission of the Flame*, Huairang responds immediately to Huineng's question, gets Huineng's approval, and then spends fifteen years serving as Huineng's acolyte.

A hybrid version of the dialogue is commonly raised as a kōan in Zen literature. Dahui Zonggao's 大慧宗杲 (1089–1163) *Treasury of the True*

*Dharma Eye* (*Zhengfayanzang* 正法眼藏, ZZ.118:104a16-b1), for example, presents it as follows:

> 南嶽讓和尚初參六祖。祖問、甚處來。曰、嵩山來。祖曰、甚麼物恁麼來。曰、説似一物即不中。祖曰、還假修證也無。曰、修證即不無、汙染即不得。祖曰、只此不汙染、乃諸佛之護念。汝既如是、吾亦如是。

Reverend Nanyue Rang visited the Sixth Ancestor. The Ancestor asked him, "Where do you come from?"

He said, "From Mount Song."

The Ancestor said, "What thing is it that comes like this?"

He said, "To say it's like any thing wouldn't hit it."

The Ancestor said, "Then does it depend on practice and verification?"

He said, "It's not that it lacks practice and verification, but it can't be defiled by them."

The Ancestor said, "Just this 'not defiled' is what the buddhas bear in mind. You're also like this, I'm also like this."

**when the bright comes, the bright does it; when the dark comes, the dark does it** (*meitō rai meitō ta, antō rai antō ta* 明頭來明頭打、暗頭來暗頭打): A tentative rendering of a vexed saying, variously read, "When it comes (or they or I come) in the bright, I hit in (or with) the bright . . . ." Our translation treats the verb *ta* 打 ("to hit") simply as a generic predicate marker ("to do," "to deal with," etc.) and takes the saying to mean something like, "when it's clear, then it's clear; when it's obscure, then it's obscure." The saying is attributed to the Chan monk Puhua 普化 (dates unknown) in the *Discourse Record of Chan Master Linji Huizhao of Zhenzhou* (*Zhenzhou Linji Huizhao chanshi yulu* 鎮州臨濟慧照禪師語錄, T.1985.47:503b20). The version recorded in Dōgen's *Shōbōgenzō* in Chinese script (*shinji Shōbōgenzō* 眞字正法眼藏, DZZ.5:136-138, case 22) reads as follows:

> 鎮州普化和尚〈嗣盤山〉居常入市、振鈴鐸云、明頭來、明頭打、暗頭來、暗頭打。四方八面來、旋風打、虚空來、連架打。一日臨濟、令僧捉住云、或遇不明不暗來時如何。師拓開云、來日大悲院裡有齋。僧廻舉似齋。齋云、我從來疑著這漢。

Reverend Puhua of Zhenzhou (heir to Panshan) always went into the market, ringing a bell and saying, "When the bright comes, the bright does it. When the dark comes, the dark does it. When the four quarters and eight sides come, the whirlwind does it. When empty space comes, the flail does it."

One day, Linji had a monk take hold of him and say, "How about when neither bright nor dark come?"

*Supplementary notes to the translation* 553

The Master [Puhua] broke free and said, "There's a maigre feast in the Dabei Cloister tomorrow."

When the monk reported this to [Lin] Ji, Ji said, "I've always had my doubts about this guy."

**whether from a wise friend, whether from a sūtra scroll** (*waku jū chishiki, waku jū kyōkan* 或從知識或從經卷): Fixed expressions occurring together several times in the *Shōbōgenzō*; possibly reflecting the *Great Calming and Contemplation* (*Mohe zhiguan* 摩訶止觀, T.1911.46:10b20-24) by Tiantai Zhiyi 天台智顗 (538–597):

名字即者。理雖即是日用不知。以未聞三諦全不識佛法。如牛羊眼不解方隅。或從知識或從經卷。聞上所説一實菩提。於名字中通達解了。知一切法皆是佛法。是爲名字即菩提。

Identity in words: Although [the preceding identity in] principle is like this, in everyday life, we do not know it. Because we have yet to hear of the three truths and are completely unaware of the buddha dharma, we are like cattle and sheep, whose eyes do not understand the directions. When we hear, whether from a wise friend, whether from a sūtra scroll, the one true bodhi and penetrate and fully understand it in words, we know that all dharmas are buddha dharmas. This is called "the bodhi of identity in words."

A "wise friend" (*chishiki* 知識), short for *zen chishiki* 善知識 (S. *kalyāṇa-mitra*), is a common term for a Buddhist teacher. A "sūtra scroll" (*kyōkan* 經卷) is a text containing a sermon of Buddha Śākyamuni. Together, those represent the two primary sources of Buddhist teachings.

**whether in fields or in villages** (*nyaku den nyaku ri* 若田若里): An allusion to a passage in the *Lotus Sūtra* (*Miaofa lianhua jing* 妙法蓮華經, T.262.9:46b27-46c6), in which Buddha Śākyamuni explains that, after his entry into nirvāṇa, if there is anyone who hears the *Lotus Sūtra* and responds with sympathetic joy (*zuiki* 隨喜), and who then goes out from the dharma assembly and energetically propagates what he or she has heard to parents, family, friends, or colleagues, and if any of those people in turn experiences sympathetic joy and passes on the teachings to another, and so on down through fifty such propagations, the merit (*kudoku* 功德) resulting from the sympathetic joy of even the fiftieth person in line will be vast and incalculable. In making this case, the Buddha states that those who propagate the *Lotus Sūtra* may do so anywhere, "whether in monks' quarters" (*nyaku sōbō* 若僧坊), whether in vacant spaces (*nyaku kūkanchi* 若空閑地), whether in walled cities (*nyaku jōyū* 若城邑), along streets and lanes (*kōbaku* 巷陌), in settlements (*juraku* 聚落), or fields and villages (*denri* 田里)." The use of the final phrase as a shorthand reference to the entire argument was well established prior

554 DŌGEN'S *SHŌBŌGENZŌ* VOLUME VIII

to Dōgen, as was its juxtaposition with a saying from the *Nirvāṇa Sūtra*, **"whether on trees or on rocks."**

**whether on trees or on rocks** (*nyaku ju nyaku seki* 若樹若石): An allusion to the story of the so-called "boy of the Snowy Mountains [i.e., Himalayas]" (*Sessen dōji* 雪山童子), also known as the "bodhisattva of the Snowy Mountains" (*Sessen daishi* 雪山大士), which was part of the common lore of Buddhism in Song-dynasty China and Kamakura-period Japan. The story is frequently mentioned in both Tendai and Zen texts, but the *locus classicus* is the *Nirvāṇa Sūtra* (*Da banniepan jing* 大般涅槃經, T.374.12:450a12-451b5), where it is framed as a first-person account given by Buddha Śākyamuni about one of his own previous lives as a bodhisattva. The protagonist of the story, who is not actually called either the "boy of the Snowy Mountains" or the "bodhisattva of the Snowy Mountains" in any extant version of the *Nirvana Sutra*, is a brahman who began his bodhisattva career in a long-ago age when the "buddha sun (*butsunichi* 佛日) [i.e., Buddhism] had not yet appeared in the world." Reading all the scriptures of other paths (*gedō* 外道), he follows their rules of ascetic restraint and maintained mental purity, resides alone in the Snowy Mountains (*sessen* 雪山), subsists on fruits, and assiduously practices seated meditation, but he does not hear of a tathāgata appearing in the world or even the name of a Mahāyāna sūtra. Nevertheless, Indra (*Shakudaikan'in* 釋提桓因) and various other devas are alarmed by his practice, fearing a loss of their own influence if he were to attain awakening. In order to test the ascetic's mettle, Indra takes the form of a man-eating demon (*rasetsu* 羅刹; S. *rākṣasa*). Descending to the snowy mountains, he stands near the ascetic and, in a beautiful refined voice, recites the first half of a verse that has been preached by former buddhas:

諸行無常、是生滅法。

All things are impermanent: this is the law of arising and ceasing.

Upon hearing this "half verse" (*hange* 半偈), the ascetic is overjoyed, "like a drowning person who suddenly encounters a boat, like a thirsty person who comes across clear cool water..., like a person who has been long chained and suddenly learns of his release..., like a traveler who is able to return home.... " He looks around for the one who had recited the verse but sees only the demon. Nevertheless, he asks to hear the rest of the verse and offers to become the demon's disciple for the rest of his life if the demon will tell him. The demon, however, says that he is too famished to do so. When the ascetic asks what he needs to eat, he replies, "The warm flesh of some human, and to drink, some human's hot blood." The ascetic replies, "If you tell me the rest of the verse, after hearing it I will give you my body as nourishment." Accordingly, the devil recites the second half:

*Supplementary notes to the translation*　　　555

生滅滅已、寂滅爲樂。

When the arising and ceasing have ceased, their cessation is ease.

Upon hearing this, the ascetic deeply contemplates its meaning. Then he "inscribed this verse here and there, whether on rocks (*nyaku seki* 若石), whether on walls (*nyaku heki* 若壁), whether on trees (*nyaku ju* 若樹), whether on roads (*nyaku dō* 若道)." Finally, to pay the price for the verse, he climbs a tall tree and, after an exchange with the tree spirit who asks him what he is doing, jumps to what he intends to be his death. While he is still in midair, however, the demon assumes its original form as Indra, catches his falling body and sets him safely on the ground. Then Indra and the other devas bow their heads in worship beneath his feet and praise him as a true bodhisattva. The Buddha concludes the story by explaining that, "As the karmic result of my past action of discarding this body for half a verse, I was able to leap over twelve kalpas [of rebirth], and obtain *anuttara-samyak-saṃbodhi* before Maitreya."

The use of the expression "whether on trees or on rocks" as shorthand for this story was well established prior to Dōgen. So was its association with the line, "**whether in fields or in villages**." The *Record of the Teachings and Career of the Sage of Siming* (*Siming zunzhe jiaoxinglu* 四明尊者教行録, T.1936.46:908a11-13) by the Tiantai master Zhili 知禮 (960-1027), for example, contains a reference to "the *Lotus Sutra's* 'Whether in fields or in villages' (*Hokke nyaku den nyaku ri* 法華若田若里) and the *Nirvana Sutra's* 'Whether on trees or on stones' (*Nehan nyaku ju nyaku seki* 涅槃若樹若石)."

The verse featured in this story is known as the *Verse of the Snowy Mountains* (*Sessen ge* 雪山偈), or more commonly, the *Verse of Impermanence* (*Mujō ge* 無常偈):

諸行無常、是生滅法、生滅滅已、寂滅爲樂。

All things are impermanent: this is the law of arising and ceasing.

When the arising and ceasing have ceased, their cessation is ease.

The verse has a long history of use in East Asian Buddhism. It appears, for example, in the "Lotus repentance" (*Hokke senbō* 法華懺法) of the Tendai school and in Chan "rules of purity" (*shingi* 清規) dating from the Yuan dynasty down to the present, in the context of funeral services for monks. In Sōtō Zen today, this verse is written on four white banners (*shirohata shiryū* 白幡四流}, one phrase on each banner, which are used in the funerals of deceased monks (*bōsō sōgi* 亡僧喪儀).

556 DŌGEN'S *SHŌBŌGENZŌ* VOLUME VIII

**whisk** (*hossu* 拂子; S. *vyajana*): The Sanskrit term *vyajana* refers to any implement, such as a palm frond, used as a fan or whisk. In the context of early Buddhist and Jain ascetic practice, the original function of the *vyajana* was to brush away insects without killing them, so the monkish implement in question was not a device used for fanning oneself, but rather a "whisk," as the Chinese translation indicates. The finer ones were made by attaching a bundle of hairs from the tail of a horse, ox, deer, or yak to a wooden handle, but the material used could be also yarn, strips of cloth, straw, etc. In India and Central Asia, the "white whisk" (*byakuhotsu* 白拂; S. *vāla-vyajana*), or "chowry," made from the tail hair of the white Himalayan yak (S. *chāmara*) attached to a costly decorated handle, was an insignia of high social class or royalty. In Chinese Buddhist texts translated from Sanskrit, eminent brāhmaṇas, kings, and occasionally bodhisattvas are described as holding a "white whisk."

In East Asian Buddhism, the whisk became an emblem of authority that was held by senior monks in certain ritual settings. It seems that during the Tang dynasty, in formal doctrinal debates between two eminent monks of equal status, the speaker would raise their whisk to signal that they were holding forth, then lower it to allow their opponent a chance to speak. Paintings that depict the layman Vimalakīrti debating Mañjuśrī (a famous scene from the *Vimalakīrti Sūtra*) show him wielding a whisk in that way. In what was perhaps a vestige of that earlier form, the abbots of major monasteries in Song- and Yuan-dynasty China would hold a whisk when they mounted the high seat in the dharma hall to engage in public question and answer with the assembled monks. The whisk thus became part of the formal regalia of an abbot, and the mortuary portraits of eminent monks frequently depicted them holding one. The expression "wield the whisk" (*hinpotsu* 秉拂) also came to mean "preside over a convocation in the dharma hall."

In Zen literature, abbots are sometimes depicted using their whisks in unorthodox ways, such as holding them up in silent response to a question, referring to them as props in debate, or using them to hit their disciples. In the *Extensive Record of Chan Master Yunmen Kuangzhen* (*Yunmen Kuangzhen chanshi guanglu* 雲門匡眞禪師廣錄, T.1988.47:556a7-9), for example, Yunmen Wenyan 雲門文偃 (864-949) uses his whisk in the following manner:

舉一宿覺云、六般神用空不空、一顆圓光色非色。師拈起拂子云、者箇是圓光、是色非色。喚什麼作色。與我拈將來看。

[Someone] raised the case of the overnight awakening [of Yongjia Xuan-jue 永嘉玄覺 (675–713)], saying, "The spiritual action of the six senses is emptiness that is not empty; the one circular light [i.e., the halo about the head of a buddha] has a form that is not form."

Supplementary notes to the translation | 557

The Master [Yunmen] held up his whisk and said, "This is one circular light; it is the form that is not form. What would you call it to make it form? Come on, try taking that up with me!"

According to the *Collated Essentials of the Five Flame Records* (*Wudeng huiyuan* 五燈會元, ZZ.138:528b3-6), Touzi Yiqing 投子義青 (1032-1083) used his whisk in the following manner in an exchange with his disciple Furong Daokai 芙蓉道楷 (1043–1118):

乃問、佛祖言句如家常茶飯。離此之外、別有爲人處也無。子曰、汝道、寰中天子敕、還假堯舜禹湯也無。師欲進語。子以拂子摵師口曰、汝發意來、早有三十棒也。師即開悟。

[Daokai] asked, "The words and phrases of the **buddhas and ancestors** are like **everyday tea and rice**. Apart from those, is there a separate place from which to help people, or not?"

Yiqing said, "You tell me: when 'within the imperial domain, the son of heaven issues commands,' does he still avail himself of [the ancient emperors] Yao, Shun, Yu, and Tang, or not?"

The Master [Daokai] wanted to say something, but Yiqing took his whisk and hit the Master's mouth, saying, "If you bring forth intention, you already deserve thirty blows." The master immediately awakened.

**wooden stake** (*bokuketsu* 木橛; also *mokketsu*): The glyph 橛 (*ketsu*) may be translated as "peg," "nail," "spike," or "stake." Zen texts refer to both "wooden stakes" (*mokketsu* 木橛) and "iron stakes" (*tekketsu* 鐵橛). The items in question can be "stakes" driven into the ground for the purpose of tethering an animal or anchoring a tent, etc., or "pegs" or "nails" used to join pieces of wood. Metaphorically, the image of a "stake" has at least two attested meanings in Zen literature.

In the first place, a "stake" is any name or concept that has become the object of deluded attachment. In the *Discourse Record of Chan Master Dahui Pujue* (*Dahui Pujue chanshi yulu* 大慧普覺禪師語錄), for example, Dahui Zonggao 大慧宗杲 (1089–1163) says: "'Old Man Śākya' is a donkey-tethering stake" (*kero ketsu* 繫驢橛, T.1998A.47:847b6-7), and "'bodhi' and 'nirvāṇa' are donkey-tethering stakes" (T.1998A.47:879c6). In Zen literature, ignorant students are called "donkeys" (*ro* 驢): i.e., animals that resemble horses but are not suitable for riding. The entry for Yaojing Hankuang 樂淨含匡 (dates unknown) that appears in the *Jingde Era Record of the Transmission of the Flame* (*Jingde chuandeng lu* 景德傳燈錄, T.2076.51:404b5-7) contains the following exchange:

因普請打籬次有僧問、古人種種開方便門、和尚爲什麼却攔截。師曰、牢下橛著。

When driving bamboo fence [posts] during communal labor, there was a monk who asked: "The ancients opened all sort of gates of skillful means. Why do you, Reverend, fence things off?"

The Master [Yaojing] said, "[Your] corral is staked down."

Yaojing's retort implies that the monk has imprisoned himself in a conceptual "corral" (*rō* 牢), or cattle pen, that is "staked down" (*kaketsu* 下橛) by his own deluded conceptualizing.

Secondly, "setting a stake in empty space" (*kokū chū kaketsu* 虛空中下橛) is a metaphor for attempting something that is futile, such as trying to pin down what really exists by using words. In the *Extensive Record of Chan Master Yongjue Yuanxian* (*Yongjue Yuanxian chanshi guanglu* 永覺元賢禪師廣錄, ZZ.125:422a11-13; X.1437.72:395a23-b1), for example, we find the following:

竪拂云、只如這裏、是結耶是解耶。是有生滅耶、是離生滅耶。有事不如無事好。莫向空中重下橛。喝一喝、下座。

[At a convocation in the dharma hall, Yuanxian] raised his **whisk** and said: "As with this here, is it bondage, or is it release? Is it the presence of arising and ceasing, or is it freedom from arising and ceasing? Having concerns is not like the ease of having no concerns. Do not, in the middle of empty space, repeatedly drive in stakes." Shouting a single shout, he got down from the seat.

**Yaoshan's not thinking** (*Yakusan fushiryō tei* 藥山不思量底): The nickname of a kōan that appears several times in Dōgen's writings, involving Yaoshan Weiyan 藥山惟儼 (751-834) and an unnamed monk interlocutor. The story is found in a number of Chan sources, such as the *Jingde Era Record of the Transmission of the Flame* (*Jingde chuandeng lu* 景德傳燈錄, T.2076.51:311c26-28), as well as in Dōgen's *Shōbōgenzō* in Chinese script (*shinji Shōbōgenzō* 眞字正法眼藏, DZZ.5:196, case 129). The version of the story on which Dōgen comments at the opening of his "Needle of Seated Meditation" ("Shōbōgenzō zazen shin" 正法眼藏坐禪箴, DZZ.1:103) reads as follows:

藥山弘道大師坐次、有僧問、兀兀地思量什麼。師云、思量箇不思量底。僧曰、不思量底、如何思量。師云、非思量。

Once, when the Great Master Hongdao of Yaoshan was sitting [in meditation], a monk asked him, "What are you thinking of, [sitting there] so fixedly?"

The Master answered, "I'm thinking of not thinking."

The monk asked, "How do you think of not thinking?"

The Master answered, "Non-thinking."

*Supplementary notes to the translation*　　559

The monk's initial question to Yaoshan contains an implicit criticism of the practice of sitting in meditation; see "**sit fixedly**." Yaoshan's first answer might also be rendered, "I'm thinking the unthinkable," and his final remark could be read, "It isn't thinking"; the translation chosen here follows the usual Sōtō interpretation.

In the Buddhist tradition at large, the term "non-thinking" (*hi shiryō* 非思量; S. *acintayitvā*) indicates a mental state, or "sphere of cognition" (*kyōgai* 境界), that is "unconditioned" (*mui* 無爲) in the sense of being beyond language. This is explained, for example, in the *Sūtra of the Inconceivable Sphere of Cognition of a Buddha, as Explained by Mañjuśrī* (*Wenshushili suoshuo busiyi fo jingjie jing* 文殊師利所説不思議佛境界經, T.340.12:108a28-b3):

> 佛言、童子、無爲者非思量境界。文殊師利菩薩言、世尊、非思量境界者是佛境界。何以故。非思量境界中無有文字。無文字故、無所辯説。無所辯説故、絶諸言論。絶諸言論者、是佛境界也。

The Buddha said, "Young postulant, the unconditioned is the sphere of cognition that is non-thinking." Mañjuśrī Bodhisattva said, "World-Honored One, the sphere of cognition that is non-thinking is the sphere of cognition of a buddha. Why is that? Because within the sphere of cognition that is non-thinking there is no existence of scriptures. Because there is no existence of scriptures, there is no subject of eloquent speech. Because there is no subject of eloquent speech, verbal arguments are cut off. The cutting off of verbal arguments is the sphere of cognition of a buddha."

In the Zen tradition, the expression "non-thinking" is found in the *Inscription on Faith in Mind* (*Xinxin ming* 信心銘, T.2076.51:457b17) attributed to the Third Ancestor, Sengcan:

> 非思量處、識情難測。

[As for] the place of non-thinking, deluded consciousness finds [it] difficult to fathom.

The expression is best known, however, from the kōan "Yaoshan's not thinking."

**you're also like this, I'm also like this** (*nyo yaku nyo ze, go yaku nyo ze* 汝亦如是、吾亦如是): Words attributed to the Sixth Ancestor, Huineng 慧能, in a famous dialogue with Nanyue Huairang 南嶽懷讓 (677-744) that is cited throughout the *Shōbōgenzō*. The version recorded in Dōgen's *Shōbōgenzō* in Chinese script (*shinji Shōbōgenzō* 眞字正法眼藏, DZZ.5:178, case 101) reads as follows:

> 嶽山大慧禪師〈嗣曹溪、諱懷讓〉參六祖。祖曰、從什麼處來。師曰、嵩山安國師處來。祖曰、是什麼物恁麼來。師罔措。於是執侍八年、方省前話。乃告祖云、懷讓會得、當初來時、和尚接某甲、是什

麼物恁麼來。祖云、爾作麼生會。師曰、説似一物即不中。祖曰、還假修證否。師曰、修證即不無、染污即不得。祖曰、祇此不染污、是諸佛之所護念。汝亦如是、吾亦如是、乃至西天諸祖亦如是。

Chan Master Dahui of Mount Nanyue (descendant of Caoxi, named Huairang) visited the Sixth Ancestor. The Ancestor asked him, "Where do you come from?"

The Master said, "I come from the National Teacher An on Mount Song."

The Ancestor said, "**What thing is it that comes like this**?"

The Master was without means [to answer]. After attending [the Ancestor] for eight years, he finally understood the previous conversation. Thereupon, he announced to the Ancestor, "Huairang has understood what the Reverend put to me when I first came: 'What thing is it that comes like this?'"

The Ancestor asked, "How do you understand it?"

The Master replied, "To say it's like any thing wouldn't hit it." The Ancestor said, "Then does it depend on **practice and verification**?"

The Master answered, "It's not that it lacks practice and verification, but it can't be defiled by them."

The Ancestor said, "Just this '**not defiled**' is what the buddhas bear in mind. You're also like this, I'm also like this, and all the ancestors of Sindh in the West [i. e., India] are also like this."

In this dialogue, the expression, "You're also like this, I'm also like this" is clearly an affirmation of Huairang's awakening and suitability to serve as Huineng's dharma heir. What it means to be "like this" (*nyo ze* 如是), in this context, is to engage in practice and verification in a manner that is not defiled by attachment to it. For another version of the dialogue and a discussion of its overall meaning, see "**what thing is it that comes like this?**"

**Yunmen's three phrases** (*Unmon no sanku* 雲門の三句): *The Eye of Humans and Devas* (*Rentian yanmu* 人天眼目, T.2006.48:312a7-10), a collection of Zen lore compiled in 1188, contains the following entry under the heading "Yunmen Lineage" and the sub-heading "Three Phrases":

師示衆云、函蓋乾坤、目機銖兩、不渉萬縁。作麼生承當。衆無對。自代云、一鏃破三關。後來德山圓明密禪師、遂離其語爲三句。曰、函蓋乾坤句、截斷衆流句、隨波逐浪句。

The Master [Yunmen] addressed the assembly saying, "It boxes and covers heaven and earth; it eyeballs and estimates pennyweight and tael; it is not concerned with the myriad involvements. How do you take it?"

The assembly had no response.

He said on their behalf, "A single arrowhead pierces three barriers."

*Supplementary notes to the translation* 561

Later, Chan Master Yuanming Mi of Deshan by separating the words formed three phrases: the phrase "boxing and covering heaven and earth"; the phrase "cutting off all flows"; and the phrase "chasing the waves and following the billows."

What is odd about this account is that it actually gives two different versions of the "three phrases" of the Yunmen Lineage, one attributed to Yunmen Wenyan 雲門文偃 (864-949) himself, and another attributed to a disciple of his, Deshan Yuanmi 德山緣密 (dates unknown).

The biography of "Great Master Yuanmi Yuanming, Ninth Abbot of De-shan [Monastery] in Langzhou" in the *Jingde Era Record of the Transmission of the Flame* (*Jingde chuandeng lu* 景德傳燈錄, T.2076.51:384c22-25) says:

師上堂示衆曰、僧堂前事時人知有、佛殿後事作麼生。師又曰、德山有三句語。一句、函蓋乾坤。一句、隨波逐浪。一句、截斷衆流。

The Master [Deshan] addressed the assembly at a convocation in the dharma hall, saying, "When there is an event in front of the saṃgha hall, people know that it exists. What about an event in the rear of the buddha hall?"

The Master also said, "I, Deshan, have a saying in three phrases. One phrase is 'boxing and covering heaven and earth.' One phrase is 'chasing the waves and following the billows.' And one phrase is 'cutting off all flows.'"

This record attributes the three phrases to Deshan alone, without mentioning Yunmen.

Nevertheless, the same three phrases are attributed to Yunmen in an appendix to the *Extensive Record of Chan Master Yunmen Kuangzhen* (*Yunmen Kuangzhen chanshi guanglu* 雲門匡眞禪師廣錄T.1988.47:576b17-29), in a section entitled "Verse Commentary to Yunmen's Three Phrases, by his follower Great Master Yuanming, abbot of Deshan [Monastery]":

函蓋乾坤
　　　乾坤并萬象、地獄及天堂。物物皆眞現、頭頭總不傷。
截斷衆流
　　　堆山積岳來、一一盡塵埃。更擬論玄妙、氷消瓦解摧。
隨波逐浪
　　　辯口利舌問、高低總不虧。還如應病藥、診候在臨時。

"Boxing and covering heaven and earth."

Heaven and earth join together the **myriad forms**,
From the hells to the halls of heaven.
Every single thing has its real appearance,
And every single being is unharmed.

"Cutting off all flows."

> When high mountains and obstructing peaks come,
> Every single one is reduced to motes of dust.
> When, likewise, theories become abstruse,
> The ice melts and the bricks are pulled apart and smashed.

"Chasing the waves and following the billows."

> With an articulate mouth and eloquent tongue, he inquires;
> High or low notwithstanding, he is never deficient.
> His response is like a medicine that is appropriate to the disease;
> His diagnosis of the condition meets the needs of the occasion.

Whoever authored them, the meanings of the three phrases are far from clear, and Deshan's verse comments on them are of limited help.

The expression "box and cover" (*kangai* 函蓋), which appears in the first phrase, can be read as a compound verb that takes "heaven and earth" as its object, or it can be read as two nouns meaning "a box and its lid." Most interpreters go with the former reading; DDB (s.v. 三句), for example, translates the first phrase as "contains and includes the universe." ZGDJ (p. 77, s.v. うんもんさんく), however, glosses the first phrase as meaning that "there is a perfect fit between master and student in their question-and-answer exchange." That interpretation evidently takes the close way a box and its lid fit as a symbol of good communication between master and disciple. The expression "all flows" (*shuru* 衆流), which appears in the second phrase, is glossed in DDB (s.v. 三句) as "all flow of reincarnation" (*ruten* 流轉), but it could also be a reference to "worldly customs" (*zokuru* 俗流) or the "four raging currents" (*shi bōru* 四暴流) of desire (*yoku* 欲), existence (*u* 有), ignorance (*mumyō* 無明), and views (*ken* 見). Deshan's verse comments on the third phrase, "chasing the waves and following the billows," glosses it as a metaphor for skillful means.

"Yunmen's three phrases" became well known and were frequently raised as kōans by subsequent Zen masters and students, either singly or as a set. The biography of Senior Seat Rifang 日芳上座 (dates unknown) that appears in the *Additional Records of the Transmission of the Flame* (*Xu chuandeng lu* 續傳燈錄, T.2077.51:479b13-16) provides a good example of the latter:

僧問、如何是函蓋乾坤句。師竪起柱杖。僧曰、如何是截斷眾流句。師橫按拄杖、僧曰。如何是隨波逐浪句。師擲下拄杖。僧曰、三句外請師道。師便起去。

A monk asked, "What about the phrase 'boxing and covering heaven and earth'?"

The Master [Rifang] raised up his **staff**.

The monk said, "What about the phrase 'cutting off all flows'?"

The Master held his staff horizontally.

The monk said, "What about the phrase 'chasing the waves and following the billows'?"

The Master threw down his staff.

The monk said, "Please, Master, speak about what is apart from the three phrases."

The Master immediately got up and left.

# Works Cited

## Primary works

*Abhidharma-koṣa.* See *Apidamo jushe lun* 阿毘達磨俱舍論.

*Abhidharma-nyāyānusāra-śāstra.* See *Apidamo shun zhengli lun* 阿毘達磨順正理論.

*Abhidharma-vibhāṣa-śāstra.* See *Apitan piposha lun* 阿毘曇毘婆沙論.

*Abhiniṣkramaṇa-sūtra.* See *Fo benxing ji jing* 佛本行集經.

*Additional Biographies of Eminent Monks.* See *Xu gaoseng zhuan* 續高僧傳.

*Admonitions for the Chef.* See *Tenzo kyōkun* 典座教訓.

*Āgama of Combined Discourses.* See *Za ahan jing* 雜阿含經.

*Analects of Confucius.* See *Lunyu* 論語.

*Ancestors Hall Collection.* See *Zutang ji* 祖堂集.

*Ankokuron gokan yurai* 安國論御勘由來, NDGZ.

*Anthology of Commentaries on the Nirvāṇa Sūtra.* See *Da banniepan jing jijie* 大般涅槃經集解.

*Apidamo dapiposha lun* 阿毘達磨大毘婆沙論, T.1545.

*Apidamo jushe lun* 阿毘達磨俱舍論, T.1558.

*Apidamo shun zhengli lun* 阿毘達磨順正理論, T.1562.

*Apitan piposha lun* 阿毘曇毘婆沙論, T.1546.

*Artha-vargīya.* See *Yizu jing* 義足經.

*Asabashō* 阿娑縛抄, T.3190.

*Avataṃsaka-sūtra.* See *Da fangguang fo huayan jing* 大方廣佛華嚴經.

*Ayuwang jing* 阿育王經, T.2043.

*Azuma kagami* 吾妻鏡, Hayakawa Junzaburō 早川純三郎, editor.

"Baika shisho" 梅花嗣書, facsimile, ESST.4.

*Bailun shu* 百論疏, T.1827.

*Baizhang Huaihai chanshi yulu* 百丈懷海禪師語錄, *Sijia yulu* 四家語錄, ZZ.119, X.1321.

*Baojue Zuxin chanshi yulu* 寶覺祖心禪師語錄, ZZ.120, X.1343.

*Baoning Renyong chanshi yulu* 保寧仁勇禪師語錄, ZZ.120, X.1350.

*Baozang lun* 寶藏論, T.1857.

*Bendō hō* 辦道法. DZZ.6, Kosaka Kiyū 小坂機融, editor.

*Bendōwa* 辦道話 (1788 xylograph), facsimile, ESST.4.

*Bendōwa* 辦道話 (Shōbōji 正法寺 manuscript), facsimile, *Shōbōgenzō zatsubun: Shōbōji-bon.*

566 DŌGEN'S *SHŌBŌGENZŌ* VOLUME VIII

*Benevolent Kings Sūtra.* See *Renwang jing* 仁王經.

*Bhaiṣajyaguru-pūrva-praṇidhāna-sūtra.* See *Yaoshi benyuan jing* 藥師本願經.

*Biyan lu* 碧巖錄, T.2003.

*Blue Cliff Record.* See *Biyan lu* 碧巖錄.

*Book of Changes.* See *Zhouyi* 周易.

*Book of Liezi.* See *Liezi* 列子.

*Book of the Way and its Virtue.* See *Daode jing* 道德經.

*Bore boluomiduo xin jing* 般若波羅蜜多心經, T.251.

*Bore shin jing zhujie* 般若心經註解, ZZ.42, X.575.

*Brahmajāla-sūtra.* See *Fanwang pusa jie jing* 梵網菩薩戒經.

*Brahma's Net Bodhisattva Precepts Sūtra.* See *Fanwang pusa jie jing* 梵網菩薩戒經.

*Buddha Treasury Sūtra.* See *Fozang jing* 佛藏經.

*Buddhāvataṃsaka-sūtra.* See *Da fangguang fo huayan jing* 大方廣佛華嚴經.

"Busshō" 佛性 (Ejō 懷奘 holograph), facsimile, ESST-D.

*Busso shōden bosatsu kai kyōju kaimon* 佛祖正傳菩薩戒教授戒文, DZZ.6, Suzuki Kakuzen 鈴木格禅, editor.

*Busso shōden bosatsu kai sahō* 佛祖正傳菩薩戒作法, DZZ.6, Suzuki Kakuzen 鈴木格禅, editor.

*Busso shōdenki* 佛祖正傳記. ZSZ.Jishi-Shiden 寺誌・史傳.

*Buxu gaosengzhuan* 補續高僧傳, ZZ.134, X.1524.

*Cantong qi* 參同契, *Jingde chuandeng lu* 景德傳燈錄, T.2076.

*Caoan ge* 草庵歌. See *Shitou heshang caoan ge* 石頭和尚草庵歌.

*Chang ahan jing* 長阿含經, T.1.

*Chanlin leiju* 禪林類聚, ZZ.117, X.1299.

*Chanlin paoxun* 禪林寶訓, T.2022.

*Chanlin sengbao juan* 禪林僧寶傳, ZZ.137, X.1560.

*Chanmen zhuzushi jisong* 禪門諸祖師偈頌, ZZ.116, X.1298.

*Chanyuan qinggui* 禪苑清規, ZZ.111, X.1245.

*Chanyuan zhuquan ji douxu* 禪源諸詮集都序, T.2015.

*Chanzong songgu lianzhu tongji* 禪宗頌古聯珠通集, ZZ.115, X.1295.

*Chanzong zaduhai* 禪宗雜毒海, ZZ.114, X.1278.

*Chart of the Master-Disciple Succession of the Chan Gate that Transmits the Mind Ground in China.* See *Zhonghua chuanxindi chanmen shizi chengxi tu* 中華傳心地禪門師資承襲圖.

*Chengshi lun* 成實論, T.1646.

*Cheng weishi lun* 成唯識論, T.1585.

*Chiji shingi* 知事清規, See *Eiheiji chiji shingi* 永平寺知事清規.

*Chinsim Chiksŏl* 眞心直説, T.2019A.

*Chixiu Baizhang qinggui* 勅修百丈清規, T.2025.

*Chrestomathy from the Ancestors Hall*. See *Zuting shiyuan* 祖庭事苑.

*Chuanfa zhengzong ji* 傳法正宗記, T.2078.

*Chuanfa zhengzong lun* 傳法正宗論, T.2080.

*Chuanxin fayao* 傳心法要, T.2012A.

*Chuci* 楚辞, KR.4a0001.

*Chunqiu zuozhuan* 春秋左傳, KR.1e0001.

*Chushi fanqi chanshi yulu* 楚石梵琦禪師語録, ZZ.124, X.1420.

*Cishou huaishen chanshi guanglu* 慈受懷深禪師廣録, ZZ.126, X.1451.

*Classic of Filial Piety*. See *Xiao jing* 孝經.

*Collated Essentials of the Five Flame Records*. See *Wudeng huiyuan* 五燈會元.

*Collected Records of Chan Master Fozhao Deguang*. See *Fuzhao Deguang chanshi zouduilu* 佛照德光禪師奏對録.

*Collection of the Essential Teachings of Our Lineage*. See *Zongmen tongyao ji* 宗門統要集.

*Collection of Verse Comments on Old Cases of the Sŏn*. See *Sŏnmun yŏmsong chip* 禪門拈頌集.

*Commander of the Barrier*. See *Guanlingzi* 關令子.

*Commentary on the Procedures of the Four-Part Vinaya*. See *Sifen lü xingshi chao* 四分律行事鈔.

*Commentary on the Sūtra of Humane Kings*. See *Renwang huguo bore boluomiduo jing shu* 仁王護國般若波羅蜜多經疏.

*Commentary on the Vimalakīrti Sūtra*. See *Weimojing chao* 維摩經抄.

*Commentary on the Vinaya Pratimokṣa*. See *Lü jieben shu* 律戒本疏.

*Comments on the "Collection of Gems of Wisdom from All Quarters"*. See *Nian Bafang Zhuyu Ji* 拈八方珠玉集.

*Compendium of Meanings of the Great Vehicle*. See *Dasheng yi zhang* 大乘義章.

*Complete Chronicle of the Buddhas and Ancestors*. See *Fozu tongji* 佛祖統紀.

*Congrong Hermitage Record*. See *Congrong lu* 從容録.

*Congrong lu* 從容録, T.2004.

*Continued Transmission of the Flame*. See *Xu chuandeng lu* 續傳燈録.

*Da banniepan jing* 大般涅槃經, T.374.

*Da banniepan jing jijie* 大般涅槃經集解, T.1763.

*Da baoji jing* 大寶積經, T.310.

*Da biqiu sanqian weiyi* 大比丘三千威儀 T.1470.

*Da bore boluomiduo jing* 大般若波羅蜜多經, T.220.

*Da fangdeng daji jing* 大方等大集經, T.397.

*Da fangguang baoqie jing* 大方廣寶篋經, T.462.

*Da fangguang fo huayan jing* 大方廣佛華嚴經, T.278.

*Da fangguang yuanjue xiuduoluo liaoyi jing lüeshu* 大方廣圓覺修多羅了義經略疏, T.1795.

*Dafan tianwang wen fo jueyi jing* 大梵天王問佛決疑經, ZZ.87, X.26.

"Da Fu shumi dier shu" 答富樞密第二書, *Dahui yulu* 大慧語錄, T.1998A.

"Dahui Pujue chansi taming" 大慧普覺禪師塔銘, *Dahui Pujue chansi yulu* 大慧普覺禪師語錄, T.1998A.

*Dahui Pujue chanshi yulu* 大慧普覺禪師語錄, T.1998A.

*Dahui Puzue chanshi zongmen wuku* 大慧普覺禪師宗門武庫, T.1998B.

"Daigo" 大悟 (Ōsu Bunko 大須文庫 manuscript), facsimile, Ishii Shūdō 石井修道, editor, 2015b.

*Dahui yulu* 大慧語錄. See *Dahui Pujue chanshi yulu* 大慧普覺禪師語錄.

*Daji jing* 大集經, See *Da fangdeng daji jing* 大方等大集經.

*Damamūka-nidāna-sūtra*. See *Xianyu jing* 賢愚經.

*Daming gaoseng zhuan* 大明高僧傳, T.2062.

*Daode jing* 道德經, KR.5c0046.

*Dapin bore jing* 大品般若經, T.223.

*Da piposha lun* 大毘婆沙論. See *Apidamo da piposha lun* 阿毘達磨大毘婆沙論.

*Daśabhūmika-bhāṣya*. See *Shidi jing lun* 十地經論.

*Da sazhe niqianzi suoshuo jing* 大薩遮尼乾子所説經, T.272.9.

*Dasheng bensheng xindi guan jing* 大乘本生心地觀經, T.159.

*Dasheng qishin lun* 大乘起信論, T.1666.

*Dasheng ru lengqie jing* 大乘入楞伽經, T.672.

*Dasheng suizhuan xuanshuo zhufa jing* 大乘隨轉宣説諸法經, T.652.

*Dasheng yi zhang* 大乘義章, T.1851.

*Dasheng zhuangyan jing lun* 大乘莊嚴經論, T.1604.

*Datang daci'ensi sanzang fashi chuan* 大唐大慈恩寺三藏法師傳, T.2053.

*Datang xiyuji* 大唐西域記, T.2087.

*Dazhidu lun* 大智度論, T.1509.

*Da zhuangyan jing* 大莊嚴經. See *Fangguang da zhuangyan jing* 方廣大莊嚴經.

*Da zhauanyan lun jing* 大莊嚴論經, T.201.

*Denkōroku* 傳光錄, T.2585.

*Dharmaguptaka-vinaya.* See *Sifen lü* 四分律.

*Dharmapāda.* See *Faju jing* 法句經; *Faju piyu jing* 法句譬喻經.

*Dharma Phrase Sūtra.* See *Faju jing* 法句經.

*Dharma Treasure Platform Sūtra of the Sixth Ancestor.* See *Liuzu dashi fabaotan jing* 六祖大師法寶壇經.

*Diamond Prajñā Sūtra.* See *Jingang bore boluomi jing* 金剛般若波羅蜜經.

*Diamond Sūtra.* See *Jingang bore boluomi jing* 金剛般若波羅蜜經.

*Dīrghāgama.* See *Chang ahan jing* 長阿含經.

*Discourse Record of Chan Master Baojue Zuxin.* See *Baojue Zuxin chanshi yulu* 寶覺祖心禪師語錄.

*Discourse Record of Chan Master Benji of Mount Cao in Muzhou.* See *Muzhou Caoshan Benji chanshi yulu* 撫州曹山本寂禪師語錄.

*Discourse Record of Chan Master Dahui Pujue.* See *Dahui Pujue chanshi yulu* 大慧普覺禪師語錄, T.1998A.

*Discourse Record of Chan Master Fayan.* See *Fayan chanshi yulu* 法演禪師語錄.

*Discourse Record of Chan Master Huanglong Huinan.* See *Huanglong Huinan chanshi yulu* 黃龍慧南禪師語錄.

*Discourse Record of Chan Master Huihui of Jingci.* See *Jingci Huihui chanshi yulu* 淨慈慧暉禪師語錄.

*Discourse Record of Chan Master Liangjie of Mount Dong in Ruizhou.* See *Ruizhou Dongshan Liangjie chanshi yulu* 瑞州洞山良价禪師語錄.

*Discourse Record of Chan Master Lingyou of Mount Wei in Tanzhou.* See *Tanzhou Weishan Lingyou chanshi yulu* 潭州潙山靈祐禪師語錄.

*Discourse Record of Chan Master Linji Huizhao of Zhenzhou.* See *Zhenzhou Linji Huizhao chanshi yulu* 鎮州臨濟慧照禪師語錄.

*Discourse Record of Chan Master Mazu Daoyi of Jiangxi.* See *Jiangxi Mazu Daoyi chanshi yulu* 江西馬祖道一禪師語錄.

*Discourse Record of Chan Master Mingjue.* See *Mingjue chanshi yulu* 明覺禪師語錄.

*Discourse Record of Chan Master Wuben of Mount Dong in Junzhou.* See *Junzhou Dongshan Wuben chanshi yulu* 筠州洞山悟本禪師語錄.

*Discourse Record of Chan Master Yuanwu Foguo.* See *Yuanwu Foguo chanshi yulu* 圓悟佛果禪師語錄.

*Discourse Record of Chan Master Yuanzheng of Mount Cao in Muzhou.* See *Muzhou Caoshan Yuanzheng chanshi yulu* 撫州曹山元證禪師語錄.

*Discourse Record of Layman Pang.* See *Pang jushi yulu* 龐居士語錄.

*Discourse Record of Reverend Longmen Foyan of Shuzhou.* See *Shuzhou Longmen Foyan heshang yulu* 舒州龍門佛眼和尚語錄.

*Discourse Record of Reverend Rujing.* See *Rujing heshang yulu* 如淨和尚語錄.

*Discourse Record of Reverend Yangqi Fanghui* . See *Yangqi Fanghui heshang yulu* 楊岐方會和尚語錄.

*Discourse Record of Reverend Xutang.* See *Xutang heshang yulu* 虛堂和尚語錄.

*Discourse Record of Reverend Zhaozhou.* See *Zhaozhou heshang yulu* 趙州和尚語錄.

*Discourse Record of Xuefeng.* See *Xuefeng yulu* 雪峰語錄.

*Discourse Records of Past Venerables.* See *Guzunsu yulu* 古尊宿語錄.

*Dongming ji* 洞冥記, KR.310097.

*Dōgen oshō kōroku* 道元和尚廣録, DZZ.3–4, Kagamishima Genryū 鏡島元隆, editor.

*Dōgen oshō kōroku* 道元和尚廣録 (Monkaku 門鶴 manuscript), facsimile, Ōtani Tetsuo 大谷哲夫 and Watanabe Kenshū 渡部賢宗, editors.

*Dongshan dashi yulu.* See *Dongshan Wupen chanshi yulu* 洞山悟本禪師語錄.

*Dongshan Wupen chanshi yulu* 洞山悟本禪師語錄, T.1986A.

*Dongshan yulu* 洞山語錄. See *Dongshan Wupen chanshi yulu* 洞山悟本禪師語錄.

*Eihei Gen zenji goroku* 永平元禪師語録, DZZ.5, Sakai Tokugen 酒井得元, editor.

*Eiheiji chiji shingi* 永平寺知事清規, DZZ.6, Kosaka Kiyū 小坂機融, editor.

*Eiheiji koku chiji mon* 永平寺告知事文, DZZ.7, Itō Shūken 伊藤秀憲, editor.

*Eihei kōroku* 永平廣録. See *Dōgen oshō kōroku* 道元和尚廣録.

*Eihei kōroku* 永平廣録 (1672 xylograph), facsimile, Ōtani Tetsuo 大谷哲夫, editor.

*Eihei Monastery Rules of Purity for Stewards.* See *Eiheiji chiji shingi* 永平寺知事清規.

*Ekottarāgama.* See *Zengyi ahan jing* 增一阿含經.

*Empty Hall Collection.* See *Xutang ji* 虛堂集.

*Erru sixing lun* 二入四行論, Yanagida Seizan 柳田聖山, editor, 1969.

*Essentials for Monastics.* See *Shukke taikō* 出家大綱.

*Explanation of Phrases from the Lotus Sūtra.* See *Lianhua jing jujie* 法華經句解.

*Explanation of the Profound Meaning of the Lotus.* See *Fahua xuanyi shiqian* 法華玄義釋籤.

*Extended Collection of the Essential Teachings of Our Lineage.* See *Zongmen tongyao zhengxu ji* 宗門統要正續集.

*Extensive Record of Chan Master Hongzhi.* See *Hongzhi chanshi guanglu* 宏智禪師廣錄, T.2001.

*Extensive Record of Chan Master Xuansha Shibei.* See *Xuansha Shibei chanshi guanglu* 玄沙師備禪師廣錄.

*Extensive Record of Chan Master Yongjue Yuanxian.* See *Yongjue Yuanxian chanshi guanglu* 永覺元賢禪師廣錄.

*Extensive Record of Chan Master Yunmen Kuangzhen.* See *Yunmen Kuangzhen chanshi guanglu* 雲門匡眞禪師廣錄.

*Eye of Humans and Devas.* See *Rentian yanmu* 人天眼目.

*Fahua chanfa* 法華懺法, T.2417.

*Fahua cidi chumen* 法界次第初門, T.1925.

*Fahua wenju* 法華文句. See *Miaofa lianhua jing wenju* 妙法蓮華經文句.

*Fahua wenju ji* 法華文句記, T.1719.

*Fahua xuanyi* 妙法玄義. See *Miaofa lianhua jing xuanyi* 妙法蓮華經玄義.

*Fahua xuanyi shiqian* 法華玄義釋籤, T.1717.

*Fahua yishu* 法華義疏, T.1721.

*Fahua zhuanji* 法華傳記, T.2068.

*Fajie cidi chumen* 法界次第初門, T.1925.

*Faju jing* 法句經, T.210.

*Faju piyu jing* 法句譬喻經, T.211.

*Fangguang da zhuangyan jing* 方廣大莊嚴經, T.187.

*Fanwang jing* 梵網經, T.1484.

*Fanwang pusa jie jing* 梵網菩薩戒經. See *Fanwang jing* 梵網經.

*Fayan chanshi yulu* 法演禪師語錄, T.1995.

*Fayuan zhulin* 法苑珠林, T.2122.

"Fengling song" 風鈴頌, *Rujing heshang yulu* 如淨和尚語錄, T.2002A.

*Fenyang yulu* 汾陽語錄, T.1992.

*Flower Garland Sūtra.* See *Da fangguang fo huayan jing* 大方廣佛華嚴經.

*Fo benxing ji jing* 佛本行集經, T.190.

*Foguo chanshi yulu* 佛國禪師語錄, T.2551.

*Foguo ji* 佛國記. See *Gaoseng Faxian zhuan* 高僧法顯傳.

*Foming jing* 佛名經, T.441.

*Fomu dakongque mingwang jing* 佛母大孔雀明王經, T.982.

*Fo sheng daolitian wei mu shuo fa jing* 佛昇忉利天爲母説法經, T.815.

*Fo shuo ba da lingta minghao jing* 佛説八大靈塔名號經, T.1685.

*Fo shuo guan wuliang shou jing shu* 佛説觀無量壽經疏, T.1750.

# 572 DŌGEN'S *SHŌBŌGENZŌ* VOLUME VIII

*Fo shuo hai ba de jing* 佛説海八德經, T.35.

*Fo shuo hailongwang jing* 佛説海龍王經, T.598.

*Fo shuo shili jing* 佛說十力經, T.780.

*Fo yijiao jing* 佛遺教經, T.389.

*Fozang jing* 佛藏經, T.653.

*Fozhao chanshi zoudui lu* 佛照禪師奏對録, *Guzunsu yulu* 古尊宿語録, ZZ.118, X.1315.

*Fozhi biqiu liuwu tu* 佛制比丘六物圖, T.1900.

*Fozu tongji* 佛祖統紀, T.2035.

*Fuzhao Deguang chanshi zouduilu* 佛照德光禪師奏對録, *Guzunsu yulu* 古尊宿語録, ZZ.118, X.1315.

*Fu fazang yinyuan zhuan* 付法藏因緣傳, T.2058.

*Fukaki hōshiden* 不可棄法師傳, DNBZ.115.

*Fukan zazen gi* 普勧坐禪儀, DZZ.5, Suzuki Kakuzen 鈴木格禅, editor.

*Fukan zazen gi senjutsu yurai* 普勧坐禪儀撰述由來, DZZ.5, Suzuki Kakuzen 鈴木格禅, editor.

*Fushukuhanpō* 赴粥飯法, DZZ.6, Kosaka Kiyū 小坂機融, editor.

*Fuzi* 傅子 See *Yilin* 意林.

*Gakudō yōjinshū* 學道用心集, DZZ.5, Sakurai Shūyū 桜井秀雄, editor.

*Gaoseng Faxian zhuan* 高僧法顯傳, T.2085.

*Gateless Barrier*. See *Wumen guan* 無門關.

*Genben shuo yiqie youbu baiyi jiemo* 根本説一切有部百一羯磨, T1453.

*Genben shuo yiqie youbu pinaiye zashi* 根本説一切有部毘奈耶雜事, T.1451.

"Genjō kōan kikigaki" 現成公按聞書, *Shōbōgenzō kikigakishō* 正法眼藏聽書抄, facsimile, ESST.11.

*Genkō shakusho* 元亨釋書, DNBZ.101.

*Giso rokujō* 義楚六帖, ZTS.6B.

*Golden Light Sūtra*. See *Jin guangming zuishengwang jing* 金光明最勝王經.

*Goyuigon kiroku* 御遺言記録, DZZ.7, Ishikawa Rikizan 石川力山, editor.

*Goyuigon kiroku* 御遺言記録 (Eifukuan 永福庵 manuscript), facsimile, Ishii Shūdō 石井修道, editor, 2015b.

"Gozan jissatsu zu" 五山十刹圖, *Zengaku daijiten* 禅学大辞典, *Bekkan* 別巻.

*Great Adornment Discourse Sūtra*. See *Da zhauanyan lun jing* 大莊嚴論經.

*Great Calming and Insight*. See *Mohe zhiguan* 摩訶止觀.

*Great Master Yongjia Zhenjue's Song of Realizing the Way*. See *Yongjia Zhenjue dashi zhengdao ge* 永嘉眞覺大師證道歌.

*Great Perfection of Wisdom Sūtra.* See *Da bore boluomiduo jing* 大般若波羅蜜多經.

*Great Treatise.* See *Dazhidu lun* 大智度論.

*Great Tang Record of Travels to Western Lands.* See *Datang xiyu ji* 大唐西域記.

*Grouped Sayings from the Chan Tradition.* See *Chanlin leiju* 禪林類聚.

*Grove Record.* See *Linjian lu* 林間錄.

*Guanghongming ji* 廣弘明集, T.2103.

*Guangqingliang chuan* 廣清涼傳, T.2099.

*Guanlingzi* 關令子. Not extant.

*Guan wuliangshou jing* 觀無量壽經, T.365.

*Guanzi* 管子, KR.3c0001.

*Guihai yuheng zhi* 桂海虞衡志, KR.2k0115.

"Gujin dayi" 古今大意, *Jingde chuandeng lu* 景德傳燈錄, T.2076.

"Guijing wen" 龜鏡文, *Chanyuan qinggui* 禪苑清規, ZZ.111, X.1245.

*Gulin qingmao chanshi shiyi jisong* 古林清茂禪師拾遺偈頌, ZZ.123, X.1413.

*Guoqing bailu* 國清百錄, T.1934.

*Guoqu xianzai yinguo jing* 過去現在因果經, T.189.

*Guoqu zhuangyanjie qian foming jing* 過去莊嚴劫千佛名經, T.446.

*Guzunsu yulu* 古尊宿語錄, ZZ.118, X.1315.

*Hanyuan xinshu* 翰苑新書, KR.3k0038.

*Heart Sūtra.* See *Bore boluomiduo xin jing* 般若波羅蜜多心經.

*Hengchuan xinggong chanshi yulu* 橫川行珙禪師語錄, ZZ.123, X.1411.

*Heroic March Sūtra.* See *Shoulengyan jing* 首楞嚴經.

*Hidden Meaning of the Lotus Sūtra.* See *Miaofa lianhua jing xuanyi* 妙法蓮華經玄義.

*Hōkyōki* 寶慶記, DZZ.7, Suzuki Kakuzen 鈴木格禪, editor.

*Hōkyōki* 寶慶記 (Zenkyūin 全久院 manuscript), facsimile, Ishii Shūdō 石井修道, editor, 2015b.

*Hongzhi chanshi guanglu* 宏智禪師廣錄, T.2001.

*Hongzhilu* 宏智錄 (ca. 1201 xylograph), facsimile, Ishii Shūdō 石井修道, editor, 1984–1986.

*Hōsakushō* 寶册鈔, T.2453.

*Hotsu bodaishinron kuketsu* 菩提心論口決, T.2293.

*Hotsu ganmon* 發願文, DZZ.7, Itō Shūken 伊藤秀憲, editor.

*Huainan zi* 淮南子, KR.3j0010.

*Huanglong huinan chanshi yulu* 黃龍慧南禪師語錄, T.1993.

*Huanglongshan Nan chanshi shuchi ji* 黃龍山南禪師書尺集, ZT.2.

*Huayan jing* 華嚴經. See *Da fangguang fo huayan jing* 大方廣佛華嚴經.

*Huayan jing tanxuan ji* 華嚴經探玄記, T.1733.

*Hufa lun* 護法論, T.2114.

*Hyakurenshō* 百錬抄, *Shintei zōho kokushi taikei.*

*Imperial Edition of Baizhang's Rules of Purity.* See *Chixiu Baizhang qinggui* 勅修百丈清規.

*Incremental by One Āgama.* See *Zengyi ahan jing* 增一阿含經.

*Inscription on Faith in Mind.* See *Xinxin ming* 信心銘.

*Jiangxi Mazu Daoyi chanshi yulu* 江西馬祖道一禪師語錄, ZZ.119, X.1321.

*Jianzhong Jingguo Era Continued Record of the Flame.* See *Jianzhong jingguo xudeng lu* 建中靖國續燈錄.

*Jianzhong jingguo xudeng lu* 建中靖國續燈錄, ZZ.136, X.1556.

*Jiatai pudeng lu* 嘉泰普燈錄, ZZ.137, X.1559.

*Ji gujin fodao lunheng* 集古今佛道論衡, T.2104.

*Jingang bore boluomi jing* 金剛般若波羅蜜經, T235.

*Jingang jing* 金剛經. See *Jingang bore boluomi jing* 金剛般若波羅蜜經.

*Jingang sanmei jing* 金剛三昧經, T.273.

*Jingci Huihui chanshi yulu* 淨慈慧暉禪師語錄, ZZ.124, X.1428.

*Jingde chuandeng lu* 景德傳燈錄, T.2076.

*Jinglü yixiang* 經律異相, T.2121.

*Jin guangming jing* 金光明經, T.663.

*Jin guangming zuishengwang jing* 金光明最勝王經, T.665.

"Jinshang shu" 進上書, *Jiatai Pudeng lu* 嘉泰普燈錄, ZZ.137, X.1559.

*Jinshu* 晉書, KR.2a0015.

*Ji Ryōnen dōsha hōgo* 示了然道者法語, facsimile, Ishii Shūdō 石井修道, editor, 2015b.

*Jukakushin kaimyaku* 授覺心戒脈, DZZ.6, Suzuki Kakuzen 鈴木格禪, editor.

*Junzhou Dongshan Wuben chanshi yulu* 筠州洞山悟本禪師語錄, T.1986A.

*Jūroku rakan genzuiki* 十六羅漢現瑞記, DZZ.7, Itō Shūken 伊藤秀憲, editor.

*Kaimokushō* 開目抄, NDGZ; T.2689.

*Kairitsu denraiki* 戒律傳來記, T.2347.

*Kaiyuan shijiao lu* 開元釋教錄, T.2154.

*Kaizan gyōjō narabi ashikaga reifu* 開山行狀并足利靈府, Nakao Ryōshin 中尾良信, 1987b.

## Works cited

*Kanke kōshū* 菅家後集, *Gunsho ruijū* 羣書類從 9.

*Karuṇā-puṇḍarīka-sūtra*. See *Peihua jing* 悲華經.

*Kenzeiki* 建撕記 (Zuichō 瑞長 manuscript; and 1754 xylograph), Kawamura Kōdō 河村孝道, editor, 1975.

*Konkōmyō saishōōkyō chūshaku* 金光明最勝王經註釋, T.2197.

*Konkōmyō saishōōkyō genso* 金光明最勝王經玄樞, T.2196.

*Kōroku* 廣録. See *Dōgen oshō kōroku* 道元和尚廣録.

*Kōzen gokokuro* 興禪護國論, T.2543.

*Kujakkyō ongi* 孔雀經音義, T.2244.

*Kyōju kaimon* 教授戒文. See *Busso shōden bosatsu kai kyōju kaimon* 佛祖正傳菩薩戒教授戒文.

*Kyōkijikokushō* 教機時國抄, NDGZ.

*Lalitavistara*. See *Fangguang da zhuangyan jing* 方廣大莊嚴經.

*Laṅkāvatāra-sūtra*. See *Ru lengqie jing* 入楞伽經; *Dasheng ru lengqie jing* 大乘入楞伽經.

*Laozi huahu jing* 老子化胡經. Not extant.

*Lengqie abaduoluo bao jing* 楞伽阿跋多羅寶經, T.670.

*Lengqie jing* 楞伽經, T.671.

*Lengqie jing* 楞伽經, See *Dasheng ru Lengqie jing* 大乘入楞伽經; *Ru lengqie jing* 入楞伽經.

*Liandeng huiyao* 聯燈會要, ZZ.136, X.1557.

*Liangshu* 梁書, KR.2a0018.

*Liang zhao Fu dashi song Jingang bore jing* 梁朝傅大師頌金剛般若經, T.2732.

*Lianhua jing jujie* 法華經句解, ZZ.48, X.604.

*Lianhuamian jing* 蓮華面經, T.386.

*Liaoan qingyu chanshi yulu* 了菴清欲禪師語, ZZ.123, X.1414.

*Lie xian zhuan* 列仙傳, KR.5a0306.

*Liezi* 列子, KR.5c0124.

*Linjian lu* 林間録, ZZ.148, X.1624.

*Linji lu* 臨濟録, T.1985.

*Lin jing* 麟經. See *Chunqiu zuozhuan* 春秋左傳.

*Liu tao* 六韜, KR.3b0002.

*Liuzu dashi fabaotan jing* 六祖大師法寶壇經, T.2008.

*Liuzu tanjing* 六祖壇經, T.2008.

*Lotus Sūtra*, See *Miaofa lianhua jing* 妙法蓮華經.

*Lü jieben shu* 律戒本疏, T.2788.

*Lunyu* 論語, KR.1h0005.

*Lüezhu jinglun nianfo famen wangsheng jingtuji juanshang* 略諸經論念佛法門往生淨土集卷上, T.2826.

*Lüshi chunqiu* 呂氏春秋, KR.3j0009.

*Lüxiang gantong zhuan* 律相感通傳, T.1898.

*Lüzong xinxue mingju* 律宗新學名句, ZZ.105, X.1107.

*Madhyamāgama*. See *Zhong ahan jing* 中阿含經.

*Mahā-kāruṇā-sūtra*. See *Peihua jing* 悲華經.

*Mahā prajñā-pāramitā sūtra*. See *Da bore poluomiduo jing* 大般若波羅蜜多經.

*Mahāsāṃghika Vinaya*. See *Mohesengqi lü* 摩訶僧祇律.

*Mahāsaṃnipāta-sūtra*. See *Da fangguang baoqie jing* 大方廣寶篋經.

*Mahāvibhāṣa*. See *Apidamo dapiposha lun* 阿毘達磨大毘婆沙論.

*Mahāyāna Awakening of Faith*. See *Dasheng qixin lun* 大乘起信論.

*Maka hannya haramitsu monge* 摩訶般若波羅蜜聞解, SCZ.1.

*Master Lü's Spring and Autumn Annals*. See *Lüshi chunqiu* 呂氏春秋.

*Mazu Daoyi chanshi yulu* 馬祖道一禪師語錄, ZZ.119, X.1321.

"Memorial to the Throne on the Essence of Mind." See *Xinyao qian* 心要牋.

*Mengqiu* 蒙求, KR.3k0010.

*Miaofa lianhua jing* 妙法蓮華經, T.262.

*Miaofa lianhua jing wenju* 妙法蓮華經文句, T.1718.

*Miaofa lianhua jing xuanyi* 妙法蓮華經玄義, T.1716.

*Middle-Length Āgama*. See *Zhong ahan jing* 中阿含經.

*Miji lishi daquan shenwang jing ji song* 密跡力士大權神王經偈頌, T.1688.

*Mind-King Inscription* . See *Xin wang ming* 心王銘.

*Mingjue chanshi yulu* 明覺禪師語錄, T.1996.

*Mingzhou Damei Fachang chanshi lu* 明州大梅法常禪師錄, *Kanazawa bunko shiryō zensho* 金沢文庫資料全書 1.

*Mohe bore boluomi jing* 摩訶般若波羅蜜經, T.223.

*Mohe Amituo jing zhonglun* 摩訶阿彌陀經衷論, ZZ.32, X401.

*Mohemoye jing* 摩訶摩耶經, T.383.

*Mohesengqi lü* 摩訶僧祇律, T.1425.

*Mohe zhiguan* 摩訶止觀, T.1911.

*Mon'yōki* 門葉記, T.3216.

*Most Excellent King Sūtra*. See *Jin guangming zuishengwang jing* 金光明最勝王經.

*Mūla-sarvāstivāda-vinaya*. See *Pinaiye zashi* 毘奈耶雜事.

*Mūla-sarvāstivāda-vinaya-vibhaṅga*. See *Genben shuo yiqie youbu pinaiye* 根本説一切有部毘奈耶.

*Myōhō rengekyō shakumon* 妙法蓮華經釋文, T.2189.

*Myōzen gusoku kaichō* 明全具足戒牒, SK.1.

*Myōzen kaichō okugaki* 明全戒牒奥書, DZZ.7, Ishikawa Rikizan 石川力山, editor.

*Myōzen oshō ryakuden* 明全和尚略傳, facsimile, ESST-D.

*Muzhou Caoshan Benji chanshi yulu* 撫州曹山本寂禪師語錄, T.1987B.

*Muzhou Caoshan Yuanzheng chanshi yulu* 撫州曹山元證禪師語錄, T.1987A.

*Naishō buppō sōshō kechimyakufu* 内證佛法相承血脈譜, *Dengyō daishi zenshū* 傳教大師全集 1.

*Nanyang heshang tan yu* 南陽和尚壇語, B.25; Hu Shih 胡適, editor, 1930.

*Nanyue Lanzan hoshang ge* 南嶽懶瓚和尚歌, *Jingde chuandeng lu* 景德傳燈錄, T.2076.

*Nanzong dunjiao zuishang Dasheng mohe boruo boluomi jing Liuzu Huineng Dashi yu Shaozhou Dafansi shifa tan jing* 南宗頓教最上大乘摩訶般若波羅蜜經六祖慧能大師於韶州大梵寺施法壇經, T.2007.

*Neishao zhong chanshi yulu* 内紹種禪師語錄, CBETA.J.B306.

*Nian Bafang Zhuyu Ji* 拈八方珠玉集, ZZ.119, X.1310.

*Ni jiemo* 尼羯磨, T.1810.

*Nirvāṇa Sūtra*. See *Da banniepan jing* 大般涅槃經.

*Nittō guhō junrei gyōki* 入唐求法巡禮行記, B.95.

"Ode to the Wind Chime" See *Fengling song* 風鈴頌.

*One Hundred Records of Guoqing*. See *Guoqing bailu* 國清百錄.

*Pang jushi yulu* 龐居士語錄, ZZ.120, X.1336.

*Peihua jing* 悲華經, T.157.

*Pearl String Collection of Verses on Old Cases from the Chan Lineage*. See *Chanzong songgu lianzhu tongji* 禪宗頌古聯珠通集.

*Perfection of Wisdom Sūtra*. See *Xiaopin bore boluomi jing* 小品般若波羅蜜經.

*Pinaiye zashi* 毘奈耶雜事, T.1451.

*Piposha lun* 毘婆沙論. See *Apidamo da piposha lun* 阿毘達磨大毘婆沙論.

*Platform Sūtra* (Dunhuang manuscript). See *Nanzong dunjiao zuishang Dasheng mohe boruo boluomi jing Liuzu Huineng Dashi yu Shaozhou Dafansi shifa tan jing* 南宗頓教最上大乘摩訶般若波羅蜜經六祖慧能大師於韶州大梵寺施法壇經.

*Platform Sūtra* (Yuan-dynasty edition). See *Liuzu dashi fabaotan jing* 六祖大師法寶壇經, T.2008.

578 DŌGEN'S *SHŌBŌGENZŌ* VOLUME VIII

*Pointers for Regulating the Mind in Seated Meditation.* See *Zazen yōjin ki* 坐禪用心記.

*Preface to the Collected Writings on the Source of Chan.* See *Chanyuan zhuquan ji douxu* 禪源諸詮集都序.

*Profound Commentary on the Vimalakīrti Sūtra.* See *Weimojing xuanshu* 維摩經玄疏.

*Proper Deportment of Jeta Grove.* See *Qiyuan chengyi* 祇園正儀.

*Pusa dichi jing* 菩薩地持經, T.1581.

*Putidamo Nanzong ding shifei lun* 菩提達摩南宗定是非論, B.142.

*Qian shou qian yan guanshiyin pusa dayuanman wuai dabeixin tuoluoni jing* 千手千眼觀世音菩薩廣大圓滿無礙大悲心陀羅尼經, T.1060.

*Qianshouyan dabeixin zhou xingfa* 千手眼大悲心呪行法, T.1950.

*Qingjing faxing jing* 清淨法行經 (partial), Ochiai Toshinori 落合俊典, editor.

*Qinglong Commentary.* See *Yuzhu Gingang jing shu xuanyan* 御注金剛經疏宣演.

*Qingyi lu* 請益錄, ZZ.117, X.1307.

*Qingyi Record.* See *Qingyi lu* 請益錄.

*Qiyuan chengyi* 祇園正儀, ZZ.111, X.1233.

*Ratnakūṭa-sūtra.* See *Ta baoji jing* 大寶積經.

*Record of Buddhist Countries.* See *Foguo ji* 佛國記.

"Record of Deeds." See *Xingye ji* 行業記.

*Record of Seeking the Profound [Meaning] of the Flower Garland Sūtra.* See *Huayan jing tanxuan ji* 華嚴經探玄記.

*Record of the Teachings and Career of the Sage of Siming.* See *Siming zunzhe jiaoxinglu* 四明尊者教行錄.

*Records that Mirror the Axiom.* See *Zongjing lu* 宗鏡錄.

*Rentian yanmu* 人天眼目, T.2006.

*Renwang huguo bore boluomiduo jing shu* 仁王護國般若波羅蜜多經疏, T.1709.

*Renwang jing* 仁王經, T.245; T.246.

*Reverend Shitou's Song of the Thatched Hut.* See *Shitou heshang caoan ge* 石頭和尚草庵歌.

*Ribenguo Qianguang fashi citangjì* 日本國千光法師祠堂記, *Zoku gunsho ruijū* 續羣書類從 9A.

*Rites of Zhou.* See *Zhouli* 周禮.

*Ruizhou Dongshan Liangjie chanshi yulu* 瑞州洞山良价禪師語録, T.1986B.

*Rujing heshang yulu* 如淨和尚語録, T.2002A.

*Ru lengqie jing* 入楞伽經, T.671.

*Rules of Purity for Stewards*. See *Eiheiji chiji shingi* 永平寺知事清規.

*Rules of Purity for the Chan Park*. See *Chanyuan qinggui* 禪苑清規.

*Ryūsen tsūgen zenji sōki* 龍泉通幻禪師喪記, ZSZ.2.Shingi 清規.

*Saddharma-puṇḍarīka-sūtra*. See *Miaofa lianhua jing* 妙法蓮華經.

*Sado gosho* 佐渡御書, NDGZ.

*Sāgara-nāga-rāja-paripṛcchā-sūtra*. See *Fo shuo hailongwang jing* 佛説海龍王經.

*Saishōōkyō kaidai* 最勝王經開題, T.2199.

*Samantapāsādikā*. See *Shanjianlü piposha* 善見律毘婆沙.

*Saṃyuktāgama*. See *Za ahan jing* 雜阿含經.

*Saṃyukta-ratna-piṭaka-sūtra*. See *Zabaozang jing* 雜寶藏經.

*Sanqian weiyi jing* 三千威儀經. See *Da biqiu sanqian weiyi* 大比丘三千威儀.

*Sanso gyōgōki* 三祖行業記, SZ.Shiden 史傳 1.

*Santendai godaisanki* 參天台五臺山記, B.174.

*Seng jiemo* 僧羯磨, T.1809.

*Sequenced Introduction to the Dharma Realm*. See *Fajie cidi chumen* 法界次第初門.

*Shaku makaenron kanchū* 釋摩訶衍論勘注, T.2290.

*Shaoshi liumen* 少室六門, T.2009.

*Shari sōdenki* 舍利相傳記, DZZ.7, Ishikawa Rikizan 石川力山, editor.

*Shanjianlü piposha* 善見律毘婆沙, T.1462.

*Shasekishū* 沙石集. *Nihon koten bungaku taikei* 85, Watanabe Tsunaya 渡邊綱也, editor.

*She dasheng lun shi* 攝大乘論釋, T.1598.

*Shengmanbao ku* 勝鬘寶窟, T.1744.

*Shier shi ge* 十二時歌, *Zhaozhou yulu* 趙州語錄, ZZ.118, X.1315.

*Shiji* 史記, KR.2a0001.

*Shijiamouni rulai wubai dayuan jing*, Narita, "Kōzanji shozō *Shaka norai gohyaku daigan kyō* no kenkyū 高山寺所藏「釋迦牟尼如來五百大願經」の研究."

*Shijing* 詩經, KR.1c0001.

*Shiji sōjōge* 師資相承偈, SK.1.

*Shimen's Grove Record*. See *Shimen linjian lu* 石門林間錄.

*Shimen linjian lu* 石門林間錄, ZZ.148, X.1624.

*Shi niu tu song* 十牛圖頌, ZZ.113, X.1269.

*Shishi liutie* 釋氏六帖. See *Giso rokujō* 義楚六帖.

*Shishi yaolan* 釋氏要覽, T.2127.

*Shisong lü* 十誦律, T.1435.

*Shitou heshang caoan ge* 石頭和尚草庵歌, *Jingde chuandeng lu* 景德傳燈錄, T.2076.

*Shittan ryakki* 悉曇略記, T.2704.

*Shiwu jiyuan* 事物紀原, KR.3k0014.

*Shixuan tan* 十玄談, *Jingde chuandeng lu*, T.2076.

*Shōbōgenzō* 正法眼藏, DZZ.1–2, Kawamura Kōdō 河村孝道, editor.

*Shōbōgenzō* 正法眼藏 (Chinese), DZZ.5, Ishii Shūdō 石井修道, editor.

*Shōbōgenzō* 正法眼藏 (Himitsu 祕蜜 manuscript), facsimile, ESST.1.

*Shōbōgenzō* 正法眼藏 (Honzan 本山 edition), T.2582.

*Shōbōgenzō* 正法眼藏 (Jōkōji 成高寺 manuscript), facsimile, ESST.1.

*Shōbōgenzō* 正法眼藏 (Kanazawa Bunko 金澤文庫 manuscript), facsimile, ESST.1; Ishii Shūdō 石井修道, editor, 2015b.

*Shōbōgenzō* 正法眼藏 (Kenkon'in 乾坤院 manuscript), facsimile, ESST.1.

*Shōbōgenzō* 正法眼藏 (Ryūmonji 龍門寺 manuscript), facsimile, ESST.2.

*Shōbōgenzō* 正法眼藏 (Shōbōji 正法寺 manuscript), facsimile, ESST.1.

*Shōbōgenzō* 正法眼藏 (Tokuunji 德雲寺 manuscript), facsimile, ESST.4.

*Shōbōgenzō* 正法眼藏 (Tōunji 洞雲寺 manuscript), facsimile, ESST.6.

*Shōbōgenzō* 正法眼藏 (Yōkōji 永光寺 manuscript), facsimile, ESST.1.

*Shōbōgenzō kikigakishō* 正法眼藏聽書抄, facsimile, ESST.11–14.

*Shōbōgenzō monge* 正法眼藏聞解, SCZ.

*Shōbōgenzō shinzo* 正法眼藏陛座, ZSZ.1.Shūgen hoi 宗源補遺.

*Shōbōgenzō shō* 正法眼藏抄, SCZ.

*Shōbōgenzō shōten zokuchō* 正法眼藏涉典續貂, SCZ.

*Shōbōgenzō zuimonki* 正法眼藏隨聞記, DZZ.7, Azuma Ryūshin 東隆眞, editor.

*Shōichi kokushi nenpu* 聖一國師年譜, DNBZ.95.

*Shōkō shōninden* 聖光上人傳, *Zoku gunsho ruijū* 續羣書類從 9A.

*Shoulengyan jing* 首楞嚴經, T.945.

*Shoulengyan sanmei jing* 首楞嚴三昧經, T.642.

*Shoulengyan yishu zhujing* 首楞嚴義疏注經, T.1799.

*Shukke taikō* 出家大綱, Fujita Takuji 藤田琢司, editor.

*Shuzhou Longmen Foyan heshang yulu* 舒州龍門佛眼和尚語錄, *Guzunsu yulu* 古尊宿語錄, ZZ.118, X.1315.

*Sifen lü* 四分律, T.1428.

*Sifen lü hanzhu jieben shu xingzong ji* 四分律含注戒本疏行宗記; ZZ.62, X.714.

*Sifen lü xingshi chao* 四分律行事鈔, T.1804.

Works cited

*Sifenlü xingshichao zichiji* 四分律行事鈔資持記, T.1805.

*Sijia yulu* 四家語錄, ZZ.119, X.1321.

*Siming zunzhe jiaoxinglu* 四明尊者教行錄, T.1936.

*Si nianchu* 四念處, T.1918.

*Si shamen xuanzang shangbiaoji* 寺沙門玄奘上表記, T.2119.

*Siyi fantian suowen jing* 思益梵天所問經, T.586.

*Sōkishū* 喪記集, ZSZ.2.Shingi 清規.

*Song Biographies of Eminent Monks.* See *Song gaoseng zhuan* 宋高僧傳, T.2061.

*Song gaoseng chuan* 宋高僧傳, T.2061.

*Sŏnmun yŏmsong chip* 禪門拈頌集, K.1505.

*Spring and Autumn Annals.* See *Chunqiu zuozhuan* 春秋左傳.

*Songshi* 宋史, KR.2a0023.

*Straight Talk on the True Mind.* See *Chinsim Chiksŏl* 眞心直説.

*Suishu* 隋書, KR.2a0023.

*Śuraṅgama-samādhi-sūtra.* See *Shoulengyan sanmei jing* 首楞嚴三昧經, T.642.

*Śuraṅgama-sūtra.* See *Shoulengyan jing* 首楞嚴經.

*Sūtra of Adamantine Absorption.* See *Jingang sanmei jing* 金剛三昧經.

*Sūtra of Perfect Awakening.* See *Yuanjue jing* 圓覺經.

*Sūtra of the Bequeathed Teachings of the Buddha.* See *Fo yijiao jing* 佛遺教經.

*Sūtra of the Collection of the Past Acts of the Buddha.* See *Fo benxing ji jing* 佛本行集經.

*Sūtra of the Conversion of the Northern Foreigners.* See *Laozi huahu jing* 老子化胡經.

*Sūtra on the Entry into Laṅka.* See *Lengqie abaduoluo bao jing* 楞伽阿跋多羅寶經; *Lengqie jing* 楞伽經.

*Sūtra of the Inconceivable Sphere of Cognition of a Buddha, as Explained by Mañjuśrī.* See *Wenshushili suoshuo busiyi fo jingjie jing* 文殊師利所説不思議佛境界經.

*Sūtra of the Lotus Blossom of the Wondrous Dharma.* See *Miaofa lianhua jing* 妙法蓮華經.

*Sūtra on the Names of the Buddhas.* See *Foming jing* 佛名經.

*Sūtra of the Names of the Thousand Buddhas of the Past Adornment Kalpa.* See *Guoqu zhuangyanjie qian foming jing* 過去莊嚴劫千佛名經.

*Sūtra of the Names of the Thousand Buddhas of the Present Worthy Kalpa.* See *Xianzai xianjie qian foming jing* 現在賢劫千佛名經.

*Sūtra of the Past Activities of the Buddha.* See *Fo benxing ji jing* 佛本行集經.

*Sūtra of the Prior Lives of the Bhikṣuṇī Utpalavarṇā.* See *Youboluohua biqiuni bensheng jing* 優鉢羅華比丘尼本生經.

*Sūtra of the Three Thousand Rules of Deportment.* See *Da biqiu sanqian weiyi* 大比丘三千威儀.

*Sūtra of the Unprecedented.* See *Weicengyou yinyuan jing* 未曾有因緣經.

*Sūtra of the Wondrous.* See *Xiyou jiaoliang gongde jing* 希有校量功德經.

*Suvarṇa-prabhāsottama-sūtra.* See *Jin guangming jing* 金光明經.

*Ta baoji jing* 大寶積經, T.310.

*Taiping guangji* 太平廣記, KR.3l0118.

*Taizi ruiying benqi jing* 太子瑞應本起經, T.185.

*Taizi xudana jing* 太子須大拏經, T.171.

*Tang dajianfusi gusizhu fanjing dade facang heshang chuan* 唐大薦福寺故寺主翻經大德法藏和尚傳, T.2054.

*Tang hufa shamen falin biezhuan* 唐護法沙門法琳別傳, T.2051.

*Tendai hokkeshū gishū* 天台法華宗義集, T.2366.

*Tanzhou Weishan Lingyou chanshi yulu* 潭州潙山靈祐禪師語錄, T.1989.

*Tenzo kyōkun* 典座教訓, DZZ.6, Kosaka Kiyū 小坂機融, editor.

*Tiansheng Era Extended Record of the Flame.* See. *Tiansheng guangdeng lu* 天聖廣燈錄.

*Tiansheng guangdeng lu* 天聖廣燈錄, ZZ.135, X.1553.

"Tiantongshan qianfogeji" 天童山千佛閣記, *Gongkuiji* 攻媿集, KR.4d0243.

*Tianzun shuo Ayuwang piyu jing* 天尊説阿育王譬喩經, T.2044.

*Treatise Determining the Truth About the Southern Lineage of Bodhidharma.* See *Putidamo Nanzong ding shifei lun* 菩提達摩南宗定是非論.

*Treatise on the Great Amitābha Sūtra.* See *Mohe Amituo jing zhonglun* 摩訶阿彌陀經衷論.

*Treatise on the Great Perfection of Wisdom.* See *Dazhidu lun* 大智度論.

*Treatise on the New [translation of the] Flower Garland Sūtra.* See *Xin huayanjing lun* 新華嚴經論.

*Treatise on the Stages of Yoga Practitioners.* See *Yuqie shidi lun* 瑜伽師地論.

*Treatise on the True Lineage of Dharma Transmission.* See *Chuanfa zhengzong lun* 傳法正宗論.

*Tong xuan zhen jing* 通玄眞經. See *Wenzi* 文子.

"Tsuki kikigaki" 都機聞書, *Shōbōgenzō kikigakishō* 正法眼藏聽書抄, facsimile, ESST.12.

*Utpalavarṇā-bhikṣuṇī-jātaka*-sūtra. See *Youboluohua biqiuni bensheng jing* 優鉢羅華比丘尼本生經.

*Vaipulya-mahāvyūha*-sūtra. See *Fangguang da zhuangyan jing* 方廣大莊嚴經.

*Vajracchedikā-prajñā-pāramitā*-sūtra. See *Jingang bore boluomi jing* 金剛般若波羅蜜經.

*Vajrasamādhi-sūtra*. See *Jingang sanmei jing* 金剛三昧經.

*Various Aspects of the Mūlasarvāstivāda Vinaya.* See *Genben shuo yiqie youbu pinaiye zashi* 根本説一切有部毘奈耶雜事.

*Verses and Prefaces on the Ten Buffalo-herding Scenes by Reverend Kuo'an, Abbot of Mount Liang in Dongzhou.* See *Zhu Dingzhou Liangshan Kuo'an heshang Shiniutu song xu* 住鼎州梁山廓庵和尚十牛圖頌序.

*Verses on the Sūtras of the Esoteric Strongmen [i.e., Vajra Holders] and Authoritative Deva Kings.* See *Miji lishi daquan shenwang jing ji song* 密跡力士大權神王經偈頌.

*Vimalakīrti Sūtra*. See *Weimoji suoshuo jing* 維摩詰所説經.

*Weicengyu yinyuan jing* 未曾有因緣經, T.745.

*Weimojie suoshuo jing* 維摩詰所説經, T.475.

*Weimo jing* 維摩經. See *Weimoji suoshuo jing* 維摩詰所説經.

*Weimojing chao* 維摩經抄, T.2773.

*Weimojing xuanshu* 維摩經玄疏, T.1777.

*Wenshu pusa lifo zuoguan ji* 文殊菩薩禮佛作觀偈, *Qianshouyan dabeixin zhou xingfa* 千手眼大悲心呪行法, T.1950.

*Wenshushili suoshuo busiyi fo jingjie jing* 文殊師利所説不思議佛境界經, T.340.

*Wenzi* 文子, KR.5c0118.

*Wudeng huiyuan* 五燈會元, ZZ.138, X.1565.

*Wudeng quanshu* 五燈全書, ZZ.141, X.1571.

*Wujia yulu* 五家語錄, ZZ.119, X.1326.

*Wumen guan* 無門關, T.2005.

*Wu tao* 武韜, KR.3b0002.

*Wuzhun shifan chanshi yulu* 無準師範禪師語録, ZZ.121, X.1382.

*Xiangfa jueyi jing* 像法決疑經, T.2870.

*Xiangyang ge* 襄陽歌, *Quan Tangshi* 全唐詩 166.

*Xianzai xianjie qian foming jing* 現在賢劫千佛名經, T.447.

*Xianyu jing* 賢愚經, T.202.

*Xiaojing* 孝經, KR.1f0001.

*Xiaopin bore boluomi jing* 小品般若波羅蜜經, T.227.

584 DŌGEN'S *SHŌBŌGENZŌ* VOLUME VIII

*Xingye ji* 行業記, *Hongzhi chanshi guanglu* 宏智禪師廣錄, T.2001.

*Xingzong Record of the Commentary on the Annotated Pratimokṣa of the Four Part Vinaya*. See *Sifen lü hanzhu jieben shu xingzong ji* 四分律含注戒本疏行宗記.

*Xin huayanjing lun* 新華嚴經論, T.1739.

*Xinjinwen ji* 鐔津文集, T.2115.

*Xin wang ming* 心王銘, *Jingde chuandeng lu* 景德傳燈錄, T.2076.

*Xinxin ming* 信心銘, T.2010; T.2076.

*Xinxu* 新序, KR.3a0008.

*Xinyao qian* 心要牋, *Jingde chuandeng lu* 景德傳燈錄, T.2076.

*Xiuxing benji jing* 修行本記經, T.184.

*Xiuxi zhiguan zuochan fayao* 修習止觀坐禪法要, T.1915.

*Xuansha Shibei chanshi guanglu* 玄沙師備禪師廣錄, ZZ.126, X.1445.

*Xuansha Shibei chanshi yulu* 玄沙師備禪師語錄, ZZ.126, X.1446.

*Xu chuandeng lu* 續傳燈錄, T.2077.

*Xuefeng yulu* 雪峰語錄, ZZ.119, X.1333.

*Xu gaoseng chuan* 續高僧傳, T.2060.

*Xu gu cunxiu yuyao* 續古尊宿語要, ZZ.118, X.1318.

*Xutang heshang yulu* 虛堂和尚語錄, T.2000.

*Xutang ji* 虛堂集, ZZ.124, X.1304.

*Yangqi Fanghui heshang yulu* 楊岐方會和尚語錄, T.1994A.

*Yangshan Huiji chanshi yulu* 仰山慧寂禪師語錄, T.1990.

*Yaoshi benyuan jing* 藥師本願經, T.450.

*Yijing* 易經. See *Zhouyi* 周易.

*Yilin* 意林, KR.5g0071.

*Yingan heshang yulu* 應庵和尚語録. See *Yingan tanhua chanshi yulu* 應菴曇華禪師語錄.

*Yingan tanhua chanshi yulu* 應菴曇華禪師語錄, ZZ.120, X.1359.

*Yiqie you bu baiyi jiemo* 一切有部百一羯磨, T.1453.

*Yixiang* 異相. See *Jinglü yixiang* 經律異相.

*Yizu jing* 義足經, T.198.

*Yogācārabhūmi-śāstra*. See *Yuqie shidi lun* 瑜伽師地論, T.1579.

*Yongjia Zhenjue dashi zhengdao ge* 永嘉眞覺大師證道歌, T.2076.

*Yongjue Yuanxian chanshi guanglu* 永覺元賢禪師廣錄, ZZ.125, X.1437.

*Yongming Zhijiao chanshi weixin jue* 永明智覺禪師唯心訣, T.2018.

*Youboluohua biqiuni bensheng jing* 優鉢羅華比丘尼本生經. Not extant.

*Youfangji chao* 遊方記抄, T.2089.

# Works cited

*Yuanjue jing* 圓覺經, T.842.

*Yuanjue jing lüeshu* 圓覺經略疏, T.1795.

*Yuanren lun* 原人論, T.1886.

*Yuanwu Foguo chanshi yulu* 圓悟佛果禪師語錄, T.1997.

*Yuanwu yulu* 圓悟語錄. See *Yuanwu Foguo chanshi yulu* 圓悟佛果禪師語錄.

*Yuan zhiji chanshi yulu* 愚菴智及禪師語錄, ZZ.124, X.1421.

*Yugaron gi* 瑜伽論記, T.1828.

*Yunmen Kuangzheng chanshi guanglu* 雲門匡眞禪師廣錄, T.1988.

*Yunmen yulu* 雲門語錄. See *Yunmen Kuangzheng chanshi guanglu* 雲門匡眞禪師廣錄, T.1988.

*Yupose jie jing* 優婆塞戒經, T.1488.

*Yuqie shidi lun* 瑜伽師地論, T.1579.

*Yuzhu Jingang bore boluomi jing xuanyan* 御注金剛般若波羅蜜經宣演, T.2733.

*Za ahan jing* 雜阿含經, T.99.

*Zabaozang jing* 雜寶藏經, T.203.

*Zazen yōjin ki* 坐禪用心記, SSZ.*Shūgen* 宗源 2.

*Zengyi ahan jing* 增一阿含經, T.125.

*Zhangling Shouzhou chanshi yulu* 長靈守卓禪師語錄, ZZ.120, X.1347.

*Zhaozhou heshang yulu* 趙州和尚語錄, *Guzunsu yulu* 古尊宿語錄, ZZ.118, X.1315.

*Zhaozhou lu* 趙州錄. See *Zhaozhou Zhenji chanshi yulu bing xingzhuang* 趙州眞際禪師語錄并行狀.

*Zhaozhou Zhenji chanshi yulu* 趙州眞際禪師語錄. See *Zhaozhou Zhenji chanshi yulu bing xingzhuang* 趙州眞際禪師語錄并行狀.

*Zhaozhou Zhenji chanshi yulu bing xingzhuang* 趙州眞際禪師語錄并行狀, *Guzunsu yulu* 古尊宿語錄, ZZ.118, X.1315.

*Zhengdao ge* 證道歌, T.2014.

*Zhengfayanzang* 正法眼藏, ZZ.118, X.1309.

*Zhenguan zhengyao* 貞觀政要, KR.2e0006.

*Zhengyuan lüeji buyi* 正源略集補遺, ZZ.145, X.1588.

*Zhenzhou Linji Huizhao chanshi yulu* 鎭州臨濟慧照禪師語錄, T.1985.

*Zhiguan fuxing zhuan hongjue* 止觀輔行傳弘決, T.1912.

*Zhong ahan jing* 中阿含經, T.26.

*Zhong benqi jing* 中本起經, T.196.

*Zhonghua chuanxindi chanmen shizi chengxi tu* 中華傳心地禪門師資承襲圖, ZZ.110, X.1225.

586 DŌGEN'S *SHŌBŌGENZŌ* VOLUME VIII

*Zhonglun* 中論, T.1564.

*Zhou li* 周禮, KR.1d0002.

*Zhouyi* 周易, KR1a0001.

*Zhuanji baiyuan jing* 撰集百緣經, T.200.

*Zhuangzi* 莊子, KR.5c0126.

*Zhu dasheng rulengjia jing* 注大乘入楞伽經, T.1791.

*Zhudefutian jing* 諸德福田經, T.683.

*Zhu Dingzhou Liangshan Kuo'an heshang Shiniutu song xu* 住鼎州梁山廓庵和尚十牛圖頌序, ZZ.113, X.1269.

*Zōdanshū* 雜談集. Yamada Shōzen 山田昭全 and Miki Sumito 三木紀人, editors.

*Zongjing lu* 宗鏡錄, T.2016.

*Zongmen liandeng huiyao* 宗門聯燈會要, ZZ.136, X.1557.

*Zongmen tongyao ji* 宗門統要集, ZTS.1.

*Zongmen tongyao zhengxu ji* 宗門統要正續集, P.1519.

*Zongmen wuku* 宗門武庫. See *Dahui Puzue chanshi Zongmen wuku* 大慧普覺禪師宗門武庫.

*Zuimonki* 隨聞記, DZZ.7, Azuma Ryūshin 東隆眞, editor.

*Zuishengwang jing* 最勝王經. See *Jin guangming zuishengwang jing* 金光明最勝王經.

*Zuochan ming* 坐禪銘, *Jiatai Pudeng lu* 嘉泰普燈錄, ZZ.137, X.1559.

*Zuochan yi* 坐禪儀, *Chanyuan qinggui* 禪苑清規, ZZ.111, X.1245.

*Zuochan zhen* 坐禪箴 (by Hongzhi Zhengjue 宏智正覺), *Hongzhi guanglu* 宏智廣錄, T.2001.

*Zuochan zhen* 坐禪箴 (by Wuyun Zhifeng 五雲志逢), *Jingde chuandeng lu* 景德傳燈錄, T.2076.

*Zuo zhuan* 左傳, KR.1e0001.

*Zutang ji* 祖堂集, B.144.

*Zuting shiyuan* 祖庭事苑, ZZ.113, X1261.

## Secondary and tertiary works

Abe Masao 阿部正雄 (1915–2006). 1992. *A Study of Dōgen: His Philosophy and Religion.* Edited by Steven Heine. Albany: State University of New York Press.

Abe Yasurō 阿部泰郎 et al, editors. 2013–2019. *Chūsei zenseiki sōkan* 中世禅籍叢刊. 13 vols. Kyoto: Rinsen Shoten.

Akitsu Hideaki 秋津秀彰. 2017. "Taiyō Bonsei ni kansuru kenkyū no genkyō to kadai" 太容梵清に関する研究の現況と課題. *Indogaku Bukkyōgaku kenkyū* 印度學佛教學研究 66:150–154.

———. 2018. "Chūsei ni okeru *Shōbōgenzō* no shosha-denpa ni kansuru shomondai" 中世における『正法眼蔵』の書写・伝播に関する諸問題, part 1. *Komazawa Daigaku Bukkyōgakubu ronshū* 駒澤大學佛教學部論集 49:213–231.

———. 2019a. "Chūsei ni okeru *Shōbōgenzō* no shosha-denpa ni kansuru shomondai" 中世における『正法眼蔵』の書写・伝播に関する諸問題, part 2. *Komazawa Daigaku Bukkyōgakubu ronshū* 駒澤大學佛教學部論集 50:147–167.

———. 2019b. "Honzanban *Shōbōgenzō* no ihon ni tsuite" 本山版『正法眼蔵』の異本について. *Indogaku Bukkyōgaku kenkyū* 印度學佛教學研究 68:121–126.

———. 2020. "Chūsei ni okeru *Shōbōgenzō* no shosha-denpa ni kansuru shomondai" 中世における『正法眼蔵』の書写・伝播に関する諸問題, part 3. *Komazawa Daigaku Bukkyōgakubu kenkyū kiyō* 駒澤大學佛教學部研究紀要 78:121–141.

———. 2021. "Honkoku-Chōenji hon *Eiheiji sanso gyōgōki* 翻刻・長円寺本『永平三祖行業記』. *Shūgaku kenkyū kiyō* 宗学研究紀要 34:91–124.

Akiyama Hanji 秋山範二 (1893–1980). 1935. *Dōgen no kenkyū* 道元の研究. Tokyo: Iwanami Shoten.

App, Urs. 1989. "Facets of the life and teaching of Chan Master Yunmen Wenyan (864-949)." 2 vols. Ph.D. dissertation. Temple University, Philadelphia, Penn.

*Azuma kagami* 吾妻鏡. Edited by Hayakawa Junzaburō 早川純三郎 (1872–1930). 1914. Revised (*kōtei zōho* 校訂増補) edition. 3 vols. Tokyo: Kokusho Kankōkai, 1943.

Azuma Ryūshin 東隆眞, editor. 1970. *Kenkon'in bon Denkōroku* 乾坤院本傳光録. Tokyo: Rinjinsha.

———. 1985. "Koma-shi shozō *Eiheiji sanso gyōgōki* no shōkai" 小間氏所蔵「永平寺三祖行業記」の紹介. *Shūgaku kenkyū* 宗學研究 27:1–6.

———, editor. 1990. *Shōbōgenzō zuimonki* 正法眼蔵随聞記. DZZ.7:52–151.

———. 1991. *Denkōroku: gendaigoyaku* 伝光録：現代語訳. Tokyo: Daizō Shuppan.

Barnstone, Willis. 1993. *The Poetics of Translation: History, Theory Practice*. New Haven: Yale University Press.

Bielefeldt, Carl. 1985. "Recarving the Dragon: History and Dogma in the Study of Dōgen." In *Dōgen Studies*. Edited by William R. LaFleur. Pp. 21–53. Honolulu: University of Hawaiʻi Press.

———. 1988. *Dōgen's Manuals of Zen Meditation*. Berkeley: University of California Press.

———. 1997. "Kokan Shiren and the Sectarian Uses of History," in *The Origins of Japan's Medieval World*. Edited by Jeffrey P. Mass. Pp. 295–317. Stanford, CA: Stanford University Press.

Bodiford, William M. 1991. "Dharma Transmission in Sōtō Zen: Manzan Dōhaku's Reform Movement." *Monumenta Nipponica* 46:423–451.

———. 1993. *Sōtō Zen in Medieval Japan*. Studies in East Asian Buddhism, no. 8. Honolulu: University of Hawaiʻi Press.

———. 2006. "Remembering Dōgen: Eiheiji and Dōgen Hagiography." Reprinted in *Dōgen: Textual and Historical Studies*. Edited by Steven Heine. Pp. 207–222, 267–273. New York: Oxford University Press, 2012.

———. 2007. "Dharma Transmission in Theory and Practice." In *Zen Ritual*. Edited by Steven Heine and Dale S. Wright. Pp. 261–282. New York: Oxford University Press.

———. 2009. "The Monastic Institution in Medieval Japan: The Insider's View." In *Buddhist Monasticism in East Asia: Places of Practice*. Edited by James A. Benn, Lori Meeks, and James Robson. Pp. 125–147. New York: Routledge.

———. 2011. "Zen and Esoteric Buddhism." In *Esoteric Buddhism and the Tantras in East Asia*. Edited by Charles D. Orzech, Henrik H. Sørensen, and Richard K. Payne. Pp. 924–935. Leiden: Brill.

———. 2012a. "The Rhetoric of Chinese Language in Japanese Zen." In *Zen Buddhist Rhetoric in China, Korea, and Japan*. Edited by Christoph Anderl. Pp. 285–314. Conceptual History and Chinese Linguistics, volume 3. Leiden: Brill.

———. 2012b. "Textual Geneologies of Dogen." In *Dōgen: Textual and Historical Studies*. Edited by Steven Heine. Pp. 15–41, 237. New York: Oxford University Press.

———. 2013. "Myth and Counter Myth in Early Modern Japan." *Cursor Mundi* 17:277–309.

———. 2019a. "Rewriting Dōgen." *Kokusai Zen kenkyū* 国際禅研究 4:214–302, 374–385.

———. 2019b. "Dōgen o kakinaosu" 道元を書き直す. Translated by Kanako Nao 金子奈央. *Kokusai Zen kenkyū* 国際禅研究 4:303–385.

———. 2020a. "Shamon Dōgen at Ninety. *Komazawa Daigaku Zenkenkyūjo nenpō* 駒澤大學禪研究所年報 32:59–86.

## Works cited

———.2020b. "Kyūjussai no shamon Dōgen 九十歳の沙門道元. Translated by Fujikawa Naoko 藤川直子. *Komazawa Daigaku Zenkenkyūjo nenpō* 駒澤大學禪研究所年報 32:87–113.

———. 2021. "Introduction." In *Record of the Transmission of Illumination by the Great Ancestor, Zen Master Keizan*. Edited by T. Griffith Foulk. Vol. 1, pp. 1–75, 573–594. Honolulu: University of Hawai'i Press.

Borgen, Robert. 1994. *Sugawara no Michizane and the Early Heian Court*. Honolulu: University of Hawai'i Press.

*Bukkyōgo daijiten* 佛教語大辞典. Edited by Nakamura Hajime 中村元. 3 vols. Tokyo: Tōkyō Shoseki 東京書籍, 1975. Abbreviated herein as BGDJ.

*CBETA Chinese Electronic Tripiṭaka Collection*. Edited by Chinese Buddhist Electronic Text Association (Zhonghua Dianzi Fodian Xiehui 中華電子佛典協會). Taibei, Taiwan. Buddhist texts selected from the following printed editions:

> B. Supplement (*bubian* 補編): *Dazangjing bubian* 大藏經補編. Edited by Lan Jifu 藍吉富. 36 vols. Taipei: Huayu Chubanshe, 1985.
>
> J. *Jiaxing dazang jing* 嘉興大藏經. 40 vols. Taipei: Xinwenfeng Chubanshe, 1987.
>
> P. *Yongle beizang* 永樂北藏. 200 vols. Beijing: Xianzhuang Shuju, 2000.
>
> R. Reprint: *Dai Nihon zoku zōkyō* 大日本續藏經. Kyoto: 1905-1912. Reprinted. *Wan Xuzangjing: Zangjing shuyuan ban* 卍續藏經: 藏經書院版. 150 vols. Taipei: Xinwenfeng Chubanshe, 1994.
>
> T. Taishō 大正 Edition: *Taishō shinshū dai zōkyō* 大正新脩大藏經. Edited by Takakusu Junjirō 高楠順次郎 (1866-1945), Watanabe Kaikyoku 渡辺海旭 (1872-1932) et al. 100 vols. Tokyo: Taishō Issaikyō Kankōkai, 1924-1935.
>
> X. *Xinzuan* 新纂 (revised): *Shinsan Dai Nihon zoku zōkyō* 新纂大日本續藏經. 90 vols. Edited by Kawamura Kōshō 河村孝照, Nishi Yoshio 西義雄, and Tamaki Kōshirō 玉城康四郎. Tokyo: Kokusho Kankōkai, 1975-1989.
>
> Z. *Zokuzō kyō*: *Dai Nihon zoku zōkyō* 大日本續藏經. Edited by Maeda Eun 前田慧雲 and Nakano Tatsue 中野達慧. Series 1 (*daiippen* 第一編), 95 cases (*tō* 套). Series 2 (*dainihen* 第二編), 32 cases. Series 2B (*dainihen otsu* 第二編乙), 23 cases. Kyoto: Zōkyō Shoin, 1905-1912.

Cleary, Thomas and J. C. Cleary. 1992. *The Blue Cliff Record*. Boston and London: Shambhala.

*Dai Nihon Bukkyō zensho* 大日本佛教全書. 1912–1922. Edited by Nanjō Bun'yū 南條文雄 (1849–1927) et al. 150 vols. Tokyo: Bussho Kankōkai. Abbreviated herein as DNBZ.

*Dai Nihon zoku zōkyō* 大日本續藏經. 1905–1912. Edited by Maeda Eun 前田慧雲 and Nakano Tatsue 中野達慧. Series 1 (*daiippen* 第一編), 95 cases (*tō* 套). Series 2 (*dainihen* 第二編), 32 cases. Series 2B (*dainihen otsu* 第二編乙), 23 cases. 751 vols. Kyoto: Zōkyō Shoin. Reprinted. *Wan Xuzangjing: Zangjing shuyuan ban* 卍續藏經: 藏經書院版. 150 vols. Taipei: Xinwenfeng Chubanshe, 1977. Abbreviated herein as ZZ.

Denecke, Wiebke. 2014. "Worlds Without Translation: Premodern East Asia and the Power of Character Scripts." In *A Companion to Translation Studies*, edited by Sandra Bermann and Catherine Porter. Pp. 204–216. Chichester: Wiley-Blackwell.

*Dengyō daishi zenshū* 傳教大師全集. 5 vols. Sakamoto: Hieizan Kankōkai, 1926.

*Denkōroku*. See Foulk, T. Griffith, editor. 2021. *Record of the Transmission of Illumination*. Volume 1: "An Annotated Translation of Zen Master Keizan's Denkōroku."

*Dōgen zenji nanahyaku gojikkai daionki kinen shuppan: Himitsu shōbōgenzō* 道元禪師七五〇回大遠忌記念出版：秘密正法眼藏. 3 fascicles in Japanese bindings (*wasō* 和裝), 1 case (*chitsu* 帙). With Introduction (*kaidai* 解題) by Kawamura Kōdō 河村孝道. Facsimile reproduction by Daihonzan Eiheiji Daionkikyoku 大本山永平寺 大遠忌局. Tokyo: Taishūkan Shoten, 1998.

*Dōgen zenji shinseki kankei shiryōshū* 道元禪師眞蹟關係資料集. Supplemental volume (*bekkan* 別巻). *Eihei shōbōgenzō shūsho taisei* 永平正法眼藏蒐書大成. Edited by Dai Honzan Eiheijinai Eihei Shōbōgenzō Shūsho Taisei Kankōkai 大本山永平寺内永平正法眼藏蒐書大成刊行会. Tokyo: Taishūkan Shoten, 1980. Abbreviated as ESST-D.

*Dōgen zenji zenshū* 道元禅師全集. 1988–1991. Compiled by Kagamishima Genryū 鏡島元隆 (1912–2001), Sakai Tokugen 酒井得元 (1912–1996), and Sakurai Shūyū 桜井秀雄 (1916–2000). 7 vols. Tokyo: Shunjūsha. Abbreviated herein as DZZ.

*Eihei shōbōgenzō shūsho taisei* 永平正法眼藏蒐書大成. 1974–1982. Edited by Dai Honzan Eiheijinai Eihei Shōbōgenzō Shūsho Taisei Kankōkai 大本山永平寺内永平正法眼藏蒐書大成刊行会. 25 vols. Tokyo: Taishūkan Shoten. Abbreviated herein as ESST.

*Eihei shōbōgenzō shūsho taisei sōmokuroku* 永平正法眼藏蒐書大成總目録. 1982. Supplemental volume (*bessatsu* 別册). Edited by Dai Honzan Eiheijinai Eihei Shōbōgenzō Shūsho Taisei Kankōkai 大本山永平寺内永平正法眼藏蒐書大成刊行会. Tokyo: Taishūkan Shoten. Abbreviated herein as ESST-S.

*Eihei shōbōgenzō shūsho taisei zokushū* 永平正法眼藏蒐書大成 續輯. 1992–2000. Edited by Dai Honzan Eiheijinai Eihei Shōbōgenzō Shūsho Taisei Kankōkai 大本山永平寺内永平正法眼藏蒐書大成刊行会. 10 vols. Tokyo: Taishūkan Shoten. Abbreviated herein as ESST-Z.

Enomoto Wataru 榎本渉. 2001. "Sōdai no 'Nihon shōnin' no saikentō" 宋代の「日本商人」の再検討. *Shigaku zasshi* 史學雜誌 110:211–234.

———. 2003. "Chūsei no Nihonsō to Chūgokugo" 中世の日本僧と中国語. *Rekishi to chiri* 歴史と地理 567:33–42.

———. 2004. "Chūgoku shiryō ni mieru chūsei Nihon no dochō" 中国史料に見える中世日本の度牒. *Zengaku kenkyū* 禪學研究 82:57–83.

———. 2005. "Eisai nittō engi kara mita Hakata" 栄西入唐縁起からみた博多. In *Kōryū, butsuryū, ekkyō* 交流・物流・越境, edited by Gomi Fumihiko 五味文彦. Pp. 83–108. Tokyo: Shinjinbutsu Ōraisha.

———. 2007. *Higashi Ajia kaiiki to Nitchū kōryū* 東アジア海域と日中交流. Tokyo: Yoshikawa Kōbunkan.

———. 2008. "Itawatashi no bokuseki kara mita Nissō kōryū" 板渡の墨蹟から見た日宋交流. *Tōkyō Daigaku Nihon shigaku kenkyūshitsu kiyō* 東京大学日本史学研究室紀要 12:1–12.

———. 2010. *Sōryo to kaishōtachi no higashi shinakai* 僧侶と海商たちの東シナ海. Shiriizu sensho Nihon chūseishi シリイズ選書日本中世史 4. Tokyo: Kōdansha.

———. 2013. "Ajia no naka no Kenchōji" アジアのなかの建長寺. *Zen bunka* 禅文化 228:25–33.

———. 2014. "Trade Administered by Maritime Trade Offices (*Shibosi*) in Song China and by Dazaifu in Heian Japan." *Memoirs of the Research Department of the Toyo Bunko* 72:27–55.

———. 2016. "Heian makki Tendaishū ni okeru Sōdai Bukkyō e no manazashi" 平安末期天台宗における宋代仏教へのまなざし. *Bukkyō shigaku kenkyū* 仏教史学研究 59:19–41.

———. 2021. "Nitchū kōryūshi no naka no chūsei Zenshūshi" 日中交流史の中の中世禅宗史. In *Chūsei Zen no chi* 中世禅の知, edited by Sueki Fumihiko 末木文美士 et al. Pp. 37–72. Kyoto: Rinsen Shoten.

Epp, Eldon J. 1976. "The Eclectic Method in New Testament Textual Criticism: Solution or Symptom?" *Harvard Theological Review* 69:211–257.

Era Hiromu 恵良宏. 1967. "Dazaifu Anrakuji no jikan kikō ni tsuite" 大宰府安楽寺の寺官機構について. *Ube Kōgyō Kōtō Senmon Gakkō kenkyū hōkoku* 宇部工業高等専門学校研究報告 6:87–79 (from back).

Etō Sokuō 衛藤即應 (1888–1958), editor. 1939, 1942, 1943. *Shōbōgenzō* 正法眼藏. Iwanami Bunko 岩波文庫. 3 vols. Reprint. Tokyo: Iwanami Shoten, 1959.

592 DŌGEN'S *SHŌBŌGENZŌ* VOLUME VIII

———. 1944. *Shūso toshite no Dōgen zenji* 宗祖としての道元禪師. Tokyo: Iwanami Shoten. Available online via National Diet Library Digital Collections (Kokuritsu Kokkai Toshokan Dejitaru Korekushon 国立国会図書館デジタルコレクション): http://dl.ndl. go.jp/info:ndljp/pid/1040750

———. 1959. *Shōbōgenzō josetsu: Bendōwa gikai* 正法眼藏序説: 辨道話義解. Tokyo: Iwanami Shoten.

———. 2001. *Dōgen Zenji as Founding Patriarch (of the Japanese Sōtō Zen School)*. Translated by Ichimura Shōhei. [Translation of Etō 1944.] Tsurumi, Japan: Daihonzan Sōjiji.

Faure, Bernard. 1987. "The Daruma-shū, Dōgen, and Sōtō Zen." *Monumenta Nipponica* 42:25–55.

———. 1991. *The Rhetoric of Immediacy: A Cultural Critique of Chan/ Zen Buddhism*. Princeton: Princeton University Press.

———. 1996. *Visions of Power: Imagining Medieval Japanese Buddhism*. Princeton: Princeton University Press.

Foulk, T. Griffith. 2012. "Just Sitting? Dōgen's take on Zazen, Sutra Reading, and Other Monastic Practices." In *Dōgen: Textual and Historical Studies*. Edited by Steven Heine. Pp. 75–106. New York: Oxford University Press.

———. 2015. "Dōgen's Use of Rujing's 'Just Sit' (*shikan taza*) and Other Kōans." In *Dōgen and Sōtō Zen*. Edited by Steven Heine. Pp. 23–45. New York: Oxford University Press.

———, editor. 2021. *Record of the Transmission of Illumination*. Volume 1: "An Annotated Translation of Zen Master Keizan's *Denkōroku*." T. Griffith Foulk, Editor-in-Chief; translations by T. Griffith Foulk, William Bodiford; Sarah Horton, Carl Bielefeldt, and John McRae. Volume 2: "A Glossary of Terms, Sayings, and Names pertaining to Keizan's *Denkōroku*." T. Griffith Foulk, with William M. Bodiford. Honolulu: University of Hawai'i Press.

Fujita Takuji 藤田琢司, editor. 2014. *Eisai zenji shū* 栄西禅師集. Kyoto: Zenbunka Kenkyūjo.

Gershevitch, Ilya. 1979. "The Alloglottography of Old Persian." *Transactions of the Philological Society* 77:114–190.

Girard, Frédéric. 2007. *The Stanza of the Bell in the Wind: Zen and Nenbutsu in the Early Kamakura Period*. Tokyo: The International Institute for Buddhist Studies.

———. 2008. *Vocabulaire du bouddhisme japonais*. 2 vols. Paris: Librairie Droz S.A.

Groner, Paul. 1984. *Saichō: The Establishment of the Japanese Tendai School*. Berkeley: Buddhist Studies Series.

*Gunsho ruijū* 羣書類從. 1819. Compiled by Honawa Hokiichi 塙保己一 (1746–1821). Revised, 3d edition. 29 vols. Tokyo: Zoku Gunsho Ruiju Kanseikai, 1958.

*Hanyu da cidian* 漢語大詞典. 1987. Edited by Luo Zhufeng 羅竹風. 13 vols. Shanghai: Shanghai Cishu Chubanshe. Abbreviated herein as HYDCD.

Harada Masatoshi 原田正俊. 2006. "Kujō Michiie no Tōfukuji to Enni" 九条道家の東福寺と円爾. *Nihon shisōshi* 日本思想史 68:78–97.

———. 2021. "Kamakura jidai kōki ni okeru Zenshū no taitō to nanto hokurei" 鎌倉時代後期における禅宗の台頭と南都北嶺. In *Chūsei Zen no chi* 中世禅の知, edited by Sueki Fumihiko 末木文美士 et al. Pp. 206–211. Kyoto: Rinsen Shoten.

Hattori Hideo 服部英雄. 1983. "Mirai nengō no sekai kara: Hitsuke ni mujun no aru monjo yori mita shōen no yōsō" 未来年号の世界から: 日付に矛盾のある文書よりみた荘園の様相. *Shikaku zasshi* 史学雑誌 92:1304–1331.

Heine, Steven. 2006. *Did Dōgen Go to China? What He Wrote and When He Wrote It*. New York: Oxford University Press.

———. 2014. "Ishii Shūdō's Contributions to Dōgen Studies." *Japanese Journal of Religious Studies* 41:387–404.

———. 2020. *Readings of Dōgen's Treasury of the True Dharma Eye*. New York: Columbia University Press.

Hirose Ryōkō 広瀬良弘. 1982. "*Shōbōgenzō* no tōsha to denpa" 『正法眼藏』の謄写と伝播. In Sakurai 1982, vol. 1, pp. 501–525.

———. 1988. *Zenshū chihō tenkaishi no kenkyū* 禅宗地方展開史の研究. Tokyo: Yoshikawa Kōbunkan.

Hu Shih 胡適, editor. 1930. *Shenhui heshang yiji* 神會和尚遺集. Shanghai: Yadong Tushuguan. Reprint. Taibei: Hu Shi Jinianguan, 1968.

Ikeda Rosan 池田魯参. 1993. "Kaidai: *Zuimonki*: *Shōbōgenzō* no kotobure" 解題・随聞記: 正法眼藏のことぶれ. In *Gendaigoyaku Shōbōgenzō zuimonki* 現代語訳 正法眼藏随聞記. Pp. 353–439. Tokyo: Daizō Shuppan.

Ishii Seijun 石井清純. 1991. "Kenkon'in-bon 'Senmen' to Tōunji-hon 'Senmen' ni tsuite" 乾坤院本「洗面」と洞雲寺本「洗面」について (2). *Komazawa Daigaku Bukkyōgakubu kenkyū kiyo* 駒澤大學佛教學部研究紀要 49:88–106.

Ishii Shūdō 石井修道. 1982. "Chūgoku no gozan jissatsu seido no kisoteki kenkyū" 中国の五山十刹制度の基礎的研究. *Komazawa Daigaku Bukkyōgakubu ronshū* 駒澤大學佛教學部論集 13:89–132.

———, editor. 1984–1986. *Wanshiroku* 宏智録. 3 vols. Tokyo: Meicho Fukyūkai.

———. 1985. "*Shūmon tōyōshū* to shinji *Shōbōgenzō*: shinji *Shōbōgenzō* no shutten no zenmenteki hosei" 『宗門統要集』と真字『正法眼蔵』: 真字『正法眼蔵』の出典の全面的補正. *Shūgaku kenkyū* 宗學研究 27:58–65. Reprinted in Ishii 1988, 559–576.

———. 1988. *Chūgoku zenshū shiwa: shinji "Shōbōgenzō" ni manabu* 中国禅宗史話: 真字「正法眼蔵」に学ぶ. Kyoto: Zen Bunka Kenkyūjo.

———. 1989a. "Kaidai: *Shōbōgenzō*" 解題: 正法眼蔵. DZZ.5:294-309.

———, editor. 1989b. *Shōbōgenzō* 正法眼蔵. DZZ.5:124–275.

———. 1991a. *Dōgenzen no seiritsu shiteki kenkyū* 道元禅の成立史的研究. Tokyo: Daizō Shuppan.

———. 1991b. "Saigo no Dōgen: jūnikanbon *Shōbōgenzō* to *Hōkyōki*" 最後の道元:十二巻本「正法眼蔵」と「宝慶記」. In *Jūnikanbon* Shōbōgenzō *no sho mondai* 十二巻本『正法眼蔵』の諸問題. Edited by Kagamishima Genryū 鏡島元隆 and Suzuki Kakuzen 鈴木格禅. Pp. 3–30. Tokyo: Daizō Shuppan.

———. 1996. "The *Zongmen tongyao ji* and the Distinctive Character of Song Chan Buddhism." [Originally 1996, "*Shūmon tōyōshū* yori mita Sōdai Zen no tokushoku" 「宗門統要集」よりみた宋代禅の特色.] Translated by Albert Welter. *Komazawa Daigaku Zenkenkyūjo nenpō* 駒澤大學禪研究所年報 7:236–227 (47–56).

———. 2000. "Kung-an Ch'an and the *Tsung-men t'ung-yao chi*." Translated by Albert Welter. In *The Kōan: Texts and Contexts in Zen Buddhism*. Edited by Seven Heine and Dale S. Wright. Pp. 110–136. New York: Oxford University Press.

———. 2004. "The *Wu-men kuan* (J. *Mumonkan*): The Formation, Propagation, and Characteristics of a Classic Zen Kōan Text." Translated by Albert Welter. In *The Zen Canon: Understanding the Classic Texts*. Edited by Seven Heine and Dale S. Wright. Pp. 207–244. New York: Oxford University Press.

———. 2005. "Shōgen Sūgaku no hito to shisō" 松源崇岳の人と思想. *Indogaku Bukkyōgaku kenkyū* 印度學佛教學研究 54:128–135, 1250.

———. 2006. "Shōgen Sūgaku no shūfū" 松源崇岳の宗風. *Indogaku Bukkyōgaku kenkyū* 印度學佛教學研究 55:118–126, 1195.

———. 2008. "'Busso' 'Shisho' 'Menju' kō" 『仏祖』『嗣書』『面授』考, *Komazawa Daigaku Bukkyōgakubu ronshū* 駒澤大學佛教学部論集 39:29–95.

———. 2009. "Shinji *Shōbōgenzō* no shomondai" 真字『正法眼蔵』の諸問題. *Komazawa Daigaku Zenkenkyūjo nenpō* 駒澤大學禪研究所年報 21:115–134.

———. 2012. "Dōgen no 'mitsuju shin'in yori kono kata' ni tsuite" 道元の「密受心印よりこのかた」について. *Komazawa Daigaku Zenkenkyūjo nenpō* 駒澤大學禪研究所年報 24:99–127.

———. 2015a. "Dōgen's Views on Practice and Realization and His Dream Encounter with Damei Fachang." [originally 2011, "Dōgen no reimu no naka de no Daibai Hōjō to no deai to shushōkan" 道元の霊夢の中での大梅法常との出会いと修証観.] Translated by Jeffrey Kotyk. *Journal of Buddhist Philosophy* 1:193–212.

———, editor. 2015b. *Dōgenshū* 道元集. *Chūsei Zenseki sōkan* 中世禅籍叢刊, vol. 2. Kyoto: Rinsen Shoten.

———. 2015c. "*Dōgenshū* sōsetsu" 『道元集』総説. In Ishii Shūdō 2015b, pp. 571-606.

———. 2015d. "'Ji Ryōnen-ni hōgo' kaidai" 「示了然尼法語」解題. In Ishii Shūdō 2015b, pp. 607-614.

———. 2015e. "'Shisho' kaidai" 「嗣書」解題. In Ishii Shūdō 2015b, pp. 631-642.

———. 2016a. "On the Origins of Kana 'Shōbōgenzō.'" Translated by Kristyna Cislerova. *Komazawa Daigaku Zenkenkyūjo nenpō* 駒澤大學禪研究所年報 28:280–253 (33–60).

———. 2016b. "Kana *Shōbōgenzō* wa itsu seiritsu shita ka" 仮名『正法眼蔵』はいつ成立したか. *Komazawa Daigaku Zenkenkyūjo nenpō* 駒澤大學禪研究所年報 28:256–234 (61–79).

———. 2017. "Daie Sōkō no kannazen no seiritsu ni tsuite" 大慧宗杲の看話禅の成立について. *Komazawa Daigaku Zenkenyūjo nenpō* 駒澤大學禪研究所年報 29:39–79.

———. 2019. "'Kana *Shōbōgenzō* no seiritsu katei to henshū" 仮名『正法眼蔵』の成立過程と編集. *Zenbunka kenkyūjo kiyō* 禅文化研究所紀 34:373–421.

———. 2020a. "*Eihei kōroku* seiritsu kō" 「永平広録」成立考. *Komazawa Daigaku Zenkenkyūjo nenpō* 駒澤大學禪研究所年報 32:181–211.

———. 2020b. "The Formation of Eihei kōroku." Translated by Kristyna Cislerova. *Komazawa Daigaku Zenkenkyūjo nenpō* 駒澤大學禪研究所年報 32:115–180.

Ishikawa Rikizan 石川力山 (1943–1997). 1978a. "Jōtenhon *Kenzeiki* no honkoku" 承天本『建撕記』の翻刻. *Komazawa Daigaku Bukkyōgakubu ronshū* 駒澤大學佛教學部論集 36:231–264.

———. 1978b. "*Kenzeiki* no shiryōteki kachi" (part 1). *Komazawa Daigaku Bukkyōgakubu ronshū* 駒澤大學佛教學部論集 9: 196–207.

———. 1979. "*Kenzeiki* no shiryōteki kachi" (part 2). *Komazawa Daigaku Bukkyōgakubu ronshū* 駒澤大學佛教學部論集 10: 209–226.

———. 1980. "*Kenzeiki* no shiryōteki kachi" (part 3). *Komazawa Daigaku Bukkyōgakubu ronshū* 駒澤大學佛教學部論集 11: 157-170.

———. 1981. "Dōgen zenji metsugo no Eiheiji sōdan ni tsuite" 道元禅師滅後の永平寺僧団について. In *Ejō zenji kenkyū* 懐奘禅師研究. Edited by Kumagai Chūkō 熊谷忠興. Pp. 175–201. Fukui Pref.: Sosan Sanshōkai.

———. 1982. "*Shōbōgenzō zuimonki* to Nihon Darumashū" 『正法眼蔵随聞記』と日本達磨宗. *Shūgaku kenkyū* 宗學研究 24:37–43.

———. 1983. "*Shōbōgenzō zuimonki* to Nihon Darumashū (zoku)" 『正法眼蔵随聞記』と日本達磨宗（続）. *Shūgaku kenkyū* 宗學研究 24: 43–48.

———. 1989. "*Shōbōgenzō zuimonki* to Nihon Darumashū" 『正法眼蔵随聞記』と日本達磨宗. In *Shōbōgenzō zuimonki no kenkyū* 正法眼蔵随聞記の研究. Edited by Ikeda Rosan 池田魯參. Pp. 55–90. Hiroshima: Keisuisha 渓水社.

———, editor. 1990a. *Goyuigon kiroku* 御遺言記録. DZZ.7:180–215.

———. 1990b. "Kaidai: *Goyuigon kiroku*" 解題：御遺言記録. DZZ.7:352–344.

———, editor. 1990c. *Myōzen kaichō okugaki* 明全戒牒奥書. DZZ.7:234–235.

———, editor. 1990d. *Shari sōdenki* 舎利相傳記. DZZ.7:216–218.

Itō Shūken 伊藤秀憲. 1979. "*Eihei kōroku* ni okeru jōdō ni tsuite" 「永平広録」における上堂について. *Indogaku Bukkyōgaku kenkyū* 印度學佛教學研究 28:243–248.

———. 1980. "*Eihei kōroku* setsuji nendai kō" 「永平広録」説示年代考. *Komazawa Daigaku Bukkyōgakubu ronshū* 駒澤大學佛教學部論集 11:171–197.

———. 1981. "*Shōbōgenzō* senjutsu jishū nendai kō" 『正法眼蔵』撰述示衆年代考. *Komazawa Daigaku Bukkyōgakubu kenkyū kiyō* 駒澤大學佛教學部研究紀要 39:243–256.

———. 1983. "'Dōgen zenji no zaisōchū no dōsei" 道元禅師の在宋中の動静. *Indogaku Bukkyōgaku kenkyū* 印度學佛教學研究 32:353–356.

———. 1984. "Dōgen zenji no zaisōchū no dōsei" 道元禅師の在宋中の動静. *Komazawa Daigaku Bukkyōgakubu kenkyū kiyō* 駒澤大學佛教學部研究紀要 42:97–124.

———. 1985. "*Sandaison gyōjōki* no seiritsu ni tsuite" 三大尊行狀紀の成立について. *Indogaku Bukkyōgaku kenkyū* 印度學佛教學研究 34:90–97.

———, editor. 1990a. *Eiheiji chiji shingi* 永平寺知事清規. DZZ.7:284–285.

———, editor. 1990b. *Hotsuganmon* 發願文. DZZ.7:223.

———, editor. 1990c. *Jūroku rakan genzuiki* 十六羅漢現瑞記. DZZ.7:286–287.

———. 2015. "'Daigo' kaidai" 「大悟」解題. In Ishii Shūdō 2015b, pp. 622–630.

Itō Yūten 伊藤猷典 (1889–****). 1954, 1955, 1956. "*Shōbōgenzō* 'shō-jimaki' kōso jishū no shingi ni tsuki shūgakushō no oshie o kou" 正法眼蔵生死巻高祖示衆の真偽につき宗学匠の教を乞ふ. *Aichi gakuin daigaku ronsō* 愛知学院大学論叢 1:111–116; 2:149–158; 3:99–127.

Kagamishima Genryū 鏡島元隆 (1912–2001). 1954. "Shinji *Shōbōgenzō* ni tsuite" 眞字正法眼藏について. *Indogaku Bukkyōgaku kenkyū* 印度學佛教學研究 2:440–442.

———. 1965. *Dōgen zenji to in'yō kyōten goroku no kenkyū* 道元禅師と引用経典・語録の研究. Tokyo: Mokujisha.

——— et al. 1972. *Yakuchū Zennen shingi* 訳注禪苑清規. Tokyo: Sōtōshū Shūmuchō.

———. 1973. "Nyojō to Dōgen" 如浄と道元. Reprinted in *Dōgen: shisō dokuhon* 道元：思想読本. Edited by Yanagida Seizan 柳田聖山. Pp. 115–133. Kyoto: Hōzōkan, 1982.

———. 1978. "Nyojō zenjiden kenkyū" 如浄禅師伝研究. *Komazawa Daigaku Bukkyōgakubu kenkyū kiyō* 駒澤大學佛教學部研究紀要 36:1–18.

———. 1982. "Mana *Shōbōgenzō* yori kana *Shōbōgenzō* e" 真名「正法眼藏」より仮名「正法眼藏」へ. Reprinted in *Dōgen zenji to sono shūhen* 道元禅師とその周辺, pp. 277–296. Tokyo: Daitō Shuppansha, 1985.

———. 1983. *Tendō Nyojō zenji no kenkyū* 天童如浄禅師の研究. Tokyo: Shunjūsha.

———. 1985. "Dōgen zenji no zaisōchū no gyōjitsu" 道元禅師の在宋中の行実. In *Dōgen zenji to sono shūhen* 道元禅師とその周辺, pp. 297–325. Tokyo: Daitō Shuppansha.

———. 1986a. "Dōgen zenji no in'yō tōshi goroku ichiranhyō" 道元禅師の引用燈史・語録一覧表. *Komazawa Daigaku Bukkyōgakubu ronshū* 駒澤大學佛教學部論集 17:23–69.

———. 1986b. "Shohyō: Kawamura Kōdō cho *Shōbōgenzō no seiritsu shiteki kenkyū*" 書評: 河村孝道著『正法線蔵の成立史的研究』. *Komazawa Daigaku Bukkyōgakubu ronshū* 駒澤大學佛教學部論集 18:458–460.

———. 1987. "Dōgen zenji no in'yō tōshi goroku ni tsuite (shōzen): shinji *Shōbōgenzō* o shiten toshite" 道元禅師の引用燈史・語録について (承前): 真字『正法眼藏』を視点として. *Komazawa Daigaku Bukkyōgakubu kenkyū kiyō* 駒澤大學佛教學部研究紀要 45:1–17.

———, editor. 1988a. *Dōgen oshō kōroku* 道元和尚廣録. DZZ.3–4.

———. 1988b. "Jūnikanbon *Shōbōgenzō* ni tsuite" 十二巻本『正法眼蔵』について. *Komazawa Daigaku Bukkyōgakubu ronshū* 駒澤大學佛教學部論集 19:48–63.

———. 1988c. "Kaidai: *Dōgen oshō kōroku*" 解題: 道元和尚廣録. DZZ.4:299–329.

———. 1989. "'Shōbōgenzō hachi dainin gaku' okugaki shiken" 『正法眼蔵八大人覚』奥書私見. *Komazawa Daigaku Bukkyōgakubu ronshū* 駒澤大學佛教學部論集 20:14–27. Reprinted in Kagamishima 1994.

———. 1991. "Jūnikanbon *Shōbōgenzō* no ichizuke" 十二巻本『正法眼蔵』の位置づけ. In *Jūnikanbon* Shōbōgenzō *no sho mondai* 十二巻本『正法眼蔵』の諸問題. Edited by Kagamishima Genryū 鏡島元隆 and Suzuki Kakuzen 鈴木格禅. Pp. 3–30. Tokyo: Daizō Shuppan.

———, editor in chief. 1995. *Dōgen in'yō goroku no kenkyū* 道元引用語録の研究. Edited by Sōtōshū Shūgaku Kenkyūjo 曹洞宗宗学研究所. Tokyo: Shunjūsha.

*Kanazawa bunko shiryō zensho* 金沢文庫資料全書. 2017. Kanazawa Bunko 金沢文庫, comp. 10 vols. Kyoto: Rinsen Shoten.

Kasulis, Thomas P. 1985. "The Incomparable Philosopher: Dōgen on How to Read the *Shōbōgenzō*." In *Dōgen Studies*. Edited by William R. LaFleur. Pp. 83–98. Honolulu: University of Hawai'i Press.

———. 2011a. "The Zen Tradition: Overview." In *Japanese Philosophy: A Sourcebook*. Edited by James W. Heisig, Thomas P. Kasulis, and John C. Maraldo. Pp. 135–140. Honolulu: University of Hawai'i Press.

———. 2011b. "Dōgen 道元 (1200–1253)." In *Japanese Philosophy: A Sourcebook*. Edited by James W. Heisig, Thomas P. Kasulis, and John C. Maraldo. Pp. 141–142. Honolulu: University of Hawai'i Press.

Kawamura Kōdō 河村孝道. 1974. "Shinji *Shōbōgenzō* no kenkyū 真字『正法眼蔵』の研究 (2). *Komazawa Daigaku Bukkyōgakubu kenkyū kiyō* 駒澤大學佛教學部研究紀要 32:95–138.

———, editor. 1975. *Shohon taikō Eihei kaisan Dōgen zenji gyōjō Kenzeiki* 諸本對校永平開山道元禅師行状建撕記. Tokyo: Taishūkan Shoten.

———. 1978. "Shōbōgenzō shinzo" 正法眼藏陛座. In *Sōtōshū zensho kaidai sakuin* 曹洞宗全書 解題・索引. Edited by Sōtōshū Zensho Kankōkai 曹洞宗全書刊行会. Pp. 436–437. Tokyo: Sōtōshū Shūmuchō.

———. 1986. *Shōbōgenzō no seiritsu shiteki kenkyū* 正法眼蔵の成立史的研究. Tokyo: Shunjūsha.

———. 1991. *Shinji keji* Shōbōgenzō *seiritsu, henshū, densha no yōsō* 真字仮字『正法眼蔵』成立・編輯・伝写の様相. Supplement (*bessatsu* 別冊) to *Eiinbon* Shōbōgenzō 影印本正法眼藏. Sapporo: Kyōgyōsha.

———, editor. 1991–1993. *Shōbōgenzō* 正法眼蔵. DZZ.1–2.

———. 1993. "Kaidai: *Shōbōgenzō*" 解題: 正法眼蔵. DZZ.2:673–721.

Kawazoe Shōji 川添昭二. 1988. "Kamakura shoki no taigai kōryū to Hakata" 鎌倉初期の対外交流と博多. In *Sakoku Nihon to kokusai kōryū* 鎖国日本と国際交流. Edited by Yanai Kenji 箭内健次. Vol. 1, pp. 1–34. Tokyo: Yoshikawa Kōbunkan.

Kieschnik, John. 1997. *The Eminent Monk: Buddhist Ideals in Medieval Chinese Hagiography*. Honolulu: University of Hawai'i Press.

Kikuchi Hiroki 菊地大樹. 2021. "Enni-kei no inshin kara miru Zen to Mitsu" 円爾系の印信から見る禅と密. In *Chūsei Zen no chi* 中世禅の知, edited by Sueki Fumihiko 末木文美士 et al. Pp. 135–170. Kyoto: Rinsen Shoten.

Kim, Hee-Jin. 1985. "The Reason of Words and Letters: Dōgen and Kōan Language." In *Dōgen Studies*. Edited by William R. LaFleur. Pp. 54–82. Honolulu: University of Hawai'i Press.

Kimura Kiyotaka. 1991. "The Self in Medieval Japanese Buddhism: Focusing on Dōgen." *Philosophy East and West* 41:327–340.

———. 2016. "*Uzenshō* dankan (*Hokke mondo shōgishō* shoin) no shisōteki tokuchō: toku ni *Himitsu Shōbōgenzō* daiichi 'Butsu kōjō ji', daini 'Shōji' to no kanren o megutte." 『有禅抄』断簡（『法華問答正義抄』所引）の思想的特徴: とくに『秘蜜正法眼蔵』第一「仏向上事」・第二「生死」との関連をめぐって. *Indogaku Bukkyōgaku kenkyū* 印度學佛教學研究 65:94–102.

King, Ross. 2015. "Ditching 'Diglossia': Describing Ecologies of the Spoken and Inscribed in Pre-modern Korea," *Sungkyun Journal of East Asian Studies* 15:1–19.

Kishizawa Ian 岸澤惟安 (1865–1955). 1943. "Kōchū *Shōbōgenzō* no nochi ni shosu" 校註正法眼蔵ののちに書す. In *Shōbōgenzō* 正法眼蔵, edited by Etō Sokuō 衛藤即應 (1888–1958). Vol. 3, pp. 323–329. Tokyo: Iwanami Shoten 岩波書店.

Kojima Shōsaku 小島鉦作. 1985. *Ise Jingū shi no kenkyū* 伊勢神宮史の研究. *Kojima Shōsaku chosakushū* 小島鉦作著作集, vol. 2. Tokyo: Yoshikawa Kōbunkan 吉川弘文館.

Komagamine Noriko 駒ヶ嶺法子. 2015. "*Goyuigon kiroku* kaidai" 「御遺言記録」解題. In Ishii Shūdō 2015b, pp. 660–666.

Kosaka Kiyū 小坂機融, editor. 1989. *Shingi* 清規. DZZ.6:1–167.

Kanseki Repository (Kanseki Ripo 漢籍リポ). Online: https://www.kanripo.org. Abbreviated herein as KR.

Kumagai Chūkō 熊谷忠興. 1982. "Koki fukko to Gentō Sokuchū zenji" 古規復古と玄透即中禅師. In Sakurai 1982, vol. 2: 1017–1230.

Kurebayashi Kōdō 榑林皓堂 (1893–1988). 1978. "Shōbōgenzō butsukōjōji" 正法眼蔵佛向上事. In *Sōtōshū zensho kaidai sakuin* 曹洞宗全書解題・索引. Edited by Sōtōshū Zensho Kankōkai 曹洞宗全書刊行会. P. 91. Tokyo: Sōtōshū Shūmuchō.

Lee Yeounsuk [Yi Yŏn-suk]. 2010. *The Ideology of Kokugo: National-izing Language in Modern Japan*. Translated by Maki H. Hubbard. Honolulu: University of Hawai'i Press.

Leighton, Taigen Dan and Shohaku Okumura. 2004. *Dogen's Extensive Record: A Translation of Eihei Koroku*. Somerville, MA: Wisdom Publications.

Lurie, David B. 2011. *Realms of Literacy: Early Japan and the History of Writing*. Cambridge, MA: Harvard University Press.

Morohashi Tetsuji 諸橋轍次 (1883–1982), editor. 1955–1960. *Dai kanwa jiten* 大漢和辞典. 13 vols. Tokyo: Taishūkan. Abbreviated herein as M.

Maeda Eun 前田慧雲 (1855–1930). 1900. "Bukkyō kokinhen ippan" 佛教古今變一斑. Reprinted in *Maeda Eun zenshū* 前田慧雲全集. Vol. 1, pp. 355–410. Tokyo: Shunjūsha, 1932.

Mano Shinya 真野新也. 2011. "Yōsai and Esoteric Buddhism." In *Esoteric Buddhism and the Tantras in East Asia*. Edited by Charles D. Orzech, Henrik H. Sørensen, and Richard K. Payne. Pp. 827–834. Leiden: Brill.

Masunaga Reihō 増永靈鳳 (1902–1981). 1971. *A Primer of Soto Zen: A Translation of Dogen's Shobogenzo zuimonki*. Honolulu: University Press of Hawai'i.

Matsumoto Shirō 松本史朗. 2000. *Dōgen shisōron* 道元思想論. Tokyo: Daizō Shuppan.

Miyazaki Ichisada 宮崎市定 (1901–1995). 1976. *China's Examination Hell: The Civil Service Examinations of Imperial China*. Translated by Conrad Schirokauer. New York: Weatherhill.

Mizuno Yaoko 水野彌穂子 (1921–2010), editor. 1970, 1972. "Bendō wa" 辨道話, "Shōbōgenzō" 正法眼藏, "Jūnikan shōbōgenzō" 十二卷 正法眼藏. In *Dōgen* 道元, 2 vols. Edited by Terada Tōru 寺田透 (1915–1995) and Mizuno Yaoko. *Nihon shisō taikei* 日本思想大系, nos. 12–13. Tokyo: Iwanami Shoten.

———. 1975. "*Shōbōgenzō* no denshō to sono seiritsu" 正法眼蔵の伝承とその成立. *Komazawa Tanki Daigaku kenkyū kiyō* 駒澤短期大學紀要 3:1–36.

———, editor. 1990. *Shōbōgenzō* 正法眼蔵. Iwanami Bunko 岩波文庫. 4 vols. Tokyo: Iwanami Shoten.

——— and Terada Tōru 寺田透 (1915–1995), editors. 1970–1972. *Dōgen* 道元. 2 vols. *Nihon shisō taikei* 日本思想大系, vols. 12–13. Tokyo: Iwanami Shoten. Reprint. 1990–1991. *Dōgen* 道元. 2 vols. *Genten Nihon Bukkyō no shisō* 原典日本仏教の思想, vols. 7–8. Tokyo: Iwanami Shoten.

Morrell, Robert E., trans. 1985. *Sand and Pebbles (Shasekishū): The Tales of Mujū Ichien, a Voice for Pluralism in Kamakura Buddhism*. Albany: SUNY Press.

Murai Shōsuke 村井章介. 2018. "Kikaigashima is Not So Far Away After All." *Studies in Japanese Literature and Culture* 1:19–32.

Nakamura Tsubasa 中村翼. 2010. "Kamakura chūki ni okeru Nissō bōeki to bakufu" 鎌倉中期における日宋貿易の展開と幕府. *Shigaku zasshi* 史學雜誌 119:1693–1717.

———. 2014. "Kamakura Zen no keisei katei to sono haikei" 鎌倉禅の形成過程とその背景. *Shirin* 史林 97:38–67.

Nakao Ryōshin 中尾良信. 1981. "Taikō Gyōyū ni tsuite" 退耕行勇について. *Indogaku Bukkyōgaku kenkyū* 印度學佛教學研究 29:834–836.

———. 1986. "Eisai monryū to Sōtōshū" 栄西門流と曹洞宗. *Shūgaku kenkyū* 宗學研究 28:191–204.

———. 1987a. "Chūnagon hōin Ryūzen ni tsuite" 中納言法印隆禅について. *Shūgaku kenkyū* 宗學研究 29:207–212.

———. 1987b. "Taikō Gyōyū no gyōjitsu" 退耕行勇の行実. *Sōtōshū kenkyūin kenkyū kiyō* 曹洞宗研究員研究紀要 19:39–50.

———. 1988. "Kongō Zanmaiin Ryūzen ni tsuite" 金剛三昧院隆禅について. *Indogaku Bukkyōgaku kenkyū* 印度學佛教學研究 36:614–619.

———. 2004. "Eisai monryū no Nissō tōkai" 栄西門流の入宋渡海. *Zenkenkyūjo kiyō* 禅研究所紀要 33:21–43.

———. 2005. *Nihon Zenshū no densetsu to rekishi* 日本禅宗の伝説と歴史. Rekishi Bunka Raiburarii, 189. Tokyo: Yoshikawa Kōbunkan.

———. 2014. "Eisai no shōgai to jiseki" 栄西の生涯と事蹟. *Eisai to Rinzai Zen* 栄西と臨済禅. *Taiyō bessatu* 太陽、別冊, Nihon no kokoro 日本のこころ, 215:12–35, 40–42.

———. 2020. *Eisai: Ooinaru kana, shin ya* 栄西 大いなる哉、心や. Kyoto: Mineruva Shobō.

Nakaseko Shōdō 中世古祥道 (1916–2019). 1979. *Dōgen zenjiden kenkyū* 道元禪師伝研究. Tokyo: Kokusho Kankōkai.

Narita Teikan 成田貞寛. 1979. "Kōzanji shozō *Shakamuni nyorai gohyaku daigan kyō* no kenkyū" 高山寺所藏「釋迦牟尼如來五百大願經」の研究. *Bukkyō Daigaku Daigakuin kenkyū kiyō* 佛教大學大學院研究紀要 7:1–71.

*Nichiren daishōnin gosho zenshū* 日蓮大聖人御書全集. 1954. Edited by Hori Nikkō 堀日亨 (1867–1957). Tokyo: Soka Gakkai. Abbreviated herein as NDGZ.

Nishiari Bokusan 西有穆山 (1821–1910). 1930. *Shōbōgenzō keiteki* 正法眼藏啓迪. Transcribed by Tomiyama Soei 富山祖英 (d. 1929), edited by Kurebayashi Kōdō 榑林皓堂 (1893–1988). 3 vols. Reprint. Tokyo: Daihōrinkaku, 1979–1980.

Nishio Kenryū 西尾賢隆. 2001. "Gotō Bijutsukanzō *Sanmonsho* kō" 五島美術館蔵「山門疏」考. *Nihon rekishi* 日本歴史 638:66–75. Reprint in Nishio 2011, 2–19.

———. 2002. "Itawatashi no bokuseki" 板渡の墨蹟. *Zen Bunka Kenkyūjo kiyō* 禅文化研究所紀要 26:379–397. Reprint in Nishio 2011, 20–38.

———. 2003. "Tokushiki no bokuseki" 德敷の墨蹟. *Nihon rekishi* 日本歴史 659:84-92. Reprint in Nishio 2011, 39–55.

———. 2011. *Chūsei Zensō no bokuseki to Nitchū kōryū* 中世禅僧の墨蹟と日中交流. Tokyo: Yoshikawa Kōbunkan.

Nishio Minoru 西尾實 (1889–1979). 1964. "'Shōbōgenzō genjōkōan' no kōsō" 正法眼蔵現成公案の構想. *Bungaku* 文学 32. Reprint in *Dōgen* 道元. *Nihon Meisō Ronshū* 日本名僧論集, no. 8. Edited by Kawamura Kōdō and Ishikawa Rikizan. Pp. 247–263. Tokyo: Yoshikawa Kōbunkan.

——— et al., editors. 1965. *Shōbōgenzō Shōbōgenzō zuimonki* 正法眼藏正法眼藏隨聞記. *Nihon koten bungaku taikei* 日本古典文學大系 81. Tokyo: Iwanami Shoten.

Nishitani Isao 西谷功. 2013a. "'Sōshū' to Nissōsō" 「滄洲」と入宋僧. *Purojekuto kenkyū* プロジェクト研究 8:57–72. Reprint in Nishitani 2018, 167–200.

———. 2013b. "Sennyūji to Nansō Bukkyō no jinteki kōryū" 泉涌寺と南宋仏教の人的交流. *Zengaku kenkyū* 91:95–126. Reprint in Nishitani 2018, 127–166.

———. 2015. "Zenritsu jiin ni okeru sōshiki 'shurogonju' 'segaki' girei" 禅律寺院における宋式「首楞厳呪」「施餓鬼」儀礼. *Ashita no tōyōgaku* 明日の東洋学 34:2–12.

———. 2018. *Nansō Kamakura Bukkyō bunka shiron* 南宋・鎌倉仏教文化史論. Tokyo: Bensei Shuppan.

Nishitani Keiji 西谷啓治 (1900–1990). 1987–1989. *Shōbōgenzō kōwa* 正法眼蔵講話. 4 vols. Tokyo: Chikuma Shobō.

Nomura Zuihō 野村瑞峯. 1965. "Kanazawa Bunko bon *Shōbōgenzō*: dai nijūni soku ni tsuite" 金沢文庫本正法眼蔵: 第二十二則について. *Kanazawa Bunko kenkyū* 金沢文庫研究 117:14–31.

Notomi Jōten 納冨常天. 1974. "Shunjō to Dōgen" 俊芿と道元. *Indogaku Bukkyōgaku kenkyū* 印度學佛教學研究 23:114–121.

Ochiai Toshinori 落合俊典, editor. 1996. *Chūgoku senjutsu kyōten* 中國撰述經典 2. *Nanatsudera kōitsu kyōten kenkyū sōsho* 七寺古逸經典研究叢書. Tokyo: Daitō Shuppansha.

Ogawa Takashi 小川隆 et al. 2001. "Kanazawa Bunko *Shōbōgenzō* no yakuchū kenkyū" 金沢文庫本『正法眼蔵』の訳注研究, part 1. *Komazawa Daigaku Zenkenkyūjo nenpō* 駒澤大學禪研究所年報 12:119–144. 2002. Part 2. *Komazawa Daigaku Zenkenkyūjo nenpō* 13-14:63–106. 2003. Part 3. *Komazawa Daigaku Zenken-*

*kyūjo nenpō* 15:31–77. Part 4. *Komazawa Daigaku Zenkenkyūjo nenpō* 16:31–71. Part 5. *Komazawa Daigaku Zenkenkyūjo nenpō* 17:57–96. 2007. Part 6. *Komazawa Daigaku Zenkenkyūjo nenpō* 18:1–28. 2008a. Part 7. *Komazawa daigaku zenkenkyūjo nenpō* 19:67–96. 2008b. Part 8. *Komazawa Daigaku Zenkenkyūjo nenpō* 20:87–112.

Okada Gihō 岡田宜法 (1882–1961). 1953–1955. *Shōbōgenzō shisō taikei* 正法眼藏思想大系. 8 vols. Tokyo: Hōsei Daigaku Shuppankyoku.

Ōkubo Dōshū 大久保道舟 (1896–1994), editor. 1930. *Dōgen zenji zenshū: zen* 道元禪師全集: 全. Tokyo: Shunjūsha.

———, editor. 1944. *Teihon: Dōgen zenji zenshū* 定本・道元禪師全集. Tokyo: Shunjūsha Shōhakukan.

———. 1953. *Dōgen zenjiden no kenkyū* 道元禪師傳の研究. Tokyo: Iwanami Shoten.

———. 1966. *Dōgen zenjiden no kenkyū* 道元禪師傳の研究. Enlarged edition (*shūtei zōho* 修訂増補). Tokyo: Chikuma Shobō.

———, editor. 1969–1970. *Dōgen zenji zenshū* 道元禪師全集. 2 vols. Tokyo: Chikuma Shobō.

———, editor. 1971. *Kohon kōtei Shōbōgenzō zen* 古本校定正法眼藏全. Tokyo: Chikuma Shobō.

———, editor. 1972. *Sōtōshū komonjo* 曹洞宗古文書. 3 vols. Tokyo: Chikuma Shobō.

Ōmiwa Ryūsai 大三輪龍哉 and Nishitani Isao 西谷功. 2011. "Shunjō risshi nenpu" 俊芿律師年譜. In Uramura 2011, pp. 79-82.

*Mitera Sennyūji to kaisan Gachirin daishi* 御寺泉涌寺と開山月輪大師. Edited by Uramura Teirō 上村貞郎. Pp. 79–82.

Ōtani Tetsuo 大谷哲夫, editor. 1991. *Manzan-bon Eihei kōroku: Sozanbon taikō* 卍山本永平廣録: 祖山本対校. Tokyo: Ichihosha.

——— and Watanabe Kenshū 渡部賢宗, editors. 1989. *Sozanbon Eihei kōroku: kōchū shūsei* 祖山本永平廣録: 考注集成. Tokyo: Ichihosha.

Ōtsuka Norihiro 大塚紀弘. 2012. "Tōsen bōeki no henshitsu to Kamakura bakufu" 唐船貿易の変質と鎌倉幕府. *Shigaku zasshi* 史學雜誌 121:199–226.

———. 2017. *Nissō bōeki to Bukkyō bunka* 日宋貿易と仏教文化. Tokyo: Yoshikawa Kōbunkan.

Ōuchi Seiran 大内青巒 (1845–1918), editor. 1885a. *Keizan oshō Denkōroku* 瑩山和尚傳光録. Tokyo: Kōmeisha. Available on-line, National Diet Library Digital Collections: http://kindai.ndl.go.jp/info:ndljp/pid/823387.

———, editor. 1885b. *Shōbōgenzō* 正法眼藏. Tokyo: Kōmeisha. Available on-line, National Diet Library Digital Collections: https://dl.ndl.go.jp/info:ndljp/pid/823075.

604 DŌGEN'S *SHŌBŌGENZŌ* VOLUME VIII

*Oxford English Dictionary*. Third edition. New York: Oxford University Press, 2010.

Ōya Tokujō 大屋德城 (1882–1950), editor. 1934. *Kanazawa ibun* 金澤遺文. 3 vols. Tokyo: Benridō 便利堂.

Reischauer, Edwin O. (1910–1990). 1955. *Ennin's Diary: The Record of a Pilgrimage to China in Search of the Law*. New York: Ronald Press.

Robert, Jean-Noël. 2006. "Hieroglossia: A Proposal." *Nanzan Institute for Religion and Culture Bulletin* 30:25-48.

Robson, James. 2017. "Relic Wary: Facets of Buddhist Relic Veneration in East Asia and Recent Scholarship." *International Journal of Buddhist Thought & Culture* 27:15–38.

Rodríguez García, José María. 2004. "Introduction: Literary Into Cultural Translation." *Diacritics* 34:3–29.

Sahashi Hōryu 佐橋法龍. 1995. "Sōtō shūgaku no kenkyūteki hatten o samatageru mono" 曹洞宗学の研究的発展を妨げるもの. In *Dōgen shisō no gendaiteki kadai* 道元思想の現代的課題. Edited by Ishikawa Rikizan 石川力山 and Kumamoto Einin 熊本英人. *Dōgen shisō taikei* 道元思想大系, vol. 21, pp. 307–350. Kyoto: Dōhōsha.

Sakai Tokugen 酒井得元 (1912–1996), editor. 1989. *Eihei Gen zenji goroku* 永平元禅師語録. DZZ 5.54–123.

Sakurai Shūyū 桜井秀雄 (1916–2000), editor. 1982. *Eiheijishi* 永平寺史. 2 vols. Fukui Pref.: Daihonzan Eiheiji.

———, editor. 1989. *Eihei shoso gakudo yōjinshū* 永平初祖學道用心集. DZZ.5:14–39.

Sakurai Toshio 櫻井敏雄. 1985. "Kenchōji garan no sekkei keikaku ni tsuite" 建長寺伽藍の設計計画について. *Nihon kenchiku gakkai keikakukei ronbun hōkokushū* 日本建築学会計画系論文報告集 350:95–105.

Sasaki Hikari 佐々木日嘉里. 2014. "Zenshūyō kenchiku" 禅宗様建築. *Eisai to Rinzai Zen* 栄西と臨済禅. *Taiyō bessatu* 太陽、別冊, *Nihon no kokoro* 日本のこころ, 215:146–153.

Satō Shūkō 佐藤秀孝. 1985. "Nyojō zenji jijaku no shūhen" 如浄禅師示寂の周辺. *Indogaku Bukkyōgaku kenkyū* 印度學佛教學研究 34:282–286.

———. 1990. "Shoki Sōtōshū kyōdan no Kantō shinshutsu" 初期曹洞教団の関東進出. *Komazawa Daigaku Zenkenkyūjo nenpō* 駒澤大學禪研究所年報 1:143–171.

———. 1991. "Butsuju-bō Myōzen den no kōsatsu" 仏樹房明全伝の考察. *Komazawa Daigaku Bukkyōgakubu kiyō* 駒澤大學佛教學部紀要 49:41–87.

———. 1995. "Dōgen zaisōchū no sangaku kōtei ni kansuru sho mondai" 道元在宋中の参学行程に関する諸問題, part 1. *Komazawa Daigaku Zenkenkyūjo nenpō* 駒澤大學禪研究所年報 6:93–121.

———. 1997. "Dōgen zaisōchū no sangaku kōtei ni kansuru sho mondai" 道元在宋中の参学行程に関する諸問題, part 2. *Komazawa Daigaku Zenkenkyūjo nenpō* 駒澤大學禪研究所年報 8:73–97.

———. "Tendōzan no Musai Ryōha to sono monryū" 天童山の無際了派とその門流. *Komazawa Daigaku Bukkyōgakubu ronshū* 駒澤大學佛教學部論集 39:119–223.

———. 2012. "Myōan Eisai no zaisōchū no dōsei ni tsuite" 明庵栄西の在宋中の動静について, part 1. *Komazawa Daigaku Bukkyōgakubu ronshū* 駒澤大學佛教學部論集 43:71–113.

———. 2013. "Myōan Eisai no zaisōchū no dōsei ni tsuite" 明庵栄西の在宋中の動静について, part 2. *Komazawa Daigaku Bukkyōgakubu ronshū* 駒澤大學佛教學部論集 44:99–139.

———. 2014. "Myōan Eisai no zaisōchū no dōsei ni tsuite" 明庵栄西の在宋中の動静について, part 3. *Komazawa Daigaku Bukkyōgakubu ronshū* 駒澤大學佛教學部論集 45:91–134.

Schlütter, Morten. 2008. *How Zen Became Zen: The Dispute over Enlightenment and the Formation of Chan Buddhism in Song-dynasty China*. Honolulu: University of Hawaiʻi Press.

Shiina Kōyū 椎名宏雄, editor. 2012–2016. *Gozanban, Chūgoku Zenseki sōkan* 五山版, 中国禅籍叢刊. 12 vols. Kyoto: Rinsen Shoten.

——— and Yanagida Seizan 柳田聖山, editors. 1999–2001. *Zengaku tenseki sōkan* 禅学典籍叢刊. 12 volumes. Kyoto: Rinsen Shoten.

*Shintei zōho kokushi taikei* 新訂増補国史大系. 1966. 66 volumes. Tokyo: Yoshikawa Kōbunkan.

*Shōbōgenzō* 正法眼藏. 1815. Compiled by Sodō Ontatsu 祖道穩達 (d. 1813) et al. A.k.a. *Eihei shōbōgenzō* 永平正法眼藏; *Chōkoku Eihei shōbōgenzō* 彫刻永平正法眼藏; Honzanban 本山版; Sozanban 祖山版. Xylographic edition. 21 fascicles (*satsu* 冊). Echizen (Fukui Pref.): Eiheiji.

*Shōbōgenzō chūkai zensho* 正法眼藏註解全書. 1914. Edited by Jinbo Nyoten 神保如天 (1880–1944) and Andō Bun'ei 安藤文英 (1883–1958). 11 vols. Reprint. Tokyo: Nihon Bussho Kankōkai, 1956–1957. Abbreviated herein as SCZ.

*Shōbōgenzō: Honzanban shukusatsu* 正法眼藏: 本山版縮刷. 1926. Reprint. Tokyo: Kōmeisha, 1956.

*Shōbōgenzō yōgo sakuin* 正法眼藏用語索引. 1962–1963. Edited by Katō Shūkō 加藤宗厚. 2 vols. Tokyo: Risōsha.

*Shōbōgenzō zatsubun: Shōbōji-bon* 正法眼藏雜文: 正法寺本. 2010. Edited by Shōbōgenzō Zatsubun Hensan Iinkai 正法眼藏雜文編纂委員会. Tokyo: Shunjūsha.

*Sōtōshū zensho* 曹洞宗全書. 1970–1973. Edited by Sōtōshū Zensho Kankōkai 曹洞宗全書刊行会. Revised edition. 18 vols. plus 6 vols. of supplements (*bekkan* 別巻). Tokyo: Sōtōshū Shūmuchō. Abbreviated herein as SZ.

Stevenson, Daniel B. 1986. "The Four Kinds of Samādhi in Early T'ien-t'ai Buddhism." In *Traditions of Meditation in Chinese Buddhism*. Edited by Peter N. Gregory. Pp. 45–97. Honolulu: University of Hawai'i Press.

Steineck, Raji C. 2018. "A Zen Philosopher? Notes on the Philosophical Reading of Dōgen's Shōbōgenzō." In *Concepts of Philosophy in Asia and the Islamic World*. Volume 1: China and Japan. Edited by Robert Gassmann et al. Pp. 577–606. Leiden: Brill.

Sugawara Kenshū 菅原研州. 2015. "*Busso shōdenki no kenkyū*" 仏祖正伝記の研究. *Zenkenkyūjo kiyō* 禅研究所紀要 43: 41–61.

Sueki Fumihiko 末木文美士 et al., editor. 2021. *Chūsei Zen no chi* 中世禅の知. Kyoto: Rinsen Shoten.

Sugio Gen'yū 杉尾玄有 (1928–2012). 1977. "Gokyōji aogitaki nimond-ai: menju ji datsuraku no koto oyobi *Fukan zazen gi* no shofū no koto" 御教示仰ぎたき二問題：「面授時脱落」のこと及び『普勧坐禅儀』の書風のこと. *Shūgaku kenkyū* 宗學研究 19:33–37.

———. 1978. "Dōgen ni okeru shinnyo no mondai" 道元における真如の問題. *Kenkyū ronsō: jinbun kagaku, shakai kagaku* 研究論叢: 人文科学・社会科学 (Yamaguchi Daigaku Kyōikugakubu 山口大学教育学部) 28:15–30.

———. 1986. "Dōgen zenji no banzō kokukoku issei shōmetsu no shinjin datsuraku to Aikuōji saihō" 道元禅師の万象刻々一斉生滅の身心脱落と阿育王寺再訪. *Shūgaku kenkyū* 宗學研究 28:19–24.

Suzuki Kakuzen 鈴木格禅, editor. 1989. *Fukan zazen gi* 普勧坐禪儀; *Fukan zazen gi senjutsu yurai* 普勧坐禪儀撰述由來. DZZ.5:1–12.

———, editor. 1989. *Kaihō*, *Shisho* 戒法・嗣書. DZZ.6:169–232.

———, editor. 1990. *Hōkyōki* 宝慶記. DZZ.7:2–51.

Tachi Ryūshi 舘隆志. 2014. "Kamakuraki no Zenrin ni okeru Chūgokugo to Nihongo" 鎌倉期の禅林における中国語と日本語. *Komazawa Daigaku Bukkyōgakubu ronshū* 駒澤大學佛教学部論集 45:259–286.

———. 2021. "Kamakura jidai ni okeru kenshūzen to Sōchōzen no dōnyū" 鎌倉時代における兼修禅と宋朝禅の導入. In *Chūsei Zen no chi* 中世禅の知, edited by Sueki Fumihiko 末木文美士 et al. Pp. 212–217. Tokyo: Rinsen Shoten.

Taga Munehaya 多賀宗隼. 1965. *Eisai* 栄西. Ningen sōsho 人間叢書. Tokyo: Yoshikawa Kōbunkan.

Taira Masayuki 平雅行. 2020. "Tōgoku Kamakura no mikkyō" 東国鎌倉の密教. *Chizan gakuhō* 智山學報 69:347–376.

*Taishō shinshū daizōkyō* 大正新脩大藏經. 1924–1935. Edited by Takakusu Junjirō 高楠順次朗 and Watanabe Kaikyoku 渡邊海旭. 100 vols. Tokyo: Daizōkyōkai. Vols. 1–85 available on-line: *Saṃgaṇikīkṛtaṃ Taiśotripiṭakaṃ* (The SAT Daizōkyō Database): http://21dzk.l.u-tokyo.ac.jp/SAT/. Abbreviated herein as T.

*Taiso Keizan zenji senjutsu Denkōroku* 太祖瑩山禅師撰述伝光録. 2005. Edited by Shūten Hensan Iinkai 宗典編纂委員会. Tokyo: Sōtōshū Shūmuchō.

Takahashi Shūei 高橋秀榮. 2013. "Jūyō bunkazai 'Shōbōgenzō sansui kyō' no hissha ni tsuite" 重要文化財『正法眼蔵山水経』の筆者について. *Komazawa Daigaku Bukkyōgakubu ronshū* 駒澤大學佛教學部論集 44:17–29.

Tamamura Takeji 玉村竹二 (1911–2003). 1941. "Zen no tenseki 禪の典籍." Reprinted in *Nihon Zenshūshi ronshū* 日本禪宗史論集. Vol. 3, pp. 109–212. Tokyo: Shibunkaku, 1981.

Tamamuro Taijō 圭室諦成 (1902–1966). 1940. *Kanazawa bunkobon Shōbōgenzō* 金澤文庫本「正法眼藏」. Tokyo: Dōgen Zenji Sankōkai 道元禪師讚仰會.

Tanabe Hajime 田邊元 (1885–1962). 1939. *Shōbōgenzō no tetsugaku shikan* 正法眼藏の哲學私觀. Tokyo: Iwanami Shoten. Available online via National Diet Library Digital Collections (Kokuritsu Kokkai Toshokan Dejitaru Korekushon 国立国会図書館デジタルコレクション): http://dl.ndl.go.jp/info:ndljp/pid/1220615.

———. 2011 (1939). "The philosophy of Dōgen" [originally *Shōbōgenzō no tetsugaku shikan* 正法眼藏の哲學私觀, 1939, pp. 683–688]. Translated by Ralf Müller. In *Japanese Philosophy, A Sourcebook*, pp. 554–559. Edited by James W. Heisig, Thomas P. Kasulis and John C. Maraldo. Honolulu: University of Hawai'i Press.

Terada Tōru 寺田透 (1915–1995). 1974. *Dōgen no gengo uchū* 道元の言語宇宙. Tokyo: Iwanami Shoten.

Tsunoda Tairyū 角田泰隆. 1988. "Dōgen zenji no shushōkan ni kansuru mondai ni tsuite (san)" 道元禅師の修証観に関する問題について (三)." *Shūgaku kenkyū* 宗學研究 30:245–250.

———. 1995 (1993). "Keji *Shōbōgenzō* to shinji *Shōbōgenzō*" 仮字『正法眼藏』と真字『正法眼藏』. *Komazawa Daigaku Bukkyōgakubu ronshū* 駒澤大學佛教學部論集 24:243–260. Enlarged reprint in Kagamishima 1995, 15–44.

———. 2001. "*Shōbōgenzō* saiji no shosō" 『正法眼藏』再治の諸相. *Komazawa Tanki Daigaku kiyō* 駒澤短期大學紀要 29:315–329.

———. 2007. "*Shōbōgenzō* no seiritsu ni tsuite: shishu koshahon no kōsatsu" 「正法眼藏」の成立について：四種古写本の考察. *Komazawa Tanki Daigaku kiyō* 駒澤短期大學紀要 35:87–155.

———. 2020. "Kōkai kōen: Honzanban teiho *Shōbōgenzō* ni tsuite" 公開講演 本山版訂補『正法眼藏』について. *Komazawa Daigaku*

*Daigakuin Bukkyōgaku Kenkyūkai kiyō* 駒沢大学大学院仏教学研
究会年報 53:3–13.

Tsurumi Daigaku Bukkyō Bunka Kenkyūjo 鶴見大学仏教文化研究所,
editor. 2015ff (in press). *Keizan zenji* Denkōroku: *shohon no
honkoku to hikaku* 瑩山禅師「伝光録」: 諸本の翻刻と比較.
Yokohama: Tsurumi Daigaku. Part 1 (2015); Part 2 (2016); Part 3
(2016); Part 4 (2018); Part 5 (2019); Part 6 (2020); Part 7 (2021); etc.

Ui Hakuju 宇井伯壽 (1882–1963). 1938. *Hōkyōki* 寶慶記. Iwanami Bunko
岩波文庫, 1796. Tokyo: Iwanami Shoten.

Uramura Teirō 上村貞郎, editor. 2011. *Mitera Sennyūji to kaisan Gachirin
daishi* 御寺泉涌寺と開山月輪大師. Kyoto: Hōzōkan.

von Glahn, Richard. 2014. "The Ningbo-Hakata Merchant Network and
the Reorientation of East Asian Maritime Trade, 1150–1350."
*Harvard Journal of Asiatic Studies* 74:249-279.

———. 2019. "The Maritime Trading World of East Asia from the Thirteenth to the Seventeenth Centuries." In *Picturing Commerce in
and from the East Asian Maritime Circuits, 1550–1800*. Edited by
Tamara H. Bentley. Pp. 55–82. Amsterdam: Amsterdam University Press.

Wakayama Yūkō 若山悠光. 2015. "Beppon 'Shin fukatoku' no kadai" 別
本『心不可得』の課題. *Komazawa Daigaku Zenkenkyūjo nenpō*
駒澤大學禪研究所年報 27:197–218.

———. 2016a. "Beppon 'Butsukōjōji' no seikaku" 別本『仏向上事』の
性格. *Komazawa Daigaku Daigakuin Bukkyōgaku Kenkyūkai nenpō* 駒澤大學大學院佛教學研究會年報 49:35–80.

———. 2016b. "*Eihei kōroku* kan'ichi, daijūshichi jōdō kō" 「永平広
録」巻一, 第一七上堂考. *Indogaku Bukkyōgaku kenkyū* 印度學佛
教學研究 64:653–656.

———. 2016c. "The Formation of Kana Shōbōgenzō: Tracing Back Beppon (Draft Edition) Shinfukatoku." *Komazawa Daigaku Zenkenkyūjo nenpō* 駒澤大學禪研究所年報 28:312–281 (1–32).

Wang Chunyun. 2010. *Deciphering the Historical Mystery of State Gem
Heshi Bi*. Wuhan: China University of Geosciences Press.

Watanabe Shōei 渡部正英. 1992. "*Denkōroku* ni tsuite no ichi shiten" 「伝
光録」について一視点. *Shūgaku kenkyū* 宗學研究 34:107–113.

Watanabe Tsunaya 渡邊綱也, editor. 1966. *Shasekishū* 沙石集 (1283). By
Mujū Dōgyō 無住道曉 (a.k.a. Ichien-bō 一圓房; 1226–1312). *Ni-
hon koten bungaku taikei* 日本古典文學大系, 85. Tokyo: Iwanami
Shoten 岩波書店.

Watsuji Tetsurō 和辻哲郎 (1889–1960). 1923. "Shamon Dōgen" 沙門
道元. [1] Reprint in *Nihon seishin shi* 日本精神史研究. Pp.
236–388. Tokyo: Iwanami Shoten, 1926. Available online via
National Diet Library Digital Collections (Kokuritsu Kokkai Toshokan Dejitaru Korekushon 国立国会図書館デジタルコレクシ
ョン): http://dl.ndl.go.jp/info:ndljp/pid/1020621. [2] Corrected

edition, Iwanami Shoten, 1940. Revised reprint 1970. Iwanami Bunko (paperback) Ao 青 (33)-144-7 edition, 1992. Waido (large size) Iwanami Bunko, no. 252, edtion, 2005. [3] Corrected edition (1940) reprinted in *Watsuji Tetsurō zenshū* 和辻哲郎全集. Edited by Abe Yoshishige 安倍能成 et al. 4.156–246. Tokyo: Iwanami Shoten, 1961. Reprinted 1992. Digital edition 2017, available on-line from Aozora Bunko 青空文庫: https://www.aozora.gr.jp/cards/001395/files/49905_63366.html.

————, editor. 1929. *Dōgen goroku: Shōbōgenzō zuimonki* 道元語録: 正法眼藏隨聞記. Iwanami Bunko 岩波文庫. Tokyo: Iwanami Shoten.

Welch, Holmes (1921–1981). 1963. "Dharma Scrolls and the Succession of Abbots in Chinese Monasteries." *T'oung-pao* 50:93–149.

Wenger, Michael. 2001. *Wind Bell: Teachings from the San Francisco Zen Center, 1969–2001*. Berkeley: North Atlantic Books.

Whitman, John. 2011. "The Ubiquity of the Gloss." *Scripta* 3:95-121.

Wright, Arthur F. 1954. "Biography and Hagiography: Hui-chao's Lives of Eminent Monks." Reprint in *Studies in Chinese Buddhism*. Edited by Robert M. Somers. Pp. 73–111, 150–172. New Haven: Yale University Press, 1990.

*Writings of Nichiren Daishonin, The*. 1999. Edited by the Gosho Translation Committee. [Partial translations of *Nichiren daishōnin gosho zenshū* 日蓮大聖人御書全集, 1954] Tokyo: Soka Gakkai.

Yamada Shōzen 山田昭全 and Miki Sumito 三木紀人, editors. 1978. *Zōdanshū* 雑談集 (1305). By Mujū Dōgyō 無住道曉 (a.k.a. Ichien-bō 一圓房; 1226–1312). Tokyo: Miyai Shoten.

Yamamura Nobuhide 山村信榮. 2021. "Kamakuraki no Dazaifu ni okeru Tendaishū to Zenshū" 鎌倉期の太宰府における天台宗と禅宗. In *Chūsei Zen no chi* 中世禅の知, edited by Sueki Fumihiko 末木文美士 et al. Pp. 250–256. Tokyo: Rinsen Shoten.

Yamauchi Shinji 山内晋次. 2009. *Nissō bōeki to iō no michi* 日宋貿易と「硫黄の道」. Nihonshi Riburetto 日本史リブレット, no. 75. Tokyo: Yamakawa Shuppansha, 2009.

————. 2011. "Nihonshi to Ajiashi no issetten: iō no kokusai kōeki o megutte" 日本史とアジア史の一接点 : 硫黄の国際交易をめぐって. *Kōnan bunka to Nihon* 江南文化と日本, pp. 201–211. Kyoto: Kokusai Nihon Bunka Kenkyū Sentā.

————. 2012. "Heishi to Nissō bōeki" 平氏と日宋貿易. *Kōbe Joshi Daitaku Koten Geinō Kenkyū Sentā kiyo* 神戸女子大学古典芸能研究センター紀要 6:68–82.

Yanagida Seizan 柳田聖山 (1922–2006). 1969. *Daruma no goroku: Ninyū shigyō ron* 達磨の語録 : 二入四行論. *Zen no goroku* 禅の語録 1. Tokyo: Chikuma Shobō.

————. 1980. "Tabuu e no chōsen: Dōgen" タブーへの挑戦: 道元. *Chūgai nippō* 中外日報 (1980.11.18) no. 22667; (1980.11.20) no. 22668; (1980.11.22) no. 22669; (1980.11.25) no. 22670; (1980.11.27) no. 22671; (1980.11.29) no. 22672.

―――. 1982. "Search for the Real Dōgen: Callenging Taboos Concerning Dōgen." Translated by R.F.R. [Robert F. Rhodes]. *The Young East* 8:3–19.

Yoshida Dōkō 吉田道興. 1982. "Manzan-bon *Shōbōgenzō* no henshū" 卍山本『正法眼藏』の編集. In Sakurai 1982, vol. 2: 909-915.

―――. 1992a. "Dōgen zenjiden no shiryō kenkyū: *Sandaison gyōjōki* to *Sanso gyōgōki* o chūshin ni" 道元禅師伝の史料研究：「三大尊行状記」と「三祖行業記」を中心に. *Komazawa Daigaku Zenkenkyūjo nenpō* 駒澤大學禪研究所年報 3:63–102.

―――. 1992b. "Mujaku Dōchū hitsu *Eihei zenji sanso gyōgoki* no honkoku shōkai" 無著道忠筆「永平禅寺三祖行業記」の翻刻・紹介. *Shūgaku kenkyū* 宗學研究 34:100–106.

Yoneda Mariko 米田真理子. 2008a. "Eisai no nissō" 栄西の入宋. In *Umi o wataru Tendai bunka* 海を渡る天台文化. Edited by Yoshihara Hiroto 吉原浩人 and Wang Yong 王勇. Pp. 203-224. Tokyo: Bensei Shuppan.

―――. 2008b. "*Kaihen kyōshuketsu* hakken ni yoru Eisai denki no saikentō" 改偏教主決発見による栄西伝記の再検討. *Kokusai kenkyū shūkai hōkokusho* 国際研究集会報告書 4 (Nagoya University): 345–336 (from back).

Yoshizawa Hajime 芳澤元. 2011. "Ōeiki ni okeru Totō Tenjin setsuwa no tenkai" 応永期における渡唐天神説話の展開. *Shigaku zasshi* 史學雜誌 120:1675–1696.

*Zengaku daijiten* 禪學大辭典. 1978. Edited by Zengaku Daijiten Hensanjo 禪學大辭典編纂所. New printing (*shinpan* 新版). Tokyo: Taishūkan Shoten, 1985. Abbreviated herein as ZGDJ.

*Zengaku taikei* 禪學大系. 1910–1915. Edited by Zengaku Taikei Hensankyoku. 8 vols. Reprint. Tokyo: Kokusho Kankōkai, 1977. Abbreviated herein as ZT.

*Zengaku tenseki sōkan* 禅学典籍叢刊. 1999–2001. Edited by Yanagida Seizan 柳田聖山 (1922–2006), Shiina Kōyū 椎名宏雄, et al. 14 vols. Kyoto: Rinsen Shoten. Abbreviated herein as ZTS.

*Zengo jiten* 禅語辞典. 1991. Koga Hidehiko 古賀英彦 and Iriya Yoshitaka 入矢義高. Kyoto: Shibunkaku Shuppan.

*Zenseki mokuroku* 禪籍目録. 1962. New edition (*shinsan* 新纂). Edited by Komazawa Daigaku Toshokan 駒澤大學図書館. Tokyo: Komazawa Daigaku Toshokan.

*Zoku gunsho ruijū* 續羣書類從. Compiled by Hanawa Hokiichi 塙保己一 (1746–1821) et al. Revised, 3d edition. 72 vols. Tokyo: Zoku Gunsho Ruiju Kanseikai, 1958.

*Zoku Sōtōshū zensho* 續曹洞宗全書. 1974–1977. Edited by Zoku Sōtōshū Zensho Kankōkai. 10 vols. Tokyo: Sōtōshū Shūmuchō. Abbreviated herein as ZSZ.

# The Sōtō Zen Text Project *Shōbōgenzō*

## Volume I
### The Seventy-five-Chapter Compilation, Part 1

1. The Realized Kōan  *Genjō kōan* 現成公案
2. Mahā-prajñā-pāramitā  *Maka hannya haramitsu* 摩訶般若波羅蜜
3. Buddha Nature  *Busshō* 佛性
4. Studying the Way with Body and Mind  *Shinjin gakudō* 身心學道
5. This Mind Itself Is the Buddha  *Soku shin ze butsu* 即心是佛
6. Deportment of the Practicing Buddha  *Gyōbutsu iigi* 行佛威儀
7. One Bright Pearl  *Ikka myōju* 一顆明珠
8. The Mind Cannot Be Got  *Shin fukatoku* 心不可得
9. The Old Buddha Mind  *Kobutsushin* 古佛心
10. Great Awakening  *Daigo* 大悟
11. Principles of Seated Meditation  *Zazen gi* 坐禪儀
12. Needle of Seated Meditation  *Zazen shin* 坐禪箴
13. Ocean Seal Samādhi  *Kaiin zanmai* 海印三昧
14. Sky Flowers  *Kūge* 空華
15. Radiance  *Kōmyō* 光明

## Volume II
### The Seventy-five-Chapter Compilation, Part 2

16A. Sustained Practice, Part 1  *Gyōji jō* 行持上
16B. Sustained Practice, Part 2  *Gyōji ge* 行持下
17. Such  *Inmo* 恁麼
18. Avalokiteśvara  *Kannon* 觀音
19. The Old Mirror  *Kokyō* 古鏡
20. Sometimes  *Uji* 有時
21. Prediction  *Juki* 授記
22. Full Function  *Zenki* 全機
23. The Moon  *Tsuki* 都機
24. Painted Cake  *Gabyō* 畫餅
25. Sound of the Stream, Form of the Mountain  *Keisei sanshoku* 谿聲山色
26. Beyond the Buddha  *Butsu kōjō ji* 佛向上事
27. Talking of a Dream within a Dream  *Muchū setsumu* 夢中説夢
28. Making a Bow and Getting the Marrow  *Raihai tokuzui* 禮拜得髓
29. The Mountains and Waters Sūtra  *Sansui kyō* 山水經
30. Sūtra Reading  *Kankin* 看經

## Volume III
### The Seventy-five-Chapter Compilation, Part 3

31. Do No Evil  *Shoaku makusa* 諸惡莫作
32. Transmitting the Robe  *Den'e* 傳衣
33. Sayings  *Dōtoku* 道得
34. The Teachings of the Buddhas  *Bukkyō* 佛教
35. Spiritual Powers  *Jinzū* 神通
36. The Arhat  *Arakan* 阿羅漢

37. Spring and Autumn  *Shunjū* 春秋
38. Tangled Vines  *Kattō* 葛藤
39. The Inheritance Certificate  *Shisho* 嗣書
40. The Cypress Tree  *Hakujushi* 柏樹子
41. The Three Realms Are Only Mind  *Sangai yui shin* 三界唯心
42. Talking of the Mind, Talking of the Nature  *Sesshin sesshō* 説心説性
43. The Real Marks of the Dharmas  *Shohō jissō* 諸法實相
44. The Way of the Buddhas  *Butsudō* 佛道
45. Secret Words  *Mitsugo* 密語

### Volume IV
### The Seventy-five-Chapter Compilation, Part 4

46. The Insentient Preach the Dharma  *Mujō seppō* 無情説法
47. Sūtras of the Buddhas  *Bukkyō* 佛經
48. Dharma Nature  *Hosshō* 法性
49. Dhāraṇī  *Darani* 陀羅尼
50. Washing the Face  *Senmen* 洗面
51. Face-to-Face Conferral  *Menju* 面授
52. Buddhas and Ancestors  *Busso* 佛祖
53. Plum Blossoms  *Baika* 梅華
54. Washing and Purifying  *Senjō* 洗淨
55. The Ten Directions  *Jippō* 十方
56. Seeing Buddha  *Kenbutsu* 見佛
57. Extensive Study  *Henzan* 遍參
58. The Eye  *Ganzei* 眼睛
59. Everyday Matters  *Kajō* 家常
60. The Thirty-seven Factors of Bodhi  *Sanjūshichi hon bodai bunpō* 三十七品菩提分法

### Volume V
### The Seventy-five-Chapter Compilation, Part 5

61. Song of the Dragon  *Ryūgin* 龍吟
62. The Intention of the Ancestral Master's Coming from the West
     *Soshi seirai i* 祖師西來意
63. Bringing Forth the Mind of Bodhi  *Hotsu bodai shin* 發菩提心
64. The Udumbara Blossom  *Udonge* 優曇華
65. The Entire Body of the Tathāgata  *Nyorai zenshin* 如來全身
66. The King of Samādhis Samādhi  *Zanmai ō zanmai* 三昧王三昧
67. Turning the Dharma Wheel  *Ten hōrin* 轉法輪
68. Great Practice  *Dai shugyō* 大修行
69. The Samādhi of Self Verification  *Jishō zanmai* 自證三昧
70. Empty Space  *Kokū* 虛空
71. The Pātra Bowl  *Hou* 鉢盂
72. The Retreat  *Ango* 安居
73. Reading Other Minds  *Tashin tsū* 他心通
74. The King Requests Saindhava  *Ō saku sendaba* 王索仙陀婆
75. Leaving Home  *Shukke* 出家

# Volume VI
## The Twelve-Chapter Compilation

T1. The Merit of Leaving Home *Shukke kudoku* 出家功德
T2. Receiving the Precepts *Jukai* 受戒
T3. The Merit of the Kāṣāya *Kesa kudoku* 袈裟功德
T4. Bringing Forth the Mind of Bodhi *Hotsu bodai shin* 發菩提心
T5. Offerings to the Buddhas *Kuyō shobutsu* 供養諸佛
T6. Refuge in the Treasures of Buddha, Dharma, and Saṃgha
    *Kie buppōsōbō* 歸依佛法僧寶
T7. Deep Faith in Cause and Effect *Jinshin inga* 深信因果
T8. Karma of the Three Times *Sanjigō* 三時業
T9. Four Horses *Shime* 四馬
T10. The Bhikṣu of the Fourth Dhyāna *Shizen biku* 四禪比丘
T11. One Hundred Eight Gateways to the Illumination of the Dharma
    *Ippyakuhachi hōmyōmon* 一百八法明門
T12. The Eight Understandings of the Great Person *Hachi dainin gaku* 八大人覺

# Volume VII
## Supplementary Chapters, Variant Texts

### Supplementary Chapters

S1. Talk on Pursuing the Way *Bendōwa* 辦道話
S2. Procedures for the Hall of Gathered Clouds *Jūundō shiki* 重雲堂式
S3. The *Lotus* Turns the *Lotus* *Hokke ten Hokke* 法華轉法華
S4. The Mind Cannot Be Got *Shin fukatoku* 心不可得
S5. The Four Attractions of the Bodhisattva *Bodaisatta shishōbō* 菩提薩埵四攝法
S6. Instructions to the Administration Cloister *Ji kuin mon* 示庫院文
S7. Only Buddhas with Buddhas *Yui butsu yo butsu* 唯佛與佛
S8. Birth and Death *Shōji* 生死
S9. The Way of the Buddhas *Butsudō* 佛道 (*Dōshin* 道心)

### Variant Texts

V1. Talk on Pursuing the Way *Bendōwa* 辦道話
V2. The Inheritance Certificate *Shisho* 嗣書
V3. Beyond the Buddha *Butsu kōjō ji* 佛向上事
V4. Washing the Face *Senmen* 洗面
V5. Extensive Study *Henzan* 遍參
V6. Great Awakening *Daigo* 大悟
V7. Karma of the Three Times *Sanji gō* 三時業

# Volume VIII

Introduction
Appendices
Supplementary Notes
Works Cited